Strategic Compensation in Canada

THIRD EDITION

Week 1 → ch. 1
      → ch. 2
Week 2 → ch. 3
      → ch. 4
Week 3 → ch. 5
      → ch. 6 + ch. 7 (to p. 275)

MIDTERM
week 4 → ch. 7 cont'd + ch. 8
week 5 → ch. 9
      → ch. 10
week 6 → ch. 11
      → ch. 12

FINAL

Strategic Compensation in Canada

THIRD EDITION

Richard J. Long
University of Saskatchewan

Series Editor: Monica Belcourt

THOMSON

NELSON

Australia   Canada   Mexico   Singapore   Spain   United Kingdom   United States

THOMSON

NELSON

Strategic Compensation in Canada

Third Edition

by Richard J. Long

Associate Vice President, Editorial Director:
Evelyn Veitch

Executive Editor:
Anthony Rezek

Senior Marketing Manager:
Charmaine Sherlock

Senior Developmental Editor:
Karina Hope

Permissions Coordinator:
Nicola Winstanley

Production Editor:
Anne Macdonald

Copy Editor:
Nancy Mucklow

Proofreader:
Erin Moore

Indexer:
Belle Wong

Senior Production Coordinator:
Kathrine Pummell

Design Director:
Ken Phipps

Cover Design:
Eugene Lo

Compositor:
Interactive Composition Corporation

Printer:
Thomson/West

Library and Archives Canada Cataloguing in Publication Data

Long, Richard J. (Richard Joseph)
    Strategic compensation in Canada / Richard J. Long.—3rd ed.

Includes bibliographical references and index.
ISBN 0-17-641612-9

1. Compensation management—Canada. I. Title.

HF5549.5.C67L56 2005
658.3'22'0971   C2005-904072-6

ISBN-13: 978-0-17-641612-6
ISBN-10: 0-17-641612-9

This book is dedicated to my family—Trisha, Jeffrey, Jeremy, and Michael—without whose support and forbearance it would never have been completed.

Brief Contents

Detailed Contents

Chapter 8: Evaluating the Market   311

About the Series

More than ever, human resources management professionals need the knowledge and skills to design HRM policies and practices that not only meet legal requirements but are also effective in supporting organizational strategy. Increasingly, these professionals turn to published research and books on best practices for assistance in the development of effective HR strategies. The books in the *Nelson Series in Human Resources Management* are the best source in Canada for reliable, valid, and current knowledge about practices in HRM.

The texts in this series include

- *Managing Performance through Training and Development*
- *Management of Occupational Health and Safety*
- *Recruitment and Selection in Canada*
- *Strategic Compensation in Canada*
- *Strategic Human Resources Planning*
- *An Introduction to the Canadian Labour Market*
- *Research, Measurement, and Evaluation of Human Resources*

The *Nelson Series in Human Resources Management* represents a significant development in the field of HRM for many reasons. Each book in the series (except for *Strategic Compensation in Canada*) is the first Canadian text in its area of specialization. HR professionals in Canada must work with Canadian laws, statistics, policies, and values. This series serves their needs. It is the only complete set of HRM books, standardized in presentation, that enables students and practitioners to access information quickly across many HRM disciplines. The books are essential sources of information that meet the requirements for the CCHRA (Canadian Council of Human Resource Associations) national knowledge exam for the Certified Human Resources Professional (CHRP) designation. This one-stop resource will also prove useful to anyone looking for solutions for the effective management of people.

The publication of this series signals that the field of human resources management has advanced to the stage where theory and applied research guide practice. The books in the series present the best and most current research in the functional areas of HRM. Research is supplemented with examples of the best practices used by Canadian companies that are leaders in HRM. Thus, the books serve as an introduction to the functional area for the new student of HR and as a validation source for the more experienced HRM practitioner. Cases, exercises, and references provide opportunities for further discussion and analysis.

As you read and consult the books in this series, I hope you share my excitement in being involved in the development of a profession that has such a significant impact on the workplace.

Monica Belcourt, PhD, CHRP
Series Editor
July 2005

About the Author

Richard J. Long is Professor of Human Resource Management at the College of Commerce of the University of Saskatchewan. He earned BCom and MBA degrees from the University of Alberta, a PhD from Cornell University in New York, and is a Certified Human Resources Professional. Dr. Long has been teaching, conducting research, and consulting in human resources management for more than 30 years, and has produced more than 100 publications based on his research and experience. He is currently on the editorial boards of *The International Journal of Human Resource Management* and *Relations Industrielles/Industrial Relations.*

Preface

The premise of this book is that an organization's compensation system can have a major impact on the success of that organization, but that the most effective compensation system may be very different from one organization to the next, and may even differ over time for the same organization. However, if there is no single compensation system that fits all organizations, this makes life very complicated for those who manage organizations. The purpose of this book is to reduce this complexity by providing a systematic framework for identifying and designing the compensation system that will add the most value to the organization. Chapter 1 lays out a road map to effective compensation that outlines this framework.

Achieving an effective compensation system requires a diagnostic approach. That is, to identify the most effective compensation system for a given organization, it is first necessary to understand that organization, its strategy, and its people. Part I of the book focuses on developing these understandings.

Beyond this, of course, it is equally necessary to understand the wide array of compensation choices that are available, to be able to predict their likely consequences when applied to a given organization, and to be able to select the most appropriate mix of compensation practices. Armed with this knowledge, along with an understanding of the constraints that define the parameters for the compensation system, a compensation strategy can then be formulated that has a high likelihood of success, as described in Part II.

However, the formulation of the compensation strategy does not mark the end of the compensation process. Determining actual compensation values for a given employee depends on a combination of the relative value of that employee's job to their employer, the value that the labour market places on that job, and the value of that employee's performance and capabilities. Part III covers the many technical processes necessary to convert the compensation strategy into a compensation system, including those for evaluating jobs, for evaluating the market, and for evaluating individual employees.

Part IV provides detailed guidance on the key issues in designing performance pay and indirect pay plans.

After all this, the compensation system needs to be implemented, managed, evaluated, and adapted, as Part V explains. If not handled effectively, these issues can jeopardize even the best compensation strategy.

This book was written for two main purposes: to help those wishing to learn how to create effective compensation systems, and to serve as a useful source of reference to compensation practitioners. In so doing, it attempts to fill a gap in the textual resources available in Canada. Other Canadian books on compensation have lacked an integrated strategic framework, and have tended to focus on either the behavioural principles in compensation or on the technical details of compensation. Both of these are important, but what is needed is a balanced, comprehensive, and integrated presentation of strategic, behavioural, and technical principles. That is what this book attempts to achieve.

The content of this book is based on a foundation of scientific research, informed by relevant theoretical principles and verified by actual organizational experiences. Although there is still much to learn about the design of effective reward and compensation systems, our state of knowledge about compensation has advanced to the point where effective use of the available knowledge will significantly increase the likelihood of organizational success.

To maximize its value as an effective learning tool, this book incorporates a number of features. Although based on a solid scientific foundation, the informal writing style, augmented by a variety of learning devices, is intended to smooth the road to effective learning. Another key feature is the overall organizing framework for the book—the "road map" to effective compensation. Getting to any destination is facilitated by a conceptual map of how to get there, and the entire book is organized around this conceptual road map.

While retaining the features that have made it the market-leading compensation text in Canada, the third edition of *Strategic Compensation in Canada* contains a number of significant changes designed to further enhance its value to readers.

So, what's new about the third edition? Besides the updating of content so necessary in a quickly changing profession, the structure of the text has been reorganized to bring the reader more quickly to compensation strategy formulation, while the detailed design issues for performance pay and indirect pay have been moved later in the book. Another major change is the division of job evaluation into two chapters, with the first dealing with general principles of job evaluation, and the second with the specific issues in designing a point system of job evaluation, by far the most commonly used type of job evaluation in Canada. This change provides the opportunity for a more detailed treatment of the process for designing a point system of job evaluation and for the specifics of designing a base pay structure.

A unique feature that keeps this text at the cutting edge of compensation practice in Canada is the Compensation Practices Survey, a survey of Canadian companies conducted by the author in 2000, and then repeated in 2004. Surveying the same firms at two points in time not only allows identification of current compensation practices, but also identification of key trends in compensation practice in Canada. Results from the Compensation Practices Survey are used throughout the text to inform discussion of compensation practices.

Features retained from the previous edition of this text include chapter learning objectives, extensive use of Canadian examples, extensive use of figures to provide visual representations of key concepts and specific forms, templates, and other practical tools, tables to convey information efficiently, margin definitions of key concepts, chapter summaries, listings of key terms, compensation exercises, and an appendix containing cases for analysis. The end-of-chapter material continues to include suggested websites to help readers access resources available through the Internet or simply to provide interesting avenues for further exploration. WWW icons in the margin (like the one shown here) indicate text for which a website URL has been provided. (But note that URLs frequently change, and that google.com is your best bet to track down a website that has gone missing or to find one that is even better than the one you were looking for!)

New features of the third edition include chapter opening vignettes based on real-life organizations to provide a taste of compensation issues coming in each chapter, as well as "Compensation Today" boxes to put compensation issues in a real-life context and "Compensation Notebook" boxes to highlight key points that flow from the chapter. End-of-chapter material now includes discussion questions, a "Using the Internet" feature, and specific questions keyed to cases in the Appendix.

Besides these learning features, a notable new feature is a link between the textual material contained in this book and the Required Professional Capabilities (RPCs) necessary for earning a Certified Human Resources Professional (CHRP) designation. As a part of the process needed to earn this Canada-wide designation, granted by the Canadian Council of Human Resources Associations, applicants must take two exams, which cover 203 Required Professional Capabilities, organized into eight subject areas. One of these subject areas is "Total Compensation."

All RPCs are listed on the Professional Assessment Resource Centre (PARC) website (**http://www.cchra-ccarh.ca/parc/en/section_3/ss33e.asp**). However, the RPCs are not numbered on PARC, which makes it difficult to reference them. For this reason, I have adopted a numbering system specifically for this book. For example, RPC 8.2 denotes the second RPC referenced in Chapter 8, and an RPC icon (like the one shown in the margin here) links a section of the textual material to a specific RPC. At the end of each chapter, the specific RPCs covered in that chapter are listed. Linking the content of this book to the RPCs will help students and practitioners in their preparations for the CHRP examinations.

This book can stand alone as the principal resource for a course. However, student learning can be further enhanced by accompanying it with *Strategic Compensation: A Simulation* (third edition), also published by Thomson Nelson, which provides students with the opportunity to design an entire compensation system, right from compensation strategy formulation to implementation of the new pay structure, complete with market-based actual dollars attached to the pay ranges. This simulation has been specifically designed by its authors (Richard J. Long and Henry Ravichander) to utilize all the steps along the road map to effective compensation, as described in the third edition of *Strategic Compensation in Canada*.

The revisions in structure and content that have been made to the third edition of *Strategic Compensation in Canada* make the fit between the text and the simulation even better. Also, at the end of each text chapter, there is a note cross-referencing that chapter to the appropriate section(s) in the simulation. To further enhance its utility, a new feature of the third edition of the compensation simulation is that it now gives the instructor a choice of two firms for analysis.

An instructor's manual for *Strategic Compensation in Canada* is available, along with power point slides, both of which can be downloaded directly from **http://hrm.nelson.com/**. In addition, a free four-month subscription to the online version of the *Canadian HR Reporter* from Carswell is available with the purchase of any new Nelson HR book. An access card with a subscription PIN is packaged with each book.

The objectives for this book are ambitious and it is up to readers to judge how effectively they have been achieved. The author would welcome any suggestions, comments, or other feedback from you, the reader. You can use e-mail (long@commerce.usask.ca), fax (306-966-2516), telephone (306-966-8398), or postal mail (College of Commerce, 25 Campus Drive, University of Saskatchewan, Saskatoon, S7N 5A7). I look forward to hearing from you!

Richard J. Long, PhD, CHRP
University of Saskatchewan

Acknowledgments

Many people have contributed to this book in a variety of ways. A project such as this draws on the knowledge, experience, and insights of a large number of researchers, scholars, and practitioners, each of whom has played a role in developing the body of knowledge reflected in this book. I would especially like to express my appreciation to the many practitioners with whom I spoke during the course of this project, whose insights and experiences greatly enrich the book.

Many people at the College of Commerce deserve recognition. First and foremost, I would like to thank the thousands of students I have had the opportunity to learn from over the years, many of whom are now themselves practitioners or scholars. It is truly a privilege to work with such a talented group of individuals, and they provide the inspiration for a project of this nature. I would particularly like to thank the students in my compensation courses, whose suggestions and feedback on earlier editions of the book have greatly improved it.

I would also like to express my gratitude to my colleagues and support staff at the College of Commerce, especially my research assistant, Sandra Friggstad, who was a model of resourcefulness and efficiency. The series editor, Monica Belcourt, provided the impetus for this project, along with much encouragement and support along the way. The third edition of this book has benefited greatly from reviews by Anne Hardacre, St. Lawrence College; John Hardisty, Sheridan College of Technology and Advanced Learning; Gerald Hunt, Ryerson University; Barbara Lipton, Seneca College of Applied Arts & Technology; and Geoffrey Smith, University of Guelph. The team at Nelson—including Anthony Rezek, Karina Hope, Anne Macdonald, and Nancy Mucklow—exhibited a high degree of professionalism and dedication in support of this project.

Finally, I owe my greatest debt to my wife, Trisha, without whose support and affection this project could never have been completed, and to my three sons, Jeffrey, Jeremy, and Michael, who help to provide the quality of family life necessary to energize a project like this.

Richard J. Long, PhD, CHRP
University of Saskatchewan

Chapter 1

A Road Map to Effective Compensation

Chapter Learning Objectives

After reading this chapter, you should be able to:

- Describe the purpose of a compensation system.
- Explain why an effective compensation system is so important to most organizations.
- Distinguish between extrinsic and intrinsic rewards.
- Distinguish between a reward system and a compensation system.
- Define *reward strategy*.
- Describe the two key aspects of a compensation strategy.
- Explain why a compensation system must be viewed in the context of the total reward system.
- Identify and explain the key criteria for evaluating a compensation system.
- Describe the steps along the road to effective compensation and understand how this book will facilitate that journey.

FUN AND GAMES AT THE EXHIBITION

A major soft-drink maker has a prominent booth at the Canadian National Exhibition in Toronto each summer. The company employs students at minimum wage to serve soft drinks to customers. There are no benefits, and the only opportunity for advancement is to become a shift supervisor, which pays only slightly more money. Shift supervisors are also temporary employees. The jobs are dull and repetitive—simply serving soft drinks all day. A manager with an enclosed office at the back of the booth is in charge but is frequently not around, because the booth operates 12 hours a day every day. Turnover is high on this job, with most employees not lasting the whole summer.

Management does not trust these employees and makes this clear in many ways. For example, to discourage employees from "pocketing" any receipts, they have sewn the pockets shut on all employee uniforms. As further insurance against employee misconduct, a count is kept of all the paper cups used in a day, and this is balanced against actual cash on hand.

Although employees are supposed to be friendly and courteous to customers, they frequently are not. Furthermore, when the manager is not around, horseplay is frequent. The supervisors, who are usually the same age as the servers, either tolerate or join in the horseplay. In some cases, it gets so bad that customers are discouraged from approaching the booth.

Many employees have also found a way to augment the meagre extrinsic rewards of the job by simply retrieving used cups from the trash and reusing them. In this way, the employees augment their income, while the official count of cups and the receipts still balance.

Not all employees participate in the horseplay or the cup scam, because this behaviour would violate their values—such as a strong work ethic or a strong sense of honesty—or simply because they are afraid of getting caught. Denying themselves access to the extrinsic rewards received by the other employees, these employees often quit, leaving only dishonest and/or irresponsible employees. These are the only employees for whom the ratio of rewards to contributions is balanced—and the only employees likely to come back next summer! Thus, the reward system used by this company ends up creating a workforce of dishonest, irresponsible employees.

Introduction

The situation at the CNE booth is certainly not what the soft drink company had in mind when it developed its reward system. It did not intend to create a system that retained irresponsible and dishonest employees while causing responsible and conscientious employees to quit. Yet that's what happened. Are such examples of dysfunctional reward systems unusual? As the following examples show, the answer is no.

- Green Giant wished to improve the quality of its canned vegetables, so it decided to give a bonus for the number of insect parts plucked from the processing line. The plan seemed to be enormously successful—hundreds and hundreds of insect parts were turned in, and large bonuses were paid. The only problem was that most of the additional insect parts came from the workers' backyards, where they were much easier to find, rather than from the canning line.
- In order to encourage its computer programmers to work efficiently, IBM rewarded them on the number of lines of computer code they produced. It took the company years to notice that IBM computer programs tended to be much longer and more inefficiently written that those of other companies.
- In order to encourage corporate executives to be diligent about pursuing the interests of their shareholders, many firms provide extensive stock options to their executives, through which executives benefit if company stock price rises. However, research shows that the more stock options are provided to executives, the more likely executives are to "cook the books," eventually leading to not only the detriment of the shareholders but also sometimes to the collapse of the firm.[1]

These examples show that reward systems can have a powerful effect on behaviour; but the behaviour we get is not always the behaviour we want. How can we design reward and compensation systems that produce the behaviour we want, while preventing the behaviour we don't want? Answering this question is what this book is all about.

However, there are no simple answers. First of all, in many fields, the employee behaviour that companies need has become more complex and requires higher performance than in the past. In general, the more complex the behaviour and the higher the level of performance required, the more complex the compensation system needs to be. Second, there are more choices of compensation practices available than ever before. Third, there is no "one best" compensation system that fits all firms. For every successful compensation practice described in Compensation Today 1.1, examples can be found where the same practice failed to produce the desired results. Understanding why compensation systems that are successful in some firms fail in other firms is an essential precondition to successful compensation design.

Your Compensation System: Asset or Liability?

Canadian firms typically spend 40 to 70 percent of their operating budgets to compensate their employees. For most firms, compensation is the single largest operating expenditure. Last year, according to Statistics Canada, employers in Canada spent over $600 billion on wages and salaries alone and another $77 billion on employee benefits. Are they getting their money's worth? Is this money being well spent?

Compensation Supports Strategy: From A to Z

Although many organizations regard their compensation systems as simply a cost, others believe that compensation can play a key role in helping the company achieve its goals and strategies. Here is a set of examples that span the alphabet:

- At Altamira Financial Services, a large mutual fund company, online brokers and mutual funds specialists are paid salaries rather than the commissions that are the norm in this business. The company believes that this reward system results in more objective customer advice.

- At Basell Canada's chemical plant in Sarnia, Ontario, pay is based not on the specific job an employee does, but on the number of jobs the worker is qualified to perform. The company believes that this radical departure from tradition results in a more flexible and efficient workforce.

- At Canadian Tire, management attributes a great deal of the firm's success to their employee profit-sharing plan, which they believe has led to a more committed and motivated workforce than is usual in the retail business.

- At Herman Miller, a large manufacturer of office furniture, the centrepiece of the compensation strategy is a gain-sharing plan, under which employees share in company productivity gains. This plan supports the company strategy of delegating a high amount of responsibility to employees.

- At the Royal Bank, management is integrating performance pay elements into compensation packages for all employees in order to support the firm's increased focus on customers and performance. Traditionally, virtually all employees in the banking industry were paid fixed salaries.

- At Sears, measures of customer satisfaction are being factored into all employees' pay in an attempt to make the organization more flexible and customer-oriented. Executives are compensated for customer and employee satisfaction, as well as for their financial achievements.

- At Starbucks, all employees, including part-time clerks, are given stock options. This supports the company strategy of committed service from employees. In most organizations, stock options are limited to a few top executives.

- At Vanderpol's Eggs in Surrey, British Columbia, management regards employee share ownership as a key means of supporting their managerial strategy, which is to create a partnership between owners and employees. They believe that employee owners will be more committed and productive.

- At Zenon Environmental, a developer of membrane-filtering technologies for water treatment, employees are provided a flexible benefits system in which they can transfer the value of benefits they don't need to benefits that they do need. This freedom of choice supports the company's values of high employee input and involvement.

In many cases, it is not. Some firms are spending too much. Others are spending too little. But while the amount being spent is important, it is not the key issue. The real question is: What is the organization receiving for its investment in wages, salaries, and benefits? Is the compensation system and the money devoted to it contributing to the achievement of organizational objectives in the fullest possible way? Does the firm have in place the compensation system that adds the greatest possible value to the company after taking costs into account?

A compensation system is one of the most powerful tools available to an employer for shaping employee behaviour and influencing company performance, yet many organizations waste this potential, viewing compensation as simply a cost to be minimized. Even worse, some firms not only waste this potential, but their compensation systems also serve to promote unproductive or even counterproductive behaviour. As we will see in the following chapters, problems of low employee motivation, poor job performance, high turnover, irresponsible behaviour, and even employee dishonesty often have roots in the compensation system. Problems as varied as organizational rigidity, inability to adapt to change, lack of innovation, conflict between organizational units, and poor customer service may also stem, at least in part, from the reward system.

What complicates matters further is that without any obvious warning signs, a compensation system that has worked well in the past can become a serious liability when circumstances change. Failure to adapt reward systems to changing circumstances can cause new strategies to falter, new organizational structures to collapse, new technologies to malfunction, and entire companies to founder. Ironically, because the reward system often affects behaviour in very subtle ways, many firms never identify their reward system as a major contributor to these problems.

The Premise of This Book

The thesis of this book is that organizations that treat their reward system as a key strategic variable and use it to support their corporate and managerial strategies receive more value from their compensation system than those that do not, resulting in superior company performance and higher achievement of organizational objectives. The purpose of this book is to help you learn to design and implement a reward and compensation strategy that best fits your particular circumstances—one that will add the greatest possible value to your organization. This chapter starts that process by clarifying some essential concepts and by presenting a "road map" of the steps along the path to effective compensation.

Role and Purpose of the Compensation System

How do you get organization members to do what the organization wants and needs them to do? This is a central problem that has bedevilled those in charge of organizations ever since their invention. And it is a problem that is growing more complex, especially for organizations whose products, services, and technologies are becoming increasingly complicated, whose environments are more dynamic and competitive, who operate in democratic and relatively affluent societies, and who require complicated behaviours and high performance levels from their members. Compensation is normally a key part of the solution, although there are many other important parts, all of which must fit together if the desired results are to be fully achieved.

At its most basic, the **purpose of a compensation system** is to help create a willingness among qualified persons to join the organization and to perform the tasks needed by the organization. What this generally means is that employees must perceive that accepting a job with a given employer will help

purpose of compensation system

to help create a willingness among qualified persons to join the organization and to perform the tasks needed by the organization

reward

anything provided by the organization that satisfies an employee need

extrinsic rewards

factors that satisfy basic human needs for survival and security, as well as social needs and needs for recognition

intrinsic rewards

factors that satisfy higher-order human needs for self-esteem, achievement, growth, and development

reward system

the mix of intrinsic and extrinsic rewards provided to its members by an organization

compensation system

the economic or monetary part of the reward system

total rewards

a compensation philosophy that considers the entire spectrum of rewards that an organization may offer to employees

reward strategy

the plan for the mix of rewards to be provided to members, along with the means through which they will be provided

base pay

the foundation pay component for most employees, usually based on some unit of time worked

performance pay

relates employee monetary rewards to some measure of individual, group, or organizational performance

them satisfy some of their own important needs. These include economic needs for the basic necessities of life but may also include needs for security, social interaction, status, achievement, recognition, and growth and development.

Extrinsic vs. Intrinsic Rewards

Anything provided by the organization that satisfies one or more of an employee's needs can be considered a **reward**. The types of rewards available in an organizational setting can be divided into two main categories: extrinsic rewards and intrinsic rewards. **Extrinsic rewards** satisfy basic needs for survival and security, as well as social needs and needs for recognition. They derive from factors surrounding the job—the job *context*—such as pay, supervisory behaviour, co-workers, and general working conditions. **Intrinsic rewards** satisfy higher-level needs for self-esteem, achievement, growth, and development. They derive from factors inherent in the work itself—the job *content*—such as the amount of challenge or interest the job provides, the degree of variety in the job, the extent to which it provides feedback and allows autonomy, as well as the meaning or significance of the work.

Reward vs. Compensation Strategy

Both extrinsic and intrinsic rewards are important to people, and if utilized effectively, each can produce important benefits for the organization. The mix of these rewards provided by an organization is termed its **reward system**. The **compensation system** deals only with the economic or monetary part of the reward system. But since behaviour is affected by the total spectrum of rewards provided by the organization and not just by compensation, the compensation system can never be regarded in isolation from the overall reward system. This practice of looking at the total spectrum of rewards, including career advancement opportunities, the intrinsic characteristics of the jobs, work/life balance, employee recognition programs, and the nature of the workplace culture, as well as compensation, is known as the **total rewards** approach to compensation, and this concept is becoming increasingly popular in Canada.[2]

Therefore, before a company starts developing its compensation system, it needs to establish a reward strategy. The **reward strategy** is the plan for the mix of rewards, both extrinsic and intrinsic, that the organization intends to provide to its members—along with the means through which they will be provided—in order to elicit the behaviours necessary for organization success. The reward strategy is the blueprint for creating the reward system.

The compensation strategy is one part of the reward strategy—the plan for creating the compensation system. The compensation system has three main components: base pay, performance pay, and indirect pay. **Base pay** is the foundation pay component for most employees and is generally based on some unit of time—an hour, a week, a month, or a year. **Performance pay** relates employee monetary rewards to some measure of individual, group, or organizational performance. **Indirect pay**, sometimes known as "employee benefits," consists of noncash items or services that satisfy a variety of specific employee needs, such as income security (e.g., disability and life insurance), health protection (e.g., medical and dental plans), or retirement security (e.g., pension plans).

indirect pay

noncash items or services that satisfy a variety of specific employee needs, sometimes known as "employee benefits"

There are two key aspects of a compensation strategy. One aspect is the mix across these three components, whether and how it will vary for different employee groups. The other is the total amount of compensation to be provided to individuals and groups. In short, "How should compensation be paid?" and "How much compensation should be paid?" are the two key questions for compensation strategy. While simple to state, these questions are extremely complex to answer.

The optimal choices for these two aspects of **compensation strategy** ultimately depend on the organizational context; but the most immediate determinant is the reward strategy. At one extreme, the reward strategy may include no compensation components whatsoever; at the other extreme, compensation may be the only appreciable reward provided by an organization.

compensation strategy

the plan for the mix and total amount of base pay, performance pay, and indirect pay to be paid to various categories of employees

Therefore, the first step in formulating a compensation strategy is to determine the role that compensation will play in the reward system. Assuming that organizations wish to minimize compensation costs whenever possible, we must first identify what other rewards are being provided by the organization and determine whether these alone are sufficient to elicit the necessary behaviour from organization members. For example, some voluntary organizations receive thousands of hours of labour from their members for no pay whatsoever. Intrinsic rewards alone are sufficient to motivate the needed behaviour.

Of course, most work organizations cannot expect to get away with providing no compensation to their members, even though some may try, such as the Screaming Tale Restaurant described in Compensation Today 1.2. (Of course, even at the Screaming Tale, servers still received some compensation for their work; it simply flowed directly from the customer to the server.) But the key point is that the amount of pay needed to attract and retain the appropriate workforce varies with the other rewards that the organization can offer.

For example, some organizations, such as banks, have traditionally offered high job security. This has enabled them to pay less than other organizations that do not offer job security while still attracting the same calibre of employee. However, if job security ceases to be a reward that banks can provide, they may need to increase pay or other rewards to attract and retain the same calibre of employee. In fact, because bank jobs are no longer as secure as they once were, and because needs for bank employee behaviour have changed, most Canadian banks have radically changed their compensation structures in recent years.

Some organizations provide jobs that have high intrinsic rewards, which may allow them to attract employees more easily than those that do not. Similarly, firms that enjoy a high level of prestige and public esteem often find it less necessary to offer as much pay as firms that do not enjoy such prestige. Firms that offer opportunities for learning and development may be able to offer less pay than those that do not.

Compensation Today 1.2

How About This Recipe for Low Labour Costs?

Several years ago, management at the Screaming Tale Restaurants in Port Hope and Belleville, Ontario, cooked up a great recipe for cutting labour costs: don't pay your staff! They eliminated payroll for serving staff by utilizing "volunteer" staff who worked only for the tips they receive. Aside from the obvious advantage of saving the wages that would otherwise be paid to servers, this arrangement also eliminated the mandatory benefits and payroll taxes that would have to be paid to the government (which can add nearly 20 percent to compensation costs), as well as the administrative work of calculating pay and preparing paycheques. Quite a competitive advantage!

However, after two "volunteers" complained, the Ontario Ministry of Labour launched an investigation to determine whether this arrangement was in violation of provincial employment standards legislation, which requires that a minimum wage be paid to all persons con-sidered to be employees. Under the law, money received as tips does not count toward this minimum wage.

One of the restaurant chain's owners, Aldo Mauro, said the restaurants had come under attack because they had learned to operate more efficiently by reducing labour costs. In an interview with *The Globe and Mail*, Mauro said his company specialized in rescuing distressed restaurants and turning them into profitable ones and used "volunteer" workers in the past throughout southeastern Ontario.

Brent Bowser, a manager of the chain's restaurant in Port Hope, said the restaurant provided a location where workers could act as service agents and do their business. The complaints, Bowser said, came from employees who didn't hustle.

Source: *Human Resources Management in Canada*. 1996.
"'Volunteer' Staff: One Way to Cut Costs." Report Bulletin #161: 3.

Of course, firms that do offer many noncompensation rewards may also choose to provide relatively high levels of compensation in order to attract high-calibre employees and elicit high commitment and performance. The key point here is that various combinations of intrinsic and extrinsic rewards need to be considered for developing the optimal reward strategy. It is only within this context that the most appropriate compensation strategy can be determined.

For example, if a firm is experiencing high turnover because employees find their jobs mind-numbingly dull, one solution might be to increase pay to make employees more reluctant to quit. But another approach might be to try to enrich the jobs to make them more interesting, thereby increasing intrinsic rewards. Of course, it may even be possible to dispense with these jobs by automating them, which eliminates the reward issue entirely.

The best choice depends on the relative costs and benefits of each approach. It is possible that the most cost-effective approach is simply to do nothing—that is, if the cost of turnover is less than the cost of increasing extrinsic or intrinsic rewards or of automating the jobs. However, other factors come into play in this decision-making process. For example, job enrichment may not only reduce turnover, but it may also increase work quality. This may tip the scales toward job enrichment or a combination approach, rather than simply increased pay.

Compensation Notebook 1.1

Goals of the Reward and Compensation System

1. Promote achievement of the organization's goals.
2. Fit with and support the organization's strategy and structure.
3. Attract and retain qualified individuals.
4. Promote desired employee behaviour.
5. Be seen as equitable.
6. Comply with the law.
7. Be within the financial means of the organization.
8. Achieve the above goals in the most cost-effective manner.

[Handwritten margin notes:]
Behaviour
Attract + retain
Fit
Financial means
Law
Equitable
Promote strategy
Cost effective.

Criteria for Success: Goals for the Compensation System

What should an optimal reward and compensation system achieve? There are eight main criteria, as shown in Compensation Notebook 1.1. First and foremost, a reward system must help promote the achievement of the organization's goals. Second, it must fit with the organization's strategy for achieving its goals and support its structure for implementing that strategy. Third, it must attract and retain individuals who possess the attributes necessary to perform the required task behaviours. Fourth, it should promote the entire spectrum of desired task behaviour for every organization member. Fifth, it should be seen as equitable by all organization members. Sixth, it must comply with all relevant laws within the jurisdictions in which the firm operates. Seventh, it must achieve all this at a cost that is within the financial means of the organization. Eighth, it should achieve these objectives in the most cost-effective manner possible.

In general, the **optimal reward system** will be the one that adds the most value to the organization, after considering all its costs. However, this does not necessarily mean that the optimal compensation system is the cheapest one. For example, for some firms, a high-wage compensation strategy may well be the one that maximizes overall company effectiveness. Of course, resource constraints may prevent a company from adopting what would otherwise be the optimal reward strategy. But in general, an effective reward system maximizes the value added relative to the resources devoted to the reward system.

Overall, the objective of this book is to help readers learn to create a reward system that will accomplish all of the criteria outlined in Compensation Notebook 1.1.

But wait a minute! Let's stop for a reality check. These goals sound very nice in theory, but realistically, is it really necessary for a firm to achieve all of them? We all probably know of successful organizations that violate several of these criteria. For instance, there are some successful organizations where it would be difficult to find *anyone* who believes that their reward system is equitable. So does this mean that an equitable reward system may be

optimal reward system
the reward system that adds the most value to the organization, after considering all its costs

desirable from a social and ethical viewpoint, but not from the viewpoint of organizational performance?

Not necessarily. As will be seen in Chapter 3, an inequitable reward system creates some undesirable consequences for an employer, such as increased employee turnover and reduced work motivation. But the costs of these consequences vary dramatically between employers. For some firms, these costs and consequences may be tolerable, while for others they may not. As will be discussed, a variety of factors determine how important an equitable reward system is to a given employer.

However, this book argues that in Canada, the circumstances under which an organization can afford an inequitable reward system are disappearing, and that for most organizations, an equitable reward system is actually a competitive advantage, if not a business necessity. But overall, organizations vary greatly in terms of how much reward and compensation systems affect their performance, as Chapter 2 will discuss.

Is it realistic to expect that a reward system will achieve all eight of the effectiveness criteria? Probably not. But these criteria still serve as goals and measures of progress. In today's rapidly changing work environment, continual evaluation of the effectiveness of the reward and compensation system is crucial for most organizations. As firms struggle to find the right answers to the compensation puzzle, the field of compensation attracts more and more interest in the business and popular media. Indeed, firms with comprehensive and attractive reward and compensation systems may even find themselves included among "Canada's 100 Top Employers," a significant advantage when it comes to employee recruitment.[3]

A Road Map to Effective Compensation

All this may sound pretty complicated so far. So what are the steps to an effective compensation system? Figure 1.1 provides a "road map" to follow and links each step along the road to the section of the book that provides guidance for that step.

Step I: Understand Your Organization and Your People

The first step in creating an effective compensation system is to understand the organizational context within which it will operate. The reward system is just one part of the total organizational system, and each part must fit with and support the other parts. There are several viable patterns into which these parts can be arranged, and each pattern constitutes one type of managerial strategy.

For success, each managerial strategy relies on a different reward and compensation strategy. The most appropriate managerial strategy is in turn determined by a number of key contextual factors, such as the nature of the firm's environment, its corporate strategy, its technology, its size, and, of course, its people. A key implication of this mix of factors is that whenever one factor changes, it can create a need for many other organizational

FIGURE 1.1

A Road Map to Effective Compensation

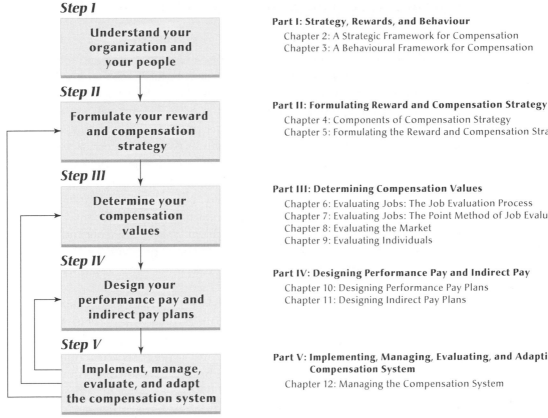

Step I
Understand your organization and your people

Step II
Formulate your reward and compensation strategy

Step III
Determine your compensation values

Step IV
Design your performance pay and indirect pay plans

Step V
Implement, manage, evaluate, and adapt the compensation system

Part I: Strategy, Rewards, and Behaviour
Chapter 2: A Strategic Framework for Compensation
Chapter 3: A Behavioural Framework for Compensation

Part II: Formulating Reward and Compensation Strategy
Chapter 4: Components of Compensation Strategy
Chapter 5: Formulating the Reward and Compensation Strategy

Part III: Determining Compensation Values
Chapter 6: Evaluating Jobs: The Job Evaluation Process
Chapter 7: Evaluating Jobs: The Point Method of Job Evaluation
Chapter 8: Evaluating the Market
Chapter 9: Evaluating Individuals

Part IV: Designing Performance Pay and Indirect Pay
Chapter 10: Designing Performance Pay Plans
Chapter 11: Designing Indirect Pay Plans

Part V: Implementing, Managing, Evaluating, and Adapting the Compensation System
Chapter 12: Managing the Compensation System

changes, including changes to the reward and compensation system. The purpose of Chapter 2 ("A Strategic Framework for Compensation") is to provide a conceptual toolkit for understanding the organizational context and identifying the compensation system that best fits that context.

Another essential concept to understand is the link between reward systems and human behaviour. There are three main behaviours desirable to an organization—membership behaviour, task behaviour, and citizenship behaviour—but the importance of each of these can vary dramatically for different organizations. It is crucial to understand what specific attitudes and behaviours are needed by your organization and the role that the reward system can play in eliciting these behaviours.

Besides understanding how reward systems can promote desired behaviours, it is also important to understand how reward systems can unintentionally generate *undesirable* attitudes and behaviours. As Chapter 3 explains, this is a surprisingly common phenomenon. The purpose of

Chapter 3 ("A Behavioural Framework for Compensation") is to provide a conceptual toolkit for understanding how compensation relates to employee behaviour.

Step II: Formulate Your Reward and Compensation Strategy

The next step in creating an effective compensation system is to formulate your reward and compensation strategy—to determine the mix of compensation components to include in your system and the total level of compensation to provide, relative to other employers. To determine the compensation mix, you must understand what compensation options are available, their advantages and disadvantages, and the consequences each produces. There are three main compensation components—base pay, performance pay, and indirect pay—and Chapter 4 ("Components of Compensation Strategy") examines these components, along with the key elements and choices available within each component. The purpose of Chapter 4 is to describe the available choices in sufficient detail to allow you to decide the mix of components and elements to include in a reward strategy that best fits your organization. The technical details for designing and implementing these components are described later in the book.

Based on the concepts provided in the first four chapters, you can identify the kinds of behaviour your organization needs and then choose the most appropriate combination of rewards (the reward strategy) to elicit this behaviour. A major purpose of the reward strategy is to define the role that compensation is expected to play in bringing about the desired behaviour. From this reward strategy, you will develop specific compensation objectives.

You can then formulate a compensation strategy that defines the mix of compensation components (along with the specific elements of these components) and the compensation level strategy that best fits your organization. But to do this effectively, you must understand the constraints on your organization that define the parameters within which choices can be made. These include legal constraints, labour market constraints, product/service market constraints, and constraints on the financial resources available to the organization. Chapter 5 ("Formulating the Reward and Compensation Strategy") guides you through this process.

Step III: Determine Your Compensation Values

Once you have formulated the compensation strategy, you must then establish the process for determining actual dollar values for jobs and for individual employees. The dollar value of compensation to be provided to a specific employee is typically determined by a combination of three factors: (1) the value of the employee's assigned job relative to other jobs in the firm, usually determined by a process called job evaluation; (2) the value of the employee's job relative to what other firms are paying for this job, usually determined by analyzing labour market data; and (3) the value of the employee's job performance relative to other employees performing the same job, usually determined by a process called performance appraisal. In some cases, the value of the employee's skills and capabilities will also be factored in, through what is known as a pay-for-knowledge system.

However, not all firms will include all these practices in their compensation strategy. For compensation strategies in which job evaluation plays a role, Chapters 6 ("Evaluating Jobs: The Job Evaluation Process") and 7 ("Evaluating Jobs: The Point Method of Job Evaluation") provide a description of the key steps and procedures in the job evaluation process. For compensation strategies in which compensation is calibrated to the "going market rates," Chapter 8 ("Evaluating the Market") describes how to gather and apply labour market data to determine these rates. Finally, for those compensation strategies that include performance appraisals or pay-for-knowledge systems, Chapter 9 ("Evaluating Individuals") describes how to design these systems.

Step IV: Design Your Performance Pay and Indirect Pay Plans

The great majority of firms include some type of performance pay in their compensation mix. Performance pay can be based on the performance of individual employees, groups or teams of employees, or the organization as a whole. Chapter 10 ("Designing Performance Pay Plans") provides guidance on designing the main types of performance pay plans.

Most firms also include some form of indirect pay (often known as "employee benefits") in the compensation mix. Chapter 11 ("Designing Indirect Pay Plans") provides specific guidance for designing an indirect pay plan that will serve company needs.

Step V: Implement, Manage, Evaluate, and Adapt the Compensation System

Once developed, the compensation system needs to be implemented and then managed on an ongoing basis. Key issues here include procedures for implementing the system, communicating the system, dealing with compensation problems, budgeting, and controlling compensation costs.

In addition, after implementation, the compensation system needs to be continually evaluated to determine whether it is accomplishing the company's objectives and whether it is doing so in the most cost-effective manner possible. If not, then some of the technical aspects of the compensation system may need to be changed, or the compensation and rewards strategy may need to be reworked entirely, as the feedback loops in Figure 1.1 illustrate.

Furthermore, if the circumstances facing the organization change, or if the technology, strategy, or structure of the organization changes, these changes may trigger a need for changes to the compensation strategy or system. In addition, the organization must have a way of detecting unintended negative consequences generated by the compensation system. The final chapter in this book, Chapter 12 ("Managing the Compensation System"), provides guidance on how to deal with all of these issues.

The Context of Compensation Management

Except for voluntary organizations, all organizations—whether large or small—must deal with compensation issues.

In small organizations, the responsibility for compensation strategy usually resides with the owner or chief executive officer, and compensation administration is often contracted out to firms that specialize in payroll management.

In larger organizations, the compensation function normally resides within the Human Resources Department, with the head of that department bearing ultimate responsibility for the successful operation of the compensation system. Typically, compensation strategy is formulated by the head of HR, based on the recommendations of the manager of compensation; but because it is such a crucial issue for most organizations, the approval of top management (and often the board) is always required for major changes to compensation strategy.

Within a large firm, there are many specialized roles for compensation specialists. These include job analysts, who develop job descriptions and conduct job evaluations; benefits specialists, who oversee the benefits plans; and compensation analysts, who evaluate market data. Compensation managers are responsible for overseeing the administration of the compensation system and recommending, designing, and implementing compensation policies. Compensation Today 1.3 gives three examples of HR jobs that require extensive knowledge of compensation, along with their pay levels.

Responsibility for specialized aspects of compensation, such as evaluating the market or managing benefits plans, is often contracted to compensation consulting firms. Compensation consulting firms have grown in number as a result of the increasing complexity of compensation systems and have become an important source of employment for compensation professionals.

In recognition of its importance within the human resources field, compensation has been designated as one of the eight main categories of professional capabilities required for the Certified Human Resource Professional (CHRP) designation in Canada. To receive this designation, a candidate must successfully demonstrate expertise in these eight categories of capabilities through a national testing process conducted by the Canadian Council of Human Resources Associations. Within the subject area of compensation, there are 31 **required professional capabilities (RPCs).** Whenever material in this book directly relates to one of these RPCs, an RPC icon will appear in the margin, keyed to a specific RPC listed at the end of the chapter.

required professional capabilities (RPCs)

a set of capabilities designated by the Canadian Council of Human Resources Associations as essential for Human Resources practitioners and required for designation as a Certified Human Resources Professional (CHRP)

Summary

This chapter explains the purpose of a compensation system, its relationship to the broader reward system of an organization, and the key elements of a compensation strategy. It discusses the goals of an effective reward and

Examples of Jobs That Require Compensation Knowledge

Compensation Analyst

Under the direction of the manager of compensation, helps design and administer company compensation programs, such as base pay, performance pay, and benefits. May conduct job analyses and job evaluations. May analyze market data to determine competitive pay levels. May analyze benefits programs to determine utility and efficiency. May supervise clerks that carry out routine compensation procedures. Requires a university degree with course work in related areas. CHRP and appropriate experience are assets.

Manager of Compensation

Under the direction of the Vice-President of Human Resources, is responsible for managing the operation of the compensation system, including staffing, performance review, staff training and development, and the technical aspects of compensation management. Is responsible for monitoring the effectiveness of compensation policies, making necessary adjustments, and recommending and implementing new compensation policies. Assists the Vice-President of Human Resources in evaluating and formulating compensation strategy. Requires a university degree with coursework in related areas and at least five years experience in the field. CHRP an asset.

Vice-President of Human Resources

Under the direction of top management, ensures the acquisition, training, motivation, and retention of personnel needed for achievement of corporate goals.

Evaluates human resource management strategy and organization design and recommends new human resource policies to top management when appropriate. Recommends the most effective recruitment, selection, training, and compensation strategies and oversees the implementation of approved policies and programs. Formulates the recommended compensation budget for upcoming year. Responsible for the selection, appraisal, and coaching of subordinate human resources managers, achieving departmental objectives, and meeting departmental budget goals. Assists top management and other departments in dealing effectively with human resource issues and problems and provides support to top management in identifying strategic issues affecting the company. Requires a university degree in business or commerce, with specialization in human resources, at least 10 years of HR management experience, and a CHRP designation.

Since this book is a compensation text, your next thought probably is (or should be): What are these jobs worth in dollars? As subsequent chapters show, there are many ways to answer this question. However, a quick and easy way is to consult a website that specializes in providing market values for various jobs. For example, Salary Wizard suggests that the typical range of cash compensation (base pay plus performance pay) for a compensation analyst is about $43,000 to $53,000 (based on a national average across Canada); for a compensation manager, $55,000 to $90,000; and for a head of human resources, $115,000 to $177,000.

compensation strategy, and presents a road map for developing an effective compensation system. The chapter concludes with a brief discussion of the context of compensation management within a firm and within the field of human resources management. This chapter sets the stage for Chapter 2, which provides a strategic framework for developing the reward and compensation system that best fits a given firm; and Chapter 3, which provides a behavioural framework for developing the reward and compensation system most likely to produce employee behaviour that the firm needs.

Key Terms

base pay, 6

compensation strategy, 7

compensation system, 6

extrinsic rewards, 6

indirect pay, 7

intrinsic rewards, 6

optimal reward system, 9

performance pay, 6

purpose of compensation system, 5

required professional capabilities (RPCs), 14

reward, 6

reward strategy, 6

reward system, 6

total rewards, 6

Web Links

For the latest information on labour income in Canada, go to Statistics Canada's website at **http://www.statcan.ca**. (p. 3)

To get a taste of compensation issues making the news, go to **http://www. hrreporter.com** and click on "compensation" or "benefits." (p. 10)

To identify employers of choice in Canada, go to **http://www.CanadasTop100. com**. (p. 10)

To check on requirements for the CHRP designation at the Canadian Council of Human Resources Associations website, go to **http://www.cchra-ccarh. ca/parc/en/default.asp**. (p. 14)

To check on pay levels for various jobs in Canada using Salary Wizard, go to **http://workingcanada.salary.com/csalarywizard**. (p. 15)

RPC Icon

RPC 1.1 Identifies and develops the philosophy, strategy, and policy of a total compensation package that is consistent with the organization's goals. This RPC is accomplished within the context of the legal, regulatory, taxation, and community framework.

Discussion Questions

1. Discuss why an effective compensation system is so important to most organizations.
2. Discuss why a compensation system must be viewed in the context of the total reward system.

Using the Internet

1. Using Salary Wizard (**http://workingcanada.salary.com/csalarywizard**), what conclusions can you draw about variations in pay level in different parts of Canada? Pick two or three different jobs to make your comparisons across the country.

2. Using Salary Wizard (**http://workingcanada.salary.com/csalarywizard**), check how much the pay ranges for the jobs in Compensation Today 1.3 have changed since 2005, the year in which this book's salary data was collected.

Exercises

1. In a small group, describe to each other the compensation system at your most recent job, in terms of base pay, performance pay, and indirect pay. Then discuss your reactions to this system. Do you believe it was equitable? What impact did it have on your motivation and commitment to the organization? How could it have been improved? Of the compensation systems described by your group members, which appeared to be the most effective, and why?

2. Consider the pay system in use for servers at the Screaming Tale Restaurant, described in Compensation Today 1.2. Do you believe that it meets the criteria for effectiveness identified in Compensation Notebook 1.1? Do you consider it an effective system for this restaurant? Is it fair to servers? Can you think of any possible disadvantages or negative consequences that this system could cause for the employer?

Case Question

1. Read "Henderson Printing" in the Appendix. What is your assessment of the compensation system in place there? Do you think it meets the criteria for an effective compensation system set out in Compensation Notebook 1.1? Which criteria does it meet, and which does it violate?

Simulation Cross-Reference

If you are using *Strategic Compensation: A Simulation* in conjunction with this text, you will find that the concepts in Chapter 1 are helpful in preparing Section A of the simulation.

Endnotes

1. Harris Jared, and Philip Bromiley. 2003. "Incentives to Cheat: Executive Compensation and Corporate Malfeasance." Paper presented at the 2003 Strategic Management Society International Conference, Baltimore, Maryland.
2. Humber, Todd. 2005. "Total Rewards: One Concept, Many Monikers." *Canadian HR Reporter*, February 14: R3.
3. Yerema, Richard. 2005. *Canada's Top 100 Employers*. Toronto: Mediacorp.

Strategy, Rewards, and Behaviour

Chapter

2

A Strategic Framework for Compensation

Chapter Learning Objectives

After reading this chapter, you should be able to:

- Explain why the same compensation system may be a success in one firm but a failure in another.
- Describe an organizational system.
- Explain how the strategic framework for compensation can be used as a tool for designing effective reward and compensation systems.
- Describe the three main sets of elements in the strategic compensation framework, and explain how they relate to one another.
- Describe the three main managerial strategies that organizations can adopt, and explain the implications for the most effective reward and compensation system.
- Describe the five main determinants of managerial strategy, and explain how they can be used to select the most appropriate managerial strategy.
- Analyze any organization to determine the most appropriate managerial strategy.
- Discuss how conditions in North America changed during the twentieth century, and explain how this has affected today's managerial and compensation strategies.

L-S Electrogalvanizing (LSE) produces corrosion-resistant sheet steel for the automotive industry. The firm receives large coils of sheet steel from steel mills, unrolls and cleans them, and then applies a coating of zinc to precise specifications. Although the process is highly automated, many things can go wrong, and mistakes are very costly. Rather than hourly pay geared to the specific task that a worker does (such as packaging or process control), which is the norm in this industry, LSE plant workers are paid salaries, with their salary level based on the number of different plant jobs that they are qualified to perform (a "pay-for-knowledge" system). To maintain their skills, workers rotate through the various plant jobs. This means that someone working at one of the traditionally lower-paying jobs, such as packaging, may be earning twice the standard industry rate for this same job. On top of this, employees receive an excellent benefits package, as well as gain-sharing bonuses based on plant productivity, and profit-sharing bonuses based on company performance. Overall, LSE pays its workers far more than its competitors. Are you surprised to learn that almost no one ever quits?

In contrast, B.C. Rogers Processors operates a plant that converts live chickens into packages of chicken parts. All work is centred around "the chain" on which the chickens are hung, which rattles past line workers at a rate of 90 birds per minute. Workers posted along the chain perform various operations on the chickens as they pass by, such as snipping their heads off or reaching in and yanking out their innards. Unlike LSE, B.C. Rogers hasn't implemented any pay innovations and simply pays workers an hourly wage not much above the legal minimum. Employee benefits are virtually nonexistent. Are you surprised to learn that employee turnover often exceeds 100 percent a year?

Introduction

Let's start this chapter with a little contest. The reward for winning? Strictly intrinsic. As you noticed, the two firms discussed above have completely different compensation systems. Here's your skill-testing question: Which compensation system is the most effective? Note that this question does not ask you to pick the system that you like the most, but the one that best fits our definition of an effective compensation system. As we discussed in Chapter 1, the most effective compensation system for a given firm is the one that adds the most value to the organization, after considering all its costs.

So back to the question. Which of these compensation systems do you think is the most effective? LSE sounds like a workers' paradise. But how can the company stay competitive when it pays its workers so much more than its competitors pay theirs? And while B.C. Rogers certainly can't be accused of overpaying its workers, wouldn't that turnover rate cause serious problems?

Aha, you think, maybe this is a trick question, and neither system is effective! But in fact, despite being so different, *both* compensation systems are effective. How can this be? The answer is that they each *fit* the organization and its strategy. If these firms were to trade compensation systems, they would both soon be as dead as the B.C. Rogers chickens.

How can a compensation system that is a great success in one organization be a miserable flop in another? And how do you know in advance whether a particular type of compensation system will be successful for your organization? These are puzzles that must be solved if you want to successfully design or redesign a compensation system.

The Concept of Fit

The solution to these puzzles is *fit*. Ultimately, the success or failure of any reward system depends on how well it fits the organizational context and total organizational system. Therefore, to successfully design, manage, and modify any reward system, you must understand this context and how it links to the reward system.

But what are the key aspects of the organizational context, and exactly how do they relate to reward strategy? The purpose of this chapter is to address that question by developing a framework that identifies the key aspects of the organizational context and then illustrates how each of them affects the reward system. This framework describes three managerial strategies an organization can adopt and shows how each of these strategies relates to an organization's structure and its best-fit reward system. The framework then identifies the determinants of managerial strategy, since these will ultimately determine the most appropriate reward strategy. Finally, the chapter ends with a discussion of trends in managerial strategies and compensation systems. But first, you need to understand some basic organizational concepts.

Organizations as Systems

As Figure 2.1 illustrates, **organizations** are systems that apply procedures to a set of resources in order to transform input materials into outputs that

organizations

systems that apply procedures to a set of resources to transform inputs into valued outputs

FIGURE 2.1

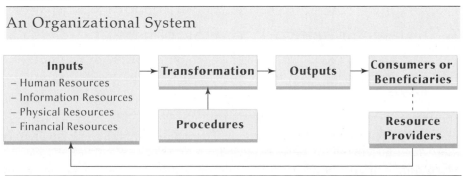

An Organizational System

Inputs
– Human Resources
– Information Resources
– Physical Resources
– Financial Resources

→ **Transformation** → **Outputs** → **Consumers or Beneficiaries**

Procedures

Resource Providers

Chapter 2: A Strategic Framework for Compensation

someone values. Automakers transform thousands of component parts into automobiles. Hospitals transform sick people into well people. An accounting firm transforms a shoebox full of receipts, invoices, and bank records into a set of financial statements. Prisons transform homicidal maniacs who are a threat to society into captive homicidal maniacs. The procedures and resources used to carry out these transformation processes constitute the **technology** of the organization.

If no one values the system output enough to be willing to provide the resources necessary for the transformation process, then the organization will cease to operate. In a business organization, the consumer of the output normally provides the resources (usually money) that can be used to acquire the other necessary resources. However, in other types of organizations, such as hospitals or public schools, the direct consumer of the output (i.e., patients or students) may provide few or none of the resources necessary for the organization to continue. But the point is that even if they themselves do not consume the output, someone or some group somewhere must value the outputs of the organization enough to provide the resources necessary for continuation. Of course, in the case of hospitals and public schools, this group is taxpayers.

Organizations typically use four types of resources in the transformation process—human, information, physical, and financial. Management's role is to acquire these resources, combine and deploy them to achieve organizational goals, and carry out the transformation process as efficiently as possible. Doing so requires some type of strategy for achievement of organizational goals. The **corporate strategy** (sometimes known as the competitive or business strategy) is the organization's plan for how it will achieve its goals. The **organization structure** is the vehicle for execution of this strategy and is composed of several structural dimensions or variables. The purpose of the organization structure is to generate the behaviours necessary to carry out the organization's strategy.

For the organizational system to be effective, the corporate strategy and organization structure must fit with certain other key variables, including the type of environment in which the organization operates, the type of technology it uses, the size of the organization, and the nature of the people employed. This is known as the **contingency approach to organization design**,[1] and it is the foundation for the strategic framework presented in this chapter.

A Strategic Framework for Compensation

> Pay is a "red phone." When it rings, employees want to find out who is on the other end and what is being said. The goal is to wire the red phone to company strategy.[2]

Sounds good. So how exactly do you do that? Properly wiring "the red phone" is more complex than it sounds. Fortunately, this chapter develops a tool to do just that. But be prepared! Initially, this tool will only seem to make things more complicated! But once you invest the effort necessary to

---

technology

the procedures and resources used by an organization to transform inputs into outputs

corporate strategy

an organization's plan for how it will achieve its goals

organization structure

the means through which an organization generates the behaviours necessary to execute its corporate strategy

contingency approach to organization design

an approach to organization design based on the premise that the best type of structure for an organization depends on the key contingencies (contextual variables) associated with that organization

FIGURE 2.2

A Strategic Framework for Compensation

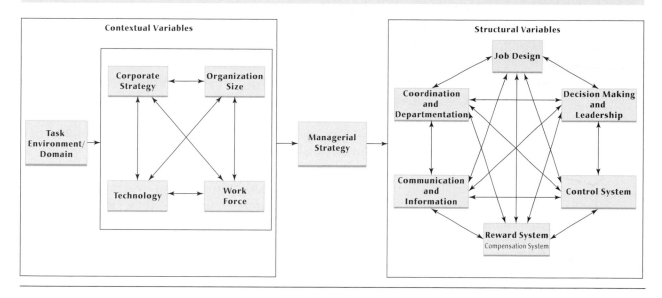

understand it, you should find it an indispensable part of your conceptual tool kit for building effective compensation systems.

Figure 2.2 presents the strategic framework. Two main sets of variables are shown—contextual and structural—linked by managerial strategy. As the diagram shows, the reward system is only one of the variables that make up the organization's structure. To be effective, the reward system must fit with the other structural variables, as well as with the managerial strategy, which must in turn fit with the contextual variables. But what do all the double-sided arrows mean? Simply that all of the structural variables are interrelated and must fit with each other if the organization is to be effective. The same is true for the contextual variables.

The first step in understanding how to use this framework is to understand each of these components.

Structural Variables

To generate the behaviours necessary to execute a corporate strategy, an organization structure needs to do two main things. It first needs to *divide* the total task into manageable subtasks (a process sometimes known as "differentiation"), and then it needs to *coordinate* the completion of these subtasks so that they fit together to accomplish the total task of the organization (a process sometimes known as "integration").

An effective organization structure serves to reduce internal and external uncertainty for the organization. It reduces internal uncertainty by structuring and directing employee behaviour. It reduces external uncertainty by creating specialized units to interpret and deal with key aspects of the firm's environment and bring appropriate information to organizational decision makers. For example, a firm may create a marketing department to learn about and

job design

a dimension of organization structure that describes the manner in which the total task of an organization is divided into separate jobs

coordination and departmentation

a dimension of organization structure that describes the methods used to coordinate the work of individual employees and subunits in an organization

decision-making and leadership structure

a dimension of organization structure that describes the nature of the decision-making and leadership processes used in an organization

communication and information structure

a dimension of organization structure that describes the nature of and methods for communication in an organization

control structure

a dimension of organization structure that describes the nature of the processes used to control employee behaviour in an organization

managerial strategy

the combination of structural variables adopted by an organization

contextual variables

factors in the firm's context that indicate the most appropriate managerial strategy and organizational structure

deal with its customers, a purchasing department to learn about and deal with its suppliers, and an economic forecasting unit to help understand economic trends and how they affect the organization.

The organization structure consists of a number of separate variables or dimensions. These variables are the *levers* that are used to produce the behaviour desired by the organization. Besides the reward system, there are five other structural variables. **Job design** describes the manner in which the total amount of work to be done is divided into subtasks that can be handled by individual workers. **Coordination and departmentation** mechanisms are the methods used to ensure that the work of individual employees fits together such that the overall task is accomplished. The **decision-making and leadership structure** comprises the mechanisms through which the organization's decisions are made and the type of leadership role played by those in managerial positions. The **communication and information structure** describes the methods used to communicate information throughout the organization and the amount and kinds of information to be transmitted. The **control structure** is the means used to ensure that organization members are actually doing what they are supposed to do.

Managerial Strategy

The structural variables described above can be arranged in a virtually limitless number of ways. However, over time, three main patterns, or managerial strategies, have emerged. Each of these managerial strategies represents a particular combination of structural variables that has proved to be successful in the right circumstances. The particular **managerial strategy** used by a given firm is the most important single determinant of what will or will not be a successful reward system for that firm. The specific linkages between managerial strategies and the structural variables, including reward systems, are discussed in more detail later in the chapter.

Contextual Variables

So what determines the most appropriate managerial strategy? The five main **contextual variables** are shown in Figure 2.2—the organization's environment, corporate strategy, technology, size, and workforce. Each of these is discussed in more detail later in the chapter, along with its relationship to managerial strategy.

But if contextual variables differ for different organizations, how are the contextual variables themselves determined? It all starts with organizational goals. When founders create an organization, they have certain goals for their organization. In a business enterprise, the goals may include making money and/or providing employment for the owner. In a governmental organization, the goal may be to satisfy some collective need, such as the need for fire or police protection, or for education. In a not-for-profit enterprise, the goal may be to address some important need not currently being met. For example, the Canadian Cancer Society was created to serve the needs of those who have cancer and to find a way to cure or prevent cancer. UNICEF was created to help serve the needs of children in poverty-stricken areas.

From the interaction between the goals of the founders and the general environment in which they are located, the organization's *domain* emerges. The **domain** defines the specific products or services to be offered by the organization. The domain also defines the **task environment,** which is the specific slice of the general environment of particular relevance to the organization. Key elements of the task environment include the customers or clients of the organization, as well as competitors, suppliers, and regulatory agencies.

Once a firm has established its goals and defined its domain, it needs to formulate a plan for achieving its goals (the corporate strategy). Decisions can then be made about the most appropriate type of technology to produce the product or service, the most appropriate size for the organization, and the nature of the workforce needed. These decisions need to be seen as interrelated, since changes in one variable affect each of the others. For example, a change in the firm's technology may necessitate changes to its corporate strategy and the nature of its workforce, as well as to the size of the firm.

The key point about contextual variables is that a change in any of them may trigger a need for a change in the reward system. Thus, a company that changes its corporate strategy, implements a new technology, grows in size, or experiences a change in its workforce may need a new reward strategy. A company attempting to introduce work teams or flexible production almost always needs to change its reward system. A firm striving to change its managerial strategy usually needs to change its reward system. As discussed earlier, failure to make the right changes to the reward system in the light of these other changes may have dire consequences. Because organizations are systems, change in one aspect of the organization almost inevitably has implications for other parts of the organization.

Managerial Strategies and Reward Systems

As organizations have evolved, three main patterns of management, or managerial strategies, have emerged.[3] Each of these strategies reflects different assumptions about employees and how they should be managed. Adherents of the **classical managerial strategy** believe that people are inherently lazy, dislike work, and would prefer to get as much as they possibly can from a work relationship while giving as little as possible. According to this perspective, the only way to get people to work is to create circumstances under which satisfaction of their economic needs becomes threatened if they do not behave as the organization wants them to. Essentially, this school of thought views employees as potentially dishonest shirkers who need to be tightly controlled if the organization is going to be sure of getting any work out of them.

Adherents of the **human relations managerial strategy** agree with the classical managers that people inherently dislike work, but they differ in that they believe people can be motivated by appealing to their social needs. They have observed that the classical school of thought frequently creates an adversarial and unpleasant relationship between management and workers and that peer groups of workers often form within the firm in order to satisfy human needs unmet or threatened by the formal organization.

domain

describes the specific products or services offered by a given organization

task environment

the portion of the general environment that has direct relevance to a given organization

RPC 2.1

classical managerial strategy

an approach to management that assumes most employees inherently dislike work but can be induced to work in order to satisfy their economic needs

human relations managerial strategy

an approach to management that assumes most employees inherently dislike work but can be induced to work in order to satisfy their social needs

Chapter 2: A Strategic Framework for Compensation

These peer groups often have more influence than management over the workers and often work against management. But by treating employees with fairness and consideration and supporting and encouraging peer groups of workers (rather than trying to break them up, which would be the classical approach), human relations managers believe that positive employee norms can develop. Employees work loyally and comply with these norms out of gratitude for the satisfying social environment the firm provides. The human relations view of employees tends toward paternalism—the organization is like a family, in which employees are like children who need to be treated kindly but firmly by a benevolent employer who knows what is best for them and the organization.

high-involvement managerial strategy

an approach to management that assumes that work can be intrinsically motivating if the organization is structured properly

The **high-involvement managerial strategy**[4] differs from the previous two schools in its belief that if jobs are structured correctly, people can actually enjoy and be motivated intrinsically by their work. Adherents believe that people are motivated by needs for interesting work, challenge, autonomy, personal growth, and professional development, and that employees can exercise self-control if the organization provides these conditions while treating employees fairly and equitably. (You should be aware that the high-involvement managerial strategy has several labels. The "mutual gains enterprise,"[5] the "high-performance work system,"[6] "open book management,"[7] and "high commitment management"[8] are all very similar to the "high-involvement" managerial strategy described here.)

Given the disparate assumptions that each of the three managerial strategies holds about employees, it is not surprising that organizations will be structured very differently, depending on their managerial strategy. Compensation Notebook 2.1 summarizes how each of the three managerial strategies compares in terms of the six main dimensions of organization structure.

Classical Managerial Strategy

Under the classical managerial strategy, thinking is completely separated from doing. Jobs are designed with only a few basic elements so they can be supervised closely and so that employees can be replaced easily if they quit or are dismissed. The specific duties and work methods for each job are planned and defined in detail by management, since employees cannot be trusted to perform effectively without doing so. Jobs are arranged in strict, hierarchical, pyramidal fashion because of the overriding need for accountability. Coordination is always handled vertically by a common superior. Employees are organized by function; for example, all engineers are put into one department, all marketers in another department, and all production staff in another department.

The major role of the supervisor is to control and evaluate subordinates, who will try to shirk and goof off if given the opportunity, according to the theory's assumptions. Decisions are made at a relatively high level in the organization, and the main leadership role is autocratic with a high emphasis on tasks. Essentially, senior management makes the decisions, middle management transmits them, and first-line management (supervisors) enforces them.

Control is exercised through close supervision and the threat of punitive action should the employee deviate from organizational policies. There is often a large body of formal rules and procedures which are strictly enforced.

humans dislike work but do it to satisy economic needs

humans dislike but do it to meet social needs

work can be intrinsically motivating if properly structured

Comparison of the Three Managerial Strategies and Their Structural Implications

Structural Variable	Classical Managerial Strategy	Human Relations Managerial Strategy	High-Involvement Managerial Strategy
Job Design	Thinking separate from doing; narrow, fragmented jobs.	Similar to classical, but job design may allow more social contact.	Joint planning and goal setting; broader, more meaningful jobs.
Coordination and Departmentation	Strict, formalized pyramidal hierarchy emphasizing accountability; vertical coordination (by superiors); departmentation by function.	Similar to classical; possibly use of some work teams.	Horizontal coordination (by employees) in addition to vertical coordination; use of work teams; departmentation by product, customer, project, or matrix.
Control	External—through supervision, rules, punishments, and some extrinsic rewards.	External—through use of social or peer pressure, rules, some extrinsic rewards.	Internal—through intrinsic rewards from the work itself, self-control through internalized commitment.
Communication	Formal and vertical; restricted.	Use of formal and informal (grapevine) communication; some restriction.	High amount of vertical and horizontal communication; less formal; climate of open communication.
Decision Making and Leadership	Autocratic decision making; task-oriented; controlling supervisory role.	Autocratic decision-making with minor consultation; employee-oriented; controlling supervisory role.	Participative or democratic decision style; both task- and employee-oriented; facilitator supervisory role.
Reward Systems	Extrinsic economic rewards related to individual output (e.g., piece rates, commissions) or to time worked (e.g., hourly pay).	Extrinsic economic rewards, unrelated to performance; liberal fringe benefits (indirect pay) and loyalty rewards; social rewards.	Intrinsic rewards from job itself; pay for knowledge; extrinsic rewards focusing on group/organization performance (e.g., gain sharing, profit sharing, stock ownership.)

Control is also frequently embedded in the technology or the work process itself, as in the case of assembly lines, which do not allow deviation from the standard procedures.

Communication is quite low, with an emphasis on a downward vertical flow, and tends to be formal. Informal communication (i.e., the "grapevine") is discouraged, although, ironically, the grapevine usually flourishes as employees attempt to fill in the information gaps. Generally, management disseminates as little information as possible, in the belief that information is power. Communication upwards from employees is not generally sought, and when sought, is likely minimal and distorted, due to the adversarial relations.

Since management's key task is to minimize variations in employee behaviour from the specified behaviour, the reward system is quite simple—an extrinsic (economic) reward. Wherever feasible, a system that ties pay directly to output—such as piece rates or sales commissions—is used. Where this is not feasible, pay is tied directly to hours of work. In both cases, pay is no higher than absolutely necessary to attract a sufficient flow of job applicants. Little indirect pay is used, because it is not tied to individual performance, and management does not see much value in incurring large benefits costs in order to promote loyalty and reduce turnover. This is because classical organizations are structured to minimize the cost of turnover: with narrow jobs, workers are easy to replace, train, and supervise. Compensation Today 2.1 illustrates how one firm, Electronic Banking System Inc., has taken the classical strategy about as far as anyone could take it.

One exception to the general rule about poor compensation in classical organizations occurs in unionized classical firms. Because of the low consideration for worker needs in most classical firms and their adversarial worker–management relations, workers in these organizations often become unionized in an attempt to protect their interests. These unions are often able to win substantially higher compensation packages than management would wish to provide, often including extensive benefits packages. This often causes non-union classical firms to provide more compensation than they would wish, in order to attract employees and serve as a union-avoidance tactic. Ironically, these classical firms may end up paying very well indeed, which is precisely the opposite of their compensation goal!

Human Relations Managerial Strategy

The human relations approach is similar to the classical approach in terms of job design, although management attempts to arrange jobs to allow social interaction among employees. This approach is also similar to the classical school in the way it coordinates employees. But the supervisor's role is much more complicated than it is in the classical school. Leadership is still autocratic in the sense that senior management makes all the important decisions; but there is a much greater attempt to "sell" the decisions, something the classical manager does not bother with.

Human relations managers understand that people like to feel they have some control over their work lives, and so they attempt to provide a *feeling* that employees have some influence over company decisions (although employees typically have little *real* influence). Therefore, employees are sometimes asked for their opinions on decisions, or they are permitted to make a number of minor, inconsequential decisions. In addition to attempting to sell decisions, the supervisor also has the added task of exhibiting a high concern for people and fostering a pleasant atmosphere. Overall, the role of the leader is controlling but employee-oriented.

In the human relations school of thought, control is still external but is preferably exercised through the work group. The human relations

Compensation Today 2.1

Control Is an Art Form at EBS

Because classical organizations don't believe that employees can be trusted to put in an honest day's work on their own volition, they often go to great lengths to structure themselves to constrain workers from doing anything except the desired behaviour. Ron Edens, president of Electronic Banking System Inc. (EBS) of Hagerstown, Maryland, has refined "control" to an art form.

EBS offers a type of financial service known as "lockbox processing." Firms contract with EBS to process, record, and deposit incoming payments and donations. For example, EBS processes donations for organizations such as Mothers Against Drunk Driving, Greenpeace, and the National Association for Women.

Inside the plain brick building that houses the company, long lines of women sit at spartan desks, each performing a small fragment of the total work process. Some women open envelopes and sort their contents, others compute figures, and still others key information into the computer. Strict quotas are maintained. Workers who open envelopes must process three envelopes a minute, and data entry workers must key at least 8500 strokes an hour.

The work is deliberately structured to avoid the use of any high-level skills. "We don't ask these people to think—the machines think for them," Edens says. "They don't have to make any decisions." At the end of each day, the computer produces a printout of the productivity and error rate for every woman, which management uses to weed out workers who don't meet quota.

The work floor itself resembles an enormous classroom in the throes of exam period. Desks point toward the front, where a manager keeps watch from a raised platform that workers call "the pedestal" or "the birdhouse." Other supervisors are positioned toward the back of the room. "If you want to watch someone," Edens explains, "it's easier from behind because they don't know you're watching." The room is silent. Talking is forbidden. The windows are covered. "I'm not paying people to chat. I'm paying them to open envelopes," he says. Of the blocked windows, Edens adds: "I don't want them looking out—it's distracting. They'll make mistakes."

In his office upstairs, Edens sits before a TV monitor that flashes images from eight cameras posted through the plant. "There's a little bit of Sneaky Pete to it," he says, using a remote control to zoom in on a document atop a worker's desk. "I can basically read that and figure out how someone's day is going." At EBS, workers handle thousands of dollars in cheques and cash, and Edens says cameras help deter would-be thieves.

The company does not believe in fancy pay innovations. Pay for clerical staff is based on an hourly rate starting at the minimum wage and ranging no more than a couple of dollars above it. Minimal benefits are provided. Turnover is high. But that is not a major problem since it takes little time to recruit and train a new worker. EBS runs smoothly, like a well-oiled machine, and business is booming. All in all, Edens has reason to be pleased with how his organization works.

Source: Horwitz, Tony. 1994. "9 to Nowhere: These Six Jobs are Dull, Dead-End, Sometimes Dangerous." *The Wall Street Journal*, December 1: A1–A8. Reprinted by permission of *The Wall Street Journal*. Copyright © 1994 Dow Jones & Company, Inc. All Rights Reserved Worldwide.

---

organization devotes a considerable effort toward developing loyal employees who are dedicated to the norms of the organization. Pressure from the work group is expected to make individual members conform to the expectations of the organization. If this fails, the supervisor is then expected to step in. However, punishments are not extensively used, out of fear that they will disrupt the social harmony.

Communication within informal work groups is encouraged, and management often attempts to utilize the grapevine for communication. Management also makes considerable effort to facilitate social communication (such as when an employee marries or has a baby). However, the flow of work-related communication tends to be low, whether up or down the hierarchy. Like the classical school, management still tries to restrict the flow of what it considers to be important information. However, unlike the classical school, they often make use of suggestion systems and newsletters.

The human relations strategy calls for rewards that are mainly extrinsic and focus on loyalty to the organization. Salaries (rather than hourly pay) are often used to foster a feeling of permanence. Seniority increases are also likely provided to encourage workforce stability. In addition, liberal employee benefits may be provided, again to develop employee loyalty. A number of noneconomic rewards may also be provided, such as five-year pins and employee-of-the-month citations, to show the interest of the organization in its employees. Management expects employees to find the positive social environment in these firms rewarding.

One firm that is famous for its use of the human relations strategy is Kodak, as described in Compensation Today 2.2, although the firm has in recent years been attempting to move to a more high-involvement strategy to adapt to its increasingly dynamic task environment.

High-Involvement Managerial Strategy

Compared to the previous two managerial strategies, job design under the high-involvement model is very different. Here, a major effort is made to create jobs that are both interesting and challenging and that provide workers with considerable autonomy over the planning and execution of the work activity, as well as job-based feedback on how well they are performing. Therefore, jobs are broader, involve more elements, and attempt to include a meaningful cycle of work activity. Joint employee–management planning and goal setting are also often used. In contrast to the classical approach, a conscious effort is made to *combine* the thinking and the doing.

Coordination is horizontal as well as vertical. In fact, horizontal coordination, whereby workers coordinate directly with one another in task completion, is preferred to vertical coordination. Jobs are often arranged in clusters, in which a group of employees has the responsibility for coordinating the completion of a set of tasks among themselves. These clusters, or teams, often consist of people from various specialties mingled together. Departmentation is based on the product, customer, or project, not functional groupings.

In addition, the role of the supervisor in a high-involvement organization is very different from that in the other two schools. Rather than primarily a controller and evaluator, the supervisor is a facilitator. His or her job is to remove barriers to effective performance and to provide adequate resources and other assistance to enable subordinates to perform effectively. Since employees are assumed to be able to exercise self-control and self-motivation, the supervisor does not need to perform a control function. Moreover, because employees are assumed to be self-motivated and competent, decisions can be made at the lowest possible level in the organization. The overall leadership style is participative or democratic in nature.

Moreover, control is internal (within the individual). Employees are expected to exercise self-control, because of their identification with the goals

Compensation Today 2.2

Does Human Relations Still Work for Kodak?

Eastman Kodak, the huge photographic products firm, is renowned for the fierce loyalty it generates among its employees. But this doesn't happen by accident. Historically, Kodak's management practices have included rigid adherence to a "promote-from-within" policy, an excellent compensation package with large profit-sharing bonuses, and a "no layoff" policy to maintain employment security. Its benefits package is truly remarkable, including everything from an excellent pension plan to generous sick leave entitlements (employees receive full pay for the first 52 weeks of sick leave), and even free noontime movies. As a result, Kodak has attracted top-notch employees.

Although most companies in its industry are unionized, there has never been any interest in unionization among Kodak employees, and the company is non-union to this day. The company has many long-term employees who are committed to the traditional "Kodak way" of doing things, which has proved successful for many years. A classic illustration of Kodak's tradition mentality was the case of a supervisor who recently retired. Upon his retirement, it was discovered that he had kept employment records from as far back as the 1930s in his office drawer "because they had always been there."

Management style at Kodak could best be described as patient and paternalistic, with an extensive system of written rules, policies, and procedures. Decisions percolate to the top for even minor issues. For instance, the head of photographic and information products could be called on to make a decision on any one of 50 000 products.

Although the company has had many years of success with this human relations managerial strategy, coming to dominate the world market for many photographic products, it started to encounter problems in the 1980s, resulting in financial difficulties by the end of the decade. Profit-sharing bonuses shrank to nothing, and the company was forced to sell divisions, close plants, and lay off thousands of employees, the first such layoffs in the company's history. What happened?

Several things. New competitors, such as Fuji, had entered the film market, a high-margin market dominated by Kodak for decades. In addition, technological change in the photographic business had increased dramatically, and Kodak wasn't able to keep up, despite spending billions on research and development. For example, Kodak didn't believe that 35 mm cameras or video cameras would amount to much and delayed entry into these fields until they were dominated by others. When Kodak did introduce new products, such as the disc camera and a CD system to view snapshots on a television screen, these new products flopped.

In late 1993, Kodak brought in a new CEO, George Fisher, who had previously been head of Motorola (a highly innovative and effective producer of communications technology) to try to get the company back on track. Shortly after his arrival, Fisher attempted to move toward a high-involvement managerial strategy in those areas of the business that depended on innovation. However, Kodak's problems continued, resulting in layoffs in 1998 that reduced the company's workforce from 100 000 to about 84 000 employees; and continuing reductions decreased total employment to 80 000 by mid-2000. While this did improve the company's bottom line, it didn't seem to make the firm any more flexible or innovative. That prompted some commentators to argue that Kodak should give up on innovation entirely, and hive off the innovative portions of its business—such as digital imaging—into a separate business not under the control of Kodak management.

By 2005, when continuing reductions had reduced the workforce to about 65 000 employees, the company still had not done so; but it had announced a plan to lay off another 12 000 to 15 000 employees by 2007. Also in 2005, Antonio Perez, the company's new CEO, warned that Kodak had no more than two years to find its place in digital photography "to avoid fading into history."

Sources: (1) Jacoby, Sanford M. 1997. *Modern Manors: Welfare Capitalism since the New Deal*. Princeton, NJ: Princeton University Press. (2) Robbins, Stephen P. 1990. *Organization Theory: Structure, Design, and Applications*. Englewood Cliffs, NJ: Prentice-Hall: 514–515. (3) Maremont, Mark. 1995. "Kodak's New Focus." *Business Week*, January 30: 62–68. (4) Coy, Peter. 2000. "The Myth of Corporate Reinvention." *Business Week*, October 30: 80–82. (5) Dobbin, Ben. 2005. "Perez to Replace Carp as Kodak CEO." *Business Week Online*: May 11.

of the organization and the intrinsic rewards flowing from the work itself, and because they have sufficient training and knowledge to behave responsibly. Because of this internalized commitment, little supervision is necessary, and formalized rules and regulations can be kept to a minimum.

Full disclosure of information is essential, since decisions are being made at all levels throughout the organization. Without adequate information, poor decisions would result. The high-involvement firm recognizes this, so communication is a major focus of management attention. Great effort is made for communication to flow vertically (both up and down the organization), horizontally, and diagonally.

For these reasons, a high-involvement organization uses a wide variety of both intrinsic and extrinsic rewards. Employees are expected to receive substantial intrinsic rewards directly from performing their jobs and participating in decision making. Extrinsic rewards are geared toward fostering good performance rather than controlling substandard output; and they tend to focus on the work unit, rather than the individual, since tasks are usually complex and require teamwork.

Base pay tends to be salary, augmented by profit- and gain-sharing plans of various types, as well as employee stock ownership. Pay is often person-based (i.e., pay for knowledge) rather than job-based, in order to promote skills acquisition and flexibility within the organization. Because of the complex behaviour and high performance levels required in high-involvement organizations, reward and compensation systems are usually more complex than those in firms using the other two managerial strategies.

Compensation Today 2.3 illustrates how one high-involvement firm, Gennum Corporation, puts all of this together.

Interrelationships among Structural Variables

It should now be apparent that there are strong interrelationships among the structural variables. Some elements are *complementary* and must occur together for any of them to be effective. For example, pushing decision making down to lower-level employees in the organization is dangerous if they have not been provided adequate information with which to make informed decisions, a knowledge base to understand this information, and a reward system that creates a strong sense of identity with the company. But creating knowledgeable, well-informed employees with a financial stake in the firm's performance and then not allowing them input in decision making creates employee frustration.

Research has also shown that some structural elements can serve as *substitutes* for others. For example, a Canadian study has shown that profit-sharing and gain-sharing systems can serve as substitutes for managerial control.[9] This study found that firms that had profit- or gain-sharing systems (or preferably both) were able to operate with 31 percent fewer managers and supervisors and significantly fewer rules and regulations than firms without these systems. These firms, like Gennum Corporation, substitute internal (self-) control for external control. On the other hand, Electronic Banking System, which makes no attempt to generate self-control, must depend heavily on external management control.

Compensation Today 2.3

High Involvement at Gennum Corporation

Based in Burlington, Ontario, Gennum Corporation designs and produces miniature integrated circuits used in a variety of special applications. For example, a large proportion of the hearing aids produced worldwide incorporate Gennum circuits. The firm has about 650 employees, a large proportion of them professionals and highly skilled technicians. Because of rapidly evolving technologies, the company is continually working at the frontiers of knowledge.

When first established in 1973, the firm's founders believed that three characteristics would be key to their success: an atmosphere of innovation and challenge, a commitment to egalitarianism, and the participation of all employees in the company's financial success. Their managerial philosophy is illustrated by this quote from founder Doug Barber:

> The company really is its people ... It is clear that we need not just the hands and bodies, but the minds and ideas of everyone. We believe in teamwork and interdependence. It is important that everyone feels they are playing a significant role, and that they personally have opportunities to develop. We like to challenge people to take on new responsibility to develop them to their fullest potential.

Sounds good, but how does the company actually achieve all this? Essentially, by applying virtually every element of the high-involvement model. Jobs are broad. The company has few supervisors, and their role is employee support, not control. Employees are expected to speak up if they believe they have a better way of doing something. In the words of one employee: "In some places they say 'Do it this way,' even if you don't believe it's going to work. Here, you have a free hand." As Barber explained during a 1997 interview, "When you have a lot of skilled people in the company, to think that one or two or three people should tell them what to do is crazy."

At many firms, employees are told that they can exercise initiative and try new things, but woe to them if they fail! So most employees just play it safe. But not at Gennum. As one employee puts it, if employees think they

see a better way to do something, "You suggest it. Fine. It's your idea. Do it. If it doesn't work, that's fine. If you try something and it doesn't work, it's not held against you." To support this, employee knowledge about the total business and communication is crucial. According to president Barber: "We deliberately try to keep employees mixing. We encourage interdisciplinary team problem solving."

So what kind of reward and compensation system do you think would best fit this organization? In fact, consistent with theory, the firm uses a complex mix of intrinsic and extrinsic rewards. Intrinsic rewards stem from the broad nature of the tasks and the freedom employees are given in performing them, as well as the high degree of learning and development the company fosters. Extrinsic rewards include a policy of job security for all employees who are competent performers, and opportunities for social interaction and career development.

In addition, all three components of compensation are used. All employees, including production workers, are on salary, rather than hourly pay. The company uses market surveys to set base pay within a competitive salary range each year. Annual salary increases are based on performance.

There are many different types of performance pay in place. All employees, regardless of job category, are eligible. First, everyone is eligible for the profit-sharing plan, which pays 6 percent of pre-tax profits into a deferred profit-sharing trust, which is structured as a Registered Retirement Savings Plan. The total profit-sharing funds available are allocated 60 percent according to salary and 40 percent equally to all employees. (This is in contrast to many profit-sharing plans, where the entire profit-sharing bonus is allocated by salary level.)

A second element of performance pay is the firm's incentive compensation plan. If return on average equity exceeds 5 percent, then an additional amount is allocated to every employee for each percentage point above that level. (During the past 10 years, return on average equity has never been less than 10 percent.) The growth in annual corporate revenue also affects performance pay. This money is allocated according to salary and level of responsibility. Senior employees are required to take a portion of this bonus in company stock, which is held in escrow and released over a four-year period. This incentive is intended to reward profitable growth and to maintain a long-term perspective on company performance.

Two other incentive plans were introduced in recent years to attract, retain, and provide differentiation for top contributors. The Stock Option Plan was introduced in 2000, and the Special Incentive Plan, a stock grant that vests in three years, was introduced in 2003. Once again, every employee is eligible to receive these awards, but grants are reserved for the top 10 to 20 percent of employees that senior management believes will contribute the most to company success.

Another element of Gennum's performance pay strategy is an employee stock plan. Employees are permitted to use up to 5 percent of their earnings to purchase company stock (traded on the Toronto Stock Exchange); the company then provides another share of stock for every two that the employee purchases. Most employees take full advantage of this offer, and virtually all employees own company stock.

For indirect pay, the company provides a benefits package that matches its competitors (with the exception of a pension plan), on a cost-shared basis, in which the employees pick up a portion of the costs of each benefit. Every employee (including top management) receives equal benefits. Because it has no pension plan, the company relies on the deferred profit-sharing plan to help employees generate retirement savings. Payments from the incentive compensation plans can also be placed directly into the registered retirement savings plan. To help employees plan their retirement funds, the company brings in financial advisers every year at no cost to employees.

Sources: (1) Innes, Eva, Jim Lyon, and Jim Harris. 1991. *The Financial Post 100 Best Companies to Work for in Canada*. Toronto: Harper-Collins: 58–59. (2) Personal communication with company officials, May 2005.

All of this suggests that organizations that consistently adopt a single managerial strategy, no matter what that managerial strategy is, are usually more effective than those that have an inconsistent mix of structural elements. MacDuffie refers to internally consistent practices as "human resource bundles"[10] and presents evidence that firms that use these "bundles" perform better than those that do not.

Indeed, it should be noted that even within a given managerial strategy, there are different possible combinations of human resource policies. For example, a firm may choose to hire only experienced workers, or it may hire inexperienced workers and train them. Hiring experienced workers usually costs more in compensation; but hiring inexperienced workers costs more in training costs, and there is the risk of losing them once they are trained.

But different managerial perspectives have different preferences. Because of high turnover, classical organizations would prefer not to incur high training costs. So their tendency is to hire experienced, trained workers, where jobs require training. (Their preferred course of action, of course, is to fragment tasks into small pieces, so that little training is necessary.)

Other human resource policies, such as recruitment, must fit into the managerial strategy. Because high-involvement organizations need workers who have high potential for growth, self-control, and motivation by higher-order needs, they have the most comprehensive selection processes. In contrast, because classical organization demands are simple task performance, they have the least sophisticated recruitment and selection procedures. Human relations organizations fall in between because they want to screen out people who would disrupt the social environment of the firm.

Part I: Strategy, Rewards, and Behaviour

Before we leave organization structure, there is one other concept that is relevant—organizational culture. "**Organizational culture** is the set of values, guiding beliefs, understandings, and ways of thinking that are shared by members of an organization."[11] Organizational culture can be considered the informal structure of the organization.

A strong culture can play a major role in shaping and directing behaviour within the organization. Culture can supplement the formal structure of the organization, or it can substitute for it. For example, because of their need to stay flexible, high-involvement organizations like to use as little formal structure as possible, so a strong organizational culture is important to them. Classical firms, on the other hand, prefer to depend on the formal structure, so they focus very little on organizational culture. Human relations firms use both formal structure and culture to shape behaviour.

A given culture may be beneficial to one organization, but detrimental to another, depending on whether it fits with the managerial strategy. However, some cultures are simply detrimental. For example, employees in many classical organizations develop a strong anti-management culture, which may include norms such as "never cooperate with management," "never go beyond your minimum work requirements," and "ignore the rules when the supervisor is gone." In human relations firms, a culture of avoiding conflict, never criticizing the company or a fellow employee, valuing tradition, and doing things the way they have always been done tends to develop. Remember the Kodak employee who kept 50-year-old employment records in his desk drawer because they "had always been there"? In contrast, key cultural values in high-involvement organizations like Gennum include honesty, trustworthiness, open communication, and acceptance of risk taking.

How does an organization shape culture? By its actions. For example, a firm that says it values initiative and risk taking but punishes every employee initiative that fails teaches employees not to exercise any initiative. The reward system is critical in shaping culture. A firm that says it values cooperation and teamwork but then promotes an employee who isn't a team player is signalling a very different message. If a company's top management is fond of talking about how "we are all partners in this enterprise" but doesn't share gains when the firm is successful and lays off employees at the first sign of trouble, then employees will not feel much like "partners."

Both human relations and high-involvement organizations typically spend considerable effort developing their cultures. But culture is most important to high-involvement organizations because they depend on it to substitute for the formal structure. It is no accident that organizational culture, as a concept, came into prominence with the rise of high-involvement organizations.

Determinants of the Most Appropriate Managerial Strategy

If the most appropriate reward system is determined by the managerial strategy, then it is important to understand the factors that determine the most appropriate managerial strategy. Of course, the answer lies in the five key

organizational culture
the set of core values and understandings shared by members of an organization

Workforce
Environment
Size
Technology
Strategy

contextual variables identified in Figure 2.2—the environment, corporate strategy, technology, size of the organization, and nature of the workforce. But simply knowing the names of these variables is not very useful if you do not know how each relates to managerial strategy.

The purpose of this section is first to show how each of these contextual variables can be categorized into types, and then to show how each type relates to managerial strategy. At the end of this section, a template is provided as a tool to help identify the most appropriate managerial strategy (and hence, reward strategy) for any given organization.

Of course, just because the contextual variables point to a particular managerial strategy doesn't necessarily mean that the organization has actually adopted that managerial strategy. In some cases, firms may be using a managerial strategy that doesn't match their contextual variables, and in some cases firms really have no distinct managerial strategy.[12] But in either case, company performance will be lower than it should be, and company survival could even be threatened if competitors have adopted the most appropriate managerial strategy.

Finally, in some cases an organization may have a mixed set of structural dimensions and thus appears to have no definite managerial strategy, but it is actually in a planned transition from one managerial strategy to another. This transition may be very appropriate if this change is driven by the need to respond to changes in the firm's contextual variables, although successful transitions from one managerial strategy to another (such as from classical to high involvement) are actually very difficult.

Environment

Of the five contextual variables, the most important is the environment that faces a given firm. The first question to ask is whether the firm's environment is stable or unstable. An unstable (dynamic) environment exists where product or service life cycles are short, where product or service demand is volatile, where customer needs change quickly and unpredictably, where technologies are changing rapidly, where new competitors frequently enter the field, and where the regulatory environment is unpredictable. Firms generally have little control over the degree of stability in the task environment. Because of their rigidity, classical and human relations firms have great difficulty operating successfully in dynamic, unstable environments.

The second question to ask is whether the firm's environment is simple or complex. A firm's environment is complex if the firm has numerous distinct product or service domains, where the product/service provided is complicated, where the technology is complex, and where there are many different factors that can influence the firm's success. While firms do not have much control over the degree of stability in their environments, they do have some control over the *complexity* of their task environments. For example, a firm that chooses to operate in a number of unrelated product/service domains creates a more complex environment for itself than a firm that operates in only one product/service domain. Thus, the complexity of a firm's environment depends in part on how broadly it defines its domain(s). But certain domains (e.g., designing micro-circuits) are inherently more complex than others (e.g., processing chickens).

However, even if a task environment is complex, *as long as it is stable*, a classical or human relations approach can be effective. If the complexity stems from operating in many domains, either a classical or human relations approach should work. But if the complexity is due to the domain itself, then a human relations approach may work best. This is because complex domains often require high levels of expertise among employees, and the high turnover that typifies a classical organization will be very costly in these circumstances.

But when task environments are dynamic, then complexity compounds the uncertainty facing the organization. Neither classical nor human relations organizations are able to adapt quickly to environmental change. In general, a high-involvement approach is needed whenever environments are highly unstable or dynamic and is even more essential when the environment is also complex.

Corporate Strategy

Although there are a number of ways to classify types of corporate strategy, one useful categorization has been developed by Miles and Snow.[13] They suggest that company strategies can be divided into three main types (defender, prospector, or analyzer), with a residual type (the reactor) to cover firms that do not practise any distinct overall strategy.

The **defender strategy** entails taking a fairly narrow product or service segment and excelling in it, based on a combination of product quality and price. A defender firm may not always be the low-cost leader, but it will always try to provide the best possible quality/price tradeoff, so that its products offer the best value to customers. The byword for this strategy is *consistency*. The key need is to identify the most efficient process for providing the product or service and then to lock it in. For defenders, the classical or human relations approaches are most suitable. In general, classical works well for manufacturing, and human relations for service enterprises, where there is extensive contact with customers.

defender corporate strategy
focuses on dominating a narrow product or service market segment

The **prospector strategy** is the complete opposite of the defender. It focuses on identifying new product and market opportunities and being the first to exploit them. However, prospectors tend to move on to other new products or services as competitors enter the market. These competitors can copy the product and mass produce it at a lower cost than the prospector can because the competitors do not have to include development costs or costs of failed products in their pricing structures. The byword for the prospector strategy is *speed*. The key need is to have a process for identifying new opportunities quickly and an organization flexible and dynamic enough to get them to market before anybody else. Clearly, a high-involvement approach is essential.

prospector corporate strategy
focuses on identifying and exploiting new opportunities quickly

The **analyzer strategy** is the most complex of the three corporate strategies because it attempts to combine both the prospector and defender strategies. This strategy entails being able to both identify and exploit new product or service opportunities at a relatively early stage—not long after the

analyzer corporate strategy
focuses on exploiting new opportunities at a relatively early stage while maintaining a base of traditional products or services

low–cost corporate strategy

a corporate strategy that depends on providing low–cost products or services to a broad range of customers

focused low-cost corporate strategy

a corporate strategy that depends on providing low–cost products or services to a narrow range of customers

differentiator corporate strategy

a corporate strategy that depends on providing unique products or services to a broad range of customers

focused differentiator corporate strategy

a corporate strategy that depends on providing unique products or services to a narrow range of customers

long-linked technology

divides the total task of producing a product or service into a series of small sequential steps performed by different employees

mediating technology

uses standardized transactions to connect parties wishing a mutually beneficial relationship

intensive technology

requires that each item or case be dealt with individually, depending on the specific nature of each case

prospectors—while also maintaining a firm base of traditional products or services. The byword for the analyzer strategy is *balance*. The key need is to be able to balance stability and flexibility. This often requires a hybrid or dual organization structure: one that promotes speed and flexibility for new product development and one that promotes stability and consistency for the established products. Typically, analyzer firms are not first with new products or services, but they do enter these markets early, after the prospectors have identified them. They are generally less efficient in production than defenders, but are able to get their products on the market long before the defenders in the industry get around to doing so.

Analyzers would likely operate best with something close to a high-involvement approach for new product development and a classical approach for the traditional products. But since it is very difficult to practise two such divergent managerial strategies in the same firm, analyzers often seem to end up practising a compromise human relations strategy across the board. This can be successful as long as the environment is not too dynamic.

A second way of classifying corporate strategy has been developed by Michael Porter.[14] Porter suggests that competitive strategies can be categorized on two dimensions, based on whether the firm is seeking to be the low-cost producer of standard products or whether it is attempting to differentiate itself by having unique products or services, and on whether the firm caters to a narrow customer base (a "focus" strategy) or a broad customer base. These distinctions result in four types of corporate strategy—the **low-cost strategy,** the **focused low-cost strategy,** the **differentiator strategy,** and the **focused differentiator strategy.** Overall, because it is dependent on innovation and creativity, the differentiator strategies seems best suited to the high-involvement managerial strategy, while the low-cost strategies seems best suited to the classical managerial strategy, due to its emphasis on tight cost controls.

Technology

The organization's technology can be classified in a variety of ways. One way is to classify it according to the type of production process. Thompson suggests three main types: long-linked, mediating, and intensive.[15] A **long-linked technology** divides the total task into many small sequential steps, with each step performed by a different employee, such as in an automobile assembly line. This is the technology used at Electronic Banking System and the B.C. Rogers chicken-processing plant.

A **mediating technology** uses standardized transactions to connect two parties who wish to have some kind of mutually beneficial relationship. Banks connect people who want to lend money with people who want to borrow it. Transportation companies connect people who have an item with people who want that item. Retailers connect manufacturers of a product with people who wish to purchase the product. Real estate agents connect people who want to sell houses with people who want to buy houses.

An **intensive technology** requires that each item or case be dealt with individually, based on feedback from the client or the object being worked on. Examples of organizations with intensive technologies include general hospitals, custom home builders, tailors who produce made-to-order suits, auto repair shops, legal firms specializing in criminal law, and consulting firms.

Clearly, an intensive technology requires a high-involvement structure, while a long-linked technology would suit a classical structure. Because most mediating technologies involve considerable contact with people (in contrast to manufacturing, where the main interaction is with objects, such as dishwashers or vacuum cleaners), the human relations strategy is usually the most appropriate for them.

Another approach to classifying technology concerns the degree to which it is routine or nonroutine.[16] There are two aspects in determining this: how many exceptions or different types of problems are involved in a particular task, and whether there is a standardized process for dealing with these exceptions. A **routine technology** is defined as a technology in which there are relatively few exceptions to the standard work processes; and where these exceptions do occur, a standardized process for solving these problems is already in place. Examples include an electrical utility or a plant that manufactures washing machines.

A **nonroutine technology,** on the other hand, has many exceptions inherent in the work, and there is no standardized way to deal with these exceptions. Examples include consulting firms, aerospace engineering firms, and pharmaceutical firms attempting to discover new drugs. In these firms, the key need is not so much the production of goods or services but of new ideas. Gennum Corporation uses a nonroutine technology, since the firm's lifeblood is the production of new ideas and innovations in micro-circuitry.

Between routine and nonroutine are two other types, the craft technology and the engineering technology. The **craft technology** has relatively few exceptions, but there is no standardized way to solve these exceptions when they occur—solutions depend on the judgment and intuition of the worker. Specialty glass-blowing is one example. Comedians, such as Jerry Seinfeld, would be another example. You can buy one of his books, with all of his joke material in it; but would anybody be willing to pay you $30 million a year to tell them?

The **engineering technology** has many exceptions, but there is always a standardized way for dealing with them. Examples include an accounting firm, in which every client is different, but standardized procedures (i.e., GAAP—generally accepted accounting principles) are used to generate the necessary financial reports; or an engineering firm that designs bridges, each of which is different, but for which there is a standardized way of designing them.

Clearly, a firm that uses a nonroutine technology requires a high-involvement managerial strategy, while a firm that uses a routine technology can use a classical or human relations approach. Firms with craft or engineering technologies generally depend on the judgment of relatively skilled employees, who prefer autonomy in performing their job duties. It may not be essential to have a full high-involvement structure for the engineering technology, but a strict classical structure would tend to alienate these employees. For the craft technology, something close to a high-involvement approach is

routine technology

few exceptions occur during the production process, and those exceptions that do occur can be dealt with in a standardized way

nonroutine technology

many exceptions are inherent in the production process, and there is no standardized way to deal with these exceptions

craft technology

few exceptions occur in the production process, but there is no standardized way to deal with them when they do occur

engineering technology

many exceptions occur in the production or service delivery process, but there are standardized ways of dealing with them

probably necessary, since the organization depends on the intuitive judgment of its employees.

One final typology can provide some useful insights. Woodward suggests that manufacturing technologies can be divided into three main types: unit/small batch, mass/large batch, and process.[17] A **unit/small batch technology** produces one-of-a-kind items, or small batches of them, and is analogous to the intensive technology. A **mass/large batch technology** produces large amounts of a single item in a standardized way, and is analogous to the long-linked technology. The **process technology** produces the product in a continuous flow, such as an oil refinery, chemical plant, or electrical power plant, and has no equivalent in the typologies already discussed. It is different from the long-linked technology because of the continuous product flow, which usually makes these firms highly capital-intensive, and because workers are focused on monitoring and maintaining this flow. The key task of these workers is to either prevent or respond effectively to problem situations when they arise. Therefore, these employees need to be both highly knowledgeable and highly diligent in their work, which requires at least a human relations structure, and possibly a high-involvement structure, as in the case of L-S Electrogalvanizing.

Organization Size

Because of the need to coordinate and control large numbers of people, large organizations generally use classical or human relations strategies, although these strategies can be found in organizations of all sizes. In general, it is easier to implement high involvement in a small- to medium-sized organization, because the larger the organization, the greater the need for some formal structure. However, some large organizations have resolved this problem by segmenting their organization into a series of relatively small units and then practising high involvement in these units. Hewlett-Packard, the computer products firm, has traditionally used this approach.

Size also affects structure in at least one other way. As organizations get larger, the impact of technology on their structure lessens. Indeed, some large organizations may use a number of different technologies. This diversification may call for different managerial strategies in different parts of the organization, which can be very difficult to manage, since top management tends to prefer one particular managerial strategy (the one consistent with their assumptions about people).

The Nature of the Workforce

The nature of the people employed by the organization—their skills, educational characteristics, and expectations—also has a major impact on the choice of managerial strategy. In general, highly skilled, well-educated, or professional employees are more suited to the high-involvement school. Indeed, a high-involvement strategy requires these characteristics because of the broad jobs and decision-making responsibility expected of employees.

On the other hand, classical organizations are specifically designed to utilize employees with relatively low skills; and because of their approach to

---

unit/small batch technology

manufacturing technology that produces one-of-a-kind items or small batches of unique items

mass/large batch technology

manufacturing technology that produces large amounts of single items in a standardized way

process technology

manufacturing technology that produces a single product in a continuous flow

WESTS

Workforce Environo Technno Strategy

Compensation Notebook 2.2

Template for Selecting the Most Appropriate Managerial Strategy for an Organization to Utilize

Contextual Variable	Classical	Human Relations	High-Involvement
Environment			
• Stability	Stable	Stable	Unstable
• Complexity	Simple	Simple or Complex	Complex
Corporate Strategy			
• Miles and Snow Typology	Defender *(dominant product/service)*	Analyzer	Prospector
• Porter's Typology	Low Cost	Focused Differentiator	Differentiator
Technology			
• Thompson's Typology	Long-linked	Mediating	Intensive
• Perrow's Typology	Routine	Routine or Engineering	Craft or Nonroutine
• Woodward's Typology	Mass	Process	Process or Unit
• Product Transformed	Things	People	Ideas
Size			
• Number of Employees	Any Size	Any Size	Small/Medium
Workforce			
• Skills/Education	Low	Moderate	High
• Economic Circumstances	Poor	Moderate	Good

motivation and control, these organizations are most suited to workers who badly need the money the job provides. Their motivational approaches work best in poor economic circumstances and in areas with high unemployment and a low standard of living. (This helps to explain why many classical firms move their production operations to Third World countries, where living conditions make their managerial strategy effective.) In contrast, human relations organizations can often utilize relatively low-skill workers, but do not need to depend on poor economic circumstances for their motivational policies, since they offer both economic and social rewards.

Tying It All Together

From this discussion, it can be seen that contextual variables must align not only with managerial strategy but also with each other. For example, using a long-linked technology or a defender strategy in an unstable environment is courting disaster, because the organization may not be able to respond quickly to change. Compatible combinations would be those that are consistent with a given managerial strategy. Thus, a defender strategy, a stable environment, a long-linked technology, a relatively low-skilled workforce, and a large organization would be a good combination, well suited for the classical managerial strategy. Compensation Notebook 2.2 illustrates these combinations and provides a template for selecting the most appropriate managerial strategy for a given organization to utilize. (Of course, where the contextual variables are out of alignment with each other, there can be no ideal managerial strategy and no ideal reward strategy.) Compensation Notebook 2.2 also helps solve the mystery why some firms do quite nicely without adopting pay innovations, and why compensation systems that work well for some firms are completely inadequate in others.

Let's use this template to revisit some of the organizations you learned about earlier in the chapter. Let's start with B.C. Rogers chicken processors. But before doing so, you need a little more background on chicken processing, which Compensation Today 2.4 provides. After reading Compensation Today 2.4, you will probably know more about chicken processing than you ever really wanted to know!

Now, let's compare B.C. Rogers Processors with the characteristics in the template. Rogers has a stable, simple environment, uses a defender strategy (where low-cost production is crucial) and a long-linked technology, requires low-skilled employees, and is located in a region where economic conditions are generally poor. Perfect for a classical structure! Although turnover is high, *it doesn't matter*, because employees are easy to replace and train. Employee commitment is not needed because control is easy, with the technology itself ("the chain") providing most of the necessary control. Given all this, the sole purpose of the compensation system is to assure a sufficient flow of applicants so that the chain is always staffed at the lowest possible cost.

Let's take a closer look at L-S Electrogalvanizing, which pays top dollar to its employees. Because of overcapacity in their industry and stagnant demand for their products, the environment can be considered quite unstable, although relatively simple, since LSE specializes in a narrow range of products. The firm uses a defender strategy, with a focus on high-quality products. Process technology is used. The plant is relatively small, with only about a hundred production workers. But because of the complexity of the production process, the skill levels required by workers are high. The cost of errors is potentially high, as is the cost of downtime due to equipment failures and other problems. Economic conditions in Cleveland, where the plant is located, are moderately good, supported by the presence of many high-paying industrial jobs.

When you compare these points to the template in Compensation Notebook 2.2, you can see that the case of LSE is not as clear-cut as the chicken plant case, with various contextual variables pointing toward different managerial strategies. Indeed, you can find examples of each of the three managerial strategies in the steel industry, although the classical approach predominates. But LSE has obviously chosen a high-involvement strategy. Worker tasks and responsibilities are broad. There are few supervisors in the plant, and each shift crew operates as a team to handle whatever needs to be done to maintain production and quality. Each team is delegated a lot of decision-making power regarding the operation of the plant. To make such decisions, the employees need to be knowledgeable, informed, and committed to the goals of the organization. They must also be flexible enough to work together to prevent and

Anyone for Chicken Fingers?

If chickens don't have fingers, then where do chicken fingers come from? One story is that a marketer was trying to come up with a name for the company's new chicken product when there was an accident on the processing line. An employee had two fingers lopped off, which fell into the boxes of chicken parts. As workers shouted, "Get the fingers from the chicken!" inspiration struck the marketer! But whether or not this story is really true, safety on a chicken-processing line is no joking matter, and accident rates are high in this line of work.

The demand for poultry has been growing by leaps and bounds in North America. Because turnover is high in poultry companies—often exceeding 100 percent a year—these companies are hiring constantly, and they don't waste time being choosy about whom they hire. Writing an article on the poultry industry, Tony Horwitz, a reporter with the *Wall Street Journal*, decided to see for himself what work was like in a chicken-processing plant.

At a B.C. Rogers Processors Inc. plant in Morton, Miss., the first this reporter visited in search of work, the plant manager, Jerry Duty, barely glanced at an application that listed my university education and Dow Jones & Co. (publisher of this newspaper) as my employer. "It's tough work and will make you sore as hell," he said, offering a job starting the next day at $5.10 an hour. "But it won't kill you—only the chickens."

On the factory floor—a noisy, wet expanse of chutes and belts loosely linked by the ubiquitous chain—a supervisor pointed me to a space along a conveyor belt where workers frantically weighed chicken parts and crammed them into cardboard boxes. "Show him the ropes," he shouted at no one in particular, and no one ever did.

Each job carries its own hazards and hardships. By common acclaim, the toughest is held by "live hangers," who hitch incoming birds to shackles at a rate of 25 or more a minute. So strenuous that only a few can do it, live-hanging exposes workers to struggling birds that scratch, peck and defecate all over them. Some hangers spend breaks in the bathroom, coughing up feathers and dust.

After the birds have been stunned with electric current, slaughtered and plucked—largely by machine—they are re-hung, dangling headless and upside-down for their journey through the plant. At one station, a worker who calls herself a "butthole cutter" slits open the bird so a "gut-puller" can reach in and yank out the animal's innards. Others lop off limbs, pull skin or separate organs.

Packed tightly and working quickly with knives and scissors, workers often cut themselves and others. At break times I would find fat globules and blood speckling my glasses, bits of chicken caught in my collar, water and slime soaking my feet and ankles and nicks covering my wrists.

While foremen circulate, joining in the work or urging employees to speed up, the labour is effectively self-supervising. As in many factories, the conveyor belt sets the pace and anyone who flags creates more work for those farther down the line. So workers tend to vent their fatigue and frustration on each other, shouting at colleagues to do a better job. "Someone's putting thighs in the leg boxes!" rang the refrain of a self-appointed coxswain near me. "And I'm going to kick some butt if people don't close those boxes tight!"

Source: Horwitz, Tony. 1994. "9 to Nowhere: These Six Growth Jobs Are Dull, Dead-End, Sometimes Dangerous." *The Wall Street Journal*, December 1: A1–A8. Reprinted by permission of *The Wall Street Journal*. Copyright © 1994 Dow Jones & Company, Inc. All Rights Reserved Worldwide.

cope with production problems. This means they must have broad knowledge of the entire production process, rather than just a tiny part of it.

Clearly, the pay-for-knowledge system, gain- and profit-sharing systems, and high indirect pay amount to a compensation strategy that supports the high-involvement managerial strategy. But how can LSE get a payback from this very expensive compensation strategy? In several ways. First, because of employee flexibility, the plant has eliminated the specialized maintenance personnel most plants must have on hand in case of a breakdown. Second, because of delegation of decision making and use of employee self-control, fewer supervisors are needed, which keeps salary costs lower. In addition, LSE operates its plant with fewer workers than comparable plants using conventional management practices, which reduces labour costs. Third, turnover is low, which reduces recruiting and training costs. Fourth, and probably most important, the presence of multiskilled personnel reduces plant downtime and improves product quality. When the system does go down, everybody can play a role in getting the plant up and running again in a minimum amount of time. In this business, plant downtime is the single biggest driver of cost, followed only by production of an unusable coil of steel, each of which may be valued at $25,000 or more.

Once all of this is factored in, guess what happens? You guessed it! The LSE plant actually turns out to be *more* profitable than its lower-paying competitors.

Remember Ron Edens and his firm, Electronic Banking System, from Compensation Today 2.1? Let's use the strategic template to classify EBS. EBS is a firm that uses low-skill labour and a routine, even long-linked, technology. The firm deals with things, not people, and certainly not ideas. The environment is simple and relatively stable, because of high demand. The firm uses a defender strategy to compete on the basis of low-cost production.

From this information, we can predict that Edens could use a classical managerial strategy very successfully, which, of course, he does. Given this, his pay system is a perfect fit with the circumstances his firm faces. We may not like Edens, and we can predict that his employees probably don't either, *but that doesn't matter!* Whether by accident or design, he has created an organizational system that matches the conditions facing his firm, with a simple reward system that matches his organization's needs.

In contrast, Kodak illustrates what can happen when circumstances change and what was once a highly effective management strategy no longer fits these circumstances. Conditions used to fit the human relations strategy well. Kodak has always had a complex environment, as evidenced by the vast array of products it makes; but the dominance of the firm created a relatively stable environment. In the 1970s and 1980s, it tended to practice a defender strategy for some products and an analyzer strategy for others. Technology was routine for most products. Except in the research and development areas, only moderate employee skills and education were required.

But as competitors entered the field and product innovations occurred, Kodak could not change rapidly enough to adjust to these changes. It was too slow-moving, and its overloaded hierarchical decision-making systems did not have the capacity to judge its environment accurately. This problem was compounded by the firm's acquisition of unrelated companies, such as Sterling Drug in 1988.

Kodak's organizational culture of stability, which had once been an asset, became a liability when the firm tried to move toward a prospector strategy.

The company has undertaken several measures to try to deal with these problems, such as reducing environmental complexity (through sale of noncore divisions) and moving toward a high-involvement strategy in areas of the business that depend on innovation. But as Compensation Today 2.2 suggests, these changes have not necessarily borne fruit. Moving from a human relations organization to a high-involvement organization is a very difficult and long-term process, especially for large organizations with well-entrenched cultures.

Finally, let's consider Gennum Corporation. It is an excellent example of fit. Look at how its high-involvement managerial style fits the company's context: unstable, complex environment, prospector strategy, intensive technology (many of Gennum's products are made to order for specific customers), relatively small size, highly educated workforce, operating in a relatively prosperous region. Instead of formal structure, the organization cultivates a culture of commitment, egalitarianism, teamwork, and risk-taking. And look at how the reward system fits with and supports the company's strategy!

Therefore, according to our strategic framework, Gennum should be very successful. So let's do a reality check, and look at the actual results. In the past 10 years, sales have tripled, from $42 million to $136 million. During this period, despite the high-tech meltdown in 2001, the firm has always shown a profit and has never provided an annual return on average equity of less than 11 percent per annum. Shareholders (many of whom are employees) also have another reason to be happy with the firm—company shares are worth about six times their value in 1995!

Trends in Managerial and Compensation Strategies

All three managerial strategies can be effective if used in the right context. But how are circumstances changing in North America, and how will these changes affect the optimal choice of managerial strategy? This is an important question for those designing reward systems, since the most appropriate reward system depends on the managerial strategy that is used. To get a handle on this question, you need to understand how conditions and managerial strategies have evolved over time. As discussed at the end of this section, these changes also help to explain some of the recent trends in compensation practices.

The Evolution of Managerial Strategies

Initial Dominance of the Classical Approach

Historically, there is no question that the classical managerial strategy, when fully implemented, has been an extremely successful approach. Of the most successful firms in the first half of the twentieth century, virtually all were classical. The largest and most successful company in the world in 1950 was General Motors, and it is no coincidence that GM had the most fully developed classical system anywhere. Although Henry Ford had pioneered the modern classical organization, with its strict division of labour into tiny fragments, Alfred P. Sloan of General Motors had taken the concept and applied it more fully, adding other structural elements. By 1960, this approach to management allowed the big three automakers (GM, Ford, Chrysler) in the United States to virtually control the North American automobile industry.

Why were these firms so successful? It is no mystery. Look at their contextual variables: long-linked technology, stable environment, defender strategy, large size, and a large pool of unskilled labour. Perfect for the classical managerial strategy.

But while classical organizations have great advantages flowing from their high division of labour and strict control, they also have numerous disadvantages. One of these disadvantages is a very high cost of coordination and control, especially as the firm gets larger. (Even at a relatively small firm, such as Electronic Banking System, look at the costs of all those supervisors and all that surveillance equipment!) Another disadvantage is that people do not enjoy fractionated work under tight control. They tend to develop negative work norms, and the negative assumptions that this school holds about workers tend to be self-fulfilling. In order to exert more control over their working lives and to protect their own interests, workers in classical organizations are very likely to form strong adversarial unions.

Classical managers are strongly opposed to unionization because they know that unionization weakens their basis for control of employees (i.e., power) in a variety of ways, most notably by making it harder to dismiss workers. With this threat diminished, management must resort to more inspectors and supervisors, rules, and procedures to control employee behaviour. Unionization increases labour costs in three ways: first, the additional inspectors and controls add costs; second, more workers are needed, because the union imposes controls on the amount of work that can be extracted from workers and on the ways workers can be deployed; and, third, because of the strong anti-management solidarity of the workers, the union is usually able to win higher wages and benefits than it would otherwise.

Not surprisingly, the result is lower profitability, as research has shown.[18] Research has also shown that unionized Canadian companies experience lower employment growth than non-union firms,[19] probably due to their lower profitability.

Rise of the Human Relations Approach

The disadvantages of the classical approach were apparent to perceptive employers as far back as the 1920s, as they asked themselves if there was some way to maintain the advantages of the classical system, especially its high division of labour and well-developed hierarchy for coordination and control, while avoiding the bitter and adversarial labour–management relationship normally found in classical organizations.

Their solution was the human relations school of management, in which employees would be treated with high consideration by management. Pay and benefits would be relatively good, job security would be high, other security needs would be addressed (i.e., through pension and health insurance plans), and the company would play a role in satisfying social needs. All this would create positive group norms that would augment and support the formal structure. Since the company would make every effort to satisfy

Part I: Strategy, Rewards, and Behaviour

employee needs, workers would see no need for a union. Indeed, twentieth-century companies that used the human relations model seldom became unionized, and employees often felt a fierce loyalty toward the company. Turnover was low, with the result that these firms had low recruiting and training costs, and a highly knowledgeable and experienced workforce.

By the 1960s, companies practising the human relations model had begun to supplant classical firms as the model for a well-managed firm. Companies like Kodak and Sears began to dominate their industries, along with IBM, often considered in the 1960s and 1970s to be the best-managed company in the world. IBM practised all the key elements of the human relations school, with a few elements of the high-involvement approach tacked on. These companies truly seemed to have overcome the disadvantages of the classical school while still capturing its advantages and were rewarded with great success.

However, as long as environmental conditions are favourable, it is possible for firms that practise the human relations strategy and firms that practise the classical strategy to coexist in the same industry. If practised well, there may be room for both. But when conditions become adverse, the firms with the approaches least suited to the conditions, or least well executed, will be the first to suffer.

Changing Conditions

The most serious shortcoming of the classical system did not turn out to be its poor employee–management relationship, but rather, its rigidity. Classical organizations spend huge sums to discover the "one best way" of doing something, to develop specialized technology and job structures, and then to lock the behaviour in. Obviously, employee "innovation" is discouraged; if a company already has the best system, then, by definition, any deviation is inefficient. And despite their kinder employee relations, human relations organizations are as rigid and inflexible as classical organizations.

This rigidity at the workplace level is compounded by a decision-making structure that requires all major decisions go to the top of the organization for resolution. This causes three problems. First, decision making is slow. Second, decision implementation is slow, since classical organizations resist change. Third, decision makers at the top of the organization can be seriously out of touch with the problems they are trying to solve and may end up making poor decisions. This is partly due to the poor communication that usually exists in these firms.

Of course, rigidity is not a problem when there is no need to change. In fact, if the organization has truly discovered the "one best way" of doing things, rigidity is an asset. But when the nature of the market, the environment, or technology starts to change quickly, and that "best way" is no longer the best, what had been the key advantage of the classical organization becomes a huge liability.

By the 1980s, the environment in many industries was becoming much more dynamic. For the auto industry, it started with the oil crisis of the 1970s, coupled with the emergence of foreign competition. In computers, it started with the invention of the microchip. For established retailers, it started with the recession of 1981–82 and the emergence of large-scale discount stores. For cameras and photo supplies, it started with the invention of new camera technology (the easy-to-use 35 mm camera and the video camera) coupled with foreign competition.

By 1990, the same North American companies that had once been so admired had become the subject of ridicule and scorn, even being labelled "dinosaurs."[20] GM watched as its North American market share underwent a steady 50-year decline, going from 50 percent in the 1960s to 25 percent in 2005. In a radical departure from its no-layoff policy, IBM cut 140 000 jobs in the early 1990s. Sears was forced to sell its landmark headquarters in Chicago (the Sears Tower), close dozens of stores, and lay off thousands of employees.

What are the options available to classical and human relations firms to get them back on track? Before discussing this question, it should be noted that many fundamental socioeconomic changes have taken place in Canada, that have created conditions that are more suitable for high-involvement organizations and less suitable for classical and human relations organizations. Since the first half of the twentieth century, when these two managerial strategies were first developed, educational levels have increased, economic and social security has improved, and social values have become more democratic and egalitarian. At the same time, products and services have become more complex, along with the technologies used to produce them, all of which generally calls for greater skill, initiative, and motivation from employees. Rapid discovery of new knowledge causes older knowledge to quickly become obsolete, and it is not uncommon for new employees in many firms to understand far more about the firm's technology than their bosses. All of these conditions work against classical and human relations organizations.

Finally, one other development warrants a special note. The emergence of sophisticated information technology (IT) has had a major impact on organizations and has the potential for an even greater impact. Some observers fear that the technology will be used to control employees and reinforce the classical management system. Look, for example, at how Ron Edens has used technology to enforce control at EBS. But other observers argue that IT will be used to facilitate the use of high-involvement management by serving as a vehicle to disseminate the information necessary for the decentralization of decision making.

So how will IT affect managerial strategy? No one knows for sure, but one plausible scenario is that organizations will attempt to use IT to reinforce their existing managerial philosophy, whatever that is. For example, classical organizations will use IT to facilitate control, while high-involvement organizations will use IT to decentralize decision making. Although the empirical evidence on this is not conclusive, Canadian studies have found that in general, firms that use more IT practise more employee involvement[21]; that most employees who had been computerized reported increased satisfaction with the intrinsic characteristics of their jobs[22]; that the majority of employees believe that introduction of computers had made their jobs more interesting[23]; and that computerization upskills more jobs than it downskills.[24]

The Reaction of Human Relations Firms

Human relations companies have been forced to react to late-twentieth-century changes in one of three ways. First, they could try to become more classical, eliminating job security, cutting wages and benefits, and cutting staff—in other words, undoing the very managerial practices that had made them so successful. However, while this "lean and mean" approach may prolong their survival, it does nothing to deal with their fundamental problem: their inability to cope with change. Paradoxically, there is considerable evidence that such actions actually make the organization more resistant to and/or incapable of change. The best employees end up feeling betrayed and seek jobs elsewhere, while the remainder try to keep their heads down. The high stress levels caused by the "lean and mean" approach are also antithetical to effective change. Interestingly, there is evidence, based on samples of Canadian firms, that downsizing generally does not increase future profitability[25] and actually decreases worker efficiency.[26]

A second option is to retain the human relations school of thought but attempt to shift to markets that are less dynamic. In other words, if your environment no longer fits your management strategy, find an environment that does. This course of action frequently requires major surgery, with entire divisions being sold or closed down. However, for those parts of the organization that remain, there are no major changes to managerial strategy or to the reward system. Some organizations have used this approach, known as *downscoping*, very successfully. Sometimes simply reducing the number of disparate markets served is an effective strategy for reducing environmental complexity. Both Sears and Kodak have used downscoping as a part of their turnaround strategies, with Sears now focusing only on retailing and Kodak only on photographic products and imaging technology.

The final option for coping with environmental change is to retain the current domain but attempt to become flexible and innovative—that is, to become a high-involvement organization. Converting to the high-involvement approach is in many ways the toughest road, but it is probably the only one that will lead to long-term success if the firm chooses to stay in a dynamic environment. (Indeed, environments that are not dynamic are becoming increasingly scarce.) This approach has major implications for all aspects of the organizational system. As Figure 2.2 showed, virtually every structural variable—including the reward system—must undergo dramatic change to make this conversion.

Compensation Today 2.5 shows how Sears has tried to move away from its human relations approach toward a high-involvement approach.

The Reaction of Classical Firms

Classical organizations that find themselves facing a dynamic environment are in an even worse position than human relations organizations. Since they are already "lean and mean," there is not much fat that can be easily trimmed, and tough unions may prevent them from becoming as mean as they would like to be. Seeing unions as a threat to their power, some firms have attempted

Can the Circus Help Sears?

It is 9:00 on a Friday morning in November 1995, and 900 employees are packed into the auditorium at Sears' head office in Chicago. None of them knows exactly what to expect.

Suddenly, a spotlight stabs through the semi-darkness, revealing a ringmaster. "Welcome to the Sears PSE Circus," he says. "It's eye-popping. Death defying. Larger than life. Well, not death defying." Then out comes Jim La, the clown, in orange hat, turquoise-and-pink jacket and plaid pants. After telling a few corny jokes, he breaks into a rap song, ending with "We work real hard; now it's time to play. Hey, hey, what do you say?"[27]

In the early 1990s, Sears was in big trouble. Low customer satisfaction, a fierce, competitive environment, declining sales, and high costs had added up to huge losses. So under new CEO Arthur Martinez, the company launched an ambitious program to move away from their famous human relations strategy—which Martinez believed no longer fits their environment—toward a high-involvement model. But Martinez was not pinning all his hopes to change the rigid Sears culture on Jim La, the clown, and his musical comedy act.

The first thing to go was the policy manual (a 29 000-page manual of rules, policies, and procedures), replaced by a 35-page folder entitled "Freedoms and Obligations." The many changes to the managerial system included decentralizing decision making, starting at head office and going all the way to the sales staff. But for that to be effective, employees needed a common frame of reference and a solid understanding of the business and its goals.

So Sears launched a multifaceted training program, including sessions like the PSE circus. (Once Mr. La finished, at about 9:20 a.m., the session transformed into a more serious learning environment, in which "PSE" was translated to mean "Pure Selling Environment.") Other training mechanisms included a "learning map" that all Sears employees journeyed around in 1995 and 1996, and a management training institute dubbed "Sears University."

Moreover, in a reversal of the traditional policy of high job security, the 100 top managers were told to "change or leave," and many managers who couldn't or wouldn't grasp the new concepts were replaced.

A key part of these changes include revisions to the compensation system, starting right at the top, where the top 200 senior executives were no longer compensated only on financial measures. Revenue growth, return on assets, and operating margins now determine half of their annual bonus, while the other half depends equally on customer satisfaction and employee ratings of Sears as an employer. The firm believes (as it always has) that disgruntled employees do not give good customer service. So the challenge was to create a work system that was both motivating and satisfying.

All employees were expected to boost their performance, and every employee's compensation now included a measure of customer satisfaction. This augmented the profit-sharing program that Sears has always had, which seemed to boost employee loyalty, but not employee performance.

In the decade since these changes were made, Sears' performance has improved, although not to the extent that investors had hoped. In 2004, in an attempt to remedy this shortfall, Sears announced a merger with struggling retail giant K–Mart (a low-price chain), making the combined firm the third-largest retailer in the world. The jury is still out on the wisdom of this move.

to destroy or at least weaken their unions. They then have a freer hand to cut costs by cutting pay and benefits, reducing staffing levels, and increasing workloads. Other firms have attempted to circumvent the union by contracting out as much work as possible to non-union or weak-union firms. Another tactic is to shift production to regions or countries where unions are not strong or economic conditions are poor. Sometimes simply threatening to do so may be sufficient to get the union to agree to various concessions.

However, some classical firms have chosen the opposite approach—to work with the union to develop a more cooperative problem-solving atmosphere. Recent Canadian research suggests that, on average, the cooperative approach is more effective in improving company performance than the "lean and mean" approach.[28] Some firms have gone so far as to include labour as partners in management, moving to a high-involvement approach in the process. The most prominent example of this is the Saturn Division of General Motors, which was designed from the ground up as a high-involvement organization.[29]

Classical firms that have chosen to move to a high-involvement management approach have an even tougher task than human relations organizations, because they are starting off with very poor and adversarial employee–management relationships, and the key ingredient for movement to a high-involvement school of thought—trust—is sorely lacking. Furthermore, classical structural characteristics are the exact opposite of what is needed for a high-involvement organization. It often takes a major crisis, coupled with visionary leadership, in order to successfully make the transition.

A key part—perhaps the most crucial part—of making the transition to high involvement is changing the reward and compensation system. The compensation system can be a powerful tool for change or a powerful inhibitor of change, as will be seen in Chapter 3. There is considerable evidence that business firms attempting to move to high-involvement management find their success short-lived if their reward and compensation system does not support the new managerial strategy.[30] Even if employees value high-involvement management for its intrinsic rewards, failure to spread the extrinsic rewards generated by the new management system to all employees can create a sense of inequity that destroys the foundation of trust and goodwill necessary for high involvement to be successful.

An exception to the need for extrinsic rewards can occur in not-for-profit organizations. Where the organization generates no financial surpluses that can be shared, employees may be willing to accept high-involvement management (and even welcome it) on its intrinsic rewards alone. But even here, it is unlikely that high involvement can survive long unless organization members perceive that whatever extrinsic rewards are available are being distributed in an equitable manner. Overall, reward equity, to the extent that it is within the organization's control, is a critical foundation of the high-involvement approach, as is discussed further in Chapter 3.

Current Incidence of High Involvement

To what extent have Canadian companies actually adopted the high-involvement model? This is one of the questions addressed in a major survey of compensation practices in Canadian firms conducted by the author of this text in 2000 and repeated in 2004. Each survey covered about 250 medium to large Canadian companies from a wide variety of business sectors, and the companies surveyed employed over 450 000 Canadians. About half of the firms in the 2004 survey are the same firms as those surveyed in 2000, and all results described in this book will pertain to this sample of identical firms. (For convenience, this survey will be referred to throughout this book as the **Compensation Practices Survey (CPS).**)

Results indicated that in 2004, about 27 percent of the sample resembled high-involvement firms, in that at least three of the five structural dimensions (not including reward structure, which will be discussed separately) shown in Compensation Notebook 2.1 were consistent with a high-involvement structure. However, only about 2 percent of firms were consistent with high-involvement management on all five dimensions. Comparing only the same companies in 2000 and 2004, the survey shows little change, suggesting that existing companies did not make any appreciable movement toward high-involvement management in the first part of this decade. It is not clear whether the tumultuous events of the first few years of the new millennium, such as the 2001 high-tech meltdown, the 2001 World Trade Center terrorist attack, overall dampened economic growth, and intensified global competition have affected the advance of high-involvement in North America.

Trends in Compensation Systems

The strategic framework presented in this chapter helps to explain some of the trends that took place in Canadian compensation systems during the latter part of the twentieth century. The underlying trend has been toward more complicated pay systems. When classical firms dominated, pay systems were simple, based on output or hourly pay, as illustrated by Electronic Banking System Inc. Then, as human relations firms came to the fore, indirect pay made extrinsic rewards more complex, as more and more benefits were added to increase employee security, as illustrated by Kodak. Finally, as some firms began to practise high-involvement management, with a need for complex employee behaviour and high employee performance, compensation systems became yet more complex, as illustrated by Gennum Corporation. Overall, the Compensation Practices Survey shows that high-involvement firms are more likely to use a whole range of compensation practices than are other firms.

General compensation trends over the past two or three decades have included a major increase in the adoption of pay-for-performance systems—especially those aimed at organizational performance, such as profit-sharing and employee stock plans.[31] There has also been an increase in group- or team-based incentive systems, and more firms have also experimented with pay-for-knowledge systems in place of traditional job-based pay systems. Flexible benefit plans have also increased in popularity, and there has been a gradual movement away from hourly pay to the use of salary. However, as will be seen in Chapter 4, many of these trends appear to have stalled in the first few years of the twenty-first century.

Not all trends have been driven by a movement toward high-involvement management. The 1980s and 1990s saw wage freezes and rollbacks and the increased use of two-tier wage structures (under which new employees are hired under a lower pay structure than existing employees). However, use of these practices declined as economic conditions improved in the late 1990s. In adopting these practices, some firms were attempting to deal with their problems by simply cutting the amount of compensation they provided to employees. These tended to be either classical organizations or human relations organizations attempting to survive by simply growing meaner.

Another change that had direct implications for compensation was the increased use of part-time, temporary, and contract workers (often known as "contingent workers") that occurred during the 1980s and 1990s (although this trend appears to have levelled off in recent years). While there were a number of reasons for this trend, as will be discussed in Chapter 5, a major advantage of contingent workers is that they are often much cheaper to employ than regular full-time employees, because of lower wages and employee benefits. Organizations can also dismiss contingent workers without demonstrating cause or providing severance pay, which not only provides flexibility but also fits well with the classical management philosophy. Another reason that classical organizations like these workers is that they are easier to manage because of their economic insecurity. As conditions have become more difficult for classical organizations, many have continued to look to contingent workers as one way of helping their classical system continue to function.

However, it should be noted that some high-involvement organizations have also increased their use of contingent workers, although for different reasons. A prime reason is to help provide employment security for their core workforce, by using contingent workers as a buffer to deal with demand fluctuations. In many of these high-involvement firms, contingent workers are compensated on the same basis as permanent employees, because the motivation for using them is not to cut costs.

Summary

This chapter provides a strategic framework for identifying the reward and compensation system that will best fit an organization's strategy and structure. To achieve this, the compensation system must be developed in the context of the total reward system, which in turn must be developed in the context of the organization's structure and managerial strategy.

The three managerial strategies identified in this chapter—classical, human relations, and high involvement—each call for a different reward and compensation system. Since the most appropriate managerial strategy (and therefore the most appropriate reward and compensation system) for a given organization depends on certain key factors in that organization's context, it is important that you understand what these factors are and how they relate to managerial strategy. Compensation Notebook 2.2 provides a template to help you select the managerial strategy that best fits the five main contextual factors (the organization's environment, its corporate strategy, its technology, its size, and the nature of its workforce) and therefore should fit a firm the best. However, you should note that not all firms actually utilize the managerial strategy that best suits their contextual variables, and the way to determine which managerial strategy a firm is *actually* using is to examine the structural dimensions of the organization, as summarized in Compensation Notebook 2.1.

Overall, conditions in recent years have generally become much less favourable for the human relations and classical managerial strategies, and the shift to high involvement is creating a change in the nature of reward systems. Although there are still circumstances under which a classical or human relations strategy remains viable, these circumstances are likely to become increasingly scarce. Organizations with a suboptimal managerial strategy can often continue to survive for a period of time, but only as long as market conditions are favourable, or as long as none of their competitors is managed any better than they are. (Of course, if they have no competitors at all, as in the case of a monopoly, they may be able to survive for an indefinite period of time even with an inappropriate managerial strategy.)

Indeed, not all organizations have a conscious managerial strategy. In fact, for most organizations, managerial strategy is implicit, rather than explicit; but it still serves to govern managerial behaviour in their organizations. Of course, the degree of development and refinement of managerial strategies varies enormously across firms. However, for some firms, there is no consistent managerial strategy at all. What this means is that there is no ideal reward and compensation system for these firms. When there is no coherent managerial strategy, you cannot design a compensation system to support that strategy. In these cases, you cannot start designing an optimal reward and compensation system until you have sorted out these underlying organizational problems.

But enough about strategy and compensation for now! The next milestone on your journey to effective compensation is to add to your conceptual tool kit a framework that helps you understand how reward systems link to human behaviour.

Key Terms

analyzer corporate strategy, 39

classical managerial strategy, 27

communication and information
 structure, 26

Compensation Practices Survey (CPS), 54

contextual variables, 26

contingency approach to organization
 design, 24

control structure, 26

coordination and departmentation, 26

corporate strategy, 24

craft technology, 41

decision-making and leadership structure, 26

defender corporate strategy, 39

differentiator corporate strategy, 40

domain, 27

engineering technology, 41

focused differentiator corporate strategy, 40

focused low-cost corporate strategy, 40

high-involvement managerial strategy, 28

human relations managerial strategy, 27

intensive technology, 40

job design, 26

long-linked technology, 40

low-cost corporate strategy, 40

managerial strategy, 26

mass/large batch technology, 42

mediating technology, 40

nonroutine technology, 41

organizational culture, 37

organizations, 23

organization structure, 24

process technology, 42

prospector corporate strategy, 39

routine technology, 41

task environment, 27

technology, 24

unit/small batch technology, 42

Web Links

To get a taste of some of the latest trends and issues in compensation, go to **http://www.worldatwork.org** or **http://www.hrreporter.com**. (p. 54)

RPC Icons

RPC 2.1 Designs and evaluates total compensation strategies to ensure that they reflect the organization's goals, culture, and external environment.

Discussion Questions

1. "If a compensation system works well for one business, that same compensation system should also work well for other businesses." Discuss whether this statement is true.
2. Discuss why it is important to understand which managerial strategy a firm is practising before designing a compensation system for that firm.
3. Discuss recent trends in compensation practices taking place in North America and explain what may be causing those trends.

Using the Internet

Go to the website for the *Canadian Human Resources Reporter* **http://www. hrreporter.com**, and click on *compensation*. From the stories that have been published in recent months, what seem to be the key themes and concerns in compensation?

Exercises

1. Take an organization that you know well, such as a current or former employer, and apply the template in Compensation Notebook 2.2 to determine the most appropriate managerial strategy for that firm. Does this match the managerial strategy actually in use? If not, why not? Do you agree with what the template indicates as the best managerial strategy? Would you consider this firm to be an effective organization? Does the organization's reward system match its managerial strategy?
2. In a group of five or six people, share the results of your analysis from Exercise 1. Compare the organizations that were considered to be effective with those that were not. Were the firms that matched strategy with contextual variables rated better than those that did not? Discuss why or

why not. If you find some organizations that seem effective despite a poor fit between contextual variables and managerial strategy, discuss why this might be.

3. Compensation Today 2.5 discusses how Sears has tried to move toward a high-involvement strategy. Using the template in Compensation Notebook 2.2, analyze whether this is the right move for the company to make. Based on your analysis, what advice would you give to top management at Sears? Discuss your conclusions with your group. In the process, ask any group members who have worked in retail to discuss their experiences and the managerial strategies these firms seem to use.

Case Questions

1. The "Achtymichuk Machine Works" in the Appendix is having a lot of trouble motivating and retaining its cleaners. To get as many ideas as possible for solving this problem, they have hired three different consultants. One is an adherent of the classical managerial strategy, one is an adherent of the human relations managerial strategy, and one is an adherent of the high involvement managerial strategy. Each consultant works separately, and provides a separate set of recommendations for solving the problem. All of their recommendations include changes to the compensation system for cleaners, but these changes are all different. Knowing what you do about the three managerial strategies, what do you think the recommendations of each consultant were? Which do you think would be the most effective solution?

2. Read "The Fit Stop" case in the Appendix and determine which managerial strategy would be most effective for this firm. Given what you know about Susan Superfit, which managerial strategy do you think she would prefer to use? Does this match your choice?

3. Read the "Multi-Products Corporation" case in the Appendix and determine the managerial strategy that would be most effective for this firm. What reward and compensation strategy would fit this managerial strategy? What problems might you encounter in using this managerial strategy?

Simulation Cross-Reference

If you are using *Strategic Compensation: A Simulation* in conjunction with this text, you will find that the concepts in Chapter 2 are helpful in preparing Sections A, B, and C of the simulation.

Endnotes

1. Daft, Richard. 2001. *Organization Theory and Design*. Cincinnati: Southwestern Publishing.
2. Turnasella, Ted. 1994. "Aligning Pay with Business Strategies and Cultural Values." *Compensation & Benefits Review*, 26(5): 65.
3. Miles, Raymond E. 1975. *Theories of Management: Implications for Organizational Behavior and Development*. New York: McGraw-Hill.
4. Lawler, Edward E. 1992. *The Ultimate Advantage: Creating the High Involvement Organization*. San Francisco: Jossey Bass.
5. Kochan, Thomas A., and Paul Osterman. 1994. *The Mutual Gains Enterprise*. Boston: Harvard Business School.
6. Betcherman, Gordon, Kathryn McMullen, Norm Leckie, and Christina Caron. 1994. *The Canadian Workplace in Transition*. Kingston: IRC Press.
7. Case, John. 1995. *Open Book Management: The Coming Business Revolution*. New York: Harper Business.
8. Wood, Stephen. 1996. "High Commitment Management and Payment Systems." *Journal of Management Studies*, 33(1): 53–77.
9. Long, Richard J. 1994. "Gain Sharing, Hierarchy, and Managers: Are They Substitutes?" Proceedings of the Annual Conference of the Administrative Sciences of Canada, Organization Theory Division, 15(12): 51–60.
10. MacDuffie, John Paul. 1995. "Human Resource Bundles and Manufacturing Performance: Organizational Logic and Flexible Production Systems in the World Automobile Industry. *Industrial and Labor Relations Review*, 48(2): 197–221.
11. Daft, Richard. 2001. *Organization Theory and Design*. Cincinnati: Southwestern Publishing: 1314.
12. Hodson, Randy. 2001. "Disorganized, Unilateral, and Participative Organizations: New Insights from the Ethnographic Literature." *Industrial Relations*, 40(2): 204–30.
13. Miles, Raymond E., and Charles Snow. 1978. *Organizational Strategy, Structure, and Process*. New York: McGraw-Hill.
14. Porter, Michael E. 1980. *Competitive Strategy: Techniques for Analyzing Industries and Competitors*. New York: Free Press.
15. Thompson, James D. 1967. *Organizations in Action*. New York: McGraw-Hill.
16. Perrow, Charles. 1967. "A Framework for Comparative Analysis of Organizations." *American Sociological Review*, 32: 194–208.
17. Woodward, Joan. 1965. *Industrial Organization: Theory and Practice*. London: Oxford University Press.
18. Addison, John T., and Barry T. Hirsch. 1989. "Union Effects on Productivity: Has the Long Run Arrived?" *Journal of Labor Economics*, 7(1): 72–105.
19. Long, Richard J. 1993. "The Impact of Unionization on Employment Growth of Canadian Companies." *Industrial and Labor Relations Review*, 46(4): 691–703.
20. Looney, Carol J. 1993. "Dinosaurs?" *Fortune*, May 3: 36–42.
21. Long, Richard J. 1993. "New Information Technology and Employee Involvement." *Proceedings of the Administrative Sciences Association of Canada, Organizational Behaviour Division*, 14(5): 161–70.
22. Long, Richard J. 1993. "The Impact of New Office Information Technology on Job Quality of Female and Male Employees." *Human Relations*, 46(8): 939–61.
23. Lowe, Graham S. 1992. *Human Resource Challenges of Education, Computers, and Retirement*. Ottawa: Statistics Canada.
24. Lowe, Graham S. 2000. *The Quality of Work*. Don Mills, ON: Oxford University Press.
25. Mentzer, Marc S. 1996. "Corporate Downsizing and Profitability in Canada." *Canadian Journal of Administrative Sciences*, 13(3): 237–50.

26. Wagar, Terry H. 1998. "Exploring the Consequences of Workforce Reduction." *Canadian Journal of Administrative Sciences*, 15(4): 300–9.

27. Dobrzynski, Judith H. 1996. "Sears Goes to the Circus to Motivate Employees." *The Globe and Mail*, January 10: B16.

28. Wagar, Terry H. 1997. "The Labour–Management Relationship and Organization Outcomes: Some Initial Findings." *Relations industrielles/Industrial Relations*, 52(2): 430–47.

29. Rubenstein, Saul. 2000. "The Impact of Co-Management on Quality Performance: The Case of the Saturn Corporation." *Industrial and Labor Relations Review*, 53(2): 197–218.

30. Lawler, Edward E. 1992. *The Ultimate Advantage: Creating the High Involvement Organization*. San Francisco: Jossey Bass.

31. Chaykowski, Richard, and Brian Lewis. 1995. *Compensation Practices and Outcomes in Canada and the United States*. Kingston: IRC Press.

Chapter 3

A Behavioural Framework for Compensation

Chapter Learning Objectives

After reading this chapter, you should be able to:

- Identify the three main types of reward problems that can afflict organizations.
- Define the three key employee behaviours desired by employers.
- Identify three key job attitudes and explain their role in determining employee behaviour.
- Describe the causes and consequences of reward dissatisfaction.
- Explain how to generate membership behaviour.
- Outline the process through which task behaviour is motivated.
- Explain how to generate organizational citizenship behaviour.
- Discuss the role that managerial strategy plays in determining the type of employee attitudes and behaviour needed by an organization.
- Understand the integrated model for human behaviour and explain how it helps us to design effective reward systems.

CLOUDY VISION AT BAUSCH AND LOMB

Bausch and Lomb is a major producer of contact lenses, sunglasses, and other optical products. In order to promote product sales, the company instituted large bonuses for sales managers who met their monthly and quarterly targets, but severe penalties for those who did not. Managers lived in fear of "red ball" days, named for the red dots marking the end of fiscal quarters on B&L calendars. Red ball days also fell at the end of each month.

Managers resorted to various tactics for meeting their "red ball" targets. If they were coming up short, they offered large discounts in the two or three days preceding red ball days. Customers learned to wait for these periods and seldom booked orders unless they could receive a hefty discount. In other cases, managers threatened to cut off distributors unless they took far more of the product than they wanted. Managers also offered deferred payment plans to their distributors, since a product was counted as being sold when it was shipped, not when payment was received. In some cases, sales managers simply shipped product that had not been ordered at all.

Among the problems created by this system were major cost inefficiencies. As a *Business Week* investigative report found:

> The lumping of orders into a few frantic days each month also made B&L's distribution operations woefully inefficient. Its sunglass distribution centre in San Antonio, Texas, stayed open around the clock the last few days of every month in recent years. That meant hiring up to 35 temporary workers, while staffers racked up huge overtime. "We'd ship 70 percent of the month's goods in the last three days," says a former operations manager. "The hourly workers must have thought we were nuts."

Source: Maremont, Mark. 1995. "Blind Ambition: How the Pursuit of Results Got Out of Hand at Bausch and Lomb." *Business Week*, October 23: 78–92.

Introduction

On the surface, the reward system used for managers at Bausch and Lomb seems to make sense. Sales are important to the firm, so set high sales targets and reward managers for meeting them. However, while the reward system did increase sales, in the short run at least, it also created many unanticipated problems, such as reduced profit on sales, alienated customers, and inefficient distribution. But surely, such undesirable reward systems are scarce? Well, consider the following examples before answering that.

- Sears wanted to increase sales in its service department, and so it started paying a commission to its auto mechanics on the amount of service work done. This did increase sales dramatically, but many customers found that much of the work done was unnecessary. When word of this hit the newspapers, it caused serious damage to the firm's reputation.
- In order to boost book sales in its college division, a major Canadian publisher introduced a plan that would pay bonuses to its sales reps if annual sales exceeded a target set by the regional sales manager. The plan seemed to have no effect on sales whatsoever and was eliminated within a year.
- A manufacturer of consumer products had the following system for rewarding its three main units: marketing was evaluated on volume of sales; production was evaluated on production costs; and research and development was evaluated on number of patents registered. Not only did this system cause enormous conflict between the three units, but the company also found it almost impossible to bring new products to the market on a timely basis. Those that did reach the market either did not achieve customer acceptance or were not profitable.
- For years, purchasing officers at Canadian National Railways were evaluated on the basis of reducing item costs in comparison to the previous year. For example, one key part of a boxcar is the axle, a round bar of steel on which the wheels are mounted. Since thousands of axles are used in a year, a purchasing officer who could reduce the cost of each axle by even 2 or 3 percent was regarded as a hero. But it turns out that by spending slightly *more* on each axle, and ordering them slightly thicker, they would last much longer. However, under the previous reward system, any purchasing officer who bought the longer-lasting axles would have been penalized.
- A Canadian auto retailer wished to create a more cooperative "team" atmosphere among its sales staff by having experienced sales personnel take more responsibility for training new sales staff. Compensation for sales staff was straight commission on volume sold. Management couldn't understand why, despite their exhortations, senior sales personnel showed little interest in training new sales staff.

These examples serve to illustrate that reward systems may have a powerful effect on behaviour, but that the behaviour we get is not always the behaviour we want. Could we have predicted any of these outcomes? Why do people behave as they do? Why do they often not behave as we want them to? How can we get them to behave as the organization needs them to behave? What role can reward systems play in influencing their behaviour?

As any manager knows, the answers to these questions are not obvious. But finding these answers is crucial for designing an effective reward system. The purpose of this chapter is to develop a conceptual framework that can be used to find these answers.

We will start by identifying three main categories of reward problems: failure to produce desired behaviour; production of desired behaviour and undesirable consequences; and production of reward dissatisfaction. Then we will look at three types of desired employee behaviour: membership behaviour, task behaviour, and organizational citizenship behaviour. Since reward systems can generate these behaviours only through their impact on employee attitudes, we will focus on the job attitudes that generally lead to these behaviours. From there, we will move on to the issue of reward dissatisfaction, examining the possible consequences and causes of this potentially devastating phenomenon.

After that, we will examine each of the three desired employee behaviours in depth, and consider how the reward system can help to generate these behaviours. The culmination of all this will be an integrated model of behaviour that can be used as a tool to design reward systems that will generate the employee behaviour the organization needs and wants.

RPC 3.1

Types of Reward Problems

As the B&L case shows, a multitude of different reward problems can occur. To get a better handle on these problems, we can organize them into a few basic types. The first type of problem occurs when the reward system fails to produce the desired behaviour. The second type occurs when the reward system does produce the desired behaviour but also produces undesirable consequences. The third problem occurs when the reward system produces a state of reward dissatisfaction among employees.

Failure to Produce Desired Behaviour

A common problem occurs when a reward system simply has no impact on behaviour, as in the case of the publisher described above. (While we don't know the details, a possible cause was that the sales targets were set too high, and we know that unrealistic goals do not motivate behaviour.) Obviously, if the behaviour the organization needs isn't occurring, or if it is occurring only for certain employees, this can be a serious problem. However, there can be an even more harmful variation of this problem. In some cases, the reward system not only fails to produce the desired behaviour, but also produces undesirable behaviour, or behaviour that leads to negative consequences. For example, the Green Giant reward system (Chapter 1) did not produce significantly cleaner product but it did produce higher costs.

Production of Desired Behaviour and Undesirable Consequences

Another type of problem occurs when the reward system does indeed generate the desired behaviour, but there are also unanticipated negative consequences. The new reward system for Sears service technicians did cause them to generate increased sales; but Sears hadn't wanted them to do it by cheating the customers. The Bausch and Lomb system did produce higher sales, but also lower profits, dissatisfied customers, and higher shipping costs. The reward system used at CN Rail did reduce per-item purchasing costs, but it also discouraged examination of other potentially more valuable approaches to cost savings.

The reward system at the consumer goods company did motivate marketing to increase sales, production to minimize costs, and research and development (R&D) to develop new products. However, while the R&D department did secure many patents, most of these products either had no market or were difficult to manufacture. The production department did minimize costs, but they did so by using poor-quality materials and oversimplifying the product. Marketing did try to sell these products but found that the only way to do so was by making outlandish promises or by cutting prices, which put even more pressure on the production department to reduce costs. These behaviours resulted in low cooperation and high conflict among the departments. Marketing blamed the R&D department for developing "useless" products and production for producing poor-quality products. R&D blamed production for destroying "good product designs" and blamed marketing for not knowing how to sell. Production accused both R&D and marketing of incompetence.

In short, the more that each department tried to meet its own reward goals, the less successful the company was. By rewarding mutually incompatible goals in a situation where interdependence is high and cooperation essential, the company was guaranteeing failure. Thus, a reward system that looks reasonable when viewed in a narrow (departmental) context may in fact be very damaging for the organization as a whole.

A slightly different variation of reward problem occurs when the reward system does generate the rewarded behaviours, with no obvious negative consequences, but also serves to suppress other desirable behaviours that are not measured or rewarded. The case of the auto retailer illustrates this problem. If the sales staff are paid only on the basis of their individual sales, why would they want to spend time training possible competitors? When an organization rewards only one aspect of a job, is it really surprising that the other aspects are neglected?

So why do companies reward only certain aspects of a job? As numerous studies have shown, companies tend to reward job aspects that are easy to measure—aspects that are highly visible and for which objective data are available—while hoping that employees will also perform job tasks that are not measured or rewarded.[1] In fact, some conscientious employees may indeed perform all of the desired job aspects; but if they do, it is in spite of the reward system, not because of it.

Production of Reward Dissatisfaction

A final type of problem is not specifically related to any single aspect of the reward system but is potentially very serious. When employees believe that the rewards they receive are not consistent with the contributions they are making to the organization, or when they believe that the reward system is unfair, they will experience *reward dissatisfaction*. Reward dissatisfaction can result in a variety of negative consequences, such as poor work performance, high turnover, poor customer service, and even employee dishonesty. Because reward dissatisfaction can be such a serious problem, its causes and consequences will be examined in depth later in the chapter. But before doing so, we need to focus briefly on the other side of the coin—what outcomes *should* the reward system produce?

Desired Reward Outcomes

Three Key Employee Behaviours

An effective reward system should not only avoid causing undesirable behaviour but also promote desired behaviour. There are three general sets of behaviours most organizations find desirable. **Membership behaviour** occurs when employees decide to join and remain with a firm. **Task behaviour** occurs when employees perform the specific tasks that have been assigned to them. **Organizational citizenship behaviour** occurs when employees voluntarily undertake special behaviours beneficial to the organization that go beyond simple membership and task behaviour, such as extra effort, high cooperation with others, high initiative, high innovativeness, extra customer service, and a general willingness to make sacrifices for the good of the organization. Organizational citizenship behaviour is sometimes known as "contextual performance" in contrast to "task performance."[2]

Three Key Employee Attitudes

So how do you create a reward system that will generate these behaviours? This question is complicated by the fact that reward systems do not affect human behaviour directly. They first affect employee perceptions and attitudes, which then drive behaviour. So this brings us to another question. What are the key employee attitudes that need to be created in order to generate the employee behaviour we desire?

The three key attitudes are job satisfaction, work motivation, and organizational identification. **Job satisfaction** can be defined as the attitude one holds toward one's job and workplace, either positive or negative. **Work motivation** can be defined as the attitude one holds toward good job performance, either positive or negative. Essentially, it is the strength of an employee's desire to perform his or her job duties well. **Organizational identification** consists of three interrelated elements: a sense of shared goals and values with the organization, a sense of membership or belongingness, and an intention to remain a member of the organization. This third element is sometimes known as "organizational commitment."

Each of these attitudes can lead to behaviour that is beneficial to the organization in different ways. Job satisfaction leads to membership behaviour, work motivation leads to task behaviour, and organizational identification leads to citizenship behaviour, although it also contributes to the other two behaviours. Figure 3.1 illustrates these relationships.

You will notice that Figure 3.1 has arrows leading from organizational identification to both job satisfaction and motivation. That is because organizational identification can have a positive impact on each of these elements. For example, a sense of membership and belongingness can help to

membership behaviour

occurs when employees decide to join and remain with a firm

task behaviour

occurs when employees perform the tasks that have been assigned to them

organizational citizenship behaviour

occurs when employees voluntarily undertake special behaviours beneficial to the organization

job satisfaction

the attitude one holds toward one's job and workplace

work motivation

the attitude one holds toward good job performance

organizational identification

a sense of shared goals, belongingness, and desire to remain a member of the organization

Part I: Strategy, Rewards, and Behaviour

FIGURE 3.1

How Rewards Affect Employee Behaviour

satisfy social needs, which then enhances job satisfaction. A sense of shared goals and the positive group norms that develop from shared goals can increase employee motivation.

But wait a minute! Isn't there an arrow missing? Shouldn't job satisfaction also increase motivation and task behaviour? In the past, many people believed that job satisfaction was virtually synonymous with work motivation. But we now know that this is not true. (Of course, classical managers, such as Ron Edens of EBS in Compensation Today 2.1, have always known that it is possible to get a lot of work out of employees without providing much job satisfaction!)

Satisfied, happy workers are not necessarily more productive workers. But they are less likely to quit, to be absent, or to submit grievances, and more likely to be pleasant with other employees and customers. Satisfied employees also suffer less work stress, which then reduces errors and accidents and produces fewer health problems that would cause absenteeism.

Because of low turnover rates, organizations with high job satisfaction have lower recruiting and training costs and more knowledgeable employees, who more often develop cordial relationships with customers than firms with low job satisfaction. So although high job satisfaction does not automatically bring high productivity, it certainly can bring a number of real benefits. As with the other two key employee attitudes, the reward system can have a major impact on job satisfaction.

Figure 3.2 summarizes some of the specific consequences of each job attitude. As just discussed, the consequences of job satisfaction include decreased turnover, absenteeism, and grievances, reduced stress, and positive group norms. Work motivation leads to job effort, which should in turn lead to task performance. Organizational identification leads to positive group norms,

FIGURE 3.2

Key Employee Attitudes and Their Consequences

cooperative behaviour, innovative behaviour, and increased job effort, along with decreased turnover, absenteeism, and grievances.

Clearly, all three of these attitudes are desirable. But exactly how important they are to a given firm varies enormously. Consider the example of B.C. Rogers chicken processors, described in Compensation Today 2.4. From the point of view of Rogers' management, employee job satisfaction and organizational identification would probably be nice to have, but they are certainly not essential. The firm doesn't need innovative or cooperative behaviour from its employees, nor does management care if turnover is high, since employee replacement costs are so low. It doesn't even need particularly high motivation, since the "chain" dictates productivity. What the firm needs is simply enough physical job effort from each employee to keep up with the chain. No more, no less. In return for this minimal expectation, the firm provides minimal rewards. All that the reward system needs to accomplish is a flow of new employees sufficient to replace those who quit. Under current conditions, while very simple and exclusively extrinsic, the company's reward system appears to be appropriate. It fits the firm's classical managerial strategy, which in turn fits the firm's contextual variables.

Of course, for many firms, such minimal employee contributions would be wholly inadequate and their reward systems would need to be much more sophisticated to promote the full range of desired behaviours. As a general rule, the more complex the desired behaviour—and the higher the performance

Compensation Today 3.1

Rewards Support Strategy at Toyota

At its Kentucky assembly plant, Toyota uses a carefully conceived reward system to support its managerial strategy, which focuses on three central concepts: employee loyalty and commitment to the firm, teamwork, and high performance. So how do you create the attitudes necessary to generate these behaviours?

The reward system includes all three compensation components. Base pay is reasonable, but not high for the industry. But to create a feeling of cohesion among production workers, all employees receive the same pay once they have completed 18 months of service. Although Toyota provides an extensive array of benefits to employees, including childcare and on-site recreational facilities, they are not out of line for the auto industry, which is famous for the benefits its unions have won.

What is unusual is that benefits are structured identically for all employees, from assembly workers to the plant manager. There are no executive dining rooms, preferred parking, or private offices for executives. The company believes that egalitarianism is necessary to avoid the division between workers and managers that is so common in this highly unionized industry. (Toyota employees have never voted to unionize.)

When Toyota uses performance pay, it is not based on the individual. For example, annual bonuses, based on company performance, make up a big chunk of earnings for all employees. Special award money is distributed to groups or teams that have made suggestions that result in safety, cost, or quality improvements. This money is distributed equally among group members and usually consists of gift certificates that can be used at local retailers. The purpose of this program is threefold: to make sure that this money simply doesn't get lost in the paycheque; to create family involvement; and to make the reward more tangible. For example, every time the employee looks at her new VCR, purchased with these certificates, she will be reminded why she received it. In addition, PT (personal touch) money is made available to team leaders to support team social activities, such as a summer picnic, monthly team lunches, or trips to ball games.

As a part of its reward strategy, the company offers numerous rewards beyond compensation, one being job security. According to Besser, "Of all the rewards an organization can offer, the one which was seen as most important by nearly all my informants was the job security offered them by Toyota. Every American interviewee mentioned job security in one form or another as either the reason they took a job with Toyota and/or the reason they would remain, even if offered a better paying job."

Another key pillar of the reward system is training and promotion opportunities. The company has a promote-from-within policy and invests heavily in training for its employees. Toyota focuses on bringing in top-calibre employees with the potential to grow and develop. However, to keep them interested in what is essentially routine and repetitive work is a challenge. Toyota deals with this challenge by providing job enrichment, team-based decision making, job rotation, and the possibility of advancement to other jobs.

Finally, there are a number of recognition rewards, such as plaques for a perfect safety record. These rewards are valued by employees for the symbolic meaning behind them rather than for any economic value. But they must be seen in the context of the total reward system. As one observer notes: "Certainly, these tokens alone would be insufficient, perhaps even insulting to employees. However, in conjunction with the other rewards already discussed, they encourage employees to believe that they will not be 'fools for busting their butts for the company.'"

The result of all this? A tightly knit, team-oriented workplace, with very low turnover, high productivity, and high quality.

Source: Adapted from Besser, Terry L. 1995. "Rewards Support Strategy at Toyota." *Journal of Management Studies*, 34(1): 383–399. Reprinted with permission of Blackwell Publishing.

level required—the more complex the reward system will have to be, as we have already seen at Gennum Corporation (Compensation Today 2.3).

Compensation Today 3.1 illustrates this point further by describing the multifaceted reward system at Toyota Motors. For Toyota, all three job attitudes are important. High job satisfaction is important because the firm wants to develop a stable and loyal workforce with cohesive work teams. Employee motivation is important because Toyota expects very high employee job performance. Organizational identification is important because the firm depends on employee initiative for constantly improving the production process and on employee self-control to reduce the need for costly inspection and supervision. Positive group norms are also important to motivate and direct employee behaviour. As this example shows, it takes a complex combination of extrinsic and intrinsic rewards to produce the kinds of attitudes and behaviour Toyota needs for its high-involvement managerial strategy to work.

By now, it should be apparent that the three managerial strategies will require different behaviours and different attitudes, so let's summarize here. Classical organizations need only provide sufficient rewards to create some degree of membership behaviour. They don't really need job satisfaction because very little membership behaviour is really needed. Motivation for task behaviour can be achieved through rewards tied directly to the needed behaviours, or through the use of control systems, with the underlying threat of dismissal providing the basic motivation. Classical organizations pay a price for not having job and reward satisfaction, or organizational identification, but they are structured to minimize this price.

In contrast, human relations organizations rely on job satisfaction and positive work norms and must ensure that they have equitable reward systems that generate job satisfaction and a substantial degree of commitment. They depend on high membership behaviour and adequate task behaviour. Organizational identification, while desirable, is not essential, since a high degree of organizational citizenship behaviour is not essential.

Because high-involvement organizations typically require the most complex behaviour from their employees and the highest level of performance, they generally require the most complex reward systems. They need to generate all three job attitudes and behaviours. The key job attitude for them is organizational identification, which generates the organizational citizenship behaviour so important to these firms and plays a major role in generating membership and task behaviour. Work motivation needs to be high. And job satisfaction must also be high enough to help generate the high membership behaviour that the firm needs. Clearly, a key element in maintaining these attitudes is employee satisfaction with the reward system.

RPC 3.1

Causes and Consequences of Reward Dissatisfaction

Reward dissatisfaction can cause many undesirable consequences for organizations. But first, what causes reward dissatisfaction?

Causes of Reward Dissatisfaction

Four main factors play a role in causing reward dissatisfaction, as Figure 3.3 illustrates. These are violation of the psychological contract, perceived inequity, relative deprivation, and lack of organizational justice.

FIGURE 3.3

Causes of Reward Dissatisfaction

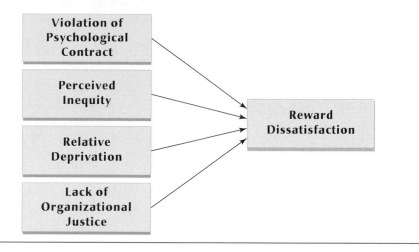

Violation of the Psychological Contract

When people decide whether to join a firm, they do so based on their expectations about the rewards they will receive and the contributions they will have to make. This is known as their **psychological contract**.[3] Similarly, an organization hires someone based on the expectation that the individual will make certain contributions to the organization, in return for certain rewards. In some cases, these psychological contracts will also include legal contracts, enforceable under law, spelling out the rewards to be provided and the contributions to be made. In most cases, they do not.

When an employee accepts an offer and joins a firm, problems with the psychological contract can occur for two main reasons: (1) there has not been accurate communication about the nature of the rewards provided and/or contributions required, and these turn out to be different from the employee's expectations; and (2) the employer unilaterally changes the "contract" in a way that the employee perceives as detrimental.

Morrison and Robinson label these two possibilities "incongruence" of expectations and "reneging" and argue that either can lead to a perceived violation of the psychological contract.[4] They cite evidence showing that perceived violation can cause employees to have less trust in their employer, decreased job satisfaction, reduced citizenship behaviour, and decreased work performance, and can lead to increased turnover, theft, or even sabotage.

Besides these two possibilities, psychological contracts are related to reward dissatisfaction in at least two other ways. One such situation occurs when employee perceptions of the fairness of the "contract" change. Employees may come to see the original contract as being unfair (even though it is being honoured) in the light of new information they receive. Another

psychological contract
expectations about the rewards offered by a given job and the contributions necessary to perform the job

situation occurs when employees feel compelled to accept a "contract" even though they believe it to be unfair right from the outset. In all four of these cases, reward dissatisfaction will likely occur.

In the 1980s and early 1990s, economic conditions caused many firms to reduce their reward structures in violation of long-standing psychological contracts. For example, Lucero and Allen note that reductions in employee benefits have a negative impact on the psychological contract.[5] But the impact of these violations depends on the nature of the firm. For human relations firms, the costs of contract violations can be especially high, since employee satisfaction and trust in management form the glue that holds these organizations together. These problems will be particularly severe if the cuts appear to be unnecessary—if, for example, cuts are made even in the face of acceptable company profitability, a previously rare practice that became more common in the 1990s.

Compensation Today 3.2 illustrates the consequences that can arise when an organization makes promises for a fundamentally new type of psychological contract but is perceived to be violating these promises, as management at the CAMI auto plant in Ontario found out.

Perceived Inequity

Individuals use at least two perceptual screens to decide whether the rewards/contributions balance is fair. The first is an internal calculus, based on their own valuations of the rewards received and contributions made. The second is a comparison with the rewards/contributions ratio of relevant others, a process explained by **equity theory**.[6]

equity theory

employees base perceptions of equity (fairness) on a comparison of their contributions/rewards ratio to the ratios of others perceived as similar

Equity theory helps to explain a number of mysteries, such as why a person making over $5 million a year doing a job he has coveted all his life may bitterly proclaim that he is under-rewarded and even threaten to quit, while another person earning $40,000 a year at a job she never particularly wanted is quite satisfied with her rewards. Sound farfetched? Not if the first person is the highest scoring hockey player in the National Hockey League, and the second is an accounting clerk with a high school education, employed by a firm that provides high job security. The accounting clerk may look around and see that most people with performance, education, and job security similar to what she has are earning less than she is; the hockey player may look around and see six players who score less earning more.

Equity theory also helps to explain why, for two employees working side by side at the same job, each making $50,000 per year, one may believe this arrangement to be equitable, while the other regards it as highly unfair. Why? The dissatisfied employee believes that his or her contribution is much greater than the contribution of the other employee, yet both are receiving the same rewards.

Thus, the essence of equity theory is simple: people make comparisons between the ratio of contributions they make to the firm and the rewards they receive, and the ratios of relevant others, mostly co-workers. They are often

Compensation Today 3.2

Violating the Psychological Contract at CAMI

Perceived violation of the psychological contract helped to derail an attempt to create a collaborative union–management relationship at CAMI Inc., a joint GM–Suzuki venture that was established in 1988 to manufacture small cars in Ingersoll, Ontario. Before the new plant opened, it agreed to a voluntary recognition of the union (the Canadian Auto Workers). The union agreed to accept somewhat lower wages and benefits than were offered by the big three automakers in return for a nonclassical approach from management, in which workers would be treated with respect and dignity, and their ideas and inputs would be valued.

To reinforce this image of equality, time clocks, executive parking spaces, and executive cafeterias were eliminated, and production was organized into teams. Hourly employees were known as production associates, team leaders, and maintenance associates. However, despite the titles, relatively few changes were made to the nature of the work itself. Perhaps most significantly, no changes were made to the usual reward system for hourly employees, and no rewards were provided for productivity or performance. Part of the reason may have been that the Canadian Auto Workers is philosophically opposed to performance pay, although it is not clear that the company actually pushed for group or organizational performance rewards.

Consequently, despite all the symbolic changes, workers soon came to believe that the promise of a fundamentally different relationship was an empty one, and that all the changes were simply superficial changes oriented toward manipulating workers to higher productivity. Workers pointed to extremely lean staffing levels, which put great pressure for production on the employees.

As a result of this perceived violation of the psychological contract, and the nonappearance of the intrinsic rewards the employees were expecting, union–management relationships became bitter, culminating in 1992 in the first and only strike at any Japanese "transplant" in North America. Prominent among the strike issues were reducing workloads and narrowing the wage/benefit gap between CAMI and other big three plants, concessions that were made by the company.

Following the strike, a psychological contract more in line with the North American auto industry appears to have emerged, in which workers believe that the firm is "just another car factory" and do not really expect treatment different from the industry norm. Since then, there have been no new major strikes, and in 1998 CAMI was selected as lead plant for the production of two new sport utility vehicles. However, this decision was likely prompted more by the plant's relatively new production technology than by any special union–management relationships. An example of the continuing tense relationships occurred on May 30, 1999, when workers refused to report to work in protest over the firing of a union steward involved in an altercation with a supervisor. In response, the company replaced the termination with a suspension, and work resumed.

Since that time, the company and the employees appear to have come to a mutual understanding on the nature of the psychological contract, and affairs are now running smoothly at the plant. Indeed, in 2005, within the context of a $2.5-billion investment in its Canadian plants, GM announced a $500-million investment in the CAMI plant so that it can re-tool and expand to start producing the new Pontiac Torrent compact SUV, with an eventual increase of 400 workers at the plant.

Source: Rinehart, James, Christopher Huxley, and David Robertson. 1997. *Just Another Car Factory?* Ithaca, NY: ILR Press.

more concerned about the perceived fairness of this comparison than the absolute level of the rewards received. For example, research has found that employee satisfaction is determined more strongly by their relative pay than by the absolute amount of pay they receive[7] (much to the astonishment of economists).

A key issue in equity theory is the selection of the comparison other.[8] For example, managers of a veterinary hospital at a Canadian university were astonished when they discovered that their veterinary hospital technicians considered themselves underpaid, even though their pay and working conditions were considerably better than those of technicians employed by private veterinary hospitals. It turns out that rather than comparing themselves with their private-sector colleagues, veterinary technicians at the university were comparing their pay and working conditions with those of the professors and research scientists with whom they were working.

As another example, in recent years, the gap between the earnings of rank-and-file employees and top executives has been widening dramatically. For example, between 1980 and 1995, executive pay in the United States increased from 42 times the average worker's pay to 141 times.[9] By 2002, the average compensation of chief executive officers in publicly traded U.S. corporations reached 531 times the average pay of a factory worker.[10] Although workers may recognize that the job of a top executive is not similar to theirs, they may still believe that it is inequitable for their CEO to be receiving 531 times as much as they receive. This is particularly true in cases where workers are being asked to make sacrifices in their rewards, while executives are receiving increases.

Relative Deprivation

Crosby suggests that employees experience dissatisfaction with their pay level under six conditions: (a) when there is a discrepancy between the outcome they want and what they actually receive; (b) when they see that a comparison other receives more than they do; (c) when past experience has led them to expect more than they now receive; (d) when future expectancies for achieving better outcomes are low; (e) when they feel a sense that they are entitled to more; and (f) when they absolve themselves of personal responsibility for the lack of better outcomes.[11]

To check on the validity of this theory, a research team examined four separate samples of American employees.[12] They found strong support for Crosby's theory. While actual pay level did predict pay satisfaction (the higher the pay, the greater the satisfaction), in every sample, Crosby's six conditions cited were at least three times as important as the pay level in predicting pay satisfaction. Three conditions were of particular importance: social comparisons (condition b or equity theory), the discrepancy between desired and actual pay (condition a), and sense of entitlement (condition e).

Lack of Organizational Justice

distributive justice

the perception that overall reward outcomes are fair

procedural justice

the perception that the process for reward determination is fair

The concept of organizational justice[13] is also useful in understanding how people judge the fairness of their rewards. Organizational justice has two main components. **Distributive justice** is the perception that overall reward *outcomes* are fair, which is what equity theory is all about. **Procedural justice** is the perception that the *process* through which rewards are determined is fair. Unless people believe that both of these are fair, they will not feel that the reward system is fair.[14]

Part I: Strategy, Rewards, and Behaviour

For example, suppose an individual has no faith in the process through which rewards are determined, regarding the process as arbitrary or even capricious. Even if the actual outcome turns out be fair in a given instance (distributive justice), the employee may still feel dissatisfied with the reward system, because he or she has little confidence that the outcome will be fair next time. On the other hand, if the employee believes that the process is fair (procedural justice), even if the reward outcome is less than the employee believes to be warranted, the employee will be *less* dissatisfied with that outcome.

As an example, suppose a firm is facing extreme financial pressure, and the total salary bill must be cut by 10 percent. At the moment, company employees are fairly compensated compared with industry standards. If the employees view the process by which it is determined that a 10 percent cut is necessary as reasonable, and if the cut is distributed in a fair way, they are much less likely to feel reward dissatisfaction.

A research study on the impact of distributive and procedural justice was conducted by Scarpello and Jones.[15] They found that although both distributive and procedural justice had an impact on employee satisfaction with the pay system (including pay level), distributive justice had by far the stronger effect.

Interestingly, these findings were reversed when employee satisfaction with the supervisor was examined: apparently employees strongly blame their supervisor for unfair pay procedures but only mildly blame them for perceived lack of fairness in the total amount of pay they receive (distributive justice). When organizational commitment—the degree of attachment to the firm expressed by employees—was examined, only procedural justice had an impact. An earlier study also found that procedural justice had the greatest impact on trust of the supervisor and organizational commitment, while distributive justice had the greatest impact on pay satisfaction.[16] In a later study, Tremblay and Roussel found in a sample of Canadian managers that while both distributive and procedural justice influenced pay satisfaction and job satisfaction, distributive justice had a greater impact on pay satisfaction, and procedural justice had a greater impact on job satisfaction.[17]

In practical terms, Theriault argues that the procedural justice is achieved if the pay system meets the following conditions. The pay system must be:

- consistent—procedures are applied uniformly to different jobs and time periods;
- free of bias—personal interests do not enter into application of the procedures;
- flexible—there must be procedures for employees to appeal pay system decisions;
- accurate—application of procedures must be based on factual information;
- ethical—accepted moral principles must guide application of the procedures;
- representative—all affected employees must have an opportunity to express their concerns, which are given serious consideration by the organization.[18]

FIGURE 3.4

Consequences of Reward Dissatisfaction

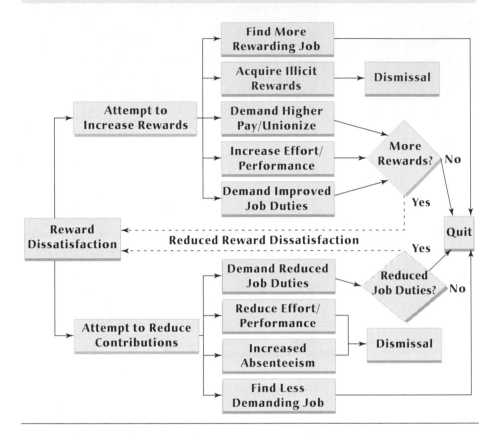

In general, when an organization is faced with a need to make changes to the psychological contract that might be unfavourable to employees, management can reduce the negative impact of these changes by practising principles of both distributive and procedural justice.

Consequences of Reward Dissatisfaction

What happens if employees experience reward dissatisfaction—if they perceive that the balance between rewards and contributions is unfair? Figure 3.4 provides a schematic illustration of some of the possible consequences. As can be seen, employees have two main options to redress the imbalance: to increase the rewards they receive or to reduce the contributions they make.

Attempt to Increase Rewards

If employees choose to try to increase their rewards, they have a number of options. One option is to quit the organization and take a more rewarding job. Of course, this is only an option if a more rewarding job is available to the employee.

Another alternative is to simply demand higher extrinsic rewards, either individually (i.e., asking for a raise) or collectively through a union

Compensation Today 3.3

The Devil Made Me Do It! (Or Was It Reward Dissatisfaction?)

"The devil made me do it!" This was a trademark line used by an old-time comedian to explain any malfeasance he committed. But it is not a very scientific explanation. In the grocery industry, theft by employees can be a serious problem. For instance, in one U.S. study, supermarket employees admitted stealing an average of $168 of merchandise a year.

Rather than the devil, a sense of reward dissatisfaction or inequity can account for this situation. As one survey respondent noted: "During the last couple of years, the company has kept raising the standards and cutting back on the hours allotted for keeping those standards up. If you don't work *off the clock* the job won't get done. Some people steal as a way to get even."

The relationship between reward dissatisfaction and employee theft has been supported by a more scientific study in manufacturing plants conducted by Greenberg.

Employee theft was measured before, during, and after a temporary 10-week pay cut caused by a decrease in orders. Greenberg found that theft increased dramatically during the rollback, but it returned to normal levels once the normal pay level was restored. Interestingly, the increase in theft was less pronounced in a plant where management explained the need for pay cuts in a candid way, and where they expressed concern for the well-being of employees.

Sources: (1) Third Annual Report on Theft in the Supermarket Industry (Rosemont, IL: London House, 1992), cited in Johns, Gary. 1996. *Organizational Behaviour: Understanding and Managing Life at Work*. New York: HarperCollins: 176. (2) Greenberg, Jerald. 1990. "Employee Theft as a Reaction to Underpayment Inequity: The Hidden Cost of Pay Cuts." *Journal of Applied Psychology*, 75: 561–68.

(i.e., demanding wage increases during the next round of collective bargaining). If no union exists, employees may attempt to form one if enough of them perceive an unfair rewards/contributions balance. If more rewards are forthcoming, then reward dissatisfaction is reduced, as Figure 3.4 illustrates. But if more rewards are not forthcoming, employees may simply quit, or they may attempt to even the balance in another way.

Some employees may resort to illicit means to increase their rewards, such as padding their expense accounts or stealing the firm's property or money. As you recall, this was how some employees at the Canadian National Exhibition (see opening vignette in Chapter 1) reacted to their reward dissatisfaction. Such behaviour may be rationalized by employees on the belief that since the company is shortchanging them, they are perfectly justified in "evening the score." In some sectors where rewards are low, and many illicit reward opportunities exist (such as in retailing), employee theft can be a serious problem, as Compensation Today 3.3 illustrates.

In some instances, employees may actually increase their work performance in response to reward dissatisfaction, but only if they are quite certain this will lead to significantly increased rewards. For example, if a promotion provides a job in which their rewards and contributions are balanced, and increased performance has a high probability of leading to this promotion, then the employee may attempt to improve performance, even though, in the short run, this worsens the rewards/contributions imbalance. But this is not the most likely response to reward dissatisfaction.

Finally, some employees may seek to even the balance by increasing their intrinsic rewards. For example, they may seek improvements to their job duties such that their work becomes more intrinsically satisfying. Their reasoning may go like this: "I may not be getting the pay I deserve, but at least I will now have a job I enjoy doing."

Attempt to Reduce Contributions

If rewards cannot be increased in some way that is significant to the employee, the employee may remain with the firm but redress the imbalance by reducing their contributions. This may be done formally or informally. For example, employees may formally request that their job duties be reduced. They may ask to be relieved of duties that require them to spend weekends away from home or that cause them to put in unpaid overtime.

This reduced contribution may also take the form of reduced effort or longer coffee breaks. It may also involve reducing the quality of customer service or eliminating any voluntary work activities. Organizational citizenship behaviour is one of the first things to go if employees seek to reduce their contributions. This is a major reason why reward dissatisfaction can be particularly damaging to high-involvement organizations.

In addition, reduced contribution may take the form of increased absenteeism. Some employees may even resort to negative behaviour, such as sabotage, as a means of evening the balance. Of course, such behaviours can result in dismissal, but this may not be seen as much of a loss by the employee.

If the perceived imbalance cannot be evened out somehow, then an employee may seek a less demanding job in a different firm, even if it pays no more than the current job. If able to find such a job, the employee will quit. But even if there are no other employment opportunities available, some employees may still quit, preferring unemployment to an intolerable imbalance and the stress it causes.

Predicting Employee Reactions

But exactly how will a given employee respond to reward dissatisfaction? Individual reactions are difficult to predict, because they depend on the personal characteristics and circumstances of the employee as well as the specific characteristics of the situation. Are alternative jobs readily available? Can the employee afford to be unemployed? Does the employee have strong values about honesty or a strong work ethic, which would prevent that person from using illicit rewards or reducing work performance?

In some instances, certain options are simply not available to employees, because organizations deliberately structure themselves to prevent them. For example, at Electronic Banking System (Compensation Today 2.1), employees handle a lot of cash. But with the cameras and other surveillance procedures, augmenting income with some of this cash is nearly impossible. And how would you really reduce work performance at the chicken-processing plant? About the only way is by not showing up for work. But if you don't show up, you simply don't get paid, so absenteeism doesn't get you very far.

So at these classical firms, there is not much employees can do to increase rewards or decrease contributions other than to threaten to quit. But that would be unlikely to be effective either, because turnover is not costly at these firms. Clearly, classical organizations are much more able to tolerate reward dissatisfaction than are human relations or high-involvement firms.

Of course, the response taken by the employer when the employee raises concerns has a strong influence on what further actions the employee takes. Employee reactions also depend on their tolerance for stress and perceived inequity. For example, some employees are high in **equity sensitivity**, which is a focus on maximization of personal rewards and a predisposition toward perceiving inequity, whether imagined or real.[19] These employees are more likely to resort to drastic action to reduce their perceived reward imbalance.

The specific nature of the factor causing the reward dissatisfaction may help to predict an employee's response to reward dissatisfaction. For example, the addition of new job duties may trigger demands for more pay in recognition of increased employee contribution. A wage cut may lead to increased illicit rewards, reduced work contributions, or withdrawal from the organization, depending on the personal values of the employee. Reduction in job security may cause employees to seek employment where greater job security exists, or to seek higher pay to compensate for their increased risk of job loss.

equity sensitivity

a personality trait that entails a high predisposition toward perceiving personal inequity

Understanding Membership Behaviour

 3.1

Why would anyone choose to pull chicken guts for a living? In fact, why would a person choose to engage in paid employment at all? Not everyone does. Of the potential Canadian labour force (defined as persons aged 15 years or older), just under 63 percent are currently engaged in paid employment or self-employment, according to Statistics Canada. Approximately 5 percent of the potential labour force are not employed, but are seeking employment.

That leaves about 32 percent who are choosing not to seek paid employment at this time. The majority of these people consist of retirees, spouses who stay at home to handle family responsibilities, students pursuing their educations, and single parents. Overall, the proportion of adults not choosing employment has been declining steadily over the past 50 years, primarily due to women entering the labour force during the 1960s and 1970s. The proportion not choosing employment may decrease even further as mandatory retirement is eliminated. Thus, more people are choosing to engage in paid employment than in the past.

So back to our question. Why do people work? Basically, people accept employment (1) if they have unsatisfied needs, (2) if employment is seen as the best vehicle to satisfy these needs, and (3) if they are able and willing to do the things that the employment requires. Put another way, people accept a job if the inducements or rewards associated with that job exceed the costs of the contributions they have to make to secure and retain that job. If there are several job opportunities available that fit the above criteria, people tend to choose the one in which the value of the rewards exceeds the cost of the contributions to the greatest extent.

That part is simple. The complicated part is that people can value the same rewards, costs and contributions differently, depending on their personal characteristics and circumstances. Thus, when three people are each presented with the same two job offers, one person may choose the first offer, another may choose the second offer, and a third person may reject both. The integrated model of behaviour, presented later in the chapter, sheds more light on the way people make these decisions.

Causes of Membership Behaviour

Let's assume that an individual has selected an employer. What factors determine whether she stays with that employer long-term? Although many factors can play a role, two job attitudes—job satisfaction and organizational identification—play a pivotal role, as discussed earlier in the chapter.

In general, job satisfaction occurs when one's important needs are satisfied through the job. One well-known model suggests that there are five main "facets" to job satisfaction: satisfaction with pay, promotion, supervisors, co-workers, and the job itself.[20] Although the weighting of each of these facets varies from person to person, each facet likely plays some role in overall job satisfaction.

Satisfaction with pay means that economic rewards meet employee needs and are considered fair. Satisfaction with promotion is the extent to which advancement opportunities are available. Satisfaction with supervisors means that supervisors are seen as supportive, helpful, and fair in the treatment of employees. Satisfaction with co-workers is the extent to which co-workers are viewed as friendly, sociable, helpful, cooperative, and supportive. Satisfaction with the job itself is defined as the extent to which the job contains various intrinsic rewards.

But the above list of facets is not necessarily complete. For example, one important omission is job security. Researchers have found that for most employees, the degree of job or employment security provided by the organization plays a major role in their level of job satisfaction.[21] Other important employee needs have to do with work motivation, which is discussed later in this chapter.

organizational commitment

the strength of the individual's attachment to his or her organization

affective commitment

attachment to an organization based on positive feelings toward the organization

continuance commitment

attachment to an organization based on perceived lack of better alternatives

While job satisfaction is a positive contributor to ongoing membership behaviour, it is not the only important factor. The strength of an individual's attachment to an organization is known as his or her level of **organizational commitment**. However, there are two main types of commitment: affective commitment and continuance commitment.

In **affective commitment**, individuals remain with the organization because of a sense of belongingness and loyalty to the organization, as well as an identification with the goals of the organization. In **continuance commitment**, individuals stay with an organization because they would lose too much by quitting: they cannot find another job that would be comparable in terms of the ratio of rewards to contributions. Continuance commitment implies nothing about an employee's level of emotional attachment to the employer or that employee's level of job satisfaction. Instead, it is simply a hardheaded calculation that "I have no better alternatives available to me."

It's even possible that an individual might have high continuance commitment but extremely low levels of job satisfaction and affective commitment. Studies have shown no relationship between continuance commitment and affective commitment[22] or between continuance commitment and job satisfaction.[23] However, affective commitment and job satisfaction *are* related, and an analysis of 155 studies found that affective commitment and job satisfaction have equal influence on reducing turnover.[24] Other studies have shown that continuance commitment also has an additional, separate effect on turnover.[25]

Rewards, Satisfaction, and Commitment

So the key question now is this: What role can the reward system play in generating job satisfaction and organizational commitment? Since a reward is anything provided by the organization that satisfies a person's needs, rewards clearly have a direct impact on job satisfaction. Of the five facets of job satisfaction discussed earlier, four are extrinsic and one (the job itself) intrinsic. Two of the facets are compensation-related: pay satisfaction and promotion satisfaction.

To generate organizational commitment, the key issue is not so much what individuals receive from their jobs, but the relationship between employees and the organization as a whole. Psychological contracts, trust, and organizational justice—especially procedural justice—play a major role in organizational commitment. For example, research has found a strong relationship between procedural justice and affective commitment.[26] Another study found that organizations perceived to be concerned about employee welfare had higher affective commitment than other organizations.[27] Employee benefits can help to create this perception; and rewards geared to organizational performance, such as profit sharing and employee stock plans, help create a feeling of belongingness and shared goals, leading to organizational identification and affective commitment.

Job security has also been found to relate to both job satisfaction and affective commitment. However, the impact of job security may vary, depending on its source. For example, some unionized employees have a high level of job security built into their contracts. This should enhance job satisfaction. But it may not enhance affective commitment if the employer is seen to be granting the job security grudgingly. For job security to have a positive impact on affective commitment, it needs to be seen as something granted willingly by the employer. Employees need to feel "I am a valued and loyal employee and the firm is recognizing this by giving me job security," not "They'd love to fire me, but they can't."

To generate continuance commitment, several types of compensation policies can be used. Seniority-based rewards are a cornerstone, including seniority increases in pay and benefit packages that increase with continued employment (especially if they are not entirely portable). Of course, simply having higher pay levels than competitors increases the costs of quitting (thus increasing continuance commitment) and reduces employee turnover.[28]

But if a high pay level is the only strategy a firm adopts to decrease turnover, it may be a very costly one. For example, one study found that higher pay levels did decrease quit rates somewhat, but it concluded that "raising wages to reduce turnover would be profitable only if turnover costs were enormous."[29] This finding is not surprising, since we have seen that pay level is only one of many factors affecting turnover. Indeed, researchers examining the impact of pay *level* satisfaction (distributive justice) and pay *system* satisfaction (procedural justice) on affective commitment found that satisfaction with pay *level* had absolutely no impact on affective commitment, while satisfaction with the pay *system* was strongly related to affective commitment.[30]

Is Low Turnover Always Good?

You have no doubt noticed that most of the foregoing discussion assumes that employee turnover is a bad thing. Certainly, turnover can very costly. But is a very low turnover rate *always* a good thing? For example, low turnover may not be a sign of organizational health if it is due only to continuance commitment. If the firm focuses on continuance commitment (by, say, providing high wages) but neglects job satisfaction and affective commitment, it risks ending up with a workforce of dissatisfied, uncommitted employees *who will never quit*.

Excessively low turnover can also cause stagnation in an organization, especially when the organization is not expanding. Some firms have launched early-retirement programs specifically to provide opportunities to younger employees. Finally, it should be noted that turnover rate by itself does not always tell the whole story. Two firms may have identical turnover rates, but this does not mean they have equally good reward and compensation systems. The key question is *who is quitting*? Are they employees who are not really a good fit with the organization, or are they valuable employees the firm sorely needs? Recall the soft-drink company described in the Chapter 1 opening vignette, whose reward system served to retain only dishonest, irresponsible employees, while causing honest, conscientious employees to quit.

Understanding Task Behaviour

Have you ever watched somebody do something and then wondered, "Now, why did they do that?" To understand a person's behaviour, you need to understand the person's *motivation*. Over the past few decades, two useful sets of motivation theory have emerged—content theories and process theories—that can help us better understand motivation.

content theories of motivation

theories that focus on understanding motivation by identifying underlying human needs

Content theories of motivation focus on identifying and understanding underlying needs, based on the commonsense notion that people behave in ways they think will help them satisfy their key needs. For example, a basic human need is the need for survival—for food and shelter. In modern society, this translates to a need for money. But content theories cannot predict the precise behaviours that different people will undertake in order to satisfy their needs for money. For example, some people will seek paid employment.

Part I: Strategy, Rewards, and Behaviour

Some will buy lottery tickets or go to the racetrack. Some will seek a rich spouse. Some will rob banks.

If we all have the same basic needs, but can pursue different avenues in attempting to satisfy those needs, what determines how each person will go about satisfying them? **Process theories of motivation** help us understand the process through which different people choose different courses of action in pursuit of the same needs.

Content Theories of Motivation

What are the important needs that human beings seek to satisfy? Using a variety of classification systems, psychologists have identified dozens of specific needs that drive behaviour. However, for our purposes, it is useful to group these needs.

Maslow's Hierarchy of Needs

Maslow suggested that people have five sets of needs, which are arranged in a hierarchy,[31] as shown in Figure 3.5. There are two key points to his theory. First, lower-order needs must be satisfied before higher-order needs come into play. Second, a satisfied need no longer motivates behaviour.

Thus, once when a person's immediate physiological (survival) needs for the basic necessities of life—food and shelter—are satisfied, that person will become concerned about the next level—safety and security needs: that is, how to satisfy their survival needs tomorrow and the next day and the day after that. People like the security of knowing that their basic needs will be satisfied in the future.

Once safety and security needs are met, people then become concerned about satisfying their needs for companionship and positive social regard by others, a need to be with and be accepted by other humans. Once these social or belongingness needs are met, people then become concerned with ego or

process theories of motivation

theories that focus on understanding motivation by determining the process humans use to make choices about the specific actions they will take

Maslow's hierarchy of needs

content theory of motivation that groups human needs into five main levels and states that humans seek to satisfy the lowest-order needs before satisfying higher-order needs

FIGURE 3.5

Maslow's Hierarchy of Needs

esteem needs—for accomplishment, achievement, and mastery or competence. Finally, if these needs are satisfied, the final set of needs is activated—the need for self-actualization. This is the need to maximize one's human potential, the need for continued learning, growth, and development. Maslow argues that self-actualization is the ultimate motivator, because, unlike the other needs, it can never be satisfied.

But is Maslow correct? Does human motivation really work the way he suggests? So far, research has not been able to confirm the theory precisely as outlined by Maslow. Some researchers have collapsed Maslow's five categories into three: existence (corresponding to Maslow's lower two need levels), relatedness (corresponding to Maslow's middle or social need level), and growth (corresponding to Maslow's upper two levels).[32] Research has shown that lower-order needs do not have to be completely satisfied before the other needs come into play, and that people can be motivated by more than one level of needs simultaneously.

To illustrate the possible variation in needs, consider the most basic need—the need for survival. Most people would view the need for survival as the most important need. But even here there are dramatic variations. If the basic need for survival dominates all else, then why did the electrical crew of the *Titanic*—faced with certain death from drowning if they did not leave—stay at their stations deep in the bowels of the ship to keep the vital electrical system operating even as the ship slid beneath the waves? Of course, it is possible that they believed that the ship really was unsinkable, and this is why they stayed at their stations. But what about secret service agents who willingly accept the duty to shield their heads of state from an assassin's bullet with their own bodies? And what about those cases where people intentionally take their own lives?

The reality is that people differ greatly in the strength of their various needs. And the same individual may vary over time in the strength of her or his different needs. For example, a single person may have relatively low economic needs but relatively high social needs. Therefore, that person will turn down opportunities to earn overtime in order to socialize with friends. But suppose that person gets married, buys a house, and has children. Economic needs may increase, reducing the importance of social needs. That person will then be more likely to be motivated to work overtime.

But even though Maslow's theory is unable to predict an individual's motive pattern, it is still useful because it does appear to describe group or aggregate behaviour very accurately. For example, as the income of a group or society increases, there tends to be a greater concern for satisfying higher-order needs. Thus, in a relatively wealthy society, such as Sweden, where the social welfare system ensures that lower-order needs are met, it is difficult to entice people to work at jobs that do not satisfy their higher-order needs.

In the 1960s and 1970s in Canada, when jobs were plentiful and income was steadily rising, people also became more concerned with the intrinsic qualities of their jobs. A "good job" was one that allowed autonomy, self-expression, and personal growth. Then as jobs became more scarce in the 1980s and 1990s and income stagnated, lower-order needs became more predominant, a "good job" became one that has good pay and benefits and job security. Although economic conditions have improved since then, real earnings have not really grown for most employees, and in the eyes of many people, a "good job" is still a job that is secure and has good pay and benefits.

The Two-Factor Theory of Motivation

In an attempt to determine the most important factors causing job satisfaction or dissatisfaction, Frederick Herzberg asked a sample of employees to list factors that made them feel good about their jobs and then list those that made them feel bad about their jobs. He was surprised to find that the factors mentioned in the two lists were completely different. He had expected many of the same items to appear on both lists, except reversed. For example, he expected high pay to make people feel good about their job, and low pay to make people feel unhappy about their jobs.[33]

Instead, while he found that low pay did indeed make people dissatisfied, high pay did not make them enthusiastic about their work. Factors that made them feel good about their work had more to do with job content—mastering a difficult task, learning a new skill, or completing a major job accomplishment. Factors that made them dissatisfied were low pay, a poor relationship with their supervisor or co-workers, and poor working conditions.

Subsequently, Herzberg realized that he was really dealing with two different concepts—job satisfaction and work motivation.[34] The factors that caused job dissatisfaction he labelled "hygienes," and the factors that made people feel good about their work he labelled "motivators." He concluded that job satisfaction was caused by extrinsic (hygiene) factors and motivation by intrinsic (motivator) factors. He suggested that to have both satisfied and motivated employees, an organization had to provide both extrinsic (hygienes) and intrinsic (motivators) rewards. Hertzberg's theory fits well with Maslow's theory, since the hygienes correspond to the lower-order needs and the motivators to the higher-order needs.

Job Characteristics Theory

Richard Hackman and Greg Oldham extended Herzberg's work by attempting to identify the specific job characteristics that cause intrinsic motivation and by developing a method to calculate the amount of intrinsic motivation in a particular job.[35] They identified what they call five *core job dimensions*—task identity, task significance, skill variety, autonomy, and feedback—and suggested that jobs high in these dimensions are intrinsically motivating: people enjoy doing these jobs for the satisfaction they derive from performing them, rather than the extrinsic rewards they receive from them.

Task identity is defined as the extent to which a worker is able to perform a complete cycle of activities, from start to finish, rather than only one small part of the job cycle. **Task significance** is the perceived importance of the job in the general scheme of things. For example, the job of heart surgeon would carry more task significance than that of a hot dog vendor. **Skill variety** is the extent to which a substantial number of skills are required for task completion. **Job autonomy** is the extent to which workers are able to decide for themselves how to perform their jobs. **Job feedback** refers to the level of feedback

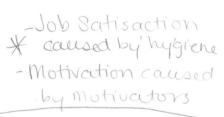

two-factor theory of motivation

argues that intrinsic factors influence work motivation, while extrinsic factors influence job satisfaction

task identity

the extent to which a worker performs a complete cycle of job activities

task significance

the perceived importance or social value of a given task

skill variety

the variety of skills required for task completion

job autonomy

the degree of freedom workers have in deciding how to perform their jobs

job feedback

the extent to which the job itself provides feedback on worker performance

on work quantity and quality that an individual receives from the job itself. For example, a typist using a spellcheck program gets feedback on the quality of work from the job itself. A bomb disposal expert does not need outside feedback to know if he or she has been successful in a job!

Although Hackman and Oldham originally hypothesized that jobs high in these characteristics would be motivating only for persons with a high growth need, subsequent research has shown that most people respond favourably to jobs with these characteristics. For example, Fried analyzed 79 studies and found that the core job dimensions were significantly related to higher work performance and even more strongly related to employee satisfaction.[36]

job enrichment

the process of redesigning jobs to incorporate more of the five core dimensions of intrinsically satisfying work

A conscious effort by organizations to redesign their jobs to include higher amounts of the five core dimensions is known as **job enrichment**; and many organizations, especially high-involvement firms, have job enrichment programs. As long as employees do not perceive the enrichment as simply an attempt to load more work on them, most will probably respond favourably to job enrichment. However, some organizations forget that if employees are expected to perform at a higher level, the compensation system should recognize this, or perceived inequity and reward dissatisfaction will result, which would undo the otherwise favourable effects of job enrichment.

Although job characteristics theory is a separate theory, it fits well with the other content theories of motivation. As Figure 3.6 illustrates, the intrinsic job characteristics identified by Hackman and Oldham correspond to the motivators identified by Herzberg and address the higher-order needs specified by Maslow. The figure also shows how these content theories relate to the three managerial strategies.

FIGURE 3.6

Content Theories of Motivation and Their Relationship to Managerial Strategy

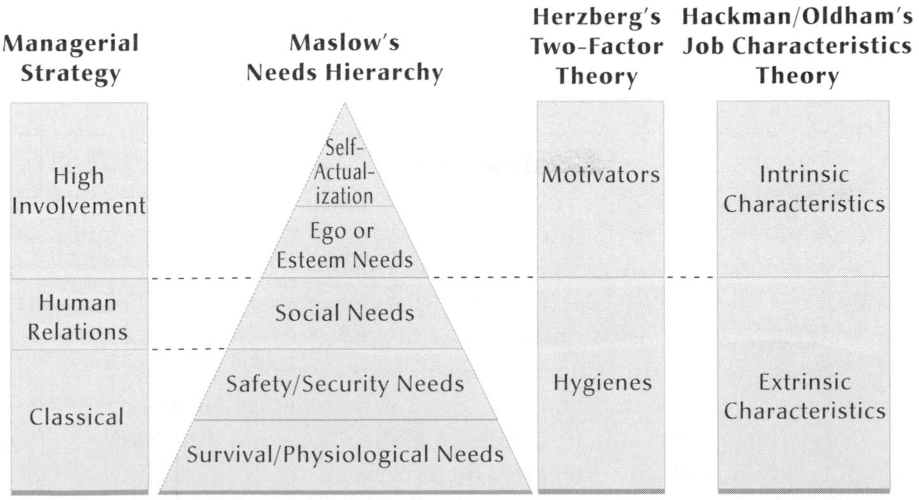

Managerial Strategy	Maslow's Needs Hierarchy	Herzberg's Two-Factor Theory	Hackman/Oldham's Job Characteristics Theory
High Involvement	Self-Actualization / Ego or Esteem Needs	Motivators	Intrinsic Characteristics
Human Relations	Social Needs		
Classical	Safety/Security Needs / Survival/Physiological Needs	Hygienes	Extrinsic Characteristics

Money as a Motivator

According to Herzberg and many other experts,[37] money itself is not a motivator. But is this really true? Before answering this question, consider that money itself is not technically a need, but rather a generalizable resource that can be used to acquire things to satisfy needs. However, money also has a symbolic value and represents status and accomplishment to many people. In this way, the need for money can be considered a need in itself.

In organizations, the amount and manner in which one is paid sends important signals about how one is regarded by the employer. For example, if a person receives a slightly smaller raise than a co-worker, even if the raise itself is generous, that person may infer that the co-worker is more highly regarded and has the inside track on the next promotion. And we have already seen how perceptions of relative inequity can have a greater impact on employee satisfaction than the absolute value of compensation received.

The multifaceted nature of money as a motivator adds complexity to the compensation process, as does the fact that people vary in their "money ethic"—the inherent value they place on money.[38] But one thing is clear: for many people, money is an important motivator. However, the type of motivation money produces is different from the type of motivation intrinsic rewards produce, as you will see when we discuss attribution theory later in the chapter.

Salience of Needs

Before leaving our discussion of human needs, we need to consider the issue of **need salience**. The salience of a particular need determines the extent to which an individual is compelled to satisfy that need. For a reward to be motivating, it must address a salient need. Clearly, different needs are salient for different people. As Figure 3.7 shows, two sets of factors—personal characteristics and personal circumstances—interact with basic human needs to determine need salience.

How does this process work? Two key factors determine the salience of a need for a given person at a given point in time: the *amount of need deprivation* and *the importance of the need*. Need deprivation is the difference between how

need salience

the degree of urgency an individual attaches to the satisfaction of a particular need

FIGURE 3.7

How Need Salience Is Determined

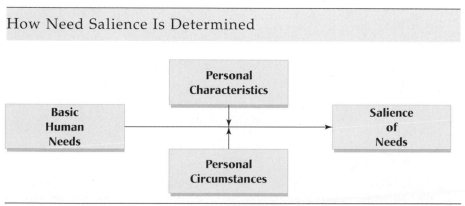

Chapter 3: A Behavioural Framework for Compensation

The Klondike (1896–98) was the greatest gold rush in Canada's history. Almost overnight, Dawson City went from an unpopulated, mosquito-infested mud flat in the middle of Yukon Territory to the largest city west of Winnipeg and north of Seattle. But those who struck gold found themselves in an odd position: there was nothing to buy, not even labour. At this time in the rest of North America, top wages for a working man were $1.50 a day. In Dawson, it was difficult to find someone who would work for 10 times that much.

But as economic needs became less salient, other needs became more so. Because of the isolation, aspects of life that would have had little or no value elsewhere commanded exorbitant prices. For example, "when one man drifted in with an ancient newspaper soaked in bacon grease, he was able to sell it for fifteen dollars"—equivalent to about $1,000 today. With their economic needs satisfied, the needs of grizzled miners changed dramatically. Because of their isolation, a need that became highly salient was for news of the outside world.

Source: Berton, Pierre. 1972. *Klondike: The Last Great Gold Rush 1896–1899*. Toronto: Penguin Books: 373.

much a person currently has and how much he or she requires to satisfy a particular need. Need deprivation is strongly influenced by personal circumstances. For example, if a person needs several close friendships to satisfy social needs but currently lives in an isolated area and has no friends at all (personal circumstances), there is high need deprivation. As another example, if a family requires about $50,000 a year to maintain what they consider a suitable standard of living, but actual family income is $25,000, then there is considerable need deprivation. Clearly, personal circumstances, such as dependants, financial obligations, and current financial conditions (e.g., no savings), affect the degree of need deprivation for money.

Need salience is also determined by the importance the individual places on the need. For example, someone may have a high deprivation of a certain need; but if that person does not consider it an important need, it may be less salient than a more important need for which there is less deprivation. Personal characteristics tend to determine the relative importance of a given need. For example, some individuals value self-actualization more than any other need and pursue this need regardless of whether their other needs are satisfied. The classic example is the "starving artist." On the other hand, some people are high in "money ethic" and have a much higher tendency to change jobs if they perceive that so doing will increase their financial rewards.[39]

So a combination of high importance and high deprivation adds up to high need salience. The higher the need salience, the higher the value placed on things that satisfy that need. Compensation Today 3.4 illustrates the role that personal circumstances play in this process.

Process Theories of Motivation

Different individuals can choose different paths or behaviours to satisfy exactly the same need. Process theories of motivation attempt to explain the process by which individuals choose to pursue one path over another to satisfy a need.

Reinforcement Theory

The simplest process theory is **reinforcement theory**,[40] sometimes called behaviourism, operant conditioning, or behaviour modification. The underlying premise of this theory is that an individual will repeat behaviours that have led to need satisfaction in the past and will discontinue behaviours that do not contribute to need satisfaction. This theory is based on learning theory. As young children, human beings all experiment with a variety of behaviours. They learn to repeat behaviours that have positive consequences and discontinue behaviours that have negative consequences.

For reinforcement theory to work, the individual must perceive a link between the behaviour and the consequence. For example, if children grow up in a household where rewards and punishments are provided in a capricious or arbitrary manner, then they learn that there is little connection between behaviour and consequences. They also tend to develop a personality trait known as an "external locus of control"—as adults, they will tend to believe that they have very little control over outcomes. In the work setting, these individuals tend to believe that the degree of job effort they exert has very little influence on the degree of performance they achieve or on the rewards they receive.

According to reinforcement theory, the key to understanding how a person will behave in the future is to understand how that person and others around them were reinforced for various types of behaviour in the past. As an example, if someone grows up in an environment where most people are unemployed, and those who are employed never earn more than minimum wage, that person may come to regard employment as a very unlikely way to satisfy the need for money. If the same person sees local drug dealers driving around in big cars and wearing fancy clothes, that person may perceive drug dealing as a much more viable way to satisfy the need for money.

Reinforcers can be of two types: positive and negative. Positive reinforcement takes place when a reward follows a valued behaviour; negative reinforcement takes place when an undesirable consequence occurs whenever the valued behaviour does not occur. This undesirable consequence can be either the removal of something valued (such as docking a day's pay for an unauthorized absence) or the imposition of something not wanted (such as assigning an employee to the least desirable job in the plant on the day following an absence).

For those who are designing a reward system, the guidelines offered by reinforcement theory are quite clear. Desired behaviours for each employee need to be clearly specified. Then each time that behaviour occurs, it is followed by a reward of significant value to the recipient. The closer in time the reward is to the behaviour, the better. Behaviour modification theory also states that unrewarded behaviours eventually disappear, so this can be a way of dealing with undesirable behaviours. It is very important that undesirable

reinforcement theory

a theory that states that a behaviour will be repeated if valued outcomes flow from that behaviour, or if performing the behaviour reduces undesirable outcomes

behaviours not be inadvertently rewarded, as was the case at Bausch and Lomb (opening vignette).

However, the practical application of this theory is problematic. One problem is that reinforcement theory assumes that all desired behaviours are measurable and that it is practical to identify and respond to every instance of the behaviour. As we have seen, rewarding only a portion of the range of behaviours desired from an employee can cause serious problems.

The second problem is that reinforcement theory considers only those rewards that the organization can control. For example, an autoworker who welds pop bottles into car rocker panels is not receiving any kind of company-based reward for doing so, but may be receiving psychological rewards for "outsmarting" the company. In other words, behaviourism is an extrinsically based theory: it does not recognize differences in how individuals value rewards, or how they evaluate the costs of alternative behaviours. It also does not recognize intrinsic rewards or the possibility of altruism.

Third, there is the issue of what happens when rewards stop—will the desired behaviour cease? Reinforcement theory predicts it eventually would, so behaviour needs to be continually rewarded under this system.

Some critics argue that behaviourism takes away employee responsibility for their actions, making them incapable of self-control,[41] and removes intrinsic motivation.[42] It can also make many employees feel manipulated, like powerless pawns, and can cause resentment toward the punisher, and even the rewarder in some cases. However, there is no doubt that application of reinforcement principles can change human behaviour.[43] Reinforcement theory appears to work best for simple behaviours and short-term behavioural change.

Expectancy Theory

Although reinforcement theory is important, it does not help us understand the thought process that takes place when individuals choose a particular behaviour from the virtually infinite possibilities. The main theory to explain this process is known as the *expectancy theory of motivation*.[44]

FIGURE 3.8

Expectancy Theory of Motivation

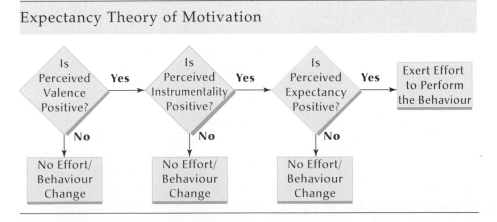

The $50,000 Hamburger

Picture this. It is a beautiful summer day. You are sitting on a park bench, eating your lunch. Suddenly, your reverie is interrupted by an elderly stranger sitting next to you, who offers you $10 if you will run to the hamburger stand two kilometres away and bring him back a "Big Mike" sandwich. But there's a catch. He will only pay you the $10 if you can bring it back within 10 minutes, because he has to leave then. Would you do it? Let's use expectancy theory to predict your reaction.

First, you would likely consider whether the net value (valence) of the outcome is positive, once the costs are subtracted from the rewards. For example, getting the hamburger will make you late for work, and your boss has warned you that one more late appearance could cost you your job. You are pretty sure that you would not be fired for getting back a few minutes late, but you are not positive about that. The boss would certainly be angry, and who needs that? Given the small size of the reward, the net valence of the outcome is probably negative, and you will probably not go any further in considering whether to perform the desired behaviour.

But suppose that the stranger bumps the reward up to $50,000. You might then conclude that the size of that reward outweighs the risk of job loss, and the valence is now positive. So would you now get the hamburger? Probably not. Why not? You are likely not convinced that the behaviour (getting the hamburger) would actually lead to the reward (would the stranger really give you $50,000?). In other words, you perceive a low instrumentality.

But let's suppose that the stranger reveals himself to be an eccentric billionaire well known for such bizarre acts as paying $50,000 for a hamburger. He also shows you that he has more than $50,000 in his billfold. You now believe that it is very probable you would receive the $50,000 if you brought back the hamburger (instrumentality is high). Now would you go get the hamburger? Of course! You'd be crazy not to!

Well, that depends on your expectancy that you could actually perform the behaviour—that is, bring the hamburger back within 10 minutes. You are at the centre of the park, the sidewalks are crowded, and you would probably have to stand in line for at least five minutes. In high school, your best time for running the 1000 metres was three minutes, and that was quite a few doughnuts ago! If you believe that there is no chance of bringing back the hamburger within the 10 minutes (zero expectancy), you will still not be motivated to attempt to perform the behaviour.

How could the stranger attempt to motivate you at this point? What if he made the reward $1 million? This would have no impact on your behaviour. When either instrumentality or expectancy is zero, the size of the reward is irrelevant. So the only thing he could do would be to somehow change the expectancy—for example, by lending you a bicycle or increasing the time allowed for task completion.

Expectancy theory suggests that the likelihood of performing one behaviour or another is dependent on three things: (1) the net value (valence) of the consequences of that behaviour, (2) the perceived likelihood that the behaviour will actually lead to those consequences (instrumentality), and (3) the perceived likelihood of actually being able to perform those behaviours (expectancy). As Figure 3.8 indicates, valence, instrumentality, and expectancy must all be positive before a person exerts effort to perform a behaviour.

In essence, individuals ask themselves three questions before acting. Is the task worth doing—do the rewards exceed the costs (valence)? Will I actually receive the rewards if I perform the task (instrumentality)? Am I actually able to do the task (expectancy)? Only when the answers to all three questions are positive will the person attempt the task. Compensation Today 3.5 provides an illustration of this process.

expectancy theory

a theory which states that individuals are more likely to attempt to perform a particular behaviour if they believe that behaviour will lead to valued consequences and if they expect they can perform the behaviour

The implications of this theory for reward systems are quite clear. First, make sure that the net valence for performing a behaviour is positive *in the eyes of the person expected to perform the behaviour*. This involves maximizing the person's rewards while minimizing their costs of performing the behaviour. To do so, you need to understand the needs and personal values of the people you are attempting to motivate. But motivating a group becomes much more complicated if they all vary in their needs and values. For this reason, many firms have an implicit preference for a homogeneous workforce and tend to hire "clones"—employees who are very similar to those they have now.

Second, make sure that instrumentality is strong. Employees must clearly understand that performance of the desired behaviours leads to the specified rewards. Trust and credibility may be an important issue here. Have you promised rewards in the past that failed to materialize?

And third, make sure that employees have confidence in their ability to perform the desired behaviours. This may involve providing the physical and mental tools necessary to get the job done and creating the right context.

Attribution Theory

Expectancy theory does not distinguish between extrinsic and intrinsic rewards in determining the valence for performing a particular behaviour. It assumes that rewards simply add up: thus, people are more motivated to perform a behaviour that has both intrinsic and extrinsic rewards, all other factors being equal.

However, there is one theory that argues that provision of extrinsic rewards may actually destroy or cancel out intrinsic rewards. This is known as **attribution theory**.[45] The premise of attribution theory is that human beings are active creatures, continually engaging in a variety of activities, without necessarily having a conscious understanding of their motives before performing these activities. But after performing any activity, people often feel compelled to try to understand why they performed that activity—"Now why did I do that?" In other words, people seek to attribute some motive to that activity. If there is an "obvious" reason for so doing, they will attribute our activity to that motive. The following story may help to illustrate this concept:

> An elderly man who lived next to a vacant lot had enjoyed his peace and quiet until the neighbourhood children selected the site for various noisy games every day after school. After vainly trying a number of approaches, such as admonishing them to be quiet or trying to convince them to play elsewhere, he tried a new approach. He gathered the children around one day and announced that he had come to enjoy the sound of their play so much that he wanted to reward them. He told them that he would give each of them 50 cents for each day they would come and play at the vacant lot.

attribution theory

theory of motivation arguing that humans often act without understanding their motives for their behaviour and afterwards attempt to attribute motives for their actions

The children thought this was great, and the noise actually increased! However, after several days the old man regretfully announced that since he was not a wealthy man, he would have to reduce their payment to 25 cents a day. Although the children grumbled, they accepted this. He subsequently lowered their pay to 10 cents and then 5 cents, at which point the children announced that they would not be coming back to play anymore. It was simply not worth it for a nickel a day!

This story indicates how the man replaced intrinsic motivation with extrinsic motivation, which he then extinguished by removing the extrinsic rewards. Research studies in laboratory settings involving intrinsically interesting activities such as doing a puzzle have confirmed this result. Subjects usually are children, and half of them are told that they will be paid for the number of puzzles that they complete in 30 minutes. The other half are simply told to complete as many puzzles as they can in 30 minutes, with no mention of money. At the end of the 30 minutes, both groups are told that they now have some free time, and can do whatever they want. Almost invariably, the nonpaid group continues to do more puzzles, while the group that had been paid stops doing them. This is taken as evidence that the extrinsic reward has destroyed the intrinsic motivation for the paid group.

However, Wiersma analyzed 20 studies and found that in work behaviour simulations in which extrinsic rewards are not removed, extrinsic rewards add to intrinsic rewards to create greater task behaviour.[46] Yet most of Wiersma's studies were simulated in a laboratory and were short-term in nature. Perhaps in other situations, intrinsic motivation would be extinguished over time by extrinsic rewards, as Deci has argued.[47]

So what are the implications of attribution theory for reward systems? Deci argues that pay should not be related to output, and that intrinsic rewards should be used to motivate performance. Of course, this plan assumes that there is intrinsic motivation in the first place. But if there is not, either intrinsic motivation must be generated by enriching jobs, or extrinsic means must be used.

So does this mean that you should never provide extrinsic rewards for good individual performance if it is already intrinsically motivated? Not necessarily. Some researchers argue that providing extrinsic rewards as recognition for accomplishment can actually increase feelings of equity and satisfaction without damaging intrinsic motivation, but only if rewards are not seen as driving, controlling or evaluating behaviour.[48]

For example, consider the case of volunteers who work at a UNICEF gift shop. Suppose UNICEF decides it would like to recognize their services by providing one dollar an hour as a token of appreciation. Volunteers would fill in time cards, which would be verified by a supervisor. Would this increase motivation? Likely not. We can predict that the volunteers will be insulted by the implication that they are involved with the organization to serve their own self-interest, that their time is worth just one dollar an hour, and that they cannot be trusted. But on the other hand, if dedicated service is recognized by paying a volunteer's expenses to a valued national

Chapter 3: A Behavioural Framework for Compensation

convention, this would not likely decrease intrinsic motivation and may enhance overall commitment.

Economic Theory

A final theory of work motivation is based on economic theory. Although economic theory can be a useful predictor of behaviour of some employees, it represents a much narrower version of motivation theory. Essentially, economic theory assumes that people are motivated only by extrinsic (economic) rewards, and they will always seek to maximize these rewards while minimizing their contributions to the organization. This theory sees all work as being inherently distasteful and assumes that whenever given the opportunity, people will seek to do as little of it as possible.

agency theory

agents (employees) will pursue their own self-interests rather than the interests of their principals (employers) unless they are closely monitored or their interests are aligned with the interests of their principals

One of the most prominent economic theories is known as **agency theory**.[49] This theory makes a key distinction between principals (those who own the enterprise) and agents (those who work on their behalf within the organization). Agency theory assumes that the interests of principals and agents will be divergent, and that faced with a choice between advancing the principal's interests or their own, agents will always seek to further their own interests. As a result, principals need procedures to monitor agent behaviour to minimize agent pursuit of their own interests at the expense of the principal. However, this monitoring is expensive, and principals seek to reduce these costs whenever possible. Therefore, principals tend to favour reward systems that closely tie individual rewards to specific behaviours desired by the principals, especially individual performance pay.

Overall, economic theory represents a simplified view of employee behaviour. It assumes that all people are fixated at the lowest level of Maslow's needs hierarchy, that personal values such as honesty and strong work ethics do not exist, and that intrinsic rewards have little or no relevance to behaviour. Of course, these are all classical beliefs, and classical organizations tend to favour economic theory as the foundation for their managerial systems. In general, economic theory is only useful if the employees of the organization actually match these assumptions. When they do, it can be a useful model of behaviour in designing reward systems. But when they do not, it can result in the development of reward systems that are suboptimal, ineffective, and counterproductive.

Understanding Organizational Citizenship Behaviour

 3.1

Organizational citizenship behaviour is a relatively new concept which describes voluntary or discretionary behaviours that go beyond task and membership behaviour. At a broad level, it is a "willingness to cooperate" in the pursuit of organizational goals. It is no coincidence that this concept has emerged simultaneously with the emergence of high-involvement organizations. Because of the nature of this managerial strategy and the conditions of high uncertainty and dynamism in which these firms operate, they greatly value organizational citizenship behaviour, in contrast to human relations firms and especially classical firms.

Although concepts of citizenship behaviour are continuing to evolve from their original formulation,[50] current theories suggests five main dimensions.[51] *Altruism* is the willingness to offer help to a co-worker, supervisor, or client without any expectation of personal reward for so doing, and without any negative repercussions if the help had been withheld. *General compliance* is the extent to which conscientiousness—in terms of attendance, use of work time, and adherence to policies—goes beyond the minimum necessary standards. *Courtesy* is the practice of "touching base" with people before taking actions that could affect their work. *Sportsmanship* is the ability to tolerate, with good grace, the minor nuisances and impositions that are a normal part of work life. *Civic virtue* is the extent to which individuals take an interest and participate in the broader governance and operation of the organization.

Causes of Citizenship Behaviour

The prime source of citizenship behaviour is organizational identification. Two causes of organizational identification are (a) shared organizational goals and (b) feelings of membership (or belonging).

There are two ways in which shared organizational goals may affect organizational identification. In the first way, which Argyris refers to as "organizational integration,"[52] the interests of both the individual and the organization are congruent: "If the organization is successful, I will share in the rewards." An example would be a firm in which employees are also significant shareholders. The second way through which shared goals affects organizational identification occurs when the goals of the organization match important values of the individual employee. Some researchers refer to this as "moral" or "normative" commitment. For example, people might join UNICEF because they want to help fight child poverty. For another example, a person might choose to work in a hospital because of a desire to help heal the sick.

The second cause of organizational identification is a feeling of membership or belongingness. If people feel that they are valued and respected members of their organization, then they are much more likely to engage in citizenship behaviour. Their citizenship behaviour is also connected to perceptions of justice, fair treatment, and reciprocity in the organization: "The organization does whatever it can to look after my interests, and I will therefore do the same for the organization."

Employees with high organizational identification seek to further organizational goals in any way possible, ranging from increasing job effort to making innovative suggestions. Employees also promote a spirit of cooperation within the organization, since this also furthers organizational goals. Other results of organizational identification are decreased turnover, absenteeism, grievances, and other negative behaviours.

A key value of organizational identification is that it acts as a counterweight to narrow self-interest. In the Green Giant case discussed at the beginning of Chapter 1, employees pursued their own self-interest at the expense

Chapter 3: A Behavioural Framework for Compensation

of the interests of the company by "cheating" on the payment system. But if organizational identification had been high, this result would have been much less likely.

Creating Citizenship Behaviour

So how can organizational identification be created, and what role can the reward system play in this process? First of all, several preconditions are necessary for the development of citizenship behaviour. One of these is employment security. Employers cannot reasonably expect employees to be loyal to an organization that shows no loyalty to them. Trust is another key precondition—if employees do not trust management, little citizenship behaviour will take place.

In addition, research also shows that an organization that shows genuine concern for the needs of its employees—for example, through benefits that help employees successfully mesh their work and family lives—provides more fertile ground for organizational citizenship.[53] Another precondition is a sense of both distributive and procedural justice within the organization, and the sense that the organization is attempting—within the means available—to provide as fair a psychological contract and reward structure as possible. Moorman found that procedural justice was a key determinant of organizational citizenship,[54] while Konovsky and Organ cited supervisory fairness as a key determinant.[55] Janssen found that worker innovation was reduced by perceived unfairness in the reward system.[56]

One way of creating identification is by developing reward systems in which both employees and the organization benefit when organizational goals are met. These may include gain sharing, goal sharing, profit sharing, or employee stock plans. Another way the reward system can foster shared goals and values is by attracting and retaining employees who already possess compatible values. The employer identifies the needs of people who already share organizational goals and values and then gears the reward system to those needs.

Participation in decision making, especially in goal setting, has also been shown to foster organizational identification. People with a role in setting organizational goals are much more likely to be committed to those goals. In addition, employee participation in developing the company reward system will likely produce reward systems that are consistent with employee needs and result in more trust in the system itself. But all types of participation in decision making have been shown to create greater commitment to the decisions that are made, as well as providing a sense that employees are true "citizens" in the organization, and that their views are valued and respected.

A good example of using employee participation to create organizational identification is Byers Transport, a trucking company in western Canada that was purchased from its corporate owner by its employees.[57] In addition to the change in ownership, management style became more open, with information sharing and participative management. In short, the firm moved from a classical to a high-involvement managerial style. After employee purchase, many employee attitudes and behaviours changed almost overnight. Group norms, which had been somewhat poor under corporate ownership, improved dramatically. Losses resulting from "shrinkage" (employee theft) declined dramatically, as did customer damage claims and employee turnover. Grievances disappeared. A new attitude of commitment and cooperation permeated the company. Truck drivers made great efforts to satisfy customers, and everyone, whatever their position, was always on the lookout for potential new customers. The result? A dramatic increase in profitability, which had been absent in the years prior to employee purchase.

An Integrated Model of Behaviour

Now that we've looked at the individual pieces of the human behaviour puzzle, it's time to put them together. The rather intimidating-looking Figure 3.9 does just that.

As Figure 3.9 shows, all behaviour starts with human needs. But individuals vary in their need salience (which is crucial for reward systems), depending on their personal circumstances and personal characteristics. Personal characteristics combined with salient needs strongly influence employee perceptions of the valence, instrumentality, and expectancy of a particular behaviour.

FIGURE 3.9

An Integrated Model of Motivation and Behaviour

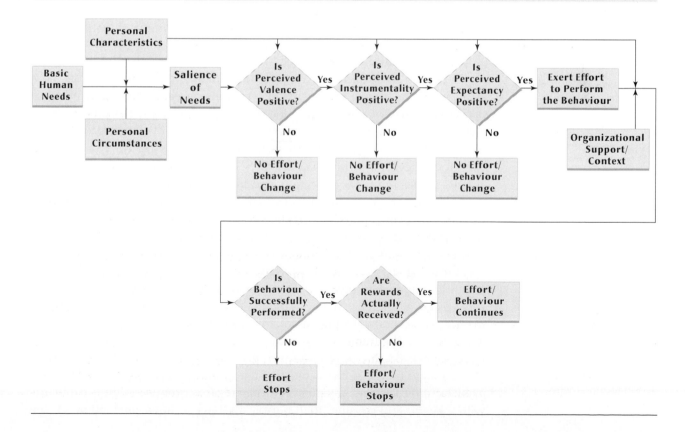

If these perceptions are all positive, then people will attempt to perform the target behaviour. But whether they are actually able to perform the behaviour depends on their individual attributes and the organizational context, including the organizational support provided. If the behaviour is successfully carried out, and the expected rewards follow, the behaviour is reinforced and will likely continue. If the expected rewards do not materialize, the behaviour will cease.

That's the model in a nutshell. It is actually not as intimidating as it may appear at first glance. But to really understand it and its implications for reward systems, we still need to work our way through it, focusing on parts that have not received much attention so far.

Personal Characteristics

Personal characteristics are one part of the equation that has received little attention so far. **Personal characteristics** include the beliefs, values, competencies, personality, demographic characteristics, and perceptual frame of reference of a given individual. The nature of these personal characteristics is a result of a person's experiences and learning in combination with inherent individual differences.

Personal beliefs reflect people's understanding of how the world around them works, based on their experiences and learning, both formal and informal. Major sources of beliefs are parents, teachers, and peer groups. But beliefs change throughout life, depending on further experiences and encounters with new people. In contrast, **personal values**—core beliefs about appropriate and inappropriate behaviour—form early in life and endure over time. Examples of personal values include the importance of honesty, altruism, loyalty, friendship, and the work ethic.

Personal competencies comprise a person's particular abilities and skills—physical, verbal, and mental. **Personality characteristics** are a person's particular behavioural and emotional tendencies (traits). Personality traits include pessimism vs. optimism, extroversion vs. introversion, passivity vs. aggressiveness, risk tolerance vs. risk aversion, cynicism vs. trust, and internal vs. external locus of control. **Demographic characteristics** include such items as age, gender, ethnicity, education, and marital status.

The **personal frame of reference** is the set of perceptual filters that people use in interpreting and understanding the world around them. The world is a complicated place, bombarding people with many more perceptual cues than they are able to assimilate and interpret. Instead of responding to all stimuli, human beings practise *selective perception*—a largely unconscious process of selecting only certain perceptual cues for interpretation. An individual's personal frame of reference determines which cues to select and how to interpret them. As a general rule, people tend to select cues that reinforce their preexisting beliefs. The frame of reference results from the person's previous experiences, beliefs, values, personality type, and demographic characteristics.

How are personal characteristics relevant to reward systems? Here are a few examples. A person high in cynicism regards promises of future rewards with skepticism, causing that person to have a low perception of the

personal characteristics

a person's beliefs, values, competencies, personality, demographic characteristics, and perceptual frame of reference

personal beliefs

a person's understanding of how the world around them works

personal values

a person's core beliefs about appropriate and inappropriate behaviour

personal competencies

a person's physical, verbal, and mental skills

personality characteristics

a person's behavioural and emotional tendencies

demographic characteristics

a person's age, gender, ethnicity, education, marital status, and similar characteristics

personal frame of reference

the perceptual filters that people use in interpreting and understanding the world around them

instrumentality of a particular behaviour (and thus low motivation). Or a young employee may not even "hear" the presentation about pension benefits during the employment interview; so an employer trying to attract young employees with a generous pension plan may be trying the wrong strategy. And, of course, personal values and personality type play a major role in determining which needs are salient for a given employee and therefore what rewards will likely motivate him or her.

Personal Circumstances

Personal circumstances influence a person's level of need deprivation, which then affects that person's need salience. For example, someone who has a million dollars in the bank likely has less financial deprivation than a person whose total financial assets amount to 10 dollars. Of course, need deprivation is a function of not only how much a person currently possesses, but also how much the person needs. Someone with three young children to support has a higher financial need than a childless person, all other things being equal. In addition, people living in jurisdictions where health care is free have lower financial needs than those living in jurisdictions where it is not.

Other personal circumstances are also relevant. Does the person have high student loans to pay off? Are his or her skills in high demand? Are there many alternatives open to that person?

Moreover, how much need satisfaction will be "enough" for a person depends on many factors. Personal experience also affects the desired satisfaction level. For example, people accustomed to a high standard of living likely set higher threshold levels than those accustomed to a lower standard of living. People who grew up in poverty during the Great Depression and who experienced great uncertainty about their very survival likely have a very high threshold for security needs. In cases where people have a very high threshold for satisfaction of a particular need, it is almost impossible for them ever to fully satisfy this need, and many people remain fixated on this need throughout their lives, often to the detriment of other needs.

Evaluating Valence

Need salience plus personal characteristics determine how a person will calculate the valence of a particular behaviour. Need salience is particularly important in evaluating the rewards flowing from a behaviour. Will performing this behaviour help to satisfy salient needs? In considering this question, an individual takes into account both the short- and long-term extrinsic and intrinsic rewards. For example, the current extrinsic rewards for unknown actors to perform in a television show may be low (i.e., they don't get paid much!); but the future value of this performance may be high if it leads to additional roles in television or movies.

Personal values and competencies play a key role in determining how individuals evaluate the costs of a behaviour. There are four main types of "costs": tangible costs, physical costs, psychological costs, and opportunity costs.

Let's take a specific behaviour—accepting a job rather than continuing to remain unemployed. There are some obvious *tangible costs*, such as transportation costs. There are also *physical costs*, such as fatigue or possible health risks. *Psychological costs* may include stress and frustration, or the need to violate one's personal values in order to perform the job. A person strongly opposed to smoking may consider a job in a tobacco factory much more objectionable than would a smoker. Some people may find the loss of autonomy and freedom inherent in accepting a job to be a high psychological cost. Finally, there are the *opportunity costs* of taking this job. Performing any behaviour at a point in time means that the opportunity to perform other behaviours is lost. So accepting a job means less time available to spend with children or other family members. Certainly, accepting a job means less time for leisure or social activities.

Personal values and personal competencies determine how a person weighs these costs. For example, personal values determine what costs a person assigns to physical activity (Are you an active person who likes physical activity or not? How highly do you value your health?). Personal competencies also play a role: if a job requires competencies that you do not have (e.g., physical strength, manual dexterity, good communication skills), you will likely find the job more draining than someone else might.

Personal values also affect psychological costs. For example, a person is offered a well-paying job selling fur coats; but if that person believes that trapping animals to produce fur coats is inhumane, there will be psychological costs to taking the job. Another person could be offered a good job in a distillery but is strongly opposed to the consumption of alcohol. Or someone who values his or her autonomy very highly could be offered a highly paid job working on an assembly line. These kinds of mismatches cause frustration and stress, increasing the costs of accepting these types of jobs (and increasing the rewards necessary to induce people to accept them).

Similarly, personal values may play a key role in evaluating opportunity costs. Accepting a job takes a young parent away from his or her preschool-aged children. Some people may consider this a very severe cost, while others may not consider it a cost at all, but in fact a reward! A newly hired employee may have to give up some volunteer work that she or he finds fulfilling. Of course, opportunity costs are also a function of personal circumstances—some people may not have many opportunities to forego by accepting a job. It depends on what else is happening in their lives.

Evaluating Instrumentality

If the balance of perceived costs and benefits nets out to a positive valence, the next question individuals will ask is: "What is the likelihood that the promised rewards will actually materialize?" If a person performs the behaviour (i.e., to accept and perform the job), will that person really receive all the promised rewards? For example, a firm may promise pay of $10 an hour, with a raise to $12 after six months, and to $14 after a year, subject to satisfactory performance. It may also promise lucrative opportunities for overtime pay, as well as profit-sharing bonuses contingent on good company performance.

But a major issue here is one of credibility: can this employer be trusted to carry through with the rewards that have been promised? Has the firm been in financial difficulty? Does it have a history of laying off employees on a thin pretext just as they are about to receive an increase in pay? A person's perception of the likelihood of promised rewards materializing is conditioned by both past experiences and personality. Has he or she been associated with a previous employer whose promises never materialized? Is he or she high or low in the personality trait of cynicism? A person high in cynicism may have a predisposition not to trust promises of future rewards.

Evaluating Expectancy

If employees do believe that the promised rewards will materialize, what is their likelihood of being able to successfully perform the necessary behaviour? Their sense of personal competencies, along with personality and past experiences, affect perceived expectancy. For example, if they have been able to perform the behaviour successfully in the past, their expectancy of being able to do it again will be high; if they believe that they have the skills and competencies necessary to perform the job, this increases their expectancy. If they are high in the personality trait of optimism, their expectancy increases.

Two main factors determine whether effort actually leads to successful performance of the behaviour in question: individual attributes, and organizational context and support. Individual attributes comprise the abilities, knowledge, and skills necessary to successfully perform the job. Organizational context means the circumstances in which the behaviour will take place. For example, if the behaviour is selling sporting equipment, the quality and price of the products will have a great deal to do with success.

Organizational support consists of the resources, training, and tools the organization needs to provide for successful job performance. Before attempting to perform the job, an individual must perceive that there is enough organizational support to make successful performance and achievement of the behaviour highly likely. This perception directly affects perceived expectancy.

Achieving the Desired Behaviour

 3.1

Of course, actual performance is a function not only of effort but also of personal characteristics and organizational context; and these factors determine whether effort actually leads to the desired behaviour. If the expected behaviour does not take place, rewards will not follow and effort will cease. If the behaviour takes place, but the expected rewards are not perceived to follow, effort will again cease.

As you may have noticed, we've reached the last element in our model for understanding and predicting human behaviour. So what are the implications of this model for designing reward systems? Compensation Notebook 3.1 distils these implications into nine steps that will produce a reward system that generates the behaviour an organization wants and needs.

Compensation Notebook 3.1

Steps in Designing a Reward System that Produces the Desired Employee Behaviour

1. **Define** the behaviour that is really needed.
2. **Determine** the employee attributes and qualifications needed to perform these behaviours.
3. **Identify** the needs that individuals possessing these qualifications are likely to find salient.
4. **Develop** rewards that will address these salient needs.
5. **Ensure** a positive valence for needed behaviours.
6. **Make it clear** that performance of the behaviour will lead to the rewards.
7. **Be sure** that employees *perceive* that effort will very likely lead to the desired behaviour.
8. **Provide conditions** that make it likely that effort *actually will* lead to the desired behaviour.
9. **Make sure** that rewards are actually provided as promised.

Summary

This chapter has shown you how reward systems can affect behaviour in organizations. You have learned how reward systems may not only fail to produce the desired employee behaviour but actually create undesirable consequences, some of which could even threaten the survival of the organization. You now know the potentially high costs of reward dissatisfaction—from low motivation and low employee satisfaction to high turnover and even employee theft. You also know some of the causes of reward dissatisfaction, including violation of the psychological contract, perceived reward inequity, discrepancy between desired and actual reward levels, and a perceived lack of distributive and procedural justice.

You have learned that there are three main sets of desired employee behaviours—membership behaviour, task behaviour, and citizenship behaviour—and that these behaviours are valued more by some firms than others. Task behaviour is the only one of the three valued by classical firms, while human relations firms value task and membership behaviour, and high involvement firms value all three. You also learned that these behaviours can only be induced by generating three key job attitudes—job satisfaction, work motivation, and organizational identification—and learned the role that reward systems can play in fostering these attitudes.

You now understand how the managerial strategy of your firm affects the way you will tailor the reward system. Classical organizations need to provide only enough rewards to create a tolerable psychological contract that results in a minimal degree of membership behaviour. They can achieve work motivation through rewards tied directly to the needed behaviours, or through the use of control systems, with the underlying threat of dismissal providing the basic motivation. Classical firms pay a price for lacking job and reward satisfaction and organizational identification, but they are designed to minimize this price.

In contrast, human relations organizations rely on job satisfaction and positive work norms. In a human relations firm, you must ensure that the reward systems are equitable and that they generate job satisfaction and a substantial degree of commitment. Organizational identification, while desirable, is not essential.

And finally, high-involvement organizations generally require the most complex reward systems, because they typically require the most complex and high-level behaviour from their employees. These reward systems need to be seen as equitable and as adhering to principles of organizational justice. Of the three managerial strategies, reward dissatisfaction is most damaging to high-involvement firms, because this dissatisfaction undermines the foundation of trust needed for successful utilization of this strategy.

In addition, this chapter has presented you with an integrated model for understanding and predicting human behaviour, including the nine key steps to creating an effective reward system, as summarized in Compensation Notebook 3.1. You are also aware of several other principles that can affect reward system success. For example, be cautious when using extrinsic rewards (especially individual rewards) to motivate specific behaviours, since unrewarded behaviours will likely be neglected, and your reward system may generate negative consequences (such as lack of concern for the performance of other employees or of the organization as a whole). At the same time, use individual extrinsic incentives only in limited circumstances, as will be discussed in the following chapters. Whenever possible, choose intrinsic rewards over extrinsic rewards. But note that extrinsic rewards tied to group and organizational performance are beneficial for many organizations.

Having developed an understanding of how rewards link to behaviour in this chapter and how strategy links to rewards in the previous chapter, you have now finished the first two steps along your road to effective compensation. The next step is to understand the spectrum of compensation components that are available, so that you can choose the combination of components that results in a compensation strategy that will best fit your organization.

Key Terms

affective commitment, 80

agency theory, 94

attribution theory, 92

content theories of motivation, 82

continuance commitment, 80

demographic characteristics, 98

distributive justice, 74

equity sensitivity, 79

equity theory, 72

expectancy theory, 91

job autonomy, 85

job enrichment, 86

job feedback, 85

job satisfaction, 66

Maslow's hierarchy of needs, 83

membership behaviour, 66

need salience, 87

organizational citizenship behaviour, 66

organizational commitment, 80

organizational identification, 66

personal beliefs, 98

personal characteristics, 98

personal competencies, 98

personal frame of reference, 98

personality characteristics, 98

personal values, 98

procedural justice, 74

process theories of motivation, 83

psychological contract, 71

reinforcement theory, 89

Web Links

To examine trends in the labour market, go to **http://www.statcan.ca/english/ Subjects/Labour/LFS/lfs-en.htm**. (p. 79)

To estimate the costs of employee turnover, go to **http://www.isquare.com/ turnover.cfm**. (p. 82)

To identify specific values and personality characteristics that affect employee motivation and ways to test for them, go to **http://queendom.com**. (p. 98)

RPC Icons

RPC 3.1 Evaluates the total compensation strategy to ensure it is consistent with the objectives of attracting, motivating, and retaining qualified people required to meet organizational goals.

Discussion Questions

1. Discuss the three main types of reward problems. Have you ever encountered any of these problems?
2. Discuss how employee job attitudes serve as the link between reward systems and employee job behaviour.
3. Discuss how reward systems can be used to generate task behaviour, membership behaviour, and citizenship behaviour.

Using the Internet

1. Employee turnover can be expensive, and it is just one possible consequence of reward dissatisfaction. Using your most recent full-time job, or that of a friend or relative, go to **http://www.isquare.com/turnover. cfm** to estimate the specific costs of turnover for that job.
2. Go to **http://queendom.com** and browse through the free personality and values tests. Identify at least one test that would be relevant to employee motivation, and take that test. Discuss what it tells you about your own motivation pattern, and how it might relate to the reward strategy that would best motivate you.

Exercises

1. In a group of four to six people, discuss situations in which employees experienced reward dissatisfaction. What caused that dissatisfaction? How did people react to it? What were the consequences for the organization? Were they serious consequences? Why or why not?

2. This chapter contained two examples of auto companies—Toyota (Compensation Today 3.1) and CAMI (Compensation Today 3.2)—that apparently wanted to adopt a high involvement managerial strategy. This was not successful at CAMI, but very successful at Toyota. Are there any concepts from this chapter or previous chapters that could help explain this result? Assuming that management at CAMI really wanted to move away from the classical school, what should they have done differently?

3. Think of an important decision that you recently made. Then use the integrated model for understanding behaviour to analyze your decision-making process. Is the decision that you actually made consistent with what the model predicted you would make? If not, then why not? Get together in a small group and share your results and conclusions.

Case Questions

1. Analyze the "Henderson Printing" case in the Appendix. Why do you think there is such a high turnover of new employees? What concepts may help to explain employee reactions to the compensation system? Do you think that the compensation system is fair? Is it effective? What principles for effective reward systems does it violate? What changes should be made?

2. Read the "Plastco Packaging" case in the Appendix. The Plastco machine operators appear to be suffering from low job satisfaction and motivation. Develop a plan for solving these problems by redesigning these jobs to add more intrinsic rewards. Besides these changes to job design, can you recommend any other changes to the various dimensions of organization structure (including the reward structure)?

Simulation Cross-Reference

If you are using *Strategic Compensation: A Simulation* in conjunction with this text, you will find that the concepts in Chapter 3 are helpful in preparing Sections A, B, and C of the simulation.

Endnotes

1. See Kerr, Steven. 1995. "On the Folly of Rewarding A, While Hoping for B." *Academy of Management Executive*, 9(1): 7–14. See also "More on the Folly." 1995. *Academy of Management Executive.* 9(1): 15–16.

2. See Van Scotter, James R., Stephan J. Motowidlo, and Thomas C. Cross. 2000. "Effects of Task Performance and Contextual Performance on Systemic Rewards." *Journal of Applied Psychology*, 85(4): 526–535. See also Gellatly, Ian R., and P. Gregory Irving. 2001. "Personality, Autonomy, and Contextual Performance of Managers." *Human Performance*, 14(3): 229–243.

3. See Rousseau, Denise M. 1995. *Psychological Contracts in Organizations: Understanding Written and Unwritten Agreements*. Thousand Oaks, CA: Sage. See also Rousseau, Denise M., and Violet T. Ho. 2000. "Psychological Contract Issues in Compensation." In Sara L. Rynes and Barry Gerhart, eds. *Compensation in Organizations: Current Research and Practice*. San Francisco: Jossey Bass.

4. Morrison, Elizabeth W., and Sandra L. Robinson. 1997. "When Employees Feel Betrayed: A Model of How Psychological Contract Violation Occurs." *Academy of Management Review*, 22(1): 228–56.

5. Lucero, Margaret A., and Robert E. Allen. 1994. "Employee Benefits: A Growing Source of Psychological Contract Violations." *Human Resource Management*, 33(3): 425–46.

6. Adams, J. Stacy. 1965. "Inequity in Social Exchange." In L. Berkovitz, ed., *Advances in Experimental Social Psychology*, vol. 2. New York: Academic Press.

7. Clark, Andrew E., and Andrew J. Oswald. 1996. "Satisfaction and Comparison Income." *Journal of Public Economics*, 61: 359–81.

8. Miceli, Marcia P., and Matthew C. Lane. 1991. "Antecedents of Pay Satisfaction: A Review and Extension." *Research in Human Resources Management*, 9: 235–309.

9. Pratt, Nancy C. 1996. "CEOs Reap Unprecedented Riches While Employees' Pay Stagnates." *Compensation and Benefits Review*, 28(5): 20–24.

10. Farrell, Christopher. 2002. "Stock Options for All!" *Business Week Online*: September 20.

11. Crosby, F. 1976. "A Model of Egoistical Relative Deprivation." *Psychological Review*, 83: 95–113.

12. Sweeney, Paul D., Dean B. McFarlin, and Edward J. Inderrieden. 1990. "Using Relative Deprivation Theory to Explain Satisfaction with Income and Pay Level: A Multistudy Examination." *Academy of Management Journal*, 33(2): 423–36.

13. Greenberg, Jerald. 1990b. "Organizational Justice: Yesterday, Today, and Tomorrow." *Journal of Management*, 16(2): 399–432.

14. Tremblay, Michel, Bruno Sire, and David Balkin. 2000. "The Role of Organizational Justice in Pay and Employee Benefit Satisfaction and Its Effects on Work Attitudes." *Group and Organization Management*, 25(3): 269–90.

15. Scarpello, Vida, and Foard F. Jones. 1996. "Why Justice Matters in Compensation Decision Making." *Journal of Organizational Behavior*, 17: 285–99.

16. Folger, Robert, and Mary A. Konovsky. 1989. "Effects of Procedural and Distributive Justice on Reactions to Pay Raise Decisions." *Academy of Management Journal*, 32(1): 115–30.

17. Tremblay, Michel, and Patrice Roussel. 2001. "Modelling the Role of Organizational Justice: Effects on Satisfaction and Unionization Propensity of Canadian Managers." *International Journal of Human Resource Management*, 12(5): 717–37.

18. Theriault, Roland. 1992. *Mercer Compensation Manual*. Boucherville, PQ: G. Morin Publisher.

19. Huseman, R.C., J.D. Hatfield, and E.W. Miles. 1985. "Test for Individual Perceptions of Job Equity: Some Preliminary Findings." *Perceptual and Motor Skills*, 61: 1055–64.

20. Smith, P.C., L. Kendall, and C. Hulin. 1969. *The Measurement of Satisfaction in Work and Retirement*. Chicago: Rand McNally.

21. Ashford, Susan J., Cynthia Lee, and Philip Bobko. 1989. "Content, Causes, and Consequences of Job Insecurity: A Theory-Based Measure and Substantive Test." *Academy of Management Journal*, 32(4): 803–29.

22. Gellatly, Ian R. 1995. "Individual and Group Determinants of Employee Absenteeism: Test of a Causal Model." *Journal of Organizational Behavior*, 16: 469–85.

23. Cramer, Duncan. 1996. "Job Satisfaction and Organizational Continuance Commitment: A Two Wave Panel Study." *Journal of Organizational Behaviour*, 17: 389–400.

24. Tett, Robert P., and John P. Meyer. 1993. "Job Satisfaction, Organizational Commitment, Turnover Intention, and Turnover: Path Analyses Based on Meta-Analytic Findings." *Personnel Psychology*, 46(2): 259–93.

25. Jaros, Stephen J., John M. Jermier, Jerry W. Koehler, and Terry Sincich. 1993. "Effects of Continuance, Affective, and Moral Commitment on the Withdrawal Process: An Evaluation of Eight Structural Equation Models." *Academy of Management Journal*, 36(5): 951–95.

26. Masterson, Suzanne S., Kyle Lewis, Barry M. Goldman, and M. Susan Taylor. 2000. "Integrating Justice and Social Exchange: The Differing Effects of Fair Procedures and Treatment on Work Relationships." *Academy of Management Journal*, 43(4): 738–39.

27. Finegan, Joan E. 2000. "The Impact of Personal and Organizational Values on Organizational Commitment." *Journal of Occupational and Organizational Psychology*, 73: 149–69.

28. Delery, John E., N. Gupta, Jason D. Shaw, G. Douglas Jenkins, and Margot L. Ganster. 2000. "Unionization, Compensation, and Voice Effects on Quits and Retention." *Industrial Relations*, 39(4): 625–45.

29. Powell, Irene, Mark Montgomery, and James Cosgrove. 1994. "Compensation Structure and Establishment Quit and Fire Rates." *Industrial Relations*, 33(2): 229–48.

30. Miceli, Marcia P., and Paul W. Mulvey. 2000. "Consequences of Satisfaction with Pay Systems: Two Field Studies." *Industrial Relations*, 39(1): 62–87.

31. Maslow, A.H. 1954. *Motivation and Personality*. New York: Harper and Row.

32. Alderfer, C. 1972. *Existence, Relatedness, and Growth*. New York: The Free Press.

33. Herzberg, Frederick, B. Mausner, and B.B. Snyderman. 1959. *The Motivation to Work*. New York: John Wiley.

34. Herzberg, Frederick. 1966. *Work and the Nature of Man*. Cleveland, OH: World Publishing.

35. Hackman, J. Richard, and Greg Oldham. 1980. *Work Redesign*. Reading, MA: Addison-Wesley.

36. Fried, Yitzhak. 1991. "Meta-Analytic Comparison of the Job Diagnostic Survey and Job Characteristics Inventory as Correlates of Work Satisfaction and Performance." *Journal of Applied Psychology*, 76(5): 690–97.

37. Kohn, Alfie. 1993. *Punished by Rewards: The Trouble with Gold Stars, A's, Praise, and Other Bribes*. Boston: Houghton-Mifflin.

38. Tang, Thomas L., Jwa K. Kim, and David S. Tang. 2000. "Does Attitude toward Money Moderate the Relationship between Intrinsic Job Satisfaction and Voluntary Turnover?" *Human Relations*, 53(2): 213–45.

39. Tang, Thomas L., Jwa K. Kim, and David S. Tang. 2000. "Does Attitude toward Money Moderate the Relationship between Intrinsic Job Satisfaction and Voluntary Turnover?" *Human Relations*, 53(2): 213–45.

40. Skinner, B.F. 1953. *Science and Human Behavior*. New York: Macmillan.

41. Kohn, Alfie. 1993. *Punished by Rewards: The Trouble with Gold Stars, A's, Praise, and Other Bribes*. Boston: Houghton-Mifflin.

42. See Deci, E.L. 1975. *Intrinsic Motivation*. New York: Plenum Press. See also Deci, E.L., and R.M. Ryan. 1985. *Intrinsic Motivation and Self-Determination in Human Behavior*. New York: Plenum Press.

43. O'Hara, K., C.M. Johnson, and T.A. Beehr. 1985. "Organizational Behavior Management in the Private Sector: A Review of Empirical Research and Recommendations for Further Investigation." *Academy of Management Review*, 10: 848–64.

44. See Vroom, Victor V. 1964. *Work and Motivation*. New York: Wiley. Or see Lawler, Edward E. 1973. *Motivation in Work Organizations*. Monterey, CA: Brooks/Cole.

45. See Deci, E.L. 1975. *Intrinsic Motivation*. New York: Plenum Press. See also Deci, E.L., and R.M. Ryan. 1985. *Intrinsic Motivation and Self-Determination in Human Behavior*. New York: Plenum Press.

46. Wiersma, Uco J. 1992. "The Effects of Extrinsic Rewards in Intrinsic Motivation: A Meta-Analysis." *Journal of Occupational and Organizational Psychology*, 65: 101–14.

47. Deci, E.L. 1975. *Intrinsic Motivation*. New York: Plenum Press.

48. Harackiewicz, J.M., and J.R. Larson. 1986. "Managing Motivation: The Impact of Supervisor Feedback on Subordinate Task Interest." *Journal of Personality and Social Psychology*, 51: 547–56.

49. See Jensen, M., and W. Meckling. 1976. "Theory of the Firm: Managerial Behavior, Agency Costs, and Ownership Structure." *Journal of Financial Economics*, 3: 305–60. See also Eisenhardt, Kathleen. 1989. "Agency Theory: An Assessment and Review." *Academy of Management Review*, 14(1): 57–74.

50. Bateman, T. S., and D.W. Organ. 1983. "Job Satisfaction and the Good Soldier: The Relationship between Affect and Employee Citizenship." *Academy of Management Journal*, 26: 587–95.

51. Organ, Dennis W. 1990. "The Motivational Basis of Organizational Citizenship Behavior." *Research in Organizational Behavior*, 12: 43–72.

52. Argyris, Chris. 1964. *Integrating the Individual and the Organization*. New York: Wiley.

53. Lambert, Susan J. 2000. "Added Benefits: The Link between Work-Life Benefits and Organizational Citizenship Behaviour." *The Academy of Management Journal*, 43(5): 801–15.

54. Moorman, Robert H. 1991. "Relationship between Organizational Justice and Organizational Citizenship Behaviors: Do Fairness Perceptions Influence Employee Citizenship?" *Journal of Applied Psychology*, 76(6): 845–55.

55. Konovsky, Mary A., and Dennis W. Organ. 1996. "Dispositional and Contextual Determinants of Organizational Citizenship Behaviour." *Journal of Organizational Behavior*, 17: 253–66.

56. Janssen, Onne. 2000. "Job Demands, Perceptions of Effort-Reward Fairness, and Innovative Work Behaviour." *Journal of Occupational and Organizational Psychology*, 73: 287–302.

57. Long, Richard J. 1995. "Employee Buyouts: The Canadian Experience." *Canadian Business Economics*, 3(4): 28–41.

Formulating Reward and Compensation Strategy

Chapter 4

Components of Compensation Strategy

Chapter Learning Objectives

After reading this chapter, you should be able to:

- Define base pay and discuss its advantages, disadvantages, and applicability.
- Define performance pay and discuss its advantages, disadvantages, and applicability.
- Define indirect pay and discuss its advantages, disadvantages, and applicability.
- Identify and differentiate between the three main methods for establishing base pay.
- Define market pricing and discuss its advantages and disadvantages.
- Define job evaluation and discuss its advantages and disadvantages.
- Define pay for knowledge and discuss its advantages and disadvantages.
- Identify and differentiate between the three main categories of performance pay.
- Define and discuss the applicability of the four main types of individual performance pay.
- Define and discuss the applicability of the three main types of group performance pay.
- Define and discuss the applicability of the three main types of organization performance pay.

Traditionally, banking compensation systems have used only base pay with virtually no performance-related pay. However, in recent years, many banks have added a performance-contingent component to virtually every job, and some jobs are even paid entirely on commission. For example, at the Royal Bank, customer service representatives (tellers) are now included in profit sharing plans, as well as employee stock plans. In addition, personnel in areas like mobile banking and registered retirement funds now have the option of selecting straight commission as their primary compensation. The bank hopes that these changes will focus employee attention on performance and create a greater understanding of the link between employee performance and organizational performance.

These policies for base and performance pay are part of a "total rewards" compensation philosophy. The other key components of "total rewards" include extensive indirect pay, with benefits ranging from pensions to work-life support programs, learning and career development opportunities, and a commitment to provide a workplace culture that supports each employee's unique needs, work style, and preferences.[1]

Introduction

Why does the person who cuts your hair get paid per head, while the person who pumps your gas gets paid per hour? In fact, why use time-based pay at all? Some compensation systems do not. For example, realtors get paid only when they sell a house, auto salespeople are paid only when they sell a car, and stockbrokers are paid only when they make a trade. Carpet installers are paid for each square metre of carpet laid, long-haul truck drivers are paid per kilometre driven, and dentists are paid for each tooth drilled. Why not pay everybody this way?

That's a good question—and one that will be addressed in this chapter. In designing any compensation strategy, we must address two key questions. First, what role should each of the three compensation components (base pay, performance pay, indirect pay) play in the compensation mix? Second, what total level of compensation should be provided?

The second question will be addressed in Chapter 5. The purpose of this chapter is to provide a foundation for answering the first question, by examining in depth the advantages and disadvantages of each of the three pay components and their key elements, along with the circumstances in which each is most appropriate. The goal here is not to describe how to design any of these compensation components, but to provide you with enough

FIGURE 4.1

Compensation Mix Choices

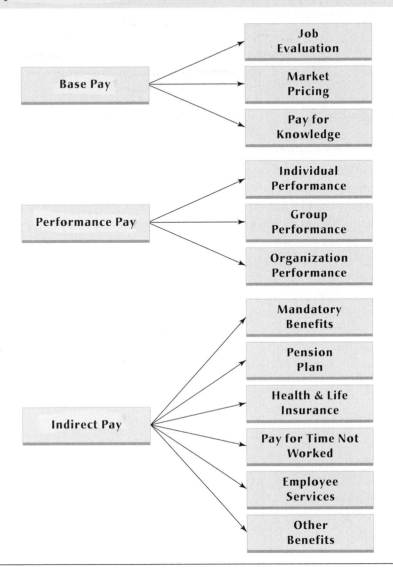

information to decide the role that each should play in your firm's compensation strategy. Figure 4.1 shows the "menu" of choices for a firm's compensation mix.

Fundamental Components
of the Compensation Mix

RPC 4.1

As Figure 4.1 suggests, the first strategic decision is the relative proportion of base pay, performance pay, and indirect pay to include in the compensation mix. Three other sets of strategic choices follow—the method for establishing base pay, the performance pay plans, and indirect pay elements. Later parts of the chapter discuss base pay choices and performance pay choices. The detailed choices surrounding indirect pay are not discussed until Chapter 11 because of the complexity of these decisions.

Base Pay

base pay

the portion of an individual's compensation that is based on a unit of time worked

Base pay is the portion of an individual's compensation that is based on time worked, not on output produced or results achieved. For the great majority of employees in Canada, base pay serves as the largest component of their compensation package. According to the 2004 Compensation Practices Survey (CPS) of medium to large Canadian firms conducted by the author for this book, base pay accounted for 79 percent of total compensation for the typical employee, performance pay for about 6.5 percent, and indirect pay (benefits) for about 15 percent. As Table 4.1 shows, this represents very little change since 2000 in the proportion of base pay, although the proportion of performance pay has dropped slightly, and proportion of indirect pay has increased slightly. The declines in performance pay represent a break in the recent trend towards increasing performance pay and may be due in part to the difficult economic circumstances in the first few years of the new millennium.

Base pay is "guaranteed" by the employer: if a person works for a certain amount of time, he or she is paid a pre-specified amount of money. In some cases, this amount is calculated on an hourly basis (e.g., $10 per hour); in

TABLE 4.1

Compensation Mix in Canadian Firms

COMPENSATION COMPONENT	2000			2004		
	PROPORTION OF TOTAL COMPENSATION (ALL FIRMS)	PROPORTION OF FIRMS USING	PROPORTION OF TOTAL COMPENSATION (USERS ONLY)	PROPORTION OF TOTAL COMPENSATION (ALL FIRMS)	PROPORTION OF FIRMS USING	PROPORTION OF TOTAL COMPENSATION (USERS ONLY)
Base Pay	79.4%	96%	82.7%	79.1%	98%	80.2%
Individual Performance Pay	6.8%	44%	15.5%	4.6%	41%	13.2%
Group Performance Pay	1.1%	19%	5.5%	1.1%	16%	6.9%
Organizational Performance Pay	1.3%	26%	5.0%	0.8%	24%	3.8%
Indirect Pay	11.4%	79%	14.6%	14.5%	95%	15.3%

Source: Compensation Practices Survey.

others, daily (e.g., $200 per day); in others, weekly (e.g., $1,000 per week), monthly (e.g., $4,000 per month), or annually (e.g., $50,000 per year). When calculated on an hourly basis, base pay is known as a **wage**; when calculated on a weekly, monthly, or annual basis, it is known as a **salary**.

Why Use Base Pay?

Why use base pay at all? Wouldn't it be more efficient just to use output-related pay? Why not simply eliminate base pay, as some employers have done? The answer is that output-related pay cannot always be used, thus forcing the use of base pay. In addition, base pay is sometimes preferable to output-related pay, even where output-related pay is feasible.

First of all, for some organizations, output-related pay is simply impractical. Substitution of output-related pay for time-based pay is only feasible for jobs in which the output is (1) easy to measure, (2) easy to price in terms of its value to the employer, (3) easy to attribute to individual employees, (4) controllable by the individual employee, and (5) not highly unstable. Obviously, most jobs do not meet all these criteria; and attempts to use output-related pay in such jobs can cause serious problems.

In some organizations, output-related pay is possible, but it is not desirable because of the unintended consequences. For example, some mines do not use output-related compensation because of a concern that this might lead to a high push for production at the expense of safety. In the retail sector, salespeople may become too aggressive or may resort to unethical sales practices in order to maximize their commission income. Jobs that combine some measurable outputs with nonmeasurable outputs are also not good candidates for a pay system based only on output, since employees tend to focus on the measured behaviours and neglect other behaviours.

In still other organizations, output-related pay may be practical and desirable from the employer's point of view, but not from the employee's point of view. In general, people prefer certainty in their rewards and thus prefer a large component of base pay in their compensation package. Trade unions have worked for many years to make wages more certain and have generally pushed for base pay as the primary pay component.

Indeed, because of the general preference among employees for base pay, it may be necessary to offer higher total pay in order to induce employees to accept jobs in which all pay is performance-contingent. This may actually result in higher total compensation costs, as employees demand a premium for the additional risk.[2] If the performance-contingent pay plan does not boost output sufficiently to cover the additional pay costs, then a firm would be better off with a time-based pay system.

So far, base pay has been portrayed as something to be used simply because no other alternative is viable, and this is indeed the major motivation to use it. But base pay can also be used for more positive reasons. One reason is flexibility. With time-based pay, the employer is essentially buying time from the employee. Within certain limits, this time may be directed in many ways and redirected as need arises. Base pay doesn't confine employee attention to only one or two behaviours, as output-based pay tends to do.

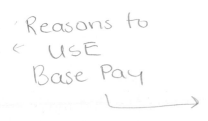

Reasons to USE Base Pay

A second reason is that base pay allows the employer to recognize and encourage important non-output-based job behaviours, such as skill development. Third, base pay can signal the relative importance of jobs within the organization. Fourth, base pay demonstrates a commitment on the part of the employer to the employee, creating a greater likelihood of employee commitment to the employer. Fifth, depending on the method used to set up a base pay strategy, it can support a particular managerial strategy. Finally, one very important reason for the use of base pay is simplicity—it is usually much simpler to implement and administer than an output-related system.

Disadvantages of Base Pay

What are the disadvantages of base pay?

1. Base pay represents more of a fixed employer commitment than performance-contingent pay, especially if salaries are used. For example, base pay is not linked to variability in an employer's ability to pay in the way that performance-contingent pay is.
2. While base pay does contribute to membership behaviour, it does not directly motivate task behaviour, nor does it signal key task behaviours.
3. Since base pay does not relate organizational success directly to individual success, it does not directly contribute to citizenship behaviour.
4. Base pay is not self-correcting. In an output-related system, employees who do not perform up to standard tend to voluntarily remove themselves from the organization because they are unable to earn enough money. But time-based pay provides no such mechanism.

Of course, time-based pay and output/performance-related pay are not mutually exclusive and can be combined. In this way, managers can capture the advantages of both while minimizing their disadvantages. Indeed, in recent years, there has been a trend away from compensation systems that rely solely on either base pay or performance pay. Many firms that have traditionally relied only on base pay are starting to add some performance-contingent elements to their pay systems (such as those in the banking industry, as discussed in the opening vignette), while others that have traditionally relied only on performance pay (such as stock brokerage firms) are starting to add base pay to their compensation systems (such as at Altamira Financial Services, as discussed in Compensation Today 1.1).

Performance Pay

performance pay

any type of financial reward provided only when certain specified performance results occur. These results may be based on the performance of individual employees, a group or team, or an entire organization

Performance pay can be defined as any type of financial reward provided only when certain specified performance results occur. It is sometimes known as "performance-contingent pay," "variable pay," or "at-risk pay." Pay-for-performance plans can be classified into three main categories, depending on whether the performance relates to the individual employee, the group or work team, or the entire organization. *Individual performance plans* include piece rates, commissions, merit pay, and targeted incentives. *Group* *performance plans* include productivity gain-sharing plans, goal-sharing plans, and other types of team-based pay. *Organizational performance plans* include employee profit sharing plans, employee stock plans, and other organizational pay plans.

Paying employees only when the desired performance takes place sounds like a wonderful idea—if you are an employer. Indeed, the latter part of the twentieth century did see a dramatic growth in performance pay, particularly group and organizational performance pay. Yet many employers still choose not to use performance pay at all, and among those who do use it, it generally constitutes a relatively small proportion of total compensation, as Table 4.1 has shown. What are the reasons for choosing performance pay?

Why Use Performance Pay?

Performance pay plans have several advantages. Properly designed, they signal key behaviours and motivate employees to achieve them. Moreover, they reduce the need for other types of mechanisms for controlling employee behaviour. They raise employee interest in performance and provide employees with information about their current performance levels. They can be used to support specific managerial strategies and thereby promote achievement of the organization's goals.

Finally, performance pay plans make pay more variable and therefore help to link compensation levels to the firm's ability to pay. This linkage helps stabilize an organization's employment levels,[3] lessening the need to lay off employees in difficult times only to rehire them when business improves. This employment stability has advantages for both employers and employees, since employers risk losing employees whenever they are forced to lay them off, and employees prefer reduced-pay employment to layoffs.

Disadvantages of Performance Pay

It is difficult to generalize about the disadvantages of performance pay plans because the types of plans differ radically, and each has its own specific advantages, disadvantages, and limitations. But one general drawback is that employees generally prefer predictable and certain rewards to unpredictable and uncertain rewards. Of course, employees usually do not object to performance pay if it is clearly an add-on, to top off base pay and indirect pay. But employees will generally resist *substitution* of performance pay for base pay or indirect pay.

In order to induce employees to accept this substitution, it may be necessary to offer higher total compensation than would otherwise be necessary. Some organizations that rely heavily on performance pay appear to pay a very steep price for so doing. For example, *The Globe and Mail* reported that some stock traders received as much as $800,000 in gross pay several years ago. Is it really necessary to pay this much? Is it really efficient to pay this much? Research in the United States indicates that workers on incentive systems average about 20 percent more earnings than comparable workers on time-based pay systems.[4]

In addition, as discussed in previous chapters, performance pay may cause employees to focus only on aspects of behaviour that are being measured, ignoring other unmeasured but still important behaviours. If poorly designed, performance pay can have unanticipated negative consequences. Getting performance pay to work right is usually not an easy matter, and base pay is frequently much simpler and more flexible.

Just how difficult it is to get performance pay to work effectively is illustrated by data from the Compensation Practices Survey. According to the CPS, depending on the type of performance pay plan, 15 to 78 percent of firms abandoned their performance pay plans during the 2000–2004 period. Overall, only four of the 13 performance pay plans examined in this survey had a discontinuation rate (the percentage of firms with a given plan in 2000 that had abandoned it by 2004) of 33 percent or less.

Indirect Pay

At Calgary-based Imperial Oil, employees receive a pension plan, life and accident insurance, disability benefits, three to six weeks' annual vacation, free tuition on any work-related course they want to take, and payment of tuition fees for dependent children—all at no cost to the employees. The company also offers shared-cost benefits, such as supplemental medical coverage, dental coverage, additional life insurance, long-term income protection, 75-percent payment of any approved physical fitness programs taken by an employee, and a savings plan in which the company matches employee contributions. These features cost Imperial a lot of money. So why provide them? Many companies don't. Why not keep things simple and just use direct pay?

In Canada, indirect pay constitutes a major expenditure for many firms. In the past, indirect pay was known as "fringe benefits," but as the extent and costs of these benefits increased, they became known simply as "benefits." In this book, the term "indirect pay" is preferred, because this term acknowledges that benefits are in fact an integral part of total compensation for many firms and should be considered a component of employee pay in the same way as base pay and performance pay. In many cases, employees and even employers underplay the role indirect pay plays in the total pay package, and this needs to change, given the cost of benefits and the strategic role they play in the compensation system.

According to the Compensation Practices Survey, indirect pay averaged 15 percent of total compensation in private-sector firms, although this ranged from 17 percent in the manufacturing sector down to 10 percent in the accommodation/food industry, where many employers don't provide any benefits beyond the statutory minimum. In her sample of larger Canadian organizations, Baarda found benefits constituted an average of 19.7 percent of total compensation.[5] Baarda's sample also included public-sector organizations, which traditionally have provided more benefits, on average, than private-sector firms.

So what do employers hope to gain from these expenditures? Why do some employers invest heavily in indirect pay, while others provide only the minimum required by law? In fact, why bother to provide indirect pay at all?

Major Categories of Indirect Pay

1. Benefits mandated by law, including employer contributions to the Canada/Quebec Pension Plan, Employment Insurance, and Workers' Compensation Benefits;

2. Deferred income plans, more commonly known as retirement or pension plans;

3. Life, medical, dental, disability and other types of health benefits;

4. Pay for time not worked, such as paid holidays and leaves;

5. Employee services, ranging from psychological counselling to food services;

6. Miscellaneous benefits, which may range from provision of company cars to purchase discounts on company products or services.

Is indirect pay a costly frill, or can it play a significant role in furthering key compensation objectives? This section of the chapter provides the foundation for addressing these questions.

What kinds of items are classified as indirect pay? Basically, **indirect pay** can be anything that costs the employer money, addresses some type of employee need (thus conferring some type of "benefit" on the employee), and is not included as part of base or performance pay. There are six main types or categories of indirect pay, as shown in Compensation Notebook 4.1.

Beyond the specific items included, indirect pay systems vary in other ways. One key variation is choice: whether employees can choose what benefits they receive (a flexible benefit system) or whether they cannot (a fixed benefit system). Another variation is responsibility for the costs: whether the employer covers all costs, or whether employees are required to share in the cost. Yet another important difference is whether coverage varies for different employee groups. These issues will all be discussed in more detail in Chapter 11.

indirect pay

any type of employer-provided reward (or "benefit") that serves an employee need but is not part of base or performance pay

Why Use Indirect Pay?

Why do firms provide indirect pay? There are seven main motives.

1. A major motive for using indirect pay is competitive pressure. If competitors are offering benefits that are important to the people the firm wants to hire, then an employer may need to offer similar benefits to attract these employees. For example, some employees would never dream of working for an employer who does not provide an adequate pension plan.

2. In order to satisfy the security needs of their members, unions have always bargained strongly for comprehensive employee benefits, and unionized firms have had to respond to these pressures. Non-union firms may match the packages won by unions at other firms in order to remove one possible incentive for unionization; although they do not always do so. On average, employees in unionized firms

receive about 45 percent higher benefits than comparable non-union Canadian employees.[6]

3. Certain types of indirect pay receive more favourable income tax treatment than direct pay (as will be discussed in Chapter 11). In these cases, a firm may use indirect pay to provide a higher total amount of after-tax compensation to employees than it would if the firm had paid out the same number of dollars in the form of direct pay.

4. Many benefit items—such as medical or dental coverage—can be purchased more cheaply by the employer than the employee, due to economies of scale in purchasing these items. (Indeed, in some cases, certain employees, such as those with serious health problems, might not even be able to acquire such insurance on their own.) Again, this provides a higher level of reward to employees for the same amount of company money.

5. Benefits can provide a way of protecting the financial security and peace of mind of employees, which may help to maintain employee performance. When employees have concerns about their ability to deal with health expenses, or what would happen should they become disabled, or even personal problems, they may have difficulty focusing on good job performance.

6. Many employers feel a genuine sense of responsibility for the welfare of their employees and want to help protect them from adversity. Others may not have the same concern but still do not want to appear hardhearted when employees encounter financial or health problems. The benefit system provides a systematic way for dealing with these types of problems.

7. Benefits can reinforce a particular managerial strategy. For example, the human relations strategy relies on a stable workforce. Since benefits for employees usually increase as their tenure increases, benefits can encourage membership behaviour. They can also create a sense of gratitude and obligation by employees toward their employer—a key feature of the human relations strategy. It is no coincidence that the boom in benefit plans started during the 1950s and 1960s, when human relations firms were becoming preeminent. Indeed, employee benefits were commonly known as "employee welfare plans" in the 1950s. (In addition, other circumstances in the 1950s, including good economic conditions, low unemployment, and the efforts of unions, had begun to turn employee attention toward benefits rather than focusing only on direct pay.) But indirect pay can be used to reinforce other managerial strategies as well. For example, because high-involvement companies focus on employee learning and development, they generally provide generous tuition reimbursement and educational leave plans. This helps provide the intrinsic rewards upon which these organizations rely for employee retention and motivation.

8. Specific benefits can also be used to promote consequences beneficial to the organization. For example, subsidizing fitness classes or

providing supplemental medical coverage may result in healthier employees who miss less work due to sickness. In addition, employee assistance programs may help employees resolve personal problems that could have a negative impact on work performance. Provision of company cars may reinforce a particular image for the sales force. Purchase discounts on company products may prevent the potential embarrassment of company employees purchasing products from a competitor and help give employees direct knowledge of the company's products. Compensation Today 4.1 gives more examples.

Disadvantages of Indirect Pay

So if indirect pay can provide these advantages, why doesn't every firm use it? There are several disadvantages of indirect pay. First and foremost, of course, is the issue of cost, which can be very substantial. Second is rigidity. Indirect pay is generally a fixed cost. Once a firm commits itself to providing certain benefits (such as a pension plan), it is liable for the costs of maintaining these benefits, even if the firm is not performing well. Also, once a benefit is provided, it becomes very difficult (and sometimes even illegal) to eliminate it; and even if the benefit is not highly valued by employees, simply eliminating it (without replacing it with something else) is likely to cause negative employee reaction. Moreover, where benefits are part of the terms and conditions of employment, as they are in union contracts, to unilaterally discontinue them may be illegal. Third, it is often difficult to develop a benefits package that successfully meets the true needs of employees and does not waste money on benefits that are not valued highly by employees. Fourth, administration and communication of a benefits program can be much more costly than simply providing higher direct pay. This is particularly relevant for smaller firms, which do not have economies of scale in purchasing the benefits and administering them.

A fifth disadvantage is the generally weak link between indirect pay and specific employee task behaviour. Since most or all employees in a firm are typically covered by benefits, regardless of employee performance, and the amount of the benefits received does not vary with performance, indirect pay is the opposite of performance pay and is not a good motivator for task behaviour.

Sixth, a benefit program may succeed too well at creating employee stability, causing unhappy employees to remain with the firm simply because they do not want to forgo the generous benefits package. Seventh, certain specific benefits or the means of administering them may actually promote undesirable behaviour. For example, an excessively generous or poorly designed sick leave policy may actually encourage absences by increasing the attractiveness of not coming to work and may also serve to penalize those who do come to work by requiring them to do the work of the absentees.

Finally, despite the large amount of money expended on benefits, not a lot is known about the impact of indirect pay on employee and company performance. More than a decade ago, two prominent experts complained that "the state of knowledge about the influence of benefits on employee attitudes and behaviours is dismal."[7] Since then, not much has improved. While we know that satisfaction with benefits is an important component of overall reward satisfaction,[8] no research explains whether simply eliminating the benefit system and adding the equivalent amount to salaries would actually make a greater contribution to reward satisfaction. In theory, a properly designed benefit system that provides valued benefits to employees *should* deliver more reward satisfaction than simply adding extra pay, due to the tax advantages of benefit plans and to the economies of scale in purchasing benefits. However, this proposition has never been effectively tested.

But even if it is true that benefits are preferable to extra direct pay, there must be a point beyond which the value of additional indirect pay declines below the value of additional direct pay. Many employers apparently believe that this point has now been reached. After a steady upward trend since the 1960s,[9] benefits costs peaked in 1995 at 21.4 percent of total compensation[10] and gradually edged down every year until 2000, settling at 19.7 percent of total compensation in large firms,[11] and lower than that in smaller firms. However, since 2000, benefits costs may have begun edging up again due to the increased costs of health benefits, particularly prescription drug plans.[12]

In general, indirect pay is not a good investment for classical firms, since it provides no task motivation. Perhaps the only circumstance in which it may be a good investment is situations involving high training costs. Since a classical firm is usually not a very satisfying organization to work for, the company needs some means of retaining its investment in trained employees; thus, using indirect pay to tie the employee to the firm may be good strategy for protecting this investment. Of course, this commitment will likely be of a grudging, continuance type.

Thus, classical organizations normally strive to minimize the use of indirect pay, except for retaining key employees. But ironically, much to the dismay of classical managers, many classical firms have ended up with very extensive benefit programs as a result of unions and the collective bargaining process. Most of these firms are probably aware that they receive very little value from these programs, and some have likely attempted to use flexible benefits as a ploy to cut costs.

If a classical organization must provide benefits, either as a result of the collective bargaining process or as an effort to match benefits of competitors, a traditional fixed benefit system would probably fit best, with employees sharing the costs of the benefits payouts (such as paying a proportion of every dental claim) to discourage frivolous use of the system. In situations where pay is tied to seniority and where employee productivity drops with age, generous pension plans may be desirable in order to encourage highly paid employees to retire.

In contrast, for human relations firms, indirect pay is a cornerstone of the managerial strategy, which is designed to show high concern for employees and to encourage high membership behaviour. As discussed earlier, human relations strategies appear to be losing popularity due to changes in the work environment. But in firms where human relations is still an effective managerial strategy, indirect pay remains a key part of the compensation strategy, although efforts will be made to contain costs of benefits. While these benefit systems may include some flexible elements, a fully flexible benefit system does not fit well with this approach.

In contrast, high-involvement firms face a dilemma regarding indirect pay. In some ways, indirect pay does not fit with the high-involvement concept because it does not relate to company performance. However, the key asset of any high-involvement firm is its members, so it needs to be sure that the absence of a benefit system doesn't cause employees to leave. It also needs to offer sufficient benefits that employees' lower-order needs for security are satisfied so that they can be motivated by their higher-order needs.

Since a high-involvement organization requires a high level of commitment from its employees, its benefit system also needs to recognize and facilitate this commitment. For example, family-friendly benefits, such as childcare, eldercare, and flexible work schedules, help employees deal with family commitments. High-involvement firms also have a genuine concern for the well-being of their employees and strive to help employees deal with unforeseen problems.

In general, high-involvement organizations tend to structure benefits to reinforce the employer-employee partnership. Thus, a flexible benefits system with cost sharing on the individual benefits is a good fit. But fixed benefits that encourage highly desired behaviours, such as tuition reimbursement and educational leave plans, also have a role. A key point is that benefits programs in high-involvement companies are not focused on continuance commitment. A high-involvement organization does not aim to "trap" people who don't fit with the organization.

Compensation Notebook 4.2 summarizes the advantages and disadvantages of the three fundamental compensation components.

Advantages and Disadvantages of the Compensation Mix Components

Component	Advantages	Disadvantages
Base Pay	• flexibility • can recognize valued job behaviours • can signal relative importance of jobs • demonstrates commitment to employee • can support managerial strategy • simplicity	• fixed pay commitment • does not motivate task behaviour • does not encourage citizenship behaviour • not self-correcting
Performance Pay	• signals key behaviours and motivates action • reduces need for control mechanisms • create employee interest in performance • can support managerial strategy • relates pay to firm's ability to pay	• employees prefer predictable rewards • may require higher compensation • may cause focus only on rewarded behaviours • may cause unanticipated consequences • usually more complex than base pay
Indirect Pay	• can help attract employees • matches unionized firms • favourable tax treatment • economies of scale in purchasing • can provide valued rewards for no cash • provide employee peace of mind • helps employer deal humanely with problems • can help promote company products • can support managerial strategy	• cost can be substantial • rigidity • difficult to develop efficient benefits package • administration and communication costly • does not motivate task behaviour • may cause excessive employee stability • may encourage undesirable behaviour

RPC 4.1

Methods for Establishing Base Pay

Suppose, like most employers, you have decided to include base pay in your compensation system. But how do you determine the value of each job to the organization so that it can be compensated accordingly? There are three main methods. The first method—**market pricing**—is to simply offer the lowest possible wage that will attract a qualified person to join the firm. The second method—**job evaluation**—is to systematically rank all jobs in the organization in terms of their value to the employer and then calibrate this system to the labour market. The third method is to develop a system based on the total value of the skills and competencies that each employee has acquired, known as a **pay-for-knowledge system** (PKS).

Market Pricing

Market pricing is the simplest of the three methods, and is the most common one used in small firms. The method is straightforward: if you need a

market pricing

establishing base pay by determining the minimum amount of pay necessary to attract qualified individuals from the labour market

job evaluation

establishing base pay by ranking all jobs in the firm according to their value to that firm

secretary or a machinist, you observe what other firms are paying for these jobs and then make similar offers. If you need exceptional performance from your employees and you can afford it, you may pay somewhat above the "going rate" in order to attract the most qualified individuals. But if you don't need exceptional performance and are prepared to put up with higher turnover, you may decide to pay somewhat less than the going rate.

As the labour market changes over time, the employer simply adjusts the pay levels of current employees and the starting pay levels for new employees in accordance with these changes. To simplify the process of determining the "market rates" for each job, some companies use compensation consulting firms that specialize in collecting these data and making them available to clients on a commercial basis. Data are also available through governmental agencies (such as Statistics Canada), industry associations, organizations such as the Conference Board of Canada, and websites.

Advantages of Market Pricing

There are two key advantages to market pricing. The first is simplicity: other methods of determining base pay are much more complicated, and ultimately, all other pay systems must include some market pricing to calibrate their system to the market. For example, the job evaluation method depends on the use of formalized and complex job descriptions. But many firms do not have such job descriptions and do not want to develop them. While these job descriptions are not needed in pay-for-knowledge systems, pay-for-knowledge systems are complex to develop and administer, and they do not necessarily fit all jobs and all organizations. As a result, market pricing is usually a much cheaper system than either of the alternatives.

The second advantage of market pricing is that it keeps all jobs in the organization aligned with market conditions. This prevents turnover caused by uncompetitive wages and makes recruiting easier.

Disadvantages of Market Pricing

Market pricing has a number of drawbacks. The first problem is that it is not as simple as it sounds. There are numerous difficulties in carrying out market pricing. One such difficulty is that identifying one specific "going rate" for a given job can be very elusive. Different wage surveys turn up different results, because they make different judgments about which jobs to survey and how to define different labour markets. Labour markets can be defined several ways—in terms of industry type, occupational group, and geographic areas, as well as firm size. So market pricing often does not result in standard, usable information.

Another difficulty with the market pricing method is job definitions. Different employers define jobs differently. For example, a "secretary" in some firms serve mainly as a typist or receptionist, while in other firms, "secretaries" serve more as executive assistants or even as office managers. Thus, one firm may report that it is paying its "secretaries" $20,000 per annum, while another pays $40,000. For this reason, a wage survey that

pay-for-knowledge system (PKS)

establishing base pay according to the total value of the skills and competencies an employee has acquired

Chapter 4: Components of Compensation Strategy

indicates an "average" pay of $30,000 for "secretaries" may be seriously misleading.

Finally, market pricing is difficult because there is strong evidence that there is no such thing as a standard "market wage" for a given job.[13] Gomez-Mejia and Balkin found that even in a single geographical area, wage rates for the same job titles vary dramatically.[14] For many job titles, some employers paid two to three times what other employers did. Of course, some of this discrepancy may be due to inconsistencies in job definition or to differences between industries. However, research shows that there can often be wide discrepancies in pay for identical jobs in a single industry and geographic area.[15]

Although this result is often mystifying to economists, it should not be to human resources specialists. We know that membership behaviour is motivated by the total mix of rewards from a job, not from pay alone; and these "identical" jobs likely vary considerably in the total package of rewards. Compensation surveys often do not adequately account for performance pay, such as profit sharing, and usually do not take indirect pay into account at all. Moreover, they take no account of the other extrinsic rewards (such as job security or opportunities for promotion) and intrinsic rewards (such as job autonomy or skill variety). Given that the total spectrum of rewards varies widely across firms, it would be extraordinary if there were *not* wide differences in cash compensation across firms. All of this illustrates the problems inherent in comparing compensation statistics across firms.

The second major problem of market pricing is that it does not address internal equity. When market-pricing jobs, organizations make little or no attempt to weight the value of each job to the firm. Thus, jobs that are vital to the organization's success may pay less than jobs of lesser importance, simply because of data from the labour market. Furthermore, if a firm is geographically dispersed, market conditions may vary in different parts of the country, causing the same job to be paid differently in other parts of the company. These differences can cause employee resentment.

A related problem with market pricing is lack of control. In essence, when using only market pricing, a firm allows competitors to set its compensation policy. It does not tailor compensation to suit its own strategy and needs, thereby forgoing the opportunity to use compensation as a source of competitive advantage.

Finally, critics of market-based pay argue that the market does not necessarily produce pay systems that are equitable from a societal point of view. They point to a "pay gap" between jobs that have been traditionally performed by women and those that have been performed by men. They argue that the market has systematically undervalued work performed by women; and that when a firm adopts market-based pay, it perpetuates these inequities. In response, many Canadian jurisdictions have passed "pay equity" legislation (as will be discussed more fully in later chapters), which requires that jobs of "equal value" be compensated equally, regardless of what the market may suggest. Firms in these jurisdictions must include some elements of job evaluation in their compensation systems.

Job Evaluation

Job evaluation (JE) systems involve analyzing job descriptions and then comparing all jobs in the organization in a systematic manner. The most common approach is to identify a number of key factors (compensable factors) and then evaluate each job according to how much of each factor is present. This creates a ranking of all jobs, known as a "hierarchy of jobs." Exact pay levels for each job are determined by relating certain "key jobs" or "benchmark jobs" to the external market, and then interpolating the rest.

Job evaluation first gained popularity in the 1920s and 1930s as large classical organizations began to dominate industry. For them, job evaluation provided a method for centralizing and controlling compensation costs. Before this time, compensation was handled in a haphazard, often chaotic manner, with individual supervisors and managers having the authority to pay employees as they saw fit. Lack of control over such a key element of cost was a major frustration to top management in classical firms, and job evaluation was seen as a way of both gaining control and ensuring that compensation costs would be no higher than they had to be. Job evaluation also fit perfectly with the narrowly structured jobs that these types of organizations tend to have.

Job evaluation was also enthusiastically received by the human relations firms in the 1940s and 1950s. They regarded it as an important tool for fostering a sense of reward equity and fairness among employees, keeping employees loyal and satisfied, and forestalling unionization. While it was used as a vehicle for cost control, its ability to serve also as a vehicle to foster equity was probably seen by human relations firms as its most valuable feature. As in the case of classical firms, job evaluation also fit well with the narrow jobs and centralized policies preferred by human relations firms.

Advantages of Job Evaluation

Job evaluation presents several major advantages, especially in the context of the managerial practices prevailing at the time the method was first developed.

First, it provides the ability for centralized control of compensation costs to ensure that compensation costs are minimized. Second, by linking pay level to the importance or value of the job to the organization, job evaluation provides a way of signalling the importance of jobs to employees and provides an incentive to motivate people to seek promotions. Third, it provides a systematic way to promote equitable pay within the organization, diminishing the role of factors like favouritism and nepotism. When used effectively, job evaluation should also eliminate gender-based pay inequities. Fourth, the system of standardized jobs makes it easier to determine market values for jobs. Fifth, job evaluation provides a systematic way to determine pay for new jobs.

Sixth, over time, a number of consulting firms that specialize in job evaluation have emerged, with well-established technologies for conducting job evaluation, which organizations can use when implementing job evaluation programs. Finally, job evaluation fits with and reinforces both the classical and human relations managerial strategies.

Disadvantages of Job Evaluation

Job evaluation has numerous disadvantages, some related to the process itself, and others related to the organizational rigidity it creates. Ed Lawler, one of the most vocal critics of job evaluation, argues that job evaluation retards the transformation of classical and human relations organizations to high-involvement organizations.[16] He advocates the use of pay-for-knowledge systems instead. Another prominent expert argues that market pricing systems "are far better than traditional job evaluation and can be installed and administered at a far lower cost."[17]

One disadvantage of job evaluation programs is that they require the use of comprehensive job descriptions, which many organizations may not have. Development and continuous updating of job descriptions is an onerous process, although job descriptions can have value beyond the role they play in job evaluation. When accurate and up-to-date, job descriptions inform employees about their roles in the organization and guide recruiters in hiring new employees. In addition, they provide some assurance that nothing is "falling between the cracks"—that all important tasks are being done. They also allow for tight control of employees, if that is part of the firm's managerial strategy.

But job descriptions have many drawbacks. First, they are costly to develop and maintain and involve continual updating as jobs change. For organizations operating in dynamic environments, this can be a significant problem. And, of course, job evaluation does not entirely eliminate the need for market pricing, which still must be done for some benchmark jobs in order to align the JE system with the market.

In addition, evaluating jobs can also become an adversarial process, since it is in the financial interests of employees to inflate their jobs whenever possible. If job inflation occurs, it not only inflates costs of the pay system, but also causes real inequity between inflated jobs and jobs more honestly evaluated. Although job evaluation is presented as a fair and scientific way of achieving equitable pay, most employees realize that there is still substantial subjectivity in the process. Indeed, in the past, job evaluation systems, along with market pricing systems, have been accused of perpetuating rather than combating gender-based pay inequity.[18] However, this is not a problem inherent in job evaluation; rather, it's the result of the way job evaluation has been used.

But perhaps the most important criticism of job evaluation systems is that they inhibit change, flexibility, and skill development.[19] Job descriptions tend to create a "not my job" syndrome, as some employees use their job descriptions to avoid taking on extra duties. They also inhibit change. When circumstances change, job descriptions can slow organizational adaptation, because employees remain unwilling to change until their current job description changes.

There is also no incentive for employees to learn jobs that are not in the direct line of advancement. If advancement to better jobs is not possible, there is no extrinsic incentive to learn additional skills. Because of this rigidity, many firms don't bother with job descriptions at all, especially those with a need for frequent reorganization.

TABLE 4.2

Use of Base Pay Methods by Canadian Firms

TYPE OF BASE PAY	Mean Incidence 2000 (%)	Mean Incidence 2004 (%)	Discontinuations %	Discontinuations (# OF FIRMS)	Adoptions %	Adoptions (# OF FIRMS)
Job Evaluation	73	77	15	(14 firms)	56	(19 firms)
Broad Banding	30	32	58	(22 firms)	28	(25 firms)
Pay for Knowledge	23	22	76	(22 firms)	21	(20 firms)

Source: Compensation Practices Survey.

Recently, some companies, such as General Electric, have replaced job evaluation programs with "broad banding"—the practice of reducing the dozens of job grades to as few as six large job bands.[20] Some supporters of job evaluation argue that broad banding can solve the rigidity problems caused by job evaluation.[21] But others point out that it is illogical to go to all the trouble of making fine distinctions between jobs and then to throw jobs together into large bands.[22] As a result, some firms that adopt broad banding simply eliminate job evaluation altogether.

Despite these disadvantages, Table 4.2 shows that according to the 2004 CPS, the great majority of medium to large Canadian firms (77 percent) use job evaluation, which represents a slight increase from 73 percent in 2000. This increase is due to a relatively low discontinuation rate (as only 15 percent of firms that had job evaluation in 2000 had discontinued it by 2004) coupled with a relatively high adoption rate (56 percent) among firms that previously had not had job evaluation. Pay equity legislation, which requires the use of a systematic method to compare job value within organizations, probably accounts for some of this popularity.

About 32 percent of Canadian firms use broad banding, and most (about 80 percent) of these firms also use job evaluation. Interestingly, while the majority of firms (58 percent) that used broad banding in 2000 had abandoned it by 2004, this decrease was balanced by the number of firms adopting it, so the net effect was very little change in overall incidence.

Overall, these data suggest that the majority of medium to large Canadian firms seem to believe that the advantages of job evaluation outweigh its disadvantages. Clearly, job evaluation poses more problems when the organization is faced with rapid change, and therefore it seems most viable for firms using classical or human relations managerial strategies. Interestingly, however, the CPS indicates that high-involvement firms are actually *more likely* than other firms to use job evaluation. This finding is quite surprising and may indicate that job evaluation is really not incompatible with high-involvement management. It is possible that high-involvement firms see job evaluation as a way to maintain equitable and fair pay relationships, which are essential for these firms.

As a result of the 1982 Tylenol poisoning tragedy [where persons unknown had tampered with bottles of Tylenol tablets, resulting in numerous deaths], Johnson & Johnson decided to completely redo its Tylenol packaging to add greater security. At the time, it had two packaging plants: one skill-based, the other job-based. The skill-based plant quickly installed the new technology and got back into production. Not so with the other traditional job-based, seniority-driven plant. Seniority rights and traditional pay grades reduced employee flexibility in adapting to the new technology. In addition, unlike the skill-based plant, the traditional plant did not have a history of providing training, valuing personal growth, and encouraging employees to do new things. Thus, the transition to new packaging equipment was a major challenge at this plant.

Pay for Knowledge

The third method for determining base pay is radically different from job evaluation. It involves basing pay on the capabilities of individuals rather than on the characteristics of jobs. It is often called *person-based pay*, as opposed to *job-based pay*. There are various labels for this method, including pay for knowledge, competency-based pay, and skill-based pay, and these are often used interchangeably.

However, competency-based pay, which focuses at the managerial and professional level, is distinct from skill-based pay, which focuses on the operational level. The term *pay for knowledge* includes both competency- and skill-based pay, but most of the research has focused on skill-based pay. Competency-based pay, as discussed further in Chapter 9, is an unproven concept of questionable validity. Most of the discussion here focuses on "skill-based pay."

Advantages of Pay for Knowledge

The underlying premise of pay-for-knowledge systems (PKS) is that employees are paid according to their set of skills, knowledge, and competencies, regardless of the job they happen to be doing at the time. Two of the most important advantages of pay-for-knowledge systems relate to skills development and flexibility. PKS provides a major incentive for employees to learn a variety of skills, which then makes it easier to shift employees from one job to another as needed. Furthermore, PKS avoids the disincentive to movement caused by traditional job evaluation systems, which result in strictly defined jobs that are "owned" by the people currently doing them. Under traditional pay systems, if a nut on a machine needs tightening, someone has to call a mechanic, because maintenance is not part of the machine operator's job description. However, under PKS, an operator simply grabs a wrench and tightens the nut.

This flexibility is especially beneficial for organizations for which production and service processes peak and ebb unpredictably. For example, a company may have a big customer order that needs expediting or is experiencing a parts shortages in particular production processes: in both situations, PKS allows employees to move from idle functions to active functions. Of course, PKS also makes it easier to cover employee absences and vacations. Because the system relies on flexible skills, PKS companies must use job rotation, and job rotation itself has been shown to be beneficial for some organizations.[23]

Compensation Today 4.2 illustrates how PKS can facilitate flexibility and change, whereas traditional job evaluation can inhibit change.[24]

A major advantage of PKS over job evaluation is that it does not need job descriptions, thereby avoiding many of the problems of job descriptions. This is a major advantage for organizations facing rapid change.

Jobs in PKS companies are also broader and provide more intrinsic rewards. This advantage has other related advantages. For example, knowledgeable employees performing broader jobs may be more effective at customer service, since they understand more of the business. As Schuster and Zingheim put it: "Skill-based pay prepares employees to handle a wider range of customer issues without switching the customer from place to place. This is more efficient for the organization and for the customer."[25]

Although the earliest adopters of pay-for-knowledge tended to apply it to production employees (especially in firms with process technologies, such as chemical plants), firms have also successfully applied PKS to service employees. Because PKS allows individuals and teams to be more self-managing, and because it uses the workforce more efficiently, a firm using PKS should be able to operate with a smaller labour force. This staffing reduction results from a reduced need for managerial, supervisory, and inspection positions, as well as specialty positions, such as maintenance mechanics or electricians.

A key advantage of PKS is that it supports behaviours needed by high-involvement firms. When employees are knowledgeable about their organization, they can make more effective decisions, exercise good judgment, and take quick action when necessary. For example, when Shell Canada wanted to build a new, high-involvement chemical plant, the company saw that this would be difficult if not impossible using traditional pay methods, and made pay for knowledge a central part of this process, as Compensation Today 4.3 describes.

Not only does PKS fit with a high-involvement management strategy, but it also helps promote change to high-involvement practices. As Ledford puts it:

> [Pay for knowledge] can be a powerful force in helping an organization live up to a commitment to become a high-involvement organization. This is because employees, acting in their own self-interest, begin to exert pressure for greater training, information, and control over job rotation and other key decisions. In short, they begin to demand that the organization behave more like a high-involvement organization.[26]

Disadvantages of Pay for Knowledge

A major disadvantage of pay for knowledge is that it can give rise to situations where employees are "overpaid" relative to competitor companies. In fact, this is quite likely, especially if PKS has been in place for some time and has

Pay for Knowledge Finds Good Chemistry at Basell Canada

One of the first organizations in Canada to implement pay for knowledge was the Shell Chemical plant in Sarnia, Ontario (now known as Basell Canada Ltd.), which opened in 1978. The plant produces polypropylene and isopropyl alcohol in a 24-hour continuous process operation. The plant produces 75 grades of state-of-the-art plastics in pea-sized pellets. It then sells these versatile polymers worldwide for use in such products as compact discs, car-door panels, carpets, toys, and pop bottles. Consistently high product quality is essential. However, the production process is very complicated, and many things can go wrong during the multi-staged production process.

Quick and accurate reactions to production problems are essential at a major production plant. But in the past, traditional plant design had made problem solving very difficult. Production processes were usually divided into distinct departments, within which each employee had a narrowly specified job. Few employees understood the entire production process and the complex interrelations between the various production phases.

Shell had noticed numerous problems in their traditional plants, including slow responses to production problems, underutilization of employees, high boredom levels, employee dissatisfaction, and employee turnover. To prevent these problems in the new plant, Shell decided to base their new plant on the high-involvement model. At the same time, the company also wanted to develop a collaborative relationship with the union (the Communications, Energy, and Paper Workers Union) by involving it in the plant design process as well as in the continuing operation of the plant.

The new design eliminated department separations and created 20-person "shift teams" to operate the plant during each shift. These shift teams were supported by a craft team of electricians, pipe fitters, and other specialized personnel, who were present only during the day shift or during emergency situations. Each member of the shift team was expected to learn to perform all necessary tasks in the production process.

The company recognized at the outset that the traditional approach to compensating operators, which defined jobs narrowly and had a different pay grade for each job, would not be compatible with this new system. Therefore, job categories on each shift team were reduced to one: shift team member. To foster employee multiskilling and flexibility, a pay-for-knowledge system was developed.

Today, the system is still in place. When new employees start at the plant, they receive the training needed to perform a basic set of shift functions and are paid a base rate. To increase their pay rate, workers need to demonstrate competence in one additional job knowledge cluster and in four modules of a "specialty skill." (For the purposes of training and compensation, the "operations" area of the complex is divided into 10 job-knowledge clusters.) Each specialty skill (e.g., instrumentation, electrical, pipefitting) is further divided into 40 skill modules, and every worker is expected to select one specialty skill. Thus, there are 10 levels in the pay progression system, and workers make the top pay when they have mastered all 10 job knowledge clusters and all 40 modules of their specialty skill. On average, this takes about six years.

How well does the system work? When interviewed in 2001, company officials indicated that the original pay-for-knowledge system, implemented more than 20 years previously, has shown such success that it has been carried forward with very few changes since then.

Sources: (1) Halpern, Norm. 1984. "Sociotechnical Systems Design: The Shell Sarnia Experience." In J.B. Cunningham and T.H. White, eds., *Quality of Working Life: Contemporary Cases*. Ottawa: Labour Canada, 31–75. (2) HRDC. 1994. "Moving Parts and Moving People: Sociotechnical Design of a New Plant." In *Labour Management Innovations in Canada*. Ottawa: Human Resources Development Canada, 72–76. (3) Personal communications with company officials.

resulted in most employees earning the top pay level ("topping out"). In general, employees operating under PKS earn considerably more than employees not working under this system. However, PKS companies feel that the flexibility gained outweighs the cost disadvantage.

Other difficulties with PKS have to do with topping out and reaching skill ceilings. Once an individual is earning the top pay level, what is the incentive to continue learning and updating skills? Moreover, skills become out of date, so there needs to be a system to require topped-out employees to reskill. Furthermore, if employees are not rotated through jobs regularly, then their skills atrophy. However, senior employees may resent spending some of their time doing the less-advanced jobs in order for less-senior employees to perform the more advanced jobs. As Milkovich and Newman put it (a bit whimsically): "At some point, having all chefs and no dishwashers (and having to pay chef wages to those who are assigned to scrub pots and pans) is uncompetitive. And probably dissatisfying to certified chefs with dishpan hands."[27]

In addition, pay-for-knowledge systems lead to increased training costs, both in terms of the cost of training itself and the need to take employees off the job for training. For example, at L-S Electrogalvanizing (LSE) in Cleveland, a "fifth shift" had to be created in order to provide the necessary time off the job for training, even though the plant could run with four shifts. At LSE, training costs run at about 12 percent of payroll, compared with less than 1 percent in conventional firms in the same industry.

As another weakness, pay-for-knowledge systems are more complex to administer than job-based pay systems, due to the need for certification procedures (to determine whether an employee is entitled to be paid for a new skill). Adjusting pay-for-knowledge systems to the market may also be more difficult than for a job evaluation system if there are no other firms with skill-based pay systems to use as a comparison. Moreover, for many firms, applying PKS to all jobs is not feasible, creating a need to maintain dual skill- and job-based systems.

In addition, PKS is generally harder for employees to understand than other base-pay methods. Moreover, not all employees may have the ability or desire to learn multiple jobs; and unions might resist PKS because wages are based on skill levels instead of seniority.

Pay-for-knowledge systems may also appear to violate some pay equity laws, which generally stipulate that employees should be paid for what they actually do rather than for their capabilities.[28] Thus, a woman performing a bagging operation in a dog food plant who receives lower pay than a man doing the same job may appear to be unfairly treated. However, most pay equity laws do make exceptions for factors such as skill levels and relevant experience, as long as these are applied consistently to both male and female employees.

A final major disadvantage of PKS is a potentially high failure rate. Although pay-for-knowledge systems grew rapidly in popularity at the end of the twentieth century, starting from a base of virtually zero in the 1970s, their popularity may now be levelling off. For example, a study of 114 mostly large Canadian firms conducted in 1990–91 indicated that 17 percent had pay-for-knowledge systems, although these systems generally covered only a small percentage of employees.[29] By 2000, the CPS indicated that 23 percent of medium to large Canadian firms used pay-for-knowledge systems. However, as Table 4.2 shows, there was virtually no change in mean incidence between 2000 and 2004.

Chapter 4: Components of Compensation Strategy

But this apparent lack of change actually masks a high degree of instability of PKS use in Canada. Table 4.2 shows that 76 percent of firms that had used pay-for-knowledge systems in 2000 had ceased using them four years later. But this decrease was offset by the adoption of PKS among other firms between 2000 and 2004. Taken together, these findings seem to suggest that most of the firms that adopt pay-for-knowledge systems do not find them beneficial and therefore drop them; but this has not stopped new firms from trying out the concept.

In a way, these rather dramatic findings are not surprising. Given all the complexities and disadvantages of pay for knowledge, it is likely to be beneficial only for certain companies, particularly those that need a highly flexible workforce. These would primarily be firms with complex technologies or unpredictable production or service demands. Moreover, investing in more knowledgeable employees pays off only if the organization is structured in such a way as to use this knowledge. Clearly, classical and human relations organizations would not receive much value from a pay-for-knowledge system.

Data from the CPS indicates that high-involvement firms are most likely to use pay for knowledge. Moreover, in a study of 15 U.S. firms that had implemented pay-for-knowledge systems, Wallace concluded that high-involvement management was a key success factor for PKS compensation systems:

> It is important to note that skill-based pay is not so much a compensation system as it is a radical departure from traditional organizational design. It works best in work systems where there is a high level of employee involvement, where work has been organized in self-managed teams . . . and where there is a commitment to high levels of investment in human capital.[30]

Despite these caveats, some research has found that even traditional unionized organizations can benefit from PKS, but only if both management and the union are willing to adopt new, collaborative roles.[31] Overall, research indicates that PKS can be highly successful, but that many attempts to use it are unsuccessful.[32] The keys to success appear to be implementation in the right circumstances, along with effective plan design and effective implementation. All these issues are discussed in more detail in Chapter 9.

Compensation Notebook 4.3 summarizes the advantages and disadvantages of the three methods for establishing base pay.

ⓇⓅⒸ 4.1   Individual Performance Pay

Figure 4.2 shows the "menu" of performance pay choices that may be included in a compensation strategy. There are four main types of individual performance pay, two of which may substitute for time-based pay, and two of which are always used in conjunction with base pay.

Rather than being paid by the amount of time worked, an employee may be paid according to the amount of output produced. There are two main methods for output-related pay: *piece rates* and *commissions*. Of course, piece

Advantages and Disadvantages of the Methods for Base Pay

Method	Advantages	Disadvantages
Market Pricing	• simplicity and cost • keeps jobs aligned with market conditions	• "going rate" not always easy to identify • job definitions may vary from the market data • does not address internal equity • lack of control of compensation strategy • may violate pay equity legislation
Job Evaluation	• centralized control of compensation costs • signals importance of different jobs • promotes internal equity • makes calibration to the market easier • systematic way to determine pay for new jobs • availability of packaged plans from consultants • fits well with classical and human relations • low discontinuation rate	• may impede high involvement • more costly to develop than market pricing • need for job descriptions • may become an adversarial process • costly to maintain • can inhibit flexibility and skill development
Pay for Knowledge	• incentive for employee skill development • no disincentive to movement • high work force flexibility • does not require job descriptions • jobs are broader with more intrinsic rewards • may improve customer service • supports high involvement management	• may raise labour costs • "topping out" problem • resistance by senior employees to rotation • higher training costs • complex to develop and administer • may also need to maintain job-based system • may be difficult to calibrate system to market • not all employees may have desire or capability • unions may resist because not based on seniority • high discontinuation rate

rates and commissions need not supplant base pay entirely and can also be used in combination with base pay, which is probably the most common arrangement. The other two types of individual incentives—*merit pay* and *targeted or special-purpose incentives*—are always used in conjunction with base pay. Merit pay can be further differentiated into merit raises (which increase base pay) and merit bonuses (which do not increase base pay).

Table 4.3 shows the incidence of various types of performance pay in Canada. Merit raises are by far the most common form of performance pay, followed by sales commissions and merit bonuses. Special incentives are used by about a fifth of Canadian firms, while piece rates are used by only about 12 percent of firms. The table also shows that in recent years, sales commissions have become more popular, special incentives have become less

FIGURE 4.2

Performance Pay Choices

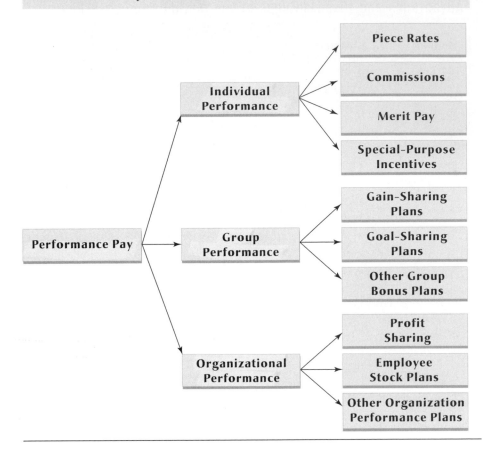

popular, and other plans have stayed about the same. It is interesting to note that piece rates, merit bonuses, and special incentives show high discontinuation rates: 47 to 62 percent of firms using these plans in 2000 no longer did so by 2004.

Piece Rates

piece rates

a pay system under which individuals receive a fixed sum for each unit of output they produce

In a **piece rates** system, an employee receives a fixed sum for each unit of output produced. The objective of piece rates is to maximize individual productivity by linking output and reward. Piece rates are commonly associated with the manufacturing sector, but they are also used in the service sector. Barbers are paid per head, tree planters are paid per tree, freelance journalists are paid per column inch, and physicians are paid per procedure. In the service sector, market pricing is generally used to set the piece rate, although medical doctors use a negotiation process between provincial governments and provincial colleges of physicians and surgeons.

But in the manufacturing sector, where the concept of piece rates was developed and popularized by Frederick Winslow Taylor at the beginning of the twentieth century, the process is more complicated. First, a job analyst or

TABLE 4.3

Use of Performance Pay by Canadian Firms

TYPE OF PERFORMANCE PAY	Mean Incidence 2000 (%)	Mean Incidence 2004 (%)	Discontinuations %	Discontinuations (# OF FIRMS)	Adoptions %	Adoptions (# OF FIRMS)
Individual Performance Pay						
Piece rates	12	12	47	(7 firms)	7	(8 firms)
Sales commissions	30	36	29	(11 firms)	21	(19 firms)
Merit raises	77	80	15	(15 firms)	63	(19 firms)
Merit bonuses	33	34	53	(23 firms)	28	(24 firms)
Special incentives	26	20	62	(21 firms)	14	(13 firms)
Group/Team Performance Pay						
Gain sharing	14	7	78	(14 firms)	5	(5 firms)
Goal sharing	18	12	65	(15 firms)	8	(8 firms)
Other group/team plans	16	9	76	(16 firms)	7	(7 firms)
Organizational Performance Pay						
Profit sharing	28	23	33	(12 firms)	7	(6 firms)
Stock bonus plans	5	2	71	(5 firms)	1	(1 firm)
Stock purchase plans	19	20	42	(10 firms)	11	(12 firms)
Stock option plans	8	9	30	(3 firms)	4	(5 firms)
Other organizational plans (LTIs)	5	5	67	(4 firms)	4	(5 firms)

Source: Compensation Practices Survey.

methods engineer times how long a particular task or job typically takes to perform, allowing for factors such as operator fatigue, rest breaks, worker ability, and unavoidable delays. The result is a *production standard*—that is, the number of units that could be produced in an hour by a typical worker. At the same time, the employer establishes the average amount of money a worker with the skills and abilities to perform these tasks should earn hourly. This amount is based on several factors, including the prevailing wage in the industry. Then, this hourly amount is divided by the production standard. The result is the *piece rate* or dollar payment per piece produced. This type of piece rate is the simplest and is known as a **straight piece rate**. A more complicated type of piece rate is the **differential piece rate**, in which an employee receives a lower rate if the production standard is not met.

straight piece rate
the same fixed sum is paid for each piece produced, regardless how many pieces are produced

differential piece rate
a lower sum per piece is paid if employee production does not meet the production standard

Advantages of Piece Rates

Piece rate systems have several advantages. First, if designed correctly and used in the right circumstances, they are highly motivational. Second, they reduce the need for external control of employees. Third, they link compensation to output, and therefore link compensation to employer ability to pay, thus reducing employer risk. Finally, they provide specific information about the "standard" level of output expected.

Disadvantages of Piece Rates

The first problem with piece rates is that they can be applied in only a limited number of circumstances. Jobs with a high degree of interdependence are not good candidates for piece rates, since an individual cannot control the rate of production, nor can responsibility for productivity be attributed to a specific individual. In jobs with diverse activities and tasks, keeping track of progress in specific areas would be very difficult. Moreover, jobs where quality cannot be monitored are also not good candidates for piece rate systems, nor are jobs in which only some tasks can be measured.

Jobs for which tasks are continually changing, or tools, materials, and technologies are rapidly changing are also not amenable to piece rates. Piece rates need to be re-calculated each time a major change occurs, which is an onerous task. But the largest problem with change is that each change provides an opportunity for friction between employees and management. For example, if a better machine is purchased, and a worker can now produce twice as much, it makes sense to cut the piece rate in half. Although workers may understand this rationale, they are unlikely to be pleased if their piece rate is cut. Moreover, where there is little trust between management and workers, workers may suspect that management is simply using new technology as an excuse to cut the piece rate.

Indeed, setting the piece rate is not nearly as "scientific" a process as it seems. For example, timing jobs depends on worker participation. When jobs are first timed, employees will probably not perform the work in the shortest possible time, for fear that it only helps to establish a high or "tight" rate. So experienced industrial engineers compensate for these tendencies by guessing how much the workers are slowing their normal speed. Thus, the "scientific process" has already deteriorated into a guessing game—and it's one that pits workers against management. In addition, the allowances made for factors such as faulty materials and machine breakdowns are often arbitrary at best. Thus, standards may only be very rough estimates, with some jobs having very "tight" rates and others having very "loose" rates.

Despite the motivational potential of piece rate systems, they frequently do not motivate maximum effort because of social forces within the work group. Since production is an important part of the activity of the work group, it is likely that group norms will develop to define acceptable rates of production. The quality of the worker–management relationship largely determines whether these norms are positive or negative. Unfortunately, the very type of organization most likely to look favourably on piece rates—the classical organization—is most likely to have poor labour–management relationships.

Furthermore, if management has laid off workers whenever productivity has increased, work groups will not look favourably on high production. Few workers want to work themselves out of a job. Moreover, while a few members of the work group may be able to produce far above standard, most will not, and they will exert pressure on the high producers to moderate their production levels. High producers are known as "rate busters" because other workers fear that management will note their high performance and then cut the piece rate. Of course, if management has had a history of cutting piece rates, workers will not be motivated to increase productivity.

In some cases, the system also creates conflict and lack of cooperation among workers. Workers may all vie for the "loose" jobs and attempt to avoid the "tight" ones. There is also little incentive to advise or help new workers, or to do any job that does not relate directly to production, such as maintaining equipment or keeping the work area clean.

But even when the system does serve to promote productivity, it can create other problems. One has to do with product or service quality. Since the emphasis is on quantity, workers may be tempted to cut corners on the quality, which necessitates increased inspection and monitoring. And even with inspection or monitoring, quality is not likely to be much above minimum acceptable levels. Furthermore, inspection/monitoring and record keeping can increase overall production costs considerably.

There may also be problems with equipment and material usage. For example, workers might find that they can reach the production standard on a drilling job more easily if they replace their drill bits more frequently or run their machines at high speed. But drill bits are expensive, and machines burn out more quickly at higher speed. Unless these costs are somehow incorporated into the pay system, the worker is unlikely to be concerned about these problems. Yet incorporating these extra costs increases the complexity of the system.

Finally, piece rates have been blamed for encouraging accidents and safety violations. For example, many mines do not use piece rates for fear that miners may sacrifice safety for productivity. In addition, on-time delivery incentives for pizza delivery drivers have been found to be related to reckless driving.

As a practical matter, to make piece work successful in a manufacturing setting requires trust between management and workers. This trust facilitates rate setting and rate changes and assures workers that management will not attempt to arbitrarily cut rates. Piece rate systems also require job security so that workers can be sure that increased productivity will not put them out of a job. The irony is that the firms most likely to want to use piece rates—classical firms—are the firms least likely to provide these conditions. It should not be surprising, then, that most manufacturing firms have abandoned piece rates over the years.[33] Compensation Today 4.4 provides an interesting exception to this trend.

Applicability of Piece Rates

In sum, when would piece rates be a viable option? Suitable jobs are those where workers each control their own production, interdependence between workers is low, each unit of production can be easily measured and priced, individuals perform a limited number of tasks (all of which can be compensated with piece rates), tasks do not change frequently, increased productivity will not cause layoffs, and monitoring of quality standards is easy.

Compensation Today 4.4

Piece Rates Spark Productivity at Lincoln Electric

Lincoln Electric, based near Cleveland, Ohio, is the world's largest producer of arc welders. While it is an acknowledged industry leader in its field, the company often attracts more attention for its reward system. The company provides no base pay and very little indirect pay to its production workers; instead, all are paid on an intricate piece rate system. The firm offers no paid sick days and only the minimum paid holidays allowed by law. Lincoln employees have to pay their own health insurance and have no choice about accepting overtime work and unexpected job assignments. If older workers decrease in productivity, they earn less. Management also does not take seniority into account for promotions. The firm has no union to protect the interests of the company's 3 400 employees.

This sounds like a classical manager's dream. But what worker would want a job at a sweatshop like this if he or she could find something better? Think of the employee turnover there must be! Imagine all the problems that there must be with conflict over piece rates and adversarial relations between workers and management.

But in fact, productivity is very high at this company, and hardly anyone ever quits. Workers and management have an excellent relationship. Whenever jobs become available, there are hundreds of applicants. Over the past 50 years, the company has never lost money. What is going on? Doesn't this example contradict research into the problems with piece rates?

In fact, this case actually reinforces the key points about piece rates. In reality, Lincoln is not a classical organization, nor is it a human relations organization. Consider some of the other policies of the firm. First, job security. The company makes it a policy never to lay off employees. According to a company spokesperson, "We don't lay off anyone unless he steals, lies, fights, or has a record of very low productivity." The firm guarantees workers at least 30 hours of work a week, even in lean times. So workers don't have to worry about working themselves out of a job.

Employees don't have to worry about cuts to the piece rate either. If workers think up a way to improve productivity, the company never cuts piece rates. But doesn't this system cause employees to think only about them-selves, rather than the best interests of the firm? To avoid self-centred motivation, the firm also provides profit sharing to all employees, which is distributed according to employee merit. In some years, this bonus can approach 100 percent of regular earnings. Another feature is an employee stock purchase plan under which employees own a large chunk of the company's shares. Profit sharing and employee stock ownership balance the self-centred perspective caused by the piece rates and encourage citizenship behaviour, with job security as the foundation. Extrinsically, the result is production workers who are among the most highly paid in the United States. Intrinsically, the result is employees who are highly committed to their employer. Because of the self-control these features generate, the company has very few supervisors.

Trust between management and employees is the foundation of this system, accompanied by a system of open communication. For this reason, the company has an elected advisory board of employees that meets with top management twice a month. (There is no union, although this type of manufacturing is normally unionized.) Mutual trust also allows adjustments to the piece rates to be made in a nonadversarial way without the conflict that normally accompanies this process.

One reason for the good employee–management relationship is the pay system for managers. Managers are not treated much differently from workers. They too depend heavily on profit sharing for their income. They receive no executive "perks"—no cars, no executive dining room, no club memberships, and no reserved parking. When new MBAs join the firm, they must spend eight weeks on the welding line so that they truly come to understand and appreciate Lincoln's unique shop-floor culture. Recruitment of both managers and workers is a lengthy process, the key criterion being their "fit" with the high-involvement managerial strategy.

Sources: (1) Chilton, Kenneth W. 1994. "Lincoln Electric's Incentive System: A Reservoir of Trust." *Compensation and Benefits Review*, 26(6): 29–34. (2) *The Globe and Mail*, October 21, 1996. (3) Johns, Gary. 1996. *Organizational Behaviour: Understanding and Managing Life at Work*. New York: HarperCollins.

Sales Commissions

Sales commissions are used to compensate sales personnel in many industries, ranging from automobiles to real estate to stock brokerage. Typically, salespersons receive a certain percentage of their gross sales, and the commission rate typically varies according to the products sold. In contrast to piece rates, commissions have remained a popular payment system, although they are more popular as a complement to base pay rather than as a complete substitute.

sales commissions

pay that is geared to the dollar volume of sales or transactions conducted

Advantages of Commissions

There are several reasons for the popularity of commissions. First, commission rates are relatively easy to set and measure. Second, there is usually less interdependence among sales employees than among production workers, which means their work output is more distinct. Third, in theory, there is an almost unlimited number of sales that can be made without creating a need to reduce the sales force. Fourth, the use of commissions reduces the need for other types of control mechanisms, such as supervision or internalized commitment. In many businesses where selling takes place off the business premises, direct control and supervision are difficult; so output-based control is a good option, especially if the sales force does not have internalized commitment to the company. Fifth, commissions can serve as a source of feedback and as a self-correcting mechanism—sales personnel can easily see whether their performance is adequate and tend to leave the organization if they are unsuccessful. Sixth, commissions reduce employer risk, since worker pay is linked directly to sales revenue.

Finally, and most important, the use of sales commissions does increase sales. From a motivational perspective, it is easy to see why. The necessary behaviour (making sales) is clearly defined. The valence of successful behaviour (earning more money) is very positive compared with the valence of unsuccessful behaviour (earning less money). In addition, instrumentality is high (successful behaviour leads to rewards). So commissions fit well with motivation theory.

Disadvantages of Commissions

Nonetheless, we should recognize some problems associated with using commissions. First, income to the salesperson may be highly variable, making personal financial planning difficult. Since most people prefer more predictable pay, it may be difficult to attract high-calibre applicants. Sole reliance on commissions may also cause high turnover. Some of these problems are illustrated by the following quote from a sales representative who works on straight commission for a firm that sells consumer telecommunications equipment:

> If I go on vacation, I lose money. If I'm sick, I lose money. If I am
> not willing to drop everything on a moment's notice to close with
> a customer, I lose money. I can't see how anyone could stay in this
> job for long. It's like a trapeze act and I'm working without a net![34]

In this person's company, half of all sales reps quit within six months of joining. However, because costs of recruitment and training are quite low, the company is willing to accept this turnover level, especially since those who quit tend to be low performers. But to attract and retain top performers, firms like this one that use individual commissions often end up providing a higher total pay than would be necessary if a different compensation mix were used. Other drawbacks to commission sales include the following:

1. Under poor economic conditions, commission income may drop precipitously, through no fault of the sales worker. This may cause good salespeople to leave the firm due to financial necessity.
2. During the period when they are learning the business and developing customer contacts, new sales workers receive little income, which may cause them to leave.
3. A salesperson may resist doing work that does not directly contribute to new sales, such as training new salespeople, keeping up records, or servicing clients.
4. Straight commission may encourage salespeople to be overly aggressive, to make misleading claims about the product to encourage sales, and to attempt to sell more units or more expensive units than the customer really needs.
5. Commission systems often produce intense competition among salespeople, resulting in a lack of cooperation.
6. Apportioning responsibility for making sales can be a major problem. Customers may be "sold" by one salesperson, but after taking a few days to "think it over," they may place the order with a salesperson who happens to be available. This can create perceptions of inequity and cause conflict among the sales workers. To avoid this problem, companies often have to devise a system for apportioning customers or establishing sales territories. But establishing sales territories may be difficult to do fairly, and use of fixed territories also creates rigidity if conditions change and territories need to be altered later on.

Using straight commissions may also cause some subtle shifts in behaviour on the part of the employer. For example, since the sales rep—not the firm—is absorbing the risk of poor performance, the employer may be less careful in recruitment and selection. When certain salespeople are not performing well, rather than attempting to assist them to improve, possibly through training and coaching, management may be tempted to just let them "sink or swim" and simply hire other salespeople to replace them.

But all these practices may have hidden costs. First, although the firm is not paying the sales rep when he or she makes no sales, the firm is also not receiving any sales revenue. Second, these practices may encourage high turnover, such that recruiting and training new salespeople becomes a significant cost. Third, customers may be disconcerted by a continuing turnover of salespeople, and they may tire of always having to deal with someone new.

Fine-tuning the commission system to create the desired behaviour is difficult. Employers should not be surprised when salespeople work the system to maximize their own income rather than company welfare. Under straight commission, the employer is showing very little commitment to the salesperson and is implicitly saying that the only attachment between the firm and the salesperson is a financial one. Salespeople will also be resistant to changes in the system, since they then need to learn all over again how to maximize their income from it.

Furthermore, when the system needs to be changed, sales workers may be suspicious of management motives and may see the changes as simply a disguised attempt to reduce their earnings. The following incident illustrates the lengths to which one company went to try to deal with this problem:

> In one case . . . the vice president of sales for a multi-media communications company hired a professional wrestler to pose as a salesperson at the company's annual sales meeting. When the sales VP announced the change in the compensation plan and started to go through the details, the wrestler-cum-salesperson charged the front of the room, lifted the sales VP off the ground, held him over his head, and threatened to toss him to the back of the room if he didn't leave the compensation plan well enough alone. At this point, the company's regional sales managers rushed up to the front of the room to calm the "angry" salesperson by explaining the virtues of the new plan.[35]

Interestingly, although this ruse did forestall questions and angry debate from the sales reps, it did not eliminate the grumbling about the new plan.

A final problem is that commissions on sales volume focus attention on gross revenue generation, not profitability of sales. Sales personnel may be tempted to focus on selling low-margin, fast-moving items, or to cut prices excessively. Recall all the problems caused by a bonus system based on gross sales at Bausch and Lomb, discussed in Chapter 3. To avoid these problems, some companies are basing their commissions on different indicators. For example, IBM has shifted to a system in which the commissions are no longer based on sales revenues,[36] but rather, on profitability of sales (60 percent) and customer satisfaction (40 percent). For this system to work, IBM recognizes that they have to provide information on profit margins to each sales rep, information that had traditionally been a closely guarded secret.

Some of the other problems with commissions can also be solved with system changes. To deal with fluctuating income, a company can provide a base salary with commissions on top. This dual system also serves to "pay" the individual for work not directly related to sales. A variation of this is a "draw" system, in which an employee receives regular advances against future commissions to smooth out income fluctuations. Managers can also vary commission rates to reflect the profitability or the selling ease of particular products. In addition, they can reduce excessive competition among sales personnel by apportioning potential customers on a systematic basis, such as by geographic district or customer type. Of course, the most important way of avoiding problems is not to use commissions in circumstances where they are not suited.

Criteria for Choosing a Commissions System

What are the circumstances under which commissions are appropriate? To help answer this question, Coletti and Chicelli have suggested three key dimensions: degree of independence, degree of persuasive skills required, and length of sales cycle (the time between meeting a new customer and closing the deal).[37] The more that each salesperson works independently of others, the higher the degree of persuasive skills required, and the shorter the length of the sales cycle, the greater the proportion of commission relative to base pay should be.

Coletti and Chicelli also distinguish four types of selling, based on whether the product and customer are new or established. **Maintenance selling** is selling established products to existing customers; **conversion selling** is selling established products to new customers; **leverage selling** is selling new products to existing customers; and **new market selling** is selling new products to new customers. Coletti and Chicelli suggest that because new market selling requires the most initiative on the part of the sales rep, it should have a high incentive opportunity (high ratio of commission to base pay); while conversion selling and leverage selling should have a moderate incentive opportunity; and maintenance selling should have a low incentive opportunity.

The managerial strategy of the firm is another important criterion in selecting commission systems. For example, in high-involvement firms, the self-control that these firms generate may make extrinsic output-based controls like commissions unnecessary; and therefore, commission programs are unlikely to be beneficial. In contrast, classical firms need output-based control wherever direct control is not feasible; for this reason, classical firms tend to use straight commissions. Similarly, human relations firms must show they value employee loyalty by providing base pay; but they can also provide some commissions to supplement behaviour control in circumstances where there is no cohesive group to exert social control, as in cases where sales reps work alone.

One Canadian study of commission sales systems found that commissions were seldom used for (a) sales jobs that were highly programmable (i.e., behaviours could be easily observed but where individual sales could not be easily measured); (b) jobs that involved working inside the office; (c) jobs that included important nonselling tasks or that required cooperation in closing sales; and (d) jobs in large organizations. They also found that organizations that used a higher proportion of base pay had lower employee turnover than those which relied more heavily on commissions.[38]

Merit Pay

The objective of merit pay is to recognize and encourage continuing good performance by individual employees. Types of merit pay include merit raises, merit bonuses, and promotions. These incentives are always used in combination with base pay.

Merit Raises

Merit raises represent a permanent increase to base pay. Thus, merit raises are extremely expensive for the employer, especially when given to young

---

maintenance selling

selling established products to existing customers

conversion selling

selling established products to new customers

leverage selling

selling new products to existing customers

new market selling

selling new products to new customers

merit raise

an increase to an employee's base pay in recognition of good job performance

employees, who may benefit from the same raise for 30 years or more. This expense is increased even more if indirect pay—such as pension benefits—is geared to direct pay levels, which is the usual practice. Merit raises are normally based on employee performance during the previous year; but in order to justify the permanent cost increase, managers hope the increased performance level will be permanent. This is, of course, difficult to predict, and most organizations simply grant the increase and hope for the best.

Merit raises offer a way for employees to advance their pay within their pay ranges. Of course, there are other ways to advance through the pay range as well, such as raises based on seniority or skills. Surveys have shown that North Americans believe that being paid according to merit is a good idea, as long as performance standards are fair and objective, and as long as performance appraisals help improve job performance.[39] While most organizations claim to use merit pay, research indicates a high degree of skepticism among both managers and employees about the extent to which pay is truly related to meritorious performance.[40] However, despite this skepticism, a review of 42 studies by Heneman actually did show a positive relationship between merit increases and previous performance.[41]

Since merit raises are generally based on appraised performance, they can take into account overall employee performance, rather than just a slice of it. They can also provide feedback to employees on how they can improve their performance, so as to warrant a merit raise in the future. By increasing the pay of outstanding performers, merit raises can also help to retain high-calibre employees.

However, the practice is fraught with difficulties. The first problem is performance measurement. As will be discussed in Chapter 9, performance appraisal is not an exact science. Studies have shown that both managers and employees frequently have little confidence in the results of performance appraisal.[42] This may help to explain why many managers are reluctant to differentiate among employees in terms of pay: they have doubts about the validity of the data on which these differentiations are to be based. Of course, they may also be concerned about antagonizing subordinates.

The second problem is that in many companies professing to use merit pay, the pay raises given to above-average performers are not very different from those given to average performers. To be motivating, the difference in pay increase between a person performing at a high level and a person performing at an average level must be perceived as significant. However, exactly how much this difference should be is not always clear.

Another problem with merit raises is that once an employee rises to the top of his or her pay range, there are no more merit raises. No organization can afford to continue to provide merit pay raises indefinitely for a given job: there is only so much an organization can afford to pay a bookkeeper or a junior supervisor, no matter how meritorious the individual. At that point, what motivation is there for the employee to continue to improve performance, or to even maintain the high performance level that has earned the merit raises?

Traditionally, the answer is the carrot and the stick—the carrot of promotion to a higher-paying job, and the stick of dismissal. However, it is legally difficult to dismiss someone who is performing at an acceptable level, even if they are being paid to perform at a superior level. Even if possible, such action would tend to destroy the motivational value of the system if receipt of merit raises is seen as increasing vulnerability to dismissal.

As for promotions, as organizations become flatter, and as many firms experience slow or even negative growth, promotion opportunities have become increasingly rare. But even for those organizations that do have promotional opportunities, rewarding outstanding performance in a lower-level position through promotion to the next higher position is not necessarily a wise policy, as will be discussed in Chapter 10.

As a result, if merit raises are the only element of performance pay an organization uses, there is no longer any element of performance pay for employees once they reach the top of their pay range. An organization could rely on intrinsic motivation and organizational identification to maintain performance (in a high-involvement organization), or possibly social norms (in a human relations organization); but classical organizations would not have these to depend on. One solution may be the use of merit bonuses, discussed in the following section.

There are several other problems with merit raises. Because they are usually based on a judgment by a superior, they may cause antagonism between the superior and the other employees. Merit raises can also cause divisiveness within the work group itself and can build resentment against employees receiving a merit raise.

Rewarding only one or two employees when effective performance is really dependent on effective cooperation among all employees can exacerbate divisiveness and lead to reduced cooperation. This problem is especially severe if the amount of money for merit raises is fixed for a given department, or if the supervisor is allowed to provide merit raises to only a fixed proportion of the subordinates. What this creates is a zero-sum game—if you get more, I get less or none at all. This is certainly not a system to encourage cohesiveness and cooperation among employees! Of course, if an organization does not need cooperation among its employees, then resentment is not a big problem.

In sum, although the idea of rewarding individuals through merit raises is appealing, for many organizations the disadvantages may outweigh the advantages. Indeed, for some firms where close collaboration between employees is necessary and separating out individual performance is not possible, even the idea may not be a good one, as Toyota concluded for its production workers (see Compensation Today 3.1). Fortunately, there are many other ways to motivate and reward good performance.

Merit Bonuses

merit bonus

a bonus provided to recognize good employee performance that does not increase base pay

Merit raises have numerous problems, including the topping-out problem and the risk of providing a long-term future reward for short-term past performance; but **merit bonuses** avoid these problems since they are granted only for the period in which good performance occurs, and good performance must be repeated each year in order for employees to continue to receive them. Merit bonuses can also be used in conjunction with a merit raise system.

For example, for those employees no longer eligible for further merit raises, an opportunity to obtain an annual merit bonus may keep them focused on performance.

Beyond these advantages, merit bonuses also have the advantage of not being a fixed amount; thus, they can be varied from year to year depending on the financial circumstances of the employer. They can also be paid out in lump sums, either quarterly or annually, and they may have more visibility as a result. Many firms like to prepare completely separate cheques to reinforce this visibility.

But merit bonuses still have many of the disadvantages of merit raises. They still depend on reliable and accepted performance measures, which may not exist. Managers and employees alike may also have little faith in the available measures. In addition, bonuses can cause poor relations between supervisors and their subordinates and between employees and their co-workers, especially if the bonus pool is limited. Merit bonuses are also not suited for work that depends on collaboration and cooperation. Since they apply only for one year, they may be seen as less valuable than merit raises and may need to be much higher to attract an equivalent amount of attention from employees.

One key issue is how to set the amount of the total available bonus pool. If it is simply an arbitrary decision by top management, then it may cause dis-satisfaction, especially if it results in low bonuses or limited numbers of bonuses. Many firms are now tying the bonus pool to some measure of orga-nizational performance, such as profit sharing, and then allocating this amount to employees based on individual merit.

Another major issue in the use of merit bonuses is defining the behaviours that will be rewarded. Merit bonuses can be based either on the overall per-formance of the individual or on specific behaviours or indicators. Frequently, they are based on meeting a quota or goal. Research has shown that employees who work to challenging but attainable goals—especially when they have had a role in formulating these goals—outperform those without specific work goals.[43] So goal-based bonus systems can be very successful.

These goals can range widely. In some cases, they are geared to produc-tivity: produce a certain number of units or serve a certain number of clients and receive a bonus. Some organizations are starting to give bonuses to employees who score high in customer service ratings. A bonus may also be provided for minimizing errors or for low scrap rates. As seen in Chapter 3, bonuses can be provided for finding insects during vegetable processing. Book sales reps can be given a bonus for finding new authors. Baseball players can be given a bonus if they score a specified number of home runs. Bonuses can be given for making creative suggestions, or even for just showing up at work consistently, as discussed later in Chapter 10.

The possibilities are endless. This flexibility is one of the most attractive features of bonuses. But whenever bonuses focus on only a subset of the total behaviour expected from an individual, extreme caution must be exercised to ensure that the other "unbonused" aspects of the job are not neglected. Of course, care must also be taken that the behaviours being rewarded are actu-ally the behaviours that are wanted, as has been discussed in Chapter 3.

Advantages and Disadvantages of Individual Performance Pay Plans

Plan	Advantages	Disadvantages
Piece Rates	• can be highly motivational • may reduce need for external control of employees • reduces employer risk by relating pay to output • can make expected levels of performance clear	• are applicable only in limited circumstances • may not be as "scientific" as they appear • may pit workers against management • social forces may constrain employee effort • product/service quality may suffer • may cause conflict among employees • may cause abuse of equipment or tools • may cause accidents
Sales Commissions	• relatively easy to set and measure • unlimited opportunity for sales • reduces need for employee control • can serve as source of feedback • reduces employer risk by linking pay to sales • highly motivational to increase sales	• uncertain employee income may cause turnover • pay may be higher due to employee risk • low earnings for new sales workers • workers may avoid tasks unrelated to sales • may encourage overly aggressive sales staff • may cause conflict among sales workers • may cause neglect of good HR practices • may focus attention on sales volume not profitability
Merit Raises	• focuses attention on overall performance • provides feedback to employees • a means for advancement through the pay range • helps to retain outstanding employees • can foster perceptions of equity	• very expensive since they are permanent raises • requires an effective employee appraisal system • need to ensure a noticeable difference in pay • employees will eventually "top out" • may cause antagonism towards supervisor • may inhibit collaborative behaviour • not suitable where work is highly interdependent
Merit Bonuses	• more flexible because they are not permanent • can be related to financial conditions of firm • can serve as solution to "topping out" problem	• need valid performance measures • not suitable where work is highly interdependent • bonus amount may need to be higher
Special Incentives	• focuses attention on key employee behaviours • depends on specific nature of plan	• employees may focus only on rewarded behaviours • depends on specific nature of plan

Special-Purpose (Targeted) Incentives

targeted incentive

an incentive designed to motivate a specific type of employee behaviour

In order to foster certain behaviours that are of special importance to an organization, or to counteract behaviours that are causing problems for the organization, some firms have developed **targeted incentive** programs. An example would be the Green Giant insect bonus plan. Although targeted incentives could be used for variety of purposes, the most common are suggestion programs (to encourage creativity) and attendance programs (to discourage absenteeism). Although the advantages and disadvantages of targeted incentive plans vary depending on the specific nature of the plan, their overall advantage is that they focus employee attention on a behaviour of key importance to the firm; while the overall disadvantage is that they focus attention only on the specific behaviour being sought, potentially causing employee neglect of other important behaviours. These types of plans will be discussed in more detail in Chapter 10. Compensation Notebook 4.4 summarizes the advantages and disadvantages of the five individual performance pay plans.

Group Performance Pay

ⓇⓅⒸ 4.1

In this section, we will examine the oldest and best-known group performance plan—productivity gain-sharing, followed by goal-sharing plans, and other group/team pay plans. As Table 4.3 shows, group/team performance pay plans are generally much less common than individual pay plans and appear to have declined in popularity in recent years, with high discontinuation rates during the period 2000 to 2004. This decline follows a period of rapid expansion during the latter part of the twentieth century.

Gain-Sharing Plans

In **gain-sharing plans**, whenever employees in a work group are able to improve productivity, these gains are systematically shared among all the employees in the work unit. Improved quality, decreased waste, and improved methods of working are all ways of increasing productivity. A key aspect of gain-sharing programs is that they depend on a historical base line of productivity to determine whether productivity has increased, and if so, by how much.

gain-sharing plan

a group performance pay plan that shares cost savings or productivity gains generated by a work group with all members of that group

Advantages of Gain-Sharing Plans

From an employer's point of view, undoubtedly the most attractive feature of gain-sharing plans is that, if properly designed, they are self-funding. That is, the plans themselves produce the funds from which the gain-sharing bonuses are paid. Proponents argue that gain sharing results in improved productivity and efficiency, greater labour–management cooperation, and increased employee acceptance of change.[44] They maintain that improved productivity stems from several sources. One source, perhaps the least important, is the direct incentive: people work more productively because they expect to receive a share of the financial benefit. However, as critics point out, this source of motivation is limited at best, since the extent to which an individual's increased effort will be reflected in their overall income is small.

A more important source of productivity is that gain sharing can help create social norms favourable to productivity. Positive social norms can enhance productivity by stimulating work effort, promoting cooperation among employees and with management, and reducing the need for supervisory control. These norms occur because gain sharing promotes internalization of company objectives and therefore self-control. Those employees not capable of self-control can still be controlled by social norms (under behavioural theory) or mutual monitoring (under agency theory).

Since external controls are costly, reducing them should produce significant savings for the firm. In a study of 44 large Canadian manufacturing firms, Long found that firms with gain sharing or profit sharing had significantly less formal hierarchy, with about 31 percent fewer managers than firms without these plans.[45] Thus, even if gain sharing produced no direct gain in employee productivity, it could still help by diminishing the costs of hierarchy and management.

Another advantage of gain sharing is increased employee commitment, which reduces costs due to turnover and absenteeism. In addition, cost-saving suggestions and innovations generated by gain sharing systems add more value, as well as other more general benefits, such as increased employee awareness of the business and improved communication between management and employees. One final advantage of gain sharing over other types of group programs, such as profit sharing or employee stock ownership, is that gain sharing can be applied to not-for-profit and government organizations.

Disadvantages of Gain-Sharing Plans

What are the potential disadvantages of gain sharing? First, there are some obvious ones, such as the costs of establishing and administering the program. There are also the costs of the managerial and employee time devoted to the program, including time consumed in meetings, as well as in preparing for meetings, evaluating suggestions, and communicating about the program. In many cases, to make gain sharing work well, additional employee training is necessary.

Another important disadvantage of gain sharing is that it is not very amenable to rapidly changing circumstances because of its reliance on a historical base line to gauge productivity changes. If products or technology are frequently changing, then it is very difficult to determine whether productivity gains (or losses) are due to increased worker input or to other factors. Management will not want to pay out productivity bonuses if cause and effect cannot be clearly defined.

Another possible problem is that workers may focus only on what they can do to maximize their bonus, even if these actions have negative implications for the organization as a whole. For example, a shipping team may pack their shipments very quickly, but in such a way that more breakage occurs. A customer service team may handle more customer calls by reducing the quality of their assistance.

Moreover, critics claim that group-based payment systems can actually be detrimental to motivation and productivity. In collective reward systems, any additional effort expended by an individual employee has only a negligible effect on the reward she or he receives. But the employee shares in the benefits of the cumulative effects of other employees. Therefore, an individual may "shirk" and become a "free rider."[46] If everyone does this, collective reward systems actually serve to reduce productivity, especially if heightened hierarchical controls are needed to prevent shirking.

Gain sharing may also exacerbate labour–management conflict, since it provides additional matters to disagree and argue about. Improperly or inappropriately implemented, gain sharing can become a dissatisfier and a demotivator rather than a motivator. Even in firms where there is a reservoir of trust between management and workers, this trust can be sorely tested by all of the adjustments and changes necessary to get just about any gain-sharing system working right. As a result, few gain-sharing systems are wholly successful on the first try.

Overall, getting these plans to work effectively is difficult, as the high discontinuation rate indicates. As Table 4.3 shows, 78 percent of the firms that used gain-sharing plans in 2000 no longer had them four years later. Although some firms did adopt gain sharing over the 2000–2004 period, more firms dropped it, which caused the mean incidence of gain sharing to drop from 14 percent to 7 percent in that time period.

This discontinuation rate is much higher than in earlier studies. For example, another Canadian study found that 17 percent of firms that had gain sharing in 1980 no longer had it in 1985.[47] Similarly, a 1992 sample of North American firms showed a 20.4 percent discontinuation rate;[48] and another U.S. study conducted in the late 1980s showed a 15.1 percent discontinuation rate.[49] These results suggest that gain sharing may have been adopted by firms for which it was unsuited; or that the pace of industrial change has been increasing, making gain sharing less viable.

Experience and Applicability of Gain Sharing

The evidence is clear that gain sharing can lead to positive results,[50] but it does not always do so. Kim found that gain sharing is generally less successful in unionized settings,[51] a finding also reported by Cooke.[52] In fact, Cooke found that while nonunion firms benefited significantly from gain sharing, unionized firms showed no benefit whatsoever. Like many other pay elements, gain sharing fits best with only certain managerial strategies. Classical firms generally do not look favourably on gain sharing because it doesn't allow individual accountability and it permits free riding. However, human relations organizations may find gain sharing attractive because it fits in with their concept of group cooperation. Some of the foundations for effective gain sharing would likely already be in place at human relations firms, such as trust between managers and employees. Strong and favourable social norms may also be able to prevent free riding, and job security may allay fears of layoff due to productivity increases.

But in high-involvement organizations, the potential payoff for gain sharing is greatest, since virtually all the conditions for success are already in place, including a participative culture, trust, communications, training, broad-based jobs, and reasonable job security. These organizations are also likely be favourably disposed toward these plans, since gain sharing fits their managerial philosophy of encouraging teamwork, participation, innovation, and problem solving. Gain sharing also fits with and supports the use of work teams, which are often a prominent feature of high-involvement firms.

However, a problem with gain sharing for high-involvement firms is that change can occur so quickly that developing valid performance baselines may be difficult, and the package of performance measures may need to continually change. Under these conditions, gain sharing is unlikely to be effective. Indeed, analysis of data from the Workplace and Employee Survey (WES) conducted by Statistics Canada in 2001 indicated that there was no relationship between use of group pay (the survey did not distinguish types of group pay) and workplace profitability in firms pursuing an innovator business strategy; but the survey did show a strong positive relationship between group pay and profitability in firms that were not pursuing an innovator business strategy. This survey also indicates that group pay is a low-risk innovation; it never seemed to actually decrease profitability.

Goal-Sharing Plans

goal-sharing plan

a group performance pay plan in which a work group receives a bonus when it meets prespecified performance goals

In plans involving **goal sharing**, management sets goals on one or more performance indicators for each work group or team, to be met within a specified time period; if the goals are met, all team members then receive a bonus.[53] Goal-sharing plans are quite different from gain-sharing plans. In gain sharing, cost savings are quantified and then shared between the company and the group; unlike goal sharing, there are no set goals other than to simply improve as much as possible relative to the historical baseline. Thus, goal sharing is much more of an "all or nothing" type of plan than gain sharing. That is, under gain sharing the employees receive a portion of any productivity gain, but under goal sharing employees receive nothing at all until the productivity goal is met.

Like gain sharing, goal sharing is a group pay plan that gained popularity rapidly in the last two decades of the twentieth century but may now be waning in popularity. As Table 4.3 indicates, the mean incidence of goal sharing fell from 18 percent in 2000 to 12 percent in 2004. Moreover, nearly two-thirds of those firms that had goal sharing plans in 2000 had discontinued them by 2004, although this was partly offset by a number of firms that adopted goal sharing plans during this period. Still, goal sharing remains the single most popular type of group pay plan.

Advantages of Goal Sharing

Goal-sharing plans have several advantages over gain-sharing plans. First, they are much simpler to develop and are much more flexible. They can therefore be applied in a much broader set of circumstances. They can also be tied to specific objectives that support company strategy. In addition, meaningful performance increases must take place before any bonus is paid out. Thus, the company retains 100 percent of gains below the bonus-targeted level.

When goal-sharing plans work, they can produce many of the same advantages as gain-sharing plans. Group norms valuing high productivity may develop (as long as negative consequences, such as layoffs or reductions in valued overtime, do not result from this increased productivity). These favourable group norms lead the group to police itself by encouraging lower-producing workers to improve their performance. Group members are also motivated to help new employees learn their jobs quickly and effectively. A collaborative attitude results, and workers who develop better ways of performing their jobs are more likely to share their knowledge.

Disadvantages of Goal Sharing

However, because goal-sharing plans are flexible, they can be much more arbitrary than gain-sharing plans. Goal levels necessary to qualify for a bonus and sizes of bonus paid are often the result of arbitrary management decisions. In addition, goal-sharing plans may be modified or dropped at any time. None of these characteristics is desirable for enhancing motivation. For example, if employees perceive goals to be unrealistic (low expectancy), they will not exert extra effort to meet them. If they do not think the bonus is sufficiently attractive relative to the effort required (low valence), again, they will not exert the extra effort. If employees believe the program can be modified or ended at any time, they will be skeptical whether the promised rewards will actually materialize or continue once goals are met (low instrumentality). If management modifies the goal-sharing system frequently, then employees may consider it a "flavour of the month" to be simply ignored.

Goal sharing also has equity issues. Goal-sharing systems often have no established basis for judging the value of meeting a particular goal, and no fixed, mutually agreed-upon basis to apportion gains between the company and employees. Thus, employees may feel that the company is trying to "rip them off" by providing token rewards for major gains in productivity. As a result, goal-sharing programs may be less motivational than gain-sharing programs, under which the gains to be shared are a prespecified proportion of measurable productivity increases.

Goal sharing can also produce conflict. A work team may become frustrated if one or two workers unwilling or unable to perform at the necessary levels prevent the group from attaining their output goals. Alternatively, if the group believes the productivity goal is set unrealistically high, they will not be motivated to strive for the goal, even if some members may wish to try. And even if the goal is reached, there is no incentive to surpass it, and workers may slack off after reaching their goal.

Employee dissatisfaction may occur if everyone worked hard but didn't quite reach the goal and therefore received no reward. Managers may be tempted to redress this resentment by lowering the goal and providing the reward anyway; but this action would only teach employees that goal attainment is unnecessary for reward attainment. Another problem is that many situational factors also affect goal achievement; so using the identical goals for different work teams may be highly unfair. But attempts to correct this unfairness by developing "easier" goals for some work teams simply builds resentment elsewhere.

Many of these problems are surmountable. Extensive employee participation in the development of these plans can help to create realistic goals. Indeed, research has shown that employee participation significantly increases employee motivation for goal achievement. Multi-tiered goals can be used to recognize different goal achievement levels to reduce frustration if a team can't meet a top goal. Management can also quantify the value of the specified goals in order to give some assurance of equity in determining reward size. All the same, as Table 4.3 indicates, the discontinuation rate for goal sharing is high.

Experience and Applicability of Goal Sharing

Unlike individual goal-setting plans, group goal-sharing plans have not been well researched. However, most experts suggest that to work well, group goal-sharing plans must be designed with input from employees; they should clearly communicate factors affecting goal achievement and ways that employees can influence these factors; and they should communicate progress toward meeting goals on an ongoing basis.[54] The key factor for success is a high level of trust between management and employees. Thus, goal sharing is most effective in high-involvement organizations, somewhat effective in human relations organizations, and ineffective in classical organizations. A caveat to this is that goal-sharing plans may not work well in highly dynamic firms, where the setting of realistic goals may be difficult or impossible.

Other Types of Group Performance Pay Plans

Besides gain or goal sharing, there are numerous other types of group bonus plans; and Table 4.3 showed that about 9 percent of Canadian firms use one or more of these. As with gain- and goal-sharing plans, this statistic represents a drop in popularity since 2000. There is also a high (76 percent) discontinuation rate.

competitive bonus plan is the **competitive bonus plan**. For example, many real estate firms with multi-office operations encourage competition between sales offices by providing a bonus to all sales personnel in the highest-producing office each month. In retail chains, all employees in a particular store may receive a bonus if their store has the highest customer satisfaction ratings in the chain in a given time period.

Competitive bonus plans are most suited to circumstances in which the groups do not need to work closely with one another. In general, competitive bonus systems that pit one group against another should be used only when the groups are truly independent and never need to cooperate with one another. These plans do not fit well with the philosophy of human relations organizations or high-involvement firms.

Another type of team-based reward system is **pooled performance pay.** One example of pooled performance pay is **group commissions**, where the pay for a group of sales reps is based on the total sales the group generates, with each member receiving an equal share of the resulting commissions. Another example is **group piece rates**, in which group members get paid based on the number of completed products or components produced by the group. For example, tree planters might get paid according to the total number of trees planted by a team of planters, with the money being shared equally among members of the planting team.

The value of these plans is that each group member wants the other group members to succeed, and each shares tips and techniques for better performance. In other words, this type of plan encourages teamwork. The danger with

competitive bonus plan
a group pay plan that rewards a work group for outperforming other work groups

pooled performance pay
a pay plan in which the performance results of a group are pooled, and group members share equally in the performance bonus

group commissions
a performance pay plan in which the commissions of a group of sales workers are pooled and then shared out equally among members of the group

group piece rates
a performance pay plan in which group members get paid based on the number of completed products produced by the group

Advantages and Disadvantages of Group Performance Pay Plans

Plan	Advantages	Disadvantages
Gain Sharing	• self-funding if designed properly • can stimulate higher productivity • may enhance labour-management cooperation • may create positive group norms • may improve employee cooperation • may reduce need for external control • may increase employee commitment • may generate cost-saving suggestions • can increase employee knowledge of the business	• costs of establishing and administering plan • costs of employee and managerial time • not amenable to changing circumstances • may focus attention on group's interests only • may create "free riders" • may create more opportunities for conflict • may become a dissatisfier • high discontinuation rate
Goal Sharing	• simple to develop • more flexible than gain sharing • only rewards major productivity gains • may create positive group norms • may encourage cooperation • may reduce need for external control	• can be arbitrary in goal levels and bonus amounts • less continuity than gain sharing • difficulty in establishing realistic and equitable goals • may not meet criteria for good employee motivation • may cause frustration if some do not contribute • may cause frustration if efforts fall slightly short • no incentive to surpass goal • high discontinuation rate
Other Group Plans	• competition between groups can be motivational • may encourage group members to assist others • depends on specific nature of plan	• can cause conflict between work groups • may encourage free riders • high discontinuation rate • depends on specific nature of plan

these plans is that they may encourage "free riding" or "social loafing." However, this may not be a problem if the groups are kept relatively small, and if members understand that their well-being is maximized when all perform to the best of their abilities.

Finally, another way of encouraging teamwork while discouraging social loafing is through the use of **team-based merit pay**.[55] Team-based merit pay provides rewards to individuals based on their contributions to the team. For example, at Johnsonville Foods, team leaders and members rate each member's contribution to team goals, communication with other team members, willingness to work with other team members, and attendance and timeliness at group meetings.[56] From this information, management calculates a merit pay bonus for each team member. Compensation Notebook 4.5 summarizes the advantages and disadvantages of group performance pay plans.

team-based merit pay

a performance pay plan that rewards individuals on the basis of their contribution to a group or team

Organization Performance Pay Plans

Organization performance pay plans consist of profit sharing, employee stock plans, and other plans, often known as long-term incentives. Although both profit-sharing and employee stock plans experienced growing popularity in the latter decades of the twentieth century, Table 4.3 suggests that their popularity may have levelled out in the last few years, with profit sharing actually showing a decline in popularity. Overall, profit sharing and stock plans are about equal in popularity, as 23 percent of firms report profit sharing, and 24 percent report having at least one stock plan.

Profit Sharing

employee profit-sharing plan

a formal pay program in which a firm provides bonus payments to employees based on the profitability of the firm

current distribution plan

a profit-sharing plan that distributes the profit-sharing bonus to employees in the form of cash or shares, at least annually

deferred profit-sharing plan (DPSP)

a profit-sharing plan in which the profit-sharing bonuses are allocated to employee accounts but not actually paid out until a later date, usually on termination or retirement

combination plan

a plan that combines the current distribution and deferred profit-sharing plans by paying some of the profit-sharing bonus on a current (cash) basis and deferring the remainder

To be recognized as having an **employee profit-sharing plan**, a firm must have a formal program in which payments are made to a wide cross-section of employees on at least an annual basis, based on a formula relating the size of the bonus pool to the profitability of the business. While it is not considered necessary that all employees or groups be included, plans that restrict profit sharing to managers are generally not considered "true" profit-sharing plans.

Profit-sharing plans may take one of three forms. The **current distribution plan** (also called a "cash plan") pays a share of company profits to employees in cash or occasionally in company stock. (When stock is used, it is also considered a type of employee stock plan.) In most firms, the distribution is annual, but it can also be more frequent, depending on the availability of profit data.

In a **deferred profit-sharing plan (DPSP)**, an employee's share of the profit bonus pool is placed in a trust fund to be distributed at a future date, usually on the employee's retirement or termination of employment. This type of plan is often used as a type of retirement savings plan. A **combination plan** provides both cash (or stock) and a deferred component. The objective of a combination plan is to take advantage of the provisions for tax deferral in federal tax legislation to help build some retirement income, while also providing a more visible incentive to employees through the cash portion.

Advantages of Profit-Sharing Plans

As part of a study on profit sharing, researchers asked a business owner whether his firm had employee profit sharing.[57] In response, he exclaimed, "Give away my profits to employees? Why would I want to do *that*?" Why, indeed, would employers want to share their profits with their employees?

Advocates of profit sharing argue that there are many sound business reasons to do so.[58] First, when the interests of employees and the employer are aligned, employees may be more motivated to help improve productivity. Profit sharing can also contribute to the development of favourable group norms, improved cooperation among employees and between employees and management, improved labour–management relations, and greater organizational identification, which may lead to more organizational citizenship behaviour. These improved norms can in turn reduce the need for supervision,

3 forms of Profit sharing

thereby reducing costs. Profit sharing also fits with and supports a move to high-involvement management for firms moving in that direction.

In a major Canadian study, chief executive officers said that they saw profit sharing as a way either to increase company performance (through improving employee motivation, promoting teamwork, or helping employees understand the business) or to provide better rewards to employees, thereby improving employee commitment and loyalty.[59] Most CEOs said that they believed profit sharing had helped their companies achieve these goals.

Other advantages stem from the fact that profit sharing is a reward related to ability to pay. By providing profit sharing, an employer is able to offer a more attractive compensation package but does not have to continue payments when business conditions are unfavourable. Moreover, for some organizations, it is the only way they can afford to offer a retirement plan. Profit sharing may also reduce the need for layoffs in poor economic circumstances, since labour costs are automatically adjusted downward.

At the societal level, some commentators have called for widespread profit sharing as a way to increase employment levels and stability, while others have seen profit sharing as a way of reducing labour–management conflict.[60] Still others have seen it as a way of increasing the competitiveness of businesses in the global marketplace. From an employee point of view, profit sharing can improve job security by reducing the need for layoffs and improving company performance. Employees may also gain greater job satisfaction working in an environment where there is harmony.

Finally, compared with plans such as gain sharing, profit sharing is far simpler to set up and administer. Profit measures are readily available: there is no need to compute baselines or to try to quantify the value of cost savings. Administration is also relatively simple, and the plan and results are relatively easy to communicate to employees.

Disadvantages of Profit Sharing

The most important disadvantage of profit sharing is that it may not pay off for the employer: the costs of the profit-sharing bonus and administration of the profit-sharing system may exceed the benefits. Some critics even argue that as a collective reward system, profit sharing may actually reduce employee performance by causing "free riding," just as in group-based pay systems. In fact, because the connection between individual performance and the expected reward for that performance is more tenuous, profit sharing actually has a weaker "line of sight" between performance and reward than group pay and so may have little direct impact on employee performance. So many factors intervene between worker performance and company profitability that worker performance can improve dramatically while profits actually go down or even disappear due to market conditions or poor management decisions.

The arguments about general employee aversion to uncertain rewards also apply; and with only one exception,[61] studies in Canada have shown a negative link between unionization and the presence of profit sharing[62]—that is, few unionized companies have profit sharing. Besides the concern about uncertain rewards, unions worry that profit sharing results are subject to manipulation, and also that by increasing worker commitment to the company, profit sharing might weaken worker allegiance to the union.

A final drawback of profit sharing in the eyes of some employers is that it requires employers to share financial information about the company.

Applicability of Profit Sharing

The impact of profit sharing on company performance has been studied extensively. A major U.S. study found that the adoption of profit sharing is associated with productivity increases averaging 4.3 percent (although 25 to 33 percent of firms showed no productivity increase whatsoever).[63] Other U.S. studies have shown similar results.[64] A Canadian study also found that profit sharing improves productivity.[65] These results fit well with a U.S. study (described in Compensation Today 4.5) that found that companies that made extensive use of organization-based performance rewards, such as profit sharing and employee stock plans, showed a much higher five-year survival rate than firms that did not use organization-based performance pay. Interestingly, while these data strongly supported the importance of organization-based pay in predicting future company success, the stock analysts and investors at that time seemed to think the opposite! This difference suggests that the positive effects of organization-based performance pay are not well understood in the investment sector. Studies have also shown that profit sharing improves employment stability.[66]

Which types of firms are most likely to want to adopt profit sharing? The only common factor found in three Canadian studies of this issue was the practice of high-involvement management.[67] This conclusion fits in with a U.S. finding by Kim that profit sharing had significant positive effects on profitability only in high-involvement firms.[68] Overall, profit sharing seems particularly important in companies where a high level of cooperation is needed across company units, between management and employees, and among employees. Profit sharing helps to promote internalization of company goals, as well as providing a mechanism for keeping employees informed about the financial state of the business.

Yet profit sharing may be useful in human relations organizations to the extent that it serves as an additional means of cementing loyalty to the firm and fostering positive work norms. However, the impact of profit sharing is not likely to be dramatic, since the participative culture necessary to maximize the contribution of profit sharing is not generally in place at human relations firms.

For classical firms, profit sharing would yield few benefits. Profit sharing is not philosophically compatible with the classical managerial philosophy, in which workers and management are seen as adversaries and where control requires that individuals be accountable for their own performance. In a situation of low trust, profit sharing simply becomes another source of conflict: employees believe that management is somehow attempting to cheat them out of their rightful share of the profits or trying to use profit sharing to reduce other compensation or to weaken union allegiance. Reluctance of management to release financial information also fosters mistrust and makes it difficult for

How Many Stock Analysts Does It Take to Change a Light Bulb?

How many stock market analysts does it take to change a light bulb? The answer: None. If the bulb really needed changing, the market would have already changed it.

The humour in this joke relies on stock market analysts' belief in the "infallibility of the market"—the notion that the stock market takes account of all information about a company and accurately incorporates it into the valuation of the company's stock. Yet the "infallibility of the market" is in fact a fiction. Through their own individual actions, stock analysts continually pass collective judgment on the decisions of company management and influence changes in the firm's stock price. Investors *are* the market!

Management decisions in publicly traded corporations are evaluated in terms of whether they "add value" to a company—whether they cause a company's share price to go up or down. So researchers have started to examine the quality of management decisions in terms of the market's reaction to them. But is the market always right? Or does the market sometimes act on erroneous assumptions?

An interesting study by Theresa Welbourne and Alice Andrews examined the five-year survival rate of firms that were first listed on a stock exchange in 1988. The study then related this rate to the extent to which these firms had organizationally-based performance rewards, such as profit sharing and employee stock plans. Their results were impressive. They found that the use of organizationally based performance rewards significantly increased the likelihood of company survival.

This is an interesting finding in its own right; but the researchers also made another interesting discovery. They examined whether the stock market had valued the shares of companies with organizational rewards more highly than those firms without organizational rewards at the time of the initial public offering. It should have, since these firms ended up with a higher survival rate.

But it did not. In fact, firms with organizational rewards were valued significantly *lower* than firms without these rewards. The researchers concluded that "investors seem to respond negatively to a factor that actually has a positive impact on survival chances." They also found that despite believing that organizational rewards had played some role in their company's success, the top executives of survivor companies substantially undervalued the role that organizational rewards had actually played in company survival. This suggests that business culture itself may have a tradition of discounting the impact of organizational rewards.

Source: Welbourne, Theresa M., and Alice N. Andrews. 1996. "Predicting the Performance of Initial Public Offerings: Should Human Resource Management Be in the Equation?" *Academy of Management Journal*, 39(4): 891–919.

employees to understand how they could contribute to profitability. In addition, a major potential benefit of profit sharing—the ability to operate with less hierarchy and fewer supervisors—is not viable in classical firms.

What are the desirable conditions for profit sharing? First, there must be some expectation of profits in at least the first one or two years of the plan. And the profitability level should be sufficient to afford an annual payout that amounts to at least 3 to 5 percent of base pay for each employee.[69] Firms with highly unstable profits and a weak line-of-sight between employee performance and profitability are not ideal candidates. For profit sharing to be successful, companies need reasonably good relationships between management and employees; and management must be willing to share financial information and value employee input.

Although economists argue that profit sharing would have more impact if it substituted for base pay, consultants and practitioners universally oppose this practice.[70] Instead, they argue that competitive base pay and an equitable compensation system are preconditions to successful use of profit sharing. In fact, research indicates that profit sharing is usually used as an "add-on," rather than as a substitute for base pay, and that employees in profit-sharing firms earn more than in comparable firms without profit sharing.[71]

Employee Stock Plans

An **employee stock plan** is any type of plan through which employees acquire shares in the firm that employs them. There are three main types of employee stock plans. An **employee stock bonus plan** is very simple in concept—an employer provides company shares to employees at no cost to the employee, either by outright grant or in conjunction with some other performance pay plan, such as profit sharing. In an **employee stock purchase plan,** employees provide some kind of direct payment in return for company shares, but they usually do not have to pay full market price for these shares. In an **employee stock option plan**, employees are provided with options to purchase company stock at some future time at a set price, which they would exercise if the market price rises to exceed this price.

Employee stock plans enjoyed rapid growth in popularity during the latter part of the twentieth century, but their popularity appears to have levelled off during the last few years, as Table 4.3 shows. This is not surprising in the light of down-market conditions during the first few years of the new millennium and the controversy about whether employee stock option plans are beneficial to investors. As Table 4.3 shows, stock purchase plans are the most common plans, followed by stock option plans, and stock bonus plans. Compensation Today 4.6 describes two fairly typical stock purchase plans, one in a private corporation and one in a public corporation.

Advantages of Employee Stock Plans

The objective of most stock ownership plans is to get employees "to think like owners"—that is, to align the goals of employees with those of the owners. This may encourage internalization of company goals and lead to enhanced citizenship behaviour and membership behaviours. Large-scale employee ownership plans, in which employees acquire a significant portion of the ownership, can serve as a catalyst in a shift to a more flexible and entrepreneurial, high-involvement type of organization.

Stock ownership may also encourage decision makers within the firm to look at ways of maximizing share value. In addition, it may serve as a spur toward improved management, because stock-owning employees hold managers to a higher performance standard than other employees. These plans are also intended to promote cooperation among employees and between employees and management and to create a stronger understanding of and concern for overall company performance. These plans improve the compensation package, making it easier to attract and retain employees. They can also serve as a retirement plan. Some companies also adopt them for philosophical reasons, on the grounds that employees should benefit financially from the success of the firm, since they have helped to create that success.

Ownership Eggs on These Employees

At Vanderpol's Eggs in Abbotsford, British Columbia, most employees are shareholders in this privately held firm. A typical employee may hold $75,000 worth of company shares, and many own much more than that. Most of this ownership results from employees choosing to invest their allocations from the company profit-sharing plan in company stock. (Because the company wishes to preserve working capital, their other alternative for the profit-sharing payout is to lend it back to the company, which pays interest of prime plus 1 percent on these funds.) Although the company provides no discount on the shares that are purchased with profit-sharing money, the British Columbia government does provide a 20-percent tax credit on funds so invested. Employees are allowed to remove their funds at retirement or termination. The company finds that stock ownership creates a keen interest among employees in company performance.

Similarly, the Royal Bank of Canada, a publicly traded firm, has for many years had an employee savings program under which employees may purchase bank stock. All employees with at least six months' service have the option of placing up to 10 percent of their annual earnings in a savings plan that may be invested in deposit accounts, mutual funds, or bank stock. The bank matches the shares by 50 percent, up to a limit of 3 percent of the employee's annual earnings. That is, if an employee invests 6 percent of his or her earnings, that person receives additional bank shares amounting to 3 percent of his or her gross earnings at no extra cost. If the employee's annual RRSP allowance is not used up, these shares are placed in a deferred profit-sharing plan, and there is no income tax liability until redemption. If the RRSP allowance is used up, the shares are placed in an employee profit-sharing plan, and income taxes are not deferred.

This philosophical position may also have a practical slant. In recent years, the earnings of CEOs have soared relative to the earnings of other employees, mainly due to stock options. By 2000, chief executive pay in the United States had reached an average level of 475 times the pay of an average worker,[72] up from 209 times in 1996,[73] and 42 times in 1960.[74] Most of this gain can be attributed to stock ownership. In contrast, real wages in the United States and Canada have hardly budged in the last 20 years. So for some companies, the creation of employee stock plans, especially stock options, can help redress this apparent inequity.

Stock plans also have some practical advantages. One is that stock plans do not require the company to lay out any cash. Thus, for companies that are cash-poor and cannot afford pay raises, shares may be one way to reward employees. In a very limited number of cases, shares have been used to help compensate for pay reductions. For publicly traded companies, another practical advantage is that mechanisms for stock plans are already in place because of the pricing and trading of shares; and since the company already has to provide profit information to shareholders, extending this information to employees is not difficult.

For employees, there are five main benefits.

1. Employee stock can mean financial gains. For example, thousands of Microsoft employees are millionaires due to the employee stock plans at that firm.

2. Employee stock plans can provide a vehicle for retirement savings.
3. If employee ownership enhances company performance, greater job security can result. For example, at Spruce Falls Pulp and Paper in Kapuskasing, Ontario, conversion to employee ownership saved the company, along with the jobs of those employed there.
4. Stock ownership, particularly if accompanied by employee participation, can provide employees with a say in the enterprise and a sense of control over their own destiny.
5. Stock ownership can foster a sense of pride and membership among employees.

Disadvantages of Employee Stock Plans

Employee stock plans have some general disadvantages and some specific disadvantages pertaining to each type of plan. First of all, establishing and administering these plans carries a cost. Second, if share prices decline, especially due to poor management decisions, employee dissatisfaction may result. Third, if employees want to participate in decision making to improve company performance but are not supported by management, then backlash may result. Fourth, for plans in which employees do not purchase their shares at full value, there is some dilution in the equity held by other owners. Fifth, there is a risk that the expected advantages of employee ownership will not materialize.

Employee stock plans for privately held corporations are more difficult than those for publicly traded corporations, because many necessary mechanisms are not in place and have to be created. Procedures for issuing, pricing, selling, and trading shares need to be developed, as well as procedures for shareholder voting and communicating financial information. However, these problems are not insurmountable; and although stock plans are most common in publicly traded corporations, many privately held corporations do adopt them.

For employees, the main disadvantages of stock plans are that gains are very uncertain, and that by investing in one's employer, employees are at risk for losing not only their jobs but also their investment in the company shares. Of course, an obvious disadvantage for share purchase plans is that the employee must come up with the necessary funds to make the purchase, even if shares are sold on a discounted or subsidized basis. The risks of investment may also be greater when the employer is a private corporation, because there is no established market through which to price and liquidate holdings. In addition, in private corporations where employees hold less than 50 percent of the voting shares, employees may have little real say in the operation of the enterprise; and coupled with the inability to easily liquidate their shares, this situation can make them very vulnerable to adverse decisions by the majority owner.

Applicability of Employee Stock Plans

What is the evidence on the effects of employee stock plans on company performance? Although no large-scale studies of this subject have been conducted in Canada, numerous studies have been conducted in the United States. In general, the results range from moderately positive to neutral (but rarely negative), when employee ownership is considered on its own.[75]

However, when combined with employee participation, employee stock ownership can lead to dramatic results. For example, one U.S. study found that firms that introduced employee ownership and practised employee participation in decision making grew 11 to 17 percent faster than their competitors, while firms that simply introduced employee ownership showed no difference from their competitors.[76] Other studies have shown similar results.[77] Moreover, firms that combine ownership with employee participation were also found to provide a significantly greater financial return (including both employment earnings and stock earnings) to their employees than comparable conventional firms.[78]

What about the results of introducing employee stock options? A major study conducted by researchers at Rutgers University, using a matched sample longitudinal design, found that firms that adopted broad-based stock option programs were more productive—by about 6.3 percent—than comparable firms even before they adopted their programs. However, in the period subsequent to adoption of their stock option programs, stock option companies more than doubled their productivity advantage (to 14 percent) over their competitors.[79]

However, some market analysts have argued that extensive use of stock options can dilute the returns enjoyed by other stockholders if those options are eventually exercised (if not exercised, they have no impact, of course). But the Rutgers team also addressed this question and found that returns to shareholders were not reduced in companies with extensive use of broad-based stock options. In fact, some of the analyses indicated that returns on assets were greater in firms with stock options than in other firms. (However, these positive results do not always hold true for executive stock option plans, as will be discussed in Chapter 5.)

One further issue is the impact of stock option plans on employee earnings. Many stories circulate about how new dot-com companies attract employees by providing stock options in lieu of competitive salaries. To what extent do broad-based stock options substitute for conventional employee earnings? The Rutgers team found that employees in firms that adopted stock options actually earned more (about 8 percent more) than those in comparable companies that did not adopt stock options, a difference that prevailed even before they had adopted stock options. Thus, employees did not give up any conventional earnings in return for the stock options. Since there was no net substitution effect, any employee gains from their stock options would serve to further increase the difference in total employee earnings between stock option firms and other firms.

As with profit sharing, employee stock plans fit best with high-involvement organizations. In fact, the idea of ownership fits even better with high-involvement organizations than profit sharing does, because it connotes a greater degree of unity of purpose between employees and the other owners. It also carries expectations about information and control rights. In addition, employee ownership has the potential to deliver to employees three of the four elements Lawler deems essential for a high-involvement organization: power, information, and rewards (the other key element is knowledge).[80]

For human relations organizations, employee stock plans may hold some benefits, especially if these plans are regarded by employees as an attractive part of the compensation system. They may help to retain employees and foster positive group norms. But because these organizations are not likely to provide opportunities for participation, nor the information and training needed for effective participation, the positive consequences are likely to be limited. There is also the risk of damage to morale if stock prices drop.

In classical organizations, given the adversarial nature of employee–management relations, employee stock ownership is not likely to be offered, nor would it be greeted with much enthusiasm by employees, especially if they are required to give up something in exchange. Unless the stock plan is very generous, there is not likely to be much interest among employees. If stock bonuses or options are granted outright, employees in a classical firm would likely sell their shares at the first possible opportunity.

Employees in classical firms who do retain their shares and who attempt to improve company performance are likely to experience hostility from their peers, since co-workers are likely to be concerned that productivity increases may lead to negative consequences such as layoffs. Attempts to increase employee involvement in decision making will likely be met by indifference or resistance from classical managers, since these managers are unlikely to believe that the workers are capable of making useful suggestions or participating responsibly in the decision-making process. These attitudes would likely lead to frustration on the part of employee-owners.

Other Organization Performance Plans

In recent years, many companies have been experimenting with other reward plans based on organization performance. The most prominent of these is known as **long-term incentives (LTIs)**. In the past, LTIs were generally limited to top management, on the assumption that "only high level executives are in a position to significantly impact the long-term financial performance of the corporation."[81] In essence, these plans are set up so that a payout is contingent on the achievement of three- to five-year performance goals.

Long-term compensation has traditionally involved stock options and stock grants. But LTIs may use performance units rather than shares. A **performance unit plan** grants an organizational member (usually an executive) a number of performance units, each of which carries a monetary value to be realized if certain performance targets are met. There are two ways to establish a value for these units. One way is to issue units where the value of each unit is constant, but the number of units actually payable depends on the degree of attainment of targeted goals. The second way is to vary the value of each unit based on the degree of goal attainment.

long-term incentives (LTIs)

a type of performance pay in which the incentives are tied to an organizational performance horizon that ranges beyond one year, often three to five years

performance unit plan

a long-term incentive in which the bonus amounts are expressed in units for which the monetary value will fluctuate, depending on degree of goal accomplishment

Part II: Formulating Reward and Compensation Strategy

Advantages and Disadvantages of Organizational Performance Pay Plans

Plan	Advantages	Disadvantages
Profit Sharing Plans	• may contribute to higher employee productivity • may foster increased cooperation • may improve labour-management relations • may increase organizational identification • can reduce need for employee supervision • may help employees understand the business • may result in more attractive compensation package • ties compensation to ability to pay • may help employment stability • may be used as a retirement plan • relatively simple to set up and administer • relatively low discontinuation rate	• may not pay off • may not motivate due to weak "line of sight" • subject to the "free rider" problem • employees like predictable rewards • may be opposed by unions • administrative costs
Employee Stock Plans	• aligns interests of employers and employees • may stimulate improved management • may increase employee-management cooperation • foster employee interest in firm performance • can improve perceptions of equity in firm • can make compensation more attractive • does not require firm to lay out cash	• possible dilution of stockholder equity • cost of establishing and managing plan • employee dissatisfaction if share prices decline • more difficult to establish in private corporations • employees may not have funds to purchase shares • employees have "all their eggs in one basket"
Long Term Incentives	• encourages a long term focus • can encourage better understanding of business	• difficulty in establishing realistic long term goals • "line of sight" may be weak

A **performance share plan** uses company shares instead of units. Depending on the degree of goal attainment, the individual receives a certain number of company shares at the end of the performance period. This plan has a double-barrelled incentive: to meet targeted goals and to increase company share value.

As with stock options, LTIs were originally granted only to the three or four top executives. But in 1996, a major departure from this practice occurred when apparel giant Levi Strauss announced a six-year, long-term incentive plan that included *all* employees.[82] Unfortunately, by 1999 the company was so far away from meeting the LTI goals that the program was cancelled.[83] Nonetheless, it appears that the Levi Strauss LTI example may have caused some firms to follow suit. According to Table 4.3, about 5 percent of Canadian firms had adopted broad-based LTIs by 2000. Growth levelled off during the

performance share plan

a long-term incentive in which the bonus amounts are expressed in company shares

subsequent four years; but in 2004, LTIs were still being used by 5 percent of Canadian companies.

Because use of LTIs as broad-based employee performance pay plans is so new, not much is known about the effects of these plans on corporate performance. One challenge for researchers is to separate out the impact of LTIs from other factors that affect firm performance. But in general, most of the advantages and disadvantages of goal sharing can be expected to apply to LTIs, with a particular disadvantage being the difficulty of estimating realistic goals for the three- to five-year period that long-term incentives cover. Realistic goals are hard enough to estimate for the one-year period that goal sharing programs typically cover, let alone a longer period.

Compensation Notebook 4.6 summarizes the advantages and disadvantages of the main types of organizational performance pay plans.

Summary

The purpose of this chapter was to provide you with a menu of compensation options, so that you can select the most appropriate mix of compensation components to include in the compensation strategy for a particular organization. You now know the roles of base, performance, and indirect pay within a compensation system, along with motives for their use and their advantages and disadvantages. Although base pay remains the largest component in most pay systems, there has been a trend towards supplementing it with performance pay. At the same time, some firms that traditionally have not used base pay are adding it to their compensation mix.

You also now understand the advantages and disadvantages of indirect pay and know why a properly designed indirect pay component can play a significant role in meeting compensation objectives. However, the role to be played depends on the characteristics of the firm, most notably managerial strategy.

You have learned about the three methods for establishing base pay (market pricing, job evaluation, pay-for-knowledge) and the advantages and disadvantages of each. You have also learned that some of these fit different managerial strategies better than others; and all of this information should help you decide which base pay method (if any) will provide the best foundation for your compensation system.

You have learned about the three categories of performance pay and understand that pay can be contingent on individual performance, group/team performance, or organizational performance. Each type of performance pay has distinct advantages and disadvantages, tends to serve different objectives, and produces different consequences. Individual performance pay—which includes piece rates, sales commissions, merit pay, and targeted incentives—generally focuses on promoting task behaviour. Group performance pay—which includes gain sharing, goal sharing, and pooled performance plans—promotes task behaviour, as well as positive social behaviour within groups/teams, and favourable group norms. Organization performance pay—which includes profit sharing, employee stock plans, and long-term incentives—tends to promote organizational citizenship behaviour and membership behaviour, as well as positive group norms. But keep in mind that within each of the three main categories of performance pay, there are many variations; and each variation may produce different results in different circumstances.

Be aware also of the factors that influence the appropriateness of each type of performance pay. Key factors for individual performance pay include the extent to which individuals have exclusive control over the desired performance outcomes and whether performance is dependent on collaboration with others in the organization. Another factor is the ability to separate out, measure, and price individual performance outcomes.

Group performance rewards are appropriate where good individual performance is not really possible without effective cooperation from other members of the work group or team, and where it is difficult or not practical to measure the performance of individuals. Organization-based performance pay plans are most appropriate when there is a need for cooperation between various segments of the organization. They are intended to foster a holistic perspective among organization members and focus attention on the good of the organization as a whole.

In general, individual performance pay fits best with the classical managerial strategy, although it can cause a variety of unintended negative consequences for these organizations. Because many types of individual incentives tend to foster an adversarial employee–employer relationship, you need to constantly watch for loopholes in the plan and develop ways to close them. But this frequently requires increased inspections, monitoring, and record keeping, the costs of which may outweigh any positive benefits of the incentive. Given these problems, it is not surprising that many classical firms have moved away from individual incentives and output-based control systems and have chosen to regulate behaviour directly through rules and supervision.

However, by combining group compensation elements with individual incentives, you may be able to cancel out or moderate disadvantages while maintaining advantages. You may even want to use certain individual incentives to promote cooperation and teamwork—for example, by basing an individual's merit bonus partly on his or her teamwork.

In general, keep in mind that classical organizations tend to benefit very little from group- and organization-based performance rewards because these firms do not provide the context in which employees are willing and able to significantly affect organizational performance. Although human relations firms may realize some benefits from group- and organization-based performance pay, high-involvement firms benefit the most from these pay systems, since these organizations provide conditions that translate the increased employee interest in performance generated by these systems into increased organizational performance. These conditions include well-trained, knowledgeable employees who have ready access to the information they need to allow them to identify various actions beneficial to the organization and who are empowered to take these actions.

Key Terms

base pay, 114

combination plan, 156

competitive bonus plan, 154

conversion selling, 144

current distribution plan, 156

deferred profit-sharing plan (DPSP), 156

differential piece rate, 137

employee profit-sharing plan, 156

employee stock bonus plan, 160

employee stock option plan, 160

employee stock plan, 160

employee stock purchase plan, 160

gain-sharing plan, 149

goal-sharing plan, 152

group commissions, 154

group piece rates, 154

indirect pay, 119

job evaluation, 124

leverage selling, 144

long-term incentives (LTIs), 164

maintenance selling, 144

market pricing, 124

merit bonus, 146

merit raise, 144

new market selling, 144

pay-for-knowledge system (PKS), 125

performance pay, 116

performance share plan, 165

performance unit plan, 164

piece rates, 136

pooled performance pay, 154

salary, 115

sales commissions, 141

straight piece rate, 137

targeted incentive, 148

team-based merit pay, 155

wage, 115

Web Links

To get a taste of current issues in benefits management, check the websites of three publications: *Benefits Canada* at **www.benefitscanada.com**, *Benefits and Pensions Monitor* at **www.bpmmagazine.com**, and the *Canadian Human Resources Reporter* at **www.hrreporter.com/home**. (p. 121)

For more information on profit sharing, check the website of the Profit Sharing Council of America, based in Chicago: **http://www.psca.org**. (p. 125)

For Canadian information on employee stock plans, go to the ESOP Association of Canada web site, based in Toronto: **http://www.esop-canada. com**. (p. 157)

RPC Icons

RPC 4.1 Considering the total compensation strategy, develops a compensation program with respect to base pay, variable pay, profit and gain sharing, incentive pay, and stock options, and recommends the best mix.

Discussion Questions

1. Discuss why it is not always desirable or even possible to use output-based pay.

2. Discuss why organizations would ever want to use indirect pay.
3. Discuss why organizations might prefer job evaluation to market pricing.
4. Pay for knowledge appears to work very well at Basell Canada (described in Compensation Today 4.3). Why does it work so well there?
5. Discuss the different circumstances that would fit each of the following: individual performance pay, group performance pay, and organizational performance pay.

Using the Internet

Implemented for the right reasons, an employee stock plan can be an effective organizational pay plan. Using the ESOP Association of Canada website (**http://www.esop-canada.com**), explain the four main motives for implementing employee stock ownership plans in Canada.

Exercises

1. Form small groups of four to six people. Each group member will contact one local retailer and find out about its pay system for its sales staff. Compare the systems and discuss whether any of these systems are linked to the type of product sold and the type of sales activity. Do they fit with the advice offered in this chapter? Do they fit with the firm's managerial strategy, as far as you can determine? Get together with other groups and share your conclusions.
2. In a small group, discuss how important benefits will be to you in choosing your next job. Then everyone should identify the three benefits that are of most importance to them. Do these vary across individuals in your group? If so, discuss why.
3. Three firms are briefly described below. For each firm, identify the role (if any) that you believe indirect pay should play in the compensation system, and give examples of specific benefits to offer. Explain your choices.
   a) A company offers lawn maintenance and yard clean-up services in the summer and snow removal services in the winter. It employs about 600 people at peak season (in the summer) and has branches in major cities across the prairies.
   b) A retail clothing chain offers personalized service and caters to upscale customers. It is located in major cities across Canada and employs approximately 600 sales staff.
   c) A computer software firm develops customized software for specialized applications for individual clients. Located near Ottawa, it employs about 1000 people.

Case Questions

1. Analyze the "Fit Stop Ltd." case in the Appendix and determine whether base pay should be an important component of compensation for the sales staff. If so, identify the most appropriate method for determining base pay for their sales staff. What factors did you consider in making these decisions?
2. Analyze the "Multi-Products Corporation" case in the Appendix and determine what would be the most appropriate method for determining base pay. What factors led you to the choice you made?
3. Do you think that the Fit Stop in the Appendix would be a suitable organization in which to implement an organization performance pay plan? Explain why or why not. If the Fit Stop is suitable, what type of organization performance plan would be most appropriate? Describe the key elements of this plan, as applied to the Fit Stop.
4. Analyze the pay system at Alliston Instruments in the Appendix. Why is the new pay system apparently not working? Do you think that the individual production bonus system could work if some changes were made? What changes? Is individual performance pay suitable to this company? If management insists on some type of individual performance pay system, what type would you recommend?
5. Suppose that management at Alliston Instruments in the Appendix has decided to scrap the current individual performance pay system. However, they have not decided what, if anything, will replace it and have called you in to advise them. They want you to examine the group and organization performance plans available and recommend the one that fits best with Alliston and the problems they are facing. In preparing your report, be sure to include the pros and cons of each approach and reasons why your recommended approach is the best.

Simulation Cross-Reference

If you are using *Strategic Compensation: A Simulation* in conjunction with this text, you will find that the concepts in Chapter 4 are helpful in preparing Sections C, D, and E of the simulation.

Endnotes

1. Humber, Todd. 2004. "RBC Organizes Pay, Benefits, Training, Work Environment, into a Single Package". *Canadian HR Reporter*, February 23: G1, G13.
2. Mitchell, Daniel J.B., David Lewin, and Edward E. Lawler. 1990. "Alternative Pay Systems, Firm Performance, and Productivity." In Alan S. Blinder, ed., *Paying for Productivity: A Look at the Evidence*. Washington, DC: The Brookings Institution, 15–87.
3. Gerhart, Barry, and Charlie O. Trevor. 1996. "Employment Variability under Different Managerial Compensation Systems." *Academy of Management Journal*, 39(6): 1692–1712.

4. Mitchell, Daniel J.B., David Lewin, and Edward E. Lawler. 1990. "Alternative Pay Systems, Firm Performance, and Productivity." In Alan S. Blinder, ed., *Paying for Productivity: A Look at the Evidence*. Washington, DC: The Brookings Institution, 15–87.

5. Baarda, Carolyn. 2000. *Compensation Planning Outlook 2001*. Ottawa: Conference Board of Canada.

6. Renaud, Stephane. 1998. Unions, Wages, and Total Compensation in Canada. *Relations Industrielles/Industrial Relations*, 53(4): 710–29.

7. Gerhart, Barry, and George T. Milkovich. 1992. "Employee Compensation: Research and Practice." In M.D. Dunnette and L.M. Hough, eds., *Handbook of Industrial and Organizational Psychology*. Palo Alto, CA: Consulting Psychologists Press, 484–569.

8 Judge, Timothy A. 1993. "Validity of the Dimensions of the Pay Satisfaction Questionnaire: Evidence of Differential Prediction." *Personnel Psychology*, 46: 331–55.

9. McKay, Robert J. 1996. *Canadian Handbook of Flexible Benefits*. New York: John Wiley and Sons.

10. Carlyle, Nathalie B. 1996. *Compensation Planning Outlook 1997*. Ottawa: Conference Board of Canada.

11. Baarda, Carolyn. 2000. *Compensation Planning Outlook 2001*. Ottawa: Conference Board of Canada.

12. Brown, David. 2005. "Benefits Providers Strive to Meet Clients' Wellness Needs." *Canadian HR Reporter*, 18(6): 6–7.

13. Rynes, Sara L., and George T. Milkovich. 1986. "Wage Surveys: Dispelling Some Myths about the Market Wage." *Personnel Psychology*, 39(1): 71–90.

14. Gomez-Mejia, Luis, and David Balkin. 1992. *Compensation, Organizational Strategy, and Firm Performance*. Cincinnati, OH: South-Western.

15. Foster, K.E. 1985. "An Anatomy of Company Pay Policies." *Personnel*, September, 66–72.

16. Lawler, Edward E., Susan A. Mohrman, and Gerald E. Ledford. 1995. *Creating High Performance Organizations*. San Francisco: Jossey-Bass.

17. Sibson, Robert E. 1990. *Compensation*. New York: American Management Association: 115.

18. Weiner, Nan J. 1991. "Job Evaluation Systems: A Critique." *Human Resource Management Review*, 1(2): 119–32.

19. Gupta, Nina, and G. Douglas Jenkins. 1991. "Practical Problems in Using Job Evaluation Systems to Determine Compensation." *Human Resource Management Review*, 1(2): 133–44.

20. Ledford, Gerald E. 1995. "Designing Nimble Reward Systems." *Compensation and Benefits Review*, 27(4): 46–54.

21. Milkovich, George T., and Jerry N. Newman. 1996. *Compensation*. Chicago: Richard D. Irwin.

22. Ledford, Gerald E. 1995. "Designing Nimble Reward Systems." *Compensation and Benefits Review*, 27(4): 46–54.

23. Cheraskin, Lisa, and Michael A. Campion. 1996. "Study Clarifies Job-Rotation Benefits." *Personnel Journal*, 75(11): 31–38.

24. Lawler, Edward E. 1990. Strategic Pay: Aligning Organizational Strategies and Pay Systems. San Francisco: Jossey-Bass: 161.

25. Schuster, Jay R., and Patricia K. Zingheim. 1992. *The New Pay: Linking Employee and Organizational Performance*. New York: Lexington Books: 108.

26. Ledford, Gerald. 1991. "The Design of Skill Based Pay Plans." In Milton L. Rock and Lance A. Berger, *The Compensation Handbook*. New York: McGraw-Hill, 199–217.

27. Milkovich, George T., and Jerry N. Newman. 1996. *Compensation*. Chicago: Richard D. Irwin: 193.

28. Barrett, Gerald. 1991. "Comparison of Skill-Based Pay with Traditional Job Evaluation Techniques." *Human Resource Management Review*, 1(2): 97–105.

29. Long, Richard J. 1993. "The Relative Effects of New Information Technology and Employee Involvement on Productivity in Canadian Companies." *Proceedings of the Administrative Sciences Association of Canada (Organizational Theory Division)*.

30. Wallace, Marc J. 1991. "Sustaining Success with Alternative Rewards." In Milton L. Rock and Lance A. Berger, *The Compensation Handbook*. New York: McGraw-Hill, 147–57.

31. Mericle, Kenneth, and Dong-One Kim. 1999. "From Job-Based Pay to Skill-Based Pay in Unionized Establishments: A Three Plant Comparative Analysis." *Relations industrielles/Industrial Relations*, 54(3): 549–80.

32. See Long, Richard J. 1989. "Patterns of Workplace Innovation in Canada." *Relations industrielles/Industrial Relations*, 44(4): 805–26. See also Wallace, Marc J. 1991. "Sustaining Success with Alternative Rewards." In Milton L. Rock and Lance A. Berger, *The Compensation Handbook*. New York: McGraw-Hill, 147–57. See also Long, Richard J. 1993. "The Relative Effects of New Information Technology and Employee Involvement on Productivity in Canadian Companies." *Proceedings of the Administrative Sciences Association of Canada (Organizational Theory Division)*. See also Jenkins, G. Douglas, Gerald E. Ledford, Nina Gupta, and D. Harold Doty. 1993. *Skill-Based Pay: Practices, Payoffs, Pitfalls and Prescriptions*. Scottsdale, AZ: American Compensation Association. See also Parent, Kevin J., and Caroline L. Weber. 1994. "Does Paying for Knowledge Pay Off?" *Compensation and Benefits Review*, 26(5): 44–50. See also Murray, Brian, and Barry Gerhart. 1998. "An Empirical Analysis of a Skill-Based Pay Program and Plant Performance Outcomes." *The Academy of Management Journal*, 41(1): 68–78.

33. Peck, Charles. 1993. *Variable Pay: Nontraditional Programs for Motivation and Reward*. New York: The Conference Board.

34. Harrison, David A., Meghna Virick, and Sonja William. 1996. "Working without a Net: Time, Performance, and Turnover under Maximally Contingent Rewards." *Journal of Applied Psychology*, 81(4): 331–45.

35. Keenan, William. 1994. "Beyond the Basics." In William Keenan, *Commissions, Bonuses, and Beyond*. Chicago: Irwin, xv–xviii.

36. Sagar, Ira. 1994. "IBM Leans on Its Sales Force." *Business Week*, February 7: 110.

37. Coletti, Jerome A., and David J. Chicelli. 1991. "Increasing Sales Force Effectiveness through the Compensation Plan." In Milton L. Rock and Lance A. Berger, eds., *The Compensation Handbook*. New York: McGraw-Hill, 290–306.

38. Tremblay, Michel, Jerome Cote, and David Balkin. 1997. "Explaining Sales Compensation Strategy Using Agency, Transaction Cost Analysis and Institutional Theories." Paper presented at the Academy of Management Annual Meetings, Boston.

39. Heneman, Robert L. 1990. "Merit Pay Research." *Research in Personnel and Human Resources Management*, 8: 203–63.

40. Kerr, Steven. 1995. "On the Folly of Rewarding A, While Hoping for B." *Academy of Management Executive*, 9(1): 7–14.

41. Heneman, Robert L. 1992. *Merit Pay: Linking Pay Increases to Performance Ratings*. Reading, MA: Addison-Wesley.

42. Lawler, Edward E. 2000. *Rewarding Excellence: Pay Strategies for the New Economy*. San Francisco: Jossey-Bass.

43. Bartol, Kathryn M., and Edwin A. Locke. 2000. "Incentives and Motivation." In Sara L. Rynes and Barry Gerhart, eds., *Compensation in Organizations: Current Research and Practice*. San Francisco: Jossey-Bass, 104–50.

44. Graham-Moore, Brian, and Timothy L. Ross. 1995. *Gainsharing and Employee Involvement*. Washington, DC: BNA Books.

45. Long, Richard J. 1994. "Gain Sharing, Hierarchy, and Managers: Are They Substitutes?" *Proceedings of the Administrative Sciences Association of Canada (Organization Theory Division)*, 15(12): 51–60.

46. See Olson, M. 1971. *The Logic of Collective Action*. Cambridge, MA: Harvard University Press. See also Jensen, M., and W. Meckling. 1973. "Theory of the Firm: Managerial Behavior, Agency Costs and Ownership Structure." *Financial Economics*, 3: 305–60.

47. Long, Richard J. 1989. "Patterns of Workplace Innovation in Canada." *Relations industrielles/Industrial Relations*, 44(4): 805–26.

48. Kim, Dong-One. 1999. "Determinants of the Survival of Gainsharing Programs." *Industrial and Labor Relations Review*, 53(1): 21–42.

49. Markham, Steven E., K. Dow Scott, and Beverly L. Little. 1992. "National Gain Sharing Study: The Importance of Industry Differences." *Compensation and Benefits Review* (August): 36–40.

50. See GAO. 1981. *Productivity Sharing Programs: Can They Contribute to Productivity Improvement?* Washington, DC: United States General Accounting Office. See also Schuster, Michael. 1984. "The Scanlon Plan: A Longitudinal Analysis." *Journal of Applied Behavioural Science*, 20(1): 23–38. See also Schuster, Michael. 1985. "Models of Cooperation and Change in Union Settings." *Industrial Relations*, 24: 382–94. See also Wallace, M. 1990. *Rewards and Renewal: America's Search for Competitive Advantage through Alternative Pay Strategies.* Scottsdale, AZ: American Compensation Association. See also Bowie-McCoy, Susan W., Ann C. Wendt, and Roger Chope. 1993. "Gain Sharing in Public Accounting: Working Smarter and Harder." *Industrial Relations*, 32(3): 432–45.

51. Kim, Dong-One. 1996. "Factors Influencing Organizational Performance in Gainsharing Programs." *Industrial Relations*, 35(2): 227–44.

52. Cooke, William N. 1994. "Employee Participation Programs, Group-Based Incentives, and Company Performance: A Union-Nonunion Comparison." *Industrial and Labor Relations Review*, 47(3): 594–609.

53. Belcher, John G. 1996. *How to Design and Implement a Results Oriented Variable Pay System.* New York: American Management Association.

54. Belcher, John G. 1996. *How to Design and Implement a Results Oriented Variable Pay System.* New York: American Management Association.

55. Heneman, Robert L., and Courtney von Hippel. 1995. "Balancing Group and Individual Rewards: Rewarding Individual Contributions to the Team." *Compensation and Benefits Review*, 27(4): 63–68.

56. Stayer, Ralph. 1990. "How I Learned to Let My Workers Lead." *Harvard Business Review*, 68(6): 65–72.

57. Long, Richard J. 1992. "The Incidence and Nature of Employee Profit Sharing and Share Ownership in Canada." *Relations industrielles/Industrial Relations*, 47(3): 463–88.

58. Tyson, David E. 1996. *Profit Sharing in Canada: The Complete Guide to Designing and Implementing Plans That Really Work.* Toronto: John Wiley and Sons.

59. Long, Richard J. 1997. "Motives for Profit Sharing: A Study of Canadian Chief Executive Officers," *Relations industrielles/Industrial Relations*, 52(4): 712–33.

60. Weitzman, Martin L. 1984. *The Share Economy.* Cambridge, MA: Harvard University Press.

61. Long, Richard J. 1997. "Motives for Profit Sharing: A Study of Canadian Chief Executive Officers," *Relations industrielles/Industrial Relations*, 52(4): 712–33.

62. See Long, Richard J. 1989. "Patterns of Workplace Innovation in Canada." *Relations industrielles/ Industrial Relations*, 44(4): 805–26. See also Betcherman, Gordon, Norm Leckie, and Anil Verma. 1994. "HRM Innovations in Canada: Evidence from Establishment Surveys." Working Paper Series QPIR 1994-3. Kingston: Industrial Relations Centre, Queen's University. See also Wagar, Terry H., and Richard J. Long. 1995. "Profit Sharing in Canada: Incidence and Predictors." *Proceedings of the Administrative Sciences Association of Canada (Human Resources Division)*, 16(9): 97–105. See also Long, Richard J. 2002. "Performance Pay in Canada." In Michelle Brown and John S. Heywood, eds., *Paying for Performance: An International Comparison*. Armonk, NY: M.E. Sharpe.

63. Kruse, Douglas L. 1993. *Profit Sharing: Does It Make a Difference?* Kalamazoo, MI: W.E. Upjohn Institute.

64. Doucouliagos, C. 1995. "Worker Participation and Productivity in Labour-Managed and Participatory Capitalist Firms: A Meta-Analysis." *Industrial and Labor Relations Review*, 49(1): 58–77.

65. Magnan, Michel, Sylvie St-Onge, and Marie-Pierre Lalande. 1997. "The Impact of Profit Sharing Plans on Firm Performance: An Empirical Investigation." *Proceedings of the Administrative Sciences Association of Canada (Human Resources Division)*, 18(9): 106–17.

66. See Chelius, James, and Robert S. Smith. 1990. "Profit Sharing and Employment Stability," *Industrial and Labor Relations Review*, 43(3): 256–74. See also Gerhart, Barry, and Charlie O. Trevor. 1996. "Employment Variability under Different Managerial Compensation Systems." *Academy of Management Journal*, 39(6): 1692–1712.

67. Wagar, Terry H., and Richard J. Long. 1995. "Profit Sharing in Canada: Incidence and Predictors." *Proceedings of the Administrative Sciences Association of Canada (Human Resources Division)*, 16(9): 97–105. See also Long, Richard J. 1997. "Motives for Profit Sharing: A Study of Canadian Chief Executive Officers," *Relations industrielles/Industrial Relations*, 52(4): 712–33. See also Long, Richard J. 2002. "Performance Pay in Canada." In Michelle Brown and John S. Heywood, eds., *Paying for Performance: An International Comparison*. Armonk, NY: M.E. Sharpe.

68. Kim, Seongsu. 1998. "Does Profit Sharing Increase Firms' Profits?" *Journal of Labor Research*, 19(2): 351–70.

69. Tyson, David E. 1996. *Profit Sharing in Canada: The Complete Guide to Designing and Implementing Plans That Really Work*. Toronto: John Wiley and Sons.

70. Tyson, David E. 1996. *Profit Sharing in Canada: The Complete Guide to Designing and Implementing Plans That Really Work*. Toronto: John Wiley and Sons.

71. Kruse, Douglas L. 1993. *Profit Sharing: Does It Make a Difference?* Kalamazoo, MI: W.E. Upjohn Institute.

72. *Economist, The.* 2000. "Chief Executives' Pay." September 30: 110.

73. Reingold, Jennifer. 1997. "Executive Pay: Special Report." *Business Week*, April 21.

74. Byrne, John A. 1995. "Why Executive Compensation Continues to Increase." In Thomas Hall, ed., *Compensation: Present Practices and Future Concerns*. New York: The Conference Board, 19–20.

75. Doucouliagos, C. 1995. "Worker Participation and Productivity in Labour-Managed and Participatory Capitalist Firms: A Meta-Analysis." *Industrial and Labor Relations Review*, 49(1): 58–77. Or see Blasi, Joseph, Douglas Kruse, James Sesil, and Maya Kroumova. 2000. "Broad Based Stock Options and Company Performance." *The Journal of Employee Ownership Law and Finance*, 12(3): 69–102.

76. Rosen, Corey, and Michael Quarrey. 1987. "How Well Is Employee Ownership Working?" *Harvard Business Review*, 65: 126–30.

77. Logue, John, and Cassandra Rogers. 1989. *Employee Stock Ownership Plans in Ohio: Impact on Company Performance and Employment.* Kent, OH: Northeast Ohio Employee Ownership Center. See also Kardas, P.A., K. Gale, R. Marens, P. Sommers, and G. Winther. 1994. "Employment and Sales Growth in Washington State Employee Owner-ship Companies: A Comparative Analysis." *The Journal of Employee Ownership Law and Finance*, 6(2): 83–131.

78. Kardas, P.A., A.L. Scharf, and J. Keogh. 1998. "Wealth and Income Consequences of Employee Ownership: A Comparative Study from Washington State." *The Journal of Employee Ownership Law and Finance*, 10(4): 3–52.

79. Blasi, Joseph, Douglas Kruse, James Sesil, and Maya Kroumova. 2000. "Broad Based Stock Options and Company Performance." *The Journal of Employee Ownership Law and Finance*, 12(3): 69–102.

80. Lawler, Edward E. 1992. *The Ultimate Advantage: Creating the High Involvement Organization*. San Francisco: Jossey-Bass.

81. Peck, Charles. 1995. *Long-Term Unit/Share Programs*. New York: The Conference Board.

82. *Star-Phoenix*. 1996. "Keep Your Pants On! Levi Offers Huge Employee Bonus." Saskatoon, June 13: C11.

83. Schoenberger, Karl. 2000. "Levi Strauss Stitches Together Turnaround Plan." *The Globe and Mail*, July 4: B11.

Chapter 5

Formulating the Reward and Compensation Strategy

Chapter Learning Objectives

After reading this chapter, you should be able to:

- Identify the four key understandings necessary for formulating compensation strategy.
- Describe the constraints that limit the design of a compensation strategy.
- Explain the compensation strategy formulation process and describe each step.
- Discuss the considerations in deciding whether to adopt a lead, lag, or match compensation-level policy.
- Describe utility analysis and explain how it can be used.
- Apply the compensation strategy formulation process to specific organizations.
- Explain how to evaluate a compensation strategy prior to implementation.
- Discuss the special issues involved in compensating contingent workers, new employees, executives, and international employees.

[handwritten annotations: CPCC; labour market, legislation, products + services; — Behaviours, Role, Mix, level, Evaluate; — which level is right; BAFFLE PC]

FORMULATING COMPENSATION STRATEGY AT WINDSOR FACTORY SUPPLY

Picture the following scenario for establishing a compensation strategy: All employees of the firm attend a one-day meeting on compensation each year. Attendance is compulsory. During this meeting, the staff carefully studies the firm's financial results. Then, employees vote on how much of the net profits for the year should go to shareholders, how much should go for employee bonuses, and how much should be allocated to retained earnings. The group decides what salaries and benefits will be provided for the coming year, and whether there will be any change to the compensation strategy. Evaluation committees, elected earlier in the year, provide input on individual employee performance; and each department decides the amount of bonus each employee will receive for the year just completed and how much of a raise each will receive for the coming year.

Sounds ridiculous? How could employees be trusted to make responsible decisions? Surely no firm could survive long with a system like that! Well, tell that to Windsor Factory Supply, a highly successful company in Windsor, Ontario, that uses precisely this system. It works for them; but it wouldn't work for every firm.

So why does employee determination of the compensation strategy work at Windsor Factory Supply? The answer lies in the nature of the firm itself.

Windsor Factory Supply is an industrial wholesaler of a wide variety of parts associated with the automobile industry and does about $90 million worth of business annually (up from $30 million five years ago). The firm is completely owned by its 135 employees, who completed the purchase of the firm from the original owners in 1995. The firm has no job titles and no formal hierarchy. The board of directors is elected by employee-owners each year. All employees have access to all company information, and key performance indicators come up on everyone's computer screen every morning. Employees have a wide degree of latitude in how they do their jobs, although they must be accountable for results. The firm pays higher salaries than its competitors, but it is still more profitable, due to high employee motivation and commitment.

In this high-involvement firm, employee participation in all aspects of the business, including compensation policy, is a given. Employees are committed to organizational goals, they understand the organizational context and the kind of behaviour that is required, and they certainly understand employee needs. Mix in some employees who understand the compensation options and legal constraints facing the firm, and all the ingredients for good compensation decision-making are in place.

Introduction

Of course, a more conventional approach is that the CEO sits in his or her office, looks over the financial results, and simply decides what the compensation strategy will be for the coming year; and this may be a viable approach for some organizations. But no matter who develops the compensation strategy, they must possess an understanding of the organization, the nature of the employees, the compensation options available to them, and the constraints facing the organization.

As you will recall from Chapter 1, the *reward strategy* is the plan for the mix of rewards that the organization intends to provide to its members—along with the means through which they will be provided—in order to elicit the behaviours necessary for organization success. The *compensation strategy* is one part of the reward strategy and consists of two main aspects: the *mix* of base pay, performance pay, and indirect pay to be used, and the *total amount or level* of compensation to be provided to employees. In other words, the two key questions for compensation strategy are *"How* is compensation to be paid?" and "How *much* compensation is to be paid?"

The Compensation Strategy Formulation Process

To answer these questions effectively is not a simple process. First, we need to define the employee behaviours necessary for organizational success and identify the characteristics and qualifications of people who will be able to perform these behaviours. Second, within the total organizational system that the firm creates to generate these behaviours, we need to define the specific role that the reward and compensation system will play in so doing. Third, we need to determine the most appropriate mix across the three compensation components. Fourth, we need to develop policies for establishing the total amount of compensation that employees will receive. Fifth, we need to conduct a pre-implementation evaluation of the proposed strategy to verify that it meets our criteria for success. This process is illustrated in Figure 5.1.

Four Key Understandings

To successfully carry out this process, four key understandings are essential. The first four chapters of this book were devoted to developing three of these understandings; the fourth will be covered here.

1. Understand Your Organizational Context

To understand what behaviours are needed and how the reward system can best support corporate and managerial strategies, you need to understand the organizational context in which the reward system will be applied. Chapter 2 provides a strategic framework for this understanding.

2. Understand Your People

To understand how behaviour can best be motivated, and the role that rewards and compensation can play in so doing, you must understand the

FIGURE 5.1

The Compensation Strategy Formulation Process

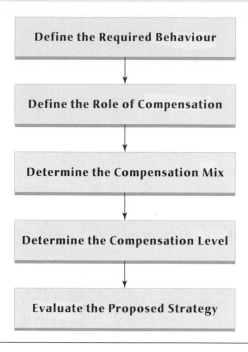

factors that drive human behaviour, as well as the specific needs and characteristics of the people who will be performing the required behaviour. Chapter 3 provides a behavioural framework as a basis for this understanding.

3. Understand Your Compensation Options

To develop an efficient compensation system that generates the required behaviour, you need to understand the compensation options available. Chapter 4 provides this information, describing the role that base, performance, and indirect pay play in shaping behaviour.

4. Understand Your Compensation Constraints

Even if you have successfully mastered the first three understandings, one remains: organizational constraints. Employers cannot simply do whatever they want when deciding compensation. There are in fact a number of constraints that define the parameters or boundaries within which the compensation system must be designed. These constraints are of four main kinds: legal/legislated constraints, labour market constraints, product/service market constraints, and financial constraints. It is essential to understand these constraints before formulating the compensation strategy. The first part of this chapter provides a foundation for understanding these constraints.

Constraints on Compensation

Remember the Screaming Tale Restaurant from Chapter 1 (Compensation Today 1.2)? The owners of this Ontario restaurant had the wonderful idea of cutting labour costs by not paying their employees. The firm claimed it had no employees, just "volunteer workers" or "commission agents" working only for the "tips" that customers provided, thus relieving the firm of the need to pay at least minimum wages or any of the mandatory benefits. But guess what? It turned out that this arrangement was illegal, and the restaurant closed just as it was being investigated for violations of the Ontario Employment Standards Act.

As the Screaming Tale case illustrates, employers cannot simply do whatever they want in regard to compensation, even if they can find employees willing to accept the compensation arrangements. In this case, the employer ran afoul of legislated constraints, specifically minimum wage laws.

Legislated Constraints

In Canada, jurisdiction for labour market legislation is split between the federal government and the provinces. The federal government is empowered to pass labour legislation covering all federal employees (including those in federal Crown corporations) and workers in a number of specified industries, including transportation, communications, defence, uranium mining, and firms engaged in interprovincial or international trade. In addition to employees of the federal government and its agencies, federal labour law covers about 10 percent of private-sector employees. All other employees are covered under provincial legislation.

There are four main types of legislation affecting compensation systems. First, every province has an Employment Standards Act, which defines minimum standards for wages, hours of work, vacation, statutory holiday and leave entitlement, termination benefits, and minimum age levels for employment. (The equivalent federal legislation is known as "The Canada Labour Code.") Second, all jurisdictions have human rights acts, which prohibit employment discrimination based on factors such as gender, race, or age. As an offshoot of this, some jurisdictions also have specific pay equity legislation, aimed at redressing past pay inequities experienced by female employees.

Third, all jurisdictions have legislation relating to unionization and collective bargaining. This legislation affects compensation in unionized firms by requiring that all compensation arrangements be approved by the union. It also has an indirect effect on compensation, as some non-union firms match settlements achieved at unionized competitors in order to reduce the incentive for unionization. Finally, all jurisdictions have income and corporate tax laws, which can have a major influence on the type of compensation offered.

Employment Standards Legislation

Employment standards legislation stipulates the minimum standards for pay and other conditions of employment by which every employer must abide. These standards relate to such matters as paid time off, maximum hours of

employment standards legislation

legislation that sets minimum standards for pay and other conditions of employment

work before overtime pay provisions take effect, minimum levels of overtime pay, and minimum wage levels. Currently, the minimum hourly rate that must be paid ranges from $6.40 in New Brunswick to $7.75 in Ontario. (For up-to-date information on employment standards, click on **http://www.hrsdc. gc.ca/asp/gateway.asp?hr=en/lp/spila/clli/eslc/01Employment_Standards_ Legislation_in_Canada.shtml&hs=lxn.**)

Although minimum wage legislation applies to most workers, there are some exceptions. Some jurisdictions exclude domestic servants, in-home babysitters, some types of farm labourers, and students in training programs; and in some jurisdictions, minimum wage rates are somewhat lower for certain classes of workers (i.e. students under 18 years of age in Ontario working less than 28 hours a week) and are somewhat higher for other classes (i.e., for employees who work from their homes in Ontario). Employers do not have to pay minimum wages (or other mandatory benefits) to persons who are classified as contractors or agents, since they are exempted from employment standards legislation.

So a key question is: What constitutes a contractor? One labour standards expert offers this definition:

> An independent contractor differs from an employee in that the contractor sets the hours of work, maintains control over work done, provides own equipment and tools, and is subject to minimal company supervision. An important additional distinction is that an independent contractor has the ability to perform work for other employers, as long as this does not compromise any existing contractual agreement.[1]

By this standard, "volunteer workers" at the Screaming Tale Restaurant clearly have to be classified as employees, rather than as commission agents. Moreover, although restaurant employees must declare gratuities for income tax purposes, gratuities do not count toward employee earnings to help satisfy minimum wage requirements. Thus, employers must always pay employees the minimum wage, regardless of any gratuities that employees may receive.

So where does this leave employees who are paid only on commissions or piece rates? For example, what happens if sales personnel who are compensated only by commission—such as automobile salespeople—achieve very few or no sales in a given period? The procedure to check if minimum wage is being paid is to take the total amount earned by an employee during a workweek, then divide that by the number of hours worked. If that amount comes out to less than the minimum wage, then the employer is required to pay the difference to the employee.

Another important issue covered by employment standards legislation is overtime pay rates. Employment standards legislation normally requires higher rates of pay (normally 1.5 times normal earnings) for hours worked in excess of stipulated limits—generally eight hours per day, and 40–48 hours per week, depending on the jurisdiction. However, there are many exemptions from this part of employment standards legislation, such as professionals, supervisors, managers, students, and farm labourers, although commission salespeople and piece-rate workers are covered.

Rather than hiring new employees, many firms use overtime when additional production is needed. This avoids the cost of hiring new employees and prevents the problem of layoffs if the amount of available work declines. However, employees cannot be forced to work overtime, nor can any employee who is covered by the Employment Standards Act waive the right to receive overtime pay. Employers are also not allowed to adjust the pay rates for non-overtime hours downwards to be in technical compliance with the overtime rules. However, some employers do attempt to limit application of overtime rules by classifying their employees as professional or managerial. One rule of thumb commonly used is that hourly-paid employees are covered by the overtime provisions, while salaried employees are not.

Another important provision included in employment standards or equivalent legislation—employee layoff and severance—is discussed in Chapter 11, along with other aspects of legislation that affect indirect pay.

Human Rights Legislation

Even if employers comply with employment standards legislation, they are still not free to pay each employee what they want. Every Canadian jurisdiction has passed legislation prohibiting discrimination in hiring and employment on the basis of race, ethnic origin, religion, gender, marital status, or age (within specified age ranges—normally 18 to 65 years of age). Some jurisdictions include sexual orientation in this list as well.

To prove compliance with human rights legislation, employers must be able to demonstrate that differences of pay between employees are related only to factors such as job duties, experience, qualifications, seniority, or performance. For example, if a member of one racial group is paid significantly less than another employee with similar job duties, the employer must be able to prove that this difference is due to one or more of the factors described above.

All jurisdictions in Canada have some form of equal pay legislation aimed at dealing with the issue of wage inequality between male and female employees. This legislation prohibits employers from paying male and female employees differently if they do "identical, similar or substantially similar work." The federal legislation—The Canadian Human Rights Act—goes one step further and stipulates that male and female employees must receive equal pay for work of *equal value*, even if the work is not substantially similar. (The Canadian Human Rights Act is administered by the Canadian Human Rights Commission. Go to **http://www.chrc-ccdp.ca/default-en.asp?lang_update=1** to see their website.)

Numerous provinces have enacted pay equity legislation specifically intended to redress gender pay inequities, although in some of these provinces (Manitoba, New Brunswick, Nova Scotia, and Prince Edward Island), the legislation applies only to governmental bodies and their agencies. Ontario and Quebec have enacted pay equity legislation that applies to all employers with 10 or more employees. In essence, pay equity schemes require the employer to divide the workforce into job classes designated either as male or female. (A job class is designated male or female if at least

human rights legislation
legislation that prohibits discrimination in hiring or employment on the basis of race, ethnic origin, religion, gender, marital status, or age

60 or 70 percent [varying by jurisdiction] of the occupants of that job class are male or female.) After that, a gender-neutral job evaluation system is applied to each job class.

If a female-dominated job class that is evaluated equally to a male-dominated job class has lower compensation than the male class, the imbalance must be redressed. Although it is theoretically possible to redress this imbalance by reducing wages in the male-dominated classes, this practice is prohibited. As Compensation Today 5.1 indicates, employers have substantial limitations on how they attempt to deal with the imbalance, once it is formally identified. (Compliance with pay equity legislation will be covered in more depth in Chapter 6.)

trade union legislation

legislation that defines the rights of parties involved in a collective bargaining relationship

Trade Union Legislation

If a group of company employees is represented by a union, any changes to pay, hours of work, and working conditions are mandatory subjects of negotiation. In other words, employers cannot make changes to these matters unless these changes have been agreed to by the union representing these workers. Employers also cannot make separate compensation arrangements with individual members of the bargaining unit. The practical result is that a unionized firm that wants to change its compensation system must first convince the union to accept these changes. This can be a long process and, in many cases, can rule out certain types of pay practices, such as profit sharing, that unions have traditionally opposed. (For more detail on legislation surrounding collective bargaining, go to **http://www.hrsdc.gc.ca/asp/gateway.asp?hr=en/ lp/spila/clli/irlc/01industrial_relations_legislation_canada.shtml&hs=czc**.)

Studies have shown that unions have a significant impact on both the structure and level of employee compensation.[2] In general, unionized employees are more likely to work under a seniority- rather than performance-based pay system. They also tend to receive a more extensive array of employee benefits and to enjoy wages about 10 percent higher than those of comparable non-union employees, although this varies greatly across industries.

Tax Legislation

The final way that legislation can influence the pay system is through income and corporate tax legislation, which encourages certain pay approaches and discourages others. For example, over the years, tax legislation has played a significant role in the movement away from direct pay (which is fully taxed) and toward indirect pay (which often is not). However, this role may have diminished in recent years, as employee benefits have increasingly become subject to income tax. On the other hand, recent changes to tax legislation are likely to encourage use of stock options (as will be discussed in Chapter 10).

As a final note, changing a worker's status from "employee" to "independent contractor" can have some significant income tax benefits. As an employee, an individual can apply very few tax deductions against income. But an independent contractor has many more possible deductions. For example, if employees use a portion of their home for an office, there is no tax deduction; but if independent contractors do the same, the contractor can deduct all costs related to that space. Employees cannot deduct the cost of transportation to and from work; but independent contractors can deduct automobile expenses for any work-related travel. Thus, "independent contractor" relationships may be attractive to some employees.

Labour Market Constraints

Another key constraint on compensation decisions is the labour market. The labour market is simply the available pool of labour from which employers choose their employees. Labour markets are normally segmented by occupational type and geographical area. In a given geographical area, both supply of and demand for a particular type of labour may be high or low. Each combination of supply/demand factors creates a unique situation for employers. For example, when demand is high but supply is low, the labour market is considered *tight*, which means it is difficult to attract qualified employees without raising compensation levels. Of course, when demand is low and supply is high, the labour market is considered *loose*, making it much easier to attract employees at compensation levels favourable to the employer.

Labour markets vary by region; thus, firms that operate on a national level must decide whether to adjust compensation based on the local labour market or to keep standard compensation across the country. For example, a bank may determine pay for customer service representatives based on the market rate for these employees in Toronto, where the firm's head office is located. But in many local labour markets, such as a small town in Nova Scotia, attracting the necessary employees may be possible for much less than what is being offered to Toronto employees. Should the bank therefore pay lower rates to its Nova Scotia employees than its Ontario employees? Is this fair? Is it worth the trouble? This is one of the questions that needs to be resolved when setting compensation level policy.

As discussed in Chapter 4, the issue of identifying "market pay" is more complex than it sounds. But the labour market poses a real constraint for firms, since a compensation system that is too far below market will not attract the necessary employees; and one that is too far above market will

labour market constraints
constraints on compensation strategy flowing from the relative levels of demand and supply for particular occupational groups

unduly increase costs. Paying above market is particularly a problem when product/service markets are highly competitive.

Product/Service Market Constraints

product/service market constraints

constraints on compensation strategy caused by the nature of the product or service market in which the firm operates

Another key constraint for organizations is the nature of the market for their products or services. Is demand low and supply high? If so, this results in a highly competitive business environment; and firms that pay more for their labour than competitors may be at a serious competitive disadvantage unless they are also more productive.

These competitive constraints are especially severe in industries that are highly labour-intensive, since labour costs constitute a higher proportion of total costs in these firms. These constraints are even more severe if competitors are able to move their production to labour markets where the cost of labour is much lower, or where legislated constraints, such as minimum wage laws or mandatory benefits, are less onerous. In contrast, firms in markets where demand for their product is high, supply is low, and competitors are few have much more latitude in designing their compensation systems.

Another aspect of the product/service market affecting compensation is its volatility. Firms that experience severe swings in demand for their product/service need to be able to adjust their organizational systems to deal with this fluctuation. Some firms react by using a high proportion of contingent workers, who are subject to different compensation constraints than core employees; while others react by including more variable pay in their compensation systems.

Financial Constraints of the Organization

Regardless of conditions in their labour or product/service markets, many organizations have specific financial constraints affecting their compensation system. In the private sector, the financial performance of the organization is usually the cause of these financial restraints: unprofitable firms are much more limited in their compensation options than profitable firms. The company's stage of growth can also create constraints: new firms or fast-growing firms often have a shortage of cash.

For public-sector organizations, financial constraints usually result from funding limitations placed on them by those providing the funds. Many public-sector organizations, such as hospitals, postsecondary educational institutions, and the Canadian military, face funding restrictions that severely limit the compensation they can offer.

Of course, rather than simply accepting all these financial constraints, organizations can and do try to change them. Public institutions can seek additional sources of funding. Some firms may attempt to escape mandatory benefits by classifying employees as independent contractors. In addition, firms may relocate operations to areas where labour is more plentiful or where employment standards are less costly. Finally, some firms attempt to escape union constraints by weakening the union or by contracting work to non-union enterprises.

Formulating the Compensation Strategy

Now that you understand your organization, people, compensation options, and compensation constraints, you are finally in a position to formulate your compensation strategy. This section takes you through the five steps depicted in Figure 5.1 and discusses who should be involved in the process of formulating compensation strategy.

Defining the Required Behaviour

The first step is to define the behaviour that your organization needs. As you will recall from Chapter 3, organizations need three main types of behaviour: membership behaviour, task behaviour, and citizenship behaviour. But the importance of these behaviours varies for different organizations. For membership behaviour: What are the costs of turnover? Is affective commitment necessary, or is continuance commitment sufficient? For task behaviour: Are tasks simple or complex? Do employees work under supervision? And are high performance levels required? For citizenship behaviour: How important is cooperation for each company unit and the individuals within it? And to what extent can extra employee initiative or ideas make a difference to organizational performance?

For some firms, high levels of membership, task, or citizenship behaviour may be nice but not worth the cost; for others, high levels of one or more of these are essential. To understand the relative importance of the three types of behaviour, you need to understand the organizational context, the most important aspect of which is the managerial strategy. As discussed in Chapter 2, classical organizations need only minimal membership behaviour, only adequate task behaviour, and no citizenship behaviour; human relations organizations need high membership behaviour, adequate task behaviour, and some citizenship behaviour; and high-involvement organizations require high levels of all three.

While every organization needs its employees to perform task behaviours, the nature of these behaviours can vary enormously. Obviously, gutting a chicken is different from designing a computer program, piloting an airplane, writing a newspaper editorial, or performing surgery. Tasks vary in terms of complexity, skill, performance level, material (i.e., things or people), and consequences of errors. Packing a chicken wing in a box of chicken legs is an error, as is removing a patient's healthy left kidney instead of a diseased right kidney (as actually happened at a Swedish hospital in 1997); but the consequences of these two errors differ dramatically.

In addition, the nature of the task behaviour required has implications for the type of organizational and reward systems needed to produce these behaviours. Compensation Notebook 5.1 lists 16 different dimensions of task behaviour. In general, the first choice in each of these dimensions (e.g., tasks that are simple, procedural, low-skilled, narrow, have low interdependence and individual output) are suited for reward systems consistent with the classical school of thought; whereas tasks characterized by the second choice in each dimension (e.g., tasks that are complex, creative, highly skilled, broad,

Dimensions of Task Behaviour

Jobs that match the first characteristic of each pair are more suited for a classical compensation system. Jobs that match the second characteristic of each pair are more suited to a high involvement compensation system.

1. Are tasks simple or complex?
2. Procedural or creative?
3. Low or high skill requirements?
4. Narrow tasks or broad?
5. Low or high task interdependence?
6. Individual or team-based output?
7. Low or high cost of errors?
8. Adequate or high performance required?
9. Low or high employee risk-taking desired?
10. Low or high customer contact?
11. Low or high impact on organizational performance?
12. Low or high employee discretion over work process?
13. High or low ability to supervise employees?
14. Individual output identifiable or not?
15. Short-term or long-term results?
16. Tasks deal with things or human beings?

have high interdependence and team-based output) are suited to reward systems associated with the high-involvement management strategy.

Interestingly, organizations often do not appear to understand their real behavioural needs and have recruiting systems that work at cross-purposes to these needs. For example, many a fresh university graduate has been told by recruiters that the firm is seeking creative, innovative, free-thinking employees, only to discover that what the organization really wants are people who will simply do what they are told in a reliable manner. It may be that recruiters believe statements about creativity and innovation to be effective in drawing high-quality recruits, without considering the potential costs of creating disillusioned employees who are likely to quit when they discover the discrepancy between their expectations and those of their bosses (or even worse, disillusioned and disgruntled employees who do *not* quit).

Once the required behaviours are defined, you need to identify the characteristics of employees able to perform these behaviours, such as skills and education. People who match these criteria are the ones the organization must attract, retain, and motivate, so it is important to understand their needs. Without understanding the needs of these employees, the organization may end up providing rewards that these people do not value highly, a result that is both ineffective and costly.

Of course, rewards are only one part of the picture when it comes to attracting employees. Table 5.1 provides the results of a major international study that identified the factors human resource officers believe to have a "great deal of impact" on highly qualified workers' choices of employer. As the table shows, the top-ranked factor was career development/advancement opportunities, followed closely by the nature and level of direct compensation. Factors such as the company's reputation in the community, its management style, corporate culture, and profitability were also cited as important by more than half of the respondents. Indirect pay (the benefits package) was

TABLE 5.1

Characteristics That Define an Employer of Choice*	
1. Career development/advancement opportunities	68 percent
2. Compensation plan/level	65 percent
3. Company reputation in community	61 percent
4. Management/leadership style	59 percent
5. Corporate culture	56 percent
6. Profitability	51 percent
7. Ethical standards	46 percent
8. Type of industry	44 percent
9. Benefits package	39 percent
10. Technology	38 percent
11. Geographic location	38 percent
12. Training programs	34 percent

*Ranked by percentage of human resource officers believing this factor to have a "great deal of impact" on the selection of employer by highly-qualified employees.

Source: Conference Board of Canada. 1996. "The Pursuit of High Quality Workers." *HR Executive Review*, 3(4): 5–12.

ranked ninth in importance, cited by only a minority of respondents (39 percent) as an important factor.

One of the implications of these findings is that organizations with various negatives, such as a poor reputation in the community or an undesirable geographic location, need to rely more heavily on their compensation systems to attract employees. This is especially true for employers who do not offer advancement opportunities, either because they are not experiencing growth, or because they don't have a "promote from within" policy. As Table 5.1 suggests, a "promote from within" policy can be an important extrinsic reward for employees. Moreover, firms that do not have such a policy risk being seen as inequitable by their employees.

But as many firms become flatter and experience slower growth, they need to develop other types of rewards (including compensation) to make up for the loss of advancement opportunities. As discussed in earlier chapters, some firms have turned to pay-for-knowledge systems, while others have created **technical ladders**, which is a defined progression of skills development and workplace movement intended to keep work interesting (and provide higher compensation) by allowing the employee to master new jobs and work activities.

technical ladder
defined progression of skills development to keep work interesting and provide opportunities for higher compensation

Defining the Role of Compensation

All organizations must have some system for generating the behaviour they require. As discussed in Chapter 2, there are three main organizational systems (managerial strategies) that can be used to generate the required behaviour, and the reward system plays a different role within each system.

NELChapter 5: Formulating the Reward and Compensation Strategy 187

Classical organizations tend to focus on economic needs as the main motivator of behaviour; human relations organizations tend to focus on social needs; and high-involvement organizations focus on employee needs for participation, growth, and development.

The first issue at this point is to examine to what extent intrinsic vs. extrinsic rewards can be used to motivate behaviour. An assessment needs to be made of the intrinsic rewards offered by the organization. These may be extensive or nonexistent. (Of course, where intrinsic rewards are nonexistent, it may be possible to create them through employee participation in decision making or work redesign, as was discussed in Chapter 3.) Where intrinsic rewards are not available, the compensation system needs to be relied on more heavily to motivate behaviour, depending on the extent to which extrinsic rewards other than compensation are available.

Tradeoffs are possible between compensation and other rewards. For example, some firms want to hire employees who are fully equipped with the skills and experience to perform the needed behaviours immediately upon joining the firm. Other firms are willing to hire employees who possess the ability to develop the necessary skills and then train them to perform the needed behaviours. This training may be seen by potential employees as an intrinsic reward (an opportunity for learning and growth) or as an extrinsic reward (since it will likely lead to a better-paying position) or both. Training programs make it possible to attract employees for less compensation than would otherwise be necessary. In contrast, hiring fully skilled and experienced employees requires much higher compensation, although this may be offset by lower training costs and more immediate productivity.

Table 5.2 provides examples of ways the role of compensation varies in different organizational settings. The first example, a gift shop operated by UNICEF to generate funds to help Third World children provides no role for compensation at all. Membership and task behaviour are motivated by intrinsic rewards, including the knowledge that volunteers are helping to save young lives, and a high degree of congruence between organizational goals and personal goals, which also stimulates organizational citizenship behaviour. Clearly, this type of organization suits the high-involvement managerial strategy.

Task behaviour itself (serving customers, ringing up sales) does not necessarily contain many intrinsic rewards (although volunteers are given considerable autonomy in how they perform their roles), so the direct motivation from the task itself is moderate at best. But task behaviour is motivated by the knowledge that performing these mundane tasks is helping to save the lives of third world children. Membership behaviour may also be motivated by the extrinsic social rewards (from mingling with other volunteers, for example) that result from membership in this organization. Of course, the success of this reward strategy depends on the availability of people who have time to contribute, whose goals and needs are congruent with those of the organization, and whose economic needs have already been met by other means.

The second example is a chicken-processing plant, similar to the one described in Compensation Today 2.4. At this organization, there are absolutely

TABLE 5.2

Role of Compensation and Intrinsic/Extrinsic Rewards in Producing Behaviour for Different Organizations

REQUIRED BEHAVIOUR	ROLE OF INTRINSIC REWARDS	ROLE OF EXTRINSIC REWARDS OTHER THAN COMPENSATION	ROLE OF COMPENSATION
UNICEF Store (Cashiers/clerks)			
Membership behaviour	High role	Moderate role	No role
Task behaviour	Moderate role	No role	No role
Citizenship behaviour	High role	No role	No role
Chicken-Processing Plant (Production-line workers)			
Membership behaviour	No role	No role	High role
Task behaviour	No role	No role	No role
Citizenship behaviour	No role	No role	No role
Tree-Planting Firm (Tree planters)			
Membership behaviour	Low to moderate role	Low to moderate role	High role
Task behaviour	Low to moderate role	No role	High role
Citizenship behaviour	No role	No role	No role
Vacation Resort (Service workers)			
Membership behaviour	High role	Moderate role	Moderate role
Task behaviour	Moderate role	No role	Moderate role
Citizenship behaviour	High role	No role	No role
Hospital (Nursing staff)			
Membership behaviour	High role	Moderate role	Moderate role
Task behaviour	Moderate role	No role	No role
Citizenship behaviour	High role	No role	No role
High-Tech Electronics Firm (Design engineers)			
Membership behaviour	Moderate role	Moderate role	Moderate role
Task behaviour	High role	Moderate role	Low role
Citizenship behaviour	Moderate role	Moderate role	High role

no intrinsic or extrinsic rewards other than compensation for production-line workers, so the only way to motivate membership behaviour is through pay. However, because costs of turnover are so low, there is no need to offer compensation beyond the minimum level necessary to attract a sufficient stream of applicants who are able to perform the necessary task behaviours. The compensation system is not used to stimulate task behaviour; that is done directly by the technology and supervisor. Compensation-based behaviour control (such as piece rates) is not really viable due to the interdependent nature of the work. This classical firm is not concerned about citizenship behaviour, and so it does not waste money promoting this behaviour.

The third example is a tree-planting firm, which has contracts with major forestry firms to undertake reforestation work. While there may be some intrinsic motivation for individual tree planters, who may see reforestation work as socially valuable and who may enjoy the autonomy and task identity the job provides, this alone would never motivate the necessary membership and task behaviour. Since tree planters work and live together in camps in remote areas, some may perceive some extrinsic social rewards. On the other hand, because of the remote locations, many tree planters experience negative social rewards due to isolation from friends and family members.

Clearly, the key motivator in this case is money. Pay can be used both to foster the necessary membership behaviour and to direct task behaviour. Both of these can be accomplished through piece rates, where tree planters are paid according to number of trees planted. Their output is identifiable, and tasks are not interdependent. This approach fits with a classical managerial strategy.

The fourth example is a very popular vacation resort that employs seasonal service workers. The work itself does not provide many intrinsic rewards, although there may be some satisfaction in helping guests to enjoy their stay. But there are high extrinsic rewards, because the locale in which the resort is located has many attractions, and the resort allows free use of recreational facilities when employees are not on duty. The resort also encourages friendly social relations among staff. The role of pay in attracting employees is moderate. Pay also plays a moderate role in motivating task behaviour through the tips that workers receive from guests, and small bonuses that the firm provides to employees who receive outstanding service ratings from guests. This firm practises a human relations strategy.

The fifth example is a hospital. Nursing staff receive many intrinsic rewards from the role they play in their organization, because of the work they do and the congruence between their goals and those of the organization. However, there are few extrinsic rewards and many undesirable features of the work, such as shift work. Along with intrinsic rewards, compensation is used to elicit membership behaviour. But it is not used to direct task behaviour or foster citizenship behaviour; intrinsic rewards serve this purpose. This approach fits best with a high-involvement strategy.

The sixth example is a firm that designs and manufactures high-tech electronics products. This firm practises a high-involvement strategy because the success of any new product depends on creativity, innovation, and cooperation among all parts of the organization. For design engineers, there is considerable intrinsic satisfaction in designing a successful product, and some extrinsic rewards result from advancing their own expertise and knowledge through the extensive training provided by the firm. The firm also provides a substantial degree of job security. The primary purpose of compensation is to motivate membership and to foster citizenship behaviour through profit sharing and employee share ownership programs.

Once the role of compensation has been defined, organizations can develop specific behavioural objectives for the compensation system. These objectives flow from the analysis just completed and may be either rudimentary or comprehensive. For example, the chicken-processing firm may be perfectly happy if the compensation system generates a minimum level of membership behaviour, as task behaviour will be shaped by other means. The tree-planting firm goes a step further, relying on its compensation system not only to attract employees but also to direct and control employee task behaviour.

In contrast, the electronics firm views its compensation system as an important part of the rewards it offers to attract high-calibre, committed employees. The firm also views it as a major part of its rewards strategy to foster high organizational citizenship and team-oriented behaviours. The firm may also use compensation to promote learning and development (through a pay-for-knowledge system or payment of tuition fees) and to promote risk-taking behaviour. But unlike the tree-planting firm, it will not depend on its compensation system to promote specific task behaviours. As discussed in Chapter 3, using the compensation system to promote specific task behaviours is a risky process and is suitable in only a very limited number of circumstances.

Table 5.3 illustrates the behavioural objectives that each of the six organizations might set for its compensation systems, along with some indicators of goal achievement.

Determining the Compensation Mix

Once an organization has identified the required behaviours and defined the role that the compensation system will play in generating those behaviours, the next step is to identify the mix of compensation components that will elicit that behaviour in the most effective and efficient way. (Figures 4.1 and 4.2 in Chapter 4 have summarized the choices available.)

A number of questions must be addressed. What role will be played by base pay, performance pay, and indirect pay? And how will each component be structured? For example, will the foundation for base pay be job evaluation, market pricing, or pay for knowledge? Will performance pay be linked to individual, group, or organizational performance? What specific benefits or services will be included in indirect pay, which benefits will be shared-cost, and what degree of choice will employees have in the benefits they receive?

The correct answers to these questions depend on the behaviours the firm requires, the organizational context (especially managerial strategy), the needs of the employees being sought, and the constraints facing the organization. Unfortunately, there is no simple formula for finding these answers: management must rely on a high degree of informed judgment at this point in the process. A further complication is that the mix of main compensation components also needs to be considered in the context of the total level of compensation to be provided. For example, the greater the variable portion of the compensation, the greater the total compensation generally necessary to compensate employees for the uncertainty and risk in their compensation.

TABLE 5.3

Sample Behavioural Objectives for Compensation Systems

COMPENSATION OBJECTIVE	INDICATOR
UNICEF Store (Cashiers/clerks)	
• None (no compensation system)	• None
Chicken-Processing Plant (Production workers)	
• Attract job applicants able to perform basic tasks	• Flow of willing applicants exceeds terminations by 10 percent
Tree-Planting Firm (Tree planters)	
• Attract applicants to staff initial needs and replace turnover	• Number of applicants exceeds requirements by 100 percent
• Maintain high retention	• Turnover during planting season less than 10 percent
• Motivate tree-planting behaviour	• Average production exceeds 200 trees per hour
Vacation Resort (Service workers)	
• Attract applicants to staff initial needs	• Number of applicants exceeds requirements by 100 percent
• Maintain reasonable retention	• Turnover during season less than 20 percent
• Promote friendly guest service	• Customer surveys
	• Less than 2 percent of customers make complaints
Hospital (Nursing staff)	
• Attract applicants to exceed turnover and maintain quality	• Number of applicants exceeds vacancies by 200 percent
• Maintain moderate to high retention	• Annual turnover less than 12 percent
High-Tech Electronics (Design engineers)	
• Attract top-quality applicants well in excess of needs	• Number of applicants exceeds vacancies by 300 percent
	• 75 percent acceptance rate of job offers
• Maintain very high retention	• Turnover less than 5 percent
• Promote creativity and risk-taking	• Number of new projects proposed per engineer
	• Number of suggestions pertaining to department
• Promote high citizenship behaviour	• Employee surveys
	• Number of suggestions extending beyond department
• Promote learning and development	• Improvement in employee qualifications

Determining Compensation Level

How much compensation should be offered? Within the constraints discussed earlier, policies need to be established for determining the total amount of compensation that individuals or groups of employees will receive. In general, the question to be asked is: Will we lead, lag, or match our relevant labour market in terms of total compensation levels?

Lagging the Market

Of course, the first question is: Do we have a choice? In some cases, the organization's financial or budgetary circumstances are such that there is no choice but to lag the market. If so, a key question is whether the organization can offer noncash rewards (perhaps including some indirect pay items) to make up for this lag. For example, the organization may sweeten its total package by offering items that cost the firm little or no cash, such as purchase discounts on company products. Or these firms may offer flexible schedules to employees or useful training. When cash is short, provision of other extrinsic rewards, along with intrinsic rewards, becomes even more important.

It is common for small, rapidly growing firms to have cash shortages. To entice crucial employees, these firms frequently offer company stock, which has no current cash cost. They may also offer other types of performance pay payable only when and if the company can afford to pay. To make this worthwhile in the eyes of employees, the future payout typically needs to be set quite high, in order to compensate employees for the risk of not receiving anything at all. Another potentially valuable reward this type of firm can offer is advancement opportunities, in addition to intrinsic rewards such as task variety or participation in decision making.

Research consistently shows that smaller firms pay less than large firms. For example, a Statistics Canada study has revealed that in the manufacturing sector, small firms paid 24 percent less than the average pay in their sector.[3] This difference may be due to a higher unionization rate in large firms (which forces wages up), tighter cost controls in small firms, or simply lower ability to pay in small firms. In fact, while their savings in labour costs might appear to be a competitive advantage, small firms appear to pay a steep price for their compensation savings. Statistics Canada also found that productivity in small firms was 32 percent lower than industrial averages. Research that indicates small firms have higher turnover rates and less-qualified employees than larger firms[4] helps to explain their lower productivity.

But what about firms that do have a choice in pay level? Many firms that could pay more make a conscious decision to pay below market. The motive for doing so is obvious—to save on compensation costs. But there are costs to this strategy. On average, firms that pay below market have a lower quality of applicants and higher turnover than other firms. Not surprisingly, employees also experience more reward dissatisfaction than employees at other firms. Unless a firm has carefully analyzed these costs, they may find that the costs of this strategy exceed the benefits. Firms that find lag strategies cost-effective are firms where the costs of both turnover and recruitment are low, where

lag compensation policy
a compensation-level strategy based on paying below the average compensation level in a given labour market

labour constitutes a high percentage of total cost, and where it is possible to contain the negative consequences of reward dissatisfaction.

Other firms that find below-market pay policies viable are those that offer other types of rewards that are highly valued by employees. With these alternative rewards, these firms may avoid the problems of poor-quality applicants, high turnover, and reward dissatisfaction.

lead compensation policy

a compensation-level strategy based on paying above the average compensation level in a given labour market

Leading the Market

Why would an organization ever choose to lead the market? There are actually many reasons. An organization may need to lead the market if it offers poor non-compensation rewards, if there are negative aspects associated with employment by this firm, or if the firm needs very high-quality applicants. Firms where recruiting costs, turnover costs, and consequences of reward dissatisfaction are all high may find this approach cost-effective. Firms that value employee stability or whose customer service needs employee stability may also favour this strategy. In addition, firms in which labour costs are low as a proportion of total costs find this strategy less costly than firms that are labour-intensive.

High compensation may be necessary to the organization's goals or its total reward strategy. Firms seeking employees who have abilities beyond those required for their entry-level jobs or who require heavy training investments may wish to secure their workforce with high compensation. For example, firms using a pay-for-knowledge system consistently pay above market. Some firms with performance pay plans, such as profit sharing, may also end up paying above the market. Many firms gear base and indirect pay to the market and then add profit sharing, which causes total pay to exceed the market in profitable years. As discussed earlier, there is evidence that employees in profit-sharing firms receive higher total compensation than employees in firms without profit sharing.

In some cases, firms do not intend to lead the market in total compensation, but end up doing so nonetheless. This can occur if the compensation structure results in increases beyond market increases, if there is no systematic assessment of market trends, or if there is a strong union. Firms can also end up paying over market if they have poorly designed compensation systems—ones that includes rewards that do not add value for the employee or the employer but still cost money.

In some cases, large firms that are geographically dispersed end up leading the market in parts of the country, even if they are only matching the market in other parts of the country. But from their point of view, the cost of determining a market-matching wage for every branch of their organization is simply not worth the effort. Furthermore, inconsistent wages for similar jobs may create perceptions of inequity and make it difficult to transfer employees to the lower-wage branches.

match compensation policy

a compensation-level strategy based on paying at average compensation levels in a given labour market

Matching the Market

Many firms settle on a "match the market" strategy as a way of "playing it safe." Their reasoning is that this strategy avoids the possible disadvantages of paying below market, while still remaining cost-competitive by not offering excessively high wages. They are simply not sure whether either a lag or lead policy will pay off, so they stick to the middle. In some cases, of course, this is the optimal solution. But this assumption cannot be confirmed without systematic analysis.

Utility Analysis

In order to help managers determine which compensation-level strategy is most appropriate—which can be a complicated process—computer-based "utility analysis" models have been developed.[5] **Utility analysis** is a method to help analyze whether a lead, lag, or match strategy would be most efficient for a given organization. Here is how it works.

utility analysis

a method used to analyze whether a lead, lag, or match compensation-level strategy is most efficient for a given organization

Suppose that you are the head of compensation at a credit union, and you are trying to decide on the pay-level strategy for your 400 tellers. Currently, your policy is to match the market. But would the bank be better off to switch to either a lead or a lag policy? Changing the policy would be expected to have an impact on turnover and on the quality of employees who would be hired. You have examined other banks that pay more or less than you do, and have found that firms that pay 20 percent more have a 10 percent lower turnover rate than you do, and that firms that pay 20 percent less have a 10 percent higher turnover rate. Your current turnover rate for tellers is running at 30 percent per year, so each year you have to replace 120 tellers.

You first need to calculate the costs of turnover. What is the cost of recruiting each teller, and what is the cost of training them? Let's assume that it costs approximately $1,000 to replace each teller, including advertising, interviewing, and the administrative costs of putting the new employee on the payroll and taking the former employee off the payroll. Let's suppose that training costs $4,000 per employee, counting out-of-pocket training costs and reduced productivity during the training period. Currently, you are paying each teller $24,000 direct pay per year, with benefits adding another $6,000, for a cost per employee of $30,000 per year. The total cost for tellers per year is the cost of their compensation (400 times $30,000 = $12,000,000) plus the costs of turnover (120 times $5,000 = $600,000) for a total of $12,600,000.

You now need to estimate the change in performance that will occur from a change in the quality of your workforce due to a lag or lead policy. If you lag the market by 20 percent, you expect that your new workforce will produce 5 percent less work and make 7 percent more errors. Considering the time needed to identify and correct the errors, you calculate that the new workforce will be 12 percent less productive. You also need to decide whether the lead pay policy would improve productivity by the same amount. Let's suppose that it does. Now, let's follow through with the analysis for the lag and the lead policy in turn.

Let's suppose we decide to lag by 20 percent. Because productivity is 12 percent less, we will now need 448 tellers. At 33 percent turnover, we will need to replace 149 tellers per year. With the 20 percent wage reduction, it will now cost us $24,000 per employee per year in salary and benefits. So the total cost will be 448 times $24,000 ($10,752,000) plus 149 times $5,000 ($745,000), which totals $11,497,000—considerably lower than our current costs.

But wait! If we have 12 percent more employees, then we need 12 percent more office space, and 12 percent more office equipment, etc. Assuming that it costs an additional $3,000 per employee per year for computer equipment and support, and $1,000 for office space and miscellaneous expenses, we can expect additional costs of $192,000, resulting in a total cost of $11,689,000. This is still a savings of nearly a million dollars per year compared to a match-the-market strategy.

Now, let's suppose we decide to lead by 20 percent. Because productivity is 12 percent higher, we will now need only 352 tellers. Approximately 95 will need to be replaced each year. So our costs would be 352 times $36,000 ($12,672,000) plus 95 times $5,000 ($475,000) for a total of $13,147,000. Even after allowing for reduced office space and equipment ($192,000), this is still the most expensive policy, at $12,955,000.

In reality, the actual calculations would be more complex than this. For example, introduction of the lag policy would normally apply only to new hires, and the pay of the existing employees would reduce gradually over time during which no scale increases would be granted. Thus, the savings in wage costs would phase in over time, along with the increases in turnover and the declines in productivity. In contrast, for the lead policy, it would be necessary to raise wages of all employees immediately. Costs would rise immediately, and the turnover rate would decline immediately, but the improved quality of employees arising from this policy would only phase in over time. Because of this complexity, computer models have been developed to do these calculations.

In this example, it does appear that adopting a lag strategy would be the most efficient, eventually generating a savings of nearly $1 million per year compared with the present "match" policy. But we have not really included intangible costs, such as customer reaction to finding a favourite teller gone. Furthermore, we have not included any costs of reward dissatisfaction other than turnover. We can predict that organizational commitment would be adversely affected; but what is the cost of that? Would cooperation with management drop? Would absenteeism increase? Would attitudes toward customers deteriorate, and what might this cost in lost revenue?

What about the cost of mistakes? We have already included the time needed to discover and correct them in our productivity calculations. But what impact does a mistake have on customers and their confidence in and satisfaction with their bank? How many bank errors would your customers tolerate?

Furthermore, what if our assumptions are wrong? Is it really reasonable that employees earning direct pay of $18,000 (and knowing that most banks pay higher wages) would have a turnover rate of 33 percent, while employees earning $30,000 (and knowing that virtually no bank pays higher wages) would still have a turnover rate of 27 percent? In our hypothetical example, the 10 percent change in turnover for a 20 percent change in pay was based on research in the United States,[6] since no Canadian data were available. Would it be the same here?

But what about economic conditions and unemployment? Were these figures calculated to include information about labour surpluses or shortages? If there is now a labour shortage, it may be virtually impossible to recruit qualified individuals at 20 percent less than market, and selection standards might need to be lowered dramatically. Furthermore, as these employees gained experience and training, the best of them would be offered jobs at other banks. Only those who couldn't get such offers would stay. How would this affect our productivity estimates? In contrast, if there were a labour surplus, there would be virtually no turnover in the leading firms, since employees would be concerned about being able to find another comparable job.

So what would happen if turnover changed by 20 percent for a 20 percent change in wages? What if productivity dropped by more than 12 percent with a 20 percent drop in wages? Furthermore, perhaps the changes are not symmetrical. For example, with a 20 percent lead policy, would the firm be able to attract all the best employees from the competitors? We all know of instances where the best employee in a unit can do much more work than the worst, sometimes twice as much. Would it be unreasonable to expect that staffing ourselves with only top-notch employees would cause a 24 percent productivity gain? (This assumes, of course, that our selection procedures are good enough to pick out the best performers from the large pool of applicants.)

Running the analysis again, we can see that changing the productivity increase to 24 percent for a lead policy results in a total annual cost of $10,970,000 (compared to $12,955,000 calculated earlier). This compares favourably with $11,689,000 for a lag policy and $12,600,000 for a match policy. Interestingly, analysis now indicates that there are savings in either a lag or a lead strategy, but that the lead strategy is now optimal from a cost perspective.

As these calculations illustrate, a major advantage of utility analysis is the ability to answer "what if" questions. Normally, the analysis is run for a whole range of estimates, including worst-case and best-case projections. Analysis also helps identify the minimum conditions necessary for a change in policy to pay off. For example, we might determine that we need a productivity gain of at least 18 percent to move to a lead policy. We can then ask: how likely is that?

But before making the final decision, we must come back to a basic point: that the pay-level strategy chosen must also support the corporate and managerial strategies and must fit the organizational context. If we are practising a high-involvement management strategy, a lag strategy may destroy in one stroke the close, carefully nurtured relationship between the organization and the employees. However, firms using a classical strategy may have no such concern and have much less to lose by choosing a lag strategy. In addition to its managerial strategy, the organization's competitive strategy might also be relevant: is the firm's strategy based on friendly, knowledgeable tellers or on low-cost service?

Given the complexity and uncertainty of this whole analytical process, is it any wonder that many firms simply throw up their hands and just stick with their current policy unless they are forced to change?

Hybrid Policies

Aside from choosing a straight lead, lag, or match strategy, firms may choose a hybrid strategy. For example, a firm could choose to lag for entry-level positions, especially if applicants are plentiful, but lead in higher-level positions

hybrid compensation policy

a compensation-level strategy that varies across employee groups or compensation components to avoid turnover of highly trained personnel. A firm may have different policies for different compensation components—for example, to lag in base pay, to lead in performance pay, and to match in indirect pay. They may also choose to have different pay-level policies for different employee groups.

Read the following scenario to test your understanding of the close interrelationship between method of pay and amount of pay.

Imagine that you are the owner of a medium-sized firm in the service sector, and you have hired two different compensation consultants to devise a compensation strategy for you. Both have come up with plans in which employees will receive an average $4,000 per month in total compensation, but there are some differences between the plans. You then submit each plan to a different independent expert for evaluation.

One expert reports that you are very lucky you consulted her, because $4,000 per month is too high a pay level! But the other expert reports that a $4,000 pay level is just fine. In confusion, you submit their reports to your next-door neighbour, who happens to be compensation manager for a prominent local firm. He tells you that both independent experts are right! What is going on here?

As it turns out, one compensation plan calls for the $4,000 to be distributed 67 percent to base pay and 33 percent to indirect pay. But in the second plan, the distribution is 50 percent base pay, 25 percent performance pay, and 25 percent indirect pay. On analysis, the second plan is projected to produce value for the organization in excess of $4,000 per employee; but the first plan is projected to produce value of less than $4,000 per employee. Thus, the *nature* of the compensation mix affects the *amount* of compensation that you can afford to pay.

RPC 5.3

Evaluating the Proposed Strategy

Compensation Notebook 1.1 in Chapter 1 listed eight goals for the effectiveness of a compensation system. At this point, before implementation, it is important to review the proposed strategy against these criteria. Three of these criteria—affordability, legality, and employee attraction—can be considered screens through which the strategy must pass. If it can't pass all of these, the strategy is a nonstarter.

Clearly, if a compensation strategy results in costs beyond the financial means of the organization, it can go no further. To determine whether the compensation strategy passes this screen, management needs to project the cost of the system and then compare it with what the organization can afford. However, this is often not a clear-cut process, since both the costs of the system and the funds available are often difficult to determine in advance. In many cases, the success of the compensation strategy itself plays a major role in determining whether the funds are available to meet payroll. In a business organization, future revenues and profitability can be difficult to predict, especially for firms in turbulent environments. And although public-sector organizations may be able to predict their budgets more accurately, many of them are prone to sudden budget cuts, which have a direct impact on what they can afford.

Before making the final decision on adopting the new compensation strategy, you need to derive some estimate of the cost of the new compensation system. This requires knowledge of the number and type of employees who will be employed over the next year. To make these estimates, you need to project the volume of business or service to be provided over the coming year. Once you have done this, multiply the projected total compensation for each employee by number of employees. The resulting number should indicate whether the program is affordable.

Although there can be areas of ambiguity, legality is more straightforward to determine than affordability. Does your plan meet the minimum standards under the employment standards act in your jurisdiction? If piece rates or commissions are used, do they meet the standards for minimum pay and overtime under the relevant employment standards legislation? Does your plan comply with human rights legislation and pay equity legislation? If your firm intends to use independent contractors, do they meet the necessary criteria to be so classified? If there is any uncertainty at all, many experts recommend getting an advance ruling from the appropriate government ministry.

Finally, when coupled with the other rewards the organization will offer, will the system really be able to attract employees with the necessary qualifications? There are numerous ways of testing the labour market to assess this, as will be discussed in Chapter 8.

After passing through these basic screens, you need to review the other criteria. Will the resulting behaviour contribute toward achievement of organizational goals? Could the system end up promoting behaviour detrimental to goal achievement? Might the system promote some behaviours at the expense of other important behaviours? Does the compensation system fit with your managerial strategy and organizational structure?

Another issue is equity. Will the system be seen as equitable by those in it? Of course, no system will be considered completely equitable by all employees. But to what degree is it considered equitable and by how many employees? A major issue to consider here is the value of an equitable system to the organization. As discussed earlier, some organizations can tolerate perceived inequities in their compensation systems, and others cannot. To those organizations that cannot, equity is another screen through which the strategy must pass before final approval. One way of checking for equity is to present the proposed plan to focus groups of employees.

Finally, even if the compensation strategy meets all these criteria, one question remains: Is it the most efficient or cost-effective strategy for meeting all these criteria? The only way to answer this is to identify all the viable alternative compensation strategies and to evaluate them against these same criteria. But given the complexity of this process, few firms have the resources or energy to do so. This is why many of them rely on compensation consultants; however, there is no guarantee that consultants will come up with the optimum plan either.

Once the strategy is implemented, it needs ongoing evaluation to determine whether it is performing as planned and whether adjustments need to be made. It is a rare compensation system that doesn't have some wrinkles to iron out. And, as discussed earlier, even a strategy that was optimal when implemented can become ineffective if circumstances change. This issue of evaluation and adaptation of ongoing compensation systems is discussed in Chapter 12.

Who Develops the Compensation Strategy?

If compensation is to serve as a strategic tool, it needs to dovetail with and support the organization's corporate and managerial strategy. For this to happen, those developing the compensation strategy must have a clear understanding of the organizational context. In fact, to develop an optimal compensation strategy, the body developing it must have all four of the key understandings discussed at the beginning of this chapter.

This suggests that the body charged with developing the overall compensation strategy should be the same one responsible for the other strategic decisions in the organization. In many organizations, this means the chief executive officer. The key contribution that top management brings to the compensation strategy process is an understanding of the strategic context for compensation. But normally, top management does not have expert knowledge in the other three necessary understandings; thus, human resource and compensation specialists must bring this knowledge to the process. Compensation specialists must carry out the detailed design of the compensation system within the parameters set by the compensation strategy. These specialists may be in-house or outside consultants; but if outside consultants are used, it is crucial that the process be actively managed by the firm itself.

Another important issue is the stage at which broad employee representation is included in the design process. Of course, if the organization is unionized, the compensation system must be acceptable to the union members. But organizations vary greatly in the degree of employee involvement they provide prior to adoption of the proposed compensation system. In traditional classical organizations, there is usually none.

Since both understanding of employee needs and acceptance by employees are necessary for the compensation system to achieve maximum success, many compensation experts recommend extensive employee involvement right from the early stages. But this is viable only in high-involvement organizations. There are many different stages at which employees can be involved, and it is quite rare for them to be involved in the initial formation of the compensation strategy.

However, it is much more common for employees to be involved in the design of the specific elements in the compensation system. For example, employees are often involved in developing and managing employee benefits or designing and managing a profit-sharing plan, often through joint employee–management committees. In general, the more employee involvement in the development process, the more likely the plan will address important employee needs, and the more likely it will be seen as equitable.

Not all organizations are able to engender effective employee involvement. Three critical conditions are employee commitment to organizational goals, trust between management and employees, and open and effective communication and information sharing. In general, high-involvement organizations are able to work with the most employee involvement, classical organizations the least, and human relations organizations somewhere in between.

Compensation Strategy Formulation: An Example

🅡🅟🅒 5.4

All of this may sound fine in an abstract way, but it probably does not feel very real to you. Let's try to make it feel more real by putting you in the hotseat. Try to visualize the following situation.

You are president and chief executive officer of Canada Chemicals Corporation, a firm that produces industrial chemicals. Although the firm is profitable, profits have been slipping in recent years, and you see some other disturbing signs. While there could be many causes for these problems, at least part of your problem may be your compensation strategy: it may need an overhaul. But be wary: things are seldom as simple as they seem! Because formulating a new compensation strategy (and deciding whether to actually go ahead with it) is complex and requires concentration, be prepared for a whopping headache before you are done! You may find it useful to input the data into a computer spreadsheet for easier manipulation.

The Company

Canada Chemicals Corporation produces two main categories of industrial chemicals. Some of the chemicals you produce are "off-the-shelf" (OTS) products, while others are custom developed in conjunction with purchasers. Custom-developed chemicals take much longer to sell, because their specifications have to be worked out between the purchaser and your company.

The chemical sales engineer's job is to interface with customers, assess their needs, and determine whether an off-the-shelf product would suit their needs. If not, he or she must identify the technical requirements for the product and then develop preliminary chemical specifications for a product that meet these requirements. In some cases, a minor modification of an OTS product does the trick. In others, modification of a previous custom product works. In still other cases, the custom product needs to be developed from scratch.

This custom-product information is then sent to the chemistry department, which further refines the product formulation, examines whether there is a cheaper way of producing the product (e.g., modifying a custom product that the sales engineer wasn't aware of), verifies that it will meet customer needs, and then develops the production specifications. These specifications are then sent to the production department, which develops a cost estimate for the product, plus a preliminary estimate of how long it would take to produce the product. These estimates go to the vice-president of sales, who develops a price and delivery date based on these estimates and relays the date to the district sales manager. All of this information then goes back to the sales engineer, who prepares a detailed proposal for the customer.

But there may be other steps. Often this proposal is reviewed by the customer's chemists, who may suggest changes to the product formulation. If they do, the whole process needs to be repeated. Sometimes the customer balks at the price or delivery date, and it is up to the sales engineer to discuss this with the district sales manager to see whether any break on price or change in delivery date can be negotiated. If the sales manager recommends a new price, the revised proposal goes back to the vice-president of sales for approval. If it is a timing problem, the sales manager takes it up with production, which can either refuse or agree to changes in the delivery date but may impose extra costs for doing so. This all then goes back to the sales engineer, who then goes back to the customer.

Despite the complexity of the custom-product process, the company actually makes a much higher margin of profit on custom products than on off-the-shelf products because there has been increasing competition in OTS products, which has caused prices to be cut to the bone. For OTS products, production costs (including labour and materials) account for 55 percent of the final selling price, resulting in a gross margin of 45 percent. For custom products, production costs amount to 35 percent, leaving a gross margin of 65 percent.

Production for both OTS and custom products is complex, using an array of complex mixing and refracting equipment, much of it computer-controlled. Products are made in batches of varying sizes, ranging from as little as 10 litres to as much as 50 000 litres. In addition, a wide array of different production processes are used. Production employees require a considerable amount of skill and experience, and many of them have certificates from technical schools.

Production employees at this firm unionized about two years ago and are paid an hourly wage, which matches the wage levels of other unionized plants but is about 10 percent higher than two non-union chemical plants that have recently opened up. The company has a modest pension plan and some health and life insurance, but total indirect pay is relatively modest for the industry, amounting to about 15 percent of total compensation. Tasks have been subdivided into many different jobs, and pay rates for each job are set by job evaluation. Jobs are defined narrowly and are considered boring by most production workers. Turnover among production workers is about 20 percent per year, somewhat high for the industry.

Overall, the company has about 360 employees, and total compensation runs at about $18 million per annum. There are 100 sales engineers, 160 production employees, 25 chemists and lab technicians, 40 managers and supervisors, and about 15 other administrative staff. Administrative and technical staff are paid a salary that is based on job evaluation and intended to match the market. Turnover among these employees is about 15 percent per year.

The company does about $40 million of business a year, and earned a before-tax profit of about $5 million last year. The company is capitalized at $30 million and is listed on the Toronto Stock Exchange.

The Problems

Although the company's financial performance was good in the past, you are concerned about several disturbing signs. Not only has total sales revenue stagnated over the past three or four years, but profits have also been declining steadily. (They peaked at $8 million three years ago.)

The reduced profits are occurring for two reasons. First, additional competitors have entered the field for OTS products, driving prices down. Second, the proportion of custom products sold has declined from about 40 percent of sales to about 25 percent of sales over the last three years. Customers are complaining about slow service and misformulated products, and they can now go to alternative suppliers, whereas several years ago there were virtually no other suppliers. (A product's failure to meet customer requirements is very costly for Canada Chemicals, because the entire purchase price must be refunded, and sometimes damages must be paid. Almost always, the firm loses the customer.)

Sales engineers have a bachelor's degree in chemical engineering. When they join the firm, they are given a two-month intensive course on company products, ways to assess customer needs, and related skills. They are then assigned a territory to cover, under the supervision and guidance of a senior sales engineer in a nearby territory. Canada is divided into five sales regions, with a regional sales manager for each.

Currently, each sales engineer averages about $50,000 in total compensation, approximately 40 percent of which is base pay, 40 percent commission based on volume of sales, and 20 percent indirect pay. (Most sales engineers consider the free use of a company car as their most important benefit.) Base pay is $20,000, indirect pay $10,000, and commissions 5 percent on gross sales (the average annual sales per sales engineer is $400,000). This system matches industry standards.

However, you perceive problems with the current sales compensation system. First, it is becoming difficult to attract sales engineers, who are usually hired right from university. Last year, there were only 160 applicants for the 30 vacancies, and three out of every four job offers the company made were rejected.

Many of those who refused job offers cited the compensation system as a deterrent. They indicated that while the average direct compensation of $40,000 plus car sounds okay, and while they were impressed that some sales engineers earned as much as $60,000 in direct pay (the company has about 10 sales engineers in this league), most were concerned about the uncertainty of their pay, given that they had high student loans to pay off. They were concerned that pay might be low in the first couple of years (average direct pay in the first two years averaged $30,000 per year). For these reasons, most new graduates turned down the firm's offers.

Second, you are concerned about a high turnover rate of new engineers, with many leaving in their first year. In fact, of the 30 you hire each year to replace vacancies, only 10 remain after the first year. The company also loses about 10 experienced sales engineers each year. Job stress is often cited as one of the reasons for leaving.

Chapter 5: Formulating the Reward and Compensation Strategy

Third, new sales engineers report that senior sales engineers show very little interest in helping them do their jobs, even though advice and tips from the senior sales engineers would be very valuable. When badgered about this problem by their district managers, the experienced sales engineers defend themselves vigorously, arguing that the only way they can make enough money is to spend all their time selling, and they have little time to help anyone else.

Fourth, you notice that most sales engineers seem to focus on the OTS products, even though the custom-designed products carry a much higher profit margin for the company. Sales engineers report that selling custom products is just too time-consuming and frustrating, citing lack of cooperation from the other departments. As one sales engineering put it, "With friends like those (in the chemistry and production departments), who needs enemies? They don't seem to understand what it takes to sell a product, and seem to work against me more than with me. Besides, with prices dropping on the OTS products, I've got to pay most of my attention to moving these products if I want to make a living."

Fifth, high animosity and conflict among the chemists, the production department, and the sales engineers has you very concerned. Production accuses the sales engineers of always trying to cut prices on their products to stimulate sales and accuses the chemists of coming up with production specifications that are overly complex and do not meet customer requirements, resulting in wasted product. The chemists accuse the sales engineers of not taking the time to really find out the customer's needs and turning in poorly defined customer requests, which often results in the wrong type of product. They view the production department as technically incompetent, fouling up the final product. The sales engineers accuse the chemists of being too fussy in what they want, too slow to formulate the product, and too likely to misformulate products. They accuse production of overpricing the product, being too slow in delivery, and producing poor-quality product. There is also high resentment among the sales engineers against top management, who is leaning on them to sell more custom products, although there is little money in it for them, and making them scapegoats for the company's drop in profitability.

Formulating the New Compensation Strategy

In fact, you do believe that most of the problems the firm is facing are due to poor performance of the sales engineers. You call in the VP of sales and ask him to explain this poor performance. However, he repeats the party line that the problems are not his fault. Instead, they are caused by the other departments and by the poor quality of sales engineers that the human resources department is recruiting.

You then march into the human resources department and demand to know why they are failing to do their job effectively. "If we are matching the market in total compensation, why can't we find decent sales engineers? Maybe something is wrong with our recruitment and selection procedures or with our recruiters. Maybe we even need a new head of human resources!" But like everybody else, they claim that it is not their fault! So you reply, if it is not their fault, whose is it? After some hesitation, they begin to reply.

You know what they are going to say: We need to pay our sales engineers more money. More money! Always more money! Don't they know our profits are going down? But they reply that there is more to it than that. It is the whole managerial system. Aha, you reply, so now it's all *my* fault!

But after calming down, you start to realize they are making sense. They talk about how the organization seemed to function fine when the environment was stable and there were few competitors. But with the increasingly competitive environment, the classical structure just doesn't seem to be performing.

Defining the Required Behaviour

The human resources manager explains: "We have a small-batch, intensive technology. We want our competitive strategy to be more like a prospector than a defender. Most of the task behaviour that we need requires creativity, high interdependence, and high skill. We require well-educated, highly skilled people, who need to collaborate across departments. We need high membership, task, and organizational citizenship behaviour. We are a relatively small organization, so do we really need all the hierarchy and centralized decision making? Shouldn't we be moving toward a more high-involvement, flexible, collaborative managerial strategy?"

When they put it that way, you can't help but agree. So how do you get there? There are a lot of things that need to be changed, but none of them will work unless you also change your compensation system. To do that, you put together an executive task force, consisting of you, the manager of human resources (now promoted to VP of human resources, reporting directly to you rather than to the VP of finance and administration), and the VPs of sales, chemistry, production, and finance/administration.

The task force first examines the whole array of rewards—both intrinsic and extrinsic—that the organization provides and is depressed by what they find. At the moment, the only reward perceived by employees as having any value is compensation, and almost nobody is satisfied with that either. Jobs are seen as boring, promotions are rare and seem mainly based on whether top management likes a person, and training is infrequent. The VP of human resources suggests that by moving to a high-involvement strategy, the firm can offer many new intrinsic and extrinsic rewards. But it is also clear that the compensation strategy itself must also change.

Determining the Compensation Mix

To redesign the sales compensation system, you create a design task force, including you, the VPs of human resources and sales, several regional sales managers, and several sales engineers, especially several younger ones. Their first decision is to create teams of five to eight sales engineers who have the responsibility for sales in a given geographic area. Although each engineer will have her or his own territory, all are also expected to help cover the territories of other team members when they are away or need help.

Using the strategic template illustrated in Figure 5.2 as a guide to outline their options and summarize their choices, the task force formulates the following sales compensation strategy. To improve income stability, the new

FIGURE 5.2

Compensation Strategy Template

Job Family: _Sales Engineer_

Total Compensation Level: Match? _____ **Lead?** _20%_ **Lag?** _____

PROPORTION OF TOTAL PAY

1. **Base Pay**	*50%*
a. Job evaluation	~
b. Market pricing	*50%*
c. Pay for knowledge	~
2. **Performance Pay**	*30%*
a. Individual performance pay	~
i. Piece rate	~
ii. Commissions	*10%*
iii. Merit bonuses	~
iv. Special incentives _____	~
b. Group performance pay	
i. Gain sharing	~
ii. Goal sharing	~
iii. Other group pay _Group Commissions_	*10%*
c. Organization performance pay	
i. Profit sharing	*5%*
ii. Stock plan	*5%*
iii. Other organization pay	~
3. **Indirect Pay**	*20%*
i. Mandatory benefits	*8%*
ii. Pension plan	*4%*
iii. Health & life insurance	*3%*
iv. Paid time off	~
v. Employee services	~
vi. Other benefits _Automobile_	*5%*

strategy will redistribute pay between base pay and performance pay, by increasing base pay to 50 percent of compensation (from 40 percent), and reducing performance pay to 30 percent (from 40 percent). There will also be a major redistribution within performance pay, aimed at improving teamwork. Only 10 percent will now be allocated to individual commissions, and a group commission plan targeted to comprise about 10 percent of compensation will be introduced. Under the group commission plan, all members of a sales team will share equally in commissions based on the total sales of that team.

To encourage more sales of custom products, commissions will now be based half on total sales volume and half on gross margin. The actual commission rates will be as follows: individual commissions—0.75 percent of individual volume, 1.45 percent of individual gross margin; group commissions—0.75 percent of sales team volume, 1.45 percent of sales team gross margin. Thus, total commissions for each sales engineer will be 1.5 percent of volume and 2.9 percent of gross margin, compared with the previous 5 percent of total volume.

After considering the options, the task force decides to recommend profit sharing for all employees, in order to increase employee interest in the bottom line and to create greater cohesion and cooperation within the firm. It also proposes a company stock plan to further reinforce this interest. Through these organizational performance pay plans, they hope to create a commonality of goals with the organization and to serve as a source of retirement savings, since most employees regard the current pension plan as inadequate.

The design task force then sets up an employee task force to help design the specific features of the profit-sharing and stock plans. The union is cautious about participating in this process but finally agrees to allow two union officials to sit in on these meetings as "observers." However, they make it clear that this does not necessarily mean they will sign on to any plan that is developed, especially if they have to give up any direct wages. They also make it clear that their preference would be to improve the regular, defined benefit pension plan.

The proposed stock plan will allow employees to invest up to 5 percent of their total compensation in company stock, and the company will match each share one for one. If employees take full advantage of this plan, this amounts to a 5-percent increase in their total compensation. There is a minimum one-year holding period for the shares, and employees may place these shares in an RRSP. This allows them to deduct their contributions from income tax, and it also serves as a vehicle for retirement savings.

The profit-sharing plan will pay out in cash every quarter and is designed to amount to at least 5 percent of pay in a typical year. (One purpose of this plan is to provide a source of funds to invest in company stock, since many employees indicated that it would be very difficult to do so out of their current earnings.) Based on projected profits for the coming year, the rate needs to be set at 14 percent of pre-tax profits in order to amount to 5 percent of total compensation. You choke a little at this, especially when you realize that the stock plan could cost an equivalent amount if all employees participate; but you agree that there is no point in doing any of this if it does not make a noticeable difference to employees.

Determining the Compensation Level

In order to improve its ability to attract and retain top-calibre sales engineers, the company decides to lead the market in total compensation for sales engineers by 20 percent. However, 10 percent will be provided by the new profit-sharing and stock plans, so half of the 20 percent lead is certainly not guaranteed and will only be paid out if the company is successful. This reduces the risk to the company of such a high lead policy.

Chapter 5: Formulating the Reward and Compensation Strategy

 5.5

Evaluating the Proposed Compensation Strategy

This is what the typical sales engineer is projected to earn under the proposed new compensation system, in comparison with the average under the current system:

	CURRENT SYSTEM	NEW SYSTEM
Base pay	$20,000	$30,000
Individual commissions	20,000	6,000
Group commissions	–	6,000
Profit sharing	–	3,000
Stock plan	–	3,000
Indirect pay	10,000	12,000
Total	$50,000	$60,000

The firm now must assess the impact of the new plan on the company. It will cost at least $1 million more in sales compensation annually. Will it be worth it?

Answering that question is not easy. We have to make many assumptions, any of which could turn out to be wrong. But we have to try, and Table 5.4 illustrates an attempt to generate some projections. The first column represents the current system as a basis for comparison, while the next two columns provide "best guess" projections of what might happen in Years 1 and 2 under the new sales compensation plan. (Of course, we have no guarantee that the past year's results would be repeated this coming year if we don't change anything, but let's leave that issue aside for now.)

PROJECTIONS FOR YEAR 1   Our first assumption is that total sales volume in Year 1 under the new system will remain constant. This will be the result of two opposing forces. On the one side is improved employee relations: more cooperation among sales engineers; more training by senior engineers; better cooperation between sales engineers, chemists, and production; a higher calibre of sales engineer hired; and lower turnover of new sales engineers—all of which should work to increase sales. But against that, we expect sales engineers to devote more time to selling custom products, which is more time-consuming. In addition, the sales levels of senior sales engineers may drop somewhat as they spend more time helping junior sales engineers. And, of course, the new compensation system may result in the loss of some senior sales engineers, also reducing sales.

These factors will certainly reduce sales of OTS products; but by how much? We are estimating that the new system should boost the mix of custom products sold in the first year by 33 percent, from $10,000,000 to $13,300,000, and that OTS product will drop to $26,700,000, resulting in no net change in sales volume.

These predictions will depend on our turnover assumptions. We are assuming that the new pay system will cut the annual turnover of first-year sales engineers from 20 engineers to 10, and of middle-level sales engineers

TABLE 5.4

Canada Chemicals Corporation—Projected Results of New Sales Compensation System

	Current System	Proposed System Projected Results		Proposed System Pessimistic Expectations	
		YEAR 1	YEAR 2	YEAR 1	YEAR 2
Sales volume	$40,000,000	$40,000,000	$42,000,000	$36,700,000	$40,000,000
Proportion of custom products	25%	33%	40%	36%	33%
Gross Margin	$20,000,000	$20,660,000	$22,260,000	$19,175,000	$20,660,000
Sales engineer compensation	$5,000,000	$6,000,000	$6,174,245	$5,792,000	$6,000,000
Sales engineer turnover	30/100	25/100	15/100	25/100	15/100
Sales training costs	$150,000	$200,000	$120,000	$200,000	$120,000
Additional training costs	–	$100,000	$100,000	$100,000	$100,000
Recruitment costs	$120,000	$100,000	$60,000	$100,000	$60,000
Gross Margin					
(after subtracting direct sales costs)	$14,730,000	$14,260,000	$15,805,755	$12,983,000	$14,380,000
Add production cost savings	–	$386,800	$789,600	$175,250	$386,800
Net Margin	$14,730,000	$14,746,000	$16,595,355	$13,158,250	$14,766,800
Subtract administrative overhead	$9,730,000	$9,243,500	$9,501,345	$9,438,100	$9,243,500
Add additional production cost savings	–	$967,000	$1,381,800	$525,750	$967,000
Gross Profit before Taxes	$5,000,000	$6,369,500	$8,475,000	$4,245,900	$6,490,300
Subtract additional profit-sharing costs	–	$644,027	$854,280	$427,986	$654,222
Subtract additional stock plan costs	–	$644,027*	$644,027*	$644,027*	$644,027*
Net Profit before Taxes	$5,000,000	$5,081,446	$6,976,693	$3,173,887	$5,192,051

*Note: This assumes that all employees will purchase their full allotment of shares, which is unlikely. This also assumes that the shares contributed by the company are purchased on the market. However, if the company wished to conserve cash, it could issue treasury shares. This would, of course, dilute shareholder equity.

from 10 to five. But what about senior sales engineers? Under the proposed new plan, their compensation will actually drop, since their earnings are currently based mainly on high-volume, low-margin OTS products. Furthermore, part of their commissions will now be based on the average in their sales team (which is the effect of the group commissions), which will also bring down their pay. For example, consider a sales engineer currently selling $700,000 worth of OTS product and $100,000 of custom product, therefore earning direct compensation of $60,000 (i.e., 5 percent of $800,000 plus $20,000 base pay). Even if that engineer maintains these sales volumes, direct pay would drop to $57,721 under the new plan. But maintaining these sales volumes is unlikely, since senior engineers will be expected to shift more concentration to custom product, and spend more time training new sales engineers, so their income would likely drop more than this.

How will they react to this? Let's assume the worst—that we lose all 10 of our top producing sales engineers. This would increase turnover to 25 sales engineers in the first year of the new plan and exert a downward push on total sales at least in Year 1, until they are replaced by new sales engineers.

What about other costs? Currently, sales training costs about $5,000 per new engineer, most of which is the cost of base pay and benefits during the two-month training period. However, this cost will actually go up in Year 1 under the new plan, even though we only need to train 25 engineers, rather than 30. This is because base pay and indirect pay will be higher under the new plan. We may save a little on recruiting costs, which have been running at $4,000 per recruit. But in order to get the new system working, it needs to be explained to all sales engineers, and training will be needed for their new roles. Let's allocate a week to that—the cost of which will be at least $100,000, probably more.

On the positive side of the ledger, profitability of the sales is expected to go up as more custom product is sold. If we reach our 33 percent increase target for custom products in Year 1 and have no loss in total volume, gross margin will increase from $20,000,000 to $20,660,000. But after direct sales costs are included, gross margin would actually decrease from $14,730,000 to $14,260,000. Thus, if all the assumptions work out the way we expect them to, the new compensation system would decrease profits by about $470,000 in Year 1 compared with what they would have been with no change in the compensation system—not a very promising result.

But wait one minute! We haven't considered whether the new sales compensation might produce improvements in other areas, such as production costs. Currently, there is considerable time and effort wasted by chemists and production staff because sales engineers bring in sloppy custom orders where customer requirements have not been well assessed. In some cases, the result is unacceptable product, which is also costly.

Because of a higher calibre of sales engineer, lower turnover, and more motivation to sell custom products, you believe that better work from sales engineers can cut production costs by at least 2 percent in the first year. This would have the effect of increasing the net margin to $14,646,000. That means the firm would almost break even in the first year of the new compensation system—not bad when you consider that most organizational changes result in an initial dip in productivity because of the costs and turmoil involved in getting the new system up and running.

But the sales compensation system is not the only aspect of compensation being changed. We are also extending profit sharing and stock ownership to everybody (assuming the union signs on). Beyond the projected cost of the new sales compensation system (which included the costs of profit sharing and stock plans), these two plans will cost an additional $1,288,054 to extend to the other 260 employees. Can we afford this?

Well, we might be able to if we assume that profit sharing and stock ownership will together reduce turnover, improve cooperation between departments, and improve productivity among the production and administrative employees (we have already included the projected impact of these plans on the sales engineers). We estimate that this should result in a 5-percent reduction in production costs, and a 5-percent reduction in administrative costs in Year 1. This slightly outweighs the cost of these two programs, so the net effect of all this is virtually no change in profitability in Year 1.

But what if we are being too optimistic? Can we really shift attention toward custom products, with all the extra work that entails, lose some of our top-producing sales engineers, and still expect to maintain total sales volume? And what if the productivity increases and cost savings don't materialize the way we expect them to? Are we risking the company?

Let's see what would happen if we change some key assumptions to be more pessimistic. This is exactly what column 4 of Table 5.4 does. We are still assuming that the volume of custom products will increase to $13,330,000; but we are now assuming that total sales volume will drop by $3,330,000 to $36,700,000. Instead of a 2-percent drop in production costs due to better work by the sales engineers, we'll project a 1-percent reduction. Changing these two assumptions drops sales compensation to $5,792,000 (compared with $6 million in the first projection) but also drops net margin to $13,158,250—a drop of over $1.5 million compared with what it would be if we carried on with the current system.

But that's not all! Let's tone down the productivity and administrative cost savings for the nonsales employees to 3 percent from 5 percent. All of this results in a reduction of projected profit from $5 million under the current system to just over $3 million under the proposed new system. It wouldn't put us out of business, but shareholders wouldn't be too happy. But what if no cost savings at all materialized? We would still make a profit of more than $2 million. So it doesn't look as if we are risking the company, even if everything goes wrong. Of course, if everything does go wrong, you will likely be pounding the pavement looking for another job, unless you own enough shares to control the board of directors!

To sum up the results of all of these projections: if all goes well, we gain nothing; if all goes badly, we suffer reduced profits of nearly $3 million. Would you take that deal? Not likely! So far, it doesn't seem as if the new compensation strategy would be worth all the trouble and turmoil it would likely cause. But we were not expecting it to pay off in the first year anyway. Changes in behaviour take time, and getting everyone up to speed on the new system won't happen overnight. Let's do some projections for a two-year period. (Luckily, you have this all loaded on a computer spreadsheet.)

PROJECTIONS FOR YEAR 2 Column 3 of Table 5.4 provides projections for Year 2 of the new system. It assumes that turnover of sales engineers will drop to half the original level, that sales engineers will work together to help each other, and that working with the other departments will become significantly easier. Total sales are assumed to increase by 5 percent to $42 million, and 40 percent of that is assumed to be custom products. Although sales compensation by these calculations exceeds $6 million, gross margin after sales costs rises to $15,805,755. In addition, we expect more experienced sales engineers to be able to provide better custom proposals and reduce production costs by

Chapter 5: Formulating the Reward and Compensation Strategy

4 percent compared with the current system. All this results in a net margin of $16,595,355, a gain of $1.87 million from what would have happened without the new system.

For the rest of the picture, we expect administrative and overhead costs to rise by 5 percent to accommodate the higher sales volume, but then to be reduced by 7 percent as the impact of reduced turnover and more committed and cooperative employees becomes significant. For the same reasons, we expect a 7-percent drop in production costs from their pre-implementation levels. The net effect is profitability almost $2 million higher than it would have been without the new system. This should make shareholders happy, as well as employees (who will also be shareholders). What's more, we will have a more flexible, cooperative company, better suited for the contextual variables it faces.

But let's be pessimistic again. Let's see what happens in Year 2 under pessimistic assumptions. That's what column 5 in Table 5.4 shows. After the disastrous first year (shown in column 4), we are assuming that sales volume recovers to the original levels but that custom work stays steady at $13,330,000. Assuming that performance of sales engineers reduces production costs by 2 percent, the net margin is $14,766,800—virtually identical to what it would have been with no changes in compensation. Assuming other cost savings of 5 percent, total profit for Year 2 amounts to just over $5 million, similar to what it would have been without the new system. Of course, because of the nearly $2-million profit shortfall in Year 1 (under the pessimistic projections), we are behind about $2 million over the two years.

Making the Decision

So do we go ahead with the new compensation system or not? If our expected projections represent reality, then of course, yes. But there are so many assumptions that could be wrong. How much confidence do we have in our "best guess" projections? What if the pessimistic estimates are closer to the truth? Why not just play it safe and stick with the current system?

Well, there is one key assumption we have not examined. For comparison purposes, we have assumed that by doing nothing, things would stay the same, including our $5-million profit. But is that really a good assumption? Consider that profitability has been dropping a million dollars a year for the last three years. Consider all the problems that are emerging. Consider the fact that application of the strategic framework (from Chapter 2) predicts that the performance decline will continue because of a mismatch between the contextual variables and the classical school of management the organization has been practising.

If this is true, then even with the pessimistic projections, the new system looks good. All in all, it appears that the risks of not doing anything are greater than the risks of going ahead. If you fail to act because you are not completely sure about the consequences of your actions, then you will never act. In short, whatever your decision, you will lose some sleep over it. But making decisions like this is the reason why you are paid the big bucks!

There are still a few things that you need to do before going ahead. One is to develop goals and indicators for evaluating your strategy, as will be discussed next. Another is to check the legality of the new plan, even if there seem to be no obvious legal problems with it. If the position of sales engineer is a primarily male job class, and if you are in a jurisdiction with pay equity laws, you may have to modify pay levels of some of your female job classes (although this wouldn't affect many employees in this particular company), since pay is going up for your male group. However, this adjustment may not be possible until the system has been in place for a year, since you don't know whether the pay of sales engineers will actually go up, or by how much.

Setting Goals for the New Strategy

You've decided to take the plunge and go ahead. But you are still aware that this is no sure thing. You need to design a process for evaluating the success of the new compensation system once it has been implemented. To do this, you need to develop the specific goals you hope the plan will achieve, along with performance indicators for evaluating whether these goals are being achieved. This should enable you to evaluate whether modifications to the compensation plan are needed and identify what those modifications should be. Examples of possible compensation goals and performance indicators are shown in Table 5.5.

Remaining Tasks

A lot remains to be done before plan implementation. You need to identify the other factors in the managerial system need to change to make the compensation system work. You may also need to modify the compensation strategy for other employee groups in the firm. Afterwards, the most important tasks are to develop the implementation plan, create the necessary infrastructure for operating the new compensation system, and then manage it on an ongoing basis. Even a sound compensation strategy can be torpedoed by poor implementation and weak ongoing management. These issues are covered in depth in Chapter 12.

Compensating Different Employee Groups

RPC 5.6

Should the compensation strategy be different for different employee groups? Traditionally, it has been for most organizations. Normally, employees are categorized into several groups, and a separate compensation system is used for each group. There are six main groups: hourly paid employees, clerical employees, sales employees, professional employees, managerial employees, and executives. Most firms also differentiate between permanent, full-time employees, and contingent workers—workers who are part-time or temporary. Some even have separate systems for new hires and existing employees.

Traditional hierarchical organizations (which include both classical and human relations organizations) have always based compensation on hierarchical level, on the assumption that jobs (and employees) higher in the

Table 5.5

Canada Chemicals Corporation—Goals for New Sales Compensation System

GOAL	INDICATOR
Membership Behaviour	
1. Increase attraction of new sales engineers	• Increase qualified applicants from 160 to 400
	• Increase offer acceptance rate from 25% to 50%
2. Increase retention of new sales engineers	• Reduce turnover of first-year engineers from 67% to 33%
3. Increase retention of other sales engineers	• Reduce turnover from 14% to 7%
Task Behaviour	
4. Increase sales of custom product	• Increase from 25% of sales to 33% in year 1
	• Increase to 40% of sales in year 2
5. Maintain/increase total sales volume	• Maintain total sales volume in year 1
	• Increase total sales volume by 5% in year 2
6. Improve cooperation with other sales engineers	• Sales employee surveys
7. Improve quality of custom proposals	• Reduction in rejected product due to sales errors
	• Reduction in hours by chemists processing proposals
Citizenship Behaviour	
8. Increase cooperation with other departments	• Surveys of other departments
9. Increase flow of suggestions for improvement	• Number of suggestions submitted
Financial Goals (Overall Compensation System)	
10. Production costs	• Reduce by 7% in year 1
	• Reduce by 11% in year 2
11. Net profit	• Exceed $5 million in year 1
	• Exceed $7 million in year 2

organization are more valuable and thus should be compensated more highly. Classical organizations typically pay their lowest-level employees based on individual performance (piece work or commissions) if they can, or else the number of hours worked. Employees higher in the hierarchy are provided with salaries and limited indirect pay. Top management is provided base pay, indirect pay, and a large component of organizational performance pay. The logic behind providing organizational performance pay to only top management is that only they are in a position to significantly impact the success of the organization.

The compensation system in human relations firms is not much different, except that there is a greater tendency to put all employees on salary. Indirect pay is also typically more generous than in classical firms. But organizational performance pay is still confined to senior management.

However, in recent years, two major trends have emerged: a greater tendency to extend group and organizational performance pay throughout the organization, and a trend toward greater similarity of treatment for employees within the compensation system. Sales employees now often have base pay included in their compensation plans, while other employees have an element of performance pay added to their compensation. Stock options used to be provided only to senior management; now many firms provide them to all employees. Perks that were formerly restricted to top management are now either being offered widely or are being eliminated. Some firms are moving away from hourly pay toward "all salary" systems to reduce distinctions between employee groups. In many cases, these changes are being made to create a greater sense of cohesion and unity among the workforce, particularly in firms that adopt the high-involvement model.

According to the framework developed in this book, the compensation system for various employee groups should differ if the type of required behaviour differs significantly between employee groups or if the needs of the employees in the various employee groups are significantly different. If required behaviour is similar, then the compensation system should reflect this similarity. Aside from sales employees, who were discussed in Chapter 4, there are four main groups for whom the compensation system often differs dramatically from the compensation norm in the organization—contingent employees, new employees, executives, and international employees.

Contingent Workers

One trend that received a lot of notice during the 1990s was the increasing use of **contingent workers**—workers not employed on a full-time, permanent basis. For example, by 1996, approximately 19 percent of Canadian employees were part-time workers, nearly a 50-percent increase since 1976.[7] Other types of contingent workers—temporary full-time employees, independent contractors, and persons hired from temporary help agencies—also made up an increasing proportion of the workforce.[8] Some observers even wondered whether this trend heralded the end of the full-time permanent job as the standard model of employment.[9]

However, the trend toward contingent workers (sometimes known as "non-standard workers") has levelled off in some respects. For example, the proportion of part-time employees did not grow at all between 1996 and 2000;[10] and the Compensation Practices Survey (CPS) showed no change between 2000 and 2004. Moreover, the average length of time that a worker is employed by the same employer, which had decreased during the 1980s

contingent workers

workers not employed on a permanent, full-time basis

and early 1990s, had by 2000 returned to levels similar to what they had been in the 1970s.[11] On the other hand, in the past few years, the proportion of new employees hired into temporary jobs has increased from 11 percent in 1989 to 21 percent in 2004.[12] According to the CPS, another change that occurred during this time period was an increase in the outsourcing of employees: the percentage of the firm's total labour requirements that is outsourced increased from 6 percent in 2000 to 8 percent in 2004.

Why do firms employ contingent workers? In some cases, contingent workers are hired to handle highly skilled work for which the skills do not exist within the organization—such as designing a new computer system or planning a plant expansion—because the organization cannot afford to maintain or fully utilize their skills on an ongoing basis. In other cases, contingent workers are hired to assist regular employees to handle overflow work and temporary peaks in workflow. Contingent workers are also hired as temporary replacements to handle vacations, parental leaves, and other forms of leave. The key difference from regular, permanent employees is that contingent workers are used only when needed, and they are released when they are not.

However, sometimes contingent workers are hired to do the regular work of the organization on an ongoing basis. For example, retailers may hire a few full-time cashiers but have most of this work done by part-timers. Using part-timers helps deal with a workload that fluctuates with time of day, day of the week, and even day of the month. Often these employees are not really temporary at all, nor are they peripheral to the main operations of the business; but they are employed only at the will of the organization. However, some firms differentiate between casual part-time and permanent part-time employees. The latter group are not really contingent workers, since the firm makes a commitment to provide at least a certain minimal level of employment on a continuing basis.

Use of contingent workers generally frees employers from many of the legal constraints that apply to permanent employees. For example, contingent employees are typically exempt from severance pay provisions, as well as from employee benefits. Contract employees (although not part-time employees) are exempt from employment standards provisions and mandatory benefits. No cause is needed for dropping a contingent worker from the workforce, so this makes it easy to correct selection errors. Some employers, especially those from the classical school, may believe that contingent workers are easier to manage because the employer can hold the threat of dismissal over their heads.

Of course, some firms see contingent workers simply as a way of reducing the cost of labour and attempt to substitute contingent workers for regular employees whenever possible. But for other firms, the motives are somewhat more complicated. These firms see their labour force as consisting of two groups of employees. One group consists of core employees, who are committed, loyal, and highly knowledgeable, with skills and training that have taken years to acquire. They are compensated accordingly. But it is too expensive to use these core employees for routine, repetitive, low-skilled work, so

Part II: Formulating Reward and Compensation Strategy

contingent workers (the second group) are used for this type of work. Using contingent workers to do a portion of the organization's regular work also provides a buffer to protect core employees if product/service demand drops. Recent research in the United States showed that firms offering the most costly benefits to permanent employees used significantly more contingent workers than employers offering more modest benefits.[13]

Yet the Conference Board study of Canadian employers found that "controlling benefits costs" and "buffering core workers against job loss" were the two *least* important reasons for using contingent workers, as each was cited by less than 15 percent of respondents.[14] In contrast, "developing labour flexibility to meet demand fluctuations" was cited by more than 90 percent of employers as a reason, and "acquiring special expertise" was cited by about 70 percent. Nearly half cited "controlling head count," and about one-quarter cited "screening candidates for future employment."

From a compensation point of view, the key issue is how to pay these employees. If the work they are doing is the same as that of permanent employees, and the current compensation system is effective, management would want to use the same compensation system for both groups of employees. But if management believes that the compensation system has become too generous or expensive, particularly for some types of work, they may deal with this problem by using a different compensation system for contingent workers. Of course, if the behaviour expected of contingent workers is significantly different from that of regular employees, then a different compensation system may well be justified.

In organizations where contingent workers perform regular, important functions, such as in banking, the same compensation system is often extended to all employees. For example, the Royal Bank has introduced a "one employee" policy, where all employees participate in the same compensation system. But this is not the norm. In the Conference Board study, only 20 percent of respondents indicated that their firms offered the same benefits to contingent workers who worked side-by-side with regular employees; and other research has shown that contingent workers are often paid less than regular workers[15] and receive fewer benefits.[16]

According to equity theory, this discrepancy in pay should lead to perceptions of inequity, from which negative consequences might arise. Unfortunately, there has been little direct research into this issue, although studies have found that turnover is much higher among part-time workers than full-time workers,[17] and job satisfaction is lower.[18] However, a study in the United States found no difference between the task performance of contingent and permanent office workers at a large university.[19]

One factor that may influence employee reactions is whether the employees are doing contingent work voluntarily or involuntarily. For example, Marshall notes that the majority (73 percent) of part-time employees in Canada are engaged in part-time employment because they prefer it, or because their circumstances prevent them from accepting full-time employment.[20] It would be expected that involuntary part-time employees will be less satisfied with part-time work and exhibit higher turnover than employees who prefer part-time employment. But while some studies have borne out this expectation, such as studies of Canadian nurses[21] and temporary help employeees,[22] others have not.[23]

Finally, before we leave the subject of contingent work, the concept of job sharing should be clarified. On some levels, job sharing may appear to be a type of contingent work, since job sharers work less than a full workweek—generally half. But job sharing is not contingent work because job sharers are considered permanent employees, with rights similar to those of full-time employees. Under job sharing, two individuals share one full-time job, along with the pay and benefits that attach to that job.

Employers are generally motivated to allow job sharing in order to retain valued employees who do not wish to work a full workweek for various reasons. Not surprisingly, job sharers show greater satisfaction with their hours and pay than do casual part-time employees.[24] In general, research shows that job-sharing employees are at least as committed as full-time employees to their employer and may even be more productive, because they are better able to strike a balance between their home and work lives.

New Employees

One compensation practice that became popular in the early 1990s was the **two-tier wage system**, in which new employees receive lower wages than existing employees for doing exactly the same work. Of course, you could argue that seniority systems, merit pay, and pay-for-knowledge systems all produce the same result. However, the difference is that under seniority-based pay, merit pay, and pay for knowledge, new employees can eventually earn what the older employees now earn once they acquire the same seniority, performance level, or knowledge. In contrast, the intent of many two-tier systems is to ensure that new employees never earn as much as existing employees. By applying it in this way, organizations use the two-tier wage structure as a vehicle to permanently reduce compensation levels as older employees retire and new employees join the firm. Once all the former employees are gone, there will no longer be two tiers, just one lower tier.

But if the pay level is too high, why not just cut pay levels for all employees and be done with it? Of course, some firms do just that. But for unionized employees, it is legally necessary to get them to approve these reductions, which may not be easy. Since employees who haven't yet been hired have no vote, it is often easier to sell existing employees on a two-tiered system than on across-the-board cuts.

Indeed, if existing employees believe that compensation costs must be cut in order to improve the viability of the firm, they may see a two-tier system as a way to increase their own job security while creating new employment.[25] Meanwhile, management reasons that since new employees know what they are getting into when they join the firm, there is no violation of the psychological contract for them if they join at a lower pay level than that enjoyed by existing employees.

Numerous firms also use a two-tiered approach for their non-union employees, because they believe that it would not be equitable to violate the

two-tier wage system

pay system in which new employees are subject to a different (lower) pay structure than existing employees

psychological contract under which non-union employees were hired. In some cases, it may be illegal to arbitrarily cut compensation for even non-union employees. For example, an Ontario court ruled in favour of a manager who was told at the time of employment that she would be eligible for a bonus paid by a specified date. When the company refused to pay the bonus, she quit her job and took the firm to court. The court ruled that the company could not arbitrarily eliminate the bonus and ordered the firm to pay it.[26]

Some firms use a modified form of the two-tier system for new employees. Rather than creating a permanent pay cut, they offer a temporarily lower wage to new employees in order to tide the firm over difficult circumstances. For example, a firm may now be paying a flat $20 an hour to all employees. Under a temporary two-tier plan, new employees may start at $10, and take five years to reach $20. However, this does not really constitute a full-fledged two-tier system.

Very little is known about the impact of two-tier systems on either new or existing employees or on the relationship between the two groups. Equity theory suggests that once new employees learn that their pay will never match that of existing employees doing precisely the same work, they may find this inequitable. At Lincoln Electric (discussed as a high-involvement firm in Compensation Today 4.4), management did at one time push for a two-tier system. But existing employees strongly resisted it on the basis that it would be inequitable and would impede employee relationships. As a result, the plan was rescinded.

With a two-tier system, lower-tier employees may feel they are being treated as second-class citizens, which may damage their relationships with management and other employees. They may try to balance the psychological contract themselves, resulting in some of the negative consequences discussed in Chapter 3. Of course, offering a lower wage rate can be expected to reduce the quality of new recruits and increase turnover rates.

There is very little empirical evidence on the consequences of two-tier systems. One study did find that low-tier workers reported significantly lower satisfaction with pay and pay fairness than high-tier workers.[27] However, there was no difference in absenteeism and self-reported job effort between the two groups; and—even more interestingly—job satisfaction and affective commitment to the company were actually significantly lower among high-tier workers than among low-tier workers. The explanation may be that dissatisfied high-tier employees perceive no opportunity to leave the company, since their pay is significantly higher than what they could expect elsewhere. However, dissatisfied low-tier employees perceive little difficulty in obtaining comparable employment elsewhere, so they simply leave the firm, leaving behind only the satisfied low-tier employees. Thus, for high-tier employees, the pay system is apparently generating continuance commitment but not affective commitment.

As economic conditions improved during the late 1990s, two-tiered wage systems lost popularity. They have also been subjected to court challenges under human rights legislation, and some jurisdictions (notably Quebec) have amended labour standards legislation to make two-tiered wage structures illegal, although "temporary" two-tier structures are permissible.[28]

But policies to contain wage increases by targeting new employees appear to be having a significant effect, particularly for new male employees.[29] The median hourly earnings of male employees aged 25 to 64 (with at least two years seniority with their current employer) have shown very little movement (after adjusting for inflation) over the past 23 years, ending up just 4 percent higher in 2004 than they were in 1981; at the same time, the median hourly earnings of new male employees in the same age group actually declined by 13 percent. In contrast, the median earnings of female employees in the same age group with at least two years seniority with the same employer rose 14 percent, while the median hourly earnings of new female employees declined just 2 percent over the same time period.

Executives

Another issue that has been attracting a lot of attention for the past few years is executive pay. This is partly because executive pay has been escalating, while the pay of rank-and-file employees has been stagnating; partly because new disclosure laws have made executive pay more visible; and partly because some top executives have profited handsomely in recent scandals which have driven their companies into receivership. The most striking case is Enron Corporation, where mismanagement and fraudulent accounting practices caused the collapse of the firm, along with the collapse of its auditing firm, Arthur Andersen. Just before thousands of Enron employees lost their jobs, life savings and pensions, corporate executives were receiving bonuses and cashing in stock options worth millions of dollars. (For a summary of some of the major corporate scandals of recent years, go to **http://www.thecorporatelibrary.com/Governance-Research/spotlight-topics/scandals.html**.)

In the United States, which leads the world in executive pay, executive compensation had jumped from an average of 43 times the pay of an average worker in 1960 to more than one hundred times by 1990.[30] Moreover, the total annual compensation of some chief executive officers—such as Warner Communication's CEO Steven Ross—had cracked the $100-million mark. Following this trend, executive pay also soared in Canada, resulting in a doubling of the gap between workers and top corporate executives between 1970 and 1990.[31]

Coming at a time when many employers were downsizing, and coupled with evidence that executive pay often bears little or no relation to company performance, this newfound awareness of executive salaries caused a major outcry, which received extensive media coverage. As a result, in 1992, the Securities and Exchange Commission in the United States toughened its already stringent requirements for disclosure of top executive salaries in publicly traded corporations; and in 1994, they took this a step further by limiting the tax deductibility (for corporate taxes) of non-performance-related executive compensation to $1 million per year. In 1993, the Ontario government passed similar legislation, which resulted in the Ontario Securities Commission establishing the first disclosure requirements ever imposed on top executive salaries in Canada.

The outcome of all this? By 2002, the average compensation of chief executive officers in publicly traded U.S. corporations reached 531 times the average pay of a factory worker.[32] Another study found that the pay of the top five executives in publicly-traded companies more than doubled, from 4.8 percent of aggregate earnings of these firms in 1993–1995 to 10.3 percent in 2001–2003, adding up to a total $US 290 *billion*.[33] This occurred during a period when compensation for most workers had shown no real gain.

What message does this send to employees? How do you think they would react to exhortations from their CEO that "we all need to pull together" to ensure the success of "our company"? Sure, workers would likely be disgruntled; but at least managers would side with the executives.

Or would they? Listen to a manager at United Technologies, which had downsized by 30 000 employees in the previous six years. A 20-year veteran of the firm, with good performance reviews, he has done slightly better than the industrial averages, with increases of about 4 percent a year for the past three years. During this period, the net income of the company rose dramatically, by 28 percent in one year alone, a year in which shareholders received a 55-percent return on their investment:

> I used to go to work enthusiastically. Now, I just go in to do what I have to do. I feel overloaded to the point of burnout. Most of my colleagues are actively looking for other jobs or are just resigned to doing the minimum. At the same time, the CEO is paid millions, and his salary is going up faster than anyone else's. It makes me angry and resentful.[34]

In Canada, the divergence between the pay of top executives and other employees has not been as large as in the United States, and Canadian executive compensation did not rise during the 1990s to the heights enjoyed by U.S. executives. Research suggests that Canadian executives currently earn about half what CEOs in comparable U.S. firms receive,[35] compared with about 75 percent in the early 1990s.[36] Overall, the typical Canadian CEO makes about what CEOs earn in most European countries, but more than those in Japan,[37] where executives earn only about 11 times worker pay. According to one expert, the Japanese believe that morale and teamwork within the organization will be destroyed if differences between executive pay and pay of other employees become too large.[38]

One thing to note is that the salary levels enjoyed by U.S. and Canadian corporate executives are not enjoyed by top executives of all organizations. Take David Dodge, governor of the federal Bank of Canada, for example. Dodge has many years of experience in senior public-service positions, including five years as deputy minister of finance, and has a doctorate in economics from Princeton. The quality of his performance can make or break the Canadian economy and can affect the livelihood of millions of Canadians and the success of tens of thousands of businesses. His current salary range: $320,200 to 376,700. At that level, he is one of the most highly paid executives in the federal government, earning more than his boss, the minister of finance ($213,500), as well as the prime minister ($288,600).

Chapter 5: Formulating the Reward and Compensation Strategy

Compensation Today 5.2

10 Highest Paid Canadian CEOs

Name of CEO	Company	Annual Salary	Annual Bonus	Value of Benefits	Value of Stock Grants	Stock Option Gains	Total Compensation
Robert Gratton	Power Financial	$3,500,000	$ 0	$ 327,381	$ 0	$169,365,407	$173,192,788
Bernard Isautier	PetroKazakhstan	493,850	0	0	0	92,621,450	93,115,300
Gerry Schwartz	Onex Corporation	842,725	11,645,338	0	0	63,941,100	76,429,163
Frank Stronach	Magna International	260,300	52,206,679	0	0	0	52,466,979
Pierre Choquette	Methanex	452,381	650,000	8,931	2,279,200	18,599,161	21,599,161
Hunter Harrison	CN Rail	1,626,875	4,555,250	2,230,310	12,615,151	0	21,027,586
D. D'Alessandro	Manulife Financial	1,281,958	3,700,800	60,575	11,298,375	0	16,341,708
Hank Swartout	Precision Drilling	831,000	3,200,000	138,520	0	9,980,211	14,149,731
John Hunkin	CIBC	1,000,000	3,050,000	6,393	4,207,500	4,829,410	13,093,303
Tony Comper	Bank of Montreal	1,000,000	2,000,000	376,285	2,800,000	6,551,496	12,727,781

Source: *The Globe and Mail*. 2005. May 4: B8. Reprinted with permission from *The Globe and Mail*.

Dodge's pay may sound pretty good to the average Canadian wage earner, who received about $37,270 in 2005. But compare Dodge's compensation with that of John Hunkin, CEO of the Canadian Imperial Bank of Commerce, who earned $13,093,303 in 2004, and Dodge's salary doesn't seem quite so substantial. And, to be fair, Hunkin's compensation is not at the top of the corporate list.

Why Do Corporate Executives Make So Much?

So why do corporate executives make so much? A large part of the answer lies in the bonus and incentive structure of their compensation. Let's examine this by looking at the compensation of 10 of Canada's highest-paid executives, as shown in Compensation Today 5.2. Their base pay (which averaged $1,128,909), while substantial, amounted to a very small portion—just 2.3 percent—of their total earnings (which averaged $49,413,800). Income from exercise of stock options accounted for the biggest chunk of earnings, averaging 74 percent ($36,588,600), followed by earnings from the annual bonus, which averaged $3,208,904 (excluding Frank Stronach's bonus, which would skew the average too severely). Stock grants provided another $3,320,022, on average, while "other" compensation averaged $314,840 ("other" compensation includes the value of benefits received by the executive, such as car and housing allowances, interest-free loans, and insurance premiums).

What factors determine how much an executive receives? As already discussed, sector makes an enormous difference, with executives in the corporate sector receiving much more than executives in the public sector. What else? Some observers argue that executive pay should be tied to the financial performance of the corporation; but research in both the United States[39] and Canada[40] shows little or no relationship between executive compensation and company performance after excluding stock options. But once stock options are included, there is a significant relationship between firm performance (in terms of stock value) and executive compensation, although not necessarily between executive compensation and other indicators of corporate performance.[41]

The most important factor affecting executive compensation is firm size, as CEOs of large firms make more than CEOs of small firms.[42] Another important factor is whether the firm is management-controlled or owner-controlled. In many large firms with widely dispersed ownership, there is no single owner with the power to significantly affect management decisions. These firms are termed *management-controlled* firms; firms where this is not the case are termed *owner-controlled*. In general, all other things being equal, top executives in management-controlled firms earn significantly more than top executives in owner-controlled firms.[43] In other words, firms in which top executives determine their own salaries set them higher than firms where top executive salaries are set by owners.

Studies in the United States suggest two other important factors.[44] Firms with fewer hierarchical levels (after controlling for size) pay their top executives less than firms with more hierarchical levels; and more diversified firms pay their CEOs more than less diversified firms. The first factor makes sense when you consider that hierarchical organizations must increase pay at each hierarchical level in order to provide an incentive for employees to move up the hierarchy; and the second makes sense because more diversified organizations are more complex to manage than less diversified organizations.

But these factors still do not explain all of the variation in executive pay, nor all of the recent escalation.[45] One way of examining this further is to understand the process by which executive pay is set in large corporations. The board of directors strikes a compensation committee consisting of several directors. The committee then hires a compensation firm to provide data on how "comparable" chief executive officers are being compensated and then uses these data as a basis for their decisions. This sounds like a rational and reasonable process.

However, the process may not always be as "rational" as it sounds. First, the compensation consultants hired are often recommended by the CEO, and it is in consultants' best interests to keep the CEO happy if they want to do other business with the firm. Thus, when looking for appropriate comparators, the consultant will certainly not be interested in erring on the low side. Furthermore, many boards (especially in management-controlled firms) are populated by directors recommended by top management, and these directors will not wish to incur ill will by being stingy with executive pay. One prominent observer[46]—a former compensation consultant now highly critical of executive compensation practices—also points out that no board of directors wishes to believe that they have an average or below-average CEO, and that most firms attempt to pay above the median market value.[47] If the majority of firms do this, then a continually increasing executive "market" is inevitable.

Moreover, many corporate directors are often themselves CEOs and can be expected to be highly sympathetic to other CEOs. Of course, high executive salaries can be used as evidence for higher compensation when it is *their* turn to be compensated as CEOs. All told, unless someone on the compensation committee is representing the owners' interests, then there is little incentive to hold executive pay down. But perhaps this will change as shareholders become more militant and as institutional investors, such as pension funds, take a more active role in corporate affairs to push for better corporate governance, as the Ontario Teachers' Pension Fund[48] and the Canada Pension Plan Investment Review Board[49] (Canada's largest institutional investor) are already attempting to do.

Executive Pay and Performance

It was noted earlier that CEO compensation does not necessarily bear any relation to company financial performance. But should it? The obvious answer would seem to be "yes"; but is this really correct? One prominent commentator in this area argues that "contrary to much of what one reads in the academic and practitioner press, there is no sound theoretical basis to expect a strong relationship between executive pay and firm performance."[50]

To what extent can a top executive actually influence organizational performance? In the short run, not much, especially in large organizations. In most organizations, financial performance is a function of many factors, many of which are beyond the control of the CEO, especially in the short run. But research does show that CEOs have an increasing impact over a longer time period.[51] This is not surprising. In general, the role of a top executive is to formulate the strategy that best achieves organizational goals and then create an organizational system for carrying out that strategy. Particularly in large organizations, this process may take years to pay off.

Current conditions of the firm may also be an important consideration. A CEO who takes over an organization in a tailspin may be considered a great success if he or she can slow the descent in the first year and start to turn things around in the following two or three years. Does this CEO really deserve less than a CEO who takes over a prosperous firm operating in a highly favourable competitive environment?

Moreover, it may not be in the best interests of the organization or the shareholders to tie executive pay too closely to current or short-term performance. There are all kinds of tricks and manoeuvres to make short-run performance look good which could ruin the firm in the longer run. For example, a CEO could cut research and development expenditures, saving money now but causing a shortage of new products when the old ones become obsolete. A CEO could also cut employee compensation, causing the most-talented employees to gradually leave, which will affect long-term productivity. In addition, a CEO could forgo long-term investments that might be very beneficial to the firm but which would take years to pay off.

Part II: Formulating Reward and Compensation Strategy

For these reasons, long-term incentives, rather than base pay and annual bonuses, have been forming an increasing portion of the CEO's compensation.[52] There are three main types of longer-term incentives commonly used for executive pay: stock options, restricted stock, and long-term unit/share plans.

Problems with Executive Stock Options

Until the Enron debacle, stock options had been very popular, partly because they have traditionally been regarded as a virtually costless way of compensating executives. But use of stock options has come increasingly under critical scrutiny, as shareholders have come to realize that these options do have a very real cost in terms of dilution of equity.[53] Also, in a declining stock market, executives may be penalized despite good performance; in a rising stock market, they may reap windfall gains unrelated to their personal performance. Moreover, in recent years executives are increasingly turning to "zero cost collars"—hedges that tend to decouple performance of the company stocks from their financial returns, effectively reducing their risk.[54] Because hedges do not have to be publicly reported, other shareholders may not know that the CEO is decoupling his or her financial returns from those of the company. As Lavelle puts it, "An executive who hedges is a little bit like the captain of a ship who sees an iceberg up ahead and heads for his lifeboat without waking the sleeping passengers."[55]

However, the biggest problem with large-scale executive stock options is not their cost, nor even the negative impact they may have on employee morale, but their hidden incentives for mismanagement. As the final report of the court-appointed examiner for Enron stated:

> The evidence suggests that the compensation system provided what proved to be an overpowering motivation for implementing [accounting] transactions that distorted Enron's reported financial results. Evidence further shows that flawed or aggressive accounting . . . enabled the Enron officers to obtain greatly inflated bonuses and to realize substantial proceeds from the sale of Enron stock they received as part of their compensation packages. In fact, during a three-year period from 1998 through 2000, a group of twenty-one officers received in excess of $1 billion in the form of salary, bonus, and gross proceeds from the sale of Enron stock.[56]

As a result of these problems, there has been some investor backlash against the use of executive stock options. For example, the Ontario Teachers' Pension Fund, the second-largest institutional investor in Canada, has been pressing for changes so that the basis for CEO compensation depends on whether the firm outperforms competitors, not simply on whether the stock price goes up.[57] Moreover, the Canada Pension Plan Investment Board is now urging that stock option plans be discontinued entirely:

> Stock options are problematic in many areas, including their effectiveness in aligning management interests with those of the shareholders, the potential dilutive impact on existing shareholdings,

their tendency to focus management on short-term performance, their use as a cash incentive rather than an ownership incentive, and intractable accounting issues.[58]

While both prominent academics[59] and corporate executives, such as Bill Gates of Microsoft,[60] also now support the elimination of executive stock options, some experts go even farther than this. Dean Roger Martin of the Rotman School of Business at the University of Toronto has urged that the use of all stock-based compensation for executives be discontinued entirely.[61] His argument is that any type of stock-based compensation for executives is flawed, because these systems create incentives for executives to manipulate stock prices, which is relatively easy for them to do, even without resorting to overtly fraudulent practices. As Martin explains, "Stock-based compensation creates the direct and clear incentive to raise expectations of future earnings and then sell the stock before expectations fall—and then do it all over again."[62] Not all executives will succumb to this temptation; but why structure executive compensation in such a way that dishonest executives are rewarded for their misdeeds, while honest managers are penalized for their honesty? Martin suggests that executives of publicly traded firms be compensated on real, long-term earnings growth, in the same way that executives of corporations that are not publicly traded are often rewarded.

Interestingly, empirical evidence to back up Martin's perspective on executive stock options is now available. Researchers in the United States have found that the likelihood of a firm using questionable accounting practices is directly related to the amount of stock options that executives have been granted.[63] Other researchers have found that stock options were in fact a very expensive way to motivate executives, and that restricted stock is much superior.[64]

Restricted stock is an alternative to stock options. The essence of restricted stock is that executives are granted shares of company stock, but they are not allowed to actually receive these shares unless certain conditions are met. Sometimes the condition is simply a holding period, say of three years, during which period the stock is forfeited if the CEO leaves the firm. In other cases, the executive will not receive the shares unless certain performance targets are reached.

In addition, as a result of the problems inherent in stock options, long-term unit/share plans (as discussed in Chapter 4) have become increasingly popular. If structured properly, long-term unit/share plans can provide a longer-term perspective (three to five years) to counterbalance the short-term perspective that other types of incentives promote.

Of course, a more fundamental question can also be asked: Why should it be necessary to provide incentives to individuals who are already being compensated handsomely for doing their jobs? Is there a concern that without multimillion-dollar stock packages, executives will simply goof off? The response to this question usually focuses on attraction and retention. However, even here, there is room for debate. A recent study by researchers in the United States found that a CEO's total compensation relative to others in the industry had no effect on CEO retention, suggesting that when CEOs leave a company, they do so for reasons other than compensation.[65]

Other Executive Perks

Indirect pay can also be an important component of executive pay, especially for executives who are not in the top echelon of pay. Many executives receive a number of perks of considerable value, the most common of which are company cars, country club memberships, access to the company plane, free travel for family members, payment of financial planning fees, and supplemental executive retirement plans. In Canada, one significant form of indirect pay for some executives (mainly those who are lured from the United States) is the equalization of personal income taxation rates with those in the United States, so that these executives end up receiving the same amount of after-tax income as they would have if they were living in the United States. This is achieved by simply reimbursing executives for the difference between income taxes in Canada and the United States.

One controversial item of indirect pay for executives is known as the "golden parachute." Golden parachutes may be structured in many ways, but the essence is that an executive who is dismissed for any reason within a certain time frame (for example, five years) is guaranteed a large severance payment, usually amounting to about three to five years' pay. Sometimes there is no time limit on these payments, and they kick in whenever the CEO is dismissed.

Many observers argue that such "parachutes" take away the incentive for good performance, since the executive will be paid very nicely regardless of performance. Opposing observers argue that these "parachutes" are beneficial because they encourage executives not to fight takeover bids that may be beneficial to shareholders but which would cause the CEO to lose his or her job. In addition, they argue that it would be difficult to lure good executives away from highly paid jobs with other firms without some financial guarantees to protect them if things do not work out. But opponents ask: Why would you want to hire an executive who has so little faith that an ironclad guarantee is required?

Decision Issues for CEO Pay

So how should a CEO be paid? There are six decision issues:

1. the amount of performance pay relative to base pay and indirect pay;
2. the amount of short-term (annual) performance pay vs. longer-term performance pay;
3. the nature of the performance pay itself;
4. the specific performance indicators used as criteria for the performance pay;
5. the stringency of the performance criteria;
6. the time period to be used as the performance period for the incentive.

How do you decide on the best way to handle each of these decisions? As with all types of compensation, the first question is: What do we want the executive compensation system to accomplish? There are two main aspects to consider: a behavioural aspect and a symbolic aspect.

Chapter 5: Formulating the Reward and Compensation Strategy

The behavioural aspect addresses the kind of executive behaviour the company wants. Research has shown that executives, like most people, tend to pursue actions that maximize their compensation. Therefore, the compensation system should promote executive behaviour that fosters achievement of organizational goals and serves the long-term best interests of the organization.

Moreover, the way top executives are compensated influences the rest of the firm's compensation system. An executive tends to design the firm's compensation system to foster employee behaviour that in turn helps the executive to achieve his or her compensation rewards. This is known as a "cascading effect." Of course, a cascading effect in a compensation system is fine as long as both executive and employee behaviours are in line with the objectives and strategy the organization is pursuing.

The executive compensation system also has a very important symbolic value. Because of its visibility, executive pay is seen as a signal of the kinds of behaviours the organization values. The behaviours for which top executives are rewarded tend to be emulated by subordinates. Another symbolic aspect is an equity or fairness dimension. If executive pay is structured very differently from the pay of other employees, this may cause serious motivational problems and other negative consequences that result from reward dissatisfaction. Recall the manager at United Technologies who had reduced his commitment to the organization because of his dissatisfaction with top executive pay levels. Other employees at the same firm were actively seeking other jobs or were reducing their effort to the minimum for the same reason.

But the need for perceived equity is a much bigger problem in some types of organizations than in others. In classical organizations, perceived inequity is a minimal problem: as long as the cost of turnover is low, extra job effort and citizenship behaviour are not really needed, and controls constrain dysfunctional behaviour. In human relations firms, perceived equity may not be a big problem either, as long as the firm has traditionally demonstrated high concern for employees and has paid relatively well.

But excessive CEO compensation can be a huge problem for high-involvement organizations, where a sense of equity is essential to generating the cooperative and citizenship behaviour that is crucial for success. As Lawler puts it: "High involvement management requires that senior managers . . . give up some of the special perquisites and financial rewards they receive."[66] This is because extreme divergence between executive pay and that of other employees makes it almost impossible for a sense of commonality of interests to emerge.

Expatriate and Foreign Employees

As Canadian companies respond to globalization, an increasing number have established operations outside of Canada. Of course, employees of these foreign operations must be paid; but compensation practices that are suitable in Canada may not be appropriate in other countries. This is because labour market conditions, product market conditions, and legal and cultural conditions differ dramatically in other countries.

A key question is whether the employees are foreign nationals or expatriate Canadians sent to play a role in operating foreign subsidiaries. The compensation policy issues are very different for each of these groups. For firms creating compensation packages for home-country expatriates (those who are sent to foreign countries from Canada), the key issue is to create a compensation package that ensures that expatriates do not lose financially compared with their home-country peers but is still cost-effective for the company. There are four main approaches to expatriate compensation: (1) the balance sheet, (2) negotiation, (3) localization, and (4) lump sum.

The most common approach has been the **balance sheet approach**. The objective of the balance sheet approach is to create a compensation system that enables expatriates to maintain a standard of living comparable with what they would enjoy in their home country, regardless of the host country they are sent to. Expatriate expenses are broken down into four main categories: (1) income taxes, (2) housing, (3) goods and services, and (4) a "reserve" or "discretionary" component. Costs of comparable income taxes, housing, and goods and services in the host country are calculated and then converted to Canadian dollars, and the "reserve" amount is added. This total amount (paid in Canadian dollars) is the base pay for the expatriate. The "reserve amount" is calculated by determining how much a comparable Canada-based employee would have left as discretionary income. In some cases, an additional amount may be added to base pay as a "hardship allowance" to compensate expatriates who are sent to locations that have health and safety risks or other undesirable aspects.

However, there are several potential problems with this procedure. These problems include changes in the currency exchange rates in the period after conversion to Canadian dollars, as well as changes in tax rates, housing costs, or other living costs. To deal with these problems, management can use an equalization approach. For example, for income taxes, the company can deduct the cost of Canadian income taxes from the expatriate's pay and then simply pay the expatriate's actual income taxes in the host country, which could be more or less than the Canadian amount. This creates a tax-neutral treatment from the expatriate's point of view.

An equalization approach for housing expenses is similar. Reasonable Canadian costs are calculated, and this amount is deducted from the expatriate's income. The company then pays whatever it actually takes to provide comparable housing in the host country, either directly to the foreign landlord or through payment to the employee in the local currency. The same basic procedure can be followed for other living expenses. The key advantage of this approach is that expatriate employees are treated equally regardless of the host country, and that compensation does not need to change as exchange rates or local circumstances change. Employees can also be transferred from one host country to another without changing the way they are compensated.

Besides the balance sheet approach, several other approaches to expatriate pay have been developed. *Negotiation* is a process in which the employer and employee negotiate a mutually acceptable package. However, there are numerous problems with this approach. First, the employee may not be very knowledgeable about conditions in the host country and thus may find it

balance sheet approach approach to designing expatriate compensation that attempts to provide a standard of living comparable with the home country

difficult to judge whether a package is reasonable or not. Second, there is the potential for inequity if different packages are negotiated for different employees, especially if the differences are based only on the negotiating skills of the employees. Third, the packages often have no systematic procedure for changing them in response to changes in host country conditions.

Localization is the practice of paying expatriate employees the same compensation as local nationals in equivalent positions. This method fits best with assignments that are going to be long term, with companies that have extensive operations (and well-developed compensation systems) in the host country and in host countries that have higher compensation levels than Canada, as is generally the case with Canadian employees assigned to the United States. Localization to home-country (i.e., Canadian) rates is also often done for foreign nationals who have been assigned work in Canada on other than a temporary basis.

Another approach to expatriate compensation is the *lump sum approach*. This method differs from the balance sheet approach in that the various allowance amounts (such as for housing) are paid directly in home-country (i.e., Canadian) dollars to the employee, who may then decide to live in a lower standard of housing than the norm and pocket the remainder of that allowance. Problems with this approach include changes in foreign exchange or local conditions, and possible losses of some tax advantages. For example, in some countries, housing allowances are not taxed as income to the employee, although salary paid directly to the employee is.

One issue common to all approaches is the amount of premium to pay for foreign assignments. These premiums are paid over and above the standard compensation that preserves the employee's standard of living, and they vary considerably for different countries. There is no hard and fast system for determining the amounts of these premiums, and the only method may be to assess employees' degree of aversion to each country. Of course, what may be paradise to one employee may be purgatory to another, so this is a subjective process.

The usual method for paying foreign premiums is to simply prorate them and add the prorated amount to the monthly paycheques. However, this method artificially inflates monthly pay and may make employees reluctant to transfer from a high-premium country to a lower-premium country or to repatriate to Canada. To deal with this problem, some firms use "mobility bonuses"—employees are paid the premium as an up-front bonus, thus removing disincentives for transfer.

"Third-country nationals"—employees of the firm not based in the home country who are assigned to a third country—are treated somewhat differently from expatriates. For example, suppose that a Canadian firm assigns a Spanish employee from its Spanish subsidiary to its operation in Chile. Should the employee be compensated in Spanish currency using a balance sheet approach, or should the employee be localized? While the same decision rules could be used as for Canadian expatriates, this does get very complicated, especially if the balance sheet approach is used. Another problem occurs when employees from two or more foreign countries are assigned to the same third country. For one, the balance sheet approach may be most appropriate, while for another, the localization approach is best. Unless localization is used for both employees, they will have very different compensation levels, even if they perform the same work. To avoid this problem, some companies simply use the same rates as would apply to Canadian expatriates in Chile; but this may not be fair to third-country nationals from high-wage countries such as the United States. Unfortunately, there are no simple solutions.

A final issue has to do with compensation of local nationals in foreign countries. Clearly, the home-country (Canadian) compensation system would probably be inappropriate. But this is not to say that the most appropriate compensation strategy is to simply copy local competitors. The same understandings discussed earlier in the chapter—understanding your context, people, compensation options, and compensation constraints—need to be applied to the foreign subsidiary, along with the five steps in the compensation strategy formulation process. The resulting compensation system could well be different from that used in the home country and from that used by local competitors.

Because of the complexity of international compensation, the objective of this section has been to simply acquaint the reader with some of the key issues, and more detailed information is available elsewhere.[67]

Summary

After studying this chapter, you should understand the process for building an effective compensation strategy. Four key understandings form the necessary foundation of knowledge for compensation strategy formulation— understanding your organization, your people, your compensation options, and your constraints. The first four chapters of this book cover the first three understandings, while this chapter identifies four types of constraints that set the parameters for compensation strategy—legislated, labour market, product/service market, and financial constraints—and illustrates how understanding them is essential for formulating the compensation strategy.

Next, you learned about the five main steps in formulating the compensation strategy: (1) define the behaviour that the organization requires; (2) define the role the compensation system will play in eliciting that behaviour; (3) determine the best mix of compensation components; (4) determine policies for compensation level; and (5) evaluate the proposed strategy against effectiveness criteria. As part of this process, you learned who should be involved in the compensation strategy formulation process, and how to apply the five steps with the use of a detailed example in which you played the CEO.

Finally, you examined some of the issues related to compensating four special employee groups—contingent workers, new employees, executives, and international employees.

The remaining three parts of this book focus on how to convert the compensation strategy from a blueprint into an operational compensation system. Part III covers the technical processes for evaluating jobs, evaluating the market, and evaluating individuals. Part IV discusses the key issues in designing effective performance pay and indirect pay plans. Part V covers the processes for implementation, ongoing management, evaluation, and adaptation of the compensation system.

Key Terms

balance sheet approach, 229

contingent workers, 215

employment standards legislation, 179

human rights legislation, 181

hybrid compensation policy, 197

labour market constraints, 183

lag compensation policy, 193

lead compensation policy, 194

match compensation policy, 194

product/service market constraints, 184

technical ladder, 187

trade union legislation, 182

two-tier wage system, 218

utility analysis, 195

Web Links

To check on current minimum wage rates in your jurisdiction and other employment standards and labour legislation, go to **http://www.hrsdc.gc.ca/ asp/gateway.asp?hr=en/lp/spila/clli/eslc/01Employment_Standards_ Legislation_in_Canada.shtml&hs=lxn**. (p. 180)

For a variety of information on pay and benefits in each province, go to **http://search-recherche.gc.ca/cgi-bin/query?mss=canada%2Fen%2Fsimple. html&enc=iso88591&pg=q&kl=en&site=main&browser=IE&q=Pay+and+ Benefits**. (p. 180)

For information on the Canadian Human Rights Act, administered by the Canadian Human Rights Commission, to go to their website at **http://www. chrc-ccdp.ca/default-en.asp?lang_update=1**. (p. 181)

For more detail on legislation surrounding collective bargaining, go to **http:// www.hrsdc.gc.ca/asp/gateway.asp?hr=en/lp/spila/clli/irlc/01industrial_ relations_legislation_canada.shtml&hs=czc**. (p. 182)

For detailed analysis of trends for non-standard workers, go to **http://www. statcan.ca/Daily/English/050126/d050126a.htm**. (p. 216)

For a summary of some of the major corporate scandals of recent years, go to **http://www.thecorporatelibrary.com/Governance-Research/spotlight- topics/scandals.html**. (p. 220)

For information about a range of issues involved with being an expatriate employee, go to **http://www.escapeartist.com**. (p. 228)

RPC Icons

RPC 5.1 Identifies and develops the philosophy, strategy, and policy of the total compensation package to be consistent with the organization's goals. This is accomplished within the context of the legal, regulatory, taxation, and community framework.

RPC 5.2 Designs and evaluates total compensation strategies to ensure that they reflect the organization's goals, culture, and external environment.

RPC 5.3 Evaluates the total compensation strategy to ensure it is consistent with the objectives of attracting, motivating, and retaining the qualified people required to meet organizational goals.

RPC 5.4 Considering the total compensation strategy, develops a compensation program including base pay, variable pay, profit and gain sharing, incentive pay, and stock options, and recommends the best mix.

RPC 5.5 Assesses the effectiveness of the compensation program in achieving the organization's goals, and its competitiveness in attracting qualified candidates.

RPC 5.6 Establishes compensation policies and procedures based on the compensation program and compliance with the legal framework.

Discussion Questions

1. Managers need to use the four key understandings necessary in formulating an effective compensation strategy. Discuss why and how each contributes to effective compensation strategy formulation.
2. Discuss the constraints that set the parameters for the compensation strategy.
3. Discuss and explain the five main steps in the compensation strategy formulation process (Figure 5.1). Which do you think is the most difficult step?
4. Discuss specific considerations in deciding whether to adopt a lead, lag, or match compensation level policy.
5. Discuss the special issues involved in compensating contingent workers, new employees, executives, and international employees.

Using the Internet

1. How do the employment standards in your province vary from those in other provinces? Go to **http://search-recherche.gc.ca/cgi-bin/query? mss=canada%2Fen%2Fsimple.html&enc=iso88591&pg=q&kl=en&site =main&browser=IE&q=Pay+and+Benefits** and compare the employment standards in your province with those of your neighbouring provinces.
2. To what extent do you think employees in different occupations are attracted by different workplace characteristics? What about employees in the financial services industry, such as banking or insurance? Go to **http://www.towersperrin.com/tillinghast/publications/publications/ emphasis/Emphasis_2002_1/2002041805.pdf** to read the results of a survey of employees in the financial services industry. How closely do these results match the ranking shown in Table 5.1? What may be some of the reasons for the differences? How would you rank the items in Table 5.1?

Exercises

1. In your role as CEO of Canada Chemicals Corporation (described earlier in the chapter), you have just finished formulating a new compensation strategy for sales engineers. It occurs to you that given your movement toward high-involvement management, your firm may also need a new compensation strategy for production workers, administrative staff, and technical staff. Using a strategic compensation template similar to that used in Figure 5.2, formulate a compensation strategy for each of these employee groups.
2. You are a prominent compensation consultant, and you have been hired by the board of directors of Canada Chemicals Corporation to recommend a compensation strategy for the firm's top executives. In your report, be sure to provide the reasoning for each of your recommendations, along with the advantages and disadvantages of each recommended compensation element.
3. Canada Chemicals Corporation has decided to move to a high-involvement managerial strategy and has hired you as a consultant to that process. Aside from the compensation strategy, what other changes need to be made if this conversion is to be successful? Is there any way to increase the intrinsic and extrinsic rewards (besides through compensation) provided by the firm? How could this be done?

Case Questions

1. Susan Superfit, CEO in "The Fit Stop" case in the Appendix, has hired you to formulate a compensation strategy for her firm. Using the five-step compensation strategy formulation process (Figure 5.1), formulate such a strategy, and summarize it using a strategic template similar to that shown in Figure 5.2. Give your rationale for each element of the strategy.

2. Using the five-step compensation strategy formulation process (Figure 5.1), formulate a compensation strategy for production workers in the "Multiproducts Corporation" case in the Appendix and summarize it using a strategic template similar to that shown in Figure 5.2. Justify your recommendations.

Simulation Cross-Reference

If you are using *Strategic Compensation: A Simulation* in conjunction with this text, you will find that the concepts in Chapter 5 are helpful in preparing Sections C and N of the simulation.

Endnotes

1. Braun, Katherine. 1997. "Employment Standards Legislation in Canada." Unpublished report: 17.
2. Renaud, Stephane. 1998. "Unions, Wages, and Total Compensation in Canada." *Relations Industrielles/Industrial Relations*, 53(4): 710–29.
3. "Wages, Productivity Fall at Small Firms." 1996. *Star-Phoenix*. October 4: D9.
4. Evans, David S., and Linda S. Leighton. 1989. "Why Do Smaller Firms Pay Less?" *The Journal of Human Resources*, 24(2): 299–318.
5. Klaas, Brian S., and John A. McClendon. 1996. "To Lead, Lag, or Match: Estimating the Financial Impact of Pay Level Strategies." *Personnel Psychology*, 49(1): 121–41.
6. Klaas, Brian S., and John A. McClendon. 1996. "To Lead, Lag, or Match: Estimating the Financial Impact of Pay Level Strategies." *Personnel Psychology*, 49(1): 121–41.
7. Zeytinoglu, Isik. 1999. "Flexible Work Arrangements: An Overview of Developments in Canada." In Isik Zeytinoglu, ed., *Changing Work Relationships in Industrialized Countries*. Amsterdam: John Benjamins Publishing, 41–58.
8. Lebrun, Sharon. 1997. "Growing Contract Workforce Hindered by Lack of Rules." *Canadian HR Reporter*, May 19: 1–2.
9. Zeytinoglu, Isik. 1999. "Flexible Work Arrangements: An Overview of Developments in Canada." In Isik Zeytinoglu, ed., *Changing Work Relationships in Industrialized Countries*. Amsterdam: John Benjamins Publishing, 41–58.
10. Statistics Canada. 2001. *Labour Force Survey Statistics, 1996–2000*. Ottawa: Statistics Canada.
11. Picot, Garnett, Andrew Heisz, and Alice Nakamura. 2000. "Were 1990s Labour Markets Really Different?" *Policy Options*, July-August: 15–26.
12. Statistics Canada. 2005. "Are Good Jobs Disappearing in Canada?" *The Daily Online*, January 25.
13. Houseman, Susan N. 1997. "New Institute Survey on Flexible Staffing." *Employment Research*, 4(1): 1–4.
14. Lebrun, Sharon. 1997. "Growing Contract Workforce Hindered by Lack of Rules." *Canadian HR Reporter*, May 19: 1–2.
15. Zeytinoglu, Isik. 1999. "Flexible Work Arrangements: An Overview of Developments in Canada." In Isik Zeytinoglu, ed., *Changing Work Relationships in Industrialized Countries*. Amsterdam: John Benjamins Publishing, 41–58.
16. Zeytinolgu, Isik U., and Gordon B. Cooke. 2005. "Non-Standard Work and Benefits: Has Anything Changed since the Wallace Report?" *Relations Industrielles/Industrial Relations*, 60(1): 29-60.
17. Tilly, Chris. 1992. "Dualism in Part-time Employment." *Relations industrielles/ Industrial Relations*, 31(2): 330–47.
18. Bourhis, Anne. 1996. "Attitudinal and Behavioural Reactions of Permanent and Contingent Employees." *Proceedings of the Administrative Sciences Association of Canada, Human Resources Division*, 17(9): 23–33.
19. Bourhis, Anne. 1996. "Attitudinal and Behavioural Reactions of Permanent and Contingent Employees." *Proceedings of the Administrative Sciences Association of Canada, Human Resources Division*, 17(9): 23–33.
20. Marshall, Katherine. 2000. "Part-Time by Choice." *Perspectives on Labour and Employment*, 1(2): 1.
21. Armstrong-Stassen, M., M.E. Horsburgh, and S.J. Cameron. 1994. "The Reactions of Full-Time and Part-Time Nurses to Restructuring in the Canadian Health Care System." In D.P. Moore, ed., *Academy of Management Best Paper Proceedings*. Dallas, TX: 96–100.
22. Krausz, Moshe. 2000. "Effects of Short- and Long-term Preference for Temporary Work upon Psychological Outcomes." *International Journal of Manpower*, 21(8): 635–47.

23. Bourhis, Anne. 1996. "Attitudinal and Behavioural Reactions of Permanent and Contingent Employees." *Proceedings of the Administrative Sciences Association of Canada, Human Resources Division,* 17(9): 23–33.

24. Evenson, Brad. 1997. "Job Sharing Helps Balance Work, Family Life." *Star-Phoenix,* June 10: C11.

25. Martin, James E., and Thomas D. Heetderks. 1990. *Two Tier Compensation Structures: Their Impacts on Unions, Employers, and Employees.* Kalamazoo, MI: W.E. Upjohn Institute.

26. *Human Resources Management in Canada.* 1997. "Unilateral Changes to Employment Contract Costs $175,700." *Report Bulletin,* 170: 6.

27. Martin, James E., and Thomas D. Heetderks. 1990. *Two Tier Compensation Structures: Their Impacts on Unions, Employers, and Employees.* Kalamazoo, MI: W.E. Upjohn Institute.

28. Coutu, Michel. 2000. "Les clauses dites 'orphelins' et la notion de discrimination dans la Charte de droites et libertés de la personne." *Relations Industrielles/Industrial Relations,* 55(2): 308–31.

29. Statistics Canada. 2005. "Are Good Jobs Disappearing in Canada?" *The Daily Online,* January 25.

30. Bok, Derek. 1993. *The Cost of Talent.* New York: The Free Press.

31. Lohr, S. 1992. "Executive Pay Becomes a 'Hot-Button' Issue." *The Globe and Mail,* January 22: B1.

32. Farrell, Christopher. 2002. "Stock Options for All!" *Business Week Online:* September 20.

33. Bebchuk, Lucian, and Yaniv Grinstein. 2005. *The Growth of Executive Pay.* Discussion Paper No. 510, Harvard Law School, Cambridge, MA.

34. Byrne, John A. 1996. "How High Can CEO Pay Go: Special Report." *Business Week,* April 22.

35. *Report on Business Magazine.* 2000. "50 Best Paid Executives." July: 135–36.

36. Magnan, Michel L., Sylvie St-Onge, and Linda Thorne. 1995. "A Comparative Analysis of the Determinants of Executive Compensation between Canadian and U.S. Firms." *Relations Industrielles/Industrial Relations,* 50(2): 297–319.

37. *Economist, The.* 2000. "Chief Executives' Pay." September 30: 110.

38. Bok, Derek. 1993. *The Cost of Talent.* New York: The Free Press.

39. Gomez-Mejia, Luis R., and David Balkin. 1992. *Compensation, Organizational Strategy, and Firm Performance.* Cincinnati, OH: South-Western Publishing.

40. See Magnan, Michel L., Sylvie St-Onge, and Linda Thorne. 1995. "A Comparative Analysis of the Determinants of Executive Compensation between Canadian and U.S. Firms." *Relations Industrielles/Industrial Relations,* 50(2): 297–319. See also Zhou, Xianming. 2000. "CEO Pay, Firm Size, and Corporate Performance: Evidence from Canada." *Canadian Journal of Economics,* 33(1): 213–51.

41. Zhou, Xianming. 2000. "CEO Pay, Firm Size, and Corporate Performance: Evidence from Canada." *Canadian Journal of Economics,* 33(1): 213–51.

42. See Magnan, Michel L., Sylvie St-Onge, and Linda Thorne. 1995. "A Comparative Analysis of the Determinants of Executive Compensation between Canadian and U.S. Firms." *Relations Industrielles/Industrial Relations,* 50(2): 297–319. See also Zhou, Xianming. 2000. "CEO Pay, Firm Size, and Corporate Performance: Evidence from Canada." *Canadian Journal of Economics,* 33(1): 213–51.

43. Magnan, Michel L., Sylvie St-Onge, and Linda Thorne. 1995. "A Comparative Analysis of the Determinants of Executive Compensation between Canadian and U.S. Firms." *Relations Industrielles/Industrial Relations,* 50(2): 297–319.

44. Gomez-Mejia, Luis R., and David Balkin. 1992. *Compensation, Organizational Strategy, and Firm Performance.* Cincinnati, OH: South-Western Publishing.

45. Bebchuk, Lucian, and Yaniv Grinstein. 2005. *The Growth of Executive Pay.* Discussion Paper No. 510, Harvard Law School, Cambridge, MA.

46. Crystal, Graef S. 1991. In Search of Excess: The Overcompensation of American Executives. New York: W.W. Norton.

47. Colvin, Geoffrey. 2001. "The Great CEO Pay Heist." *Fortune*, June 25.

48. Macklem, Katherine. 2001. "Teachers' Pet Peeves." *Maclean's*, April 30: 32–33.

49. Canada Pension Plan Investment Board. 2003. *Proxy Voting Principles and Guidelines*.

50. Gomez-Mejia, Luis R. 1994. "Executive Compensation: A Reassessment and a Future Research Agenda." *Research in Personnel and Human Resources Management*, 12: 161–222.

51. Gomez-Mejia, Luis R., and David Balkin. 1992. *Compensation, Organizational Strategy, and Firm Performance*. Cincinnati, OH: South-Western Publishing.

52. Bebchuk, Lucian, and Yaniv Grinstein. 2005. *The Growth of Executive Pay*. Discussion Paper No. 510, Harvard Law School, Cambridge, MA.

53. Reingold, Jennifer. 1997. "Executive Pay: Special Report." *Business Week*, April 21.

54. Lavelle, Louis. 2001. "Executive Pay." *Business Week*, April 16: 76–80.

55. Lavelle, Louis. 2001. "Undermining Pay for Performance". *Business Week*, January 15: 70–71.

56. Batson, Neal. 2003. *Final Report of Neal Batson, Court-Appointed Examiner*: United States Bankruptcy Court of New York: 91.

57. Macklem, Katherine. 2001. "Teachers' Pet Peeves." *Maclean's*, April 30: 32–33.

58. Canada Pension Plan Investment Board. 2003. *Proxy Voting Principles and Guidelines*: 15.

59. Recently, Michael C. Jensen, a professor at the Harvard Business School who is regarded as the "father" of executive stock option plans, has recanted, believing them to damage corporate performance and shareholder interests. See Deutsch, Claudia C. 2005. "An Early Advocate of Stock Options Debunks Himself." *The New York Times Online*: April 3.

60. *CNN Money Online*. 2005. "Gates Regrets Paying with Stock Options." May 3.

61. Martin, Roger L. 2003. "Taking Stock: If You Want Managers to Act in their Shareholders' Best Interests, Take Away Their Company Stock." *Harvard Business Review*, 81(1): 1–19.

62. Martin, Roger L. 2003. "The Fundamental Problem with Stock-based Compensation." Rotman Management: 7-9.

63. Harris Jared, and Philip Bromiley. 2003. "Incentives to Cheat: Executive Compensation and Corporate Malfeasance." Paper presented at the 2003 Strategic Management Society International Conference, Baltimore, Maryland.

64. Hall, Brian J., and Kevin J. Murphy. 2000. *Stock Options for Undiversified Executives*. National Bureau of Economic Research.

65. Hassenhuttl, Maria, and J. Richard Harrison. 2000. "Exit or Loyalty: The Effects of Compensation on CEO Turnover." Paper presented at the Academy of Management Conference, Toronto.

66. Lawler, Edward E. 1992. *The Ultimate Advantage: Creating the High Involvement Organization*. San Francisco: Jossey-Bass: 329.

67. Tyson, John, ed. 2005. *Carswell's Compensation Guide*. Toronto: Thomson Canada.

Determining Compensation Values

Chapter 6

Evaluating Jobs: The Job Evaluation Process

Chapter Learning Objectives

After reading this chapter, you should be able to:

- Explain the purpose of job evaluation and the main steps in the job evaluation process.
- Describe the process for job analysis and the key steps in that process.
- Prepare useful job descriptions.
- Identify and briefly describe the five main methods of job evaluation.
- Describe the key issues in managing the job evaluation process.
- Describe the general process for conforming to pay equity legislation.

At a secondary school, how valuable is a school secretary relative to an audiovisual technician? What about a law clerk and an investigator at a law firm? How about a personnel manager and a service manager at a baked goods manufacturer? How about a health technician compared to a transportation worker at a hospital? Given that the jobs in each of these pairs differ considerably in the nature of their duties and necessary skills, are we not trying to compare apples and oranges when we compare the value of each job to the other?

In fact, that is precisely the kind of task that job evaluation is designed to accomplish. In Ontario, application of a gender-neutral job evaluation system, in conformance with the procedures applied under pay equity legislation in Ontario, determined that the jobs in each pair are similar in value, despite their other differences, and despite the fact that they had previously been paid significantly differently. As a result of this process, the first job in each pair (which was held primarily by females) received substantial raises to bring them in line with the pay of the second job in each pair (which was held primarily by males). The secretaries received a raise of $7,680 per annum, the law clerks received a raise of $4.28 an hour, the personnel managers received an increase of $4.65 an hour, and the health technicians received a raise of $2.79 an hour.[1]

Introduction

By now, you have formulated a compensation strategy for each of your major employee groups. This is a major milestone on your road to effective compensation. But you don't yet have a compensation *system*. The four chapters in Part III of this book describe the technical processes necessary to transform a compensation strategy into an operating compensation system.

Chapters 6 and 7 focus on how to design the job evaluation process that best fits your particular organization. Chapter 8 describes how to collect and interpret relevant labour market data to ensure that your compensation system is grounded in economic reality. Chapter 9 describes how to evaluate individual employee skills as part of a pay-for-knowledge system and how to evaluate individual performance as part of a merit pay system.

Purpose of Job Evaluation

As you will recall from Chapter 4, the purpose of job evaluation is to determine the relative contribution made by each job in an organization to the success of that organization so that each job can be remunerated accordingly. The output of job evaluation is a hierarchy of jobs, where all jobs of a similar *value* to the organization, no matter how different they may be from each other in other respects, are located at the same level on the job hierarchy. This job hierarchy provides the foundation for the development of pay grades and pay ranges.

In conducting job evaluation, key objectives are to ensure that all jobs in the organization are compensated equitably and are *perceived* by organizational members as being compensated equitably. Effective job evaluation should also ensure that jobs are not underpaid—which would make it difficult to attract qualified employees—and not overpaid—which is important from a cost and competitive viewpoint.

Steps in the Job Evaluation Process

There are five main steps in the job evaluation process:

1. *Understand* the jobs to be evaluated. Accurate and reliable job information is an essential precondition for job evaluation.
2. *Decide* how many pay structures to use. In the past, firms tended to create different pay structures for different occupational groups. But for the purposes of internal equity, the fewer the pay structures, the better.
3. *Select and apply* the most appropriate job evaluation method(s).
4. *Create* a pay structure with appropriate pay grades and pay ranges, along with procedures for moving through these ranges.
5. *Develop* procedures for evaluating and modifying the system.

Chapter 6 starts off by describing job analysis, which is the process for collecting information about the key characteristics of jobs. Next, the different job evaluation methods that are available will be described. Then, the process and issues involved with conducting and managing job evaluation will be outlined. The final section in this chapter illustrates the necessary steps for conforming to Canadian pay equity legislation, using the Ontario Pay Equity Act as a model. Chapter 7 focuses on how to design and apply the most commonly used job evaluation system—the point factor method—usually known simply as the point system of job evaluation, and how to convert the results of this into a base pay structure.

job analysis
the process of collecting information on which job descriptions are based

 6.1

job description
a summary of the duties, responsibilities, and reporting relationships pertaining to a particular job

Job Analysis

A precondition for job evaluation is accurate information about the jobs to be evaluated. The purpose of **job analysis** is to obtain this job information, which is usually summarized in the form of a job description. A **job description** is a summary of the duties, responsibilities, and reporting relationships that pertain to a particular job. Derived from the job description are the **job specifications**, which are the employee qualifications deemed necessary to successfully perform the duties involved with the job.

Beyond compensation, job descriptions can serve a wide variety of organizational purposes. These include recruiting and selection, developing training programs, providing guidance to employees and supervisors, developing

job specifications
the employee qualifications deemed necessary to successfully perform the duties for a given job

employee performance standards, and helping to ensure that all necessary organizational activities are being undertaken and that no important activities are "falling between the cracks." Of course, as discussed in Chapter 4, job descriptions are time-consuming to prepare and maintain, especially in dynamic firms where jobs and task demands change frequently, and they can cause rigidity if they are defined too narrowly or interpreted too literally.

Nature of Required Information

What information is needed for effective job evaluation? If job descriptions are accurate and up-to-date, they may provide all the necessary information for evaluating jobs. However, experience suggests that this is relatively rare, despite the fact that many organizations expend considerable effort on developing job descriptions. As one compensation practitioner puts it:

> More time, money, and patience are wasted on job or class descriptions than on any other aspect of personnel administration. [Yet,] in almost twenty-five years of consulting, my firm has never had a client lay claim to an up-to-date and complete set of job descriptions. [Moreover,] job descriptions never contain all the information required to evaluate jobs for compensation.[2]

So why is using job descriptions for job evaluation likely to prove so fruitless? First, some firms simply are not willing to devote the effort needed for the task of developing and updating job descriptions. But a bigger problem is that in many organizations, particularly those in more dynamic environments, job duties are changing all the time, often escaping notice by anyone in the human resources department. Moreover, as will be shown in this chapter,

Compensation Notebook 6.1

Basic Elements of a Useful Job Description

1. Job title, department or location, reporting relationships, and date when job analysis was originally completed or updated.
2. A brief statement of job purpose or objectives.
3. A list of the major duties of the job, in order of priority or importance. Some indication of the proportion of time spent on each duty may be useful, although this may not be feasible for some jobs. In describing these duties, be sure to include the tools, equipment, or work aids that are utilized in performing these duties.
4. An indication of responsibilities for people, results, and organizational assets, including cash, tools, equipment,

and facilities, along with the spending or budget authorities attached to the job. The consequences of error or poor performance could also be explained. Included here is the nature and extent of supervision given and received.
5. The mental and physical effort demanded by the job.
6. The conditions under which the work is performed, including the quality of the work environment and any hazards or dangers that may be involved in job performance.
7. A specification of the qualifications needed to perform the job, including skills, training, education, and abilities, as well as any certificates or licences required.

Compensation Notebook 6.2

Important Points to Remember About Job Descriptions

1. Describe all ongoing aspects of the job. Also include duties or responsibilities that you are expected to carry out, even if on an infrequent basis. For example, you prepare a report once every two months; this report is usually 20 pages or longer, requires statistical research and analysis, and takes four to six days to prepare.

2. List each job duty and its related tasks, starting with the duties that take the largest portion of time. A duty is a distinct area of responsibility; a task is a particular work action performed to accomplish the duty.

3. Include enough detail about the job. Be clear and concise. For example, "handles mail" could mean any or all of the following: receiving, logging, reading, distributing, locating background material related to the correspondence and attaching it for the reader's information.

4. Show how often, how much, or how long a task or a responsibility takes to perform.

5. Indicate the approximate amount of working time spent on each major duty, using percentages, number of hours per day, frequency (daily, weekly, monthly).

6. Explain technical terms describing processes and equipment in easy to understand language. Be specific about the degree of responsibility involved and the equipment, processes, and work aids used.

7. Ask yourself "how" and "why." This may help you more accurately describe aspects of the job. Use an alternative task statement format where there is too much information in a single sentence.

8. Define abilities that had not been previously rated or that are now being realigned due to changes in the job environment or requirements.

9. Focus on the facts. Do not overstate or understate duties, knowledge, skills, abilities, and other characteristics.

10. Avoid general references to personality, interest, intelligence, or judgment.

11. Avoid use of ambiguous or qualitative words, such as "assist" or "complex" without providing clarifying examples.

12. Begin each task statement with an action verb in the first person present tense, e.g. write, calibrate, analyze. Use the *Glossary of Active Verbs* (http://www.gov.on.ca/lab/pec/peo/english/pubs/glossaryverbs.html) to help clarify actions and tasks.

13. Exclude duties and responsibilities no longer performed, or any future requirements, in the description.

14. Exclude skills, education, or experience a staff member has or may acquire that are not required by the current position.

15. The supervisor may develop a composite position description representative of a group when two or more individuals hold the same type of position (e.g., Customer Service Clerks).

16. Employees should not assume responsibilities and authority which is not theirs. However, supervisors should make clear those responsibilities that are required.

Source: Ontario Pay Equity Commission website www.gov.on.ca/lab/pec/peo/english/casestudy/t_exreq.html. © Queen's Printer for Ontario, 2005. Reproduced with permission.

conducting job analysis effectively is an onerous task, with many obstacles to collection of valid data. In some cases, considerable effort is expended, but the resulting job descriptions omit certain pieces of information that are essential for effective job evaluation.

Compensation Notebook 6.1 lists the key elements needed for a useful job description, Compensation Notebook 6.2 gives some important considerations to keep in mind when developing job descriptions, and Figure 6.1 shows a detailed example of a job description.

FIGURE 6.1

Example of a Detailed Job Description

Space Toy Corporation

Job Title: ADMINISTRATIVE SECRETARY I   **Departments:** All

Reports to: Department Head or Division Manager   **Updated:** January 30, 2006

Summary Statement

Under the supervision of a Manager, the incumbent performs a variety of administrative support and office clerical functions for a Department Head and/or Division Manager. These duties include taking and preparing minutes, composing and typing administrative/confidential/legal documents, arranging of appointments and travel plans, and performing the general duties of a private secretary. Responsibilities may include supervising a small clerical staff.

How long have the duties and the distribution of time been substantially as below?

3 years

Major Duties and Responsibilities

1. Liaises with other departments, divisions, outside agencies, committees, or boards regarding office administrative matters pertaining to the immediate supervisor.
2. Prepares, maintains and provides letters, memoranda, reports, forms and other materials from rough draft, final working draft notes, and dictation notes for supervisor's review and signature, in accordance with department or division policy.
3. Composes and prepares correspondence of a simple and straightforward nature for the division or department.
4. Performs other secretarial and clerical functions such as assembling, taking and preparing minutes, agendas or other reports for division or department committees.
5. Answers telephones and personal inquiries. Provides information and referrals to employees and the general public, as required.
6. Develops and maintains efficient and up-to-date filing system.
7. Arranges meetings and schedules out-of-town travel for departmental or division personnel.
8. Ensures that adequate operating levels of office supplies, equipment and furniture are maintained, by preparing and processing requisitions and verifying completed purchase orders. Also prepares vouchers and billings for division services, travel requests, other reports related to revenues collected and financial or budget statements. May be required to administer and disburse petty cash.
9. Maintains accurate records of hours worked by division or department employees. Includes securing timesheets, calculating overtime and benefits accrued and preparing related payroll reports. Prepares various personnel action forms and coordinates with the Office of Employee Services to assure compliance with policies and procedures.
10. May be required to supervise clerical staff or to be lead person for secretarial staff. Assigns tasks and reviews work of subordinates.
11. Coordinates all details related to special projects and events, i.e., the annual sales conference and the quarterly division general meetings.
12. Performs other related duties as assigned.

Minimum Qualifications and Skills

1. Graduation from high school or the equivalent, and four year's work experience in an office performing secretarial or office clerical duties. Office administration training may be substituted for one year's experience if the course work is sufficient to be the equivalent.

FIGURE 6.1 *Continued*

2. Demonstrated proficiency in the use of personal computers, with a working knowledge of computer software for filing, word processing, spreadsheets, database management, and emailing. Ability to type 60 wpm net. Ability to record minutes of meetings in an accurate, efficient, and timely manner. Shorthand and speedwriting skills would be an asset.
3. A working knowledge of various standard office equipment and other specified technical equipment such as a business calculator, copying machine, fax machine, etc.
4. A working knowledge of modern office policies and procedures in a computerized and local network environment.
5. Ability to schedule appointments, develop and maintain complex filing systems, and keep orderly records.
6. Ability to relate well with co-workers, supervisors, other employees, client groups and the general public, and provide leadership and work direction to subordinates.
7. Possession of a valid driver's licence.

Mental Effort

Mental and visual concentration during computer work four or five hours daily for accuracy in data entry and editing.
- Listening and mental attentiveness in dealing with customer or public queries and manager's requirements.
- Mental effort required in multi-tasking and handling interruptions that require constant refocusing.

Physical Effort
- Performs multiple, repeated, and sustained hand–eye movements on computer keyboard and screen up to four to five hours daily.
- Lifts and shelves office supplies (up to 30 pounds) daily;
- Sits for extended periods of up to five hours daily, operating computer and other office equipment.

Working Conditions
- Works in confined space of four-feet high, minimum-grade baffled privacy station.
- Governed by concurrent and dynamic deadlines, despite conflicting priorities and frequent interruptions.
- Intermittent exposure to co-workers/clients; occasional handling of queries and calls from upset or irate people.
- Frequent exposure to glare from computer screen, printer toners, or chemicals.
- Lifting of boxes that can result in injury to back, feet, or hands.

Type of Supervision Received
- Reports to a department head or division manager. Works under general instructions to prioritize and complete assigned tasks. Assignments are periodically checked for progress by the immediate supervisor.

Type of Supervision and/or Assistance Given
- May be required to supervise clerical staff or to be lead person for secretarial staff.
- Assigns, prioritizes tasks, and reviews work of subordinate staff.

Source: Adapted from the Ontario Pay Equity Commission website www.gov.on.ca/lab/pec/peo/english/casestudy/t_exreq.html. © Queen's Printer for Ontario, 2005. Reproduced with permission.

Methods of Job Analysis

If the necessary job information does not already exist, how can it be obtained? There are four main methods: observation, interviews, questionnaires, and functional job analysis. However, the first three can be conducted only in existing organizations that already have examples of the jobs that need to be evaluated. Organizations that are just being created or that are introducing new jobs must depend on the fourth method, functional job analysis.

The job analysis process can be conducted by personnel from the human resources department or by outside consultants. In many cases, managers and supervisors may do most of the actual work, but there always needs to be some central body to ensure consistency of results.

Observation

Observation involves watching the employee as the job is performed and noting the kinds of activities performed, with whom they are performed, and utilizing what tools or equipment. The extreme version of this process is a time and motion study, as discussed in Chapter 4. On its own, observation is mainly useful for jobs in which the activities can be easily observed and for which the work cycle is short (i.e., all of the important activities of the job can be seen in a short period of observation). For most jobs, observation is useful only as a supplement to other methods.

Interviews

Interviews can be conducted with either a sample of employees, their supervisors, or both. But interviewing only one or the other of these groups has drawbacks. Interviews with employees can lead to valid information; but the employee perspective on the importance of various job duties may be different from that of the supervisor. Moreover, if employees know that the job analysis is being conducted for the purpose of job evaluation, it is in their interest to portray the job in such a way as to maximize its value. Interviewing supervisors may produce more objective information; but supervisors may not be as aware of the realities of the job as the employee.

Therefore, in the interests of accuracy, interviewing both the supervisor and a representative sample of employees for each job being analyzed is best. (Of course, it may turn out that employees who were seemingly doing the same jobs are actually doing different jobs, and it is important for the job analysis to be able to pick up this difference so the jobs can be formally differentiated.) The main drawback to interviewing so many people is the cost of the time involved, both for the job analyst and the interviewees. Use of a structured interview format helps to reduce the time requirement, as well as providing more consistent information.

Questionnaires

Questionnaires may vary on two dimensions. They may be open-ended or closed-ended, and they may be firm-specific or proprietary. An open-ended questionnaire asks the respondent (either the supervisor or the job incumbent) a series of questions, such as the purpose and main duties of the job. A closed-ended questionnaire asks the respondent to select from a list the phrases that best describe the job. In order to cover the variety of jobs in an organization, the questionnaire must contain a wide variety of possible duties and activities. Care must be taken to ensure that the questionnaire is reliable (i.e., that two independent observers would answer it in the same way) and valid (i.e., that the information collected accurately reflects reality.)

Because development of reliable and valid questionnaires is a complex process, many organizations use proprietary questionnaires developed by outside specialists. Perhaps the best known is the Position Analysis Questionnaire (PAQ) developed more than 30 years ago by industrial psychologist Ernest J. McCormick.[3] Since this instrument is commonly used, we will describe some of its key features.

The PAQ focuses on the behaviours that make up a job and utilizes 187 items (called job elements) to describe work activities. These job elements are grouped into six dimensions:

- *Information input* describes the sources of information an employee uses on the job.
- *Mental processes* describe the types of reasoning, decision-making, planning, and information-processing activities being used.
- *Work output* includes items assessing physical activities and use of tools in the work process.
- *Relationships with other persons* describes the extent to which the job involves working with other people as a part of its duties.
- *Job context* items examine the physical and social environment of the job.
- *Other job characteristics* cover other conditions of work not covered by the first five dimensions.

A specific response scale is used to assess each of the 187 elements (statements). Anyone knowledgeable about the job may complete the questionnaire, including job analysts, supervisors, and job incumbents. Multiple incumbents may also be used. The questionnaires are then sent to PAQ Services Inc. for computer processing. PAQ uses this information to derive job dimension scores, along with assessments of the required employee aptitudes necessary to perform the job. These data are especially useful for recruitment and selection, but can also be used for job evaluation. A major advantage is that the system is standardized so that it can be used to compare a wide variety of jobs.

There are other standardized instruments. For example, the Management Position Description Questionnaire (MPDQ) focuses on task-centred characteristics of managerial jobs.[4] The Executive Position Description Questionnaire (EPDQ) focuses on behaviours of senior managers.[5] Many consulting firms have also developed their own versions of standardized instruments. Some consulting firms are willing to customize their basic instruments when individual employers have special needs.

Functional Job Analysis

Functional job analysis (FJA) is an attempt to develop generic descriptions of jobs using a common set of job functions. FJA was pioneered in the United States in the 1930s when the federal government created the *Dictionary of Occupational Titles,* which has now been replaced by a system known as O-Net (with the "O" standing for occupation). A version of this system was used by the Canadian federal government to create the *National Occupational Classification,* which includes over 10 000 descriptions of jobs.

FJA has been refined over the years. The current system uses a series of task statements that contain four elements for each job: (a) who performs what, (b) to whom or what, (c) with what tools, equipment, or processes, (d) to achieve what purpose or outcome. The following is an example for the job of "Residential Counsellor" in a group home for wayward youth: "The Counsellor (a) records behaviour (b) of group home residents (c) using standardized record sheets (d) to determine the cause of undesirable behaviours."[6] FJA produces a series of statements like this one that, taken together, describe the job.

Managers can then analyze these statements to draw conclusions about the nature of the job, as well as the skills, effort, responsibility, and working conditions associated with it. However, depending on the job, it may be difficult to draw conclusions about all of these factors, such as working conditions or responsibility. Organizations will have to modify the standard job descriptions to suit their specific circumstances and the specific responsibilities they plan to attach to each job.

Identifying Job Families

For administrative purposes (such as recruitment, selection, and training), it is often convenient to identify jobs that are related to one another and then to cluster them in "job families." For example, an organization may have the following job families for nonmanagerial staff: clerical (clerks, receptionists, secretaries), maintenance (plumbers, electricians, welders), technical (lab technicians, instrumentation technicians), and food services (cooks, cafeteria workers, cashiers). However, as shown later in this chapter, evaluating job families separately for pay purposes can lead to serious inequities.

Thus, unless there is a compelling need to compensate different job families in different ways—for example, with sales personnel who are on commission—job families should be grouped together as much as possible for purposes of job evaluation. Differentiation of employee groups for compensation purposes should be based on strategic or behavioural considerations, as discussed in Chapter 5, not simply on job differences.

Pitfalls in Job Analysis

There are several possible pitfalls in the job analysis process. The first is the risk of analyzing the jobholder instead of the job. For example, the jobholder being interviewed may go above and beyond the call of duty, doing much more than the job calls for. On the other hand, some jobholders may perform

Part III: Determining Compensation Values

only a portion of the intended job duties. But the analysis of the job should not be unduly influenced by either case.

Another problem is that job descriptions have been subject to gender bias. For example, Kelly claims that "it has been well-documented that job analysts are particularly prone to allow gender bias to influence their analysis of jobs unless trained to do otherwise."[7] Traditionally, different language has been applied to duties performed by men and women even though the actual duties may be virtually identical. For example, when men direct the work of employees, they "manage" these employees; when women do so, they "supervise" employees. These types of language differences must be avoided. Also, jobs traditionally held by males are often described in technical terms that sound impressive, while female jobs are often described in simpler, less impressive language, even though the importance and difficulty of the duties are similar.

Regardless of possible gender bias, technical jargon is an impediment to effective understanding of jobs and needs to be translated into everyday language for the job description. For example, instead of "calibrates the FP 25 flow meter and adjusts circulant flow commensurate with these calibrations," try "performs simple tests of the measuring accuracy of water meters and adjusts the water flow accordingly."

But while simplifying the language as much as possible, avoid oversimplifying job duties. For example, "performs general office duties" would be more informative expressed as follows: "answers incoming telephone calls from clients and redirects to the appropriate information officer, operates word processing equipment to prepare letters and reports, utilizes spreadsheet programs to prepare drafts of department budget," and so on. In the process, it is essential to ensure that both women's and men's jobs are described accurately, using simple, straightforward, precise, and bias-free language. There should also be a check on job titles to make sure they are gender-neutral.

Another issue has to do with jobs that are dynamic. Job analysis and the information it produces is useful only as long as the job stays constant. When the job changes, this information may not only become obsolete, but it may also become misleading, causing a variety of inappropriate decisions in areas such as recruitment and selection, training, and compensation. This problem is most likely to occur in high-involvement organizations, since they tend to operate in the most dynamic environments. To avoid this problem, updating of job descriptions needs to be an ongoing process, and supervisors and workers need to be reminded to report significant changes in job duties as they occur. However, they may fail to do this, or duties may change gradually and thus may go undetected. Figure 6.2 provides an example of a form that may assist in the updating process.

Job Evaluation Methods

R P C 6.1

Over time, five major methods for job evaluation have evolved: (1) ranking, (2) classification or grading, (3) factor comparison, (4) statistical/policy capturing, and (5) the point method. In addition, compensation consulting firms

FIGURE 6.2

Form for Updating Job Descriptions

Request for Review of Job Information

1. Reason for review of job information _____ new position _____ update/review requested			

2. Incumbent's name	**3. Department**	**4. Job Title**	**5. Title Code**

6. Supervisor's name	**7. Name of person who assigns work** (if different from Box 6).

8. Directly supervises the following employees: *Name* *Job Title*	**9. List positions reporting to employee's named in Box 8:** *Number of employees* *Job Titles*

10. List any new or additional licences, certificates, degrees, or credentials that are required for the job:

11. List any new machines, tools, equipment, office appliances, or motor vehicles which are now required to do the job. (Indicate whether use is occasional, frequent, or constant):

12. List which responsibilities were added, deleted, or changed since last review:

13. List which duties were added, deleted, or changed since last review:

14. Indicate the areas where new or added skills or knowledge are now required:

15. Signature (Signatures indicate neither agreement nor disagreement with the re-classification/review requested).

Employee–I certify that the information on this form is correct and complete, and describes my job as I understand it. x _____ Signature Date	**Immediate Supervisor**–I have reviewed the statements on this form and certify to their accuracy. x _____ Signature Date

Source: Ontario Pay Equity Commission website www.gov.on.ca/lab/pec/peo/english/casestudy/t_exreq.html. © Queen's Printer for Ontario, 2005. Reproduced with permission.

have developed numerous proprietary systems, all of which use some variation of the five basic methods. For example, the Hay Plan or Profile Method, developed many years ago by Hay Associates, combines features of the factor comparison and point methods, and is intended mainly for management and executive jobs. Kelly provides a thorough description of the Hay Plan, as well as 10 other proprietary plans offered by consulting firms operating in Canada.[8] However, this chapter focuses on the five most commonly used generic methods.

These five basic job evaluation plans can be divided into two main categories—"whole job" methods, in which human judgment is the main determinant of the job hierarchy—and methods that use quantitative factors to establish the job hierarchy. Ranking and classification/grading are whole job methods, whereas the factor comparison, statistical/policy capturing, and point methods are quantitative methods.

Ranking/Paired Comparison

Simple ranking is the least complicated system for deriving an ordering of jobs. The **ranking method** involves asking a group of "judges" (e.g., managers, human resource specialists) to examine a set of job descriptions and to rank jobs according to their overall worth to the organization. The specific criteria are left up to each judge, and frequently these criteria are not formally identified. Using a group of judges is believed to cancel out individual biases in ranking.

One variant of this approach is known as the **paired comparison method,** in which each job is compared with every other job, one pair at a time. The number of times each job is ranked above another job is recorded, and these pair rankings are used as the basis for ranking the entire set of jobs. While this method is more systematic than simple ranking, one drawback to this approach is the very large number of comparisons that must be made if a large number of jobs are being evaluated.

Once a hierarchy of jobs has been created, by whatever means, new jobs can be added using a method known as "slotting." New jobs are compared with the hierarchy of existing jobs, and simply "slotted" into the most appropriate level.

Although less complex than many other systems, ranking/paired comparison methods have a number of drawbacks. First, it may be difficult to get the group of judges to agree on rankings, since the relative importance of each job factor may be weighted differently by each judge. Second, this method does not establish the *relative* intervals between jobs. For example, the ninth-, tenth-, and eleventh-ranked jobs may be quite close in terms of importance, while the eighth-ranked job may be much more important than the ninth. This method would not recognize that difference.

Perhaps most important, this method provides no explicit basis for explaining why jobs are ranked as they are, leaving the results of the plan open to charges of inequity. Indeed, because of its subjectivity, the ranking/paired comparison method is not deemed an acceptable method for job evaluation for organizations in jurisdictions covered by pay equity

ranking method of job evaluation

the relative values of different jobs are determined by knowledgeable individuals

paired comparison method of job evaluation

every job is compared with every other job, providing a basis for a ranking of jobs

legislation. Under pay equity legislation, four categories of factors must be taken into account when evaluating jobs—skill required, effort, responsibility, and working conditions—and whole job ranking does not take these factors separately into account.

This problem could be rectified by comparing each job to the others using each of the four factor categories separately, providing a separate ranking on each factor category. The factors could then be weighted in terms of importance, and then a composite score could be developed for each job. However, although this would appear to satisfy pay equity provisions, it would not be very useful for firms with large numbers of jobs, or where jobs change quickly, since a change in any job would require a new ranking for each factor category for every job in the system (although an adapted version may be acceptable, as will be discussed later in the chapter).

Classification/Grading

classification/grading method of job evaluation

the use of generic grade descriptions for various classes of jobs to assign pay grades to specific jobs

The **classification/grading method** operates by establishing and defining general classes of jobs (e.g., managerial, professional, technical, clerical) and then creating a series of grade descriptions for each class. Different grades possess different levels of knowledge and skills, complexity of duties, supervision, and other key characteristics. Organizations compare jobs using these grade descriptions within the appropriate job class and then select the pay grade that best matches them. Jobs in the same grade within a given class receive the same remuneration.

Figure 6.3 provides an illustration of a hypothetical classification guide for employees in the "nonprofessional" job class at an electrical utility. As Figure 6.3 shows, there are five pay grades, each of which carries a different pay range. Let us assume that we wish to determine the appropriate salary for the job of computer operator. The job description indicates that some training and skill are necessary, but tasks are simple, errors are easily detected, and operators work under direct supervision of the senior computer operator. Which grade would you place this job in?

Did you pick NP-2? This job description appears to match that grade most closely. Pay ranges (in terms of dollar values) for each pay grade are usually set by identifying the market rates for typical or "benchmark" jobs in each pay grade. Where employees are unionized, pay ranges are set through collective bargaining.

The number of job classes used depends largely on the nature of the organization and the variety of jobs found. Many organizations that use this system have separate classes for managerial, professional, clerical, and blue-collar jobs. The number of pay grades usually depends on the skill range and the number of jobs in each job class.

This method has the advantage of being straightforward and inexpensive, as well as being flexible enough to encompass a large number of jobs. Since the basis for a particular job rating is spelled out, the results are easier to defend than those derived by simple ranking. However, descriptions of pay grades must be fairly general in order to encompass several types of jobs, so there still may be disagreement about the exact grade placement for each job.

FIGURE 6.3

Sample Guide for Job Classification Method

Rocky Mountain Hydro Corporation

Job Classification Guide
(Nonprofessional Job Class)

Instructions: Match the job description with one of the following categories in order to establish the appropriate pay grade.

Pay Grade	Characteristics of Typical Job
NP-1	Works under direct supervision. Tasks are simple, repetitive, and require little initiative. When made, mistakes or errors are easily detected and are not costly. Minimal level of education and training required. Examples: janitor, file clerk, general labourer.
NP-2	Works under direct supervision. Tasks generally simple and repetitive, although some training is required. Little initiative is necessary. Although easily detected, some mistakes or errors can be costly. Examples: switchboard operator/receptionist, accounting clerk, trenching machine operator.
NP-3	Generally, but not always, works under direct supervision. Although most tasks are routine, some require use of discretion. Mistakes or errors may not be easily detected and can be costly. Minimum of high school education and/or substantial training required. May have direct customer contact. Examples: customer service representative, senior accounting clerk, control room monitor.
NP-4	Frequently does not work under direct supervision. Some tasks are complicated and require considerable education or training. Considerable use of independent judgment may be required. Consequences of error may be severe and/or costly. May use costly equipment and/or materials in executing job. May involve supervision of others. Examples: accountant, senior control room monitor, electrical repair crew member, safety inspector, executive secretary.
NP-5	Does not work under direct supervision, but has responsibility for the supervision of others. Tasks are varied and require independent judgment. Substantial education, training, or experience required. Responsible for detecting errors of subordinates. Errors by subordinates not detected by incumbent may be difficult to detect and/or extremely serious. Examples: electrical repair crew leader, senior safety inspector, shift supervisor (plant), trenching and cable crew leader.

As well, since this method only considers the job as a whole, no weighting is applied to different job factors, some of which may be more important than others.

Depending on the nature of the grade descriptions (whether they contain the four essential factor categories required for pay equity) and the breadth of the job classes (the broader, the better), this method of job evaluation may or may not be acceptable for pay equity purposes. However, this system has historically been very popular with government civil service organizations.

Factor Comparison Method

factor comparison method of job evaluation

assigns pay levels to jobs based on the extent to which they embody various job factors

Because of its complexity, the **factor comparison method** is used less frequently than the other methods. This method identifies several major factors against which all jobs in a job class can be assessed and then rates the extent to which each factor is present in each of a large set of "key jobs" thought to be properly compensated at the present time.

Organizations use statistical analysis (multiple regression) to determine the dollar value of varying degrees of each factor. Then they rate the remaining jobs for each factor and determine compensation by applying the dollar values derived by the multiple regression analysis. Use of these factors distinguishes this method from the previous two methods (which are "whole job methods" because they attempt to compare one whole job against other "whole jobs") because they segment jobs into factors and then evaluate these factors, rather than the "whole job." Depending whether the factors used conform to the four factor categories required under pay equity legislation, this method may be acceptable for use under pay equity legislation.

Statistical/Policy Capturing Method

statistical/policy capturing method of job evaluation

combines use of statistical methods and job questionnaires to derive job values based on prevailing external or internal pay rates

The **statistical/policy capturing method** is perhaps the most complicated method of job evaluation. This method uses questionnaires to gather information about the task elements of each job to be evaluated, as well as the typical time spent on each task and the relative importance of each task. Information is also collected about the level of skill or education required for each job, and possibly data on the quantity and quality of output expected for each job. Market data for certain jobs that match well (in terms of job characteristics) with jobs in the external market are incorporated, and multiple regression analysis is used to derive a formula for the value of the different job characteristics. This formula can then be used to evaluate the jobs that do not have good market matches.

This approach can also be used in conjunction with internal data based on current pay rates to identify possible inequities within current pay structures and to rectify them. Used properly, this method is acceptable under pay equity legislation, as confirmed by a ruling by the Ontario Pay Equity Tribunal.[9]

The Point Method

point method of job evaluation

establishes job values by the application of points to each job based on "compensable factors"

The **point method** of job evaluation (sometimes known as the "point-factor" method) is the most widely used system of job evaluation. This method identifies key job characteristics (known as "compensable factors") that differentiate the value of various jobs, weights these factors, and then determines how much of each factor is present in a given job by assigning a certain number of points to each job for that factor. The point totals are used to create a hierarchy of jobs. As discussed in the next chapter, this hierarchy of jobs is then transformed into a set of pay grades and pay ranges, based on the market rates of certain key or "benchmark" jobs. Because the point method is by far the most commonly used job evaluation system in Canada and is generally the most appropriate choice of job evaluation method for most organizations, Chapter 7 is devoted to this method of job evaluation.

Conducting and Managing the Job Evaluation Process

RPC 6.1

There are three main purposes for conducting job evaluation: to control wage costs, to create an equitable pay structure, and to create perceptions of equitable pay among those covered by the system. Whether all three of these objectives are achieved depends on the processes used to conduct job evaluations and to manage them on an ongoing basis. Organizations need to answer five main questions before setting up a job evaluation process: (1) Who conducts the job evaluations? (2) How should the process be communicated? (3) What appeals/review mechanisms are (or need to be) established? (4) How should the job evaluation results be applied? and (5) How should job evaluations be updated?

Who Conducts the Job Evaluations?

Most organizations create a job evaluation committee to oversee the job evaluation process, although some firms assign the task exclusively to their compensation manager, while others use outside consultants. When a committee is used, it typically consists of experts in job evaluation (from either inside or outside the company), the compensation manager, and a representative sample of supervisors from the departments where jobs are being evaluated. In some cases, rank-and-file employees will be included.

In unionized firms, there is usually a joint union–management job evaluation committee, although some unions may prefer not to participate in the process. However, at the least, there should be continuing two-way communication with the union in order to try to prevent misunderstandings.

Employee participation in both developing the job evaluation method and conducting the job evaluation process usually leads to greater employee satisfaction with the results. However, if this participation is attempted in a classical organization, it may not be helpful, since there is often an adversarial culture and a lack of common goals in these organizations. Employee participation is also not very effective unless committee members receive training about job evaluation and understand the goals of the process.

There are several necessary conditions for a job evaluation committee to be successful. First, the parameters and terms of reference for the committee, including authority, must be spelled out. However, this is often left vague because top management is unsure just how much authority they should delegate to the committee. This authority question will be a problem for both classical and human relations firms. Second, both technical and clerical support resources need to be made available to the committee. Third, the committee needs training in job evaluation, as well as in the process for effective group functioning, including such areas as open communication and active involvement.

Communicating the Job Evaluation Process

A key issue in conducting job evaluation is communicating the process. To foster perceptions of equity, communication is essential. In general, employees need to be given an opportunity to understand the job evaluation process that will be used and its scope and parameters, including the type of results that will likely occur. But just as important, the committee members need to know what will *not* happen. For example, job evaluation will not be used as a ploy to cut jobs or to ferret out individual employees with performance deficiencies.

A variety of methods can be used to ensure adequate communication. Of course, if employees sit on the job evaluation committee, they can serve as a conduit for information to the rest of the staff. In addition, small group meetings led by a member of the job evaluation committee can also help communicate to staff, as well as formal written reports and policy documents. Overall, it is important to establish two-way communication channels so employee concerns and questions can be received and addressed.

A question of concern to many employers is whether they should reveal the detailed results of job evaluation to employees or simply present the outcome in terms of which pay grade their job is placed within. The answer depends on the nature of the organization and the purposes of the job evaluation. If the organization is a classical one and the main objective is to develop an internal pay structure that controls labour costs, management will conduct the job evaluations and not release the detailed results. This is probably best in these organizations, since the lack of trust and poor relations that often exist would likely lead to this information being misinterpreted or used in unproductive ways.

But if perceptions of compensation equity are important, as in the case of human relations and high-involvement organizations, then more open transmission of information will be desirable. Employees will not be convinced of the fairness of the process unless they understand the workings of the system.

Developing Appeal/Review Mechanisms

One key element of procedural justice is the opportunity for an individual or group to appeal decisions they believe to be unfair. The logical body to approach first is the job evaluation committee, which can review its decisions in the light of the concerns expressed and any new information the complainant provides. Sometimes the problem is not due to the final decision itself but to misunderstandings about the process used to make the decision. At this point, effective communication may solve the problem. Of course, it may be that the complainant is actually correct, and the decision should be changed.

If the complainant does not receive satisfaction at this level, there should be at least one other avenue of appeal available. For unionized employees, the typical recourse is to initiate a grievance. In a non-union firm, it may be appropriate to designate a senior company official (often the head of human resources) to review the matter and make a final decision. However, overruling the job evaluation committee is not something to be taken lightly, because committee members may interpret such decisions as undermining their authority or showing a lack of confidence in their decisions. If the committee is frequently overruled, committee members will grow increasingly cynical about the role played by the committee, and it may become difficult to find good members willing to serve.

Updating Job Evaluations

There are at least five events that can trigger a need to reevaluate jobs:

1. Whenever the job itself changes significantly. It is important to have some procedure for identifying jobs that change, because this information may not always reach those who are charged with maintaining the job evaluation system.
2. When the strategy of the organization changes, such that certain behaviours become valued more or less highly than in the past.
3. When there are signs that the job evaluation system is no longer working effectively. These signs could include a high level of appeals, or an inability to fill certain jobs with competent individuals.
4. When labour market conditions change significantly.
5. When legislative conditions require it, such as when new pay equity legislation is introduced in a given jurisdiction.

Failure to update job evaluations is probably most likely in organizations that depended on outside consultants to develop and implement their job evaluation systems. Once the consultants leave, the tendency is to just forget about the system, especially if the consultants did not provide internal employees with the expertise to maintain the job evaluation system. As a part of any consulting contract, the organization should ensure that it provides training for internal staff so that they have a full understanding of the job evaluation system and are able to maintain it. Otherwise, provisions have to be made to retain the consultant on a continuing basis.

Conforming to Pay Equity Requirements

RPC 6.2

Up until now, we have described generic job evaluation procedures. Using them effectively *should* ensure gender equity. However, many Canadian jurisdictions do not want to leave this to chance and have imposed specific procedures on employers for ensuring pay equity. In this final section, we will address the issues in conforming with specific pay equity requirements, a subject not well understood by the general public.[10] We will focus on compliance with the Ontario Pay Equity Act to illustrate the nature of the process because Ontario is the largest jurisdiction, because other provincial legislation (i.e., that of Quebec) is patterned after Ontario legislation, and because it has broad application (covering all employers with 10 employees or more). In contrast, the other jurisdictions that have pay equity legislation (Manitoba, New Brunswick, Nova Scotia, and the federal jurisdiction, which includes federal government employees, as well as selected industries such as banking and interprovincial transportation) cover only public-sector employees. Although a task force commissioned by the federal government recently concluded that the Ontario model should be applied to all employers under federal jurisdiction,[11] this change has not yet taken place.

The following are the main steps in the Ontario process, and each will be discussed in turn. (Extensive further information is available from the Ontario Pay Equity Commission in the form of booklets or from their website.)

1. Determine what rules apply.
2. Identify female and male job classes.
3. Establish a body to conduct pay equity.
4. Select a gender-neutral job comparison system.
5. Collect job information.
6. Compare jobs.
7. Check for permissible differences
8. Adjust compensation.
9. Communicate the results.
10. Maintain pay equity.

Determine What Rules Apply

If your organization employs fewer than 10 people in Ontario (including part-time employees), Ontario pay equity legislation does not apply. It also does not apply if your organization is in the federal jurisdiction. Slightly different procedures apply to private-sector employers with 10 to 99 employees, compared with larger employers. The main effect of the size differences relates to the requirement for "posting" the pay equity plan. All public-sector employers and all private-sector employers with 100 or more employees must formalize their pay equity plan in a format outlined by the Ontario Pay Equity Act and post it where all employees may have easy access to it. Smaller private-sector employers have the option of preparing and posting a plan or not posting. If they do not post it, they have an obligation to inform any requesting employee of the process that was conducted to achieve pay equity and the results of this process.

These differences aside, the general process for pay equity is the same for all employers covered by the Act. First, the number of pay equity plans needs to be determined. If the organization is unionized, it needs one pay equity plan for each bargaining unit in an establishment, and one for all non-union employees within the same establishment. If the firm is not unionized, there will generally be only one pay equity plan. However, a single employer may differentiate employees by geographical region and thus may have two or more "establishments" within the province. This would entitle the employer to have different pay equity plans for each establishment.

Identify Female and Male Job Classes

The second step in conducting the pay equity process is to determine whether your organization has any female job classes within each pay equity plan. A job class is a group of jobs that have similar duties, require similar qualifications, are filled by similar recruitment procedures, and have the same compensation schedule. Female job classes are those in which (1) at least 60 percent of employees holding them are women, (2) females have traditionally dominated this job class, or (3) most people commonly associate the job with female employees.

Thus, even if you have no job classes that are 60 percent female, if you have jobs that are covered under points (2) or (3), then you still have a female job class. For example, if your company has two secretaries, one of whom is male, you still must consider "secretary" a female job class. Even if your organization employs just one nurse, who happens to be male, the "nurse" job class must be considered a female job class.

If your organization has no female job classes, then there is no need to go any further in the pay equity process. But if it does, the next step is to determine if there are any male job classes in the same pay equity plan. Male job classes are defined by the same criteria noted above, except that 70 percent is the minimum proportion of male jobholders necessary to be considered a male job class. If there are no male job classes in that pay equity plan, the pay equity process does not apply, unless the firm has two or more pay equity plans, and one of those has a male job class, or unless the firm is in the public sector and is allowed to use the "proxy approach" to job comparison, as discussed later in this chapter. Of course, when and if the firm creates any male job classes, pay equity would then apply.

Establish a Body for Conducting Pay Equity

If pay equity legislation does apply, the next step is to conduct the pay equity process. If there is a bargaining agent, the Act requires that the bargaining agent be fully involved in all aspects of the pay equity process. This is usually done through a joint union–management pay equity committee. Although not required for non-union employers, it is strongly recommended that they also establish a joint employee–management pay equity committee.

Some of the benefits of such a committee were discussed along with the discussion of job evaluation committees earlier in the chapter. However, because of the nature of the pay equity process, it is probably even more important to establish such a committee. The diverse viewpoints likely to be found among committee members help to ensure that potential pay inequities are identified. This body also serves as a communications mechanism and creates more employee confidence in the process and its results.

This committee should have a mix of employees who hold various jobs throughout the organization and should include both female and male members if possible. Training in the pay equity process is essential for members.

Moreover, it is useful to establish some ground rules for committee operation, covering issues such as confidentiality, decision-making processes, and the role of the committee and its members.

Select a Gender-Neutral Job Comparison System

The committee needs to identify and develop a gender-neutral job evaluation system that allows comparison of job classes on the four required factor groups—skill, effort, responsibility, and working conditions. The system most commonly used for pay equity is the point method. While the ranking and classification methods can be adapted to meet the requirements of the pay equity legislation, it is probably only worthwhile to do so if they are already in use by the organization and if the organization is happy with them.

Collect Job Information

The next step is to gather information for evaluating the jobs. This is the process of job analysis described earlier in the chapter. A key part of this process is to avoid gender biases and the potential pitfalls in the job analysis process that have been described earlier.

Compare Jobs

Once the information has been collected, the committee then applies the job evaluation system to each job class and develops a job hierarchy (one for each pay equity plan). Three main methods can then be used for comparing female and male job classes: the job-to-job approach, the proportional value method, or the proxy method (only for public-sector employers).

job-to-job method

establishes pay equity by comparing a female job class to a male class that is comparable in terms of job evaluation criteria

In the **job-to-job method**, a male job class "comparator" is sought for each female job class. This comparator male class needs to be similar to the female class by having an equal or comparable number of points as the female job class, not by job similarities. For example, if the "electrician" job class has a similar point total to the "nurse" job class, then the "electrician" can serve as the comparator class for the nurse job class. If there are two or more male comparator classes similar in point totals to one female class, the appropriate one is the lower paid. (Incidentally, neither the Pay Equity Act nor the Pay Equity Commission provide any guidance on exactly how similar the point totals have to be before the female and male job classes are considered "equal or comparable.")

The committee then compares total compensation (including benefits) for the two jobs. If the male job class (electrician) is receiving higher pay than the female job class (nurse), then pay inequity *may* exist and, if so, would need to be corrected.

What if there is no male job class at the same level in the job hierarchy to use as a comparator? In this case, if the organization has other pay equity plans at other establishments, the other pay plan(s) should be checked to see if an equivalent male comparator job class can be found there. If not, an attempt should be made to identify male job classes of lower value (according to job evaluation), but which are being paid more than the female job class. If several male job classes match this criterion, the appropriate comparator is the one with the *highest* pay rate. But what if a suitable comparator still cannot be found?

The next course of action is the **proportional value method,** which was introduced in mid-1993 to deal with the problem of lack of a male comparator, which can occur in the job-to-job method. The proportional value method requires the employer to calculate what a male job class at the same point in the job hierarchy where the female job is placed would theoretically pay, based on data only from the other male job classes.

Let's use a simple example. Suppose that an organization has one female job class (let's label it "F1") and two male job classes ("M1" and "M2"). The job evaluation points for these jobs, and hourly pay rates, including benefits, are as follows:

- M2: 800 points ($24 per hour)
- F1: 600 points ($15 per hour)
- M1: 400 points ($12 an hour)

As can be seen, there is no equivalent male comparator for the female job class, so the job-to-job method cannot be used. There is a gap in the male job hierarchy at 600 points. But proportional value fills this gap by examining classes M1 and M2 to see what a male class evaluated at 600 points would theoretically pay. Job classes M1 and M2 would be plotted on a graph, a straight line would be drawn that fits these points (very simple with just two points in this example), and then 600 points would be read from the graph, which would be $18 per hour. (In fact, in this example, no complicated calculations are really necessary to show that a male job midway between 400 and 800 points would pay $18 an hour.)

What we have apparently found is pay inequity, since class F1 is receiving only $15 an hour. This $3 inequity must be corrected, unless it is found to stem from what are known as "permissible differences." If the entire difference does result from permissible differences, it is not considered to be a pay inequity, and no pay adjustments are required.

What if the proportional value approach doesn't work either, because there are no male job classes (or only one)? For most organizations, this brings the pay equity process to a halt. But in what is known as the "broader public sector" (which includes municipal governments, colleges, hospitals, and the like), the **proxy comparison method** must then be used. In this method, the employer must select another public-sector employer that has completed pay equity procedures and collect information on the female job classes in that "proxy" organization. This information is then subjected to job evaluation, and the proportional value method is used to calibrate the employer's female job classes. The key issue in this process is, of course, selection of the proxy employer.

proportional value method

establishes pay equity where no comparator male job class exists by extrapolating a hypothetical male comparator job class based on other male job classes

proxy comparison method

establishes pay equity in public-sector organizations where neither the job-to-job method nor the proportional value method can be used

Check for Permissible Differences

Pay differences are not considered pay inequities if they are due to "permissible differences." So what are these permissible differences? In the words of the Ontario Pay Equity Commission, **permissible differences** are allowed "where the employer is able to show that the difference is the result of the following: a formal seniority system, a temporary training or developmental assignment, a merit compensation plan, red-circling, or a temporary skills shortage."[12] (The "merit compensation plan" must be based on formal criteria and be communicated to all employees to be eligible as a permissible difference.)

However, it should be noted that the use of a permissible difference does not necessarily exclude a male job class from being used as a comparator. In some cases, permissible differences will account for the entire gap between a female and male job class; but in other cases, they will only account for a portion of the difference. If this is the case, then the remaining portion must be addressed.

Besides those reasons cited above, there are two other allowable reasons for a difference between female and male pay. One is bargaining strength. Under the Act, after "pay equity has been achieved in an establishment, differences in compensation between a female job class and male job class are permissible if the employer is able to show that the difference is the result of differences in bargaining strength."[13] But just how does an employer show that? Neither the Pay Equity Act nor the guidelines provided by the Pay Equity Commission offer any guidance on that question, although they both emphasize that the onus is on the employer to prove that an exception based on bargaining strength meets the requirements of the Act. To date it appears this section of the Act has never been used successfully.

The other allowable reason is very rarely found. Where an arbitrator or other tribunal *not* related to interest arbitration (interest arbitration is used to determine pay and benefits when the union and management reach an impasse in the bargaining process) raises the pay of a male comparator job class, the employer may select a different male comparator job class and, if one cannot be found, may use the proportional value method instead. This provision can only be used after pay equity has been achieved in the first instance, and it may serve to limit the requirement to maintain pay equity over time.

There is one other possible exception in the pay equity process. An employer (in conjunction with the bargaining agent, if any) may designate certain jobs as "casual." Casual jobs do not fall under the purview of pay equity legislation. However, there are strict limitations on using this designation. A job *cannot* be designated casual when:

a. The work is performed for at least one third of the normal work period that applies to similar full-time work; or
b. The work is performed on a seasonal basis in the same position for the same employer; or
c. The work is performed on a regular and continuing basis, although for less than one third of the normal work period that applies to similar full-time work.

Given these constraints, very few jobs can, in reality, be classified as "casual."[14]

While pay equity must be applied to all except designated "casual" employees, it does not have to be applied to independent contractors. However, the conditions for this exclusion are stringent. For example, in a recent case, individuals who provided daycare for children in their own homes were deemed to be employees of an Ontario county (and thus subject to pay equity provisions): they were not deemed independent contractors, as the county had maintained. The daycare providers filed their income tax as self-employed persons, held their own general liability insurance, and purchased most of their own equipment. However, because the county had a rigorous selection process for providers, often a lengthy relationship with them, and exercised control through its placement procedures, regular mandatory orientation and training sessions, regular inspection visits, and discipline and termination procedures, the Pay Equity Tribunal deemed them to be employees, not independent contractors.[15]

Adjust Compensation

The Ontario pay equity legislation does not necessarily require employers to correct the full extent of pay inequities immediately (although the employer may well decide to do so, if it is within their financial means), as long as the employer has "posted" its pay equity plan. Essentially, this means that all employees have been provided access to the process that was conducted in determining pay equity and have been provided with their own personal copy, if they have requested it. (New employers coming under the purview of the Act are expected to correct pay inequities immediately, regardless of whether they post a pay equity plan.)

If an employer has posted a pay equity plan, it must devote at least 1 percent of the previous year's payroll toward correcting pay inequities. This must then be done every year until the inequities are corrected. If the 1 percent is not sufficient to correct the inequities, the Pay Equity Act specifies how the available money will be distributed:

- The [inequitable female] job class or classes with the lowest job rate in the plan must receive a greater adjustment than other [inequitable female] job classes in the same plan until pay equity is achieved.
- Each female job class must receive an adjustment each year until pay equity is achieved.
- All positions in a job class will receive the same adjustments in dollar terms.[16]

Finally, in case an employer may be tempted to avoid higher compensation costs, the act specifically prohibits the achievement of pay equity through the lowering of pay levels for male comparator jobs.

Communicate the Results

Once the pay equity plan has been developed, it should be communicated to employees so that they understand both the process and the results. However, the only organizations *required* to post their pay equity plans are public-sector employers and private-sector employers with at least 100 employees. In organizations that do not post their plan, employers are obligated under the Act to disclose both the process undertaken to ensure pay equity and the results of that process to any employee who requests it.

Maintain Pay Equity

Even after organizations have achieved pay equity, they are not free of their obligations under the Pay Equity Act. Employers are responsible for actively ensuring that pay equity is maintained over time. There are many changes that can occur in the employer that may have an impact on pay equity. These include the following:

- Restructuring of the organization
- Certification of a bargaining agent after a deemed-approved plan
- Changes in the gender of a job class
- New or vanishing job classes
- New male comparator job class for a female job class
- A change in the value of work performed in a job class
- A change in compensation system or compensation levels.[17]

Let us now examine each of these briefly.

Structural or Bargaining Agent Change

Various types of company restructuring may trigger a need for review of pay equity. For example, when one firm takes over or merges with another, the pay system must be reviewed for equity, looking at all jobs under the new structure. When a new bargaining agent is certified, or a bargaining agent is decertified, it will be necessary either to create another pay equity plan or to merge the previous pay equity plans.

Gender Changes

If the workforce changes such that the percentage of males and females in a particular job class changes, then this class may change from male to female, from female to male, from one of these to gender-neutral, or from gender-neutral to one of these. However, a change in the percentage of males and females does not automatically change the gender status of the job class. For example, if the percentage of secretaries who are female changes from 95 percent to 50 percent, this does not mean that the secretary job class will be reclassified as gender-neutral. In this case, "secretary" would stay a female job class because historically this has been a female job and because of the existence of a stereotype that this is a female job.

New Job Classes

Sometimes an employer creates a new job class, which then must be assessed for gender. If it turns out to be a female job class, then the process described earlier applies, where the job-to-job or proportional value approach must be used to check for inequity. If a new male job class is created, two questions need to be asked. Should this job be used as a comparator to a female job class (if the job-to-job method is used)? Does this job affect the value for jobs established through a proportional value system?

Vanishing Job Classes

Sometimes a job class will vanish. Reasons may include technological change, company restructuring, or the sale or closure of a business or unit. If a female job class vanishes, or its gender changes, "its incumbents must be paid the full amount of their pay equity adjustments owing up until the date on which the job class disappears."[18]

If a male job class vanishes, the implications depend on whether the job-to-job or proportional value method has been used. If the job-to-job method has been used, and the vanished male job class had been used as a comparator, a new comparator must be found. But if the new comparator is paid lower than the female class, compensation for the female class cannot be lowered. If the proportional value method has been used, the usual procedure is to remove that class from the male job pay line (as discussed earlier in conjunction with "proportional value method") and then reassess female jobs against the new male pay line. But if the results indicate a lower pay level for the female job class(es), their pay cannot be reduced from their original pay equity entitlement.

Job Value Changes

Sometimes a male or female job class changes in value, especially if duties or job requirements change. If the change is significant enough to warrant a change in its position in the job hierarchy (the employer determines this repositioning through its gender-neutral job evaluation process), the pay level needs to be reassessed in the manner described earlier. Then, depending on whether it is a female or male job, the procedures described above apply.

Compensation Changes

Various changes in the compensation system or compensation levels may have implications for pay equity. For example, if a male job class comparator receives a compensation increase greater than that received by the female job class, pay equity is threatened. Even if the female job class and its comparator receive equal percentage increases, if these percentages apply before the female job has achieved full pay equity, the pay increase actually widens the pay gap between the male and female jobs. In both of these cases, money must be found to reclose these gaps, and this money cannot be deducted from the 1 percent minimum of annual payroll already dedicated to eliminating pay equity gaps.

Communication about Pay Equity Plan Changes

If any of these changes occur and have pay equity implications, the employer (or, if there is a bargaining agent, the employer and the bargaining agent) must revise the pay equity plan accordingly and repost it. The only employers not required to repost changes to their pay equity plan are those employing fewer than 100 employees and those that did not post a plan originally.

Chapter 6: Evaluating Jobs: The Job Evaluation Process

Summary

The purpose of this chapter is to start developing your understanding of the key technical processes necessary to transform the compensation strategy into an operating compensation system, beginning with the process for evaluating jobs. Not all organizations will decide to use job evaluation. But for those that do, this chapter provides the fundamentals of how to develop an effective job evaluation system. It explains the process of job analysis, which provides the information (known as a "job description") that is the foundation for any effective job evaluation system. It describes various job analysis methods and outlines some possible pitfalls in the process.

This chapter has provided you with an overview of the main methods for job evaluation—ranking/paired comparison, classification/grading, factor comparison, statistical/policy capturing, and the point method. (Detailed discussion of the point method, will take place in Chapter 7.)

If a job evaluation process is to be both equitable and seen to be equitable, the process for conducting and managing job evaluation is crucial. Organizations need to work out procedures for who will conduct the job evaluation process, for how it will be communicated, for how procedural justice can be established, for how results will be applied, and how job evaluations will be updated.

Finally, many jurisdictions have specific legislation pertaining to pay equity, which mandates a specific procedure to identify jobs for which there is gender inequity in pay and to correct any inequities that are detected. Although the legislation varies somewhat in each jurisdiction, much of it is patterned after Ontario pay equity legislation. Because of this fact, and because Ontario is the largest single jurisdiction, this chapter has presented you with an overview of the process for achieving and maintaining pay equity in Ontario.

Key Terms

classification/grading method, 254

factor comparison method, 256

job analysis, 243

job description, 243

job-to-job method, 262

job specifications, 243

paired comparison method, 253

permissible differences, 264

point method, 256

proportional value method, 263

proxy comparison method, 263

ranking method, 253

statistical/policy capturing method, 256

Web Links

To check out the United States occupational classification system, go to **http://online.onetcenter.org/**. (p. 250)

To check out the Canadian National Occupational Classification, go to **http://www.hrsdc.gc.ca/en/hip/hrp/noc/noc_index.shtml**. (p. 250)

The Ontario Pay Equity Commission website has further information on avoiding gender bias in job descriptions. Go to **http://www.gov.on.ca/lab/pec/peo/english/pubs/glossaryverbs.html**. (p. 251)

To review the findings of the Pay Equity Task Force, go to **http://www.payequityreview.gc.ca**. (p. 260)

The Ontario Pay Equity Commission provides a website that describes the steps required to achieve pay equity, along with links to the specific guidelines for each step. Go to **http://www.gov.on.ca/lab/pec/peo/english/steps10/10steps.html**. (p. 260)

RPC Icons

RPC 6.1 Implements an effective procedure for describing work-related duties, establishing their relative worth, and aligning them with the organizational structure.

RPC 6.2 Establishes compensation policies and procedures based on the compensation program and compliance with the legal framework.

Discussion Questions

1. Discuss the purpose of job evaluation and the main steps in conducting job evaluation.
2. Discuss the advantages and disadvantages of job analysis.
3. Discuss the key issues in managing the job evaluation process.
4. Discuss the general process for conforming to pay equity legislation. Does legislating pay equity seem like a good idea to you?

Using the Internet

1. To trace through the steps required to create a gender-neutral job evaluation system that complies with Ontario Pay Equity legislation, go to **http://www.gov.on.ca/lab/pec/peo/english/eval/welcome.html**.
2. To test your knowledge of pay equity provisions in an interactive way, take the "Pay Equity Quiz" developed by the Ontario Pay Equity Commission. Go to **http://www.gov.on.ca/lab/pec/peo/english/quiz/start.html**.

Exercise

1. Examine the job description depicted on the next page. Using the information from Compensation Notebooks 6.1 and 6.2, assess whether this is a good job description, and what improvements could be made to it.

Beaver Manufacturing Corporation

Job Title: Drafter 1   **Department:** Engineering (Drafting Section)

Reports to: Head of Drafting   **Updated:** January 15, 2005

Job Purpose

This employee utilizes computer-aided design (CAD) techniques to produce and update drawings of plant facilities, based on rough sketches, diagrams, notes, and verbal instructions provided by design engineers.

Main Job Duties (listed duties are illustrative, not restrictive)

1. Prepare finished CAD drawings from sketches, diagrams, notes, and verbal instructions.
2. Search computer databases for existing information on which to base drawings.
3. Meet with engineers to clarify drawing requirements and to discuss revisions to drawings.
4. Assist with site verifications of existing facilities.
5. Share in filing of facilities records.
6. Assist other staff in locating physical records information.

Other Job Information

Works under the supervision of senior drafters, who check product before sending to engineers for final approval. Engineers provide final check on output. If undetected, errors can cause serious facilities damage. Basic keyboarding skills and ability to utilize computer-assisted design equipment are required. Considerable concentration is required to transform input materials into finished product. Work is mainly performed in a quiet office environment. Some exterior facilities inspection required.

Job Specifications

High school graduation plus a two-year diploma in computer-assisted design from a recognized technical institute. Ability to communicate effectively in verbal and nonverbal modes.

Case Question

1. Examine the job descriptions that are used in the "Eastern Provincial University" case in the Appendix. What are their strengths and weaknesses? What would you change about them?

Simulation Cross-Reference

If you are using *Strategic Compensation: A Simulation* in conjunction with this text, you will find that the concepts in Chapter 6 are helpful in preparing Sections D and I of the simulation.

Endnotes

1. Brown, David. 2004. "Pay Equity Impacts in Ontario." *Canadian HR Reporter*, 17(11): 3.

2. King, Ian. 1992. *Compensation Administration and Equitable Pay Programs—A Practical Guide*. Don Mills, ON: CCH Canadian Limited, 4.

3. McPhail, S.M., P.R. Jeanneret, E.J. McCormick, and R.C. Mecham. 1991. *Position Analysis Questionnaire: Job Analysis Manual*. Palo Alto, CA: Consulting Psychologists Press.

4. Tornow, W.W., and P.R. Pinto. 1976. "The Development of a Managerial Job Taxonomy: A System for Describing, Classifying, and Evaluating Executive Positions." *Journal of Applied Psychology*, 61: 410–18.

5. Hemphill, J.K. 1954. "Job Descriptions for the Executive." *Harvard Business Review*, 37: 55–69.

6. Fine, Sidney A., A.M. Holt, and M.F. Hutchinson. 1974. "Functional Job Analysis: How to Standardize Task Statements." *Methods for Manpower Analysis*. Kalamazoo, MI: W.E. Upjohn Institute for Employment Research.

7. Kelly, John G. 1994. *Pay Equity Management*. North York, ON: CCH Canadian Limited, 23.

8. Kelly, John G. 1994. *Pay Equity Management*. North York, ON: CCH Canadian Limited.

9. *Focus on Canadian Employment and Equality Rights*. 2000. "Policy-Capturing Job Evaluation Methodology Considered." 5(28): 222–23.

10. Forrest, Anne. 2001. "Pay Equity: The State of the Debate." In Y. Reshef, C. Bernier, D. Harrisson, and T.H. Wagar, eds. *Industrial Relations in the New Millenium: Selected Papers from the XXXVIIth Annual CIRA Conference*, 65–78.

11. Pay Equity Task Force. 2004. *Pay Equity: A New Approach to a Fundamental Right*. Ottawa: Department of Justice, Canada.

12. Pay Equity Commission. 1995. *Maintaining Pay Equity: Using the Job-to-Job and Proportional Value Comparison Methods*. Toronto: Ontario Pay Equity Commission, 32.

13. Pay Equity Commission. 1995. *Maintaining Pay Equity: Using the Job-to-Job and Proportional Value Comparison Methods*. Toronto: Ontario Pay Equity Commission, 33.

14. Pay Equity Commission. 1995. *Maintaining Pay Equity: Using the Job-to-Job and Proportional Value Comparison Methods*. Toronto: Ontario Pay Equity Commission, 33.

15. *Ontario Pay and Employment Equity Guide*. 2000. "Home Care Providers Entitled to Pay Equity." February: 3.

16. Pay Equity Commission. 1993. *Step by Step to Pay Equity: A Guide for Small Business: Volume I: The Workbook*. Toronto: Ontario Pay Equity Commission, 23.

17. Pay Equity Commission. 1995. *Maintaining Pay Equity: Using the Job-to-Job and Proportional Value Comparison Methods*. Toronto: Ontario Pay Equity Commission, 6.

18. Pay Equity Commission. 1995. *Maintaining Pay Equity: Using the Job-to-Job and Proportional Value Comparison Methods*. Toronto: Ontario Pay Equity Commission, 21.

Chapter 7

Evaluating Jobs: The Point Method of Job Evaluation

Chapter Learning Objectives

After reading this chapter, you should be able to:

- Describe the steps in designing a point system of job evaluation.
- Identify the possible pitfalls in designing a point system of job evaluation.
- Design a base pay structure, including pay grades and pay ranges.
- Discuss the issues involved in applying a new pay structure.

NURSES OR PAINTERS: WHO IS MORE VALUABLE TO A HOSPITAL?

Who performs work that is more valuable to a hospital, nurses or painters? Intuitively, we might think nurses. But that is not what the job evaluation system at a U.S. hospital concluded, and certainly not what their pay scales indicated, as painters were paid considerably more than nurses at that hospital.[1]

Is this really fair? How could we objectively determine which job is more valuable to a hospital? Let's compare the jobs systematically, using the four basic categories of compensable factors required under pay equity legislation:

- *Skill:* To perform the job of "nurse" requires medical skills (including a licence and postsecondary training), interpersonal skills, and communication skills. To perform the job of painter requires manual dexterity and the ability to mix paint.
- *Effort:* A nurse's job requires some physical effort, such as helping to lift patients and standing or walking for extended periods of time. Painters are required to be on their feet constantly, to climb ladders, and to exercise continuous repetitive movement over the entire duration of their shift. However, painters do not need to expend much mental effort, while nurses must be continually alert to monitor patient health and provide correct dosages of medication.
- *Responsibility:* Nurses are responsible for the health and welfare of human beings. Painters are responsible for neatly painted walls and ceilings.
- *Working Conditions:* Working conditions for painters are often smelly, unpleasant, or dangerous, especially when working at heights, such as painting ceilings. Working conditions for nurses may also be smelly, unpleasant, or dangerous, as when they need to empty bedpans, clean or bathe patients, clean up pus and vomit, and suffer the risk of contracting communicable diseases from patients. Other unpleasant working conditions of the nurse job include dealing with patients in severe pain and their distraught family members and discovering dead patients.[2]

This analysis suggests that a nurse's job should be evaluated more highly than a painter's job on all factors except physical effort, and therefore should be paid more, not less. Why didn't the hospital's job evaluation system pick this up? Because two separate job evaluation systems were used—one for nursing staff and one for maintenance staff.

Introduction

With a properly designed job evaluation (JE) system and base pay structure, inequities such as this should not occur. The purpose of this chapter is to describe how to design a job evaluation system using the point method of job evaluation, avoiding the possible pitfalls in so doing; develop a base pay structure that flows from this job evaluation system; and apply the new pay structure.

Using the Point Method to Design a Job Evaluation System

The point method of job evaluation identifies key job characteristics (known as "**compensable factors**") that differentiate the value of various jobs, develops a measuring scale for each factor ("scaling the factors"), and weights these factors according to their importance to the firm. The organization then determines how much of each factor is present in each job, thus generating a point total for each job. Then the resulting job hierarchy is tested against the market, and any necessary revisions are made to the JE system. Once the job evaluation system has been finalized, all jobs are scored on the system to derive a final hierarchy of jobs, which then serves as the foundation for the base pay structure. Each of these steps will be discussed in turn.

compensable factors
characteristics of jobs that are valued by the organization and differentiate jobs from one another

Identifying Compensable Factors

Compensable factors can be defined as "those characteristics in the work that the organization values, that help it pursue its strategy and achieve its objectives."[3] Compensable factors are based on the work performed, support the strategy and values of the organization, distinguish between jobs, and are acknowledged as significant by employees. These factors typically include job inputs (such as education, training, or experience), job requirements (e.g., mental effort, physical effort, decision making), job outputs (e.g., accuracy of output, consequences of mistakes), and job conditions (e.g., nature of work environment, hazards that may be encountered).

The variety of factors that can be used by different organizations is almost limitless, but four main categories of factors are more or less universal: skill, effort, responsibility, and working conditions. Under pay equity legislation, organizations are required to use these four categories in evaluating work. However, employers are allowed to use specific factors of particular relevance (sometimes known as "subfactors") from each of these factor categories.

For example, "skill" might be represented by the factors of "education" and "experience." "Effort" could be represented by "mental effort" and "physical effort." "Responsibility" might be represented by "consequences of errors" and "value of assets utilized." Working conditions might be represented by "unpleasantness of work environment" and "hazards to physical safety."

Compensation Notebook 7.1 provides a listing of some of the specific factors that can be used by organizations, clustered according to the four basic factor categories. As the table illustrates, the four categories can encompass

Compensation Notebook 7.1

Examples of Commonly Used Compensable Factors

Skill	Effort	Responsibility	Working Conditions
Ability to do detailed work	Attention demanded	Accountability	Attention to details
Ability to do accurate work	Concentration needed	Importance of accuracy	Cleaning up after others
Analytical ability	Mental demands: Complexity	Cash	Constant interruptions
Aptitude required	Mental demands: Continuity	Confidential data	Danger
Communication skills: Verbal	Mental demands: Intensity	Contact with public	Dirtiness
Communication skills: Written	Mental demands: Repetitive	Contact with customers/clients	Disagreeableness
Communication skills: Second language	Mental fatigue	Coordination	Exposure to accident hazard
Dexterity	Monotony and discomfort	Consequence of error	Exposure to health hazard
Education	Muscular strain	Dependability	Intangible conditions
Experience	Nerve strain	Determining company policy	Monotony
Initiative	Physical demands: Complexity	Effect on other operations	Out-of-town travel
Interpersonal	Physical demands: Continuity	Equipment and machinery	Physical environment/ surroundings
Knowledge	Physical demands: Intensity	Goodwill and public relations	Stress of multiple demands
Managerial techniques	Physical demands: Repetitive	Monetary responsibility	Time pressure
Manual quickness	Physical fatigue	Personnel	
Manual or motor skills	Pressure of work	Physical property	
Problem solving	Stress from dealing with difficult people	Quality	
Resourcefulness	Plant and services	Records	
Social skills	Visual application	Safety of others	
Versatility	Volume of work	Spoilage of materials	
		Supervision of others	

Source: Adapted from the Ontario Pay Equity Commission document "Overlooked Features of Women's Jobs." © Queen's Printer for Ontario, 1991. Reproduced with permission.

just about any characteristic that the organization would want to measure. It can also be seen that many factors are generic, while others may be more firm-specific. A customer-oriented firm might include "amount of customer contact" as a compensable factor, thus implying that jobs with more customer contact are more important than those with less. A firm in which innovation and development of new products and services are important might include a factor entitled "amount of innovative behaviour." A firm concerned with cost might have a factor entitled "responsibility for cost containment."

How many factors should be used? There is no simple answer to this question. There must be enough that they capture all the key aspects of work that are important to the organization, but not so many that they start to overlap or add very little additional value to the system. In general, the broader the group of jobs to be covered with a single job evaluation system, the greater the number of factors that will be needed. In recent years, there has been a trend toward broadening the inclusiveness of job evaluation systems, in order to ensure fairness for all employee groups and also in response to pay equity legislation. For example, Ontario legislation requires single plans for each union bargaining unit, regardless whether both blue- and white-collar jobs are included in the unit; if the organization is not unionized, the law requires that the same job evaluation system cover *all* jobs at a given establishment.

Overall, it is hard to see how a valid point system could operate with less than about eight factors (with at least one from each factor category); but systems that include more than a dozen factors may be including marginal factors that add very little to the ability to differentiate job values.

After selecting the factors, it is essential to develop a clear definition of each factor, a definition which clearly conveys the meaning of that factor and clearly differentiates it from other factors. If this cannot be done for a given factor, then that factor should be dropped from the system.

One trend has been for some firms to purposely omit certain traditional factors. For example, many firms have had a factor "responsibility for supervision of subordinates," which is based on the number of subordinates supervised. But some firms have started to drop this factor, for several reasons. For example, an assembly-line supervisor may have 30 subordinates, but these employees are effectively supervised by the technology, while a director of a research project may have four subordinates doing highly complex work, for which constant supervision, coordination, and interaction are essential. Moreover, number of subordinates implies that managers who expand their staffs will be rewarded, while those who improve efficiency and cut back their staffs will be penalized. Many firms no longer want to send this message.

Scaling the Factors

After the compensable factors have been selected and defined, a number of "degrees" (sometimes called "levels") are established for each factor, resulting in a measurement scale for every factor. These degrees represent gradations in the extent to which a certain factor is present in a particular job being rated. For example, it may be decided that there should be five possible "degrees" or levels for the factor of "consequences of error." Each degree needs to be carefully defined and arranged so that degree 2 always contains more of that factor than degree 1, and so on. Table 7.1 provides examples of two factors, with their factor and degree definitions.

How many degrees should be used? The number of degrees for a particular factor depends on the range of that factor. There is no reason for all factors in a job evaluation system to have the same number of degrees. For

TABLE 7.1

Sample Compensable Factors Illustrating Degrees

Factor: Formal Education

This factor deals with the level of formal education required to perform the job.

Degree 1: Completion of grade 9.

Degree 2: Completion of high school.

Degree 3: One year of postsecondary education.

Degree 4: Two years of postsecondary education.

Degree 5: University bachelor's degree or major professional designation.

Degree 6: University master's degree or bachelor's degree plus professional designation.

Degree 7: University/medical school doctorate.

Degree 8: Medical doctorate plus additional medical specialization.

Factor: Ingenuity

This factor deals with the need for ingenuity in dealing with problems arising from normal work assignments in this job. It includes the frequency, extent, and importance of ingenuity for successful job performance. It is limited by the amount of guidance/supervision that is available.

Degree 1: Work procedures and problems are standard; very little ingenuity required.

Degree 2: Work procedures and problems are mainly standard; occasional ingenuity required.

Degree 3: Work procedures and problems are often nonstandard; some ingenuity required.

Degree 4: Work procedures are mainly nonstandard; considerable ingenuity required, but considerable guidance available.

Degree 5: Work procedures are mainly nonstandard; considerable ingenuity required, little guidance available; consequences of poor choices of solution are not serious.

Degree 6: Work procedures are mainly nonstandard; high ingenuity required, little guidance available; consequences of poor choices of solution are moderate.

Degree 7: Work procedures are mainly nonstandard; high ingenuity required; little guidance; consequences of poor choices are very serious.

example, if relevant education ranges from elementary school to a university doctorate, then seven or eight degrees might be used. Where the range is from elementary school to completion of high school, only three or four degrees might be used. At the same time, "working conditions" might be assigned five degrees, and "experience" seven degrees, depending on the variation in working conditions in the organization and the variation in experience required by different jobs in the organization.

Weighting the Factors

The compensable factors that have been selected are not likely to be equal in importance to the firm. To recognize this variation in importance, each factor needs to be weighted according to its importance relative to the others. For example, in one firm, "education" may be viewed as the most important factor, followed by "experience," then by "customer contact," and "mental complexity," with "physical environment" considered the least important factor. If the maximum number of points that any job may receive is arbitrarily set at 1000, then the maximum points for education might be set at 350 points, experience at 250 points, customer contact at 200 points, mental complexity at 150 points, and physical environment 50 points. These points are then distributed across the degrees that were defined in the previous step. For example, if "education" has seven degrees, then degree 1 might be assigned 50 points, degree 2 might be assigned 100 points, and so on, all the way to degree 7, which would be assigned 350 points. However, there is no reason why the point intervals between degrees should be identical, and it may well be appropriate in many instances to vary the point intervals between degrees.

How are the factor weights derived? There are two methods—statistical analysis and expert judgment (sometimes known as the "a priori" method). Statistical analysis uses a sample of existing jobs that have already been rated and are thought to be paid correctly. The existing pay rate for each of these jobs (if desired, the market rate for each job can be used instead, if it is different from company pay rates) is also fed into the equation. Multiple regression analysis is used to determine the role that each factor plays in influencing the pay rate in this sample of jobs. These weights are then applied to all jobs covered by the job evaluation system.

But there are several drawbacks to this approach. The first is that it is complex and not easily understood. The second is that it assumes that the current pay structure (or the market pay structure, if used) for the sample of benchmark or criterion jobs is appropriate, and that all other jobs should be aligned with this pay structure. So what this approach does is to perpetuate existing pay practices. For this reason, this approach may be unacceptable for pay equity purposes. It is certainly unacceptable if the organization is trying to change the pay structure to reflect changes in corporate strategy.

The other alternative ("expert judgment") requires forming a panel or committee of knowledgeable individuals within the organization. These individuals must have a good understanding of the organization, its strategy, and its needs, as well as an accurate understanding of the meanings of each factor. Each individual independently derives a set of factor weightings and brings this set to the committee. If there are major discrepancies, the reasons need to be identified. For example, perhaps one or more of the factor definitions is unclear, or perhaps different individuals have different understandings of the types of behaviour that the organization needs to elicit. The committee members then rework their weightings and repeat this process until the factor weightings all converge.

Once the factors and degrees have been defined and weighted, the committee develops a summary rating chart, on which they will record the points

FIGURE 7.1

Sample Summary Rating Chart for Point Method of Job Evaluation

JOB TITLE _____	DEGREE RATING								POINTS ALLOCATED
	1	2	3	4	5	6	7	8	
a) Education	10	25	45	70	100	135	185	210	
b) Experience	0	15	35	60	90	120	150	—	
c) Mental Skill	15	35	65	100	125	—	—	—	
d) Mental Effort	15	35	60	80	100	—	—	—	
e) Physical Effort	15	30	40	50	65	—	—	—	
f) Importance of Accuracy	15	30	45	65	80	—	—	—	
g) Patient Contact	10	30	45	60	75	—	—	—	
h) Supervisory Responsibility	0	20	35	50	75	—	—	—	
i) Job Hazards	0	15	30	45	65	—	—	—	
j) Job/Work Environment	10	20	30	40	55	—	—	—	
							TOTAL POINTS FOR THIS JOB		

allocated for each factor for a given job. By the end of the job evaluation process, there will be a filled-in copy of this summary chart for every job.

Figure 7.1 provides an example of a summary rating chart based on that used by a Canadian hospital. This rating chart uses 10 factors, three from the "skill" category (education, experience, mental skill), two from the "effort" category (mental effort, physical effort), three from the "responsibility" category (importance of accuracy, patient contact, supervisory responsibilities), and two from "working conditions" (job hazards, job/work environment). Eight degrees have been established for the factor of education, seven for experience, and five for each of the remaining factors. The maximum total number of points that a job could receive is 1000, and the minimum a job could receive is 90 points. The factor weights (as indicated by the maximum points available for a given factor) range from 210 points (education) to 55 points (job/work environment). (Incidentally, although this example has a round number of points (1000) as its maximum, there is nothing inherently superior in so doing. A maximum could just as easily be, say, 1140 points, and that in itself wouldn't affect the quality of the job evaluation system.)

Applying and Testing the System

Once the job evaluation system has been established, it is then applied to all the jobs covered by job evaluation, and a "hierarchy of jobs" is thus produced. A good way of summarizing the results of job evaluation, and the resulting hierarchy of jobs, is through a table similar to Table 7.2, which incorporates the results of a hypothetical application to a set of hospital jobs, based on the job evaluation results taken from the summary rating charts shown in Figure 7.1. Of course, in rating these jobs, evaluators are working with the

TABLE 7.2

Results of Job Evaluation Applied to Jobs at a Canadian Hospital

Compensable Factors

Job Title	(a) Education	(b) Experience	(c) Mental Skill	(d) Mental Effort	(e) Physical Effort	(f) Accuracy	(g) Contact	(h) Sup. Resp.	(i) Job Hazards	(j) Job/Work Environ.	Total Points
Head of Surgery	210	150	125	100	40	80	60	75	30	30	900
Thoracic Surgeon	210	90	125	100	50	80	75	20	30	30	810
Director of Nursing	135	150	125	100	30	80	60	75	15	30	800
Staff Physician	185	60	125	100	50	80	75	0	30	30	735
Head Ward Nurse	135	60	100	80	50	80	75	35	30	30	675
Chief Pharmacist	135	90	100	80	15	80	10	75	15	20	620
Registered Nurse	135	35	65	60	40	65	75	0	30	30	535
Ward Nurse	100	15	65	60	40	65	75	0	30	30	480
Pharmacist	100	15	65	60	15	80	30	0	15	20	400
Accountant	135	35	65	60	15	45	10	0	0	10	375
Medical Lab Tech.	70	15	35	35	30	80	30	0	45	30	370
Nurse's Aide	45	0	35	35	50	45	60	0	30	30	330
Janitor/Cleaner	25	15	35	15	50	30	10	0	45	40	265
Pharmacist's Asst.	45	0	35	35	15	80	10	0	15	10	245
Orderly	25	0	35	15	50	30	30	0	30	30	245
Admitting Clerk	25	15	35	35	15	45	45	0	15	0	230
Food Prep. Worker	25	0	35	15	40	45	10	0	15	20	215
Accounting Clerk	45	15	35	35	15	45	10	0	0	10	210
Painter	10	15	15	15	50	30	10	0	30	20	195
Grounds Worker	10	0	15	15	65	15	10	0	15	20	165

actual factor and degree definitions, which are not shown in Figure 7.1, and applying them to each job description. However, as an example, for the factor of education, the factor and degree definitions shown in Table 7.1 were used.

What does the hierarchy of jobs in Table 7.2 tell us? First, among this sample of hospital jobs (normally all hospital jobs would be included rather than just some of them), the most valuable job to the organization is the head of surgery, while the least valuable job is grounds worker. According to the job evaluation system, the job of head of surgery is about 5.5 times more valuable to the hospital than the job of grounds worker. (This is determined by dividing the point total for the job of head of surgery by the point total of the job of grounds worker.) This also implies that the head of surgery job should be paid about 5.5 times as much as the grounds worker job.

You will also notice that the job of ward nurse is worth more than twice as much (2.5 times) to the hospital than the job of painter, which answers our question from the opening vignette. In fact, in this sample of hospital jobs (not every job is included here), only the grounds worker job is less valuable to the hospital than the painter job.

Are there any pay relationships that surprise you? For example, some may be surprised to see that the janitor/cleaner job is actually more valuable to the hospital than numerous other jobs, such as pharmacist's assistant or accounting clerk. We can examine this strange-looking result by looking at the factor scores. While a relatively low level of education is required for the janitor/cleaner job, it scores high on the factors of physical effort, job hazards, and job/work environment (meaning it has an undesirable work environment). Besides being exposed to infectious patients, cleaners must deal with and properly dispose of many dangerous substances, such as highly infectious body fluids, pus, blood, and vomit, and they must be meticulous in their cleaning to render all surfaces sterile and germ-free. How successful they are in doing this can directly affect the health of patients and other staff. Therefore, we would expect the job of janitor/cleaner to be valued more by a hospital than by, say, a corporate office.

However, we should not yet assume that the relationships presented in Table 7.2 are actually valid, or that the underlying job evaluation system on which they are based is valid. There is a long process to go through before we can conclude that we have reasonable assurance of the **validity** of the job evaluation system.

validity

the extent to which a measuring instrument actually measures what we intend it to

reliability

the extent to which a measuring instrument consistently produces the same measurement result when measuring the same thing

Testing for Reliability

So how do we know that the job evaluation system we have developed is actually a true measure of relative job values? The first test of the system is its **reliability**. Reliability is the extent to which a measuring instrument consistently produces the same results when repeatedly applied to the same circumstances whether applied by the same or different persons. In other words, does the job evaluation system produce the same point scores for each factor for a given job, for every evaluator who applies the system? For example, if one person applies the job evaluation system to a nurse's job and gets point scores of 125 for mental skill, 80 for mental effort, and 40 for physical effort, while a different person who independently applies the job evaluation to the nurse's job gets point scores of 65, 100, and 50 for the same factors, then the system may not be reliable. Using an unreliable job evaluation system is the same as using an elastic tape measure to measure distance; and this problem must be identified and fixed before proceeding any further.

Thus, the first step in testing is for the job evaluation system to be applied independently by a variety of raters to the same set of jobs and then to compare the results. (Incidentally, the best way of applying the system is for each rater to evaluate all jobs on the first factor, then all on the second factor, and so on, which encourages consistent treatment of each factor.) If discrepancies across raters are discovered, the precise nature of the problem needs to be identified. The problem could lie in the factor definitions, which may not be sufficiently clear, or in the degree definitions, or in the job information (i.e., the job descriptions) on which the evaluators are basing their ratings, which may not contain sufficient information for accurate rating.

By comparing the results of the different evaluators on the different factors, it is possible to identify whether certain factors are problematic. For example, if the evaluators seem to agree fairly closely on how most factors should be rated for most jobs, but there is a lot of discrepancy for, say, "mental effort," then there may be a problem with this factor. If there seem to be one or two jobs where the evaluators are diverging on most factors, then there could be a problem with the job descriptions for these jobs. Other potential pitfalls in designing and applying a points method job evaluation system are discussed in more detail later in the chapter.

Once the problems have been identified and corrected, the system should be applied again by a different set of independent raters. If discrepancies remain, they must be dealt with, and the process repeated until consistency is achieved. There is absolutely no point in going further in testing the system if reliability has not first been achieved.

Testing for Market Fit

Once reliability has been achieved, it is necessary to calibrate the system to the market, so that JE points can be related to dollars. Calibrating to the market provides yet another test of the system. The organization selects a number of "key" or **"benchmark" jobs**, each of which has a good match ("a **market comparator job**") in a set of valid market data. These benchmark jobs should be selected so that there is a spread across the range of job evaluation points. That is, some jobs with a high point total should be selected, some with a low point total, and some that fall in between. Including at least some jobs that are strongly related to the nature of the business and represent sizable numbers of employees is also desirable. The normal practice is to use about 10 to 15 percent of the total number of jobs to be evaluated.

In the case of the hospital example in Table 7.2, a reasonable choice of benchmark jobs might be head of surgery, director of nursing, registered nurse, medical lab technician, janitor/cleaner, admitting clerk, and grounds worker. However, the choice of benchmark jobs also must be made in the context of the availability of good market data for the jobs chosen. Let us assume

RPC 7.2

benchmark job
a job in the firm's job evaluation system for which there is a good match in the labour market data

market comparator job
a job in the market data that matches a benchmark job within the firm's job evaluation system

that we are using the Salary Expert compensation database at salaryexpert.com. One of the advantages of Salary Expert is that it claims to take the value of indirect pay (benefits) into account and present the average annual total compensation for each job title. This inclusion makes compensation comparisons more valid than simple hourly-pay comparisons. (Incidentally, this statement should not necessarily be taken as an endorsement of Salary Expert, as discussed in the next chapter.)

When using compensation survey data, job evaluators need to specify the geographic location to which these data refer. In our case, let us assume that the hospital is in Toronto, and therefore, we select the Toronto area as our geographic area for the compensation data. On examining our database, we discover that there are no good matches for the head of surgery, director of nursing, and grounds worker jobs, based on comparing the job descriptions of our benchmark jobs to the market comparator jobs. So we still need a high point total job and a low one. However, for the low job, "painter" has a good match. For the high job, "cardiologist" is available in the data set. So let us assume that this job is a reasonable comparator for our "thoracic surgeon" job. In order to have a little more representation from the high jobs, we add "staff physician," assuming that "family practitioner" is a good match. To balance that, we add "nurse's aide" for which the "nurse assistant" seems a good match.

We now go to salaryexpert.com and identify the average total compensation for our market comparator jobs. Table 7.3 summarizes the results of this process.

We now plot each benchmark job on a graph, with its job evaluation point score on the horizontal axis, and the compensation value (in dollars) for its market comparator job on the vertical axis. A spreadsheet program (such as

Table 7.3

Benchmark Jobs and Market Comparator Jobs for a Canadian Hospital

Benchmark Job	Job Evaluation Points	Market Comparator Job	Average Total Compensation
Thoracic Surgeon	810	Cardiologist	$191,346
Staff Physician	735	Family Practitioner	125,407
Head Ward Nurse	675	Nurse Supervisor	69,043
Registered Nurse	535	Registered Nurse	56,056
Medical Lab Tech.	370	Medical Lab Tech.	49,692
Nurse's Aide	330	Nurse Assistant	33,722
Janitor/Cleaner	265	Hospital Cleaner	27,267
Admitting Clerk	230	Admitting Clerk	36,078
Painter	195	Painter	33,549

FIGURE 7.2

Sample Market Line for a Canadian Hospital

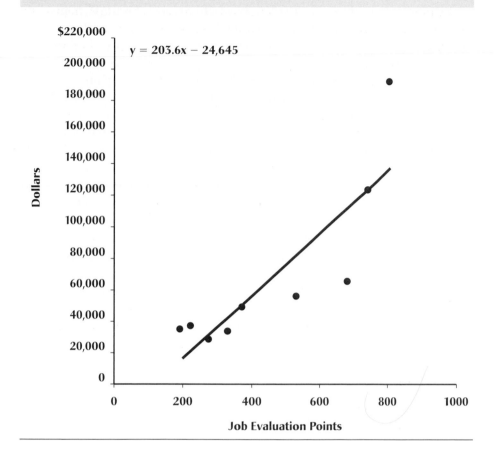

Microsoft Excel) is then used to calculate and produce a straight regression line that best "fits" the pattern of plots on the graph. Figure 7.2 shows the resulting **market line**, including the plots for our nine benchmark jobs. If we are planning to either lead or lag the market, we need to adjust the market line upwards or downwards by the percentage lead or lag to create our "**pay policy line**," which serves as the foundation of our base pay structure. If we are planning to "match the market," then our market line simply becomes our pay policy line. In this example, let's assume we are planning to match the market, so Figure 7.2 also becomes our pay policy line.

Incidentally, take note that a "match the market " strategy does not imply that every one of our jobs will actually match the market. Some jobs may be above the market, and some may be below; but the average results overall will approximately match the market. To determine what the average annual compensation would be for any job under the new job evaluation system, draw a vertical line up from the horizontal axis (at the JE point score for the job you are pricing) until it intersects the pay policy line. Draw a horizontal line from there to the vertical axis, and the amount indicated is the pay for the job.

market line

a regression line that relates job evaluation points to market pay (in dollars) for the benchmark jobs

pay policy line

the intended pay policy for the organization, generated by adjusting the market line for the intended pay level strategy of the organization

A more precise way to calculate proposed pay for a given job is to use the equation for the regression (market/pay policy) line that is generated by the computer, which is in the $y = mx - b$ format, where "y" is the dollar value of the job, "m" is the slope of the market/pay policy line, "x" is the JE points total for that job, and "b" is a constant (the constant "b" could actually be a minus or a plus, depending on where the regression line intercepts the horizontal axis). For the hospital example, the equation is $y = 203.6x - 24,645$. Therefore, the annual pay of a job with 810 points (the thoracic surgeon) would be $203.6 \times 810 - 24,645$, which equals $140,271.

As it calculates the regression (market) line, the spreadsheet program also calculates a **correlation coefficient** (sometimes called a regression coefficient) that summarizes the extent to which the plots on the graph approach a straight line. A correlation coefficient can range from +1 to –1. Either +1 or –1 occur when all the plots happen to fall in a perfectly straight line (this virtually never happens); +1 indicates a positive relationship between job evaluation points and pay rates, and –1 indicates a negative or inverse relationship between job evaluation points and pay rates. An inverse relationship would mean that pay is *lower* for jobs with *higher* job evaluation points. Needless to say, you should *never* have a minus sign in front of your coefficient!

What the coefficient indicates is the "goodness of fit" between the point values established by job evaluation and the pay rates ascertained from the market. Obviously, a coefficient that approaches zero is bad, because this says that there is little or no relationship between the value of jobs as determined by job evaluation and the value of jobs as determined by the market. If you were to stick with your job evaluation system with a low coefficient, you would find that you would be paying far more than you need to for some jobs and not enough to attract employees to others.

So then, the closer the coefficient is to 1 the better? Not necessarily. Some differences from the market line may well be justifiable if a job is more (or less) important to your organization than it is to the typical organization, or if you are using a different compensation strategy from your comparator firms. There is no hard and fast rule about exactly what the coefficient should be. But it certainly should be closer to 1 than to zero, and anything less than .80 needs to be carefully examined.

Another aspect to examine is the slope of your regression line. If it is too steep then you may end up compensating jobs at the top end of your system too much and jobs at the bottom end too little. A steep slope often means that there is not enough spread in job evaluation point scores between the lower value jobs and the higher value jobs. On the other hand, if the slope is too flat, you may be compensating jobs at the bottom too much, and jobs at the top too little. One final aspect is the average height of the pay policy line on the vertical (dollar) axis. If it is too high, you may end up paying all jobs too much; if it is too low, you may end up paying all jobs too little.

correlation coefficient

a statistic that measures the extent to which plots of two variables on a graph fall in a straight line

RPC 7.1

Exploring Solutions to Job Evaluation Problems

So if you have a coefficient problem, a slope problem, or a height problem, how do you decide exactly what needs to be modified in your system?

Part III: Determining Compensation Values

The first thing to do is to check that your benchmark jobs are actually equivalent to the market comparator jobs in the market that you have matched them with. (For example, the thoracic surgeon/cardiologist match may be questionable for our hospital sample, as might the staff physician/family practitioner match.) Compare the job descriptions carefully. You should also reexamine the nature of your market sample: are the other organizations in your market sample really appropriate comparators? (This topic is discussed further in the next chapter.)

If you are satisfied with these comparisons, then you could examine the "outlier jobs"—those that have the farthest vertical distance from the market line—to determine why they are discrepant. Have they simply been badly evaluated (e.g., their point total is incorrect, because the job evaluation system was applied poorly to that job), or are there problems with the job evaluation system itself (e.g., some factors have been weighted too heavily or too lightly)? Have the wrong factors been included in the job evaluation system, or has a key factor been omitted? There is no formula to find the right answer—it requires judgment based on studying the pattern of results. However, you must avoid the temptation to simply adjust the JE points of the outlier jobs so that the correlation coefficient looks better. Succumbing to this temptation does nothing to solve any underlying problems in your JE system, and will cause more problems later on.

In our hospital example, the correlation coefficient comes out to .87, which is acceptable. Now let us examine the outliers. You can tell which job each plot represents by looking at the JE point totals. For example, working from the left, the first plot is the "painter" job (it has the lowest JE point total of the benchmark jobs, 195 points), the second is the "admitting clerk" job, and so on. The extent to which a job is an outlier is indicated by the vertical distance that its plot is from the regression line, either above or below the line. As you can see, the greatest outlier is the "thoracic surgeon," which has a difference of about $51,000 ($191,346 – $140,271). What this result means is that while the market is paying a thoracic surgeon an average annual total compensation of about $191,000 (assuming the "cardiologist" job is actually a good match for thoracic surgeon), we are proposing to pay thoracic surgeons about $140,000. Given that difference, will we be able to attract the thoracic surgeons that we need?

RPC 7.2

The next largest outlier is the "head ward nurse" job, which we are proposing to pay nearly $44,000 above the market (the difference between $112,785 and $69,043). While we won't have any trouble attracting and retaining head nurses, can we really afford to pay so much above the market for this job? Similarly, we would pay registered nurses about $28,000 above the market, and $8,800 above the market for nurse's aides. The proposed pay for the staff physician, medical lab tech, and janitor/cleaner jobs appear to be pretty close to the market, but we are proposing to pay the admitting clerk nearly $14,000 below the market, and the painter about $18,000 below the market, a level that might not even meet minimum wage standards. Although we didn't include the grounds worker job as one of the benchmarks, given that the grounds worker job has fewer JE points than the painter, we would almost certainly be in violation of minimum wage laws for the grounds worker job.

These results suggest that we need to reexamine our job evaluation system. First, we need to be sure of the basics—that we have a valid market sample of comparator firms, that we have made a good choice of benchmark jobs, and that we have valid market comparator jobs for each benchmark job. For the market sample, salaryexpert.com unfortunately does not provide any information about the nature of its sample, nor does it allow us to structure the market sample by including only appropriate market comparator firms. But let us assume that the market sample is fine, as well as the benchmark job matches.

At this point, our main concern is the outliers. If we proceed from here, some jobs will be paid much less than the market, while some will be paid much more than the market. Of course, if being entirely in line with the market is our objective, then we needn't have gone to all the bother of creating a job evaluation system at all—we could have just used a market pricing system.

So the relevant question is whether these discrepancies are too large. It would seem that they are, so we need to examine our job evaluation system to see what is causing this problem. Since our system does seem to pay staff physicians at the market, but thoracic surgeons significantly less than the market, it appears that a specialization within medicine makes a big difference in pay. Maybe we need to increase the point difference between degrees 7 and 8 on our education factor. Or maybe we need another factor that differentiates better between the two jobs.

As for the "overpayment" of nursing staff, it may be that certain factors that they score high on are too heavily weighted, or maybe we need more degrees on these factors. As for "underpayment" of admitting clerks and painters, what factors are pulling them down? Are these factors weighted too heavily? Are the factors pulling them up not weighted heavily enough, or do we need to include an additional factor that captures the nature of the work better? Or has the market simply been "over-compensating" these jobs relative to the value of their work? Unfortunately, there is no "formula" in answering all these questions; it is simply a matter of judgment and trial and error. This helps to explain why job evaluation systems that are designed from the ground up can take years to develop.

Finally, note that any changes we make to the job evaluation system create a need to reevaluate all jobs in the JE system, not just those jobs appearing to "cause" problems for us.

Testing for Total Compensation Costs

Testing for what total compensation costs would be under the proposed compensation system is also useful. In addition to their other uses, pay policy graphs can be used to estimate the total compensation of the proposed system. For example, the rate for each job, as established by the pay policy line, can be multiplied by the number of people holding that job, thus deriving an estimate of the total compensation that would be payable under the proposed job evaluation. For an ongoing organization, this can then be compared with the current compensation cost.

It can then be determined whether the organization can afford this amount. If not, changes must be made to the pay level strategy, the job evaluation system, or other aspects of the pay structure. For example, if the JE system results in most jobs receiving high point totals, perhaps the system may not be differentiating adequately between jobs of lower and higher value.

It is also conceivable that the new plan will result in a reduction in the current payroll costs. While this may seem desirable to the employer, too large a reduction can cause perceptions of inequity among employees, which may create a higher turnover rate, particularly among the most marketable employees. Moreover, a job evaluation system that reduces the pay of most employees is not likely to be well accepted, especially the next time around. There may be many appeals of the results, and many employees may devote great effort to getting their jobs reevaluated. Chapter 12 discusses all these issues in more detail.

Possible Pitfalls of the Point Method of Job Evaluation

 7.1

The point method of job evaluation has numerous advantages, including its high degree of precision in measuring jobs. As a result, when properly designed, it can be applied with a high degree of consistency, removing one possible source of employee–management conflict. As well, this system provides not only an ordering of jobs but also the relative value of each job. This information allows jobs to be clustered in pay grades more easily, as discussed later in the chapter.

Another potential advantage of the point method is that there is a large body of knowledge that has been built up about it. There are a large number of "ready-made" plans offered by compensation consulting firms, although using these can be costly, and there is no guarantee that the consultant's system will be the best fit with the organization. For firms that cannot afford these services, there are some good guidebooks available.[4]

However, there are certainly drawbacks to point system plans. Besides the complexity of developing them, perhaps the most important drawback of point system plans is that although they may appear scientific, the process of selecting relevant factors and applying particular weights is still a subjective process. There are many opportunities for errors to enter the system, perhaps even destroying its validity, despite the massive efforts that are typically devoted to developing and maintaining the system.

There are four main categories of problems that can occur: (1) inconsistent construct formation, (2) factor overlaps, (3) hierarchical grounding, and (4) gender bias.[5] Each of these will now be examined, along with some additional pitfalls that fall outside these categories. A thorough understanding of these pitfalls is the best defence against them.

Inconsistent Construct Formation

In a point system of job evaluation, carefully established compensable factors are the key to success. Each factor must be based on a separate and well-defined construct. Factors may fail to meet this test in three areas: (1) the factor itself may be ambiguously defined, so that it is not clear to the evaluator what the factor is meant to pick up; (2) the degree or level definitions may not be consistent with the factor definition; and (3) the definitions for each degree or level may not all be degrees of the same construct.

Ambiguous Factor Definitions

Some factors may be designed in such a way that they are actually tapping numerous constructs. For example, consider the following definition of "complexity of duties":

> **Complexity of Duties:** This factor measures the complexity of duties involved, the degree of independent action, the extent to which the duties are circumscribed by standard practice, the exercise of judgment and the type of decisions made, the amount of resourcefulness and planning the job requires, the creative effort in devising new methods, policies, procedures or products, scientific discoveries, and original application.[6]

Notice how this example actually contains numerous factors. If they are all important, they need to be formed into separate factors. (Of course, if some of these are not important, they should be dropped entirely.) At least four separate factors could be extracted from this factor definition: independent action/circumscribed duties, resourcefulness, planning, and creative effort.

Inconsistent Factor and Degree Definitions

In some cases, the statements defining the different degrees of a given factor are actually measuring something other than the factor to which they ostensibly apply. Let's consider the following example for the factor of "analytical ability":

> **Analytical Ability:** This factor measures the extent to which analytical ability is required to perform job duties. Analytical ability is the ability to examine information and data, to detect patterns, explanations, and causes of various phenomena, using a variety of analytical tools and procedures.
>
> Degree 1: Little necessity for creativity in performance of job duties.
>
> Degree 2: New ideas and approaches to job duties occasionally needed.
>
> Degree 3: Frequent need to develop new approaches to job duties.
>
> Degree 4: Continually must use creativity in performing job duties.

Notice how these degree statements actually focus on creativity and innovation in performing job duties, which is not necessarily the same as analytical ability. For example, accountants may analyze financial statements to identify potential company problems, but this does not necessarily call for creative ability. On the other hand, a graphic artist in charge of developing new company logos may need considerable creativity but does not really use analytical tools and procedures in performing this job.

Inconsistent Degree Statements

In a variation of the above problem, sometimes different degree statements are actually measuring different constructs, and only some of the statements are actually focusing on the factor they are supposed to measure. Consider the following example for the factor of "supervisory responsibility":

> **Supervisory Responsibility:** This factor deals with the extent of responsibility for managing employees and overseeing their day-to-day work.
>
> Degree 1: No supervisory responsibilities.
>
> Degree 2: Responsible for supervision of one to three subordinates.
>
> Degree 3: Responsible for supervision of four to nine subordinates.
>
> Degree 4: Responsible for supervision of 10 or more subordinates.
>
> Degree 5: Responsible for development of all department policies.

Which one of these is not like the others? Clearly, the statement for degree 5 is focusing on a different construct from the other degrees. For example, it may be possible to be responsible for development of department policy with very few or even no employees.

Factor Overlaps

One problem that frequently occurs in point systems is overlapping factors. If this does occur, then some factors are being counted twice and are thus over-weighted in the job evaluation system. In some cases, this occurs because factor titles may sound different, but their descriptions are actually very similar. For example, consider the factors of "judgment" and "freedom to act":

> **Judgment:** This factor deals with the extent to which the exercise of independent judgment is required in the performance of job duties.
>
> Degree 1: Prescribed directions and rules limit the scope for independent judgment.
>
> Degree 2: Standardized work routines limit the scope for independent judgment.
>
> Degree 3: Similar procedures and methods limit the scope for independent judgment.
>
> **Freedom to Act:** This factor deals with the extent to which incumbents of this job are free to act as they see fit in performing their job duties.
>
> Degree 1: Duties are routine and specifically delineated; work is closely controlled.
>
> Degree 2: Duties are somewhat routine and clearly delineated; work is closely controlled.
>
> Degree 3: Characteristics of the position are such that activities and methods are clearly defined, and/or work is frequently reviewed.[7]

Note how these factors are virtually indistinguishable.

Hierarchical Grounding

The purpose of the point method of job evaluation is to derive a hierarchy of jobs by examining the individual components ("factors") in those jobs. However, some factors in some systems "appear to confuse the outcome with the process. That is, they say if this job is at a high level in the [organization] hierarchy, then it should be highly rated. This is circular reasoning."[8] For example, take the factor of "responsibility for action":

> **Responsibility for Action:** This factor deals with the extent to which the jobholder is expected to take independent action in addressing and solving managerial problems, and the importance of taking this action.
>
> Degree 1: Reports to the section supervisor.
>
> Degree 2: Reports to the department manager.
>
> Degree 3: Reports to the division manager.
>
> Degree 4: Reports to the vice-president.
>
> Degree 5: Reports to the president.

Notice how the degree definitions simply mimic the existing organization hierarchy, assuming that the higher the job is in the organizational hierarchy, the more responsibility for action it has. Thus, the job evaluation system is not actually deriving an independent hierarchy of jobs, which is the real goal of job evaluation. Although there is a strong tendency for jobs higher in the organizational hierarchy to pay more, this example illustrates how inequity can arise. What these degree statements are really saying is that, by definition, no one who reports to a section supervisor has any responsibility to take action, when this may not be true at all for many jobs.

Gender Bias

Gender bias occurs when a job receives a higher or lower evaluation than it should because the job incumbents are predominantly from one gender. Weiner suggests that there are at least six ways in which gender bias can operate in job evaluation:

- separate job families;
- valuing a factor when it is found in "male jobs" but not "female jobs"[9];
- confusing job content with stereotypes of inherent female attributes;
- ignoring factors found in female jobs;
- having an insufficient range of degree statements;
- biased job descriptions.[10]

In other analysis, researchers have found that insufficient rater training can also introduce unreliability and bias into the job evaluation process if raters fall back on unconscious stereotypes that have contributed to gender-based inequities in the past.[11] Let's examine each of these problems.

Part III: Determining Compensation Values

Separate Job Evaluation Systems for Different Job Families

In the past, each job family in an organization was evaluated under different job evaluation systems. However, this can defeat the purpose of job evaluation, which is to create a hierarchy of jobs within the organization using a common measure of job value. This may also cause gender bias. Even if jobs are evaluated fairly *within* job families or classes, if separate job families are used for male and female jobs, they may not be evaluated fairly *between* job classes. The opening vignette describes how nurses were shortchanged by this practice. This is why the same system of job evaluation should cover all job families that are subject to job evaluation. Indeed, in numerous Canadian jurisdictions, this is required by law.

Differential Valuation of Factors

One example of how factors can be valued differently is "visibility of dirt." Jobs carried out under dirty working conditions, such as mechanic or garbage collector, have typically been rated more highly on working conditions (in other words, they are deemed to have worse working conditions) than jobs performed in seemingly "clean" working conditions, such as hospitals or hotels. However, working conditions in hospitals and hotels may not be as "clean" as they appear, especially from the perspective of those employees, such as nurses or maids, whose job it is to create and maintain these "clean" working conditions. Conditions may be clean when nurses or maids complete their shift, but that is because of the dirt and mess they handled during their shifts!

Another example of this type of inequity is illustrated by a municipality in the United States, where the hazards of entering people's homes (e.g., being bitten by a dog; being assaulted by a resident) were factored into job evaluations for meter readers (who were male), but were not for public health nurses (who were female), who also had to enter people's homes as a part of their responsibilities.[12]

Confusing Job Content with Stereotypes

Certain jobs traditionally held by women are often considered to be "low-skill" jobs because the ability to do these jobs is considered "inherent to women." For example, in the U.S. Department of Labor's Directory of Occupational Titles, "dog pound attendant" was ranked higher than "child care worker."

When this inequity was questioned, the response given was that dog pound attendants were more highly rated because it was more difficult to acquire the necessary skills for caring for dogs than for caring for children.[13] The argument was that any skills needed to work with young children were inherent to women and therefore did not deserve to be highly rated. Of course, anybody who has actually worked with small children knows that there is considerable skill necessary to be effective, and that people (both female and male) vary greatly in these skills.

Ignoring Factors Found in "Female Jobs"

In a major study of job evaluation instruments, researchers found that although hundreds of factors had been included in these evaluation systems, many factors relevant to jobs usually performed by females had been omitted. For example, under "effort," there were rarely factors for "involuntary interruptions" (as many secretaries must cope with) or "dealing with upset people" (as complaints clerks at department stores or nurses at hospitals must do).[14] Indeed, Steinberg notes that the whole area of "emotional labour" has seldom been adequately incorporated into job evaluation plans.[15] One aspect of emotional labour is dealing with people and groups who are angry, distrustful, upset, unreasonable, psychologically impaired, or under the influence of drugs or alcohol—conditions with which nurses and social workers must contend every day. Another aspect of emotional labour is the need to stay cheerful, courteous, friendly, and helpful, even in adverse circumstances, as is the case in many service-oriented jobs. Compensation Notebook 7.2 lists a whole range of frequently omitted factors in "female jobs."

Insufficient Range of Degrees

Once a job evaluation system has all the factors necessary to accurately assess the full range of jobs, the final concern is to ensure that there is sufficient range among the degrees to make appropriate distinctions between jobs. Weiner cites the following example for "working conditions":

> **Working Conditions:** This factor deals with the physical conditions under which the job is normally performed.
>
> Degree 1: Standard office conditions.
>
> Degree 2: Inside work with possible exposure to dirt, oil, noise.
>
> Degree 3: Some exposure to disagreeable conditions, such as fumes, cold, dust.
>
> Degree 4: Constant exposure to disagreeable conditions. Continuous outside work.[16]

This example illustrates several problems. For example, "standard office conditions" does not distinguish between spacious private offices and offices that may be crowded, noisy, hot, and full of interruptions and distractions. Also, outside work (traditionally male) is assumed to be the most onerous. Is this always true? In some occupations, workers (e.g., gardeners, painters) are only outside during relatively pleasant conditions. Should outside work always be considered more onerous than working in a crowded, hot, noisy office, with constant interruptions?

Biased Job Descriptions

Finally, even if the job evaluation system itself is fair and free of bias, one possible source of bias remains—the information on which the job evaluation is based. As discussed in Chapter 6, there is evidence that descriptions of jobs traditionally performed by females have been subject to bias during the job analysis process.

Frequently Overlooked Factors in "Female Jobs"

Skill

- analytical reasoning
- communicating with upset, irate, or irrational people
- coordinating a variety of responsibilities other than "other staff or people"
- creating documents
- deciding the content and format of reports and presentations
- developing or coordinating work schedules for others
- dispensing medication to patients
- establishing and maintaining manual and auto-mated filing systems
- handling complaints
- innovating—developing new procedures, solutions, or products
- manual dexterity required for giving injections, typing, graphic arts
- operating and maintaining different types of office equipment
- providing personal services, such as arranging vacations, and handling household accounts
- reading forms
- special body coordination or expert use of fingers and hands
- training and orienting new staff
- using a variety of computer software and database formats
- writing correspondence for others, and proof-reading and editing others' work

Effort

- adjusting to rapid changes in office or plant technology
- concentrating for prolonged periods at computer terminals, lab benches, and other equipment
- frequent lifting and bending (e.g., child care work)
- frequent lifting (office supplies, retail goods, lifting or turning sick or injured adults or children)
- heavy lifting (e.g., packing goods for shipment)
- irregular and/or multiple work demands
- long periods of travel and/or isolation

- performing complex sequences of hand–eye coordination
- providing service to several people or departments, working under many simultaneous deadlines
- sitting for long periods of time at workstation (e.g., while keyboarding)

Responsibility

- acting on behalf of absent supervisors
- caring for patients, children, institutionalized people
- contacts with others—internal or external to the organization
- handling new or unexpected situations
- keeping public areas such as waiting rooms and offices organized
- managing petty cash
- planning, problem solving, setting objectives and goals
- preventing possible damage to equipment or people
- protecting confidentiality
- representing the workplace through communica-tions with clients and the public
- shouldering responsibility for consequences of error in the workplace
- supervising staff
- training and orienting new employees

Working Conditions

- adjusting to a variety of working environments continuously
- cleaning offices, stores, machinery, hospital wards
- exposure to communicable diseases
- exposure to dirt from office machines and supplies
- exposure to eye strain from computer terminals
- exposure to and disposal of body fluids
- exposure to disease and stress from caring for ill people
- physical or verbal abuse from irrational clients or patients
- stress from open office noise, crowded conditions

Source: Adapted from the Ontario Pay Equity Commission docu-ment "Overlooked Features of Women's Jobs." © Queen's Printer for Ontario, 1991. Reproduced with permission.

Other Pitfalls of Job Evaluation

Chapter 4 discussed the pros and cons of job evaluation systems in some depth. However, job evaluation is subject to a few other pitfalls not yet covered. As in the case of job analysis, there is often a tendency to evaluate the jobholder rather than the job itself.[17] For example, evaluators might think to themselves: "This is Joe's job. Joe really doesn't seem to work very hard any more. Therefore, his job does not deserve a high rating." Of course, Joe's performance is irrelevant when conducting job evaluation; it is the importance of his job that we are evaluating. But it is easy to lose sight of this distinction.

Another pitfall occurs when job evaluation becomes an adversarial process and a source of conflict between employees and management. And, of course, the biggest pitfall is that job evaluations may become out of date quickly, and continually updating them requires a never-ending commitment of time and effort. Yet if they are not updated, job evaluations can become a source of inequity rather than a source of employee satisfaction. When a job does change substantially in duties, and if the revised point total for the job warrants it, prompt reclassification from one grade to the next should take place. However, even here there is an opportunity for inequity to creep in. For example, a U.S. study found that more powerful departments in an organization were more likely to have their requests for reclassifications approved than were less powerful departments.[18] Obviously, such tendencies must be avoided if the system is to be fair.

RPC 7.3

base pay structure

the structure of pay grades and pay ranges, along with the criteria for movement within pay ranges, that applies to base pay

pay grade

a grouping of jobs of similar value to the organization

pay range

the minimum and maximum pay rates (in dollars) for jobs in a particular pay grade

Determining the Base Pay Structure

Whatever method of job evaluation has been used, by now the organization has created a hierarchy of jobs. But there is still no pay structure. A **base pay structure** normally consists of pay grades and pay ranges, along with the criteria for salary movement within the pay range. A **pay grade** is a grouping of jobs of similar value to the organization. A **pay range** provides the actual minimum and maximum pay rate, in dollar terms, for jobs in a given pay grade.

Establishing Pay Grades

In establishing a base pay structure, a fundamental issue is to decide whether to use pay grades. If the answer is yes, as it is for most firms, the number of pay grades must be decided, as well as the size of the pay grades.

Why Use Pay Grades?

Why have pay grades at all? Why not pay each job a different rate, based on what the pay policy graph indicates? There are five main reasons for clustering jobs into pay grades. First, use of grades recognizes that job evaluation is essentially a subjective process, no matter which method is used; and it makes little sense to try to make very fine distinctions between jobs. Second, pay grades make it easier to justify and explain pay rates to employees. If employees notice someone earning more money in a job that resembles their own, they may perceive inequity.

Third, pay grades simplify the administration of the pay system by eliminating the need to have separate rates and pay ranges for every job. Fourth, having jobs clustered within pay grades makes it easier for employees to move across jobs in the same pay grade. Fifth, pay grades create more stability for the pay system. For example, if a job changes, but not substantially, there is likely no need to reevaluate, unless the job is right at the boundary between two pay grades.

On the downside, pay grades do create problems with jobs on the margins of each grade. Employees with jobs on the borderline between two grades will naturally push to have their jobs placed in the higher grade. However, if this is done, then the next-lower job becomes the marginal job. No one wants his or her job to be the first one *not* included in the higher grade.

How Many Pay Grades?

How many pay grades should there be? One consideration is the total range of pay of the jobs covered by the particular job evaluation system. If the jobs in the same pay structure range from $20,000 to $300,000 per annum, there is much greater scope for pay grades than one in which the jobs range from $25,000 to $75,000. Another consideration is the width of the pay ranges used. If pay ranges are narrow, then the only way for an employee to significantly increase their pay is through promotion to a job in the next-higher pay grade. Therefore, having many pay grades in order to provide opportunities for promotion and pay raises may be desirable. Of course, the number of pay grades used is in inverse proportion to the size of the pay grades—the more pay grades, the smaller the size of the pay grades.

Establishing Pay Grade Sizes

A key question is how to establish the pay grade sizes and boundaries. In some cases, they are arbitrary. For example, suppose that job evaluation points in a particular pay structure can range from 100 to 1000, and the organization has decided to have nine pay grades. Dividing the possible range of points (which is 900) by 9 yields pay grades of 100 points. Thus, grade 1 is 100 to 200 points, grade 2 is 201 points to 300 points, and so on. This is known as the **equal interval approach**.

However, if the actual point totals for the various jobs are not evenly spread across the point range, this approach could result in very few jobs in some pay grades, and possibly even the majority in one or two pay grades. It could also lead to scarce opportunities for promotion into jobs in higher grades. Furthermore, the use of arbitrary boundaries may end up dividing a cluster of jobs that are really very similar. For example, take the example in the paragraph above. What if there were no jobs between 150 and 285 points, and no jobs between 320 and 400 points, but six jobs between 285 and 300 points, and six jobs between 301 and 315 points? Does it really make sense to arbitrarily divide this cluster of jobs, in which the jobs are very similar in value, and pay them differently? One approach which helps solve this problem is to look for the natural breaks between clusters of jobs when setting up the pay

equal interval approach
method to establish pay grade sizes, in which the point spreads are equal for all pay grades

equal increase approach

method to establish pay grade sizes, in which each pay grade increases in size by a constant number of points

equal percentage approach

method to establish pay grade sizes, in which the point spreads increase by an equal percentage

telescopic approach

method to establish pay grade sizes, in which the point spreads increase, but not by an equal percentage

broadbanding

the practice of reducing the number of pay grades by creating large or "fat" grades, sometimes known as "bands"

grades. (However, this latter approach only makes sense if you are evaluating *all* of the organization's jobs at the same time.)

Variations of the equal interval approach are the **equal increase approach** and the **equal percentage approach**. Based on the notion that jobs in higher pay grades are more complex, the width of each pay grade increases by either a constant number of points from the previous grade, or a constant percentage from the previous grade. Another variation of this is the "**telescopic approach**,"[19] in which grade widths increase for higher value jobs (in terms of their position in the hierarchy of jobs), but not necessarily by a constant percentage.

Another approach is to look at the possibility of error in the system. For example, what would be the point difference for a job if it were consistently evaluated one degree higher or one degree lower than it should be? Assume that this would result in a 200-point over or under evaluation. Then 200 points could be used as the width of the pay grades, on the logic that no job would be more than one pay grade higher or lower than it should be. However, one expert recommends dividing this maximum error by three, on the assumption that in reality two-thirds of the degree errors would cancel out.[20]

During the 1990s, many companies reduced the number of pay grades in their compensation system, thus creating large or "fat" grades. This process, known as **broadbanding**, experienced some popularity because of the flexibility it provides. However, the fewer the pay grades (sometimes known as "bands" under this system), the less meaning job evaluation results have, as jobs with very different point totals may end up in the same band, thus receiving similar pay. Moreover, broad pay grades open the door to inconsistency across departments and to the possibility of pay being determined by factors such as favouritism. Of course, broadbands also create a bigger distinction between the pay rate of a job that just makes it into a particular pay band, and a job that just falls short, ending up in the next-lower pay band. As these problems have become more apparent, the popularity of broadbanding has levelled off.

Finally, a thorny issue is what to do with jobs that end up near but just below grade boundaries. Of course, one solution is to do nothing, and just leave jobs where they fall. However, this solution invites feelings of inequity, as well as attempts by these jobholders to get their jobs reevaluated. Some firms attempt to deal with this problem by keeping job evaluation points secret, which of course can lead to other problems, such as distrust of the job evaluation system. As mentioned previously, another method is not to use arbitrary point cutoffs, but to look for "natural breaks" in the job hierarchy. But there is no ideal solution to this problem; it is inherent in the use of pay grades.

Establishing Pay Ranges

Once the pay grades have been established, the next question to decide is the pay range for each grade, in actual dollar terms. Of course, it is possible to decide to have a pay range of "zero"—that is, to pay all jobs in a pay grade the same flat rate. But this does not allow any room to recognize differential

FIGURE 7.3

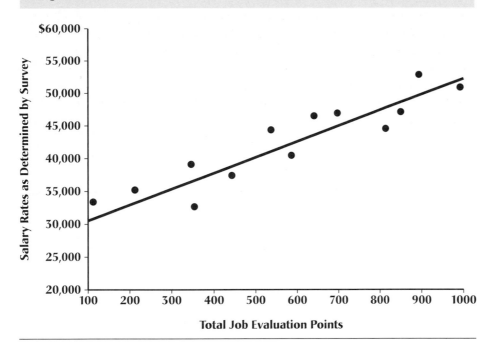

Sample Market Line

qualifications of employees as they enter a pay grade, or to provide any raises based on seniority or performance. To provide latitude for this, most organizations do use pay ranges.

There are four main questions about pay ranges. First, how are the midpoints of the ranges (in dollar terms) determined? Second, how should the range spreads be determined (i.e., the minimum and the maximum pay rates for each pay grade)? Third, should range overlaps be permitted? Fourth, how should movement through the range take place?

Establishing the Range Midpoints

As an example of how to establish the midpoint of the pay range, let's start with the graph shown in Figure 7.3, which shows a sample market line. This market line needs to be converted to a pay policy line. For example, if the compensation strategy for the employees in the job evaluation system is to pay 10 percent above market, then a new line would be drawn 10 percent above the market line. This would become the pay policy line. (Of course, if the pay strategy is to match the market, then the market line simply becomes the pay policy line.)

Once the pay policy line has been drawn, the pay grades are then marked off on the graph using vertical lines. Next, a horizontal line is drawn where the midpoint of each pay grade intersects the pay policy line. This is illustrated by the broken lines in Figure 7.4. For example, the horizontal line for pay grade 1 (which has a grade midpoint of 190 points) intersects the pay

FIGURE 7.4

Illustration of a Base Pay Structure

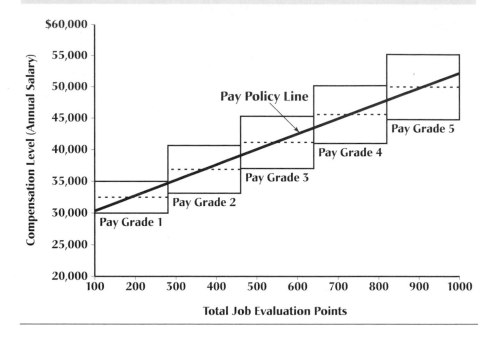

policy line at about $32,500—which is then taken as the midpoint in the pay range for this pay grade. Similarly, the horizontal line for pay grade 2 (which has a grade midpoint of 335.5 points) intersects the pay policy line at about $36,900, so this is taken as the midpoint of the pay range for pay grade 2.

The differentials in range midpoints between the grades are known as the **intergrade differentials**. Intergrade differentials may be expressed in dollars or in percentages. In dollar terms, they may be constant, or they may increase as one goes up the hierarchy of jobs. The purpose of increasing intergrade differentials is to maintain the attractiveness of promotions. For example, in the pay structure illustrated in Figure 7.4, the intergrade differentials stay constant at $4,400 throughout the structure, although the **intergrade differential percentages** actually decline. For example, the intergrade differential percentage between pay grade 1 and pay grade 2 is about 13.5 percent, but only about 11.9 percent between pay grades 2 and 3. Between grades 3 and 4, the intergrade differential percentage is 10.7 percent, and between grades 4 and 5, 9.6 percent. This means that as a proportion of pay, promotions in the higher grades are becoming relatively less attractive than promotions in the lower grades. One way to increase this percentage would be to widen the pay grades as the system goes up.

intergrade differentials

the differences between the range midpoints of adjacent pay grades in a pay structure, expressed in dollars

intergrade differential percentage

calculated by dividing the intergrade differential (expressed in dollars) of each pay grade by the midpoint (in dollars) of the previous pay grade

range spread

the difference between the maximum and the minimum pay level, in dollars, for a given pay range

Establishing the Range Spreads

Now that we have the range midpoints, we need to decide on the **range spreads**—the dollar value of the difference between the maximum and the minimum of the pay range for each pay grade. To maintain the integrity of the system, the dollar value differences between the range midpoint and the range minimum, and the range midpoint and the range maximum, need to be equal. Otherwise, you are arbitrarily moving the range midpoint, after all the work you have just devoted to establishing it!

There are no hard and fast rules in establishing range spreads, but there are several considerations. The first consideration is the extent to which the organization wants to use compensation to recognize differences between employees performing the same jobs. How important is experience? And how much can performance vary across individuals in the same job? If the organization places no value on experience, and performance does not really vary across employees, the answer is simple—no spread! Instead, the midpoint becomes the flat pay rate for the job, so all jobs in pay grade 1 would pay $32,500. Remember Rogers chicken processing plant? This is exactly what they did.

Thus, the pay range should mimic the range of performance or experience within jobs. But how do you determine this? The time it takes to become proficient at that job might be a good indicator. For example, if a job requires a person to work for four years to become fully proficient, then that job needs a much greater spread in pay range than a job which requires six months for proficiency. And even after four years when that person reaches proficiency, there may still be variations in performance that the organization wants to recognize.

Another consideration is the existence of promotional opportunities. If the organization is growing slowly or not at all, there may be few promotional opportunities for employees to use as a means to increase their pay. Or it may not be desirable to promote valued employees to management jobs just to get them a pay raise. In these circumstances, a wider pay range can be used to accommodate and retain high-performing employees.

Yet another consideration is how many steps or increments the organization intends to have in the range. The more increments it wants, the greater the range spread needs to be. In general, the range spread is wider for higher pay grades, because it is assumed that experience makes more of a difference to performance and that there is more scope for performance variation in jobs in higher pay grades. Another reason for an increasing range spread is if pay grades get larger for jobs higher in the job hierarchy, which often is the case.

Another way to set the minimum and maximum for each pay range is by referring to the labour market. Labour market data normally provide not only the midpoint or averages for each job, but also the range and quartiles. Quartiles simply indicate the pay for the lowest quarter of employees, then the second quarter, and so on. One way of setting the range minimum would be to use the top of the bottom quartile for a typical job in that pay grade as the range minimum, and the top of the third quartile as the range maximum.

Overall, the following **range spread percentages** seem typical in Canada— 10 to 25 percent for production jobs and clerical jobs, and 25 to 50 percent for professional and managerial jobs. In general, the range spreads increase for pay grades higher up the jobs hierarchy to recognize the greater complexity of these jobs. Also, the fewer the pay grades, the larger the pay ranges; the more the pay grades, the smaller the pay ranges.

range spread percentage
a percentage calculated by dividing the range spread for a given pay range by the minimum for that pay range

In our generic example, Figure 7.4 shows the minimum and maximum of the pay range for each pay grade. For example, the lower line in pay grade 1 represents the range minimum for that pay grade (which is $30,000), while the upper line represents the range maximum (which is $35,000). Overall, the graph shows that the pay ranges for the five pay grades in this example are as follows:

	POINTS RANGE FOR PAY GRADE	PAY RANGE MINIMUM	PAY RANGE MAXIMUM	PAY RANGE MIDPOINT
Pay Grade 1	100–280	$30,000	$35,000	$32,500
Pay Grade 2	281–460	$33,650	$ 40,150	$36,900
Pay Grade 3	461–640	$37,000	$45,600	$41,300
Pay Grade 4	641–820	$ 41,100	$50,400	$45,700
Pay Grade 5	821–1000	$44,600	$55,600	$ 50,100

As we develop a base pay structure, it is always useful to step back and take a hard look at what we have done so far. So how well does the pay structure depicted on Figure 7.4 work? It has five pay grades, covering 180 job evaluation points each. The minimum pay for any job is $30,000, while the maximum is $55,600. The range spread for pay grade 1 is $5,000, while the range spread percentage is about 17 percent, calculated by dividing the range spread by the range minimum ($30,000) for that pay grade. The range spread for pay grade 5 is $11,000, or 25 percent. The intergrade differential percentages vary from 13.5 percent between pay grade 1 and pay grade 2 to 9.6 percent between pay grade 4 and pay grade 5, although they stay constant in dollar terms at $4,400. (In fact, when we use equal point spreads to delineate pay grades, as we have in this example, the range midpoint for each grade will *always* be the same dollar amount higher than the range midpoint of the previous grade.)

Given that the total pay range of jobs in this pay structure is so narrow (from $30,000 to $55,000), five pay grades may be appropriate. However, if we were developing a base pay structure for the hospital example discussed earlier, this number of pay grades would be much too low, given the very large dispersion in pay and jobs at the hospital. At the hospital, 10 to 15 pay grades would likely be necessary to adequately reflect the dispersion across jobs, depending on the method used for establishing pay grade sizes. For example, increasing the size of the pay grades as jobs increase in value would allow use of fewer pay grades at the hospital (possibly 10 to 12 grades); but using equal-sized grades would probably require at least 15 grades.

Also in Figure 7.4, the intergrade differential percentages actually decline; so this may reduce the incentive for promotion to a job in a higher pay grade or reduce the perceptions of equity by those getting promotions. The final potential problem is the overlaps between pay ranges.

Part III: Determining Compensation Values

Overlaps between Pay Ranges

In Figure 7.4, the pay range for each pay grade overlaps with the previous one. When there is an overlap, an employee in a lower pay grade can actually earn more than an employee in a higher pay grade. Of course, this may be seen as a threat to the integrity of the job evaluation system. So why have overlaps?

Overlaps occur because of pay ranges. If there were very small spreads in each pay range, there would be little or no overlap. As range spreads increase, so does overlap. One purpose that overlap serves is to reduce the differences in pay between adjacent pay grades, thus reducing the difference in pay between jobs that fall on either side of the pay grade boundary. Overlaps also allow the pay of top performers in a lower grade to increase without having to promote them to a job in a higher pay grade. Finally, many people believe it would not be fair for an inexperienced employee coming into a new job to earn more than a seasoned, experienced, high-performing employee in a job in the next lower pay grade.

So when should overlap be a concern? One possible rule is that it should not be possible for a person in pay grade 1 to be making as much as a person in pay grade 3. That is, when overlap starts to cover two pay grades, it tends to negate the job values established by the job evaluation system and reduces the incentive for promotion. In addition, it can also create problems after promotion occurs. Normally, a person who has been promoted expects a raise as he/she assumes the new job. However, if that person is already earning more than the midpoint of the next higher pay grade, then he/she has to enter that pay grade above the midpoint. This severely limits the room for pay increases as the promoted individual gains increased experience and improves performance. As Figure 7.4 shows, if someone at the top of the pay range for a job in pay grade 4 is promoted to a job in grade 5, that employee would receive no increase unless he/she came in above the midpoint of their new pay range.

Clearly, excessive overlap causes problems. One way to avoid this problem is to make sure that the top of the previous pay range is always lower than the midpoint of the next one, perhaps halfway between the midpoint and the minimum. Certainly, the top of a pay range should always be lower than the bottom of the range two grades up. Note that the pay structure in Figure 7.4 meets these criteria for the lower pay grades, but not the higher grades.

Movement through the Range

Once the pay range is defined for each pay grade, criteria must be established to determine how movement within the range will occur. The three most common criteria are experience, seniority, and performance. In some cases, all three are used. For example, a person's initial placement in the pay range may be determined by previous experience. Seniority (in terms of years in the job) or performance—or both—can then be used to determine future increases within the pay range.

As one example of how to combine seniority and performance, some firms allow employees to reach the midpoint of their pay range using annual seniority increases, but to pass that point requires meritorious performance. This is known as a *split pay range*, with the midpoint serving as a "control point" to prevent pay increases unless they are based on performance. But this is just one possibility of many.

How many steps or increments should there be within a pay range? And what should the size of each increment be? Although a pay range may have as few as three or as many as 15 steps, most have six or seven.[21] To be effective, a pay raise should constitute a "**just noticeable difference (JND)**"; and if it doesn't reach that level, it may have little motivational or reward value.

just noticeable difference (JND)

the amount of pay increase necessary to be considered significant by employees receiving the increase

In times of low inflation, a JND may be 4 percent. So let's look back at pay grade 1 in Figure 7.4. The minimum is $30,000 and the maximum is $35,000. A 4 percent pay raise from the minimum would be $1,200. Since the range is $5,000, divide it by $1,200, which equals about four. Four increments would allow four raises of about 4 percent each, so this might be a reasonable number of steps for pay grade 1.

What about for the other pay grades? Let's try another, say pay grade 5. For pay grade 5, 4 percent of the minimum is $1,784. The range is $11,000, so dividing by $1,784 equals just over 6. Therefore, six increments might be used for this pay grade.

Some organizations do not use fixed steps or increments at all. Instead, they view the minimum as the entry-level pay for an employee with no experience, and the midpoint as the normal pay that a typical employee would receive. Pay raises above the midpoint will take place only if performance is above average, and pay will reach the maximum for the range at the discretion of the supervisor, who may vary both the timing and the amount of the raises. However, this procedure does not fit well with motivation theory, which suggests that motivation is maximized when the link between future performance and future pay increases is very clear. Moreover, the flexibility of this method also opens the door to inconsistency and favouritism.

Other Possible Elements of Base Pay Structure

Base pay structure can also include a number of other elements. For example, for jobs with hourly pay, overtime premiums are typically required by law when workers exceed a certain number of daily or weekly hours. However, many employers go beyond the statutory minimum, especially unionized employers. In other cases, the organization may offer shift differentials, where pay for an undesirable work shift (usually the night shift) is higher than for other shifts. Some employers may offer isolation premiums to boost the compensation of employees who work in remote areas. These are just some of the possibilities that may be incorporated into a base pay structure.

Applying Job Evaluation Results

Once the new base pay structure has been completed, the pay for some jobs will likely increase, while the pay for others will likely decrease. How to handle employees whose current pay is out of line with the new pay ranges for their jobs is an important issue for the future success and perceived fairness of the new pay structure.

Employees Below the Range

Employees who are currently paid below the new pay ranges for their jobs are known as "green-circled employees," and these employees should be moved up to at least the minimum of the pay range for their jobs as soon as possible. (Indeed, if these employees are experienced and performing well, they should be moved up well past the minimum, since new employees will be coming in at that level.) This move would normally be the first priority with the compensation funds that are available. Since new employees will come in at the minimum (or sometimes higher) of the pay range, it would be very inequitable for experienced employees to be left below them.

Employees Above the Range

A trickier problem is what to do with individuals who are currently being paid above the maximum of the new pay range for their jobs. Of course, the most direct way to address this inequity would be to simply reduce their pay to the maximum of the job's pay range. However, this approach can cause serious morale problems, since most people regard pay reduction to be unfair if it doesn't apply to everyone or if it doesn't seem necessary from an economic point of view. In this case, opposition to the new pay structure could ensue.

Moreover, unilateral reduction of employee pay is illegal for unionized employees or for employees with specific written contracts. And unilateral reduction of pay for other employees could make an employer liable under the concept of "constructive dismissal." This legal concept states that by unilaterally worsening the terms and conditions of employment, an employer is really dismissing an employee. If an employee finds the new terms of employment unacceptable and terminates his/her employment, he or she would have grounds for an unjust dismissal suit against the employer. Depending on the seniority of the employee, the nature of their job, and other factors, court-imposed settlements can be quite costly.

An employer can avoid this by offering severance pay, but this can also be costly, as discussed in Chapter 11. The only situations where an employer can avoid paying severance are at the end of fixed-term contracts or just-cause dismissals. No severance payment at all is required if it can be established that the employer has just cause for dismissing an employee.

Pay cuts are also not illegal if they are voluntarily accepted by the affected individuals, but there can be no duress—such as threatening to fire or demote the employee if he/she doesn't take a pay cut—or constructive dismissal may be charged. This employee agreement is known as "mutual rescision," where both employer and employee agree to end the current employment agreement and negotiate a new one.

Because of these legal issues, a common approach is simply to "red-circle" individuals who are being paid above their pay range and freeze their pay at their current level until salary scales catch up (due to adjustments for inflation). However, while this works quite well in times of high inflation, it doesn't work well in times of low inflation or during periods during which pay levels are static. It is particularly unsatisfactory when there are many red-circled employees and when the firm's financial viability is at stake. However, there may be no good alternatives. To avoid this problem and maintain flexibility, some employers are now attempting to free themselves from the constraints of constructive dismissal law by putting all employees on revolving fixed-term contracts.

Interestingly, although employers may feel that they are being more than generous by red-circling rather than reducing pay, this practice can still cause serious motivational problems for the affected employees. Nobody likes to look forward to a static or declining income (when inflation is considered), and there is no potential for financial reward for good performance during the period it takes for the pay scale to catch up, and possibly none even afterward, since most systems do not allow raises for employees who have reached the maximum of their pay range.

A compromise solution is to continue to grant raises based on performance, but not to adjust the base pay rate for inflation. Of course, this lengthens the period of adjustment, increases compensation costs, and prolongs inequity. Other employees may start to question why they should receive less money than somebody else who is doing the same work. Therefore, a better approach might be to simply treat red-circled individuals as if they are at the maximum of their pay range and therefore are not eligible for merit raises (or scale increases) but are still eligible for merit bonuses.

A number of other solutions may be available, depending on circumstances. For example, if some red-circled employees are close to retirement, the problem for them will be resolved as they retire. It may be desirable to hasten this process by offering early retirement incentives, thus allowing the firm to bring in a new person at the bottom of the pay range. In other cases, it may be possible to promote the red-circled employee into a job in the next-higher pay grade or to add temporary duties to their jobs that would justify their current pay level.

Still another approach is to examine employee performance levels. Perhaps red-circled employees who are performing very well can be allowed to maintain their current pay level until inflation solves the problem, or until they can be promoted to a job in a higher pay grade. Other employees might simply be offered a "buyout" severance package. But deciding who should be offered buyout packages requires careful consideration of the costs of the buyout. Chapter 11 provides some examples of what these costs might be.

Summary

This chapter showed you how to develop a point system of job evaluation and a base pay structure. You learned the four main steps in developing this method (identifying compensable factors, scaling the factors, weighting the factors, applying and testing the system), as well as the possible pitfalls in using this method.

Although the point method appears to be objective and scientific, it is still subjective and susceptible to problems that could compromise its reliability and validity. You can avoid these pitfalls, but only if you understand them well. The four main types of pitfalls are inconsistency within the factors, overlaps between factors, hierarchical grounding, and gender bias. All of these have commonly afflicted job evaluation systems (and those who were subject to these systems) in the past.

You also learned that after establishing a hierarchy of jobs by job evaluation, you must create a base pay structure. This includes developing pay grades and pay ranges, along with the criteria for movement through the range. Finally, the chapter suggested ways to adjust employees who are either below or above their new pay ranges into the new pay structure.

Key Terms

base pay structure, 296

benchmark job, 283

broadbanding, 298

compensable factors, 275

correlation coefficient, 286

equal increase approach, 298

equal interval approach, 297

equal percentage approach, 298

intergrade differentials, 300

intergrade differential percentage, 300

just noticeable difference (JND), 304

market comparator job, 283

market line, 285

pay grade, 296

pay policy line, 285

pay range, 296

range spread, 300

range spread percentage, 301

reliability, 282

telescopic approach, 298

validity, 282

Web Links

The website for salaryexpert.com is **http://www.salaryexpert.com**. (p. 284)

Prominent compensation consulting firms that do job evaluation include (p. 289): The Hay Group **http://www.haygroup.ca**, Hewitt Associates **http://was4.hewitt.com/hewitt/worldwide/canada/index.htm**, Sibson and Company **http://www.segalco.com/sibson/index.html**, Watson Wyatt Worldwide **http://www.watsonwyatt.com/canada-english**, and William M. Mercer **http://www.mercerhr.com**.

For free information on how to develop a job evaluation system based on the points method, go to the Ontario Pay Commission website **http://www.gov. on.ca/lab/pec/peo/english/about_us.html**. (p. 289)

Chapter 7: Evaluating Jobs: The Point Method of Job Evaluation

RPC Icons

RPC 7.1 Implements an effective procedure for describing work related duties, establishing their relative worth, and aligning them with the organizational structure.

RPC 7.2 Monitors the competitiveness of the compensation program relative to comparable organizations.

RPC 7.3 Recommends job price and appropriate pay ranges based on factors such as complexity of duties, nature of employment, geographic location, and supply and demand conditions in the external labour market.

Discussion Questions

1. Discuss the issue of gender bias in compensation and the ways it can affect the development of a base pay structure. In your employment experience, have you noticed possible examples of gender bias in compensation?
2. Discuss the hierarchy of jobs for a Canadian hospital shown in Table 7.2. Does everything about this ranking of job values make sense to you? Are there specific jobs that seem out of order to you? If so, which ones? Why do you think so?
3. Discuss the issue of red-circled employees and the way they should be handled. Assume that your current or most recent employer has developed a new pay structure, and 20 percent of current employees are above their new maximum pay ranges. How should you deal with this problem?

Using the Internet

1. In a small group or on your own, select benchmark jobs for the Canadian hospital in Table 7.2. Then use Salary Wizard (**http://workingcanada. salary.com/csalarywizard/layoutscripts/cswzl_newsearch.asp**) as your market database to find appropriate market comparator jobs and price them out. For the purposes of the market survey data, assume that the hospital is located in the city in which you reside. Display this information in a table similar to Table 7.3. Compare your table to Table 7.3 and discuss why it differs.
2. After completing Question 1, use Microsoft Excel to prepare a market line based on data from your benchmark jobs and market comparator jobs. Examine the resulting line, and discuss all of the possible issues surrounding its validity, including the correlation coefficient, the outliers, and the slope and height of the line.

Exercises

1. Rank the hospital jobs shown in Table 7.2 according to your own impressions of how valuable each job is to the hospital, disregarding the hypothetical job evaluation results. Share your rankings with other classmates, and discuss any differences in your rankings. Also discuss any differences from the rankings shown in Table 7.2.
2. In a small group or on your own, use Figure 7.2 to develop a base pay structure for a Canadian hospital, including pay grades and ranges, and criteria for salary movement within the range.

Case Questions

1. Using the point method and the four basic factor groups, develop a job evaluation system for "Eastern Provincial University" in the Appendix. Then apply your system to the different jobs to derive a single hierarchy of jobs. Summarize this information in a table similar to Table 7.2.
2. After completing Question 1, apply the procedures required under the Ontario Pay Equity Act to determine whether pay equity exists for the female job classes at Eastern Provincial University. The following are the annual salaries in the four job classes (as of 2004):

   - Clerk Steno I: $27,540; II: $31,692; III: $38,364 (Job class 95 percent female)
   - Draftsperson I: $34,296; II: $41,388; III: $44,976 (Job class 80 percent male)
   - Grounds Worker I: $28,848; II: $29,652; III: $32,292 (Job class 85 percent male)
   - Medical Laboratory Technologist I: $43,368; II: $45,516 (Job class 90 percent female)

Simulation Cross-Reference

If you are using *Strategic Compensation: A Simulation* in conjunction with this text, you will find that the concepts in Chapter 7 are helpful in preparing Sections D, G, H, and M of the simulation.

Endnotes

1. Weiner, Nan J., and Morley Gunderson. 1990. *Pay Equity: Issues, Options, and Experiences.* Toronto: Butterworths.
2. Weiner, Nan J., and Morley Gunderson. 1990. *Pay Equity: Issues, Options, and Experiences.* Toronto: Butterworths: 62–63.
3. Milkovich, George T., and Jerry M. Newman. 1996. *Compensation.* Chicago: Irwin, 37.

4. One of the most usable guidebooks has been produced by the Ontario Pay Equity Commission. 1996. *Step by Step to Pay Equity: A Guide for Small Business: Volume 2: The Job Evaluation System*. Toronto: Ontario Pay Equity Commission. It is also available on their website http://www.gov.on.ca/lab/pec/peo/english/about_us.html.

5. Weiner, Nan J. 1991. "Job Evaluation Systems: A Critique." *Human Resource Management Review*, 1(2): 119–32.

6. Weiner, Nan J. 1991. "Job Evaluation Systems: A Critique." *Human Resource Management Review*, 1(2): 124.

7. Based on Weiner, Nan J. 1991. "Job Evaluation Systems: A Critique." *Human Resource Management Review*, 1(2): 126.

8. Weiner, Nan J. 1991. "Job Evaluation Systems: A Critique." *Human Resource Management Review*, 1(2): 127.

9. The terms "male jobs" and "female jobs" are used to denote jobs that have been traditionally occupied mainly by males or females. These terms are used as a shorthand in pay equity literature and carry no implications about the specific nature of these jobs, nor whether males or females are more suited to these jobs.

10. Weiner, Nan J. 1991. "Job Evaluation Systems: A Critique." *Human Resource Management Review*, 1(2): 119–32.

11. Kervin, John, and Marika Elek. 2001. "Where's the Bias? Sources and Types of Gender Bias in Job Evaluation." In Y. Reshef, C. Bernier, D. Harrisson, and T.H. Wagar, eds. *Industrial Relations in the New Millenium: Selected Papers from the XXXVIIth Annual CIRA Conference*, 79–90.

12. Weiner, Nan J. 1991. "Job Evaluation Systems: A Critique." *Human Resource Management Review*, 1(2): 119–32.

13. Weiner, Nan J. 1991. "Job Evaluation Systems: A Critique." *Human Resource Management Review*, 1(2): 119–32.

14. Steinberg, R., and L. Haignere. 1985. "Equitable Compensation: Methodological Criteria for Comparable Worth." Working Paper 16. Albany: Center for Women in Government, State University of New York.

15. Steinberg, Ronnie J. 1999. "Emotional Labour in Job Evaluation: Redesigning Compensation Practices." *Annals of the American Academy of Political and Social Science*, 561: 143–57.

16. Weiner, Nan J. 1991. "Job Evaluation Systems: A Critique." *Human Resource Management Review*, 1(2): 130.

17. Weiner, Nan J., and Morley Gunderson. 1990. *Pay Equity: Issues, Options, and Experiences.* Toronto: Butterworths.

18. Welbourne, Theresa, and Charlie O. Trevor. 2000. "The Roles of Departmental and Position Power in Job Evaluation." *Academy of Management Journal*, 43(4): 761–71.

19. Thanasse, Laura. 1993. "Banding." *Human Resources Management in Canada*, February: 40, 685–88.

20. Theriault, Roland. 1992. *Mercer Compensation Manual*. Boucherville, PQ: G. Morin.

21. Theriault, Roland. 1992. *Mercer Compensation Manual*. Boucherville, PQ: G. Morin.

Chapter 8

Evaluating the Market

Chapter Learning Objectives

After reading this chapter, you should be able to:

- Discuss the key considerations in understanding labour markets.
- Identify possible sources of compensation data.
- Describe the steps for conducting compensation surveys.
- Analyze, interpret, and apply compensation survey data.

WHERE WOULD YOU CHOOSE TO WORK?

If you had to choose an industry based strictly on how much it pays its employees, which would you pick? The following are the average weekly earnings for different Canadian industries, as of March 2005, according to Statistics Canada:

Mining, oil, and gas	$1,306
Utilities	1,053
Professional, scientific, technical services	956
Finance and insurance	898
Public administration	894
Logging and forestry	890
Manufacturing	874
Construction	863
Education and related services	796
Transportation and warehousing	762
Health and social services	636
Retail trade	467
Arts, entertainment, and recreation	423
Accommodation/food/beverage services	307

Of course, all of these seem pretty miserly when you compare them with the average pay for players in the National Hockey League, which is about $45,000 a week (assuming they worked 52 weeks a year, which they do not). This is nice for hockey players; but is one week of an average hockey player's work really worth more than the combined weekly work of 71 Canadian health and social service workers? What scale would you use for judging?

Introduction

In fact, in 2004, National Hockey League employers decided that they were overpaying their players and locked out their players for an entire season in order to cut their pay. No employer, not even hockey employers, can afford to ignore market forces, as this could result in a compensation system set at a level that is unrealistically high or low. However, as discussed in Chapter 4, identifying the "going market rate" for individual jobs can be a complex process—and an elusive one, since there may be no single market rate for many jobs.

After a brief orientation to the nature of labour markets, this chapter identifies sources of compensation data, including both third-party and in-house surveys. Following that, it outlines the process for conducting a compensation survey. The chapter concludes with an illustration of the process for analyzing and interpreting compensation survey data.

RPC 8.1

Understanding Labour Markets

Why do people get paid what they do? Surely it is based on the value or importance of the job they do. Well, consider this. The Prime Minister of

Canada earns $288,600 per year. The lowest-paid hockey player with the Toronto Maple Leafs receives $600,000 per year. Is being a benchwarmer on a professional hockey team really a more important job than being Prime Minister of Canada? What's going on here?

In general, the price (wage) for a particular type of labour depends on the demand for that labour, relative to the supply for that labour, constrained by the ability of employers to pay. In theory, whenever there is a surplus of a particular type of labour, the price for that labour falls. In reality, wages seldom decline in ongoing firms unless the employer is experiencing financial difficulties and wage-cutting is seen as a necessity. This is because wage cuts often result in negative consequences for the employer, such as increased turnover and reduced employee performance, as discussed in Chapter 3. However, new firms may take advantage of a labour surplus by hiring employees at a lower rate than existing employers are paying.

In theory, faced with a labour shortage, firms in the private sector are willing to increase the price for labour until the price matches the value (in terms of revenue generated) that the firm receives from that labour. But in reality, how much an employer is willing to pay for a particular type of labour is a function of a variety of factors, including the employer's ability to pay. Key factors include company profitability, the importance of that labour to the operation of the organization, and the proportion of labour costs relative to total costs. For example, if labour is only a small portion of a firm's total costs (as in the resources industry), the firm can afford to pay much more for its labour than firms in which labour is a high proportion of total costs (as in the retail sector).

For public-sector organizations, such as hospitals, school boards, and government departments, the ability of employees to generate revenue is obviously not an issue. Instead, the employer's ability to pay is the key issue. If taxpayers (through their elected representatives on the school board) set the school district budget at $50 million, then only this amount is available for all purposes, including teacher salaries. In Canada, public-sector employees are highly unionized, so most public-sector pay is determined through collective bargaining. If the union has the right to strike, as most do, then key factors are how essential the service is, how willing public officials (and the general public) are to endure a strike, how much budget is available for pay increases, and how easy it is to obtain a budget increase. Higher pay levels can be granted without a budget increase, but the money must come from somewhere, usually a reduction in the number of persons employed by the organization.

In general, wage compression has occurred in the public sector. Public-sector employees at the lower end of the job hierarchy usually earn more than comparable employees in the private sector, while public-sector employees at the top of the job hierarchy usually earn less than they would in the private sector.[1] This differential results from the relative power of public-sector unions due to their ability to disrupt important public services. Pay equity programs, which have been in place much longer in public-sector organizations, may also play a role in increasing the pay of lower level public sector workers.[2]

Chapter 8: Evaluating the Market

However, pay for top-level government officials is constrained by the visibility of their salaries and a reluctance on the part of taxpayers to pay public employees a lot more than they themselves are earning. However, there are no such constraints on private-sector employers for their top-level employees, so the wage gap between the public and private sectors is wide for these employees.

There are several general patterns in compensation levels. On average, unionized employees receive considerably more compensation than comparable non-union employees. Male employees earn more than female employees on average;[3] employees in large firms earn more than those in small firms; employees in Alberta and Ontario earn more than those in other provinces; and, as the opening vignette showed, employees in the resources sector earn more than those in the service sector.

compensating differential

a higher compensation level offered by an employer because of undesirable aspects of employment at that employer

Aside from the relative scarcity of labour and its perceived value to the employer, pay is affected by what are known as **compensating differentials**. For example, many of the high-paying jobs in the resource sector are cyclical in nature, which means that workers in these industries often have to endure periods of unemployment. Their higher wage levels provide a differential that compensates them for this employment volatility. Likewise, the cost of living in Ontario and Alberta is higher than in most other provinces, and the higher wage rates help to compensate for this reality.

Other negative features that may trigger compensating differentials include poor working conditions and jobs for which failure rates are high. For example, many people who try selling life insurance fail, but those who are successful can earn very high compensation. Another example of a negative feature that can cause a compensating differential is a poor industry reputation: for example, an industry that is widely perceived as environmentally unfriendly, such as forestry, or an industry whose product is in social disfavour, such as tobacco production.

But does this theory really work? Are salaries in, say, the tobacco industry really higher than elsewhere? Compensation Today 8.1 tries to smoke out the truth.

ⓡ ⓟ ⓒ 8.1   Defining the Relevant Labour Market

Labour markets are complex. Luckily, an employer does not need to understand the labour market as a whole, but only that segment of the market that pertains to the specific jobs that the employer needs to fill. Essentially, what an employer needs to know is what its competitors are paying their employees.

Two kinds of competitors are relevant: competitors in the same labour market, and competitors in the same product/service market. In some cases, firms from many industries compete for the same labour—for example, an insurance company, a chemical manufacturer, and an airline may all need accounting clerks. However, in other cases, labour is so specialized that certain jobs are found only within the same industry. For example, if you are a chemical manufacturer and need chemical process-control engineers, you don't have to compete with the insurance company or the airline to hire them.

Compensation Today 8.1

Salaries Are Really Smokin' in Tobacco!

In Chapter 3, we discussed how employees take a variety of costs and benefits into account when deciding where to seek and accept employment. We also used an example of the tobacco industry, where we suggested that many people look with disfavour on the product, making them reluctant to accept employment in the industry, thus necessitating higher wages to attract them. The economic theory of compensating differentials would predict exactly the same pattern. Because of the stigma attached to the industry, salaries would have to be higher in order to entice employees into the industry.

So both behavioural and economic theory agree. All other things being equal, salaries should be higher in the tobacco industry than industrial averages. But just what are the facts? Over the years, total employment in Canada's tobacco products industry (excluding growers) has been gradually declining, from 4483 persons in 1990

to under 4000 persons today, according to Statistics Canada. At the same time, demand for the industry's product has also been declining, from 65 billion cigarettes in 1980 to less than 35 billion today. (But that still amounts to more than 1000 cigarettes per Canadian man, woman, and child per year!)

In 2005, the average wages and salaries in the Canadian manufacturing sector were $37,269. What were they in tobacco? Try $63,684, or more than $2,000 a month higher, on average! Interestingly, despite the decline in demand for tobacco employees and their product over the years, wage increases in tobacco actually outpaced increases in the industrial averages during the period 1990–2005.

So if you can stand the smoke and think you will live long enough to enjoy your money, the tobacco industry really coughs up the dough!

Labour markets and product/service markets serve as constraints to employers. If an employer is paying less than its competitors in the labour market, then it will not be able to attract and retain good employees. If the employer is paying more than its competitors in the same product/service market, then it may have difficulty offering its product or service at a competitive price.

There are two other crucial dimensions of the labour market. One is the occupational grouping; the other is the geographic scope of the market—local, regional, national, or international. But these two dimensions overlap, depending on how industry-specific and specialized the occupational grouping is.

For example, if you are looking for a secretary, the market is usually local. Virtually every organization of any size employs one or more secretaries, so they can be found in almost all labour markets. On the other hand, not every organization employs a chemical process engineer, and these employees may be very scarce in some local labour markets. In general, the more specialized the occupation, the wider the geographic scope of the market for that occupation. For example, it may be possible to hire production and office staff locally but necessary to seek technical staff across a larger region, senior managerial staff on a national basis, and specialized professional staff nationally or internationally.

Thus, before setting out to collect data, the employer needs to identify the occupational groups for which it will collect data, the geographic bounds for that group, and the industry bounds for the information. As discussed later in this chapter, the employer must also identify the specific compensation data it needs to make informed decisions.

In some cases, compensation data sources allow firms to customize the organizations that they are comparing themselves with. The selected comparator organizations are known as **market comparator firms**. The trick in putting together this sample of market comparator firms is to maintain a broad enough sample to be representative while focusing on firms as similar as possible to the target firm. Relevant characteristics in selecting this sample include the type of product or service the firm provides, whether the firm is union or non-union, the geographic area over which it operates, and the size of the firm. However, depending on the industry, even a non-union firm should include some unionized firms in its market sample to ensure wage competitiveness. Also, the market sample should include some firms in unrelated industries if they employ some of the same occupational groups. Overall, like much in compensation, there is no precise formula for selecting a market sample. Instead, it is a balancing act, informed by judgment and knowledge of our human resource needs.

market comparator firms

firms selected as comparators when constructing a sample of market data

ⓇⓅⒸ 8.2 Sources of Compensation Data

Once an organization has defined the type of labour market information it needs, it needs to acquire that information. All market information is based on compensation surveys, but organizations do not all need to conduct their own compensation surveys. There are three main "third-party" sources of compensation data: government agencies, industry groups, and compensation consulting firms. Many of these organizations have websites that include compensation data (see Compensation Notebook 8.1), although there may be a fee for accessing this information.

Third-Party Surveys

Government Agencies

A variety of governmental agencies survey employers to collect labour market information. At the federal level, these include Statistics Canada as well as Human Resources Development Canada, which maintains information on collective agreements as well as other pay information. Most provincial departments of labour also publish some data on compensation levels. Some municipal governments also publish salary surveys.

Industry Groups

Most industries have industry associations, many of which collect data on pay rates within their industries. Many professional associations also collect data on their own occupational groups.

Compensation Consultants

There are many firms for which collecting labour market information is a major business. These include large international firms such as the Hay

Group, Hewitt Associates, Sibson and Company, Towers Perrin, William M. Mercer, and Watson Wyatt Worldwide, as well as many smaller firms that operate on a local or regional basis. However, one concern is these data may come mostly from their client firms, which does not necessarily comprise a representative sample.

Free Websites

In recent years, free websites providing compensation data have emerged, most notably Salary Expert and Salary Wizard. However, a key concern with these websites is that they do not provide the nature of the sample on which they are basing their compensation values, so it is difficult to be confident about the validity of their data.

Advantages and Disadvantages of Third-Party Surveys

Using compensation data acquired from third-party sources has both advantages and disadvantages. The two most obvious advantages are ease and cost. Normally, when firms are asked to participate in compensation surveys, they are promised the results, so the only cost is the cost of the time responding to the survey. Of course, it is also much easier than designing and conducting an in-house survey.

However, there are several disadvantages. Third-party surveys may not cover the desired jobs, compensation characteristics, or employers. In addition, aggregate data are often provided, rather than company-by-company data, so that it is not possible to separate out those employers who are the most appropriate comparators for your organization.

In-House Surveys

A final option is to carry out your own compensation survey. This can be done formally or informally.

Informal Surveys

Informal approaches can range from a quick review of help-wanted ads to a question posed to a group of colleagues at an industry function to a few telephone calls to other firms. Informal surveys are usually simple and quick but may have poor reliability and validity.

Formal Surveys

Formal surveys can be undertaken by internal staff, or they can be contracted to compensation firms. The main advantage of conducting an in-house survey is that the employer controls the entire process, thereby ensuring the quality and appropriateness of the data. Of course, another advantage is that the employer avoids paying the consulting fees, which can be high, depending on the amount of customization required. However, there are numerous disadvantages to conducting your own survey. First, if the survey is to be done by internal staff, then someone with the required expertise must be available. In addition, many employers surveyed may be reluctant to reveal their compensation practices to their competitors in the absence of any intermediary organization. For these reasons, most firms prefer to contract the survey to professionals in the field.

RPC 8.2 Conducting Compensation Surveys

In conducting a compensation survey, there are four main steps: (1) identify the jobs that are to be surveyed, (2) determine the information to be collected about each job, (3) identify which employers are to be surveyed, and (4) determine the method of data collection.

Identify the Jobs to Be Surveyed

For several reasons, most organizations do not collect market data about every job they have. First, it would be very costly to do so. Second, the organization often has unique jobs for which it is hard to find matches. Third, a full-scale survey is not necessary. The usual rule of thumb is that surveying about 10–15 percent of jobs should be sufficient to calibrate the system. Moreover, it is not even necessary to survey these key or benchmark jobs every year. Instead, data can be obtained on the annual increases in pay rates, and the job rates updated on this basis.[4]

Typical Compensation Survey Questions

A. General Questions

1. Name of employer
2. Number of employees
3. Location of employees
4. Main products or services produced

B. Questions for Each Job

1. Do you have any employees performing the job described below?
   (The description for the specific job being surveyed appears here.)
2. How many?
3. Are the employees in this job union members?
4. What was the average base pay, performance pay, and indirect pay (estimate a dollar value for the benefits provided) received by employees in this job over the last year?
5. What is the minimum, maximum, and midpoint of the pay range for this job?
6. How many employees are in each quartile of the pay range?
7. On what basis do employees move through the pay range? (e.g., seniority, merit, training)
8. How long does it take a typical employee to move from the bottom to the top of the pay range?
9. What is the standard workweek for this job, in terms of hours?
10. Are these employees eligible for overtime? At what pay rate?

An essential foundation for any compensation survey is an effective method of matching an organization's jobs to those being surveyed. The most common approach is known as **key job matching**, which involves selecting certain jobs that are well understood and numerous in the job market and asking employers to compare their jobs with these jobs. Typically, a job title is provided, along with a brief job summary. Employers are then asked whether they have any of these jobs, and if so, to provide compensation data about them. In selecting these jobs, it is important to represent a variety of job families and to provide examples within each family at both the entry level and the top level.

key job matching

including jobs on a compensation survey that are well understood and numerous in the labour market, and asking respondents to supply compensation information for those jobs

Determine What Information to Collect

Simply collecting information about wage and salary levels does not generally provide an adequate basis for comparison. Information about the base pay, performance pay, and indirect pay, as well as the weekly hours of work, all need to be collected for each job in the survey. In addition to the formal pay ranges for each job, knowing where most employees actually are in the pay range is also useful. You can determine this by asking how many employees are in each quartile of the pay range. Compensation Notebook 8.2 provides a list of typical questions to ask when conducting a compensation survey. Figure 8.1 provides an actual survey form used by Koenig and Associates, a Saskatoon-based human resources consulting firm.

FIGURE 8.1

Sample Compensation Survey Form

Salary and Benefits Survey

SALARY INFORMATION

Benchmark Job Title	YOUR Job Title	Number of Incumbents	Quality of Job Match (Please Check One)			Average Annual Base Salary	Check If Job Is Bonus Eligible	Average Bonus Paid	Minimum of Salary Range	Maximum of Salary Range
			Poor (0–60%)	Good (60–80%)	Excellent (80–100%)					

1. What are wage increases based on?______ Cost of Living______ Performance______ Seniority______ Skills/Competencies______ Market Information
   _____ Other (please describe) ____________________

HOURS OF WORK AND SCHEDULING

1. What are your regular weekly business hours (e.g., 36 hours/week, 37.5 hours/week, 40 hours/week, etc.)? ______
2. Do you provide one or more alternative workweek schedules to your employees (e.g., 4.5 day week, one day off every other week or every third week, etc.) ___Yes ___No
   If yes, what is your arrangement? ____________________
3. What is the annual vacation allowance for employees? (e.g. _1_–_5_ years service earn _3_ weeks per year, etc.)
   ___–___ years service earn ___weeks per year ___–___ years service earn ___weeks per year
   ___–___ years service earn ___weeks per year ___–___ years service earn ___weeks per year
4. Do you have an allowance for paid absences due to illness and/or pressing necessity? ___Yes ___No
   If yes, what is your annual sick leave allowance? __________ How is this earned? ____________________
5. In addition to legislated statutory holidays, do you provide any other days as paid days off (e.g., Boxing Day)? ___Yes ___No If yes, how many? __________

FIGURE 8.1 *Continued*

6. Overtime is paid after _____ hours are worked in a week. At what rate is overtime paid?

   a. What groups of employees are eligible for overtime pay? (check as many as apply) _____ All _____ Admin _____ Technical _____ Professional _____ Management _____ Other _____

   b. Are employees allowed to take time off in lieu of overtime pay? _____ Yes _____ No If yes, please briefly describe policy. _____

BENEFITS

1. Please indicate (✓) which of the following benefits are provided. Detail how the cost is shared between the employer and employee (e.g. 50/50, 25/75), for each benefit listed.

2. Please indicate which of the following programs/benefits are provided. Please provide any relevant details about the design of the program in the Comments section.

BENEFIT	✓	Employer %	Employee %
Group Life Insurance			
Accidental Death & Dismemberment			
Short–Term Disability			
Long–Term Disability			
Supplementary Health Care			
Dental Plan			

BENEFIT	✓	Employer %	Employee %
Vision Care Plan			
Employee Assistance Plan			
Fitness Plan (e.g., club membership)			
Pension Plan			
Group RRSP			
Other (please list)			

Program/Benefit Offered	Available to: All	Admin	Technical	Professional	Mgmt	Other	Max Value	Comments/Details (please add additional pages as necessary)
Incentive Pay Program (e.g., share ownership, commissions, etc.)								
Personal Vehicle Allowance ($x/month)								
Company Vehicle Is Personal Use Allowed?								
Payment of Professional Dues								
Payment of Association/Society Memberships								
Other Bonus Payments (e.g., Christmas bonus, etc.)								

3. Do you provide an Education/Training Allowance to employees? _____ Yes _____ No

Source: Koenig and Associates. Reprinted with permission.

Determine Whom to Survey

Determining which employers to survey is not a simple matter. In general, firms like to survey other employers that they perceive as similar to themselves in industry type, geographic location, and size. But the sample generally varies, depending on whether the jobs being surveyed are filled by the local, regional, national, or international labour markets.

Determine How to Collect the Data

There are four main ways to collect the information: personal interviews, questionnaires, telephone interviews, and the Internet.

Personal Interviews

In general, the personal interview is thought to provide the best-quality information. In an interview, you can ensure that the jobs being surveyed are actually similar to the job data reported, and that the questions are being interpreted properly. However, this method is also very costly to use on any significant scale.

Questionnaires

By far the cheapest method of data collection is the mail survey or questionnaire. However, it is also the least reliable method, since there is no control over who is filling out the survey, and no way of knowing whether it is being done correctly. Chores such as questionnaire-filling are often delegated to the most junior member of the HR department.

Telephone Interviews

A compromise method is the telephone interview. It is much cheaper than the personal interview yet still produces a higher quality of information than the questionnaire approach, since there is an opportunity to confirm job matches and clarify survey questions. This method also provides some control over who the respondent is.

Internet Surveys

As the Internet has become ubiquitous, some organizations have started to use it for sending out surveys and collecting responses. Certainly, Internet surveys can be faster than mail surveys and can also facilitate tabulation of data. Moreover, Internet contact facilitates contact with respondents throughout the survey process. But because Internet surveys are relatively new, there is no evidence whether response rates are better or worse than mail surveys or whether the quality of information received is any different.

RPC 8.2

Analyzing and Interpreting Survey Data

After you have conducted a compensation survey, you have a set of raw data—a list of employers surveyed and what they are paying for different jobs. Hopefully, for each job, you have the minimum, maximum, and mid-points of the pay ranges, and the mean base pay, performance pay, indirect pay, and total compensation. Now what?

Analytical Procedures

The first steps in analyzing the survey data involve assessing the central tendency of pay and the variation across employers. There are two main ways to assess central tendency. Using a **mean** (sometimes known as a **simple average**), you add up the midpoints of the pay range for a given job at each company and divide them by the total number of companies. Of course, this weights all employers equally, regardless whether they employ one or one thousand of the employees performing the target job. Therefore, some firms compute a **weighted mean** (sometimes known as a **weighted average**) by weighting each employer according to how many employees that employer has performing the target job. You can also calculate a simple average or weighted average of the mean base pay, performance pay, and indirect pay across the sample of firms. A simple average mean pay gives an indication of pay policies used by a typical firm for a given job, while a weighted average mean pay gives a better indication of what the typical employee in a given job is earning.

One problem with a mean is that it can be distorted by extreme values. One way of avoiding extreme values when measuring central tendency is to use the **median**, which is the middle value in a ranking of pay levels, below which half of employers are paying less and above which half are paying more.

Dispersion of pay across employers can be assessed in several ways. One way is to look at the mean total compensation for the lowest-paying employer and then determine what percentage more the highest-paying employer is paying. For example, if the lowest-paying employer pays its secretaries a mean total compensation of $30,000, and the highest-paying employer pays its secretaries a mean total compensation of $45,000, then the dispersion in secretarial compensation across firms is 50 percent.

Another way of examining dispersion across employers is to look at **quartiles** or **deciles.** For example, the mean total compensation levels at each firm for a given job are arranged from lowest to highest, and then the list is divided into either four groups (quartiles) or 10 groups (deciles). Then, the mean total compensation within each quartile or decile is computed. This method allows an assessment of detailed pay statistics, such as what the top 25 percent of firms (using quartiles) are paying on average. Percentiles, which indicate the amount below which a certain percentage of employers would fall, can also be used. For example, if $60,000 is at the 90th percentile of total compensation for a given job, that means that 90 percent of firms pay less than that and 10 percent pay more. The **interquartile range** is the difference between the 25th percentile and 75th percentile values, divided by the 25th percentile value. If this quotient is very large, it may indicate problems with the job matching, where some of the jobs in the sample are not equivalent.[5]

mean, or simple average

a measure of central tendency of a set of values derived by summing the values and dividing by the number of values

weighted mean, or weighted average

a measure of central tendency of a set of values that adjusts the average based on the number of cases to which each value pertains

median

the middle value in an ordered list of values

quartiles or deciles

division of an ordered list of values into either four groups (quartiles) or 10 groups (deciles)

interquartile range

a measure of pay dispersion across employers, calculated by dividing the difference between the 25th and 75th percentile values by the value of the 25th percentile

A major issue in analyzing compensation data is determining whether to focus on range midpoints or actual mean compensation levels. Range midpoints and pay ranges do not actually describe what the typical employee in the job earns; and of course, pay ranges deal only with base pay, so a lot of the compensation picture could be missing. For example, most employees in the survey could be at the top of the pay range or the bottom. One way of assessing where employees are actually being paid in the pay range is to ask respondents to report the number of employees in each quartile of the pay range for each job.

A statistic that can be useful in assessing the distribution of employees within their pay range is known as the **compa-ratio**. The compa-ratio is calculated by taking the mean base pay of all employees holding a particular job and then dividing this amount by the midpoint of the pay range for that job. A compa-ratio of greater than 1 means that, on average, employees are being paid above the midpoint at that firm; a compa-ratio of less than 1 means that, on average, employees are being paid below the midpoint.

Besides analyzing the level of compensation, analyzing survey data may also give an indication of the typical structure of compensation (or pay mix) across employers. To start, you could calculate the proportion of base pay, performance pay, and indirect pay (as a percentage of total compensation) for a given job at each firm and then average these values (either a simple average, weighted average, or both). Thus, you might discover that firms in the sample pay 70 percent of their secretaries' total compensation in base pay, 10 percent in performance pay, and 20 percent in indirect pay, on average. You can also look at the percentages for each firm to examine particular compensation issues, such as variation in the use of performance pay.

Interpreting Survey Data

The best way to illustrate the issues involved in interpreting survey data is to work through a detailed example. Table 8.1 provides an example of compensation survey results for the job of "accounting clerk."

In this example, we have surveyed 10 companies and have data regarding the number of accounting clerks that each firm employs; the minimum, maximum, and midpoints of the base pay ranges; the mean amounts of base pay, performance pay, indirect pay, and total compensation paid to accounting clerks at each firm; and the distribution of accounting clerks across the pay range in each firm by quartile.

The job summary used on the survey was based on the National Occupational Classification for "Accounting and Related Clerks":

> This unit group includes clerks who calculate, prepare and process bills, invoices, accounts payable and receivable, budgets and other routine financial records according to established procedures. They are employed throughout the private and public sectors. Examples of related titles include costing clerk, ledger clerk, audit clerk, finance clerk, budget clerk, billing clerk, tax return preparer, accounts payable clerk, accounts receivable clerk, invoice clerk, deposit clerk, tax clerk, freight-rate clerk.

TABLE 8.1

Results of Compensation Survey: Accounting Clerk

Company	Total Employment	Number of Accounting Clerks Employed	Base Pay Range Minimum	Base Pay Range Midpoint	Base Pay Range Maximum	Mean Base Pay	Mean Performance Pay	Mean Indirect Pay	Mean Total Compensation	Compa-Ratio	Base Pay Quartile 1	2	3	4
A	700	5	$29,000	$32,000	$35,000	$33,400	$5,340	$6,680	$43,420	1.04	1 (20%)	0 (–)	1 (20%)	3 (60%)
B	1700	20	28,000	31,000	34,000	33,100	4,965	8,275	46,340	1.07	2 (10%)	1 (5%)	1 (5%)	16 (80%)
C	800	6	29,000	30,000	31,000	30,667	6,133	9,200	46,000	1.02	1 (17%)	0 (–)	0 (–)	5 (83%)
D	2000	25	28,000	30,000	32,000	31,560	1,578	12,624	45,762	1.05	2 (8%)	1 (4%)	1 (4%)	21 (84%)
E	700	9	6,000	30,000	34,000	31,333	3,133	9,400	43,866	1.04	2 (22%)	1 (11%)	1 (11%)	5 (56%)
F	4000	45	25,000	27,000	29,000	27,544	1,377	9,640	38,561	1.02	11 (24%)	6 (13%)	8 (18%)	20 (44%)
G	5000	65	23,500	26,500	29,500	25,923	–	7,777	33,700	0.98	20 (31%)	15 (23%)	10 (15%)	20 (31%)
H	7000	80	22,000	25,000	28,000	25,050	–	8,768	33,818	1.00	24 (30%)	18 (23%)	10 (13%)	28 (35%)
I	1000	10	21,000	25,000	29,000	25,100	–	6,275	31,375	1.00	0 (–)	7 (70%)	2 (20%)	1 (10%)
J	1000	10	21,000	24,000	27,000	24,600	3,690	6,150	34,440	1.03	0 (–)	4 (40%)	4 (40%)	2 (20%)
Simple Average			25,250	28,050	30,850	28,827	2,422	8,479	39,728					
Weighted Average			24,165	26,936	29,707	27,307	1,161	8,797	37,266					

Inspecting the Data

So what can we observe from Table 8.1? Base pay range midpoints range from $24,000 (Company J) to $32,000 (Company A). The average base pay range midpoint is $28,050, and the weighted average midpoint is $26,936. This suggests that firms that employ more accounting clerks have a lower pay range than firms that employ fewer. The median range midpoint is $28,500. (When there is an even number of cases, the median is the average of the middle two cases.)

As Table 8.1 shows, mean base pay is lowest at Company J ($24,600) and highest at Company A ($33,400). Interestingly, however, when total compensation is considered, Company I pays the least ($31,375) due to poor indirect pay and no performance pay, and Company B pays the most ($46,340). There is quite a high dispersion (48 percent) between the lowest- and highest-paying firms, which may suggest that job duties of accounting clerks may be different at these firms.

Let's examine performance pay and indirect pay. As Table 8.1 shows, three companies (G, H, I) don't offer any performance pay at all; otherwise, performance pay ranges from $1,377 (Company F) to $6,133 (Company C). Indirect pay ranges from $6,150 (Company J) to $12,624 (Company D). To examine the structure of the compensation mix, we have calculated the percentage of total compensation for each major pay component at each firm (using the data in Table 8.1):

	BASE PAY (%)	PERFORMANCE PAY (%)	INDIRECT PAY (%)
Company A	77	8	15
Company B	71	11	18
Company C	67	13	20
Company D	69	3	28
Company E	71	7	21
Company F	71	4	25
Company G	77	—	23
Company H	74	—	26
Company I	80	—	20
Company J	71	11	18
Average	73	6	21

As this table shows, companies in this sample vary considerably in their compensation mixes, in addition to their compensation levels. Base pay constitutes as much as 80 percent of total compensation, or as little as 67 percent. Performance pay ranges from as much as 13 percent of total compensation down to none, and indirect pay ranges from 28 percent down to 15 percent.

Drawing Inferences from the Data

What can we make of these substantial differences in pay policies for the same job? We can infer, from its low starting pay, that Company I may be willing to accept inexperienced and/or untrained employees and then provide them with on-the-job training. With its wide pay range, the company can reward increased experience over time. Even so, total compensation is constrained by low indirect pay and zero performance pay. So how will Company I keep its accounting clerks once they are trained?

Perhaps Company I promotes these individuals rapidly to higher jobs, such as senior accounting clerk, which may carry a considerably higher pay scale. Maybe the jobs at Company I have some intrinsic or extrinsic rewards that other firms do not offer, such as high job security. Or maybe Company I simply cannot afford to pay any more than what it pays and simply has to put up with hiring inexperienced employees who quit to take better-paying jobs once they are trained.

What about the width of the pay ranges? They vary from $2,000 in Company C to $8,000 in Company I. The mean width of the base pay range is $5,600. Beyond these facts, careful examination suggests that there may be some patterns. For example, Company C, with a pay range of only $2,000, pays a high starting base pay ($29,000). Company C also has high performance pay, which may be used to differentiate employees, since there is very little progression through the pay range.

Perhaps Company C hires only highly experienced and well-trained accounting clerks. It only employs six of them, yet expects these six to handle all the clerical accounting chores for a company of 800 employees. In comparison, Company E has nine accounting clerks for 700 employees. Of course, many factors could explain this difference in staffing, and it may not necessarily be that the accounting clerks at Company C do more work than those at Company E.

Company I (along with Company E) has the widest pay range—$8,000. However, because the firm's starting pay is so low ($21,000), it needs a wide range to keep good employees as they become more experienced. In contrast to Company C, Company I is likely using pay range to differentiate employees, since it has no performance pay.

This raises a question. What is the value of performance pay to employees? In our example, we have factored it into total compensation as if it is of equivalent value to base pay (dollar for dollar). However, is a dollar of performance pay really worth a dollar of base pay? Most financial experts would say no, because performance pay is uncertain. If the performance pay is based on individual performance and is allocated in a zero-sum way, there may be a strong possibility that an individual will not receive any performance pay in a given year. If the performance pay is based on company performance, such as a profit-sharing plan, there is no guarantee that the necessary threshold level will be reached next year, even if it was reached this year.

What about indirect pay? Because of the tax advantages of many types of indirect pay, some might argue that a dollar of indirect pay is worth more than a dollar of base pay. But that depends on the structure of the indirect pay, and the needs of the employee. Some employees may place very little value on benefits, because they don't use most of them. In fact, they may not even be aware of many of the benefits for which they are eligible.

Chapter 8: Evaluating the Market

In short, some firms may be spending a lot of money on benefits employees don't care about. (Of course, this is one of the problems that flexible benefits are intended to solve, by allowing employees to maximize their own cash value of benefits.) Thus, a dollar of benefits may be worth more than one dollar of pay to some employees and less than one dollar to others.

Let's take another angle on the data. In this survey, indirect pay averages about 21 percent of total compensation. But it is higher in larger companies than smaller companies, which is typical. For example, indirect pay averaged 26 percent of total compensation in companies with 2000 or more employees, and 19 percent in companies with fewer than 2000 employees. On the other hand, smaller firms used performance pay more heavily, as performance pay constituted 8 percent of total compensation in firms with fewer than 2000 employees, and only 2 percent in firms with 2000 or more employees. Overall, large firms paid somewhat less ($37,960) than smaller firms ($40,906). But the compensation in the larger firms was less risky, since they had higher indirect pay and lower performance pay than smaller firms.

Examining Pay Range Distribution

Finally, we need to examine the actual distribution of employees within their pay ranges. The last five columns in Table 8.1 present this information. They show that the distribution across the quartiles of top-paying firms is very different from that of the lower-paying firms, with the majority of their employees in the top (fourth) quartile.

This distribution difference is not surprising. Examine Company D, which has 84 percent of its accounting clerks in the top quartile. Although Company D does not pay the highest maximum base pay, it does provide some performance pay, and the best benefits (indirect pay). Why would anyone ever quit? No one does, so eventually most employees end up in the top pay quartile. In contrast, Companies F to J have only a minority of their employees in the top bracket. This suggests higher turnover. In addition, let's examine Company H, where just 35 percent of their clerks are in the top bracket. As Table 8.1 shows, 30 percent are also in the bottom quartile. One can infer that this firm has high turnover and is continually hiring new clerks. As these employees gain experience, they are likely able to get jobs with better-paying firms, so they quit. The table also shows a sharp drop between quartiles 1 and 2, and between quartiles 2 and 3.

In addition, Companies I and J probably cannot find acceptable employees at the low end of their pay ranges and are bringing new clerks in at the second quartile. So the bottom end of their pay ranges is really irrelevant. Because of low indirect pay at Company I, there is nothing to retain their employees as they gain experience, so they appear to quit at their first opportunity.

Inspection of the compa-ratios also gives an indication of actual base pay relative to the pay range midpoints and shows that most firms are currently paying their employees in the top half of the pay range, with the exception of companies G, H, and I, which are paying slightly below or at the midpoints.

Applying Survey Data

This example shows that interpreting survey data is a complex process. But once interpreted, how do you apply your results? If you are using a job evaluation system, you will use the survey data from key (benchmark) jobs to develop a market line and to calibrate the job evaluation system against that, as described in the previous chapter. If you are using a pay-for-knowledge system, you will need information from Chapter 9 to understand the process for using survey data to calibrate the system.

If you are using market pricing, you simply apply the market rates to your jobs, after adjusting for compensation mix strategy and compensation level strategy. You do not need to survey each job every year; if you survey one-fifth of the jobs each year, you can update the others based on estimates of annual increases. With this method, you will end up market-testing every job every five years. Of course, surveys may be done more frequently for a particular job, if there are indications that the pay level is inappropriate, such as difficulty in recruiting or excessively high turnover.

But before applying the data, you need to complete one more step. Since compensation surveys are dealing with historical data, they are always somewhat out of date. Furthermore, the pay system being planned must apply to the upcoming year, so there needs to be some consideration for the amount the market will increase in a year. So you need to adjust the survey data in a process known as **aging the data**.

There can be some thorny issues in the application of market data. For example, what happens when the pay rate indicated by job evaluation differs from that indicated by market data? Although there is not much research evidence on that question, one study[6] found that market data tended to outweigh job evaluation data in an experimental study of U.S. compensation managers. Thus, managers were inclined to abandon internal equity if it conflicted with market data. This inclination is one of the reasons why advocates argue that pay equity legislation is essential, since this inclination tends to replicate market practices even if they are not equitable.

aging the data
the process of adjusting compensation data to bring it up-to-date with the time period in which the new compensation will take effect

Limitations of Compensation Surveys

Compensation surveys are subject to numerous limitations. First, they may vary dramatically in quality of job matches and methodology. Second, they may omit important information. For example, for most firms, adequately quantifying performance pay and indirect pay is not a simple process, and some surveys may simply omit important elements. Third, unless compensation survey data are available for individual employers in the market sample (as was the case in Table 8.1 but is rare in compensation survey data), we cannot surmise anything about the compensation strategies practised by other firms. Fourth, compensation data may not fit all of the jobs an organization has, especially if these jobs are organized differently from the norm.

Furthermore, compensation surveys were developed when compensation systems were much simpler than they are today. Thus, recent extensive use of indirect pay and performance pay has complicated data gathering

Chapter 8: Evaluating the Market

enormously. For example, the value of stock options is very difficult to estimate, as are long-term incentives. In addition, some firms may provide other important benefits difficult to price out in monetary terms, such as purchase discounts or the use of company recreational facilities. To make matters more complicated, some firms include these items when reporting indirect pay, while others do not. So overall, surveys simply cannot capture the entire range of rewards—both extrinsic and intrinsic—offered by organizations.

Another issue is that there may be bias in the sample of firms responding to compensation surveys. Traditional firms with simple pay systems find it much easier to reply to compensation surveys than nontraditional firms that have nonstandard jobs and complex pay systems. Thus, compensation surveys may misrepresent actual pay trends.

Finally, while compensation surveys attempt to reflect the value placed on jobs by the labour market, use of these surveys assumes that the market values jobs fairly. As discussed in previous chapters, the market may underprice certain jobs. Underpricing puts employers in a quandary. If they wish to be fair, they may need to pay certain jobs (such as those traditionally held by women) more than the market would dictate. However, this practice may put them at a competitive disadvantage, especially if their competitors do not adjust their pay rates at the same time. For this reason, many critics of market compensation have little faith in voluntary measures to correct historic inequities and argue that pay equity legislation is essential to create a level playing field for all employers.

Summary

This chapter has explained how to evaluate the "market rate" for a given set of jobs. It discussed forces affecting "market rate" and various sources of compensation data, including third-party surveys and in-house surveys. Next, it presented the four main steps in the process for conducting a compensation survey. The chapter also presented ways to analyze, interpret, and apply compensation survey data.

The next chapter completes our discussion of the processes for determining compensation values by describing the processes for evaluating individual performance and for evaluating individual skills and competencies.

Key Terms

aging the data, 329
compa-ratio, 324
compensating differential, 314
interquartile range, 323
key job matching, 319

market comparator firms, 316
mean, or simple average, 323
median, 323
quartile or decile, 323
weighted mean, or weighted average, 323

Web Links

Updates on industry pay rates and other labour market news, updated on a daily basis, can be obtained from **http://www.statcan.ca/start.html**. (p. 312)

To learn more about the salaries of NHL hockey players, go to **www.nhlpa. com**. (p. 312)

The links for Salary Expert and Salary Wizard are **http://salaryexpert.com/** and **http://workingcanada.salary.com**. (p. 317)

RPC Icons

RPC 8.1 Identifies potential sources and the markets in which the organization competes for qualified candidates.

RPC 8.2 Monitors the competitiveness of the compensation program relative to comparable organizations.

Discussion Questions

1. Examine the list of industries and pay rates in the opening vignette. Discuss possible reasons why each industry has the relative pay level that it does.
2. Based on the concept of "compensating differentials," develop a list of job/organizational characteristics that would make you willing to work for less money. Then develop a list of job/organizational characteristics that would cause you to want more money to accept a given job. Rank each list in order of the importance to you of each characteristic. In a small group, compare your lists and discuss possible reasons for any differences.

Using the Internet

1. How should hockey players get paid? Use the website **http://www. berksiu.k12.pa.us/webquest/neiswender/default.htm** to design an effective compensation system for hockey players. Share and compare your plan with those of other class members. How do you account for the differences between these plans?
2. Take four jobs that are of interest to you and are included in both the Salary Expert and Salary Wizard databases (**http://salaryexpert.com/** and **http://workingcanada.salary.com**). Using your own geographic area as the basis for your search, identify what compensation each of these websites indicates for each of the four jobs. How close are the two websites? What are some possible reasons for the differences?

Exercises

1. Table 8.2 (on the next page) provides data from a compensation survey for the job of industrial engineer, collected from the same employers as

TABLE 8.2

Results of Compensation Survey: Industrial Engineer

Company	Total Employment	Number of Industrial Engineers Employed	Base Pay Range Minimum	Base Pay Range Midpoint	Base Pay Range Maximum	Mean Base Pay	Mean Performance Pay	Mean Indirect Pay	Mean Total Compensation	Base Pay Quartile			
										1	2	3	4
A	700	2	$50,000	$55,000	$60,000	$56,000	$6,720	$11,200	$73,920	1	–	–	1
B	1700	5	48,000	52,000	56,000	54,000	9,720	13,500	77,220	1	–	1	3
C	800	1	54,000	60,000	66,000	66,000	13,200	29,800	99,000	–	–	–	1
D	2000	12	44,000	50,000	56,000	54,666	5,467	21,866	81,999	–	1	2	9
E	700	4	50,000	58,000	66,000	62,250	9,338	18,675	90,263	–	1	2	3
F	4000	17	45,000	51,000	57,000	52,205	5,221	18,272	75,698	5	2	1	9
G	5000	21	43,000	48,000	53,000	48,095	–	14,429	65,524	8	3	2	8
H	7000	40	42,000	50,000	58,000	50,100	5,010	17,535	72,645	12	6	3	18
I	1000	4	46,000	54,000	60,000	55,250	–	13,813	69,063	1	–	1	2
J	1000	3	47,000	52,000	57,000	54,667	8,200	13,667	76,534	–	1	–	2
Simple Average			46,900	53,000	58,900	55,323	6,288	16,276	78,187				
Weighted Average			43,991	50,541	57,018	51,738	4,513	17,046	73,298				

the compensation survey for accounting clerks discussed earlier in the chapter. Assume you are managing a high-involvement firm that employs about 800 people and you employ 10 industrial engineers. Develop a compensation structure for this job, indicating the amount of base pay the job will provide (including the pay ranges) and the amount and type of performance pay and indirect pay. Assume the survey data are eight months out of date, and your new compensation structure will take effect in four months and apply to the following 12-month period.

The following job summary was used in the survey, which was based on the National Occupational Classification for "Industrial and Manufacturing Engineers":

> *Industrial and Manufacturing Engineers conduct studies and develop and supervise programs to achieve efficient industrial production and efficient utilization of industrial human resources, machinery, and materials. Industrial and Manufacturing Engineers are employed in consulting firms, manufacturing and processing companies, and in government, financial, health care and other institutions. Example titles include cost engineer, computer integrated manufacturing engineer, fire prevention engineer, plant engineer, work measurement engineers, methods engineer, industrial engineer, manufacturing engineer, quality control engineer, safety engineer, production engineer, time-study engineer.*

2. After completing Question 1, develop a compensation structure for the same firm; but this time, assume it uses the human relations managerial strategy. Then do the same for the classical managerial strategy. How do these three compensation structures differ?
3. In a large group, survey the hourly pay levels for all those group members who are currently employed or were recently employed in common jobs such as sales clerk, cashier, or fast-food worker. If there are differences in pay within the same job type, discuss why these may exist.

Case Question

1. You are the head of human resources at "Alliston Instruments" (case in the Appendix). You would like to do a compensation survey to determine whether your pay rates are in line with those in the industry. Using the steps described in this chapter, design the process for so doing.

Simulation Cross-Reference

If you are using *Strategic Compensation: A Simulation* in conjunction with this text, you will find that the concepts in Chapter 8 are helpful in preparing Section F of the simulation.

Endnotes

1. Gunderson, Morley, Douglas Hyatt, and Craig Riddell. 2000. *Pay Differences between the Government and Private Sectors: Labour Force Survey and Census Estimates.* Discussion Paper No. W/10. Ottawa: Canadian Policy Research Networks.
2. Pay Equity Task Force. 2004. *Pay Equity: A New Approach to a Fundamental Right.* Ottawa: Department of Justice, Canada.
3. Pay Equity Task Force. 2004. *Pay Equity: A New Approach to a Fundamental Right.* Ottawa: Department of Justice, Canada.
4. Sibson, Robert E. 1990. *Compensation.* New York: American Management Association.
5. Tyson, David E. 2005. *Carswell's Compensation Guide.* Toronto: Thomson Publishing.
6. Weber, Carolyn L., and Sara L. Rynes. 1991. "Effects of Compensation Strategy on Job Pay Decisions." *Academy of Management Journal,* 34(1): 86–109.

Chapter 9

Evaluating Individuals

Chapter Learning Objectives

After reading this chapter, you should be able to:

- Identify and explain the four main reasons for conducting performance appraisals.
- Explain why many performance appraisal systems fail to accurately measure employee performance.
- Identify and describe the different methods for appraising performance, along with their strengths and weaknesses.
- Explain the concept of "performance management."
- Identify the possible sources of performance appraisals, and discuss the circumstances under which each would be appropriate.
- Describe and discuss possible ways of linking pay to performance appraisals.
- Describe the key questions to consider in determining whether to apply merit pay to specific employee groups.
- Identify the key design issues in developing an effective merit system.
- Distinguish between skill-based and competency-based pay-for-knowledge systems.
- Identify and describe the key issues in developing a skill-based pay system.
- Identify and describe the key issues in developing a competency-based pay system.

TYING BONUSES TO PERFORMANCE RATINGS AT THE ROYAL BANK

Several years ago, the Royal Bank of Canada introduced a new merit bonus system—called the "quality performance incentive" or "QPI"—which it applied to virtually every employee. Under this system, the total amount of the annual bonus pool is determined by the extent to which the bank achieves certain financial objectives in each year. The specific amount received by each employee depends on his or her annual performance rating.

The system works as follows: If the company meets financial performance goals for the next year (in terms of return on equity and revenue growth), a specific sum—say $100 million—is placed in a bonus pool. This amount is increased by 25 percent if three other goals are met: if revenue growth, customer satisfaction, and employee commitment all exceed that of the competitors.

The amount each employee actually receives depends on the employee's individual performance rating. If an employee receives less than a "satisfactory" performance rating, she normally receives none of the bonus. If she receives a "satisfactory" rating, she receives 100 percent of the basic bonus amount available for her salary band. If she receives higher ratings, this amount goes to 130 percent, 170 percent, or 200 percent. For an employee in the lowest salary band, a standard payout could be $750, compared to $15,350 for an employee in the highest pay band.

Introduction

If you were an employee at the Royal Bank, how would you feel about the "QPI" plan? Your opinion would probably depend on two considerations. First, is it likely that the bank will meet its performance criteria, thus creating a bonus pool? And second, will the performance ratings measure your performance fairly, so that you receive a merit bonus consistent with your performance? Without confidence that both of these are likely, you would consider this combination organizational and individual performance pay plan irrelevant at best and demotivating at worst.

Let's suppose that your organization, like the Royal Bank, has decided to use merit pay to reward employees who display superior performance. How do you identify these employees in a fair and systematic way? Or perhaps your organization has decided to use knowledge-based pay to reward employees who have developed a superior breadth and depth of knowledge and skills. How do you judge in a fair and systematic way which employees have developed these superior skill levels? And for both types of pay systems, how can you fairly relate these judgments to actual pay decisions?

The success of merit- and knowledge-based pay systems hinges on finding the right answers to these questions, and the purpose of this chapter is to help find those answers. The first part of the chapter describes ways to evaluate the level of performance displayed by individual employees (known as **performance appraisal**) and ways to link the resulting appraisals to financial rewards. The second part of the chapter deals with ways to evaluate individual skills, knowledge, and competencies and ways to link the resulting evaluations to financial rewards.

performance appraisal
the process of assessing the performance level of individual employees

Evaluating Individual Performance

🅡🅟🅒 9.1

"I'd rather kick bricks with my bare feet than do appraisals!" says a manager at Digital Equipment Corporation.[1] Apparently, performance appraisal is not his favourite task—and many managers feel the same way. But what about their employers?

It turns out that many employers are no happier about their performance appraisal systems than are managers. For example, Pratt and Whitney, the giant manufacturer of jet engines, was dissatisfied with its performance appraisal system and made extensive changes to it. The following year, still not happy with the system, the firm made more changes. The year after that, the firm abandoned it altogether, replacing it with a completely different system.[2] Surveys have shown a continual state of flux in performance appraisal systems as companies search for an appraisal system they are satisfied with.[3]

However, the results of all this activity do not seem to have been very fruitful. At the beginning of the twenty-first century, about 90 percent of Canadian human resource managers who were surveyed said that their company's performance appraisal system needed to be modified or abolished; while even more—95 percent—of Canadian employees surveyed said the same thing.[4] Yet despite the disappointing history of performance appraisal, 90 percent of medium to large Canadian firms continued to use performance appraisals in 2004, covering 86 percent of their nonmanagerial employees and 98 percent of their managerial employees, which is about the same usage level as in 2000, according to the Compensation Practices Survey.[5]

These facts suggest two patterns in performance appraisal application. First, many companies can't seem to find a performance appraisal system that they are happy with. Second, despite their lack of success, they keep on trying to make performance appraisal work. Putting these two facts together suggests that while performance appraisal is highly valued as a concept, translating that concept into an effective practice is very difficult.

Indeed, some observers contend that translating the concept of performance appraisal into an effective practice that does more good than harm is virtually impossible. Based on their experience as consultants, Coens and Jenkins argue that performance appraisal is a fundamentally flawed concept that cannot be made to work effectively.[6] However, while agreeing that performance appraisal often does more harm than good, other commentators argue that performance appraisal can be made to work effectively if applied in the right way and in the right circumstances.[7] This chapter adopts this second viewpoint.

Why Do Performance Appraisals?

If performance appraisals are so difficult to do effectively, why do them at all? Organizations conduct performance appraisals for a wide variety of reasons, but these reasons tend to fall into four main categories—administrative, developmental, supervisory, and symbolic.

Administrative reasons include identifying individuals who are not performing to required standards and for whom dismissal may be necessary; identifying individuals who should be considered for promotion or merit increases; and monitoring overall quality of performance in the firm. A well-documented set of performance appraisals can also help deal with legal issues surrounding employee dismissal and subsequent unjust-dismissal lawsuits. The key task here is to measure individual performance accurately and consistently.

Developmental reasons include helping employees to better understand employer expectations, the key performance dimensions of their jobs, the strengths and weaknesses in their performance, and the ways they can improve their performance. The key task here is provision of useful feedback—an essential part of any learning process—that can help individuals change their behaviours in productive ways. This feedback is valuable to employees even if their performance does not need improvement, since most employees want to know how their performance is regarded by their supervisors and the organization.

Supervisory reasons include the notion that the process of conducting performance appraisals improves supervisory performance by helping supervisors to think systematically about employee performance and by encouraging communication with employees.

Symbolic reasons centre around creating the perception that management cares about good employee performance. Conducting a performance appraisal process demonstrates this concern to employees (as long as employees believe that performance is what the appraisal system truly measures, of course).

Problems with Performance Appraisal

However, for a variety of reasons, performance appraisals are not always accurate reflections of employee performance. If merit pay is to serve as a motivator for effective performance, two elements are needed: (1) a system for generating reliable and valid measures of employee performance, and (2) a system for linking these measures to pay increases so that significant financial rewards are seen as contingent on effective employee performance. If an appraisal method has reliability, two different raters, judging independently, will come up with similar ratings of a given individual. If a method has validity, then the individuals identified by performance appraisal as the most effective employees are, in fact, the best performers.

Over the years, both academics and practitioners have expended an enormous amount of effort attempting to develop reliable and valid measures of employee performance. But despite this effort, performance appraisal frequently fails to achieve its aims. Part of the problem stems from the multiple objectives of most appraisal systems; and some experts have even argued that there should be two completely separate performance appraisal processes— one for developmental purposes and one for administrative purposes. This makes a lot of sense in some ways, since not all firms want to use merit pay, but they may still want to evaluate individual performance to provide feedback about opportunities for performance improvement.

But for this feedback to be effective, it must be accepted by the employee as valid, it must identify specific behaviours that need to change (behaviours that are under the control of the employee), and it must take place within an environment where the feedback giver is seen as a trusted coach. However, when money is tied to appraisals, the appraiser is more likely to be seen as a feared judge than a trusted coach.

One advantage of tying pay to appraisals is that this link increases the probability that appraisals will be taken seriously by all involved parties. However, when appraisals are used for pay purposes in addition to developmental purposes, the focus of the appraisal process may change toward a judging role, in which appraisers must justify and defend their decisions about the granting or denial of merit pay. As a result, rather than engaging in a candid discussion of their shortcomings, appraisees focus on attempting to portray their performance as favourably as possible ("Given the circumstances, my performance was actually pretty good."), and attempting to defend themselves when the appraiser does not award high performance ratings ("My performance may have been lower than expected, but it wasn't my fault.").

Furthermore, the most accurate appraisal systems for assessing performance level may not be the best vehicles for generating useful feedback for the appraisee. But if merit pay is denied, employees will expect to be told why, and what they can do to correct the situation. Therefore, most organizations do attempt to include a developmental (feedback) element with their administrative appraisals, even though this may make it more difficult to effectively achieve either purpose.

Why would appraisal systems not produce accurate evaluations of performance? There are two main sets of reasons. One set derives from the appraisal systems themselves, which may not allow appraisers to make accurate assessments of employee performance, no matter how hard they try and how much they may want to. The second set of reasons, perhaps even more important, is that accurate measurement of performance may not in fact be the main objective of the appraiser. This insight has emerged only after many years of blaming performance appraisal problems on the appraisal systems themselves. So let's start by considering why appraisers may not want to produce appraisals that accurately mirror performance.

Intentional Inaccuracies in Appraisals

Considerable evidence supports the idea that when supervisors start the performance appraisal process, they often have certain desired outcomes in mind or certain consequences they are concerned about.[8] For example: Do I want Sally Jones to get a raise? Do I want Mike Wilson to be promoted? Do I want Greg Smith to quit? What impact will a low performance rating have on Jane Watson? Will a high or low appraisal be most likely to improve John Brown's performance?

Supervisors may see performance appraisal as a tool to help them achieve their own goals or as a fruitless or even potentially damaging exercise. But either way, they are likely to keep the broader work context in mind when conducting appraisals, as this quote from one manager illustrates:

> As a manager, I will use the review process to do what is best for my people and the division. . . . I've used it to get my people better raises in lean years, to kick a [person] in the pants if [he or she] really needed it, to pick up a [person] when he [or she] was down or even to tell him [or her] that he [or she] was no longer welcome here. It is a tool that the manager should use to help [her/him] do what it takes to get the job done . . . Accurately describing an employee's performance is not really as important as generating ratings that keep things cooking.[9]

Another manager illustrates concern for the possible interpersonal consequences of low performance ratings:

> There is really no getting around the fact that whenever I evaluate one of my people, I stop and think about the impact—the ramifications of my decisions on my relationship with the [person] and [his or her] future here. I'd be stupid not to . . . [I]n the end I've got to live with [him or her], and I'm not going to rate a [person] without thinking about the fallout. There are a lot of games played in the rating process, and whether we admit it or not we are all guilty of playing them.[10]

A very common practice in performance appraisal is for supervisors to inflate ratings, known as the "leniency" problem. This can take place for reasons that, to the supervisor, are consistent with or supportive of organizational goals, or it can take place for other reasons. For example, supervisors may inflate ratings if they lack confidence in the appraisal instrument or process. They may believe that the appraisal does not measure the right things (it is not valid), that they have had insufficient opportunity to observe employee performance to make a valid assessment, or that they do not have the expertise to adequately appraise performance. In all of these cases, it would be difficult for the appraiser to defend poor ratings; so he/she avoids the problem by simply giving high ratings.

Supervisors may have other motives for giving high ratings to everyone. They may be concerned about relationships between themselves and their subordinates if they do not give high ratings. They may also be concerned about relationships among employees, since employees who receive low ratings may resent those with high ratings. Moreover, some supervisors believe that their own reputation is damaged if their subordinates do not appear to be performing well. Furthermore, some supervisors may believe that other supervisors are giving high ratings, and that they must also do so to maintain a level playing field and to protect their department's "fair share" of the available merit money and promotional opportunities. Finally, supervisors may simply not want to put the necessary effort into producing accurate ratings, and give high ratings to forestall complaints about inaccuracy.

In some cases, supervisors may have specific motives for inflating the ratings of particular employees. For example, they may believe that accurate ratings would have a damaging effect on a particular subordinate's motivation and performance. Conversely, they may want to improve an employee's eligibility for merit raises or promotions, perhaps on the grounds that the employee has been unfairly treated in the past. They may want to protect normally good performers whose performance is suffering because of personal problems. They may want to reward employees who show great effort despite poor measurable results or who have other valued attributes not measured by the appraisal instrument. On a less noble plane, supervisors may wish to get rid of poor performers by promoting them out of the department. Finally, they may simply want to reward their friends.

Research has also found that managers sometimes (but much less often) *deflate* ratings.[11] For example, they may want to "scare" better performance out of an employee who they believe could do much more or who is in danger of being fired. Or they may wish to punish a difficult or rebellious employee. They may also want to create a strong case to justify planned firings or encourage problem employees to quit. In addition, they may be following a company order to achieve a certain distribution in ratings, and this may require deflating the ratings of some employees. Finally, they may simply be biased against some individuals.

Unintentional Inaccuracies in Appraisals

Aside from intentional manipulations of performance appraisals, numerous problems in the system itself can threaten the accuracy of appraisals. The most fundamental requirements for an accurate appraisal are an adequate opportunity to observe employee performance and an ability to draw valid conclusions about performance from these observations. In some cases, especially where a supervisor has many subordinates or where the supervisor and subordinates work separately, supervisors may have a very limited sample of behaviour on which to base their appraisals. In other cases, particularly with highly skilled or professional workers, the supervisor may lack the expertise to accurately gauge the quality of an employee's work.

In addition, numerous perceptual errors can affect appraisal accuracy. These include central tendency, halo error, recency effect, contrast effect, similarity effect, and leniency/harshness. **Central tendency** occurs when appraisers rate all employees as "average" in almost everything. Less commonly, some raters have the opposite tendency—to rate all individuals as either extremely good or extremely bad, with nobody in the middle. The **halo error** occurs when one characteristic for a given individual is judged to be either very good or very bad, which then prejudices the rater to rate all characteristics of that individual at the same level.

The **recency effect** refers to a tendency to put excessive weight on recent behaviour, with earlier employee behaviour having faded from memory. The **contrast effect** occurs when there is one employee who is either exceedingly

central tendency error

occurs when appraisers rate all employees as "average" in everything

halo error

occurs when appraisers rate an individual either high or low on all characteristics because one characteristic is either high or low

recency effect

the tendency of appraisers to overweight recent events when appraising employee performance

contrast effect

the tendency for a set of performance appraisals to be influenced upward by the presence of a very low performer, or downward by the presence of a very high performer

(next pg. for review)

similarity effect

the tendency of appraisers to inflate the appraisals of appraisees they see as similar to themselves

leniency effect

the tendency of many appraisers to provide unduly high performance appraisals

harshness effect

the tendency of some appraisers to provide unduly low performance appraisals

good or exceedingly bad, which causes the appraiser to rate other employees either worse (or better) than they really deserve. The **similarity effect** describes a tendency for appraisers to rate individuals who are similar to themselves more highly than those who are different. Finally, some evaluators tend to be inherently more lenient and rate all subordinates highly (the **leniency effect**), while others may be inherently harsh (the **harshness effect**), rating all subordinates poorly.

These perceptual errors and inconsistencies across raters can be magnified by poor rating instruments, which provide insufficient definition of the characteristics being evaluated and the scales used to rate these characteristics. Some rating instruments are better than others at controlling these errors. But despite 50 years of effort to develop valid appraisal processes, research indicates that rater bias still has about twice the weight in determining performance ratings as does actual ratee performance.[12]

A final fundamental problem with appraisals occurs when they take place under inappropriate circumstances. For example, when work is highly interdependent, separating out individual behaviour may be virtually impossible, and it makes no sense to attempt to do so. Moreover, in some jobs, there is simply not much scope for individual performance to vary. Remember our chicken plant workers in Compensation Today 2.4? It makes no sense to waste time attempting individual appraisals when so little performance variation is possible.

Methods and Instruments for Appraisal

A variety of instruments and methods have been developed over the years to help develop appraisal systems that produce accurate evaluations of performance. As the weaknesses of each instrument have been revealed, new instruments have been developed. But despite all this effort, there is no widespread consensus that any of the existing instruments provides a fully satisfactory solution to the appraisal problem.

However, depending on the setting and the objectives, some methods are more appropriate than others. This section discusses the relative merits of each instrument, in roughly the order in which they were created. The following methods will be covered:

- ranking and forced distribution
- narrative/essay
- graphic rating scale
- critical incident
- performance checklist
- forced choice
- mixed standard scales
- behaviourally anchored rating scales
- behavioural observation scales
- performance distribution assessment
- objectives- and results-based systems
- performance management
- field review
- combination approaches

Ranking and Forced Distribution

Perhaps the simplest method of performance appraisal is just to rank the performance of all individuals engaged in similar jobs, from most effective to least effective. This method has the advantage that it does not require complicated forms and procedures. Furthermore, most supervisors generally have little difficulty in determining their best and worst performers. This approach also eliminates the problems of central tendency and leniency/harshness. In addition, it fits well with a system in which management decrees that only the top, say, 10 percent, of employees will receive merit pay.

However, this system has many drawbacks. It is a highly subjective procedure, does not allow for comparisons across departments, and provides very little useful feedback to the individuals being rated. It is also subject to numerous perceptual errors, such as recency, halo, contrast, similarity, and bias, as well as inconsistency in application across supervisors, since the bases for evaluating performance are usually not made explicit. The system also implies that the distances between the ranks are the same, when in fact there may be large gaps between, say, the third- and fourth-best performers.

It is also a win-lose system—the only way a person can improve his or her ranking is to displace someone else. This may create conflict and lack of cooperation among employees. It is also highly unfair across departments, because it does not recognize that some departments may be loaded with high performers, while other departments may have very few.

Finally, this kind of ranking is difficult to do. Although it may be easy to pick out the best and worst performers, it may be very difficult to rank the large middle group. Should, for example, an employee be ranked tenth or eleventh out of 20 employees? It may also be very difficult to justify these fine differences to ratees, and these fine differences are seldom needed for administrative purposes anyway.

One method to facilitate this ranking process is the **paired comparison method.** Each individual is compared with every other individual, one at a time. The number of times each individual is judged the superior of the pair determines the rank of that employee. However, although this method does simplify the ranking process, the number of comparisons that must be made increases geometrically with the number of employees being ranked.

A modification of the paired comparison method calls for ranking employees on individual traits. The appraiser weights individual traits by importance and adds them up to arrive at an overall performance rating. This method can provide some feedback to appraisees on strong and weak areas. However, unless these traits are well defined, and unless there has been ample opportunity to observe the extent to which each employee demonstrates these traits, adding rankings of each trait may simply make the system more cumbersome and no more accurate.

Another variation of the ranking method is the **forced distribution method.** Here the rater is presented with a number of categories and is required to place a certain percentage of the appraisees into each category. For example, Merck and Company, the large pharmaceuticals firm, requires supervisors to place 5 percent of employees in the top category ("exceptional");

paired comparison method

determines the rank order of all employees in a unit by comparing each employee with each of the other employees in the unit

forced distribution method

a performance appraisal method that stipulates the distribution of employees across the performance categories

15 percent in the next category ("with distinction"); 70 percent in the middle ("high Merck standard"); 8 percent in the next lowest ("room for improvement"); and 2 percent in the lowest category ("not acceptable").[13] The company began using the system after they found that their previous rating scale was not discriminating between performance levels (almost everyone was rated at the highest level). For the same reason, IBM adopted a similar approach in 1992, requiring each supervisor to put 10 percent of employees into the highest category and 10 percent into the lowest category.

Despite a resurgence in popularity of forced distribution, it should be noted that this method still has almost all the deficiencies and problems of the ranking method. However, it is not necessary to generate a specific rank for each employee. This is a major advantage, and can simplify the appraisal process greatly. Nonetheless, this method does not fit well with either human relations or high-involvement firms.

Narrative/Essay

Another simple approach is for the appraiser to simply write out some comments summarizing the appraisee's performance. But while this approach may be useful for providing feedback to employees, it is not useful for pay purposes. It is prone to all the perceptual errors discussed earlier and does not provide a uniform basis for comparisons across employees and departments. Each supervisor may focus on different things, some of which may not be valid indicators of performance. However, this method may be useful for reinforcing ranking or rating scales or providing developmental feedback.

Graphic Rating Scale

graphic rating scale

an appraisal method in which appraisers use a numerical scale to rate employees on a series of characteristics

For many decades, the **graphic rating scale** has been one of the most widely used performance appraisal methods and likely remains the single most popular rating method, mainly because of its simplicity. First, the organization selects a number of traits or characteristics judged relevant to job performance. They typically include such characteristics as quantity and quality of work performed, initiative, responsibility, and cooperation with others. Then, immediate supervisors rate employees on the extent to which they possess each characteristic. In many cases, raters are required to make written comments in support of their ratings. These narrative comments are especially useful for feedback purposes and for justifying the ratings.

Figure 9.1 shows a graphic rating scale that has been used by a police service in a western Canadian city. Seven traits are each rated in terms of six levels of performance. Although in this example, raters are required to depend on their own judgment to define both the traits being rated and the performance level, a more effective appraisal form would also include a brief description of the traits and definitions of the performance levels, which improves consistency of application. Some rating scales also weight the traits differentially.

The graphic rating scale method has numerous shortcomings. First, in many cases, the traits or characteristics are defined very vaguely or not at all, as in Figure 9.1. As a result, different supervisors define and measure these

FIGURE 9.1

Example of Graphic Rating Scale

Name _____ Type of Duty _____
Rank and Number _____ Rating Period: From _____
Date of Appointment _____   To _____
Promoted to Present Rank _____ Date of Rating _____

Critical Standards of Performance	Inferior Performance	Acceptable Performance		Superior Performance		
	Below Standard 1	Meets Minimum Standard 2	Meets Standard 3	Exceeds Standard 4	Greatly Exceeds Standard 5	Outstanding 6
1. Work Performance	☐	☐	☐	☐	☐	☐
2. Dependability	☐	☐	☐	☐	☐	☐
3. Initiative	☐	☐	☐	☐	☐	☐
4. Relationships	☐	☐	☐	☐	☐	☐
5. Appearance	☐	☐	☐	☐	☐	☐
6. Written communications	☐	☐	☐	☐	☐	☐
7. Verbal communications	☐	☐	☐	☐	☐	☐

Rater's Signature   3. _____ Rank _____ Reviewing Officer's Signature
1. _____ Rank _____   4. _____ Rank _____ -
2. _____ Rank _____   5. _____ Rank _____ Rank _____

traits differently. Second, some characteristics are very difficult for a supervisor to directly observe, leading to guesswork. Third, the selection of traits to assess is often simply someone's opinion of what is related to job performance, and may not reflect actual job performance. Fourth, performance levels are usually defined in general terms, such as "excellent," "good," "satisfactory," or "unsatisfactory," and appraisers may differ significantly in their standards for each of these rating levels. Fifth, this method often fails to provide useful feedback to ratees.

Moreover, the graphic rating scale is vulnerable to virtually all of the perceptual errors in the rating process discussed earlier, especially leniency. Although some of these problems can be reduced by rater training and careful definition of rated characteristics and response scales, this method is generally considered to be one of the least reliable or valid approaches to performance evaluation. Indeed, many supervisors required to use this method are reluctant to put much effort into it or reliance on it because of doubts about its validity.

But many organizations use this method because of its ease, low cost, and "face" validity. That is, it looks as if it should be a valid system. Since it is an absolute system (rather than a relative system, as in the case of ranking), it does avoid certain problems of ranking systems, such as the inability to make comparisons across departments. In some cases, it may be better than no system at all, especially if it is not used for pay purposes. Use of multiple raters may also improve the utility of this method.

Critical Incident

critical incident method
appraisals are based on analysis of recorded critical incidents of employee behaviour

The **critical incident method** requires the recording of both effective and ineffective incidents of behaviour for each employee on an ongoing basis throughout the review period. The objective is to build up a database of specific employee behaviours, which the rater can then use to infer performance levels and then provide specific examples of good and bad behaviours to the employee. At the end of the review period, the rater classifies these incidents into various performance dimensions and subjectively determines a rating for each dimension.

Advantages to this approach include elimination of the recency effect, as well as provision of concrete feedback to the employee, both to explain the rating received and to allow an opportunity for the individual to see exactly what types of behaviour need to be changed.

However, there can be several problems. First, although supervisors should diligently record critical incidents as they occur throughout the review period, this task is frequently neglected until just before the review. Second, bias may still occur because a supervisor may consciously or unconsciously record only positive or negative incidents for certain employees. Third, employees may resent the supervisor for keeping what may appear to be a "little black book" on them. To avoid this pitfall, the supervisor must deal with all incidents (especially if they are negative) as they occur, in addition to simply recording them. Finally, converting the data (the recorded incidents) into an overall rating for making salary decisions is a difficult and highly subjective process, which can easily produce biased results.

Performance Checklist

performance checklist method
appraisal method based on checking off statements that apply to employee behaviour

In the **performance checklist method**, the rater simply describes employee behaviour by checking off descriptive statements (both positive and negative) that describe the typical behaviour of the employee from a list. Scoring may be a simple counting of the numbers of statements checked or a summation of their weights. The weights reflect the relative importance of the behaviours in the performance of the job in question. The numerical total of the "checked" weights provides an easy mode for linking performance to pay. An illustration of a weighted checklist is shown in Figure 9.2.

Essentially, the purpose of this method is to systematize the critical incident approach and to establish a method for which there is some confidence about reliability and validity. It also has numerous advantages over the graphic rating scale. For example, rather than asking the appraiser to rate vaguely defined traits, with ambiguity both in the trait definitions and in the response scale, it simply asks the rater to describe behaviour by checking either "yes" or "no." The behaviours that have been selected have been tested for validity, and the system improves reliability by reducing rater discretion. Since the weightings of the various items are not revealed to the rater, intentionally biasing the ratings becomes somewhat more difficult.

But a number of problems and drawbacks remain. The first is complexity—different forms need to be developed for different groups of jobs. Moreover, the checklist needs to be revised whenever the jobs undergo

FIGURE 9.2

Example of Performance Checklist

Employee name and number:_____

Rater's name:_____

Department:_____ Date: _____

Directions: Place a check mark next to each statement that accurately describes the
ratee's behaviour.

		Weight[a]
1. Generally finishes the jobs on time	_____	+ 2.5
2. Sometimes refuses to cooperate with other employees	_____	− 2.0
3. Carries out tasks without close supervision	_____	+ 2.0
4. Has good attendance record	_____	+ 2.0
5. Often makes useful suggestions	_____	+ 1.5
6. Makes frequent serious errors in work	_____	− 3.0
.		
.		
.		
40. Always treats customers courteously	_____	+ 3.0

[a]Note: These weights are provided for illustration purposes only and would not
normally appear on the rater's copy of the form.

changes. Another problem is that since the supervisors do not know the weights, they may experience frustration, since they are not sure whether they are giving highly favourable ratings to employees. This method is also not very useful for feedback purposes. Despite all the work in developing the ratings, it is still prone to bias if the supervisor tends to recall only negative or positive behaviours of a particular employee; and it is still susceptible to leniency/harshness, halo, and recency errors.

Forced Choice

In order to overcome many of the problems of the earlier methods, particularly the graphic rating scale, a number of newer methods have been developed. The **forced choice method** seeks to overcome common rating errors by presenting the rater with pairs of descriptive statements. The rater is forced to select one statement in each pair as most descriptive of the individual being rated. The statements in each pair appear equally desirable (or undesirable), but only one of them discriminates good performers from poor performers. Examples of two pairs of statements are below:

Pair A: 1. Can be relied upon to complete assignments on time.
         2. Is at ease in any situation.

Pair B: 1. Frequently does not communicate sufficiently with subordinates.
         2. The quality of work produced is not always high.

forced choice method

an appraisal method that forces raters to select the one statement that best describes employee behaviour from pairs of statements

Raters are not told which items discriminate performance, and the human resources department scores the questionnaire.

If constructed properly, the forced choice method is probably the most reliable and valid method for measuring individual performance. It eliminates most rating errors and is very difficult to intentionally bias. Because an "objective score" is obtained for employees, it can be readily used to allocate merit pay and can be used to compare employees across departments.

Ironically, this method is also one of the least-used methods. This is because it is highly complex to develop and poorly accepted by raters (and ratees). For example, in many instances, neither or both of the statements in the pair will apply to an employee, yet the rater is forced to select one. In addition, raters do not like being kept in the dark about whether they are giving high or low ratings to an individual; and this system takes away their discretion to use the performance appraisal system in a "flexible" (some might say "biased") way.

Raters may also be reluctant to defend their ratings, knowing that they cannot meaningfully explain the basis for the performance scores with their subordinates and cannot provide specific feedback on how to improve the performance scores. Finally, convincing employees of the validity of these scores may be difficult because the system is so complicated.

Mixed Standard Scales

mixed standard scales

an appraisal method that asks an appraiser to indicate whether an appraisee performs better than, equal to, or worse than specific examples of behaviour

Mixed standard scales attempt to improve on the graphic rating scale by providing a list of items that illustrate good and bad examples of different behaviours. As Figure 9.3 illustrates, the rater indicates whether the appraisee generally performs better than, equal to, or worse than each of these items.

Because these scales require the appraiser to react to specific behaviours and does not require the rater to rate their extent (but simply whether performance is above, below, or equal to the statement), they are likely more reliable than the graphic rating scale. On the other hand, they are more difficult to develop, because the pool of items may need to vary for different jobs. To have full confidence in these items, organizations need to validate these scales against actual performance in some way (which implies that they already have an accurate way of measuring performance).

Behaviourally Anchored Rating Scales

behaviourally anchored rating scales (BARS)

appraisal method that provides specific descriptors for each point on the rating scale

Behaviourally anchored rating scales (BARS) are an attempt to improve on the graphic rating scale by providing specific descriptions of behaviours for each point on the rating scale for each job dimension.

Evidence that BARS result in an appreciable improvement in the reliability and validity of ratings is mixed, although there is some evidence that BARS provide better guidance to raters in defining degrees of effectiveness. BARS have the advantage of yielding a total score for purposes of pay decisions and an evaluation in specific behavioural terms that is useful in providing meaningful feedback for developmental purposes. The major disadvantage is that different scales need to be developed for each job class (often for each job) in the organization, which can be both expensive and time-consuming. Another problem is that supervisors may disagree with the

FIGURE 9.3

Example of a Mixed Standard Scale

DIRECTIONS: Please indicate whether the individual's performance is above (+), equal to (0), or lower (−) than each of the following standards.

1. _____ Employee uses good judgment when addressing problems and provides workable alternatives; however, at times does not take actions to prevent problems. (medium Problem Solving)

2. _____ Employee lacks supervisory skills; frequently handles employees poorly and is at times argumentative. (low Leadership)

3. _____ Employee is extremely cooperative; can be expected to take the lead in developing cooperation among employees; completes job tasks with a positive attitude. (high Cooperation)

4. _____ Employee has effective supervision skills; encourages productivity, quality, and employee development. (medium Leadership)

5. _____ Employee normally displays an argumentative or defensive attitude toward fellow employees and job assignments. (low Cooperation)

6. _____ Employee is generally agreeable but becomes argumentative at times when given job assignments; cooperates with other employees as expected. (medium Cooperation)

7. _____ Employee is not good at solving problems; uses poor judgment and does not anticipate potential difficulties. (low Problem Solving)

8. _____ Employee anticipates potential problems and provides creative, proactive alternative solutions; has good attention to follow-up. (high Problem Solving)

9. _____ Employee displays skilled direction; effectively coordinates unit activities; is generally a dynamic leader and motivates employees to high performance. (high Leadership)

Source: From *Managing Human Resources*, 3rd ed. by Monica Belcourt, © 2002. Reprinted with permission of Nelson, a division of Thomson Learning: www.thomsonrights.com, Fax 800-730-2215.

ordering on the scale, or there might be two items that could be checked for a given scale.

Behavioural Observation Scales

Behavioural observation scales (BOS) were developed as an improvement to the BARS.[14] This method starts with developing behavioural statements that reflect examples of positive behaviour for each job, and then rating each employee on the frequency with which each behaviour occurs (on a "1" to "5" scale—representing "almost never" to "almost always"). Overall ratings are developed by summing the individual scores. Figure 9.4 illustrates some sample items in a BOS.

Proponents argue that this method preserves the advantages of behaviourally anchored rating scales by specifically identifying the behaviour that

behavioural observation scales (BOS)

appraisal method under which appraisers rate the frequency of occurrence of different employee behaviours

Chapter 9: Evaluating Individuals

FIGURE 9.4

Sample Items from Behavioural Observation Scales

INSTRUCTIONS: Please consider the Sales Representative's behaviour on the job in the past rating period. Read each statement carefully, then circle the number that indicates the extent to which the employee has demonstrated this *effective* or *ineffective* behaviour.

For each behaviour observed, use the following scale:

5 represents almost always   95–100% of the time
4 represents frequently   85–94% of the time
3 represents sometimes   75–84% of the time
2 represents seldom   65–74% of the time
1 represents almost never   0–64% of the time

SALES PRODUCTIVITY	ALMOST NEVER				ALMOST ALWAYS
1. Reviews individual productivity results with manager	1	2	3	4	5
2. Suggests to peers ways of building sales	1	2	3	4	5
3. Formulates specific objectives for each contact	1	2	3	4	5
4. Focuses on product rather than customer problem	1	2	3	4	5
5. Keeps account plans updated	1	2	3	4	5
6. Keeps customer waiting for service	1	2	3	4	5
7. Anticipates and prepares for customer concerns	1	2	3	4	5
8. Follows up on customer leads	1	2	3	4	5

Source: From *Managing Human Resources*, 3rd ed. by Monica Belcourt, © 2002. Reprinted with permission of Nelson, a division of Thomson Learning: www.thomsonrights.com, Fax 800-730-2215.

will be rated, while eliminating some of their disadvantages. The major advantage of BOS over BARS is that once an item is selected, there is no need to develop detailed definitions for each scale point. Furthermore, using frequency of behaviour as the rating scale ensures that two or more responses cannot be selected, as is possible for BARS.

Of course, this method also has its drawbacks. For example, frequency of a given behaviour can be hard to judge, because most supervisors have only a limited number of observations on which to base this judgment. Furthermore, some research indicates that raters generalize from a global evaluation of the individual, rather than first determining frequencies for each item.[15] In fact, these researchers conclude that BOS may actually be more subjective than other scales, such as BARS.

Performance Distribution Assessment

performance distribution assessment

appraisal method that adjusts appraisal scores for the feasibility of performance levels for each employee

Performance distribution assessment (PDA) is a more sophisticated version of the BOS approach. This is the only rating method that incorporates a formal process to correct appraisals and hold ratees accountable only for the level of performance that is feasible and under their control. The PDA response scale rates the frequency of desired behaviours relative to the feasible levels of performance.[16] It also rates the frequency of undesirable results or outcomes relative to the extent to which these can be realistically expected. It requires complex scoring but results in measures of the relative effectiveness of performance, the consistency of performance, and the frequency with which especially positive or negative outcomes are observed. However, PDA may suffer from drawbacks similar to those for BOS.

Objectives-/Results-Based Systems

An approach that first gained prominence more than three decades ago involves establishing goals and objectives for each employee, usually on a joint basis, and then measuring actual performance against these objectives. This approach is known as **management by objectives (MBO)** or sometimes "management by results." MBO is regarded by many as a highly effective approach to employee motivation because of two key elements: participation by the employee in setting the goals, and frequent feedback on goal accomplishment. Research has consistently shown that setting goals (and providing feedback on progress) increases employee performance. To be effective, goals must be significant yet realistic, and there must be a means of measuring the extent to which they are accomplished. According to the Compensation Practices Survey, 79 percent of Canadian organizations use performance appraisals based on goal setting for their managers, and 61 percent for nonmanagers. This represents a substantial increase from 2000, when 74 percent of firms used goal setting for their managers, and just 50 percent used it for their nonmanagers. As will be discussed shortly, this change is likely due to a surge of interest in the concept of "performance management," which incorporates goal setting as a central feature.

management by objectives (MBO)

an approach to management that involves setting employee goals and providing feedback on goal accomplishment

Although the motivational advantages of MBO systems can be significant, using them for determining pay levels can be difficult. One major difficulty is that not all significant goals can be easily measured in a concrete way, and goals that cannot be measured are often neglected. Another problem is that different employees set different goal levels. Should an individual who sets high goals but falls slightly short be penalized, while an individual who achieves low goals is rewarded? The following example illustrates this problem:

> A high-level manager in the start-up operations of a paper products company set stringent goals to "shoot for" regarding start-up costs. Due to the inefficiencies of outside contractors, the targets were not attained. The manager was severely penalized at Christmas bonus time and again the following February at his annual performance review. He vowed that he would not repeat the same mistake.[17]

Overall, the lesson that this manager (and his subordinates) learned from this experience was to set specific, relatively easy goals. The manager subsequently became a senior vice-president in his organization.

Performance Management

Although most practitioners and academics agreed that management by objectives was a good concept, its use waned in the 1980s as the practical problems

Key Elements of Performance Management

1. *Goals* are tied to the strategy and key success factors of the business.
2. *Measures* are the primary indicators of success.
3. *Feedback* is the data used to determine progress towards goals.
4. *Reinforcement* is the active encouragement and support for action.
5. *Rewards* are what the individual or team receives for achieving desired results.

performance management

method for improving employee performance based on goal setting, feedback, encouragement and support, and rewards for success

of making MBO work became more apparent. This decline in popularity was hastened by the emergence of the total quality management (TQM) movement in the 1980s, which eschewed the use of numerical goals, believing them to be counterproductive. However, in recent years, the concept of MBO has been resurrected under a new name—**performance management**—as part of the continuing quest to find a performance appraisal system that really works.[18]

Under performance management, the organization sets goals for individuals and groups, develops measures for goal achievement, provides feedback on progress, offers encouragement and support, and provides rewards for success.[19] When applied at the team level, performance management is really a type of goal-sharing plan (as discussed in Chapter 4). Overall, 95 percent of large Canadian employers claim to use "performance management," although only 31 percent rate it as "effective" or "very effective."[20] About 30 percent were lukewarm about the program, and 34 percent indicated that it "required improvement."

Because it has become such a widely adopted program, and because some companies do believe it to be effective, you need to understand its key elements, as listed in Compensation Notebook 9.1.[21] Although performance appraisal is an important aspect, when used properly, performance management is really more of a management system than an appraisal system.

The first element of performance management—goals—need to be "SMART"—Specific, Measurable, Achievable, Relevant, and specified in Time. Goals need to be tied to key success factors for the firm, such as customer satisfaction or product quality. However, coming up with goals that apply to individual employees can be very difficult, since results may depend the collective efforts of a number of different employees. If this is the case, some type of group goal-sharing system may be preferable.

Of course, organizations then need to develop measures of these goals that are both reliable and valid—not always easy to do. During the course of the year, employees need feedback on their progression towards goal accomplishment, as well as specific guidance on ways they could improve performance. They also need to be encouraged and reinforced as they make progress towards achieving their goals, and then appropriately rewarded when goal achievement takes place. Of course, all of this is easier said than done!

Field Review

The field review method involves a short period of direct observation of the job performance of the individual being rated, frequently by an individual from outside the department who is specially trained to conduct such reviews. This method is frequently used for jobs that are not normally under direct observation by the supervisor. Typical jobs appraised by this approach might include truck drivers and airline pilots. In the retail sector, "mystery shoppers" are often used to assess work performance of sales personnel.

A major advantage of this method is that a small number of specially trained raters may be able to rate many employees, thus increasing the consistency and reliability of the appraisals. This also provides the supervisor with a "second opinion" on the employee's performance and may reduce bias and other rating errors. Normally, this method is used in conjunction with other methods and provides supervisors with additional data for their appraisals. The main disadvantages relate to the cost of training and using specialized raters and the limited application: field reviews are only appropriate in circumstances where the behaviour can be evaluated in a short time span.

Combination Approaches

Of course, some of these methods can be used in combination with other methods. For example, at J.P. Morgan, the financial services giant, the appraisal process includes three components: core competencies important to the firm (as measured by behavioural observation scales), contribution to key business success criteria, and achievement of their individual performance objectives.[22]

Sources of Appraisals

Who should conduct the performance appraisals? In the past, the answer was obvious: the employee's immediate supervisor, often augmented with an overall review of appraisals by the next-higher level of management. But more recently, research has shown that there may be value in including others in the appraisal process, including peers, subordinates, and even customers, and that use of these alternate sources of appraisal information has expanded. However, the Compensation Practices Survey indicates that supervisory appraisals remain the mainstay of the appraisal process: 73 percent of Canadian employers use *only* supervisory appraisals for their performance appraisals. But this number is a significant decline from 2000, when 84 percent of employers used only supervisory appraisals.

Appraisal by Superiors

The traditional approach to performance appraisal involves appraisals by the immediate superior. Since supervisors are responsible for the performance of their units and of the people within their units in a classical management organization, giving them the responsibility for appraising the performance of their subordinates seems logical. This practice also reinforces the authority of the supervisor, something important for classical organizations.

But relying on the supervisor as the sole source for performance appraisals can cause a number of problems. For example, supervisors may not have had sufficient opportunities to observe behaviour, or employees may skew behaviour when they know a supervisor is observing. Supervisors may also distort ratings, both unintentionally and intentionally, as has been discussed.

The "solution" to these problems has traditionally been for the next-higher level of management to review the appraisals prepared by their subordinate managers. But while this practice may have some advantages, such as demonstrating that appraisers are held accountable for their ratings, it certainly does not solve all of the performance appraisal problems that have been discussed. Since the superior generally has even less knowledge about specific employee behaviour than the appraiser, they may be reluctant to question the results. For the same reason, the superior has to resist the temptation to tinker with individual ratings.

Peer Appraisals

To augment the information available to the manager, information is sometimes collected from employees who work at the same level as the appraisee. Overall, about 31 percent of Canadian firms use peer appraisal to supplement supervisory appraisal when deciding merit pay of managers, and 19 percent of firms do so for nonmanagerial employees, which is generally comparable to use in 2000. The rationale is that peers usually have much more contact with their coworkers than a supervisor does, and they are more likely in a position to observe typical behaviour, rather than skewed behaviour. In addition, research has shown that rating errors are usually reduced when multiple raters are used.[23]

However, when appraisals are used for pay purposes, peers may be reluctant to grade down their colleagues, and the appraisal system may informally gravitate toward a mutual admiration society, in which all can benefit if they rate each other highly. Of course, the opposite may occur if there is only a limited amount of merit pay that can be awarded, and peers may give each other low ratings in an attempt to make their own performance look better, resulting in conflict and ill will among peers.

In general, research suggests that, if anything, peers are more lenient than superiors in making their ratings. As one observer put it:

> In more than one team I studied, participants in peer appraisal routinely gave all their colleagues the highest rating on all dimensions. When I questioned this practice, the responses revealed just how perplexing and risky, both personally and professionally, evaluating peers can be.[24]

Some employees in this example feared that providing negative feedback would damage their relationships with their peers and possibly hinder their own careers. Others felt negative peer feedback was not in keeping with the supportive work environment in which they preferred to work.

Subordinate Appraisals

Appraisal of managers by their subordinates is playing an increased role in the performance appraisal process. According to the Compensation Practices

Survey, 26 percent of Canadian firms appraise managers through subordinate appraisals, covering an average of about 63 percent of their managers. The logic is that subordinates can provide valid input on the effectiveness of a manager that may not be available from a different vantage point. For example, at Ernst and Young, a Canadian professional services firm, all employees are asked to respond (anonymously) to an electronic survey question: "How well does [your manager] foster a positive work environment and help our people grow?"[25] The company believes that only employees can tell them what the atmosphere is really like "down in the trenches."

However, supervisors often have serious concerns about subordinate appraisals. They may be concerned that subordinates do not understand the full spectrum of the job demands placed on them or the constraints they are operating under. They may also fear that employees will downgrade them if they have to make unpopular decisions.

On the other hand, employees may be reluctant to be critical of their supervisor for fear of repercussions. In fact, a perverse situation could arise in which supervisors with good relationships with their subordinates—whose subordinates believe that they are free to be candid in their comments—may actually receive *less* favourable evaluations than supervisors who are perceived as vindictive tyrants, since in the latter situation, employees may be afraid that any criticism could lead to negative repercussions.

In fact, recent research has shown that subordinate appraisals are actually much less accurate in assessing managerial performance than peer or supervisory appraisals (supervisory appraisals turned out to be the most accurate of all three, even though the influence of bias was still twice as strong as that of performance in appraisee ratings).[26] In addition, subordinate appraisals clearly do not fit well with classical organizations. Nor do they fit well with human relations organizations, since nobody will want to provide any negative feedback about their well-liked supervisors. In short, subordinate appraisals can be expected to work well only in high-involvement organizations, where trust and open communication are key values.

Self-Appraisals

Including a self-appraisal component in the appraisal process may have several advantages—such as encouraging employees to critically examine their own performance and facilitating communication with superiors. However, self-appraisals are of very little value for pay purposes, since they tend to be inflated. Not surprisingly, the poorest employees tend to inflate their performance the most, as Compensation Today 9.1 shows, while some high performers may be overly self-critical.

Customer Appraisals

In some cases, customers can be included in the feedback process, which is very helpful to the organization because customer satisfaction may be a key factor in company success. At Avis Rent a Car, for example, customers can evaluate employees on a "customer care balance sheet."[27] But this approach has limitations: not all employees come into contact with customers, and

"But I'm Still Better Than Average, Right?"

One reason for employee dissatisfaction with performance appraisals (but not the only one!) is that most people tend to rate their performance as "above average" (even though this can be true for no more than half of all employees), and they don't like to be told otherwise. What heightens this problem is that not only are individuals who are performing below the norm often blissfully unaware of this fact, but they also tend to be oblivious to feedback that would help them recognize their true performance level. Research conducted by Kruger and Dunning used a series of experiments with university students to illustrate this tendency.[28]

In one experiment, subjects were given a test of grammatical ability. Before knowing their test scores, students were asked to rate their grammatical ability and estimate their test scores. Students who performed in the bottom quartile on the test estimated that they had performed at the 61st percentile, and that their overall grammatical ability was at the 67th percentile. Their actual result: the 10th percentile. Students who had performed at the second quartile also had inflated perceptions of their grammatical ability, estimating it at the 72nd percentile, when in reality it was in the 32nd percentile. Students in the third quartile (and thus actually having better-than-average grammatical ability) estimated their performance at the 70th percentile, just a few points above their actual ability, while those who were in the top quartile actually underestimated their performance, estimating it at the 72nd percentile when it was really at the 89th percentile.

Interestingly, however, not only were the students with poor grammatical skills apparently unaware of their lack of grammatical ability, but they also failed to learn from the feedback provided. After their test scores and percentile rankings were revealed to them, they were again asked to estimate their level of grammatical ability. Despite the feedback they had received, they estimated their grammatical ability at almost precisely the same inflated level they did before receiving the feedback, somehow still believing themselves "above average"!

customers may not be able to single out the performance of individual employees.

Other Appraisers

As in field reviews, professional raters may be useful for some organizations. Many firms in the service industry, including Blockbuster Video, Burger King, McDonald's, Domino's Pizza, and Taco Bell, have full-time raters (known as "mystery shoppers" when they are not identified in advance) who visit specific sites and conduct detailed appraisals that are used when evaluating the manager's performance.[29]

Multi-Source Systems/360-Degree Feedback

360-degree feedback

an appraisal system that uses feedback from superiors, peers, subordinates, and possibly customers

But any combination of these sources is also possible. A relatively new method, the "360-degree feedback" method, combines peer and subordinate appraisals (and sometimes even customer appraisals) with supervisory appraisals.[30] Due to dissatisfaction with existing appraisal systems, 360-degree feedback expanded rapidly in the 1990s, although this expansion appears to have slowed as some of its shortcomings have become more apparent. Originally intended as a tool for providing developmental feedback, this system has also been used by many organizations for pay and promotion purposes.[31] According to the Compensation Practices Survey, about 22 percent of Canadian firms are currently using 360-degree feedback for appraising their managers, and 19 percent are using it for nonmanagers (of course, for nonmanagers, it is really 270-degree feedback, since they generally have no subordinates). These numbers show slight increases since 2000.

Multi-source systems have several key characteristics. They use standardized forms that provide numerical ratings of the ratee along numerous dimensions. Individual raters (except the superior) are assured of anonymity, so they can feel free to be candid in their ratings. Importantly, the system employs several procedures to screen out invalid data. For example, in a set of ratings for a given ratee, the extreme scores (i.e. the lowest and the highest) are dropped before the scores are averaged. And if a rater is more than 40 percent discrepant from other raters, that person's ratings may be eliminated entirely.

Advocates claim that 360-degree systems have numerous advantages over traditional superior-only ratings:

1. They are fair: they have less rating inflation, and more safeguards to prevent bias.
2. They are more accurate: they have numerous raters resulting in information from a variety of perspectives.
3. They are more credible to the recipient. Ratees may believe a single rater to be wrong or biased; but could all of these raters be wrong?
4. They may be more valuable for behaviour change, since work associates are likely to be more specific about behavioural feedback.
5. They may be more motivational, since peer pressure may motivate constructive behaviour changes.[32]

However, multi-source plans are not without their drawbacks. They are subject to most of the problems with peer and subordinate ratings discussed earlier. Multi-source systems can also be complicated to set up. Forms (whether paper or electronic) have to be established that ask the right questions, and different forms may be necessary for different jobs. Employees must be willing to fill out the forms voluntarily, and it may be difficult to track those who do not submit forms because they are submitted anonymously. There need to be at least four persons in each rating group (e.g., peers or subordinates) to ensure anonymity; but this number of raters may not be available for all ratees. Moreover, rater training needs to be provided to all raters; but this is generally not practical given the number of potential raters in this system (i.e., virtually everybody!).

Are 360-degree systems effective? Unfortunately, there is very little evidence on this question, probably because of the newness of these systems. One early study indicated that 360-degree systems were somewhat more effective in fostering employee performance than other types of systems (68 percent of 360-degree users reported that their appraisal system had led to better employee performance, compared with 55 percent of users of traditional systems).[33] Moreover, 65 percent of 360-degree users believed that their systems produced valid information for promotions, compared with 55 percent of users of traditional systems. However, 360-degree systems had no real advantage over traditional systems in producing valid information for merit increases, as 69 percent of 360-degree firms believed their systems produced valid information for merit raises, compared with 65 percent of other firms.

In a more recent but small-scale study, researchers concluded that "more than half" of the 360-degree systems they examined were successful.[34] Although there is no research evidence on this, it seems probable that, like subordinate appraisals, 360-degree systems are more likely to be successful in high-involvement organizations than in classical or human relations organizations.

Linking Pay to Performance Appraisals

Besides accurate measurement of performance, the other crucial aspect of performance appraisals is having an effective way of linking to merit pay. A variety of methods can be used to make this link. The simplest way (and one of the most common) is for the supervisor to use the appraisal to determine whether an employee deserves a merit increment. In another method, supervisors rank employees according to appraisal scores, and only those above a cutoff point receive merit pay.

In some instances, a forced distribution is stipulated. For example, the top quarter of employees in a department may receive, say, a merit raise of 10 percent, the next quarter will receive 6 percent, the third quarter will receive 3 percent, and the bottom quarter will receive no merit increase at all. In still other cases, a supervisor simply receives a block of merit money to be allocated to employees as he or she sees fit, providing the wage structure is not violated.

merit pay grid
a tool for allocating merit raises, based on the performance level of the employee and the pay range quartile in which they fall

One approach to linking merit pay to performance appraisal is the **merit pay grid** (sometimes known as a *merit pay matrix*). As Table 9.1 shows, this grid has two dimensions. Across the top are employee performance ratings. Along the vertical axis are quartiles of the pay range for a particular set of employees. The numbers in each cell indicate the percentage increase that employees in that cell receive as a merit raise. For example, an employee in the second quartile of the pay range with a "good" performance rating receives a 5-percent merit increase.

As in this example, a common practice is for employees in the lower quartiles of their pay range to receive a higher percentage increase in order

TABLE 9.1

Example of a Merit Pay Grid

	Employee Performance Level			
	Unsatisfactory	Satisfactory	Good	Excellent
Fourth (highest) quartile	—	—	3%	5%
Third quartile	—	—	4%	6%
Second quartile	—	3%	5%	7%
First (lowest) quartile	—	4%	6%	8%

to bring them up to the midpoint of the range quite quickly. (Of course, increments expressed in fixed dollar amounts also amount to a higher percentage increase for employees in the lower part of the range.) The example is also designed so that employees in the third and fourth quartiles receive no merit increase for simply doing satisfactory work, although employees in the first and second pay quartiles receive 3 or 4 percent. The logic of this is that employees paid above the midpoint in their pay are already being rewarded for "satisfactory" work, and that a higher rating is necessary to trigger a merit raise for them.

Note that individuals at the top of the pay range (i.e., at the top of the fourth quartile) for their pay grade are not generally eligible for further merit raises, no matter how superior their performance. But motivational problems resulting from this situation can be eliminated by making merit bonuses available for those at the top of their ranges.

A key issue is to decide how much money to make available for merit raises in a given year. There are two main approaches. A "bottom-up approach" does not set any arbitrary amount but simply adds up all the increments and pays them. The major disadvantage of this method is that the organization has no control over labour cost increases. Because many organizations are not comfortable with that lack of control, they simply set a maximum amount available for raises (the "top-down approach") and then allocate it across departments. If this approach is used, the firm should ensure that it is making available sufficient funds to allow a reasonable number of merit increases.

Some firms gear the total amount of merit money available in a given year to the achievement of certain financial goals of the organization. The opening vignette described a system used by the Royal Bank of Canada to determine how much money is available for annual merit bonuses based on organizational performance indicators.

In addition to the total amount available for merit raises, organizations must decide how the merit money should be allocated across the different performance levels. As was discussed in Chapter 7, a raise only has motivational impact if it creates a "just noticeable difference" (JND) in the eyes of the employee. Although this amount can vary, research suggests a common rule of thumb: at least a 4-percent difference between performance levels is needed to create a perception of being differentially rewarded. This rule argues for relatively few levels of performance ratings, so that the difference in pay raises between performance levels is significant. Lawler suggests a maximum of five levels—a middle "satisfactory" level into which most employees would fall, and two levels above and two below.[35] In fact, the most common rating structures used in Canada have five levels.[36] If sufficient funds are not available to provide all deserving employees with a JND increase in a given year, the organization can provide increases only to the very top-rated performers, rather than spreading the merit money too thinly. Of course, a danger is that this practice may create perceptions of inequity among those not receiving increases.

Organizations must also decide whether persons performing at simply an adequate level should receive a merit increase at all. In general, the answer is

Suitable Conditions for Merit Pay

1. Is individual performance variable?
2. Is performance controllable by the individual?
3. Can individual performance be separated out?
4. Can an accurate measurement system be developed?
5. Will pay actually be linked to performance appraisals?

6. Will the system serve a purpose that cannot be served some other way?
7. Are any undesirable side effects readily manageable?
8. Will the system fit with the firm's culture and strategy?

no. Some firms lump all their increases together, for cost of living, experience/ seniority, and merit; and in this way everyone appears to get something. But this serves to obscure the performance–merit pay relationship.

Instead, if cost of living increases are justified, or if the labour market becomes highly competitive, increases should be provided across the board to all employees by raising base pay ranges or commission rates. If the organization wishes to reward seniority, seniority increases should also be held separate from merit increases. One option is to provide inflation/market increases to all employees, seniority increases to all employees who are performing at a satisfactory or higher level, and an additional merit increase to only those persons clearly performing at a higher-than-satisfactory level.

Conditions for Success of Merit Pay

This section addresses two key questions. First, how do you decide which employee groups (if any) should be covered under individual merit pay? Second, how do you design the right system for each group? If merit pay is to be successful, the right system must be applied to the right group.

To Whom Should Individual Merit Pay Apply?

Although most companies claim to use merit pay, it rarely applies to all employees. Nor should it. Applying merit pay to employee groups for whom it is unsuited is a recipe for frustration and failure. So how do we decide to whom merit pay should apply? Compensation Notebook 9.2 lists eight questions that can help guide this decision process. In general, all of these questions should be answered "yes" before individual merit pay is included in the compensation structure for a given employee group.

First, is performance variable? In many jobs, not much performance variation is possible or even desirable, as in the case of many routine, lower-level jobs in traditional classical organizations. If performance is not variable, why waste time and effort attempting to measure variations?

Second, is performance controllable by the individual employee? If circumstances affecting employee performance are beyond the control of the employee, then gearing pay to individual performance makes no sense.

Third, can the performance of individuals be separated out from the performance of others with whom they work? If not, an individually based merit system cannot be used, although some type of team-based performance pay might work.

Fourth, can an accurate performance measurement system be developed? Do jobs change so quickly that it is virtually impossible to come up with valid, up-to-date performance measures and standards? Does the organization have the resources to develop a reliable and valid system, and train raters in its use?

Fifth, will pay actually be linked to the appraisals in a meaningful way? Is the organization prepared to set aside sufficient funds to justify the merit process, and is it prepared to actually allocate this money so as to create meaningful differences between highly meritorious employees and other employees? If not, nobody will take the process seriously.

Sixth, will merit pay serve a purpose that cannot be better served in some other way? Ultimately, there are three main purposes for merit pay: to motivate employee performance; to maintain equity by making rewards commensurate with contributions; and to raise the pay of key performers so they will not be lured away by other firms. Can these purposes be served in other ways? As was noted in Chapter 3, intrinsic rewards are generally more effective than extrinsic rewards for motivating task behaviour. If intrinsic motivation already exists, then merit pay may not add much motivation and could even detract from motivation, especially if the merit pay system is not seen as fair.

If merit pay is intended to demonstrate equity, then the system needs to be carefully monitored to ensure that it actually does so in the eyes of the employees covered by the system. If persons perceived as undeserving receive merit increases, or if persons seen as deserving do not, a merit system may actually cause perceptions of inequity. An alternative method for recognizing employee differences is pay for knowledge.

As for retaining key employees, a wide variety of means (other than merit pay) are available to foster membership behaviour, as discussed in earlier chapters. If pay ranges are used, experience/seniority and/or skill levels can be used as vehicles for movement through the range, rather than merit raises.

Seventh, will any undesirable side effects be readily manageable? For example, one possible undesirable side effect occurs when employees concentrate only on elements of the job most visible in the performance appraisal process. For many organizations, organizational citizenship behaviour may be far more valuable than simple task behaviour; yet most performance appraisal systems focus mainly on task behaviour. In fact, there is some evidence that appraisals that focus on specific goals and performance improvements actually decrease citizenship behaviour.[37] Another side effect may be conflict or lack of cooperation among employees as they attempt to jockey for scarce merit increases.

Finally, does merit pay fit the culture and strategy of the organization? In classical organizations, merit pay for rank-and-file employees is often prohibited by union contracts, since employees in these organizations are usually skeptical about the ability of the organization to fairly administer merit systems. Indeed, while merit pay would appear to fit well with the emphasis on individual accountability practised in classical organizations, for many of the reasons already discussed, it is subject to abuse in these organizations. Most classical organizations have found direct control of behaviour and job simplification to be the most effective means of controlling and motivating behaviour. Electronic Banking System Inc. from Compensation Today 2.1 uses technology (surveillance cameras, computer monitoring) to monitor employee behaviour, so it does not need subjective performance ratings. Indeed, many classical organizations are adopting computer monitoring of employee behaviour in preference to traditional appraisal systems.

In addition, individual merit pay does not fit at all with human relations organizations either, because supervisors are concerned about social unity within the organization. Although many human relations firms do use some semblance of merit pay, the reality is that either most individuals receive high ratings and receive the same merit pay, or that there is very little distinction in merit raises between those employees receiving higher ratings and those receiving lower ratings. Interestingly, however, these practices are not necessarily dysfunctional for human relations organizations. They recognize that their main control mechanism—cohesive groups and positive work norms—could easily be subverted by an individual merit pay system.

At first glance, individual merit pay might appear to fit well with high-involvement organizations because of their emphasis on performance. But a closer look reveals that most high-involvement organizations have fluid jobs, team-based processes, a high level of interdependence between employees, and flat structures, none of which fit well with traditional performance appraisal. Ability and willingness to perform and citizenship behaviours are the keys to effective performance in these organizations. Motivation is provided by intrinsic sources and internalized commitment to the organization.

Under these circumstances, what could individual merit pay add to a high-involvement organization? It may actually cause some of the problems discussed earlier. The last thing a high-involvement organization needs is people concerned only with their own self-interests or secretive about ideas for fear that someone else might get credit for them. For high-involvement organizations, ranking or forced distribution systems are particularly destructive, because they undermine the collaborative atmosphere essential to their success. However, results-oriented appraisals or 360-degree feedback might be a good fit.

All the reasons described above may help shed light on the mystery of why, after so many years of effort, merit pay systems based on performance appraisal are so often unsatisfactory. Optimal conditions for individual merit pay are quite rare, and they may be increasingly so, as concepts like flextime and flexplace become more popular. But performance appraisal itself should not necessarily be dropped. In any organization, there needs to be some system for providing feedback to individuals and groups on their performance; and if done correctly, performance appraisal may be a satisfactory means of providing this feedback. Of course, as discussed in Chapter 3, the best feedback occurs when jobs themselves are designed to provide feedback directly.

How Would You Grade Your Professor?

Merit pay seems to be appropriate only in limited circumstances. However, university professors appear to meet many of the criteria. For the most part, they work independently, have control over their performance, and their accomplishments can usually be separated from those of others.

So how do you evaluate the performance of professors? In general, university professors are expected to perform in three main areas: teaching, research, and university and public service. Therefore, performance in each of these areas needs to be evaluated in some way.

The usual measure of research performance is the number of publications in high-quality academic journals. Why is this such a popular measure? Because it avoids virtually all of the problems inherent in more subjective appraisal systems. When a professor believes that he or she has made a useful contribution to the state of knowledge in a particular field, that professor prepares a paper describing the research results and submits it to a journal that specializes in that type of research. This journal then has the article reviewed by two or more experts in the field, using what is known as a double-blind process. That is, the reviewers do not know whose work they are reviewing, and the researchers do not know who is reviewing their work. Thus, problems of bias, halo, and the other major rating problems are avoided. Certainly, leniency is avoided, since most reputable journals accept for publication only a small minority of the work submitted to them—often as low as 5 to 10 percent of the submissions. One could therefore argue that if there is any problem with this system, it is harshness.

Compare this practice with the evaluation of teaching. The usual process is to use feedback from superiors (e.g., the department head), peers (other professors), and customers (students). But superior and peer appraisals take place for only a small sample of teaching behaviour, perhaps one class per term, and it is usual practice to inform the professor well in advance of the appraisal. This, of course, allows the faculty member to alter behaviour to impress the appraisers. On the other hand, the presence of these appraisers could make the professor nervous and detract from performance. But in any case, colleagues (department heads are normally considered as colleagues) are usually reluctant to be too critical of another colleague. In addition, since no standardized rating form is usually used, the appraisals from peers are subject to all of the errors discussed earlier in the chapter.

Students, however, have the opportunity to attend all classes and so are in a better position to judge overall behaviour. But while they are qualified to judge things like preparation and organization of material, because they are (by definition) not experts in the subject matter, students are not well equipped to judge the rigour and academic validity of what is being taught. In addition, some faculty attempt to influence student evaluations by combining lightweight material with easy tests and few assignments, in the hope of leading students to believe that they are learning a lot (as evidenced by their high grades), or simply to curry favour by making life as easy as possible for them.

With all of these problems, it is difficult to place a high degree of confidence in the evaluations of teaching. But evaluations of university and public-service accomplishments are even less systematic and just as subjective. For example, what value should be placed on serving on the university budget committee or delivering a public lecture to the Rotary Club? Given the problems of accurately measuring teaching and university/public service, is it any wonder that research performance often carries the most weight in university appraisal processes?

Interestingly, conditions in public-sector organizations may be more amenable to merit pay than in private-sector firms, where business environments are rapidly changing and where alternatives, such as gain sharing or profit sharing, are available. In contrast, jobs in public-sector organizations tend to be more stable and less subject to dramatic change. One occupational group that appears to fit many of the conditions for merit pay is university professors, as Compensation Today 9.2 illustrates.

Issues in Designing an Effective Merit System

If the circumstances in an organization are judged to be right for an individual merit pay system, the next step to tackle is designing an effective system. This means addressing the following issues:

1. What should be the objectives of the system?
2. What is the most appropriate measurement system?
3. How frequently should appraisals be conducted?
4. How are appraisals to be linked to pay?
5. How should feedback be provided?
6. How is procedural justice to be achieved?
7. How are raters to be trained and evaluated?
8. How is the system to be evaluated?

The first issue is to define what the merit pay/performance appraisal system is supposed to accomplish. Is it primarily supposed to stimulate performance, promote reward equity, retain valued performers, promote development/learning, or foster other desired behaviours? Is the focus to be task behaviour, membership behaviour, or citizenship behaviour?

The second issue is to determine the most appropriate performance measurement system. The particular appraisal method or process that should be used is largely dependent on the nature of the organization and the jobs being appraised. For example, in jobs where employees do not work under close supervision, use of objectives-based and/or field review methods may be necessary. A 360-degree feedback system might also be useful.

As a general rule, ranking and forced distribution systems should not be used (since they foster a win-lose competitive environment among employees), except possibly in instances where there is little or no interdependence between employees. These methods do not fit with high-involvement or human relations organizations. Job-based systems, such as BARS, are probably not appropriate in organizations where jobs change rapidly. Ideally, whatever method is used, it should be systematic in approach, promote consistency across various raters, and be validated in some fashion.

Third, how frequently should appraisals be done? For accuracy and feedback, the more frequent, the better. From a practical point of view, an annual basis is usually best, since merit raises are normally awarded once a year. One system that might be effective is to have two appraisals a year, with the intermediate appraisal used for feedback and development only, giving an indication of progress toward receiving a merit award.

Fourth, how should the appraisals be linked to pay? Some options were already discussed. Overall, to be effective, merit pay systems need to provide some assurance that top-rated performance will be significantly recognized. In so doing, the issue of whether and how to recognize employees at the top of their pay ranges needs to be dealt with.

Fifth, how is feedback to be provided? To be useful, appraisal results should be fully communicated to employees, with concrete feedback on what can be done to improve individual performance. As well, employees should be encouraged to identify their own strengths and weaknesses and to communicate to the supervisor their view of the appraisal results and process. While appraisal interviews held at the time of each formal appraisal usually cover basic communication, the supervisor must also provide informal performance feedback on an ongoing basis to each subordinate.

Three key factors are necessary for an effective appraisal interview—a high degree of supervisor familiarity with the subordinate's job and performance, a supportive approach, and genuine encouragement of subordinates to present their views and perceptions. In general, a friendly approach, stressing strengths as well as weaknesses and allowing subordinates to realize for themselves where behaviour needs improvement, is most effective. The supervisor should focus on specific behaviours that are undesirable rather than simply making a general statement, such as "You have a bad attitude." A statement like this is guaranteed to generate defensiveness and resistance by the subordinate and provides no real guidance on exactly what behaviour should be changed. The appraisee should leave the interview with a description of specific, concrete steps that can be taken to improve performance.

Although it is important to use a systematic and valid appraisal method, effective performance appraisal goes far beyond the appraisal method. The key is really the quality of the relationship between the supervisor and subordinates. If a climate of trust and open communication does not exist between superior and subordinate, then the effectiveness of the appraisal process will be severely hampered, no matter how good the tools. For example, a recent study showed that a positive and supportive relationship with the supervisor was just as important as the performance score itself in determining ratee satisfaction with the appraisal interview.[38] Dissatisfaction with the appraisal interview led to lower job satisfaction and lower organizational commitment.

Sixth, there need to be mechanisms for ensuring procedural justice. This may entail some type of appeals system. It could also involve employee participation in the merit process. A highly developed process used by a Canadian university is illustrated in Compensation Today 9.3.

Seventh, there need to be procedures for rater training and rater accountability. Raters need to be carefully trained to use the system, to make observations of employee behaviour, to relate them to the instrument, and to provide effective feedback. In addition, a system needs to be in place for recognizing and rewarding those supervisors who take the appraisal process seriously and do it well. Supervisors need to know that appraisals of their own performance are partly based on how well they conduct performance appraisals for their subordinates.

Finally, how should the merit system be evaluated? Organizations need to develop a process to determine whether the system is achieving its objectives and whether it is causing any undesirable side effects. Rater and ratee acceptance of the system can easily be evaluated through the use of surveys. If both raters and ratees do not accept and believe in the system, then it doesn't stand a chance. However, even if both groups accept a particular appraisal system, its weaknesses may render it ineffective or dysfunctional. Employee satisfaction with the system and its results is a key check on how it is performing.

Does This System Have Any Merit?

The University of Saskatchewan has a complex system for merit increases. Each fall, faculty members in each academic department vote on whether to have an elected merit pay committee or to delegate this function to the department head. Then, faculty who wish to be considered for a merit increment (raise) are asked to submit evidence substantiating their case. The department committee or head then reviews these submissions, ranks them, and chooses which to submit to the College Review Committee, an elected body of faculty chaired by the Dean of the College.

The College Review Committee reviews all submissions from the departments in the college and ranks them. The committee then awards merit increments (usually a half-increment, but occasionally a full increment) down the list until the available funds are exhausted. The funds available for merit increases are established through negotiations between the university and the faculty union, and they are usually sufficient to provide half-increments (which range from $1,064 to $1,215 per year, depending on rank) to approximately one-third of the faculty. There is also a special university-wide pool from which additional increments can be awarded to deserving faculty members. These funds are allocated by another elected faculty committee, the University Review Committee.

In order to ensure that teaching and university/public-service performance are not neglected because they are difficult to measure, most committees go to a special effort to make sure that some awards are made on these bases. Once the awards are official, a report listing the faculty members who have received merit awards is provided to all faculty, along with a brief explanation of the basis for each award.

If an individual does not receive a merit increase, he or she has several avenues of appeal. If the department committee or head did not recommend an increase, that faculty member may appeal to the College Review Committee. If the College Review Committee does not grant an increment, he or she may then appeal to the University Review Committee.

It should also be noted that unless faculty members are at the top of the pay range for their rank, they will receive a full increment for each additional year of service, aside from whatever cost of living increase the faculty union is able to negotiate (which is not much these days). Thus, seniority usually counts about double the value of merit, even if one is among the fortunate third who receive merit increases.

You will recognize many elements of procedural justice in this system, including openness, the election of salary committees, the opportunity to make one's own case, and the two sets of appeal processes. Interestingly, despite all of these elements of procedural justice, many faculty still feel slighted if they do not receive a merit increment and blame the system for "unfairness."

This system illustrates the difficulty inherent in developing a merit pay system that is perceived as fair by all employees. Part of the problem may be incomplete information: the brief report on merit awards that is provided to faculty typically does not portray the full spectrum of accomplishments on which the award is based; and many faculty members not receiving an award are able to point to somebody who appears to have done less then they have but were awarded a merit increment.

So is this merit system worthwhile? There is no clear answer, but it does accomplish several goals. It signals the behaviours that are important to the university, it attempts to provide some connection between contributions and rewards, it recognizes noteworthy accomplishments, and it serves as a mechanism for raising the pay of faculty members who might otherwise be lured to other universities.

Evaluating Individuals in Teams

One final topic in performance appraisal is the issue of how to evaluate the performance of individuals in teams. As tasks in organizations have become more complex and interrelated, and as the business environment has come to demand more speed and customer responsiveness, numerous organizations have come to depend on work teams. For example, the Compensation Practices Survey showed that about 19 percent of Canadian firms use work teams or project teams for their nonmanagerial employees (covering an average of 37 percent of their employees), and 22 percent have teams for their managerial personnel (covering an average of 41 percent of their managers).

The topic of teamwork raises two questions: (1) Should you attempt to recognize individual performance when that individual spends most or all of his or her time in a team? (2) If so, how can this be done? There are two schools of thought on the first question. One is that any attempt to single out individuals (except possibly on the basis of pay for knowledge) in a team context will likely do more harm than good. The argument here is that since teams are so interdependent in accomplishing their goals, singling out individuals is inherently unfair, since team success is a product of the efforts of all team members. Singling out particular team members may lead to resentment and a less cohesive and cooperative team. There is also a risk that some members will devote more energy to looking good on the appraisal system than to being an effective team player. Thus, critics of individual pay believe that team-based reward systems—such as gain sharing or goal sharing—are the best means of rewarding performance in teams.

The second school of thought argues that it is inevitable that some team members will contribute more to team success than others, and it is unfair (and possibly demotivating) to high contributors not to recognize this contribution financially. If the right behaviours are rewarded, if individual contribution level is fairly determined, and if it is used in conjunction with group-based and organization-based performance pay, then individual performance pay may play a useful role even in a team context.[39]

Which school is correct? Unfortunately, there is no definitive evidence on this issue. However, it is clear that work teams can be highly effective without the use of individual performance pay, as Toyota, Saturn Corporation, and Basell Canada have demonstrated. Whether teams at these companies would be even more successful with an element of individual performance pay is not clear. However, it is conceivable that if done right, individual performance pay might help to encourage and retain high contributors without negative repercussions for the team as a whole. But given the risks and possible pitfalls involved, it may well be that the risks outweigh the possible returns in most instances.

Nonetheless, there may be instances where identifying and rewarding individual contribution is appropriate and even necessary for team success. These instances would include teams where members do not have strong intrinsic motivation, where strong positive group norms do not exist, where group sanctions against poor contributors are ineffective, and where little member commitment to overall team or organizational goals is evident. These conditions create an opportunity for free riding and are most likely to occur in project teams that are temporary and in which membership is part-time, although they can arise in other types of teams as well. Under these conditions, recognizing individual contribution levels may be essential, not only to discourage free riding, but also to assure team members who are contributing

TABLE 9.2

Example of an Individual/Team Merit Grid

	Individual Member Contribution to Team			
	UNSATISFACTORY	EFFECTIVE	HIGH	EXCEPTIONAL
Team exceeds goals	–	8%	12%	16%
Team meets goals	–	4%	6%	8%
Team fails to meet goals	–	–	–	–

that their rewards will be different from those of the free riders. There is nothing more demoralizing to conscientious team members than the continued presence of free riders who benefit equally from team accomplishments. This can eventually result in a downward performance spiral as all members try to "cut their losses" by competing to see who can get away with contributing the least to the team.

individual/team merit grid

method for linking individual merit pay to both individual and team performance

One way of avoiding this unfortunate outcome is use of an **individual/ team merit grid** that recognizes individual contribution while still providing incentives for team-oriented behaviour.[40] Table 9.2 provides an example.

Table 9.2 uses three levels of team performance and four levels of individual performance (defined in terms of contribution to team success) to measure total performance. If the team does not meet its performance goals, there is no merit pay for anyone, regardless of individual performance. The message conveyed here is that there can be no individual success without team success. However, even if the team does meet its performance goals, there will be no merit pay for individuals who did not make at least an "effective" contribution to team success. If the team meets its goals, "effective contributors" (the norm) would receive a 4 percent raise or bonus, "high contributors" would receive a 6 percent raise or bonus, and "exceptional contributors" (these will generally be quite rare) would receive 8 percent. If the team exceeds its goals, these amounts are doubled. Overall, this system creates a common goal for team members while still recognizing individual contribution levels.

Of course, the key to success for this system is to have some way of identifying individual contribution levels that is both accurate and accepted as fair by team members. Recognizing the key individual behaviours that contribute to team success is crucial. Of course, effectively performing individual tasks assigned by the team is also important, but other behaviours that are as important, or even more important, to the team include training and coaching new team members, mediating conflict between team members, helping to create a positive team atmosphere, helping other team members with their tasks, and exercising initiative in moving the team toward its goals. It is hard to imagine how a supervisor-based appraisal could assess all these elements of team function, and therefore peer appraisal would likely play a central role in determining individual contribution levels. Team involvement in the

Part III: Determining Compensation Values

creation and ongoing operation of the appraisal system greatly increase the likelihood of its acceptance.

But if an organization cannot devise an appraisal system that the team accepts, it should not attempt to force use of an unacceptable system, since it will likely do more harm than good. However, a peer appraisal system could be used instead to identify unsatisfactory performers, so that weak team members could take steps to improve their performance or supervisors could remove them from the team. Nothing is more damaging to team morale (and, ultimately, team performance) than carrying an ineffective contributor.

Evaluating Skills, Knowledge, and Competencies

ⓇⓅⒸ 9.1

When evaluating individuals, another important dimension—besides performance—is their level of capabilities. Firms using a pay-for-knowledge system must have some systematic process for evaluating and rewarding individual skills and competencies. Let's suppose that after considering all the pros and cons of a pay-for-knowledge system (PKS), you decide that a PKS fits your organization. Now what? What are the key issues in designing pay for knowledge systems, which pay for employee capabilities rather than the specific job an employee may be performing?

But before we answer this question, you need to understand that there are really two distinct types of pay-for-knowledge systems. Skill-based pay (SBP) systems tend to focus at the production or service provision level, while competency-based pay systems focus at the managerial or professional level. Since much more is known about skill-based pay than competency-based pay, most of this section will deal with skill-based pay, while competency-based pay will be covered in the last part of this section.

There are five steps in the design of a skill-based pay system: (1) deciding whom to include, (2) designing the skill blocks, (3) linking these skill blocks to pay, (4) providing learning opportunities, and (5) certifying skill achievement.

To Whom Should Skill-Based Pay Apply?

As discussed in Chapter 4, skill-based pay fits with a high-involvement approach to management. Beyond this, the most active early adopters were continuous process operations, with products ranging from chemicals to steel to dog food. Because of their high task interdependence, high-capital intensity, and an overriding need to keep the production process running, these operations are ideal sites for skill-based pay. But increasingly, SBP has also been applied to other types of manufacturing firms and to the service sector.

Whenever the organization needs high and diverse employee skills and could benefit from high employee flexibility, then SBP may pay off. In their study of firms using skill-based pay in the United States, Jenkins and his colleagues found examples of successful SBP plans in a wide range of manufacturing industries, as well as in many service industries, including financial services, computer services, utilities, health services, and retailing.[41]

Designing Skill/Knowledge Blocks

After deciding where to implement SBP, the next step is to identify the job skills that are required for effective performance of the work system and then to "bundle" them into appropriate skill "units" or "blocks." Skills can typically be differentiated along two dimensions—horizontal and vertical. The horizontal dimension covers different *types* of skills, while the vertical dimension covers the *depth* of each skill.

Frequently, **skill/knowledge blocks** are set out in a grid, defined by these two dimensions. Table 9.3 provides an example of such a grid for a chemical plant. As the table shows, there are five horizontal skill types and four vertical skill levels, with a total of 18 skill blocks. As employees complete each skill block, they receive an increase in pay, as indicated by the dollar values shown in each skill block. (Although employees are usually expected to complete the horizontal row of skills before moving vertically to the next-higher row of skills, there may be some circumstances where it makes sense to allow some vertical skill development before the entire row is completed.) In this illustration, a fully skilled chemical plant operator will be earning $17,000 per year more than an entry-level operator just starting out with the firm.

TABLE 9.3

Example of Skill Grid for Chemical Plant

	OPERATIONS	PACKAGING	TESTING	MAINTENANCE	COORDINATION/ ADMINISTRATION
Level IV	Able to operate all production equipment for all products $1,400		Able to conduct all lab, chemical, and statistical tests $1,400	Able to diagnose and conduct major repairs on all plant equipment $1,400	Able to do all production and team coordination $1,400
Level III	Able to operate all production equipment for liquid products $1,000	Able to carry out all packaging processes $1,000	Able to conduct advanced testing and statistical analysis $1,000	Able to diagnose and repair the most common major malfunctions $1,000	Able to develop production and labour schedules $1,000
Level II	Able to operate all production equipment for dry products $800	Able to package liquid products $800	Able to analyze routine samples and do advanced quality control $800	Able to deal with minor breakdowns and conduct routine maintenance $800	Able to complete basic production and labour reports $800
Level I	Able to operate basic production equipment $600	Able to package dry products $600	Able to collect routine samples and monitor product quality $600	Able to make routine adjustments to all equipment $600	

Examples of Skill Blocks

There are many possible ways to arrange a skill-based system. The Basell Canada Sarnia chemical plant (described in Compensation Today 4.3) has 10 "job knowledge clusters" for the basic operation of the plant. In addition, it has three specialty skills (instrumentation, electrical, and pipefitting), of which all shift team members must select one. To be fully qualified in a specialty skill, team members must complete 40 training modules.

At Basell, a shift team member receives a pay increase when he or she completes one job knowledge cluster and four modules of a specialty skill. Thus, 10 pay raises are possible, beyond the entry-level base pay that each employee receives on joining the company. The amounts of these raises are determined by collective bargaining. Employees can complete the job knowledge clusters in any order, but specialty modules normally have a specified progression. Typically, it takes six or seven years for a shift team member to reach the top rate.

A system of skill blocks can range from simple to complex. A simple system was used by General Mills at a plant producing fruit drinks.[42] There were four main steps in the production process, and each step became a skill block. Within each skill block, there were three skill levels, with a raise for completion of each. Employees could start in any skill block, complete all skill levels within that block, or move to another skill block after accomplishing two levels within that block.

In contrast, a much more complex system was developed at LS Electrogalvanizing. When employees join the firm, they start as a "utility" person and receive a basic entry-level salary, determined by collective bargaining. They start in one of five plant areas (materials entry, process, inspection, delivery, or chemical plant), moving from one to another as they master each one. Completion of each of these five blocks adds one-fifth of the difference between the "utility" wage rate and the "process technician" wage rate (set through collective bargaining) to the employee's salary. Once they master all five blocks, they receive the designation "process technician."

At this point, employees are then expected to choose one of two intermediate skills: process/mechanical or electronic/instrumentation. The skills within each of these intermediate skill blocks are classified as minor skills, medium skills, or major skills. For each minor skill, there is a 2 percent increase in pay; for each medium skill there is a 4 percent increase; and for each major skill there is an 8 percent increase. Once employees have completed 80 percent of their intermediate skill, they may then start work on an advanced skill in one of three areas: mechanical, chemical plant, or electrical.

At Nortel, a much simpler skill-based pay system was used for field service technicians (whose main duty is installation of telecommunications equipment). Nortel built skill sets from existing equipment installation procedure manuals and established four skill blocks in a hierarchy. Field service technicians moved from one to the next, receiving a pay increase when each was accomplished.[43]

But Nortel used a somewhat different process to design a skill-based pay system for technical support engineers, since there was no established set of

Chapter 9: Evaluating Individuals

procedures from which to form the skill blocks. Instead, managers were asked to identify the key dimensions of this work. They came up with seven dimensions: hardware, software, customer database, documentation, network interface, written communication, and interpersonal interaction. For each dimension, they identified and ranked the specific skills needed, from simplest to most complex. They arranged these into four vertical skill blocks, with the first block including the simplest skills for each of the seven dimensions, while the second block included somewhat more complex skills for each dimension, and so on. Engineers received a pay increase on completion of each skill block.

Issues in Designing Skill Blocks

In designing skill blocks, you need to deal with numerous issues. One issue is how many skill blocks to have. In their study, Jenkins and associates found that the average number of skill blocks was 10, but there was a huge range—from 2 to 550.[44] How many skill blocks should there be? There is no clear answer, and it probably varies from case to case; but these researchers did find that the most successful plans had a slightly higher number of skill blocks (an average of 11) than "less successful" plans (an average of nine). Generally, the more complex and diverse the array of skills in a system, the more skill blocks are needed.

How long should it take to master a skill block? There is no empirical evidence on this question. But Jenkins and associates found the average was 20 weeks. This finding suggests that the average plan requires about four to five years to reach the top skill levels. Of course, the more complex the set of skills required, the longer it would take. At LS Electrogalvanizing, the first level, process technician, can be achieved in three to four years; but reaching the top of the system takes much longer. The general consensus on this matter is that for most skill-based pay plans, an employee should be able to progress through the system in no more than six to seven years.

Pricing the Skill Blocks

How are the skill blocks priced? The *relative amount* of increase for each skill block should depend on how difficult it is and/or how long it takes to complete that skill block, and on the value of that skill block to the company. But how is the *absolute amount* of the pay determined? The most common method for determining this is the **high-low method**.

high-low method

determines entry level and skill block pay amounts by pricing comparable entry-level and top-level jobs in the market and allocating the difference to the various skill blocks

Let's use the system depicted in Table 9.3 to illustrate this method. First, the firm would determine the market base pay rates for an entry-level chemical plant operator and for a job that contains all of the skills in level IV. Let's suppose these rates are $40,000 and $50,833. The firm then adjusts these amounts for its pay level strategy—for example, to pay 10 percent above the market at entry level and 20 percent above the market at top level. Thus, the entry-level pay would be $44,000, and the top-level pay would be $61,000, creating a difference of $17,000. This $17,000 would then be allocated across the skill blocks according to their relative importance or the amount of time required to master them, as shown in Table 9.3.

Of course, this process may be complicated by the fact that it is often difficult to find market data for jobs that precisely match the entry-level and top-level skill sets used under the PKS; therefore, finding a suitable match can be a complicated issue. Another question is whether to lead, lag, or match the market, and whether the same policy should apply at the entry and the top levels. In general, entry-level pay has to at least match the market in order to attract employees with the learning abilities needed to progress through the system. Typically, as the individual progresses through the system, pay levels should begin to lead the market as the value of the employee increases. A study by Jenkins and his associates revealed that on average, SBP firms paid somewhat higher than the market median for their entry-level personnel (at the 63rd percentile), and much higher for their employees at the top of the skill grid (90th percentile).[45]

Yet another question is whether all skill blocks should be priced the same. There is no inherent reason why they should be, although some firms are attracted to the simplicity of such a plan. Jenkins and associates found that 40 percent of the skill-based pay plans they examined priced all skill blocks the same.[46]

One final question is whether SBP employees should also be paid on other individual bases, such as seniority or individual merit. For seniority, the answer should almost always be no, because progression by seniority is the antithesis to knowledge-based progression. In most cases, the answer for individual merit pay should also be no, since it is at odds with the team approach that is usually essential for SBP to pay off. The exception to this rule may be where each employee works separately and independently of other employees, as in the case of the Nortel field service technicians discussed earlier.

This is not to say that performance appraisal (beyond the skill certification process) should not be used, but simply that it should generally not be linked to individual raises. In fact, performance appraisal may be useful and even essential to make sure that skill levels are being maintained and to identify and correct substandard performance. Jenkins and associates found that 45 percent of organizations with skill-based pay conducted regular performance appraisals.[47]

However, while seniority or individual merit pay does not fit well with skill-based pay, group- and organization-based performance pay fits very well, as Armstrong has noted.[48] Use of gain sharing or goal sharing can provide SBP employees with a financial reward for the increased productivity they are expected to generate; and profit sharing and stock ownership can help reinforce the citizenship behaviour so critical to the success of skill-based pay systems.

Providing Learning/Training Opportunities

Providing opportunities for employees to learn the requisite skills is essential in skill-based pay systems. Based on his experience, LeBlanc argues that this is the single most difficult issue with pay-for-knowledge plans.[49] Since pay is tied to this skill development, employees will want training opportunities.

Chapter 9: Evaluating Individuals

However, training can be very expensive, both in terms of the direct training costs, and also in terms of time away from the job. This often conflicts with the productivity of the unit, and even with other reward systems.

For example, at Nortel, LeBlanc found that managers were not using the employee training funds that they had been allocated.[50] Why? Time devoted to training reduced the efficiency measures for their departments, so those managers who encouraged the most training for their personnel received the *lowest* performance ratings! The problem was solved by revising the appraisal system so that amount of training undertaken by their subordinates became a positive managerial performance indicator.

Companies using SBP have a wide array of different training techniques to choose from. For example, at LS Electrogalvanizing, training techniques included classroom training, interactive computer-based training, and on-the-job peer training. On-the-job training is generally the largest component in most plans, especially at the lower skill levels. But a problem that frequently arises is "bottle-necking." This occurs because some skills take longer to learn than others, and for some skills there are fewer opportunities to learn them.

For example, there may be a need for only two persons to perform the product-testing function at a given time, with one of them being a skilled employee to teach the unskilled employee; and it may take six months to learn this skill. This may result in a whole queue of employees waiting to have an opportunity to learn this particular job before they can complete their current skill level. This happened at General Mills. Although it was expected that employees could reach the top rate in two to three years, the reality was four to five years, which created employee frustration.[51]

How much paid time off should be provided for off-the-job training? And should employees use some of their own time for training? In general, both are required; but if a high level of job performance and involvement is expected as part of the system, it would be unfair to consume a major portion of an employee's nonwork time for training. Often, the tradeoff made is that work time is provided for training for the lower-skill levels; but at the top skill levels, where classroom training often plays a major role, work time may not be provided, although out-of-pocket costs, such as tuition fees, are almost always covered.

Certifying Skill/Knowledge Block Achievement

A key issue for any firm using skill-based pay is to have a valid system for determining when an employee has mastered a particular skill block (a process known as **skill certification**) that is both valid and accepted as fair by employees. In some cases, an employee must spend a minimum period of time working at a particular skill before certification is granted. The purpose of this rule is to ensure proficiency in the skill and to provide enough reinforcement in that skill to make sure that it is retained.

Skill certification systems vary dramatically in their complexity and processes. Basell Canada has a relatively straightforward three-step process. All employees are provided with self-training materials indicating the certification requirements for each skill block. When employees are ready to be

skill certification

the testing process that determines whether an individual has achieved a given skill block

Part III: Determining Compensation Values

tested, they must ask a fellow employee (already certified for that skill) to confirm that they are ready. If the shift team coordinator agrees, the final checkoff is done by staff experts who specialize in the certification process.

LS Electrogalvanizing uses detailed checklists for certifying each skill block. To be certified in one of the five basic skill blocks, an employee must work for 1200 hours in that block. At 1000 hours, a formal peer review is undertaken to gauge progress and to provide feedback on areas needing improvement. After 1200 hours, an employee may apply to be certified for that skill block. To do so, he or she must receive a positive checkoff by five other certified operators and then by the process coordinator. Overall, it takes three to four years to complete the five skill blocks necessary to become a "process technician."

Nortel uses a different process to certify field service technicians. Peer assessment is not used because technicians generally work alone. Instead, at regular intervals, the supervisor conducts a four-step procedure. First is a "preassessment meeting" with the technician, during which skill accomplishments acquired since the previous review are discussed. Training and development needs for reaching the next skill block are also assessed. Next, the supervisor conducts a field assessment in which technicians demonstrate their proficiencies on the job. Third, the supervisor presents a report on these accomplishments to an assessment committee of experienced managers, who decide whether advancement to the next skill level is warranted. After this, the results are fed back to the technician in a "postassessment" meeting. If dissatisfied with the outcome, the technician may appeal to the assessment committee.

In contrast, at General Mills, the system is almost completely peer based. Peer trainers use detailed checklists to certify employees. Although there is a possible concern that employees may "go easy" on each other to avoid conflict, the company does not believe this is a major problem due to the safeguards in the system.[52] First, all team members must ratify the certification. Second, employees must requalify whenever they rotate back into the skill again. Third, if an employee is found to be unable to perform skills for which she or he is certified, the employee *and* the certifier forgo their next pay increase. And fourth, the plant manager has final authority for approving certifications, although he or she has rarely felt the need to disapprove any.

Other Skill-Based Pay Issues

Two other issues are important to the success of a skill-based pay plan. First, almost all such plans require considerable refinement after initial implementation, so it is important to monitor them on an ongoing basis. Many firms have found that the ideal vehicle is a joint employee–management committee, such as used at LS Electrogalvanizing.

The other issue is that many human resource and management practices have to fit with the skill-based pay system if it is to pay off for the organization. The example at Nortel illustrates how changing one aspect of the system (adding SBP) can be hindered by failure to change other parts (the managers' performance appraisal criteria). Another example is hiring practices, where ability to perform the entry-level job (previous experience) should not be the sole criterion for selection. Instead, the key recruitment needs are for employees with the ability to master all the necessary skills, willingness to learn, ability to help and teach others, and disposition to work cooperatively in a group setting. For this reason, many SBP firms give the group or team a major role in the hiring process. In general, the whole range of human resource practices characterized by the high-involvement managerial strategy need to be in place for SBP to realize its full potential.

Competency-Based Pay Systems

Many firms are now attempting to apply the concept of pay for knowledge to their professional and managerial personnel through the use of **competency-based pay systems**. These can vary greatly in format. For example, a defence electronics firm has a master list of more than 30 competencies that apply to professional and managerial staff, and each department selects those most relevant to its operations.[53] Pay raises are tied to achievement of each competency. In another case, a manufacturing firm pays managers for their degree of progress in mastering four managerial competencies deemed applicable to all managerial jobs. In a third case, professional and managerial employees negotiate "learning contracts" with their supervisor, and pay increases are based on accomplishment of these objectives.

In general, competency-based systems are much more problematic than skill-based systems. First of all, virtually nothing is known about their effectiveness. This lack of research is partly due to the enormous confusion and lack of precision about just what constitutes a "competency-based system." In addition, some systems appear to be little more than a trait-rating appraisal system under a new guise. For example, one list of possible "competencies" might include personality traits such as "self-confidence" and "assertiveness" as well as "flexibility" and "initiative."[54] Although personality traits can be assessed with established psychometric measures, these measures work better as part of the selection process than as part of an ongoing competency-based pay program.

Thus, part of the problem of researching competency-based systems is the wide variation in definitions of "competencies." The following definition is adopted here: "competencies are demonstrable characteristics of the person, including knowledge, skills, and behaviours, that enable performance."[55] Of course, a legitimate question is: Why not just pay people for their performance, rather than factors at least one step removed from performance? An answer is that individual performance can be difficult or even counterproductive to measure. Another answer is that identifying valid competencies can serve as the basis for an effective training and development program. When specific competencies have a dollar value, both administrative and employee attention is focused on exactly what needs to be learned; and there is no doubt that this attention can increase the rate of skill development.

In developing any competency-based pay system, there are four main issues: (1) identifying competencies that demonstrably affect performance;

competency-based pay

pay that is based on the knowledge, skills, and behaviours, rather than performance, of individual employees

(2) devising methods to measure achievement of each competency; (3) compensating each competency; and (4) providing learning opportunities. Unfortunately, many so-called "competency-based" systems fail on all four counts.

Many consulting companies sell "competency-based" systems that are simply menus of any kind of trait imaginable. Firms are expected to select "appropriate" competencies from this menu, whether or not they are valid for that employer. A sounder process is to develop a list of competencies that distinguish high performers from other employees in a particular occupational group, test all employees in that group on the presence of these competencies, and then statistically identify the competencies that differentiate the top performers from the other employees. Of course, to do this, you must already have valid performance measures for each employee. Another potential problem with this approach is that it is only valid as long as the factors that differentiated performance in the past continue to be valid.

The second issue is measurement. It may be difficult to develop reliable and valid measures for some competencies that will be perceived as fair by employees.

Third, effectively linking achievement of competencies to pay is not straightforward, because there is no generally accepted method for so doing, unlike for skill-based pay. If a statistical process has been used to identify the key competencies, these data can be used to determine the relative weighting of each competency relative to performance. However, deciding the absolute dollar value for each competency is highly subjective, because there is no external test equivalent to the high-low method used for skill-based pay. Whether to reward achievement of competencies with raises to base pay or with one-shot bonuses is another question. If a competency is likely to be enduring, then an increase to base pay seems in order; if not, a one-shot bonus would be appropriate. Overall, a simple way of linking competencies to pay is to factor achievement of competencies into an existing merit raise system.[56]

The fourth issue, providing learning opportunities, is not necessarily straightforward either, because some competencies are more inherent than learnable. But as with skill-based pay, providing opportunities to develop key competencies is essential to success of the system.

Finally, not all organizations need all employees to have the full range of competencies possessed by top performers. Thus, an overambitious competency-based pay system may cause a firm to pay for capabilities it cannot use, leading to employee frustration and higher costs to the employer.

Summary

The pay for a given employee is a function of the internal value of their job (i.e., as determined by job evaluation), the external value of their job (i.e., as determined by market surveys), and the individual's contribution to the job in terms of performance and capabilities. This chapter focused on the third element in determining compensation values. It explained how to develop processes for evaluating the performance level and the skill/knowledge level of employees so that they can then be compensated accordingly. Accurate evaluation of individual performance is essential for a successful merit pay system, while accurate evaluation of individual skills and competencies is essential for a successful pay-for-knowledge system.

You have learned how creating a reliable and valid performance appraisal system is fraught with difficulties and how many firms are dissatisfied with current appraisal processes. Part of the problem is that linking individual merit pay to performance appraisal (or even use of individual merit pay itself) is not appropriate in many circumstances. Performance appraisal can be applied effectively only where performance has scope to vary, where employees can control their performance levels, and where individual performance can be separated out and accurately assessed. In addition, you have learned that evaluating individual performance in a team context is a particularly thorny matter, although necessary in some instances.

You now understand the many threats to the accuracy of performance appraisal, some of them intentional. Managers usually view performance appraisal within the context of their overall task objectives, and accuracy of performance appraisal is often secondary to the achievement of their managerial goals.

Another potential source of appraisal problems is the appraisal method itself, of which there are many. Although no method is perfect, some methods are more reliable and valid than others; and the key is to select the method that fits best with the purpose of the appraisal system, the nature of the behaviour being evaluated, and the organizational context in which it is applied. The same is true for selecting the most appropriate individuals to actually conduct the appraisals, which may include not only superiors, but peers, subordinates, and even customers.

When pay is to be based on performance appraisal, you must develop a method for effectively linking pay to the appraisal results. But you will still have to deal with other issues before completing the design of the merit system, including the frequency of appraisals, feedback, mechanisms for procedural justice, procedures for rater training, and a system to evaluate the merit system itself.

The second part of the chapter discussed the process for creating effective pay-for-knowledge systems, noting a distinction between skill-based pay (which is focused at the production or service provision level) and competency-based pay (which is focused at the managerial or professional level). You have learned that in skill-based pay systems, the type of job or industry is less important than an organizational context in which high-involvement management is practised. To develop a successful skill-based pay system, you must do several things: design the skill blocks, price these blocks, provide learning opportunities, certify skill achievement, and ensure a context that provides complementary human resource practices.

In contrast to skill-based pay, competency-based pay is a less well-defined and less-proven concept, with little or no evidence on its effectiveness. At the moment, there are many difficulties in using it effectively for pay purposes, although numerous firms appear to be using it effectively for training and development purposes.

Key Terms

behaviourally anchored rating scales (BARS), 348

behavioural observation scales (BOS), 349

central tendency error, 341

competency-based pay, 376

contrast effect, 341

critical incident method, 346

forced choice method, 347

forced distribution method, 343

graphic rating scale, 344

halo error, 341

harshness effect, 342

high-low method, 372

individual/team merit grid, 368

leniency effect, 342

management by objectives (MBO), 351

merit pay grid (merit pay matrix), 358

mixed standard scales, 348

paired comparison method, 343

performance appraisal, 337

performance checklist method, 346

performance distribution assessment, 350

performance management, 352

recency effect, 341

similarity effect, 342

skill certification, 374

skill/knowledge blocks, 370

360-degree feedback, 356

Web Links

A set of free tools and resources for conducting performance appraisals is available at **http://www.businessballs.com/performanceappraisals.htm**. (p. 342)

To find some good examples of performance indicators that can be used in a team context, go to **http://www.zigonperf.com/**. (p. 367)

RPC Icon

RPC 9.1 Establishes compensation policies and procedures based on the compensation program, and in compliance with the legal framework.

Discussion Questions

1. One alleged problem with performance appraisal is that most employees seem to think they are above average and do not like to be told otherwise. Do you think this is actually true, and, if so, how could you design an appraisal system that might avoid this problem?

2. Take several jobs that you or other members of your class have held or are currently holding. Using the conditions that suit the use of merit pay listed in Compensation Notebook 9.2, discuss which of these jobs are suited to merit pay and which are not.

3. Discuss the key issues in designing a skill-based pay system. Which issues do you think would be the most difficult to deal with effectively?

Using the Internet

1. On the website **http://www.businessballs.com/ performanceappraisalform.pdf**, you will find a template for a performance appraisal form. Using the material in this chapter, assess the pros and cons of this form. Which type of performance appraisal method do you think that it represents?

Exercise

1. In groups of six to eight people, share your experiences with performance appraisal. Group members who have been subject to a performance appraisal system should indicate whether they believe that their performance was fairly evaluated, and, if not, why not. After that, the groups should come together and discuss the overall experience of class members with performance appraisal. How many members believe that they were fairly appraised, how many members believe that they were not fairly appraised, and what were the differences between fair and unfair appraisal systems?

Case Questions

1. "Henderson Printing" in the Appendix currently has no formal performance appraisal system. The CEO, Georgette Henderson, thinks that a performance appraisal system might be useful, and she has hired you to assess the company and recommend whether to implement one. She also wants to know whether she should link pay to the appraisals. She expects your report to include the pros and cons of each idea, along with a detailed justification for your recommendations.
2. Ms. Henderson has decided to go ahead with a performance appraisal system, and she has decided to link it to merit pay. Impressed with your earlier work for the company (see Question 1), she has hired you to design the performance appraisal system and a merit pay system that would be linked to it. She expects your report to be sufficiently comprehensive so that it could serve as the blueprint for the implementation of these systems.
3. At "The Fit Stop," described in the Appendix, CEO Susan Superfit has decided to implement a pay-for-knowledge system for her sales staff. Hearing of your excellent work from Georgette Henderson, she has hired you to design the system. She expects your report to be comprehensive and detailed, containing all the necessary steps for implementing the system and providing justification for each aspect of your proposed system.

Simulation Cross-Reference

If you are using *Strategic Compensation: A Simulation* in conjunction with this text, you will find that the concepts in Chapter 9 are helpful in preparing Sections C, E, J, and K of the simulation.

Endnotes

1. Kane, Jeffrey S., and Kimberly F. Kane. 1993. "Performance Appraisal." In H.J. Bernardin and J.E.A. Russell, eds., *Human Resource Management: An Experimental Approach*. New York: McGraw-Hill, 378.
2. Kane, Jeffrey S., and Kimberly F. Kane. 1993. "Performance Appraisal." In H.J. Bernardin and J.E.A. Russell, eds., *Human Resource Management: An Experimental Approach*. New York: McGraw-Hill, 377–404.
3. Bohl, Don L. 1996. "Minisurvey: 360-Degree Appraisals Yield Superior Results." *Compensation & Benefits Review*, 28(5).
4. *Human Resources Management in Canada*. 2000. "Performance Appraisals Get Thumbs Down." Report Bulletin 208: 4.
5. Not surprisingly, use of performance appraisal is much lower in small firms, as only 38 percent of firms with less than 100 employees reported having formal performance appraisal. See Wagar, Terry H. and Lynn Langrock. 2004. "Performance Appraisal and Compensation in Small Firms." *Canadian HR Reporter*, 17(14): 10.
6. Coens, Tom, and Mary Jenkins. 2000. *Abolishing Performance Appraisals: Why They Backfire and What to Do Instead*. San Francisco: Berrett-Koehler Publishers.
7. Lawler, Edward E. 2000. *Rewarding Excellence: Pay Strategies for the New Economy*. San Francisco: Jossey-Bass.
8. Longenecker, Clinton O., H.P. Sims, and D.A. Gioia. 1987. "Behind the Mask: The Politics of Employee Appraisal." *Academy of Management Executive*, 1: 183–93.
9. Longenecker, Clinton O., H.P. Sims, and D.A. Gioia. 1987. "Behind the Mask: The Politics of Employee Appraisal." *Academy of Management Executive*, 1: 185.
10. Longenecker, Clinton O., H.P. Sims, and D.A. Gioia. 1987. "Behind the Mask: The Politics of Employee Appraisal." *Academy of Management Executive*, 1: 183.
11. Longenecker, Clinton, and Dean Ludwig. 1995. "Ethical Dilemmas in Performance Appraisal Revisited." In Jacky Holloway, Jenny Lewis, and Geoff Mallory, eds., *Performance Measurement and Evaluation*, London: Sage Publications, 66–77.
12. Scullen, Steven E., Michael K. Mount, and Maynard Goff. 2000. "Understanding the Latent Structure of Job Performance Ratings." *Journal of Applied Psychology*, 85(6): 956–70.
13. Kane, Jeffrey S., and Kimberly F. Kane. 1993. "Performance Appraisal." In H.J. Bernardin and J.E.A. Russell, eds., *Human Resource Management: An Experimental Approach*. New York: McGraw-Hill, 377–404.
14. Latham, Gary P., and Kenneth N. Wexley. 1994. *Increasing Productivity through Performance Appraisal*. Reading, MA: Addison-Wesley, 51.
15. Murphy, Kevin R., and Jeanette N. Cleveland. 1995. *Understanding Performance Appraisal*. Thousand Oaks, CA: Sage Publications.
16. Bernardin, H. John, and Richard W. Beatty. 1984. *Performance Appraisal: Assessing Human Behaviour at Work*. Boston: Kent Publishing.
17. Latham, Gary P., and Kenneth N. Wexley. 1994. *Increasing Productivity through Performance Appraisal*. Reading, MA: Addison-Wesley, 51.
18. Weiss, Tracey B. 2000. "Performance Management." In Lance A. Berger and Dorothy R. Berger, eds., *The Compensation Handbook*. New York: McGraw-Hill, 429–42.

19. Tyson, David E. 2005. *Carswell's Compensation Guide*. Toronto: Thomson Publishing.
20. Baarda, Carolyn. 2000. *Compensation Planning Outlook 2001*. Ottawa: Conference Board of Canada.
21. Tyson, David E. 2005. *Carswell's Compensation Guide*. Toronto: Thomson Publishing, 19-3.
22. Latham, Gary P., and Soosan D. Latham. 2001. "The Importance of Performance Management to Productivity." *HR.com eBulletin*, June 11: www.hr.com.
23. Scullen, Steven E., Michael K. Mount, and Maynard Goff. 2000. "Understanding the Latent Structure of Job Performance Ratings." *Journal of Applied Psychology*, 85(6): 956–70.
24. Peiperl, Maury A. 2001. "Getting 360° Feedback Right." *Harvard Business Review*, 79(1):143.
25. Southworth, Natalie. 2001. "Managers Crucial to Curbing Turnover." *The Globe and Mail*, May 30: M1.
26. Scullen, Steven E., Michael K. Mount, and Maynard Goff. 2000. "Understanding the Latent Structure of Job Performance Ratings." *Journal of Applied Psychology*, 85(6): 956–70.
27. Kane, Jeffrey S., and Kimberly F. Kane. 1993. "Performance Appraisal." In H.J. Bernardin and J.E.A. Russell, eds., *Human Resource Management: An Experimental Approach*. New York: McGraw-Hill, 377–404.
28. Kruger, Justin, and David Dunning. 1999. "Unskilled and Unaware of It: Difficulties in Recognizing One's Own Incompetence Lead to Inflated Self-Assessments." *Journal of Personality and Social Psychology*, 77(6):1121–34.
29. Kane, Jeffrey S., and Kimberly F. Kane. 1993. "Performance Appraisal." In H.J. Bernardin and J.E.A. Russell, eds., *Human Resource Management: An Experimental Approach*. New York: McGraw-Hill, 377–404.
30. Edwards, Mark R., and Ann J. Ewen. 1996. *360° Feedback*. New York: Amacom.
31. Bohl, Don L. 1996. "Minisurvey: 360-Degree Appraisals Yield Superior Results." *Compensation & Benefits Review*, 28(5).
32. Edwards, Mark R., and Ann J. Ewen. 1996. *360° Feedback*. New York: Amacom.
33. Bohl, Don L. 1996. "Minisurvey: 360-Degree Appraisals Yield Superior Results." *Compensation & Benefits Review*, 28(5).
34. Bracken, David W., Carol W. Timmreck, John W. Fleenor, and Lynn Summers. 2001. "360 Degree Feedback from Another Angle." *Human Resource Management*, 40(1): 3–20.
35. Lawler, Edward E. 2000. *Rewarding Excellence: Pay Strategies for the New Economy*. San Francisco: Jossey-Bass.
36. Baarda, Carolyn. 2000. *Compensation Planning Outlook 2001*. Ottawa: Conference Board of Canada.
37. Findley, Henry M., William F. Giles, and Kevin W. Mossholder. 2000. "Performance Appraisal Process and System Facets: Relationships with Contextual Performance." *Journal of Applied Psychology*, 85(4): 634–40.
38. Jawahar, I.M. 2001. "Antecedents and Potential Consequences of Satisfaction with Performance Appraisal Interview." *Proceedings of the Annual Conference of the Administrative Sciences Association of Canada (Human Resources Division)*, 22(9): 45–54.
39. Zigon, Jack. 2000. "Measuring the Hard Stuff: Teams and Other Hard to Measure Work." In Lance A. Berger and Dorothy R. Berger, eds., *The Compensation Handbook*. New York: McGraw-Hill, 443–66.
40. Tyson, David E. 2005. *Carswell's Compensation Guide*. Toronto: Thomson Publishing.
41. Jenkins, G. Douglas, Gerald E. Ledford, Nina Gupta, and D. Harold Doty. 1992. *Skill-Based Pay: Practices, Payoffs, Pitfalls, and Prescriptions*, Scottsdale, AZ: American Compensation Association.
42. Ledford, Gerald E., and Gary Bergel. 1991. "Skill-Based Pay Case Number 1: General Mills." *Compensation and Benefits Review*, 23(2): 24–38.
43. LeBlanc, Peter V. 1991. "Skill-Based Pay Case Number 2: Northern Telecom." *Compensation and Benefits Review*, 23(2): 39–56.

44. Jenkins, G. Douglas, Gerald E. Ledford, Nina Gupta, and D. Harold Doty. 1992. *Skill-Based Pay: Practices, Payoffs, Pitfalls, and Prescriptions.* Scottsdale, AZ: American Compensation Association.
45. Jenkins, G. Douglas, Gerald E. Ledford, Nina Gupta, and D. Harold Doty. 1992. *Skill-Based Pay: Practices, Payoffs, Pitfalls, and Prescriptions.* Scottsdale, AZ: American Compensation Association.
46. Jenkins, G. Douglas, Gerald E. Ledford, Nina Gupta, and D. Harold Doty. 1992. *Skill-Based Pay: Practices, Payoffs, Pitfalls, and Prescriptions.* Scottsdale, AZ: American Compensation Association.
47. Jenkins, G. Douglas, Gerald E. Ledford, Nina Gupta, and D. Harold Doty. 1992. *Skill-Based Pay: Practices, Payoffs, Pitfalls, and Prescriptions.* Scottsdale, AZ: American Compensation Association.
48. Armstrong, Ann. 1991. "The Design and Implementation of Skill-Based Systems." *Proceedings of the Administrative Sciences Association of Canada, Personnel and Human Resources Division,* 12(8): 21–31.
49. LeBlanc, Peter V. 1991. "Skill-Based Pay Case Number 2: Northern Telecom." *Compensation and Benefits Review,* 23(2): 39–56.
50. LeBlanc, Peter V. 1991. "Skill-Based Pay Case Number 2: Northern Telecom." *Compensation and Benefits Review,* 23(2): 39–56.
51. Ledford, Gerald E., and Gary Bergel. 1991. "Skill-Based Pay Case Number 1: General Mills." *Compensation and Benefits Review,* 23(2): 24–38.
52. Ledford, Gerald E., and Gary Bergel. 1991. "Skill-Based Pay Case Number 1: General Mills." *Compensation and Benefits Review,* 23(2): 24–38.
53. Ledford, Gerald E., and Robert L. Heneman. 2000. "Pay for Skills, Knowledge, and Competencies." In Lance A. Berger and Dorothy R. Berger, eds., *The Compensation Handbook.* New York: McGraw-Hill, 143–56.
54. Williams, Richard S. 1998. *Performance Management.* London: International Thompson Business Press.
55. Ledford, Gerald E., and Robert L. Heneman. 2000. "Pay for Skills, Knowledge, and Competencies." In Lance A. Berger and Dorothy R. Berger, eds., *The Compensation Handbook.* New York: McGraw-Hill, 143–56.
56. Brown, Duncan. 2000. "Relating Competencies to Pay." In Lance A. Berger and Dorothy R. Berger, eds., *The Compensation Handbook.* New York: McGraw-Hill, 157–71.

PART FOUR

Designing Performance Pay and Indirect Pay

Chapter 10

Designing Performance Pay Plans

Chapter Learning Objectives

After reading this chapter, you should be able to:

- Identify and discuss the pros and cons of two important types of targeted incentives.
- Discuss the pros and cons of using promotions as an incentive.
- Identify the main types of gain-sharing plans and key issues in their design.
- Identify the main types of goal-sharing plans and key issues in their design.
- Identify the main types of profit-sharing plans and key issues in their design.
- Identify the main types of employee stock plans and key issues in their design.
- Discuss the role that nonmonetary rewards may play in motivating employees.

In the 1980s, a young, aggressive software company wanted a tool to help it attract and motivate young, dedicated employees who would be willing to stick with the firm and do whatever it takes to make the company successful. As part of their compensation strategy, they offered generous employee stock plans, where employees would acquire significant holdings in the company. At the time, no one knew whether this would end up being a bonanza or a bust for the employees. In many cases like this, the company doesn't make it, and the shares become virtually worthless.

In this case, the story had a very happy ending for employees. The company was Microsoft, and by 1996 virtually all of the company's original employees (and many of the later ones) had become millionaires. By 2005, it was estimated that Microsoft had created more than 10 000 millionaires through its employee stock plans.[1] Ironically, now that they are independently wealthy, many of these employees have left Microsoft to pursue a wide variety of their life goals, ranging from philanthropy to starting their own businesses. However, many others stay, because Microsoft pays a lot of attention to providing jobs and a work environment that are intrinsically motivating. Microsoft has always understood that there is more to motivation than money.

Introduction

Not every employee stock plan works out as well as it did at Microsoft. How can we design an employee stock plan that is likely to be successful, benefiting both the company and its employees? What are the key issues to consider in designing such a plan?

Or perhaps an employee stock plan does not fit the organization, but another type of performance pay does. This chapter identifies and discusses some of the key issues in designing performance pay plans, whether they are plans geared to organizational performance, such as employee stock plans; to group performance, such as gain sharing plans; or to individual performance.

However, because earlier chapters have covered individual performance pay plans, this chapter focuses on some of the major group and organizational pay plans, namely gain-sharing, goal-sharing, profit-sharing, and employee stock plans. The chapter also discusses employee reward programs that don't involve cash payments. As you understand by now, money is not the only valued reward an organization may offer!

RPC 10.1

Targeted Incentives and Promotions as Incentives

But first, we will examine two types of individual performance incentives that have not been extensively discussed earlier in the book, namely special purpose (targeted) incentives and the use of promotions as incentives.

Special-Purpose (Targeted) Incentives

In order to foster behaviours of particular importance to an organization or to counteract behaviours that are causing problems, some firms have developed targeted incentive programs, such as the Green Giant insect bonus plan described in Chapter 1. Although targeted incentives can be used for a wide variety of purposes, perhaps the most common are suggestion programs (to encourage creativity) and attendance programs (to discourage absenteeism).

Incentives for Attendance

Because of a concern with employee absenteeism in recent years, some organizations have started providing incentives for regular attendance.[2] For example, a 2001 collective agreement between La-Z-Boy Canada (makers of the famous recliners) and its union included a new clause providing for an attendance bonus. Employees who do not have absences in a calendar year receive eight hours of their base rate deposited into their RRSP account.

While attendance plans vary, one approach is to provide a bonus or prize to employees who have a perfect attendance record in a given time period. One interesting system was used by a manufacturing plant.[3] Each day that an employee came to work on time, he or she was allowed to draw one card from a deck of playing cards. At the end of the week, the employee with the best five-card poker hand in each department received a cash prize. This plan was found to reduce absenteeism by about 18 percent; but since the period under study was quite short, it is not clear whether this result would hold up over the longer run.

Indeed, one interesting question centres around what would happen if a firm implemented and then discontinued its attendance incentive. According to attribution theory, attendance might actually end up *lower* than before the program was instituted, since any intrinsic motivation to attend would have been eliminated by the economic attendance incentive (as in the case of the elderly man and the boisterous children discussed in Chapter 3). There is no evidence on this, but attribution theory would predict that the greater the intrinsic motivation prior to the implementation of the attendance program, the greater the negative impact of the program's discontinuation. Therefore, attendance programs are less risky for organizations in which intrinsic motivation is low in the first place. (Of course, if intrinsic motivation is high, attendance shouldn't be a problem anyway.)

There are some other more obvious drawbacks to attendance plans. First, of course, is the cost of the bonus. Second is the extra paperwork. Third, once an individual becomes ineligible for the bonus (by exceeding the number of allowable absences), he/she no longer has any incentive to curtail absences during the review period. Fourth is the issue of whether "legitimate" absences should detract from the record, and if so, how they should be defined and verified. Fifth, many employers have a philosophical objection to paying extra for something (attendance) that should be taken as a given.

But perhaps the greatest drawback is that the incentive plan may only treat symptoms without getting at the true source of the problem. If absenteeism really is a problem, a first step is to try to understand the cause. The assumption underlying attendance incentive programs is that absenteeism is caused by a lack of will to attend on the part of the employee. That may be partly true; but are there other reasons for absenteeism, and are there more appropriate solutions?

For example, we know that reward and job dissatisfaction affect absenteeism, and high absenteeism may just be the tip of the iceberg of underlying and more serious problems facing the organization.[4] One possibility is that the workplace itself may be responsible for an excessive number of accidents or injuries, or it may provide conditions that promote illness. For example, the work may be highly stressful, or employees may not want to face another day of boring, tedious, or repetitive work.

Research shows that jobs that place high demands on employees but allow them little or no control over how to respond to these demands produce high stress. It also shows that jobs with low intrinsic rewards (i.e., low levels of skill variety, task identity, task significance, feedback, and worker autonomy) are less attractive to most employees and generate higher absenteeism. In other cases, the work environment may be unpleasant, the boss unreasonable or oppressive, customers surly or abusive, and relations among co-workers poor. In addition, as discussed in Chapter 3, dissatisfaction with the compensation system may cause attendance problems. As well, any or all of these factors may also lead to negative group norms about attendance, which Gellatly and Luchak have found to have strong negative effects on individual attendance behaviour.[5] Addressing the root causes of attendance problems is likely to be more successful than simply dealing with the symptoms.

Absences can be classified into four main categories according to their root causes. First, there is absence due to sickness or injury. Second, an individual may be experiencing personal problems, such as depression or alcohol or drug abuse. Third, absences may be due to a need to deal with family responsibilities, such as a sick child. As the number of dual-income families has increased, this has become a major problem for many families. Fourth are absences for discretionary reasons, better known as "goofing off."

In some cases, sick leave policies themselves may be at fault and may actually encourage absences. For example, employees may be docked pay if they arrive late, but receive no penalty if they call in sick for the whole day. One study cited the example of a firm in which "many people make a point of using up their full sickness benefit of 10 days per year, even when they are obviously not sick."[6]

Aside from the costs of unnecessary absenteeism, a major concern is that of equity. Employees who are consistently present may actually be penalized for their good attendance by having to do the work of the absentees. This won't be much of an incentive to continue their own good attendance!

Some companies have found workable solutions to these problems. An Ontario company improved its attendance by 30 percent by lengthening the period necessary to qualify for sick pay and by providing a cash attendance bonus for absences of 12 hours or less during a given quarter.[7] Another firm improved absenteeism simply by requiring employees to speak directly to their supervisor for a brief interview if time is to be missed.[8]

One potential solution to some types of absenteeism is flextime. There are various systems under which employees can adjust their workday to allow them to take care of personal matters, such as medical appointments. Flextime systems have been shown to reduce absenteeism, and often have the side benefit of improving productivity.[9] Another possible solution is the development of employee assistance programs. Some employers have established employee health and fitness programs and have found a correlation between fitness, health, and absenteeism. For example, after Alberta Blue Cross instituted a wellness program, average annual days lost dropped from 5.5 to 4.1.[10]

Of course, an alternative way of dealing with absenteeism is to simply dismiss employees who have an excessive number of absences. But the downside is that the company loses some employees who might be valuable if their absenteeism problem could have been corrected. In some cases, establishing that absences were not legitimate can be very difficult. Recent privacy legislation has further complicated the matter of verifying the legitimacy of absences. In unionized workplaces, employees cannot be fired unless the company proves that the absences were not justified, and doing so in a non-union setting could invite an "unjust dismissal" charge. The legal doctrine of "duty to accommodate" has also greatly restricted the ability of an employer to terminate employees who are frequently absent for various health reasons, including mental health reasons.

Another approach to controlling absenteeism is to link attendance to bonus pay. (Employees on hourly pay, or piece rates, are automatically docked for absenteeism, which is seen as a major advantage of these systems.) For example, Belcher describes a gain-sharing plan in which individuals lose a portion of their group gain-sharing bonus if their attendance falls below allowable limits.[11] In one case, at an automotive plant, one day's absence (for any reason) during a six-month payout period reduced the individual's bonus allotment by 25 percent, two days by 50 percent, and three days of absence wiped it out.

While such a system may provide an incentive for attendance, it does have several drawbacks. First, if the gain-sharing system produces no bonuses for anybody in the given time period, then the penalty for absence disappears. Second, for those who miss three days, there is no incentive not to miss more. Third, it may be seen as unfair for dedicated workers to lose their entire bonus because of real illness. Fourth, gain sharing may have no meaning for any employee who misses more than two days in a six-month period. Adding the attendance rider to the gain-sharing plan decreases the perceived probability of a linkage between performance and reward; and motivation theory predicts that this will result in reduced motivation.

In short, a plan like this may end up effectively destroying the value of gain sharing without providing significant improvements in attendance. For these reasons, it is probably best to keep absenteeism control programs separate from other types of performance pay programs.

Attendance incentives are likely to suit some organizations more than others, depending on the causes of attendance problems. Of course, in some instances, attendance should not be an issue—what counts is getting the work done, and whether or not an employee physically appears at the workplace may be irrelevant. For high-involvement organizations, there will be very little voluntary absenteeism. If these companies have problems with attendance, the problems are not likely due to a simple lack of will to attend. Thus, attendance programs are likely to do more harm than good for these organizations by implying that employees are shirking their duties and by reducing intrinsic motivation.

Incentives for Creativity

suggestion system

an incentive plan through which employees receive cash bonuses for submitting money-saving suggestions

Suggestion systems are intended to promote and reward innovative thinking by employees. In general, if an employee has a suggestion that may improve organizational effectiveness, she or he submits it through the suggestion system. It is then evaluated by a committee, and if it is implemented the employee receives a percentage (usually between 10 to 20 percent) of the projected cost savings during the first year. When the savings from the suggestion are difficult to compute, a standard lump sum is awarded. Thus, suggestion systems have three components: a system through which suggestions are channelled, a systematic process for evaluating them, and an incentive for submitting usable ideas.

Many Canadian firms use such plans. A Statistics Canada survey of Canadian workplaces employing at least 100 employees indicated that 47 percent of them had suggestion plans as of 2001. However, these plans have several problematic issues. First, unless the reasons for rejecting a suggestion are fully explained to and accepted by the submitter, there may be considerable resentment and a reluctance to contribute further suggestions. Second, employees may feel that the amount of the award is not equitable. Indeed, it is often difficult to arrive at a fair reward for a given suggestion. Third, supervisors or staff specialists may resent employees who make suggestions, feeling that this reflects negatively on their own performance.

Fourth, co-workers may resent the individual making the suggestion if it disrupts former work practices. Fifth, there is the issue of who receives the credit for the idea, since it may have been developed by several individuals. In some cases, employees (including supervisors) have been accused by other employees of "stealing" their ideas. As a result, some organizations have implemented group-based suggestion and incentive schemes.

Of course, the underlying assumption of these systems is that people have useful suggestions but are currently not motivated to submit them without the carrot of the incentive. This assumption is most likely to apply to classical and, to some extent, to human relations organizations. Ironically, the problems with these systems, such as managerial or employee resentment and conflict, are most likely to occur in classical organizations, which may help to explain why many classical organizations do not bother with these incentives and do not find them useful when they do adopt them.

In a high-involvement organization, because of the internalized commitment of members and because of participation in gain-sharing, profit-sharing, and employee stock plans, employees are likely willing to submit useful suggestions regardless whether there are special bonuses. So a suggestion bonus system is probably most useful to human relations organizations.

There has been very little research evaluating the effectiveness of employee suggestion plans. However, a study based on Statistics Canada data showed that suggestion systems had a significant positive impact on workplace profitability, but only in firms not pursuing an innovator competitive strategy.[12] Rather surprisingly, among firms pursuing an innovator strategy, suggestion systems had no significant effect on profitability.

Another important result of this study was that combining a suggestion system with a group-based pay system enhanced the effectiveness of the suggestion system, but only for firms not pursuing innovator strategies. One possible reason for these results is that in firms not pursuing an innovator strategy, the key competitive factors are usually some combination of product/service quality and product/service cost, both of which can be readily influenced by employees. However, for firms pursuing innovator strategies, so many factors affect profitability that employee suggestions are less likely to play a major role in profitability.

Suggestion systems accompanied by group-based pay are generally group systems, under which all employees in a work unit or team share in the bonuses resulting from useful suggestions. McAdams compared traditional individual-based suggestion plans with team-based suggestion plans that give nonmonetary rewards (such as merchandise or travel awards) to entire teams for suggestions made by team members. He found that team-based suggestion plans resulted in a much higher employee participation rate (the percentage of employees submitting suggestions) than the traditional plans, and a much higher value of each adopted suggestion. Although many of the team plans were short-term and experienced a drop in participation rates over time, they continued to produce many more suggestions than traditional individual-based systems.[13]

Group suggestion systems are further discussed later in the chapter, in the context of gain-sharing systems, many of which formally incorporate group suggestion systems into their plans.

Promotions as Incentives

Since promotions usually bring extra pay, many organizations use them as their major reward for superior performance. They expect a "promotion from within" policy to be a key factor in motivating good employee performance. And, in fact, the great majority of employees believe "promotion from within" policies are important to recognize the contributions existing employees have made to the firm. To refuse existing employees fair consideration for promotional opportunities would be very demotivating.

However, depending on promotions as the main source of rewards for good employee performance can cause problems. First, heavy reliance on promotions in lieu of other rewards can result in a meaningless reward system if the organization has few upper-level vacancies. This is particularly a problem in firms that are expanding slowly or not at all or that are deliberately reducing their hierarchy in order to cut costs or to move toward a high-involvement managerial strategy. Even in expanding firms, only rarely do they have sufficient upper-level vacancies to reward all deserving candidates. And for some organizations (i.e., high-involvement firms), rewarding people by moving them up the hierarchy is inconsistent with their non-hierarchical managerial philosophy, even if the firm does have many promotion opportunities.

Moreover, where promotions are an important part of the reward strategy, the psychological consequences for those not promoted can be detrimental to their future motivation. For example, suppose a company has one vacancy and three deserving candidates. No matter how good they are, two will be turned down. What message do the rejected individuals receive? Probably that the firm does not value their contributions as highly as they thought. It may also shake their confidence in the fairness of the reward system. As discussed in Chapter 3, these perceptions could also cause their performance to decline.

From the organization's point of view, promoting outstanding performers to higher-level (usually managerial) positions can lead to serious problems if the attributes needed for success in the higher-level position are different from those of the lower positions. For example, an outstanding salesperson might become a very poor sales manager. The very skills and abilities that make for a successful salesperson, such as independence, competitiveness, and aggressiveness, may be undesirable in a sales manager, who must work through the recruiting, training, coordinating, and motivating of others. In addition, the sales manager loses the satisfaction of dealing directly with customers and personally closing sales, which may have been a strong motivating factor in his or her work. In circumstances such as these, promotions based on outstanding performance in a qualitatively different job can result in negative consequences for both the employer and the employee. As an employee progresses up the hierarchy, the jobs become systematically more different from those below them.

Lawrence J. Peter has summarized the results of a strict promote-from-within policy in what he has modestly dubbed the "Peter Principle": "In a hierarchy, every employee tends to rise to his [or her] level of incompetence."[14] What he means is that individuals will be promoted only if they are performing competently in their present job. If they are not performing well, they will stay where they are. Thus, "in time, every post tends to be occupied by an employee who is incompetent to carry out his or her duties." Although exaggerated, the Peter Principle does contain an element of truth.

 For all of these reasons, it seems clear that promotions should not be used as the sole component of the system for compensating superior performance. It may be preferable to base promotions on factors other than current performance, assuming that the candidate is at least competent in her or his current duties. However, this can create other difficulties, such as the perception that the organization does not care about outstanding performance.

Clearly, outstanding performers must be considered for promotions, if they wish to be. It may be possible to prepare such individuals for promotion through effective training and development programs. Failing this, management must provide the candidate with an in-depth explanation of why he or she is unsuitable for the promotion. Ideally, unsuitable candidates will, through effective discussion, reach this conclusion on their own.

In some instances, it may be desirable to place an individual in the higher position on a trial basis. If so, that person should be given every possible opportunity to succeed in order to prevent perceptions of injustice. But in this approach, a graceful way to return to the former job must be available. One way of doing this is to provide a title such as "acting department manager."

In order to avoid the problem of forcing employees to move up the managerial hierarchy simply to advance their pay levels, some companies have created dual-track programs for advancement, with a technical track (sometimes known as a "technical ladder") and a managerial track. The "technical ladder" provides a serious of steps through which employees can increase their contribution and value to the organization (and their pay) without becoming managers. Pay-for-knowledge systems also provide an avenue for advancing pay levels without requiring promotion to management.

Gain-Sharing Plans

R P C 10.1

In gain-sharing plans, whenever employees in a particular work group are able to reduce costs, a portion of these gains are shared among all the employees in the work group in a systematic way. These cost savings can be brought about in a variety of ways, such as increased productivity, improved quality, decreased waste, and improved methods of working.

Types of Gain-Sharing Plans

There are four main types of gain-sharing plans—the Scanlon plan, the Rucker plan, IMPROSHARE, and the Family of Measures plan—and countless permutations of these.

The Scanlon Plan

The **Scanlon plan** was developed by Joseph Scanlon, a United Steelworkers local president, at a financially troubled steel mill during the Great Depression. In a Scanlon plan, the organization first computes a "normal" labour cost, based on past experience and expressed as a percentage of the sales value of production. For example, labour costs may be 50 percent of the sales value of production. If workers lower this cost to 47 percent, they share this productivity gain (3 percent of sales value) with the company according to a prearranged formula. For Scanlon plans, the share traditionally has been 25 percent for the company, and 75 percent for employees, based on the notion that the workers are primarily responsible for the productivity gain; but many gain-sharing plans use a 50/50 share.

The Scanlon plan is much more than simply a financial incentive plan. According to proponents, the key to its success lies in the development of a cooperative relationship between workers, union, and management, and the establishment of a process through which workers can contribute to problem solving. Within each work unit, gain-sharing committees composed of both management and worker representatives solicit and examine suggestions for improvements

Scanlon plan

a gain-sharing plan that creates mechanisms for employee participation in developing productivity improvements and shares the financial benefits of those improvements with the employee group that generated them

made by employees and recommend either approval or disapproval. If the proposal is outside the jurisdiction of the department or involves large expenditures to implement, the committee passes it on to a plant-wide committee, where top management and union officials discuss it. Typically, all members of the gain-sharing plan share in savings from any resulting improvements.

The Scanlon plan has been modified over time. A major modification has been the inclusion of additional costs beyond labour.[15] There are two reasons for this change. First, many possible cost savings do not show up in labour costs, such as a reduction in the wastage of raw materials. Second, it is usually possible to decrease labour costs at the expense of other costs. For example, a worker may simply scrap slightly defective raw material rather than trying to work with it, since using the poorer-quality raw material would slow production and increase labour costs. As another example, a worker may discard tools that become somewhat dull because they slow down the work, even though replacements may be expensive. With the "multi-cost" approach, the share for employees is usually lower, perhaps 50 percent, because potential savings are much higher with a broader cost base.

Rucker plan

a gain-sharing plan similar to the Scanlon plan but that expresses labour costs as a percentage of value added

The Rucker Plan

Another type of gain-sharing plan was developed in the 1930s by Alan Rucker, who modified the Scanlon plan in a small but very significant way by expressing labour costs as a percentage of value added (sales value of production minus purchased inputs), rather than the sales value of production. The effect is that employees benefit from reductions in raw materials or any other purchased input and are therefore motivated to find ways to reduce these costs. This plan typically includes a worker participation component.

IMPROSHARE

a gain-sharing plan that focuses on labour hours per unit of output, and that does not usually include worker participation

IMPROSHARE

A third type of gain-sharing plan, known as **IMPROSHARE**, was developed by industrial engineer Mitchell Fein in the 1970s.[16] This plan does not use dollar values of production but rather labour hours per unit of output, usually based on the previous year's output. The plan also takes into account indirect labour hours and includes them in the base productivity factor. When productivity exceeds the base productivity factor, a bonus is paid, usually 50 percent of the labour savings.

A disadvantage of IMPROSHARE is that it does not take other cost savings into account. It also does not make employee involvement an integral part of the system (which might in fact be regarded as an advantage by classical firms). Yet although the general belief among most experts is that the participation element is fundamental to the success of gain sharing, research shows that gain sharing can be successful even in the absence of mechanisms for employee participation.[17]

family of measures plan

a gain-sharing plan that uses a variety of measures to determine the extent to which a bonus payout is justified

Family of Measures Plan

According to Belcher, the "**family of measures** category describes any gain sharing formula that uses *multiple, independent measures*. A gain (or loss) is

Compensation Today 10.1

Gain Sharing at Control Data Corporation

In the late 1980s, at Control Data Corporation, management of the Business Management Services Division—which provides computerized human resource, payroll, and related services to external clients through 40 branch offices—wanted to establish a new business strategy with more focus on the customer. They believed that a gain-sharing plan might help support this new strategy.[18]

To develop the gain-sharing plan, management selected one branch office (one of their highest-performing offices) and set up an employee team there to design the plan. The design team was aware they were breaking new ground, since no existing examples of gain sharing could be found in this industry.

The plan, which was launched in 1990, had five performance measures and two modifiers. The performance measures were the cost of processing each customer order, controllable expenses as a percentage of revenues, the number of customer credits issued, retention of customers, and number of suggestions submitted. The first two items were standard cost measures, and a historical baseline was established for each. The third item—number of credits issued—was taken as an indicator of quality of customer service, using the reasoning that each credit represented some type of error committed by the office. An analysis showed that each credit cost $80 to process, so for each credit less than the baseline, $80 was added to the bonus pool.

The fourth performance measure, customer retention, was the proportion of customers lost to competitors, and the gains from increasing this retention rate were added to the bonus pool. Finally, for each plausible suggestion made by the team at each office, $100 would be added to the bonus pool, along with another $100 if the suggestion was accepted.

The team also suggested two modifiers. The total bonus pool would be adjusted depending on (a) the level of gross profits realized at the office and (b) the results of customer satisfaction surveys. The first modifier acknowledges that without profit, there is no money to fund the bonus plan; the second modifier signifies that customer satisfaction is the way through which profitability will be achieved. This last modifier is important in preventing the office from cutting costs at the expense of customer satisfaction. For example, one way of reducing customer credits is by refusing to issue them in all but the most extreme cases. This might be tempting, if not for the customer satisfaction modifier.

calculated for each measure separately, and then aggregated to determine the size of the bonus pool."[19] The key attractions of this method are flexibility and focus. Flexibility comes from the ability to include performance measures that are particularly important to the success of that business. Focus comes from the ability to specify the types of performance that lead to bonus payouts.

For example, the performance measures might include not only labour and materials efficiency but also production schedule attainment, quality levels, customer satisfaction measures, and even accident rates. Some of these additional measures can be based on historical records, while others can be based on achievement of targets or goals set by management. In addition, some measures (known as "modifiers") may not add to the bonus but rather subtract from it. For example, some firms subtract from labour savings if there are excessive accident levels. The logic is that increased labour productivity should not come at the expense of unsafe work practices. Compensation Today 10.1 provides an example of a family of measures approach used at a service enterprise.

Issues w/Gain Sharing Plans:
- def'n of group
- establishing bonus formula
- def'n of baseline
- decide share & split
- Payout frequency
- Participation
- Comm'n

The family of measures plan has some disadvantages compared with the other types of plans. A major disadvantage is that some of the payouts are not based on calculated cost savings but on achievement of certain goals. Thus, the payout for achieving these goals may bear little resemblance to actual cost savings, since these cost savings are often hard to quantify. Consequently, employees may see the payouts as arbitrary (since there is no solid basis for them) and the goals as unrealistic. Where goals are seen as unrealistic, little effort will be made to attain them.

RPC 10.2

Issues in Designing Gain-Sharing Plans

The key steps in establishing gain-sharing plans are (a) defining the group or work unit to be included in the plan, (b) establishing the bonus formula, (c) defining the baseline against which to measure improvement, (d) deciding on the share between the company and the employees, (e) deciding on the split between employees, (f) deciding on the frequency of payout, and (g) deciding how to communicate results. Other questions to answer are whether to include certain optional design elements, and whether and how to incorporate employee participation into the process. Each of these issues, if not resolved appropriately, could cause the gain-sharing plan to founder.

Defining the Group

Defining the group or unit for a particular gain-sharing plan is not as easy as it sounds. In general, all employees who are in a position to significantly affect the results of the plan should be included.

For example, a company that distributed building materials (such as wallboard) wanted to improve the productivity of their warehousing and delivery operation. The company wanted to improve the efficiency of delivery and reduce wastage due to improperly loaded or carelessly handled material. It had warehouses in various cities across Western Canada. Originally, they decided to include just the warehouse staff and delivery drivers at each location in gain sharing. So, one gain-sharing group was the Winnipeg warehouse and delivery staff, another was the Regina warehouse and delivery staff, and so on.

Initially, the office staff at each location were not included in the gain-sharing groups. However, the company soon realized that the office staff had a significant impact on warehouse and delivery efficiency, depending how quickly they responded to customers and passed the information on to the warehouse, whether they were precise about delivery locations, and how effectively they sorted out problems. Moreover, leaving them out caused them to think that the company did not consider them important. So the plan was revised to include them in the gain-sharing groups, as well as the warehouse managers, who had also been left out on the argument that they received other types of bonuses.

Establishing the Bonus Formula

Since each gain-sharing program uses different criteria to establish its bonus formula, a company must determine which of these is appropriate for its situation. In general, the simpler the formula, the better. On the other hand, the program must at the same time capture all factors that affect performance. Thus, most plans typically include a number of performance measures, along with some modifiers to constrain undesirable behaviour. For example, the performance measure for a mining team might be tonnes produced per person-hour. To avoid abuse of equipment (by, say, changing cutting bits more often than necessary in order to maximize production), any excess equipment replacement costs could be factored into the formula. And to avoid unsafe practices, a modifier stipulating no bonus for periods in which lost-time accidents occurred could be included.

Defining the Baseline

The key to a gain-sharing plan is a historical baseline against which to compare productivity, in order to determine whether real productivity gains have actually taken place. In general, a company can use its past two to three years of productivity results and compute an average. However, this procedure is only valid if the baseline over this period does not show a markedly upward or downward trend. In some cases, stable historical baselines don't exist, especially if the product/service mix is continually changing, if raw materials are improving (or declining) in quality or ease of use, or if the production/service technology is frequently changing. If no valid historical benchmark can be set, then a gain-sharing plan is not viable, and some other option (such as goal sharing) needs to be considered.

A key question is whether to change the baseline over time. A baseline that stays constant is known as a "fixed baseline," while baselines that change are known as "ratcheting" or "rolling" baselines. A ratcheting baseline goes up each year there is a productivity gain, and last year's productivity becomes the new baseline. A rolling baseline uses a fixed period (say, a three-year period), dropping the oldest year off and adding the newest one. The result is similar to a ratcheting baseline, but it develops more slowly.

Management rationale for ratcheting or rolling baselines is to keep pushing productivity up. However, employees may find this kind of baseline just means working harder to maintain the same reward level. Moreover, depending on the measure, at some point, it becomes very unrealistic to push the baseline up further, unless the goal is to wipe out the gain-sharing plan without formally ending it. For example, if the measure is a reduction in defect rates, what happens when defect rates approach zero? Overall, ratcheting or rolling baselines are likely to be demotivational if employees start to see them as causing "long-term pain" for a "short-term gain."

This is not to say that baselines should never change. Changing them is reasonable if new capital equipment speeds up the production process without any increased worker effort, or if products are redesigned for easier production. However, in these cases, management must resist the temptation to take advantage of these changes to unduly increase the baseline. For workers to have any trust in the plan, any reasons for changes to the baseline should be clearly explained.

Deciding the Share

The "share" is the formula for dividing the bonus pool created by productivity gains between the employees and the company. Typically, the employee share ranges from 25 percent to 50 percent, although it can range as high as 75 percent in Scanlon Plans, where productivity gains are defined on a relatively small base.[20]

There are three criteria to consider in setting the share. First, the broader the bonus formula, the lower the share, since there are more opportunities for productivity gains or cost savings with a broader formula. Second, the higher the capital intensity, the lower the share. Since there are relatively fewer employees in a capital-intensive firm, a lower share can still produce high bonuses for individual employees. Third, the more demanding the baseline (i.e., the extent to which it increases), the higher the share needs to be to compensate for the increasing difficulty of productivity gains.

Deciding the Split

How should the bonus pool be split across the eligible employees? Should everyone receive an equal share? That sounds fair—but is it? What about employees who have been employed by the firm only a few days during the bonus period? What about employees who are only part-time? What about employees who have performed exceptionally well during the bonus period? What about senior employees? Do they deserve more of the pool?

The answers to these questions depend on the organization's goals for the gain-sharing plan. However, the bonus allocation method most in keeping with the underlying philosophy of gain sharing is equal allocation across employees, after adjusting for time worked during the bonus period. Gain sharing is intended to create cooperation and teamwork, and equality is an underlying condition. If singling out individuals for special treatment is necessary, companies should use other elements of the compensation system, rather than the gain-sharing plan.

Deciding the Payout Frequency

On what period should the bonus calculations be based? There are both technical and behavioural issues to consider here. For example, if productivity results fluctuate widely on a weekly, monthly, or seasonal basis, longer payout periods are required. But from a behavioural point of view, for maximum motivation, receipt of rewards should closely follow the event triggering the rewards. At the same time, the size of the reward should be at least enough to provide a "just noticeable difference," suggesting longer bonus periods, which would also reduce administrative costs. Overall, a quarterly period may be the best compromise in many cases.

Optional Design Components

A number of optional design components may be included in the plan, most commonly smoothing mechanisms, caps, and capital investment adjustments. A smoothing mechanism is intended to deal with volatility in the bonus results, where positive results occur in some quarters, but negative results in others. Smoothing may be achieved by long bonus calculation periods (such as a year) or by a deficit reserve created by holding back on full payment during high bonus periods.

The purpose of a cap (a pre-specified maximum for the bonus payout) is to provide reassurance to management that payouts will not be exorbitant if the gain-sharing plan has been badly designed. Caps are like an insurance policy; but they also limit employee motivation to make gains that would exceed the capped level.

The purpose of a capital investment adjustment mechanism is to systematically adjust the baseline to represent the impact of new capital investment. Firms may be reluctant to make capital investments if they have to share too large a portion of the returns from new capital equipment.

Communication

No compensation system will have any impact if employees do not understand how it works and how their behaviour relates to rewards. Employees also need to see whether they are making progress towards meeting the bonus criteria that have been set out, so frequent feedback about productivity results and cost savings is essential. However, communication does not happen without effort and planning; and procedures for communicating this information need to be carefully planned and implemented.

Participatory Mechanisms

Some gain-sharing plans, such as Scanlon or Rucker, explicitly incorporate a mechanism through which employees can participate in making productivity improvements. Participation is often achieved through a joint employee–management gain sharing committee, which meets on a regular basis to solicit employee suggestions and feedback. However, other plans, such as IMPROSHARE, carry no such requirements.

Overall, the research indicates that group pay systems can be successful with or without a participative employee element. For example, research shows that IMPROSHARE systems can be effective, despite not having a participative element.[21] Research based on Statistics Canada data has also found that group pay systems can be very successful in the absence of participatory mechanisms, although success was increased if these plans were accompanied by an employee suggestion program.[22] Interestingly, these results applied only to firms *not* pursuing an innovator business strategy, and group pay had no impact in innovator firms. This difference suggests that conditions in innovator firms are too unstable to provide the stable historical baselines necessary for successful gain sharing.

There has been considerable research on conditions needed for success of gain-sharing plans.[23] First, employees must regard the gain-sharing system as fair and equitable, both in terms of procedural and distributive justice. Employee participation in the development of the gain-sharing system is one way of helping to achieve this goal. Because an organization needs to make adjustments to these plans over time, it also needs a certain level of trust between management and employees, as well as a sense of job security. As with piece rates, there must be some assurance that employees will not "work themselves out of a job."

 10.1 ## Goal-Sharing Plans

Goal sharing is a group pay plan that rapidly gained popularity in the 1990s. However, like gain sharing and other group pay plans, goal sharing appears to have lost popularity in recent years, as was discussed in Chapter 4. This is a bit surprising, given that recent research shows that group-based plans can dramatically improve company profitability when adopted by firms not pursuing an innovator competitive strategy.[24] Moreover, even in firms pursuing an innovator strategy, these plans broke even on average; so there doesn't seem to be much to lose in trying them, particularly when conditions are right.

The essence of goal sharing is that work groups or teams receive a bonus when certain prespecified performance goals are met. Goal-sharing plans differ from gain-sharing plans in several fundamental ways. In gain sharing, cost savings are quantified and then shared between the company and the group. There are no set goals with gain sharing other than to simply improve as much as possible relative to the historical baseline. Moreover, in gain sharing, there is an expectation of continuity—the gain-sharing system will not be arbitrarily changed. Finally, in gain-sharing plans there is usually an explicit expectation of employee involvement in suggesting ideas for productivity gains.

In contrast, under goal sharing, goals on one or more performance indicators are set for each group or team, to be met within a specified time period, and a bonus is paid to all team members if the goal is achieved. Because of their flexibility, the continuity of goal-sharing plans is less assured than with gain sharing. Employee participation is not necessarily a component, although it can be.

Types of Goal-Sharing Plans

Because goal-sharing plans are so new and varied, they have not really evolved to the point where distinct types can be identified. However, one important distinction is whether they are single-goal plans, multi-goal plans, or financially funded plans. Single-goal plans are the simplest and focus attention on one key goal, such as customer satisfaction. Single-goal plans may cause other important behaviours to be neglected, so most firms typically use multi-goal plans to better cover the range of desired behaviour.

Financially funded plans combine two sets of criteria.[25] The total amount of goal-sharing bonus available is typically based on some indicator such as company profit, while the actual amount of the payout is based on achievement of specified goals. Although this combination of criteria prevents the problem of paying out goal sharing bonuses when the company is not profitable, it also has the effect of making the performance–reward contingency less certain, which generally diminishes motivation to meet goals.

Issues in Designing Goal-Sharing Plans

The first issue in goal sharing is to define the group to which a given goal-sharing plan will apply. In general, the smaller the group, the better the motivation; but the group must include all employees who can play a significant role in goal achievement.

Of course, a critical variable is the nature of the goals to be set. They must be important to the organization, controllable by the work group, and encompass the full range of desired behaviour. Care must be taken to ensure that the goals do not conflict. For example, in the 1990s, Continental Airlines was suffering from a very poor on-time performance record. So the company established a goal-sharing plan in which all employees who affected on-time performance, such as baggage-handlers, would receive a bonus if on-time performance improved to the point where Continental was among the five best airlines in this performance category. The plan worked: on-time performance improved and bonuses were paid out. Unfortunately, at the same time, customer complaints increased, as passenger baggage was often left behind in order to get flights out on time.[26]

Once the goals to be rewarded are identified, the organization needs to determine the levels necessary to trigger a bonus payout. This is probably the single most important factor in the success of a goal-sharing plan. Goals that are seen as too difficult do not motivate behaviour. Goals that are too easy also do not motivate, and they carry the additional penalty of paying out bonuses for no real performance gain. Moreover, with a single goal level, there is no employee motivation to surpass the target goal; in fact, it might even be undesirable to surpass it if this results in a higher target goal for the next year.

As a result, many firms have now established several levels of accomplishment for each goal. At one firm, a goal level that exceeds current performance, but not by much, is called the "standard plus" goal; the next level is called the "goal level," which is seen as realistic, but not a sure thing; and the highest level, which employees have less than a 50-percent likelihood of achieving, is the "goal plus" level. The "goal plus" level is an example of what is commonly known as a "stretch goal."

To help establish goal levels that employees will commit to, many organizations involve employees in the goal-setting process. Research has shown that employees are more motivated to attempt to reach goals that they have played a role in developing.[27]

Goals also need to be bounded by some time period. Within what time frame does the goal need to be accomplished? For most goals, a year would seem a reasonable time period. At the end of the year, new goals can be established, depending whether or not the goal was met.

Once an organization establishes the target goal levels, it must set the dollar amount of bonus for each level of accomplishment. Sometimes it can find a cost basis for so doing. For example, if a company knows how much it costs to correct a particular type of error, it could use this number to calculate a reasonable bonus for achieving a particular reduction in error rate. But in other cases, there may be no good basis for calculating the value of goal achievement—for example, the value of improved "on-time performance."

Another key issue is the basis for allocating the goal-sharing bonus across employees. The basis can be salary, seniority, individual performance, some combination of these, or equal distribution. Equal distribution is the most egalitarian; but is it really fair to more senior employees, who may feel that they contribute more to company success and who have shown long-term commitment to the firm? The advantage of salary-based allocation is that it maintains the same proportion of goal-sharing compensation in the compensation mix for all employees. One advantage of allocating the bonus on individual performance is that it confronts the free-riding problem. But the challenge here is to create an individual performance appraisal system that employees accept as fair. Finally, even where equal allocation is used, typically adjustments have to be made based on the number of days or hours actually worked during the period in which goal accomplishment took place.

RPC 10.1 Profit Sharing Plans

According to the Compensation Practices Survey, about 23 percent of medium to large Canadian firms use broad-based profit sharing. This represents a slight decline in use, from about 28 percent in 2000, as discontinuations outnumbered adoptions during the 2000–2004 period. Unlike stock plans, profit-sharing plans are equally likely to be found in both publicly traded and privately held corporations. Studies have shown that profit sharing is applicable to a wide variety of industries, as the only commonality across profit sharing firms is that they tend to be high-involvement organizations.[28]

Types of Profit-Sharing Plans

In Canada, there are two kinds of government-sanctioned profit-sharing plans: the *deferred profit-sharing plan* (DPSP) and the *employee profit-sharing plan* (EPSP). The DPSP is a tax-deferred plan. Both the employer contributions and the annual earnings of the trust are exempt from taxation until the employee actually receives the benefit. Because of this feature, DPSPs are often used as a form of pension plan, especially in many small to medium-sized companies where no other pension plan exists. The maximum tax deduction for the DPSP is tied to the unused portion of the employee's registered retirement savings plan (RRSP) contribution. "Top hat" plans (those in which only senior management is eligible) are not eligible for registration as a DPSP, as there is a requirement for wide employee eligibility.

Another taxation feature makes the DPSP even more attractive. Instead of being taxed on the full market value of the shares at the time of withdrawal, the employee is taxed only on the original value of the shares when they were placed in the plan. When the shares are sold, the difference between the original value and the selling price is considered a capital gain rather than employment income. (Note that only publicly traded shares are eligible for purchase by a DPSP.)

On the other side of the coin, there is some risk to the employee, in that even if their shares have declined in value at the time they sell the shares, they still have to pay income tax on the original amount of the profit sharing bonus. However, the decline in share value is partially offset by the capital loss this creates, which can be used to offset any capital gains that the employee may have.

The EPSP is not a tax-deferred plan. However, both employer and employee contributions to the trust can be made without limits. These plans are really a type of unsheltered company-supported savings/investment plan, and their main purpose is to provide a vehicle to accumulate savings after the tax-deferred approaches have been exhausted. They are rarely used, since there are no real advantages to registering them with the federal government, and such plans can be set up without government registration.

Besides the DPSP, the other main type of profit sharing plan is the current distribution plan (sometimes known as a "cash plan," although the form of the distribution can be either cash or company shares), in which payouts are not deferred but are paid out at least once a year. Research indicates that the majority (75 percent) of Canadian profit-sharing plans are cash-based plans, another 15 percent are deferred profit-sharing plans, and about 6 percent are combination cash/deferred plans. About 2 percent of firms pay the profit-sharing bonus in a mix of cash and company stock, and 1 percent pay out the bonus only in company stock.[29]

To provide some idea of the diversity of profit-sharing plans, Compensation Today 10.2 gives examples of profit sharing at three different Canadian companies.

Issues in Designing Profit-Sharing Plans

Besides the form of the bonus payout (deferred, cash, stock, or a combination of these), profit-sharing plans have numerous other design issues. The first is the formula for bonus determination, which can either be fixed or discretionary. Under a discretionary approach, management simply looks at the profitability at the end of the year and decides on an amount. The problem with discretionary plans is that the link between performance and reward becomes even more tenuous than otherwise, since employees do not really know to what extent (if at all) better performance will be rewarded.

For motivational reasons, fixed formula plans are strongly recommended. There are many possibilities. The simplest is simply to declare that a portion of pre-tax profit (say, 10 percent) goes into the profit-sharing bonus pool at the end of the year. Alternatively, there can be a threshold (say, a return on investment of 5 percent), and no profit-sharing bonus is paid until this threshold is exceeded. The formula may also incorporate a step function, such that the percentage of profits going to the profit-sharing bonus increases as various thresholds or "steps" are exceeded. Overall, research indicates that more than half of Canadian firms (55 percent) use a fixed percentage of annual pre-tax profits—ranging from 1 percent to 33 percent of profits—to determine the profit-sharing bonus, with the median percentage being 10 percent.[30]

Another key issue is employee eligibility. In general, the more inclusive the better, although casual and contract employees are often excluded, as are unionized employees if the union does not agree to profit sharing. In most cases, there is a time period for eligibility (usually one year). Research on

RPC 10.2

Profit Sharing at Three Canadian Companies

A company with one of the longest histories of profit sharing in Canada is Dofasco Steel of Hamilton, Ontario. A non-union firm in a unionized industry, Dofasco has always seen profit sharing as a major part of its renowned human relations managerial philosophy. The plan was started in 1938 as a pension plan and continues as a DPSP and group registered retirement savings plan.[31] Any amounts that exceed the government limits on these plans may be received in cash. The bonus pool is 14 percent of pre-tax profits from operations, and it is allocated equally to eligible employees in its 7000-person workforce. All employees with at least two years of service are included in the plan. In 2000, the company made headlines when it split a bonus pool of $53.3 million—the highest payout ever—among employees, who each received $7,906.[32]

Another company with a long-standing commitment to profit sharing is Canadian Tire. The founder of the chain, A.J. Billes, always believed in profit sharing in both a philosophical and a practical way. He believed that it was morally just that employees receive a portion of the profits they helped generate and that this would create employee commitment to the firm. The company has always had a profit-sharing plan that applies to the employees of the parent firm, and it strongly encourages profit sharing at its independently owned associate stores.

At the Canadian Tire Associate Store in Barrie, Ontario, which has 73 full-time and 94 part-time employees, the profit-sharing bonus allocation is based on salary level (40 percent), merit rating (40 percent), and seniority (20 percent). The plan is a DPSP that invests in Canadian Tire class A shares, so it is also a stock plan as well as a profit-sharing plan. Amounts that exceed the allowable government limits on DPSPs are placed in an EPSP, which pays interest at the prime rate.

Valley City Manufacturing is a maker of architectural woodwork and cabinetry located in Dundas, Ontario. Unionized by Local 1057 of the Carpenters and Joiners, the firm has about 105 full-time employees, all of whom participate in profit sharing after one year of service. The plan is a generous one, paying 27 percent of pre-tax profits. The profit-sharing bonus is allocated according to employee earnings, and the employee has the choice whether to take it in cash or place it in a DPSP. Established in 1964, the purpose of the plan is "to promote a harmonious working environment and reward success" according to Robert Crockford, the company president.[33]

Canadian firms indicates that in the majority of cases (73 percent), all full-time employees are included in the plan, while 7.5 percent of the firms exclude unionized employees, and 16 percent restrict profit sharing to designated employees only. In 39 percent of profit-sharing firms, part-time employees are included.[34]

Another issue is the basis for allocating the profit-sharing bonus. Allocation can be based on salary, seniority, individual performance, some combination of these, or equal distribution. The advantage of salary-based allocation is that it maintains the same proportion of profit-sharing pay in the compensation mix for each employee. It also tends to provide a greater reward to those employees more able to influence profits. The advantage of allocating the bonus on individual performance is that it confronts the free-riding problem. But the key here is the availability of an individual performance appraisal system that employees accept as fair. Finally, even where equal allocation is used, adjustments have to be made based on the number of days or hours actually worked during the year to which the profit sharing bonus was earned.

In fact, the most common bases for allocating the profit-sharing bonus across employees in Canadian firms are salary level or individual performance (each used in about 30 percent of firms).[35] Seniority is used in 13 percent of firms, while 17 percent use a combination of salary and seniority. Five firms (4.6 percent) allocate the bonus equally to all employees. In addition, a number of firms use multiple bases.

Payout frequency is another issue. Results must be based on financial statements, which suggests that payouts should occur no more often than quarterly. In addition, where profits fluctuate by season, an annual basis is probably best in order to smooth out these fluctuations and avoid paying profit sharing in an unprofitable year.

Research reveals three main factors that significantly affect the success of profit sharing, as perceived by Canadian chief executive officers.[36] CEOs reported better results in firms that use high-involvement management, have extensive profit-sharing communication, and allocate the bonus according to measures of individual performance.

Rather surprisingly, none of the other company characteristics or plan characteristics were very important in influencing the results of profit sharing. As a result, profit sharing can be effective for most types of companies, and various plan designs can be effective as well. One interesting caveat to this finding, however, is that while there was no major difference in results between firms that used a fixed percentage for bonus determination and those that did not (except industrial relations were more favourable in firms with a fixed percentage), for those with fixed percentage plans, success increased with the size of the bonus percentage. Overall, performance of the plan appears to improve when the bonus percentage exceeds 10 percent of profits.

Like other performance pay plans, communication is a key to the success of profit sharing. Most profit sharing firms distribute financial statements and profit-sharing newsletters on a regular basis, but some firms go beyond this. For example, Westjet holds a profit-sharing party every six months, at which employees receive their profit-sharing cheques and are treated to a company celebration.[37]

Employee Stock Plans

RPC 10.1

As discussed in Chapter 4, an employee stock plan is any type of plan through which employees acquire shares in the firm that employs them. In some plans, employees receive shares at no cost, while in other plans employees are given the opportunity to purchase stock on favourable terms. This section describes the three main types of stock plans (stock bonus, stock purchase, stock option), along with related plans that tie employee rewards to company stock performance but do not actually provide employees with the opportunity to acquire shares.

Compared with the United States, where federal legislation has provided significant tax incentives for employee share ownership since 1974, Canada's direct federal support for employee share ownership is minimal, consisting primarily of legislation surrounding deferred profit-sharing plans. One of the allowable investments for the DPSP trust fund is shares of the employer. If the company opts to invest these funds in its own shares, the normal provision requiring diversification of pension trust funds is waived.

The only other possible avenue of federal support for employee ownership is through labour-sponsored investment funds (LSIFs), through which any bona fide labour or employee group may establish a fund that can invest in qualified Canadian businesses. Employees investing through this vehicle are entitled to a deduction from their federal personal income taxes of 15 percent of the value of shares purchased (some provinces match this), up to a specified maximum value. An LSIF can be structured to allow members of the fund to invest in shares of their employer, if their employer qualifies.

Although the federal government provides minimal support, several provinces have legislation specifically designed to encourage employee stock ownership. The province of British Columbia, under its Employee Investment Act of 1989, provides a 20-percent provincial tax credit for employees purchasing shares in companies registered under the act and also has provisions for setting up a type of labour-sponsored investment fund that would invest in shares of a specific employer, which provides a 20-percent provincial tax credit and a 15-percent federal tax credit. In Manitoba, a special labour-sponsored investment fund has been established as a vehicle through which employees can purchase shares in Manitoba firms at no out-of-pocket cost.

The first province to provide a legislative framework to support employee ownership was Quebec, first through the Quebec Stock Savings Program launched in the late 1970s, then through the Fonds de solidarité set up by the Quebec Federation of Labour through the Régime d'épargne du Québec (REAQ) in the early 1980s, and finally through the Société de placements dans l'entreprise québécoise (SPEQ) created in the mid-1980s. Although none of these programs was specifically designed to encourage employee ownership, they can be used as vehicles for employee ownership.

Types of Employee Stock Plans

Employee Stock Bonus Plans

The essence of stock bonus plans is that employees receive company stock at no cost through one of several methods. One approach is simply to make stock grants to employees at periodic intervals, often annually. Another approach is to tie stock grants to the profit-sharing plan, paying out in company stock instead of paying out in cash. The employee could then put this stock into a deferred profit sharing plan, if desired. In some cases, stock bonuses are tied to certain company or individual performance criteria. As Compensation Today 10.3 shows, stock bonuses can be linked to almost any kind of criteria.

Stock bonus plans have experienced a decline in popularity in recent years, coinciding with the stock market downturn in 2001, which diminished interest in share ownership. In 2000, about 5 percent of medium to large Canadian firms had stock bonus plans, according to the Compensation

It Pays to be Green at Husky Injection Molding Systems

At Husky Injection Molding Systems, based in Bolton, Ontario, founder Robert Schad believes that capitalism can't survive without environmental protection. So he devised a plan to tie the two concepts together. Under his "GreenShares" program launched in 2000, employees receive points that can be redeemed for company shares whenever they can show community or environmental activism.[38] For example, an hour of volunteer work in the community is worth one-10th of a share. Carpooling for a month gets you one share. And if you buy a new car that runs partly on electricity, natural gas, or fuel cells, you receive one hundred shares.

Practices Survey; but by 2004, this number had dropped to about 2 percent. Unlike other share plans, these plans are equally common in publicly traded and privately held corporations.

A variation that merges the stock bonus plan with the stock option concept is **share appreciation rights**. Employees are first "allocated" a number of shares of company stock, although they do not actually receive any shares. If these "shares" appreciate over time within a fixed time period, employees receive as a bonus the number of actual company shares that this appreciation can purchase. For example, if an employee is "allocated" 1000 company shares, and the share price is $20 at the outset, and if the shares rise to the value of $25 each by the end of the specified period, then the employee would receive a bonus of 200 actual company shares (the $5,000 appreciation will buy 200 shares at $25 each), at no cost to the employee.

share appreciation rights
a plan through which employees are awarded company shares at no cost if the price of company shares rises during a specified period

Employee Stock Purchase Plans

In contrast, in an employee stock purchase plan, employees provide some kind of direct payment in return for company shares. But they often do not have to pay full market price for these shares, and firms offer many incentives to promote these purchases. Promotions include subsidized or discounted prices or matching programs in which the firm provides an additional share for each share purchased by an employee. In some cases, the company pays the brokerage fees, while in others, they provide low- or no-interest loans for stock purchase. In many cases, the company offers the convenience of payroll deduction.

Employee stock purchase plans have apparently maintained their popularity: according to the CPS, about 20 percent of medium to large Canadian firms had these plans in 2004, which represents no significant change from 2000. But stock purchase plans are far more likely to be found in publicly traded corporations than in privately held corporations: 29 percent of public corporations had stock purchase plans, compared to 12 percent of privately held corporations. Reasons for lower use in private corporations include more complicated mechanics (discussed shortly) and owner reluctance to share ownership.

Employee Stock Option Plans

Under an employee stock option plan, employees receive options to purchase company stock at a future time at a fixed price. For example, if company stock is now trading at $10 a share, then 1000 options with an exercise price of $11 a share might be issued to each employee. Half of the options might be exercisable (when options become exercisable they are considered to be "vested" in the hands of the employees) a year after they are granted, and the other half in two years, with an exercise deadline (option expiry) of three years. What this means is that one year from now, the employee has the option of purchasing up to 500 shares of company stock at a price of $11 each. Obviously, if the stock is trading at that time at, say, $9 a share, there would be no reason to exercise the options. If employees wanted the stock, they could just purchase it through a stockbroker for $9 a share.

But if the stock is trading at, say, $12 a share, employees have a decision to make. They can exercise their options and purchase 500 shares at $11. But if they do purchase the shares, there is the possibility that these shares will go down in price. Of course, they might also go up in price. It's a gamble. But employees who don't want to gamble or who don't have the money with which to purchase the shares can simply cash out by turning around and selling the shares immediately at $12, thus realizing a gain of $500 minus brokerage costs.

But they need not exercise their options at this time either. They could just continue to hold their options (for up to another two years, since that is the expiry date) in the expectation that stock prices will go up over the next two years. But if the stock price sinks below the exercise price of $11 (when the stock price is below the exercise price, the stock options are said to be "under water") and never again rises above that price (during the next two years), employees will not realize any value from their options. On the other hand, they are not out of pocket any money either, as they would be if they had purchased and held the shares as they dropped below the $11 mark.

Although stock options are not a new concept, prior to 1990, they were provided almost exclusively to top executives. What is radically new is the idea of extending stock options throughout the organization. Soft-drink maker PepsiCo Inc. started this trend in 1989, when it granted every employee bonus stock options worth 10 percent of their salary. By 1996, an estimated 2000 U.S. companies had adopted broad-based employee stock option programs;[39] and by the year 2004, it was estimated that at least 10 million U.S. workers in 4000 firms had received stock options,[40] up from less than one million in 1992.[41] As Compensation Today 10.4 illustrates, Canadian companies have not been immune from this trend.

Until 2000, the growth of employee stock option programs in Canada had been slower than in the United States because Canadian tax laws did not favour stock options the way that U.S. tax law does. However, recognizing the increasing importance of employee stock option plans in competing for and retaining employees, the Canadian federal government amended income tax legislation in 2000 to make capital gains on options taxable at the time company shares are sold, not at the time the options are exercised. The same

Options for All at Telus

In 2001, the Canadian telecommunications giant Telus Corporation granted 100 stock options to every employee not covered by existing option programs—more than 20 000 workers—and planned to do so again in each of the next two years. Many workers are eligible for more than the basic 100 options, depending on their skills and marketability. CEO Darren Entwistle said the move would help Telus recruit and retain skilled workers, motivate employees, and create a team atmosphere.[42]

legislation allowed 50 percent of the capital gain to be excluded entirely from taxation. Besides making options more attractive, these changes also encourage retention of shares after the exercise of the options, which the former tax system had discouraged.

These changes brought Canadian tax treatment of options in line with U.S. treatment and make options much more attractive to employees as a form of compensation and much more valuable to companies as a compensation instrument. At the same time, the Canadian federal government also made the overall tax treatment of capital gains more favourable, which also increases the relative attractiveness of stock plans as a compensation instrument.

Despite the less favourable tax treatment until 2000, Canada experienced a dramatic increase in the use of broad-based employee stock options during the 1990s. In 1995, about 4.4 percent of medium to large Canadian companies provided stock options to nonmanagerial employees;[43] and by 2000, this proportion had approximately doubled, according to the CPS. By 2004, this proportion still held at about 9 percent, despite the considerable bad press that options suffered in the first part of this decade.

In the early 2000s, excessive executive stock options were cited as a factor in the collapse of some major U.S. corporations and in the exorbitant increases in executive compensation that have been taking place for a number of years. Part of the problem was that due to a quirk in financial reporting systems, stock options appeared to be a virtually "costless" way of providing compensation to executives. However, when exercised, stock options can exert a very real cost to shareholders in terms of dilution of their share values. In recognition of this problem, the United States and Canada created new accounting rules that require expensing of stock option grants.

As with stock purchase plans, stock option plans are more common in publicly traded corporations than in privately held corporations. The CPS shows that 14 percent of public corporations had broad-based employee stock option plans in 2004, compared to 5 percent of private corporations.

Phantom Stock Plans

A **phantom stock plan** ties an employee's bonus to the performance of company stock, but that employee never actually receives any stock. The

phantom stock plan
a plan through which employees participate in the appreciation of company shares and any associated dividends, without ever owning any company stock

employee is granted a certain number of "units," each corresponding to a share of stock. The employee is entitled to the same dividends that accrue to the actual stock and also the appreciation in share value, both of which are paid in cash at periodic intervals.

phantom equity plan

a plan that helps retain key employees by providing rewards based on the stock performance of a portfolio of promising new high-tech firms

One new and interesting variation on a phantom stock plan is a **phantom equity plan**.[44] Professional service firms—including firms such as management consulting giants McKinsey and Company and Accenture—developed this compensation method to help them retain staff who might otherwise be drawn to high-tech companies better able to offer stock options or equity shares (which professional services firms generally cannot do, since they usually do not have a corporate ownership structure). The plan is not in fact an employee stock plan, since the shares in question are not those of the employer; instead, it is a plan in which employees are granted participation units in a pool of equities of client firms. The value of the units varies with the value of the fund. Employees are allowed to cash out only at specified intervals and on termination, when they must do so.

Compensation Notebook 10.1 summarizes the main types of stock plans available as well as the other main types of group and organizational performance pay plans.

RPC 10.2

Issues in Designing Stock Plans

The issues in designing an employee stock plan vary somewhat according to whether the employer is a publicly traded or a privately held corporation. However, for all companies, several factors differentiate more successful employee stock plans from less successful ones. The effectiveness of employee share ownership increases with the proportion of the employees who hold shares, the proportion of the firm owned by employees, and the degree of employee consultation in the development of the share plan.[45] Employees must feel that they own enough shares to make a difference to their financial well-being and must also feel a sense of real ownership in a corporate context where effective mechanisms for employee participation in decision making are in place.[46] Effective procedures for educating employees about the nature of the stock plan and communicating about company results are also essential.

Design Issues for Stock Plans in Public Corporations

Employee stock plans are simpler to implement in publicly traded corporations than privately held corporations because the public stock market provides a well-understood mechanism for the purchase and sale of company stock. However, organizations still have to decide on a number of issues before implementing the plan.

The first issue is eligibility for inclusion in the stock plan. In general, the more inclusive, the better, although temporary employees and contract employees are usually excluded. Often some minimal length of service is required, usually not exceeding one year.

Next, the criteria for allocating stock across employees must be decided. This allocation can be based on salary (probably the most common approach), seniority, employee performance, equal distribution, or some combination of these. Equal distribution is the most egalitarian; but is it really fair to more senior employees, who may feel that they contribute more to company success or who have shown long-term commitment to the firm? Salary-based allocation has the advantage of maintaining the same proportion of stock in the compensation mix for all employees. Equal allocation is the simplest method, but typically adjustments still need to be made based on the number of days or hours each employee worked in the preceding year.

The holding period is another critical issue. If the objective is to create employee-owners, then some type of holding period should be imposed. Otherwise, it is very tempting to sell the shares immediately to realize the profit in so doing. In general, the more generous the stock plan, the longer the holding period. For example, if employees are purchasing the shares at only a small discount from the market price, then only a short holding period is justified, if any. But if employees are receiving the shares at no cost to themselves, they may be required to hold the shares for up to five years.

Design Issues for Stock Plans in Private Corporations

Stock plans in private corporations must deal with the same issues as public corporations, and some others besides.[47] One key difference is that there is no external market to place a value on company shares and to serve as a mechanism for purchase or sale of the shares. Another difference is that the existing owners likely wish to prevent unfettered sale of the shares in order to maintain control of the firm. Still another difference is that as minority shareholders in private corporations, employees may have very little control or influence over what goes on the organization and no easy way to liquidate their shares if they are not happy with management or if they feel their interests are not being well represented. Employee owners in public corporations may also have very little control, but at least they have the option of easily liquidating their holdings.

To deal with these issues, an artificial "market" is often set up. At regular intervals (usually quarterly or annually), company shares are priced by an outside auditor, and employees are allowed to purchase from or sell shares to other employees at these times. If the available shares exceed the demand, the company will often agree to buy back any shares up for sale. In general, when shares are issued, the company is given "right of first refusal" so that employees must offer their shares to the company before offering them to an outside buyer. In some cases, the board of directors is required to approve sale of any of the employee shares to outside investors. In some cases, employees are not permitted to sell their shares except on termination or retirement from the firm. In many cases, employees are required to sell if they terminate their employment.

To help protect minority rights, employee shares should carry full rights to voting and information. There should be guaranteed board representation for employee shareholders and some legal protections for minority interests. For example, there could be a clause requiring a majority of employee owners to agree to major changes that might materially affect their share value, such as sale or purchase of a plant or major asset or issuance of new classes of stock to existing owners. These types of provisions are particularly important for share purchase plans, where employees must make a significant investment to purchase the shares.[48]

Nonmonetary Reward Plans

R P C 10.1

"Dump the cash, load on the praise!" This is the advice of a well-known consultant who has come up with "1001 Ways to Reward Employees," many of which do not involve money.[49] He argues that what employees really want is recognition for their achievements and affirmation as a valuable member of their organization. This recognition can take a variety of forms, ranging from simple praise to substantial prizes, such as an all-expenses-paid holiday.

Certainly, many employers find this attractive advice, since not spending money is usually popular with employers. And as we have seen, there are many problems and difficulties with individually based financial incentive plans. So it is not surprising that a majority (56 percent) of medium to large Canadian firms now use formal noncash rewards to recognize individual employee performance, up slightly (by about 3 percent) during the past four years. About 26 percent of firms have group-based recognition systems, in which all members of a team are recognized for the team's success. This represents an increase of about 4 percent over the past four years, but also masks a high discontinuation rate. About 64 percent of firms that had group recognition plans in 2000 no longer had them in 2004, compared to only 34 percent that discontinued their individual recognition programs.

What exactly is a nonmonetary recognition award? Perhaps one of the most famous examples is the "golden banana award":

> When a senior manager in one organization was trying to figure out a way to recognize an employee who had just done a great job, he spontaneously picked up a banana [which had been packed in

his lunch], and handed it to the astonished employee with hearty congratulations. Now, one of the highest honours in that company has been dubbed the "Golden Banana Award."[50]

Although some recognition rewards may have monetary value, the key to their importance is their symbolic value, as this example illustrates.

There are some important caveats on the use of nonmonetary rewards. First, such rewards do not provide a substitute for a fair and equitable pay system. Indeed, without an adequate pay system and a collaborative and trusting relationship between workers and management, employees will not likely attach much value to nonmonetary rewards. They will likely see such rewards as an attempt to manipulate them into working harder while withholding "real" (financial) rewards. And they will not value praise or recognition from managers whom they don't respect or trust.

But where there is equitable pay and employee–management trust, nonmonetary rewards can be effective, as the Toyota case (Compensation Today 3.1) illustrates. Overall, the arguments by proponents of these reward systems are consistent with Maslow's theory: once lower-order needs are satisfied, then the needs for achievement and recognition for this achievement can come to the fore. But to be effective, praise must be grounded in actual achievement, follow accomplishment closely, and come from a credible and respected source.

Given all this, nonmonetary rewards seem most suited to high-involvement organizations, although they may also have applications in human relations organizations. But because the foundation for success does not exist in classical organizations, nonmonetary rewards will likely be of relatively little value there.

Types of Nonmonetary Rewards

According to McAdams, there are five types of nonmonetary awards—social reinforcers, merchandise awards, travel awards, symbolic awards, and earned time off.[51] Social reinforcers may range from a simple pat on the back to a valued training opportunity to a company picnic. The general purpose is to demonstrate the value that the firm places on its employees.

Merchandise awards are given to individual employees to recognize performance accomplishments. Travel awards can be provided to recognize individuals or, more commonly, groups or teams for outstanding accomplishments. Symbolic awards are exemplified by the "golden banana" award. Earned time off can be used to recognize individuals or teams that have gone "above and beyond" the call of duty in finishing a project or assignment.

Issues in Designing Nonmonetary Reward Plans

RPC 10.2

A key factor in any recognition system is that the recognition must be truly deserved, and awards are not simply handed out because they are relatively cheap. In general, the more inexpensive the reward, the more judiciously it must be provided if it is to be seen as having any value at all. In addition, it is important to avoid singling out individuals for recognition if their accomplishments have been achieved in a team context or with the help of other employees. To do so will only lead to divisiveness and discord.

In general, it is best to structure these programs so that it is possible to recognize all deserving employees. For example, rather than saying that the person with the highest sales will receive a recognition award, say that "all persons who achieve a 10-percent increase in sales" will receive a recognition award. Artificially "rationing" recognition goes against the principle of these programs, which is that any employee with a significant accomplishment should be recognized.

Another major issue is determining how to identify those individuals and teams deserving of formal recognition. Of course, any manager is free to provide recognition through praise and other informal means whenever he or she wishes. However, for major recognition awards, many organizations use an elected committee of employees and managers.

At the Royal Bank, employees who wish to nominate a co-worker can go online to do so. Then the nominee's immediate manager reviews the nomination. That manager may award a small recognition on the spot or may make a recommendation to the recognition committee.[52]

While a recognition program must focus at the grassroots level and become part of the corporate culture, keeping it alive and vibrant usually requires a champion who will take the lead in promoting the program. At the Royal Bank, a five-person unit is in charge of the recognition program, constantly monitoring its health and coordinating the recognition budget. To help promote and publicize the program, the bank uses a recognition intranet page. They also have 30 "recognition counterparts" scattered throughout the organization, from all functions and departments, who act as point persons for recognition in that part of the organization and answer questions about the program. The recognition budgets for each area of the organization are funnelled through these people.

In terms of the awards themselves, the bank's recognition is in the form of "recognition points." Employees can redeem these points for a variety of awards (except cash), which enables them to select an award that is valuable to them. Employees can also accumulate recognition points in order to garner a larger recognition award.

Through this program, the Royal Bank is showing the importance it places on its employees as the key driver of business success. As earlier Royal Bank examples showed, however, nonmonetary rewards are just part of the total reward program at the bank, all of which is designed to help create a culture of employee commitment to the organization and its goals.

Summary

This chapter identified the key issues in designing performance pay plans. It started by discussing two types of special purpose incentives, namely attendance programs and suggestion systems. The key point here is that while incentive programs can be effective if they fit the situation and are properly designed, simply adopting targeted incentive programs without understanding the underlying dynamics in a given situation can be fruitless or even counterproductive.

In this chapter, you have learned about the role promotions play as incentives, noting that while a "promotion from within" policy can be an important part of a total rewards program, exclusive reliance on promotions as the main motivator of employee behaviour is unlikely to maximize employee motivation, and may even serve to do the opposite.

You are also now familiar with the four main types of group and organizational performance pay plans, namely gain-sharing, goal-sharing, profit-sharing, and employee stock plans. In addition, you have read about the four main types of gain-sharing plan—Scanlon, Rucker, IMPROSHARE, and Family of Measures—each of which uses a different formula for calculating productivity increases. Finally, you understand the key issues in designing gain-sharing plans and recognize that these plans suit stable organizations much better than more dynamic organizations.

In contrast to gain sharing, goal sharing is a much more flexible system, but it has the potential to be more arbitrary, both in the criteria for goal achievement and in the amount of the bonus for goal achievement. In designing these programs, you need to create challenging but attainable goals, which may be more difficult in dynamic organizations.

Although simpler to develop than gain sharing or goal sharing, profit-sharing plans present you with numerous design choices. To be successful, these plans need extensive communications, implementation in a high involvement setting, and allocation of the profit-sharing bonus by individual performance, where circumstances (i.e. availability of fair, accurate, and accepted individual performance measures) permit.

You also now know about the four main types of employee stock plans—stock bonus plans, stock purchase plans, stock option plans, and phantom stock plans—and have learned that although the design issues are more complex for privately held than publicly traded corporations, many private corporations do implement employee stock plans. To be successful with employee stock plans, you need to incorporate widespread implementation throughout the organization, significant ownership for employees, and mechanisms for extensive employee participation within the enterprise.

Finally, you learned about nonmonetary employee recognition programs, noting that there is more to motivation than money. To develop an effective employee recognition program, you need to ensure that all deserving employees receive recognition, that the process for determining recognition is fair, that team-based recognition is provided when warranted, and that nonmonetary rewards are not used a substitute for equitable monetary rewards.

Key Terms

family of measures plan, 396	Rucker plan, 396
IMPROSHARE, 396	Scanlon plan, 395
phantom equity plan, 412	share appreciation rights, 409
phantom stock plan, 411	suggestion system, 392

Chapter 10: Designing Performance Pay Plans

Web Links

For more information on employee suggestion systems, go to the Employee Involvement Association website at **http://www.eianet.org/**. (p. 393)

For more information on profit sharing, check the website of the Profit Sharing Council of America: **http://www.psca.org/**. (p. 407)

For the best source of information on all types of employee ownership plans, go to the U.S. National Center for Employee Ownership website: **http://www.nceo.org/**. In Canada, the association that promotes and provides information about employee ownership plans is the ESOP Association of Canada: **http://www.esop-canada.com/**. (p. 413)

For an interesting example of a successful recognition program, go to **http://www.octanner.com/news/april2000.html**. (p. 416)

RPC Icons

RPC 10.1 Considering the total compensation strategy, develops a compensation program with respect to base pay, variable pay, profit and gain sharing, incentive pay, and stock options, and recommends the best mix.

RPC 10.2 Establishes compensation policies and procedures based on the compensation program, and compliance with the legal framework.

Discussion Questions

1. Discuss the advantages and disadvantages of attendance programs and suggestion systems. What are the possible downsides in using each system?
2. Gain-sharing and goal-sharing programs have high discontinuation rates. Why do you think that may be?
3. When designing a profit-sharing plan, what do you think are the design issues that would prove to be the most difficult to decide?
4. Of the various types of employee stock plans, which do you think would best fit a privately held corporation?
5. Discuss the pros and cons of nonmonetary reward programs.

Using the Internet

Go to the website for Ethicon Incorporated (**http://www.octanner.com/news/april2000.html**) and identify the reasons for the success of their nonmonetary recognition program.

Exercises

1. Examine the three profit-sharing plans described in Compensation Today 10.2. Evaluate the possible impact of each. Which do you think will be most effective, and why do you think so? What additional information would be useful in order to draw firm conclusions?

2. In a small group, select a recent employer of one of the group members and discuss whether an attendance program, a suggestion program, both, or neither, would benefit this organization.

3. Assume you are an employee in a firm that is planning to implement profit sharing. As an employee, identify the design features you would like to see included. Then in a small group, compare your desired plans. How do they differ, and what do you think are the reasons for the differences?

Case Questions

1. You are a team of top-notch compensation consultants hired by "Alliston Instruments" in the Appendix. After analyzing the various options available, you have decided that a group pay plan would be beneficial to this organization. Select the specific group plan that would seem to work best and design it, describing specifically how you would deal with the various design issues. When you are done, the plan should be ready for implementation.

2. You have decided that "The Fit Stop" organization in the Appendix would be well suited to an organizational performance pay plan. Select the specific organization pay plan that would seem to work best and design the plan, describing specifically how you would deal with the various design issues. When you are done, the plan should be ready for implementation.

Simulation Cross-Reference

If you are using *Strategic Compensation: A Simulation* in conjunction with this text, you will find that the concepts in Chapter 10 are helpful in preparing Section K of the simulation.

Endnotes

1. Bick, Julie. 2005. "Microsoft Millionaires Branch Out." *Saskatoon Star-Phoenix*, June 3: C10.
2. Booth, Patricia L. 1993. *Employee Absenteeism: Strategies for Promoting an Attendance Oriented Corporate Culture.* Ottawa: Conference Board of Canada.

3. Lawler, Edward E. 1977. "Reward Systems." In J. Richard Hackman and J. Lloyd Suttle, eds. *Improving Life at Work: Behavioral Sciences Approaches to Organizational Change.* Santa Monica, CA: Goodyear Publishing.

4. Goodman, Paul S., and Robert S. Atkin. 1984. *Absenteeism: New Approaches to Understanding, Measuring, and Managing Employee Absence.* San Francisco: Jossey Bass.

5. Gellatly, Ian R., and Andrew A. Luchak. 1998. "Personal and Organizational Determinants of Perceived Absence Norms." *Human Relations*, 51(8): 1085–1102.

6. Booth, Patricia L. 1993. *Employee Absenteeism: Strategies for Promoting an Attendance Oriented Corporate Culture.* Ottawa: Conference Board of Canada, 8.

7. Booth, Patricia L. 1993. *Employee Absenteeism: Strategies for Promoting an Attendance Oriented Corporate Culture.* Ottawa: Conference Board of Canada.

8. Booth, Patricia L. 1993. *Employee Absenteeism: Strategies for Promoting an Attendance Oriented Corporate Culture.* Ottawa: Conference Board of Canada.

9. Zeytinoglu, Isik U. 1999. "Flexible Work Arrangements: An Overview of Developments in Canada." In Isik U. Zeytinoglu, ed. *Changing Work Relationships in Industrialized Countries.* Amsterdam/Philadelphia: John Benjamins Publishing, 41–58.

10. Booth, Patricia L. 1993. *Employee Absenteeism: Strategies for Promoting an Attendance Oriented Corporate Culture.* Ottawa: Conference Board of Canada.

11. Belcher, John G. 1996. *How to Design and Implement a Results Oriented Variable Pay System.* New York: American Management Association.

12. Long, Richard J. 2005. "Group-Based Pay, Participatory Practices, and Workplace Performance." Paper presented at the "Conference on the Evolving Workplace" Ottawa, September 28–29.

13. McAdams, Jerry L. 1995. "Employee Involvement and Performance Reward Plans." *Compensation and Benefits Review*, 27(2): 45–55.

14. Peter, Lawrence J., and Raymond Hull. 1969. *The Peter Principle.* New York: William Morrow and Company.

15. Belcher, John G. 1991. *Gain Sharing.* Houston, TX: Gulf Publishing.

16. Fein, Mitchell. 1981. *IMPROSHARE: An Alternative to Traditional Managing.* Hillsdale, NJ: Mitchell Fein Inc.

17. Kaufman, R.T. 1992. "The Effects of IMPROSHARE on Productivity." *Industrial and Labor Relations Review*, 45: 311–322.

18. Belcher, John G. 1991. *Gain Sharing.* Houston, TX: Gulf Publishing.

19. Belcher, John G. 1991. *Gain Sharing.* Houston, TX: Gulf Publishing, 83.

20. Belcher, John G. 1991. *Gain Sharing.* Houston, TX: Gulf Publishing.

21. Kaufman, R.T. 1992. "The Effects of IMPROSHARE on Productivity." *Industrial and Labor Relations Review*, 45: 311–322.

22. Long, Richard J. 2005. "Group-Based Pay, Participatory Practices, and Workplace Performance." Paper presented at the Conference on the Evolving Workplace: Ottawa, September 28–29.

23. For example, see Cooper, Christine, Bruno Dyck, and Norman Frohlich. 1992. "Improving the Effectiveness of Gainsharing: The Role of Fairness and Participation." *Administrative Science Quarterly*, 37(3): 471–90. See also Welbourne, Theresa M., David B. Balkin, and Luis Gomez-Mejia. 1995. "Gain Sharing and Mutual Monitoring: A Combined Agency-Organizational Justice Interpretation." *Academy of Management Journal*, 38(3): 881–99. See also Welbourne, Theresa M., and Daniel M. Cable. 1995. "Group Incentives and Pay Satisfaction: Understanding the Relationship through an Identity Theory Perspective." *Human Relations*, 48(6): 711–26. See also Kim, Dong-One. 1996. "Factors Influencing Organizational Performance in Gainsharing Programs." *Industrial Relations*, 35(2): 227–44.

24. Long, Richard J. 2005. "Group-Based Pay, Participatory Practices, and Workplace Performance." Paper presented at the Conference on the Evolving Workplace: Ottawa, September 28–29.

25. Belcher, John G. 1996. *How to Design and Implement a Results Oriented Variable Pay System.* New York: American Management Association.

26. Lawler, Edward E. 2000. *Rewarding Excellence: Pay Strategies for the New Economy*. San Francisco: Jossey Bass, 228.

27. Bartol, K.M. and E.A. Locke. 2000. "Incentives and Motivation." In S.L. Rynes and B. Gerhart, eds. *Compensation in Organizations: Current Research and Practice*. San Francisco: Jossey Bass, 104–150.

28. Three Canadian studies found that profit sharing was more likely in high-involvement organizations than in classical and human relations organizations. See Wagar, Terry H., and Richard J. Long. 1995. "Profit Sharing in Canada: Incidence and Predictors." *Proceedings of the Administrative Sciences Association of Canada (Human Resources Division)*, 16(9): 97–105. See also Long, Richard J. 1997. "Motives for Profit Sharing: A Study of Canadian Chief Executive Officers," *Relations Industrielles/Industrial Relations*, 52(4): 712–33. See also Long, Richard J. 2002. "Performance Pay in Canada." In Michelle Brown and John S. Heywood, eds. *Paying for Performance: An International Comparison*. Armonk, NY: M.E. Sharpe.

29. Long, Richard J. 1997. "Motives for Profit Sharing: A Study of Canadian Chief Executive Officers," *Relations industrielles/Industrial Relations*, 52(4): 712–33.

30. Long, Richard J. 1997. "Motives for Profit Sharing: A Study of Canadian Chief Executive Officers," *Relations Industrielles/Industrial Relations*, 52(4): 712–33.

31. Tyson, David E. 1996. *Profit Sharing in Canada: The Complete Guide to Designing and Implementing Plans That Really Work*. Toronto: John Wiley and Sons.

32. Kilpatrick, Ken, and Dawn Walton. 2000. "What a Joy to Work for Dofasco." *The Globe and Mail*, February 12: B1.

33. Tyson, David E. 1996. *Profit Sharing in Canada: The Complete Guide to Designing and Implementing Plans That Really Work*. Toronto: John Wiley and Sons.

34. Long, Richard J. 1997. "Motives for Profit Sharing: A Study of Canadian Chief Executive Officers," *Relations Industrielles/Industrial Relations*, 52(4): 712–33.

35. Long, Richard J. 1997. "Motives for Profit Sharing: A Study of Canadian Chief Executive Officers," *Relations Industrielles/Industrial Relations*, 52(4): 712–33.

36. Long, Richard J. 2000. "Employee Profit Sharing: Consequences and Moderators," *Relations industrielles/Industrial Relations*, 55(3): 477–504.

37. Yerema, Richard. 2005. *Canada's Top 100 Employers*. Toronto: Mediacorp.

38. McArthur, Keith. 2000. "Husky Boss Offers Equity for Activism." *The Globe and Mail*, January 21.

39. Capell, Kerry. 1996. "Options for Everyone." *Business Week*, July 22: 80–84.

40. Rosen, Corey, John Case, and Martin Staubus. 2005. "Every Employee an Owner. Really." *Harvard Business Review*, June: 1–8.

41. NCEO. 2000. "Seven to Ten Million Employees Now Eligible for Stock Options." *Employee Ownership Report*, 20(3):1.

42. Stueck, Wendy. 2001. "Telus Options Passed Down Food Chain." *The Globe and Mail*, March 2: B1.

43. Isaac, Kerry. 1995. *Compensation Planning Outlook 1996*. Ottawa: Conference Board of Canada.

44. Morrison, Helen H., and Joseph S. Adams. 2001. "New Type of Phantom Equity Plan Used to Combat Employee Defections." *The Journal of Employee Ownership Law and Finance*, 13(1): 109–26.

45. Long, Richard J. 1991. *Employee Profit Sharing and Share Ownership in Canada: Results of a Survey of Chief Executive Officers*. Toronto: Profit Sharing Council of Canada.

46. Rosen, Corey, John Case, and Martin Staubus. 2005. "Every Employee an Owner. Really." *Harvard Business Review*, June: 1–8.

47. For examples of employee ownership systems in private Canadian corporations, see Beatty, Carol, and Harvey Schacter. 2002. *Employee Ownership: The New Source of Competitive Advantage*. Toronto: John Wiley and Sons.

48. An excellent source of information on the technical aspects of designing employee share plans in Canada is Phillips, Perry. 2001. *Employee Share Ownership Plans*. Toronto: John Wiley and Sons.

49. Nelson, Bob. 1994. 1001 Ways to Reward Employees. New York: Workman Publishing. See also Nelson, Bob. 1996. "Dump the Cash, Load on the Praise." *Personnel Journal*, 75(7): 65–70.

50. Spitzer, Dean R. 1996. "Power Rewards: Rewards That Really Motivate." *Management Review*, 85(5): 48–49.

51. McAdams, Jerry L. 2000. "Nonmonetary Rewards: Cash Equivalents and Tangible Awards." In Lance A. Berger and Dorothy R. Berger, eds. *The Compensation Handbook: A State-of-the-Art Guide to Compensation Strategy and Design*. New York: McGraw-Hill, 241–259.

52. Brown, David. 2005. "RBC's Recognition Department Oversees Rewarding Culture." *Canadian HR Reporter*, 18(5): 7–9.

Chapter 11

Designing Indirect
Pay Plans

Chapter Learning Objectives

After reading this chapter, you should be able to:

- Identify the six major categories of employee benefits and the specific types of benefits included in each category.
- Discuss the advantages and disadvantages of fixed vs. flexible benefit plans and the circumstances in which each would be most appropriate.
- Describe the issues that must be addressed in designing a benefit system.

BENEFITS ARE RADICAL HERE

Picture this. It is mid-morning, and you are at the Vancouver head office of a major Canadian computer software company. Some employees are in a nearby kitchen area helping themselves to a late breakfast of bagels and cheese, cereal, or other breakfast items—all provided free to employees at a cost to the company of more than $20,000 per month. That's a lot of cornflakes! Also nearby, another employee is taking a 10-minute time-out on one of several large couches provided for the purpose, while other employees are working out in a fully equipped gym. In an employee lounge, an enormous log cabin stands, actually an in-house movie theatre.

This is the scene at Radical Entertainment, a designer of video games for companies like Sony and Microsoft, where the CEO, Ian Wilkinson, makes no apology for these expenditures. "If creating a good place to work means that people who work here will be inspired and that they will stay with us, then it's worth the cost."[1]

Introduction

Not far away, at Vancouver City Credit Union, the perks are a little more conventional. There, employees receive, at no cost to them, a pension plan, life and accident insurance, disability benefits, health and dental benefits for employees and their families, three to six weeks' annual vacation, and free tuition on any work-related course they may wish to take. The company also has a registered retirement savings plan in which the company matches employee contributions, and it also offers low-interest home loans, subsidized home insurance, subsidized childcare, discounted home computers, and discounted accommodation at the Whistler ski resort. Since the benefits plan is flexible, employees can tailor it to suit their needs and can even purchase up to five additional vacation days a year by foregoing other benefits.[2]

As discussed in Chapter 4, indirect pay can serve a variety of purposes and comprise an important component of a firm's compensation strategy. This chapter discusses the six major categories of indirect pay and the specific employee benefits included in each category. It also explains when to use flexible or fixed benefit systems and outlines the process for developing an effective employee benefit system.

RPC 11.1

Types of Employee Benefits and Services

What are the major types of benefits that can be included in the indirect pay component of a compensation system? There are six major categories of benefits: mandatory benefits, retirement income, health benefits, pay for time not worked, employee services, and miscellaneous benefits. Within each of these categories are numerous specific benefits that can be included, and Compensation Notebook 11.1 provides an overview of the benefits that will be covered in this chapter.

Common Types of Employee Benefits and Services

Mandatory Benefits

- Canada/Quebec Pension Plan
- Employment Insurance
- Workers' Compensation

Retirement Income

- Defined Benefit Plans
- Defined Contribution Plans
- Hybrid Pension Plans

Health Benefits

- Supplemental Health Insurance
- Disability Insurance
- Life and Accident Insurance
- Dental Insurance
- Health Care Expense Accounts

Pay for Time Not Worked

- Vacations, Holidays, Breaks
- Sickness, Compassionate Absences
- Supplemental Unemployment Benefits

- Parental Leaves
- Educational/Sabbatical Leaves
- Severance Pay

Employee Services

- Employee Assistance Programs
- Wellness and Recreational
- Childcare/Eldercare
- Work-Life Balance
- Financial/Legal Services
- Food Services
- Outplacement Services

Miscellaneous Benefits

- Use of Company Vehicle
- Product/Service Discounts
- Housing/Mortgage Subsidies
- Employee Savings Plans
- Tuition Reimbursements
- Work Clothing/Equipment
- Employee Expense Accounts

Mandatory Benefits

The federal and provincial governments require employers to contribute toward a number of government-provided employee benefits. Employers have no option but to participate in these programs on behalf of their employees (all except for those classed as independent contractors): the Canada/Quebec Pension Plan (CPP/QPP), Employment Insurance, and workers' compensation benefits (under which payments are made to cover treatment expenses and other costs for workers who are injured on the job). Employers must also provide minimum levels of statutory vacation, holiday, and rest breaks, and, in some provinces, they are liable for health care taxes. The amount the employer must contribute for each of these programs is based on the total cash compensation received by an employee. CPP/QPP, Employment Insurance, and workers' compensation premiums alone can amount to up to 10 percent of total compensation for lower-income employees. However, because of caps on the premiums, these programs typically amount to a much smaller percentage of compensation of more highly paid employees.

 **11.2**

mandatory benefits
government-provided employee benefits, such as pensions and employment insurance, to which employers must contribute on behalf of their employees

Retirement Income

One of the greatest concerns for many employees is securing a stream of income for the period after they retire. Therefore, many firms offer pension plans that go beyond the basic pension plans provided by the government. All citizens are currently entitled to Old Age Security, which pays a small fixed pension; low-income pensioners also receive a Guaranteed Income Supplement; and all employees qualify for the Canada Pension Plan, with the amount of their pension dependent on their credited contributions.

After mandatory benefits, company pension and retirement plans are the costliest items in most company benefits packages. There are two main types of private pension plans: defined benefit plans and defined contribution plans. Hybrid pension plans combine the two.

Defined Benefit Plans

defined benefit plans

pension plans that provide retirement income based on a proportion of the employee's pay at the time of retirement

Defined benefit plans undertake to provide a specified stream of income from the time of retirement until death. The amount is usually geared to some proportion of an employee's annual earnings, modified by the number of years the employee has been covered by the plan. For example, at Imperial Oil, employees receive 1.6 percent of the average of their best three years' earnings for each year of service. Therefore, if an employee retires after 40 years of service and has averaged $50,000 per year during his or her three best years, that person receives an annual pension of $32,000 from Imperial ($50,000 × .016 × 40), in addition to other payments from the Canada Pension Plan and Old Age Security.

Defined Contribution Plans

defined contribution plans

pension plans that provide retirement income based on the accrued value of employer and employee contributions to the plan

With **defined contribution plans** (sometimes called "money purchase plans"), the employer commits to putting a certain amount of money in an investment trust on behalf of each employee; however, at the time of retirement, the amount of annual pension is paid based on whatever amount of money is in that trust. Thus, there is no guarantee about what amount the annual pension at retirement will actually be. Contributions can be defined in two ways: either as a fixed sum of money, with the amount established each year, or as a fixed proportion of company profits. In the latter case, the plan is known as a deferred profit-sharing plan (DPSP), which has been discussed in Chapter 10.

Both defined benefit and defined contribution pension plans can be either contributory, with employees required to make an annual contribution to the plan, or noncontributory, where employees make no contribution to the plan. (The exception is deferred profit-sharing plans, which can only be noncontributory.)

Although defined benefit plans were still the most common pension plan in Canada at the start of the century,[3] there has been a continuing trend away from defined benefit plans toward defined contribution plans. By 2004, a study of medium to large Canadian firms found that only 33 percent had a defined benefits plan, while an equal proportion had a combination of defined benefit and defined contribution plans.[4] Some 22 percent had only defined contribution plans, and 12 percent had no pension plan at all.

There are several reasons for the trend towards defined contribution. An early reason had to do with inflation, which was very high in the 1970s and 1980s. As a result of inflation, the best three years of earnings would end up being far higher than the company had anticipated. As a result, money set aside over the years to fund the pension plan became insufficient to meet the obligations of the plan (this is known as an "underfunded plan"), and firms were forced to make large contributions to enable their pension plans to meet their obligations. But this problem doesn't exist for defined contribution plans, since the employer's liability is limited to the amount placed into the plan.

Why more employers use DCP.

Another source of unexpected cost for defined benefit plans occurs as life expectancies increase. This may pose a particular problem in fields in which an increasing proportion of the workforce are female, since the life expectancy of females (82.2 years at birth) is currently more than five years longer than that of males (77.1 years at birth) according to Statistics Canada.[5] For persons who reach age 65, the typical man can expect to live another 17 years, and the typical woman another 21 years.[6] This can make a big difference in the amount of money needed to fund these pensions. Moreover, if life span continues to increase, then pension liability in defined benefits plans will also increase. Compensation Today 11.1 illustrates some interesting

Compensation Today 11.1

Would You Take This Bet?

Project yourself far into the future. You are just celebrating your 90th birthday. An obnoxious relative (how did *he* get invited to my party, you wonder) who always lords it over you because he is four years younger, has the poor taste to comment that he is glad to see you enjoying your birthday party so much, because it will probably be your last!

Hotly, you tell him that you plan to be around for a few more birthdays yet. He replies that if you are so sure about that, why don't you make some money from it? He offers to pay you $1,000 if you make it to your 91st birthday, but you have to pay him $1,000 if you don't (the money to be collected immediately and held by a third party until your demise or your 91st birthday, whichever comes first—he may be obnoxious, but he is no fool!).

You stop to think. You are in normal health for a person of your age; but just how likely is it that you will see your next birthday? Should you take that bet?

You should! In fact, you should try to raise the bet! According to actuarial statistics, your chances of making it to your 91st birthday are greater than 80 percent. In fact, you could be 105 and still have a better-than-even chance of making it to your next birthday!

Overall, Canadians enjoy one of the longest life expectancies in the world. This is good news from a health perspective, but bad news from a retirement income perspective. Statistics indicate that only a minority of Canadians are putting away enough money to maintain their standard of living in retirement.[7] Less than half of Canadian employees are covered by company pension plans, and many of those who are covered will not receive pensions adequate to maintain their standard of living over the 15 to 20 years (or more) of retirement they will enjoy.

But people vary in how much they value retirement income plans. Many young employees are especially prone to not worry about retirement. Some say, why worry—I'll never even make it to retirement! But just what are the odds for a 25-year-old making it to age 65? In fact, better than 80 percent for males, and nearly 90 percent for females. And if you are in normal health at age 25, and not in a hazardous occupation, the odds are much better than that! As this realization sinks in, it is likely that companies that offer pension plans will be increasingly favoured by potential employees.

Chapter 11: Designing Indirect Pay Plans

actuarial estimates for life expectancies and the way they relate to needs for retirement income.

Of course, the actuarial projections illustrated in Compensation Today 11.1 vary for specific employee groups. Accountants will have a better chance of surviving to a ripe old age than coal miners. Making accurate actuarial predictions for a particular employee group and then incorporating them into the pension plan is a complex process, one that is not necessary for defined contribution plans. From an employer's point of view, defined contribution plans are much simpler than defined benefit plans.

A major problem with defined benefits plans since 2000 has been very low returns on invested funds. This has created a major shortfall in funding for these plans.[8] In addition, some defined benefit plans, especially for individuals with relatively high earnings, are running into difficulty with Income Tax Act regulations regarding maximum payouts permissible under the terms of a registered pension plan. Thus, many highly paid employees with long service in the pension plan are at risk of receiving much less than what the total of their own and company contributions would otherwise entitle them to. Switching to a defined contribution plan (or a hybrid plan) would avoid these difficulties.

Moreover, from an employee point of view, defined contribution plans tend to be more portable than defined benefit plans. When employees move from one employer to another, their defined benefits plan is subject to commuted values, which reduces the value of their plan, compared to maintaining employment with the firm.[9] Defined contribution plans are not subject to such commutations.

However, there are some drawbacks to defined contribution plans as well. Defined contribution plans are most beneficial to employees who enter these plans at a young age and have a long period of contributions, but may result in seriously inadequate pensions for those who join the plans later in life.[10] If long-term employment with single employers becomes less common, many employees may be subject to this problem. Furthermore, "the employee is saddled with the investment risk and the risk that annuity prices will be high at retirement."[11] In essence, defined contribution plans transfer the risk of retirement income accumulation from the employer to the employee.

One expert points out that firms are better able to manage retirement fund portfolios and the inherent risks than most employees. As she puts it: "Surely plan sponsors, with access to the various types of expertise required, investment, actuarial, and otherwise, are far better equipped to deal with these risks than are individuals."[12] Moreover, she points out that defined benefit plans offer the advantage of averaging risk over a large group of employees. Some members will terminate, die, or retire when the timing is bad for the fund, but others will do so when the timing is favourable. Such averaging is not possible under defined contribution plans.

hybrid pension plans

pension plans that combine features of the defined benefit pension plan and the defined contribution pension plan

Hybrid Pension Plans

Hybrid pension plans combine elements of both the defined benefit and the defined contribution pension plans. For example, some firms have a defined benefit plan, but they also allow employees to contribute to a defined contribution pension plan. In some cases, firms match employee contributions, to a certain maximum level. Often, these contributory plans are set up as group registered retirement plans. Employees are allowed to deduct their contributions from their taxable income, and the earnings of the plan accumulate on a tax-deferred basis. Employer and employee contributions to either defined benefit plans or defined contribution plans (both of which must be registered with the government and are known as registered pension plans) are deducted from the amounts that may be contributed to a group RRSP, which have contribution limits established by the federal government. As discussed earlier, a recent survey indicated that more than half of defined contribution plans are in fact implemented in conjunction with defined benefit plans.[13]

Experience with Pension Plans

Although not extensive, some research has been directed at examining the impact of pensions on company performance and employee job attitudes. Based on a comprehensive review of the evidence, Allen and Clark found that, on average, firms with pension plans were neither more nor less profitable than firms without pension plans, after controlling for variables such as company size.[14] Interestingly, these researchers also found that total compensation was higher in firms with pension plans and therefore concluded that firms with pension plans must be more productive than firms without them, since these greater compensation costs apparently did not reduce profitability. However, when they examined productivity, they discovered no overall difference between those firms that had pension plans and those that did not. They did discover that pensions apparently had a positive effect on productivity in industries that were not highly unionized and that had high wages, younger workers, and a stable workforce.

Research has identified several important effects of pensions. For example, firms with pensions have lower turnover, and their employees retire earlier than those at firms without pension plans.[15] This can be beneficial to two types of firms—those for whom turnover is expensive and those for whom employee productivity drops off (relative to their earnings) as employees near retirement. But recall from Chapter 3 that turnover can be low due to either affective or continuance commitment. The impact of continuance commitment is for employees to exert only enough effort to meet the minimum standards necessary to avoid being fired, whereas affective commitment can lead to positive job attitudes and behaviour. If pension plans are reducing turnover through creating continuance commitment, then this may not be much of a benefit to the firm.

This may help to explain research findings suggesting a negative impact of pensions in unionized firms—if continuance commitment is the only type of commitment generated by the firm, then high job security may allow employees to perform at the minimum standards necessary for job retention. For example, in a study of a large Canadian hospital, Luchak and Gellatly found that the pension plan generated only continuance commitment, not affective commitment. In fact, as the amount of pension that employees

Chapter 11: Designing Indirect Pay Plans

would lose by quitting went up, affective commitment actually went down.[16] What this suggests is that many employees who would prefer to quit are continuing their employment because they do not want to lose pension benefits, so they are putting in the minimum effort necessary to keep their jobs. If this is what the pension plan achieves, is it actually of much value to the firm?

This argument helps explain why classical firms, especially unionized firms, implement benefits like pensions only with great reluctance. First of all, the cost of turnover is often not high for them, so spending a lot of money on pension benefits is unlikely to pay off for the employer. Second, the job security provided by the union may make it difficult to terminate employees unless they are clearly below the minimum performance standards so the pension system may end up retaining dissatisfied employees who are able to get away with very low performance levels which the firm can do very little about.

In contrast, it is easy to see why pensions are an asset to human relations organizations, which depend on employee stability and on a sense of gratitude and obligation on the part of employees. For them, positive social norms are sufficient to maintain employee productivity at acceptable levels. Since these firms are often not unionized, a generous benefits package can also help to forestall future unionization, which they regard as a threat to the close relationships between management and employees that they like to cultivate.

Health Benefits

One of the benefits most highly valued by employees is coverage in the event of health problems, including disability and death. These benefits are usually provided through some type of insurance program and may include supplemental health insurance, dental insurance, disability insurance, life and accident insurance, and health care expense accounts.

Supplemental Health Insurance

Canadians enjoy a large number of government-sponsored medical benefits under the system generally known as "medicare." In the United States, where government-sponsored universal medical coverage does not exist, employers are expected to bear the cost of medical insurance. This cost can be staggering.

However, because of government medicare, health benefit costs for Canadian employers is much lower, resulting in much lower benefits costs. Nonetheless, many medical services are not covered by medicare, including optical/vision care, chiropractic treatments, and prescription drugs. In recent years, the cost of providing health insurance to employees has been increasing, mainly due to the rising prescription drug costs.[17]

RPC 11.4

Disability Insurance

Many employers purchase long-term disability insurance for their employees to cover disabilities arising from nonwork-related causes. (Work-related disabilities are covered under workers' compensation benefits.) This coverage typically provides for 60 to 70 percent of normal pay and carries on until the employee is able to return to work, reaches retirement age, or dies (in which case, there are usually benefits provided to the surviving spouse and/or dependent children).

Historically, most disability claims have been based on physical disabilities. However, while it appears that this cause of disability has been declining, mental disability is now driving higher disability claims.[18] Recent estimates suggest that mental disorders cost Canadian employers at least $7 billion a year, including the costs of lowered productivity, employee replacement, and disability programs.[19] To counter these problems, some of which may stem from workplace stress or work/life conflicts, many employers have launched employee assistance programs, wellness programs, and work/life balance programs.

Life and Accident Insurance

One item included in virtually all benefit plans is term life and accident insurance. The coverage is usually expressed in terms of a multiple of annual salary (e.g., two times annual salary). Frequently, employees are given the option of increasing their coverage, either at their own expense or on a cost-shared basis. In some cases, insurance coverage is also available for family members, if the employee opts to pay the premiums for this coverage.

Dental Insurance

Dental care insurance has expanded rapidly in the past few years. It has become popular because dental coverage is not provided under medicare and can be a major expense (especially for orthodontic services for dependent children). It is also a highly tax-favoured benefit.

Tax Status of Pension and Health Benefits

Table 11.1 summarizes the tax status of the various insurance and pension benefits. As the table shows, several aspects of these benefit programs have tax implications. First, how are employer contributions treated? Are they deductible from corporate taxes, and are they considered as a taxable benefit to employees on which income tax must be paid? Second, how are employee contributions treated? If employees make contributions to the benefit, are their contributions tax-deductible? Third, is purchase of the benefit subject to a premium or sales tax that may be levied by a provincial government? Fourth, in the case of pension funds, are the earnings of the fund taxable as they are accumulating? Finally, when the benefit pays out to employees, must they include it as income and pay tax on it?

As Table 11.1 shows, pension plans receive favourable tax treatment (up to the limits imposed by the Canada Revenue Agency). Employees ultimately have to pay taxes on the payouts from these plans, but not until retirement, when they are likely to be in a much lower tax bracket. Moreover, at retirement, employees can use the funds to purchase annuities, so that income tax is spread over a number of years rather than being payable in the year of retirement. However, it should be noted that because of RRSP legislation,

TABLE 11.1

Tax Status of Pension and Health Benefits

	Employer Contributions Deductible by Employer?	Employer Contributions Taxable for Employee?	Employee Contributions Deductible by Employee?	Purchase of Benefit Subject to Premium or Sales Taxes?	Fund Income Is Taxable?	Benefit Payouts Taxable for Employees?
Registered Pension Plan	Yes	No	Yes	No	No	Yes
Group Registered Retirement Savings Plans	N/A	N/A	Yes	No	No	Yes
Deferred Profit-Sharing Plans	Yes	No	N/A	No	No	Yes
Health and Dental Insurance/Health Care Expense Accounts	Yes	No[1]	No	Yes[2]	N/A	No
Short-Term Disability (Self-Insured)	Yes	No	N/A	N/A	N/A	Yes
Long-Term Disability Insurance	Yes	No	No	Yes[3]	N/A	Yes/No[4]
Group Life Insurance	Yes	Yes	No	Yes[4]	N/A	No
Group Accidental Death and Dismemberment	Yes	No[1]	No	No[5]	N/A	No

[1]Except in Quebec for provincial income tax.

[2]Applies to both insured and uninsured plans in Ontario and Quebec; only uninsured plans elsewhere.

[3]Provincial premium tax applies in all provinces; provincial sales tax in Ontario and Quebec.

[4]Yes, if premiums are paid by employer; no, if premiums are paid by employee; partially, if premiums are shared.

[5]Not subject to provincial premium tax, but subject to provincial sales taxes in Ontario and Quebec.

individual employees can now create their own retirement plans that have tax benefits similar to those of company-provided plans. In the past, this was not the case, and company-provided pension plans had dramatic tax advantages over individual retirement plans.

Insurance plans enjoy favourable tax treatment as well, especially health/dental insurance and accidental death/dismemberment insurance. In both cases, employees do not pay tax either on the employer contributions for these plans nor on the benefits that are paid out. Since employee contributions to these plans are not tax-deductible, but employer contributions are, it makes sense for the company to provide these plans.

Look at it this way. Suppose that an employer currently pays $800 per employee to purchase a dental plan. If the employer decided to instead give the $800 directly to each employee to purchase dental coverage, the employee would lose as much as $400 of this to federal and provincial income taxes, leaving only $400 to purchase the dental coverage, so they would receive much less coverage. On top of this, the employee would have to pay a higher price for the coverage they do purchase, since individual plans typically cost much more than company plans. In fact, most employees would probably not find it feasible to purchase dental coverage at all, leaving them liable to major dental bills that may arise.

So it is far more cost-effective for the employer to purchase dental coverage on behalf of employees. Indeed, if an employer is not willing to provide the coverage, employees would be much better off to have their pay reduced by the $800 and have their employer pay this money toward health or dental coverage. Compared to purchasing their own coverage, employees would save up to $400 in income taxes and would also get better coverage.

In contrast, employer-provided long-term disability insurance is not as tax-favoured. While employees are not liable for income taxes on employer contributions to these plans, they are liable for tax on any benefits received. (On the other hand, if the employees pay for these plans themselves, employee contributions are not tax-deductible, but any benefits received are not taxable.) However, since the great majority of employees will be lucky enough never to receive these payments, it is far better for them to have the employer purchase the coverage with pre-tax money than for the employee to have to purchase the coverage with after-tax money.

Another popular benefit, group life insurance, has become less tax-favoured over time as the tax rules have changed. It is the only benefit in which employer contributions are considered as a taxable benefit. There is therefore no tax advantage for the employee in having the employer purchase the coverage. However, because employers receive much more favourable rates on purchase of this insurance than would employees, a company-provided group life insurance plan (whether or not the employer or employee pays the premiums) is still beneficial to employees.

Health Care Expense Accounts

Due to quirks in the tax system, a benefit known as a **health care expense account** has become popular in recent years.[20] In this benefit plan, employers place a certain amount of money (health care expense credits) in a separate account for each employee. Employees may then draw on their individual accounts to cover a wide variety of health care expenses not covered by their other plans, including nonprescription drugs; services that are only partly reimbursed under other plans; cosmetic surgery; and even the deductible amounts from other insurance plans. The key advantage of this benefit is that while employer contributions are still fully deductible for the employer, the funds paid to each employee are not taxable at any point—not when they are placed in the health care account, and not when they are received by employees (except in Quebec, where reimbursements to employees are subject to provincial income tax). This is a very significant tax benefit.

Health care expense accounts have shown a dramatic surge in popularity in recent years.[21] Aside from the tax advantages, employers like the idea of a fixed amount set for health coverage. In conventional health insurance plans, as costs increase, the employer must either pay them, pass them along to employees, or reduce coverage—all unpopular choices. With the health care

health care expense account
a tax-favoured employee benefit that allows employees to use employer-provided health care credits to purchase a wide array of health care services

Chapter 11: Designing Indirect Pay Plans

expense account, the employer has the option of not adjusting the health care credits as health costs increase, or increasing the credits less than the full increases in health costs. Of course, the result of this may be employee discontent if the plan is no longer able to cover their needs.

Pay for Time Not Worked

pay for time not worked
an employee benefit that covers a wide array of different types of employee absences from work

This awkward-sounding but descriptive term is used to cover a variety of circumstances in which employees receive pay even though they are not actually working. As discussed earlier, some pay for time not worked is mandatory, including basic vacations, statutory holidays, and rest breaks. But many firms go beyond these mandatory levels and provide pay for additional holidays, sickness and personal leave, educational and other types of leave, and severance pay.

Vacations, Holidays, and Rest Breaks

Most major employers go beyond the two or three weeks of vacation mandated by law (depending on the jurisdiction) and the nine statutory holidays to give 11 to 13 paid holidays on fixed dates and up to three paid "floater" holidays that can be moved around from year to year. Most workplaces also give two paid rest breaks of 15–20 minutes (besides an unpaid lunch break) during a seven- or eight-hour day.

One new twist on vacations is the concept of "vacation buying or selling." Some firms allow employees to "buy" additional vacation days by forgoing the pay for these days. Conversely, employees can "sell" vacation days that they don't intend to use back to the employer. Essentially, vacation buying or selling simply provides some additional flexibility to employees.

Sickness, Compassionate, and Personal Absences

Most employers provide pay continuation for short-term absences from work due to illness or for other specified reasons, such as the death of a family member. Some firms have formal plans that allot a certain number of allowable sick days in a given period, beyond which wages will not be paid. In some cases, sick days can accumulate beyond a year; in most cases they cannot. In other cases, employers do not formally provide sick leave, but do not dock absences if the missing time is made up at some future time. In still other cases, absences may be counted against the annual vacation allotment.

One issue here is whether the only allowable paid absences are for personal illness, or whether other reasons (such as illness of a child) are allowable reasons for absence under the plan. In some cases, firms are relabelling their "sick leave" days to "personal leave" days to avoid forcing employees to claim personal illness when the actual reason is an illness or personal emergency involving a family member. In other cases, employers are simply rolling all leave days together, including vacation and sick leave, and providing these as the total allowable number of paid absences. In a few cases, employers are willing to "buy back" unused leave days, so that employees who do not use all their allotted days are not penalized relative to employees who do use all of their leave days. However, it may not be wise to buy back all of these days at full rates if this creates too strong an incentive for employees to come to work even when they are seriously ill.

Many firms also offer compassionate or bereavement leaves to permit employees to attend the funerals of close family members. Under revisions to the Canada Labour Code effective January 2004, all employers in the federal jurisdiction are required to provide unpaid compassionate care leave for employees who must be absent from work to provide support to a child, parent, spouse, or common-law partner who is gravely ill with a serious risk of death, and their jobs must be held for them until their return to work. Most major firms also provide paid leaves for jury duty. Short-term absences to give birth or attend the birth of a child are also included here. (Longer-term maternity/paternity leaves will be discussed shortly.)

Of course, one way of helping to deal with the need for short-term absences is through a flexible-hours or a flexible-workplace program. For example, IBM Canada lets some staff compress their schedules to four days and also allows them to adjust start and finish times by up to two and a half hours per day to accommodate personal needs.[22] Some employees are also permitted to work at home for several days a week.

Supplemental Unemployment Benefits

When an employee is temporarily laid off and must go on Employment Insurance, many firms offer **supplemental unemployment benefits (SUBs)**, designed to "top up" the EI benefits to some proportion of the employee's normal pay. The usual process is for the employer to set up a fund, to which they contribute regular amounts based on the number of hours worked by employees. This fund is then used to provide the supplemental unemployment benefits to eligible employees and may also include employees on maternity or paternity leave. But the firm's liability is limited to the amount in the fund. Note that these plans have to be approved and registered with the Employment Insurance Commission.

supplemental unemployment benefits (SUBs)

an employer-provided benefit that extends government-provided unemployment benefits

Parental Leaves

Some firms may also offer some period of paid maternity or paternity leave, usually in conjunction with Employment Insurance, which provides coverage for up to 50 weeks of maternity or paternity leave (but not both to the same couple at the same time). Firms may treat maternity or paternity leave in the same way as a temporary layoff and use funds from their supplemental unemployment fund to top up the employee's EI benefits to a certain proportion of normal income. Or if the firm does not have a SUB fund, they may simply have a policy for topping up EI in the case of maternity or paternity leaves.

Educational and Sabbatical Leaves

Some organizations have paid educational leave plans, in which employees are compensated while undertaking a full-time educational program. In some cases, full pay is provided, while in others some portion of normal pay is provided. There is normally an expectation that the employee will return to the employer after completing the educational program; and employees who don't return are usually expected to reimburse the employer for the cost of the leave. Because of their high cost, these plans are usually restricted to key individuals within the organization, and/or there may be some competitive process that awards a restricted number of paid leaves each year.

In some cases, firms offer unpaid sabbaticals. To facilitate sabbaticals, the Income Tax Act has created some opportunities for employees to defer income taxes while putting aside money for the sabbatical. Once an employer has registered a sabbatical leave plan with the Canada Revenue Agency, employees may put aside a portion of their earnings each year, for a period of three to five years prior to the sabbatical. For example, school teachers in Toronto may set aside a fifth of their annual income for four years, and then receive this money in the fifth (sabbatical) year. There are two tax advantages to this plan. First, the earnings from the deferred salary fund can accumulate tax-free until the funds are withdrawn. Second, the total amount of tax paid is reduced, because income is being "smoothed." Instead of being taxed for four years at a higher marginal rate (and then having zero income in the sabbatical year), income is spread evenly over the five-year period.

Severance Pay

The ultimate form of pay for time not worked is severance pay. The federal and provincial jurisdictions have statutory requirements either for notice to be provided when terminating employees without cause or for pay in lieu of this notice; but these requirements are quite minimal. For example, for employers covered by the federal jurisdiction, the only requirement is two weeks' notice, as long as an employee has been employed for at least three months. In Ontario, the requirement is generally a week's notice (or pay in lieu) for each year of service up to eight years, to a maximum of eight weeks. Unionized firms typically have a formula that goes beyond these minimums for providing a lump-sum payment to employees who receive permanent terminations. At the executive level, extensive severance packages ("golden parachutes") are often negotiated on an individual basis at the time of employment.

Technically, if an employee has been dismissed for cause, no notice or severance pay is required.[23] However, unless cause can be proven, an employer may end up with a wrongful-dismissal suit against them and be required to pay a substantial severance award if they lose the suit. There are no hard-and-fast rules specifying the minimum notice for a given employee. However, based on court settlements, the following would seem to be the minimal amounts for fair severance in cases of termination without cause: for labourers, production workers, clerical workers, administrative support staff, two weeks per year of service, two-month minimum; for technical, professional, supervisory, and middle management, three weeks per year of service, three-month minimum; and for senior management, four weeks per year of service, four-month minimum. For all groups, the maximum is 24 months.

In setting notice periods (severance amounts), courts take several factors into account: (1) the employee's age, (2) the length of service, (3) the character of the employment, (4) the availability of similar employment, (5) whether enticement was involved. Essentially, the more difficult it is for an employee to find similar employment, the longer the notice period. Beyond this, the notice period is extended dramatically if an employer had enticed the terminated employee away from secure employment in a different region of the country, and this applies even to new employees and employees who have not yet started their employment with the firm.[24] Recently, Ontario courts have awarded a month per year even to clerical employees in enticement cases, and have made sizable awards even to employees with little or no seniority with the firm.[25]

Employee Services

Employee services are often not included in traditional surveys of employee benefits but are frequently of considerable value to employees and may produce some favourable spinoffs for the organization. A major advantage of these services is that most are tax-deductible to the employer but are not subject to income tax for employees. This section discusses several of the most common and important employee services.

Employee Assistance Programs

The majority of major Canadian firms have established **employee assistance programs (EAPs)** to help employees deal with personal problems that have the potential to affect their work performance.[26] One key problem covered by EAPs is substance abuse and addiction. In these cases, the firm may contract the services of professional counsellors or other specialists, who help employees to diagnose their problems and chart a course of action for dealing with them. This course of action may include paid leave to attend alcohol or drug treatment centres and coverage of the costs of these programs. EAPs may also deal with other problems, such as stress, workplace conflict, and marital, family, or financial problems, either through the use of in-house counsellors or through referrals to outside specialists. Some organizations maintain 24-hour counselling hotlines. One interesting example of a counselling program at a trucking firm is described in Compensation Today 11.2.

employee assistance programs (EAPs)

employer-provided programs to help employees deal with a variety of personal problems

Compensation Today 11.2

Help is on the Road!

Long-haul trucking can be a solitary occupation, with a lot of time spent away from family and friends. So at Reimer Express Lines, support and counselling follows the truckers. For three months at a time, twice a year, Ken Heppner and his wife Holly, hook up their 36-foot trailer and set out from their Winnipeg home to visit the 15 locations across Canada where Reimer has terminals. At each location, they'll pull into the terminal and stay for maybe a day, maybe two weeks, depending on how many people

would like to talk to them. Sometimes people want to talk about a recently deceased parent, sometimes some other matter that is bothering them. Since Ken is also a Mennonite pastor, he is used to talking with people about matters of personal importance to them; but the advice, when offered, always stays secular.

Source: Vu, Uyen. 2004. "Spiritual Support on the Road." *Canadian HR Reporter*, 17(10): 1–4

There are obvious advantages to the employer if the EAP can help to solve these problems, since many of them have the potential to severely affect work performance or cause safety problems. Unresolved problems may also cause valued employees to quit the firm. In some cases, EAPs provide an alternative to simply firing troubled employees, an act which may be seen as hard-hearted and may be damaging to employee morale. Indeed, in order to effectively dismiss a problem employee and to avoid or win an unjust dismissal suit, a company will need to show that the firm did all it could to solve the problem, and employee assistance programs can be used as evidence that the firm attempted to do so.

Wellness Programs and Recreational Services

Some organizations purchase memberships in recreational clubs or sports facilities for employees and their families. Some organizations sponsor company sports teams or help support other types of recreational programs. In addition, some firms provide on-site fitness centres or exercise rooms. Hamilton-based steelmaker Dofasco provides a recreation and learning centre that encompasses two NHL-size arenas, a twin gym, a track, a golf driving range, tennis courts, baseball diamonds, and a playground.[27] In general, these are nontaxable benefits for employees.

Some firms provide these benefits within a broader context of a "wellness program" that typically deals with three main health issues: (a) individual health practices, such as smoking, inactivity, and unhealthy eating, (b) organizational health issues, such as job satisfaction and stress, and (c) physical work environment, such as ergonomics and musculoskeletal injury prevention.[28] Proponents argue that such programs can be beneficial to the organization in a wide variety of ways, including reduced absenteeism, reduced health benefits costs, and higher employee productivity.[29] Overall, a survey of Canadian employers undertaken in 2003–2004 revealed that about 20 percent were offering comprehensive wellness programs.[30]

Childcare/Eldercare Services

Many employees with young children have difficulty finding satisfactory childcare. As a result, over half (54 percent) of major Canadian employers have some type of program to support childcare.[31] The most common program is information and referral services, but 11 percent also provide financial assistance, 11 percent provide emergency childcare, and 14 percent provide either on-site or off-site childcare. In addition, some companies provide subsidies to childcare centres to reduce the costs to employees. These subsidies are not considered a taxable benefit. Ford Motors in Oakville, Ontario, offers an on-site daycare centre and provides a $2,000-per-child-per-year subsidy for employees using it.[32]

At the other end of the spectrum, some employees have the responsibility for care of aged parents or other elderly relatives. Nearly half (48 percent) of firms now provide some type of eldercare program, although most programs simply provide information and referral services.[33] About 8 percent provide some type of financial assistance, including provision of subsidized services.

Given the demographic trends in Canada, the issue of eldercare will be of growing importance to many employees in the future; and if not dealt with effectively, it has the potential to lead to a problems for both employee and employer, including stress-related problems and even withdrawal from the workplace.

Particularly under stress will be those employees who are responsible for both childcare and eldercare—the so-called "sandwich generation." Currently, about 10 percent of Canadians between ages 45 and 64 have both childcare and eldercare responsibilities, and 83 percent of them are also employed.[34] Given current trends toward later childbearing and increased longevity, this "sandwich generation" will only become larger in the future.

Work-Life Balance Programs

Given all the stresses of balancing work and family life, many firms have created "work-life balance" programs to minimize these stresses as much as possible.[35] Work-life balance programs typically include many of the features discussed so far, such as flexible schedules, parental and personal leave programs, health care programs, childcare and eldercare programs, and wellness programs. Indeed, many organizations view work-life balance as an essential element of a total rewards program. Human Resources Canada has an excellent website describing work-life balance programs, and ways that employers can promote this balance.

Financial or Legal Services

As retirement and financial planning becomes more and more complex, some firms are providing employees with access to financial planners in order to help them make good financial decisions. This service is most likely offered by firms with flexible benefit plans to help employees understand the ramifications of the choices they make.

In a few companies, prepaid legal services are provided. There are two main types of legal plans. Access plans provide free telephone or office consultation, document review, and discounts on fees for more complex matters. Comprehensive plans cover matters such as real estate transactions, divorce cases, and civil and criminal cases.

Food Services

Many organizations offer types of subsidized food services at company facilities. This program may be necessary on sites where food services are not readily available. An advantage of on-site food services is that employees do not need to waste scarce break time by leaving the company premises. In addition, subsidized food services constitute a taxable benefit for employees only if prices are set "unreasonably low."

Outplacement Services

Finally, some firms provide assistance to employees whose jobs are being terminated, beyond simply awarding severance pay. This assistance may include advice on how to secure new employment and how to manage financial affairs until new employment is found, as well as counselling to ease the shock of termination. Although these services will, by definition, not be used by continuing employees, employees notice whether terminated employees are being treated fairly, and this will condition their attitudes toward the employer; thus, provision of these services has a positive impact beyond the direct recipients.

Miscellaneous Benefits

Organizations can provide a wide array of other benefits, often related to the type of work an employee does or the type of industry in which the firm operates. For example, sales personnel who must travel extensively by automobile are frequently provided with a vehicle, which can also serve personal uses. Retailers may provide discounts on their products. Banks may provide subsidized loans. There are endless possibilities, and this section will briefly highlight just a few of the most common.

Use of Company Vehicle

In the past, a company-provided automobile that could be used for personal as well as business use was a major benefit. However, changes in income tax legislation have made this benefit less attractive, since employees are now required to declare the personal-use portion of the automobile as a taxable benefit. Nonetheless, since companies that lease a large number of vehicles for their employees may be able to negotiate favourable lease terms, it may still be advantageous for employees to use a company-provided vehicle for personal use. In addition, transportation to and from the job site may not be considered personal use; so even if an employee is permitted to use the vehicle only for transportation from home to the job site, and during the workday, this may still be a significant benefit—and a nontaxed one.

Product or Service Discounts

Many organizations offer their products or services to employees at a discount. For example, the City of Hamilton provides half-price bus passes to all employees. GE Canada gives employees a substantial discount on company products, including refrigerators, washers and dryers, and air conditioners.[36] Most of these benefits are non-taxable to employees, as long as they are not provided below company cost. Besides the financial benefit to employees, these policies also serve organizational objectives by making employees more familiar with company products. Moreover, employee use of company products avoids the potential embarrassment of company employees using competitors' products.

Housing or Mortgage Subsidies

Employers who require employees to relocate to remote areas frequently provide housing at a nominal rate. Some employers provide mortgage subsidies or low-interest loans to all employees. But unless the employer is a financial institution, the mortgage or loan subsidies are considered as a taxable benefit for the employee.

Employee Savings Plans

To promote the financial security of their employees, many firms offer employee savings plans. Imperial Oil offers a plan whereby employees may place up to 30 percent of their annual earnings in a savings plan. The company also provides some matching contributions, depending on length of service. After one year, the company matches 1 percent, after two years, 2 percent, and then up to 5 percent after five years. That is, for a five-year employee who contributes 5 percent of her or his pay to the savings plan, the company will also contribute 5 percent. However, unless the savings plan involves a registered retirement savings plan (which it may), and the employee has not exceeded the allowable RRSP contribution limit, the company contribution is subject to income tax.

Tuition Reimbursements

In an era of constant change, one benefit of particular value to many employees is tuition reimbursement. Some firms reimburse full tuition and book expenses for any work-related course undertaken by employees. Definitions of "work-related" vary, with some employers reimbursing virtually any course undertaken by an employee, and others reimbursing only a very narrow set of courses that are directly related to the employee's job. As long as the employer is deemed to benefit more than the employee from the training, the training subsidies are not considered a taxable benefit.

In addition, with the increased costs of education, another attractive benefit is educational assistance for dependent children. Some firms offer a fixed number of scholarships that are awarded on a competitive basis. Others undertake to provide tuition assistance to all dependent children who meet their eligibility requirements. A major advantage of these plans is that the awards are made directly to the student, rather than the parent, and are therefore taxable for the student, not the parent/employee. Since the student typically has much lower income than the parent/employee, this reduces the income taxes paid dramatically.

Provision of Work Clothing or Equipment

Firms that require their employees to wear uniforms may provide these uniforms to employees as a nontaxable benefit. Similarly, equipment or tools used in the course of performing job duties are also deemed nontaxable benefits. One highly valued piece of equipment is a home computer, and a number of major firms have implemented programs to provide them. Most are hoping that the program will encourage more computer-literate employees, and that this will eventually benefit the company.

Employee Expense Accounts

Employee expense accounts are similar to health care expense accounts, but they are used to reimburse employees for expenses they incur in the course of their employment. For example, some universities have established

employee expense account
an employer-provided benefit that provides a fund from which individual employees can draw money to cover work-related expenses

nontaxable professional allowance accounts through which faculty can be reimbursed for expenses they incur in their work. But organizations need to ensure that the system is set up to comply with tax laws. For example, if a faculty member purchases a computer for home use and is reimbursed for it, this reimbursement is taxable to the employee if the employee holds title (ownership) to the computer. But if the university holds title to the computer, the reimbursement is not taxable to the employee.

RPC 11.1

Fixed vs. Flexible Benefit Systems

How would you like to be able to pick and choose among the benefits your firm offers, selecting only the benefits of value to you, or possibly even forgoing some benefits and receiving the equivalent in cash? Some Canadian employers are now giving employees this flexibility, including such well-known firms as IBM Canada, Du Pont, Husky Oil, and the Potash Corporation of Saskatchewan. These "flexible benefit plans" have become popular in recent years, in contrast to the fixed benefits plans that held sway for many years. Both plans have their advantages and disadvantages, and one of these plans may fit a given firm much better than the other plan.

Fixed Benefit Systems

fixed benefit system

an employee benefit plan that provides a standard set of benefits to all those covered by the plan

In fixed benefit plans, which have been the norm, all employees are covered by a standard package of benefits. The advantages of this approach include simplicity, economies of scale in purchasing the benefits, relatively low administrative costs, and ease in communicating the plan to employees. But the key disadvantage of this approach is that it does not recognize differences among employees in how much they may value each benefit. Also, fixed benefit plans have a tendency to grow in cost as existing benefits escalate in cost or as new benefits are added to meet the diverse needs of the workforce. Existing benefits are seldom dropped to make way for the new benefits.

Semi-Flexible Benefit Systems

Most benefit systems are not entirely fixed. There are a variety of ways to make fixed systems more flexible. The most common approach starts with a "core" set of benefits to which employees "add on" additional levels of coverage or additional benefit options at their own expense. Another approach is the "modular plan," in which employees are given the choice between two or more fixed benefits packages, each of which is designed to be of similar cost to the company.

Flexible Benefit Systems

flexible benefit system

an employee benefit plan that allows employees to allocate employer-provided credits to purchase the benefits of most value to them

The distinguishing feature of a flexible benefit plan is employee control over the disposition of benefits funds provided by the employer, in addition to any funds that employees themselves provide. In a fully flexible approach, there is no "core" or "standard" benefits package. Instead, employees receive a set of "flexible credits" they can use to "purchase" the combination of benefits that best suits them. An example of this approach is the "Beneflex" system at telecommunications giant Telus Corporation, under which an employee can select several different levels of coverage (including none) for each of numerous benefits. Employees can also use real money (i.e., their after-tax earnings) to purchase higher levels of particular benefits after their "flexible credits" run out. If they have any unused flexible credits, they can take them in the form of cash (which however is then fully taxable as employment income).

Forces for and against Flexible Benefit Systems

Canada's first flexible benefit plan was introduced in 1984 by Cominco, a Vancouver-based mining company.[37] During the early 1990s, flexible benefit plans were the fastest-growing pay innovation in Canada;[38] and by 2000, 23 percent of medium to large Canadian firms had them, according to the CPS. Since then, they have continued to grow steadily, with 29 percent of firms using them by 2004. Compared to most pay innovations, they have shown a low discontinuation rate, as 79 percent of firms that had a flexible benefits system in 2000 still had one in 2004, and the number of firms adopting flex plans during this period was more than double the number dropping them. What have been the forces fuelling this growth?

Forces Promoting Flexible Benefits

Flexible benefits plans began in the United States, where employers found themselves subject to skyrocketing benefits costs, especially health insurance costs. Between the mid-1960s and the mid-1990s, the cost of benefits in the United States rose from 10 percent of total compensation to 29 percent.[39] If this weren't enough motivation, flexible benefit plans in the United States (although not in Canada) are tax-favoured. In response, by 1995, 85 percent of large U.S. firms had adopted flexible benefits plans.[40]

Although Canadian firms have also been subject to increasing benefits costs, this escalation has been much lower due to government-funded medicare. For example, according to the CPS, benefits costs in medium to large Canadian firms were about 15 percent of total compensation in 2004, which represented only a modest increase from 2000. However, there is concern that escalating prescription drug costs coupled with an aging work force may push up costs of the health benefits in the near future. Indeed, in a survey of Canadian HR professionals conducted in 2004, more respondents cited "pension and benefit cost containment" as their top priority than any other issue, although "attraction and retention" followed closely behind.[41] Since these two priorities may actually work against each other, HR specialists may be in quite a dilemma!

Overall, benefits costs are considerably higher in large Canadian firms, running at about 20 percent of total compensation in 2004,[42] creating more incentive for large firms to introduce flexible benefits plans. In fact, according to the CPS, nearly 40 percent of Canadian firms with a thousand or more employees had flexible benefits in 2004, compared to about 20 percent of firms with less than a thousand employees. Of course, there may be reasons other than benefits costs why large firms are more likely to adopt flexible benefits than smaller firms, such as the ability to spread the administrative costs of the plan over a larger number of employees, and the greater availability of expertise to manage flexible plans, which are much more complex than other plans.

So how do flex plans reduce costs? In some cases, firms have introduced flex plans as a smokescreen to reduce the amount they devote to benefits. Because benefits plans are so complicated and are poorly understood, it is difficult for employees to tell whether the new flexible benefits plan is really delivering the same value of benefits as their previous plan.

Not surprisingly, it didn't take long for hidden cost-reduction ploys to give the entire concept a bad name. As one observer put it, compared with the earlier days of flex plans, "the difference now is that employees are discontent when they hear they are getting flex, before they even find out what they've lost."[43] In some cases, employees have discovered that they are unable to buy back their original coverage using the available credits, while in other cases, employees can do so initially but then find that increases in credits do not keep up with increases in benefit cost.

In other cases, employers discuss the need to cut benefits costs with employees and introduce a flexible benefit plan to give employees a choice about what to cut from the benefits. In essence, employees are being given the chance to rebalance their total compensation package as they see fit in order to maintain as much value as they can. As long as employees don't regard the flex plan as the *cause* of the reduced employer contributions, they may still regard it as beneficial—a tool to help them protect their economic well-being as best they can. Arguably, this use of flex plans can create a win-win situation, in which the employer can cut benefit costs while employees are able to maintain the value provided to them by the benefit system.

Other firms do not want to reduce their benefit costs in the short term but do want to prevent future escalation of these costs. Of course, as benefit costs increase, firms could simply reduce coverage, increase deductibles, or increase employee contributions without recourse to a flexible benefits plan at all, and some firms are already doing this.[44] But flex plans allow employee preferences to play a major role in the evolution of the benefits package. At New Brunswick Power Corporation, a jointly developed flexible benefits plan reduced projected health benefits costs dramatically, to the benefit of both the employer and employees, as Compensation Today 11.3 describes.

Cutting benefits costs is not the only possible reason for implementing flexible benefits plans. A second reason is the increasing diversity of the workforce. Most traditional benefit systems were developed in an era when the typical employee was a married man with a spouse not employed outside the home and several dependent children. Indeed, as recently as 1967, two-thirds of Canadian families fit this model.[45] Because of the homogeneity of this workforce, it was relatively easy to come up with a standard benefits package that would suit this "typical" employee.

But by 1992, in 61 percent of married couples, both spouses were employed—in some cases by the same employer. Since benefit plans typically cover all members of a family, often the traditional benefits package

Compensation Today 11.3

Flexible Benefits Power Savings at the Power Company

In 1999, projections at New Brunswick Power Corporation indicated that the annual costs of its health benefits plan would rise from $5.3 million in that year to $20 million in 2009–2010. The company couldn't unilaterally change the benefits plan because 2200 of its 2700 workers are unionized. However, because of a good relationship with its union, the company was able to share this problem with the union leadership and ask for their help in solving it. Reduced health benefits costs would benefit union members, because under the collective agreement, benefits costs are shared 60–40 between the company and its workers. Over the course of a year, management and the union worked together to create a voluntary flexible benefits plan that workers could opt into if they wished. By 2003, 68 percent of workers had opted for the flexible system; and combined with a plan redesign, the projected expenditure for health benefits in 2009–2010 was reduced to $11.6 million.[46]

unnecessarily duplicates benefit coverage. In this case, it might be efficient for one spouse to drop the duplicate coverage and use the benefit credits to increase other benefits, add new benefits, or even take cash. At CUC Cable in Scarborough, Ontario, benefit costs dropped by more than one-quarter after a flex plan was implemented, largely because it allowed for better coordination of benefits between spouses.[47]

Moreover, as the workforce has become more diverse, there has been increased demand for additional types of benefits, such as childcare or eldercare, to supplement the traditional benefits. Flexible benefits are seen as one way of dealing with this diversity without raising the costs of the benefits package to the employer. The company simply makes the new benefit available, and employees who want the benefit redeploy their benefits credits from other benefits less valuable to them until they come up with the combination that best suits their personal needs. As their needs and circumstances change, they can realign their benefits accordingly. Essentially, this plan allows employees to maximize the value of the benefit system for any given level of benefits expenditure by the employer. Flexible plans can also help arrange the benefits package in the most tax-advantageous way, as Mary Smith, in Compensation Today 11.4, has discovered.

A third force in favour of flexible benefits is the desire of many employers to change the concept of employee benefits as an entitlement—something provided as a condition of employment—to the idea that benefits are really a type of pay that must be earned rather than simply granted. Flexible benefit systems can certainly help to encourage employees to understand the cost and value of the benefits being provided.

Another force is the change in managerial strategies, as discussed in Chapter 2. As human relations organizations move toward the high-involvement model or the classical model, their attitudes toward benefits tend to change. Flexible benefits are attractive to both high-involvement and classical organizations, although for opposite reasons. For high-involvement organizations, flexible benefits fit with the concept of partnership, as well as

Mary Smith Gets Her Revenge on the Tax Collector

One of your employees, Mary Smith, is annoyed that the tax collector has recently decided to declare the unpaved, muddy, parking spot provided by the company as a taxable benefit. But using your company's flexible benefits plan, she has found a way to get even.

Currently, the company pays $360 per year for the premiums on Mary's $100,000 life insurance policy. At the same time, Mary has increased her dental package to the maximum level, which requires an annual contribution from her (in after tax dollars) of $360. This current arrangement has two tax implications. First, Mary's contribution to the dental plan is not tax-deductible, so she must earn about $720 to pay for this benefit (assuming a 50-percent incremental tax bracket), since the tax collector will take about half these earnings before she can pay the company for the upgraded dental coverage. Second,

Mary will also have to pay tax on the employer's contribution to the life insurance, which will cost her about $180 per year. Thus, the overall cost to her of these two benefits is about $900 per year.

But Mary has a better idea. What if she pays for the life insurance herself and directs the company to allocate the $360 it saves to pay for the upgraded dental plan? Let's look at the tax consequences now. The money she pays for the life insurance is still not deductible, so she must use after-tax income. This means the pre-tax cost of the life insurance is $720, exactly the same as the dental upgrade would cost. But—and it is a big "but"—employer contributions to the dental plan are not taxable as income to Mary. So simply reversing the way in which the payments are made saves Mary about $180 per year in income taxes, without increasing company costs in any way.

with the belief that employees are responsible individuals capable of choosing their benefits more wisely than the firm could do for them. Flexible benefit plans are simply one more way of increasing employee involvement and self-control in the workplace. In contrast, classical organizations may simply see flexible benefits as an opportunity to cut benefits costs, although, as will be discussed shortly, flexible benefit plans may actually be less successful in classical organizations than in other types of organizations. Overall, the Compensation Practices Survey showed that high involvement firms are significantly more likely to have flex plans than other firms.

Some firms that do not currently have a benefits package may find flexible benefits appealing. These employers may have stayed away from fixed benefit plans to avoid getting enmeshed in a program where costs get out of hand. However, a flex plan can be seen as a type of defined contribution plan, in which the employer commits to making a limited sum of money available for benefits. Thus, there is less exposure for the employer if certain benefits escalate in cost.

Firms with flex plans may enjoy a competitive advantage in terms of employee recruitment and retention. First, prospective employees may find the idea of choosing their benefits appealing. Second, if the flex plan is designed and communicated properly, firms with these plans should be able to deliver more value to their employees than firms without flex plans for the same number of benefits dollars. Of course, this assumes that the flex plan is not so expensive to administer that the firm is forced to reduce the number of dollars it contributes to the plan, or to pay more for benefits because of loss of economies of scale, as will be discussed shortly. It also assumes that flex plans are seen as attractive by prospective employees, and not simply as code words for an inferior benefits plan.

Finally, there may be a type of bandwagon effect as the concept gains momentum. This effect may be based on sound reasons. For example, as knowledge accumulates about how to successfully apply the concept, it becomes easier to apply. Moreover, many benefits consultants now have considerable experience working with flex plans and can guide companies with new programs. In addition, computer software has been developed that makes the administration of the system far more efficient and user-friendly.

Forces Hindering Flexible Benefits

Several factors can hinder the adoption of flexible benefit plans. These include the cost of implementation and administration, loss of economies of scale in the purchase of benefits, possible confusion and poor decision making among employees, lack of fit with the organizational culture, and possible resistance from employees or unions.

First, one-time implementation costs in developing the flexible plan can be substantial. These involve the costs of the personnel involved in the design process, as well as the costs of consultants. Few firms have the in-house expertise to develop such a plan without the aid of consultants.

In addition, administration and communication costs are also likely to be much higher than with other benefits systems. Costing out the various options, predicting employee take-up, and pricing the benefits options fairly is a major process. Additional tasks include informing employees about their options and the tradeoffs involved and simply managing the paperwork. Add to this the fact that employees may be tinkering with their benefits packages every year, and it is clear that the additional administrative burden is substantial. However, this administrative burden may be reduced by new spreadsheet packages that allow employees to calculate their various options and costs and then submit their benefit choices. Outsourcing benefits administration to firms that specialize in so doing may also reduce administrative costs.

Another problem with flex plans is the possible loss of economies of scale in purchasing benefits from suppliers. For example, most insurance is much cheaper if purchased in volume. If there is relatively low take-up on some benefits, the costs of these benefits will be higher. Further, there is the issue of adverse selection (adverse from the point of view of the insurance company, not the employee!), where, for example, employees with large families afflicted with many dental problems may load up on dental coverage, while those with no dental problems may forgo it entirely. Or people in ill health may be the only ones purchasing medical coverage. These situations, of course, drive up the costs of these benefits tremendously. To combat this problem, some firms impose mandatory minimum levels of some benefits, but this goes against the flexibility concept. Thus, for all these reasons, flex plans may actually increase benefits costs, both to the employer and employee.

Chapter 11: Designing Indirect Pay Plans

Another drawback is that employees can become confused by the array of choices facing them. As an illustration of the scope for confusion, analysis of one firm's flex plan (which had nine benefit categories, with two to eight levels of coverage per category, and two flexible spending accounts) revealed that employees had a choice of over *two million* benefit combinations.[48] What are the odds that an employee will select the best possible combination for them? Critics of flex plans argue that this complexity could lead to poor benefits decisions and decreased satisfaction with benefits.

Another possible obstacle to flex plans is company culture. Human relations firms may be reluctant to move to flexible benefits for fear the system will be too complex for employees, or that employees will make unwise benefits choices that leave them without coverage in the event of emergencies. Flexible benefits may also be unsuccessful in classical organizations because these firms may not be willing to commit the resources necessary to effectively communicate their plans to employees, and employees may have little faith in the information they do receive. Employees and unions in classical organizations may have especially high resistance to flex plans because of fears that the flex plan is simply a way of tricking them into accepting reduced benefits.

Finally, some benefits consultants are starting to turn against completely flexible systems, arguing that they don't serve many employees well because of their complexity, and that they don't serve many employers well because of their high administrative costs, which wipes out any employer savings.[49] They argue that semi-flexible systems might be the best choice to balance employee needs and administrative complexity.

Experience with Flexible Benefit Systems

Very little research has been conducted on the cost effects of flexible benefits plans in Canada. However, data from the 2004 Compensation Practices Survey reveal some interesting results. A comparison of firms that had flex plans to those that did not showed that each devoted a virtually identical portion of their total compensation—averaging about 16 percent—to benefits. Interestingly, four years earlier, firms with flex plans devoted about 14 percent of total compensation to benefits, while firms without flex plans devoted about 15 percent of total compensation to benefits, suggesting that flex plans did not reduce employer cost, although they may have increased the value of benefits to employees.

There were 12 firms in the sample that did not have flex plans in 2000 but had adopted them by 2004. The portion of total compensation these firms devoted to benefits was about 17 percent in 2000 and about 15 percent in 2004—but this is not a statistically significant change. There were also three firms that had flex plans in 2000 but had dropped them by 2004. One firm showed a slight drop in benefits costs, one showed a slight increase, and one showed no change at all.

One must always be cautious when generalizing from a single study but taken together, these results suggest that flex plans in Canada have in fact had very little impact on benefits costs, consistent with the views of some consultants.[50] But have these plans had any impact on employee satisfaction with their compensation?

Unfortunately, evidence is also sparse on this question. But a study of three Canadian firms, one with a fixed benefit system, one with a modular benefit system, and one with a fully flexible system, found the least satisfaction with the flexible system.[51] To explain this result, the researchers argued that a key determinant of benefits satisfaction is employee understanding of their benefits package, and that this understanding is even more important for a flexible benefit system. They concluded that the firm with the flexible system had not adequately communicated the system, causing employee discontent with the plan.

Other research indicates that employee satisfaction with flexible benefits plans is dependent on whether they believe that adoption of the plan has reduced their benefits. In a survey of Canadian employees with flexible benefit plans,[52] 75 percent of employees reported that their firm had not reduced benefits in conjunction with the move to flexible benefits, while 25 percent reported that a reduction had taken place. Of those employees whose benefits had not been reduced, 87 percent had a favourable reaction to flexible benefits, with only 13 percent showing "mixed" reactions. Of these employees who had experienced a benefits reduction, just 40 percent had a favourable reaction to the flex plan. Clearly, implementing a benefits reduction along with a flex plan has a substantial negative impact on employee perceptions of the flex plan.

Still other research suggests that employee satisfaction depends on the decision-making support that the employer provides. In a study of a large U.S. firm's flex plan, researchers wanted to determine whether a computerized system to aid in benefits decision making might improve satisfaction with the benefits received in a flexible benefit system. They asked three randomly selected groups of employees to simulate the annual flex plan reenrollment process (for selecting benefits) using either a pen-and-paper approach, a computerized decision-support system, or a computerized expert system. They found that the employees using the expert system made significantly better benefits decisions than those using the other two systems, and also experienced a significantly higher level of benefits satisfaction.[53]

Designing the Benefit System

ⓇⓅⒸ 11.1

To develop an effective benefit system, organizations need to deal with five main issues. First, can the provision of benefits contribute to the achievement of compensation objectives? If so, how? What objectives should be set for indirect pay? Second, what will be the process for designing the plan? Third, what benefit system will be used, and what specific benefits will be included? Fourth, how should each individual benefit be structured regarding coverage, funding, eligibility, and flexibility? And fifth, what procedures for administering, communicating, evaluating, and adapting the benefit system are needed?

Each of these issues will now be examined. The purpose is to provide some understanding of the kinds of issues that need to be dealt with in benefit plan design. But this chapter will make no attempt to deal with all the details involved in so doing. Without doubt, the benefit system is the most technically complex aspect of the entire compensation system, and dealing with all the technical details would require an entire book. Fortunately, there are some excellent sources for this already available.[54]

Issue 1: Determine the Role of Indirect Pay in Compensation Strategy

The first issue in establishing an indirect pay system is to identify what compensation objectives it will serve beyond those that can be served by direct pay. Some organizations see no role for indirect pay at all. Recall Electronic Banking System from Compensation Today 2.1. This classical firm concluded that there was little to gain from offering employee benefits. For them, the cost of turnover was low, and the type of person they need was in plentiful supply. So why offer benefits?

Although indirect pay will not be a good investment for many classical firms, it may well be a good investment for human relations and high-involvement organizations, as discussed in Chapter 4. Before moving on to the next set of issues, the role of, and company objectives for, indirect pay must be defined. Examples of these roles to be served may include encouraging membership, retaining senior employees, satisfying lower-order needs for economic security, adding value to the compensation package, promoting specific behaviours of strategic importance to the firm, and helping to remove possible hindrances to productivity (such as through alcohol or drug abuse problems). Ideally, this all will have been done during the compensation strategy formulation process, as discussed in Chapter 5.

Issue 2: Choose the Process for Plan Design

Once an organization has decided that there is a significant role for indirect pay in its compensation system, and has defined the objectives for indirect pay, it then needs to establish a process for designing a benefit plan that will achieve these objectives. Most experts argue that employee participation in this process is highly desirable.[55] This participation achieves three main goals. First, it provides better understanding of employee needs. If the benefit system does not address real employee needs, then it will be of little value to employees, while still costing the employer money. Second, it provides more trust and acceptance of the plan. Third, it helps communicate the plan.

Firms vary enormously in how much employee participation they provide. High-involvement firms likely have extensive employee participation on the design team, whereas human relations and classical firms will rely more on staff specialists, management, and outside consultants. Besides direct employee representation on the design team, employee input can also be solicited through focus groups and benefits surveys.[56]

Issue 3: Identify the Benefit System and Benefits to Be Included

After choosing the process for designing the benefit system, the organization then needs to decide the specific benefits to provide and the type of system (i.e. flexible, semi-flexible, fixed) through which they will be provided. The design team must consider the extent to which a benefit contributes to the objectives of indirect pay, the extent to which it is valued by employees, the cost to the employer, and the net value it adds to the compensation package. Since firms have only a finite budget for benefits, these benefits must be prioritized in order of total value to the firm.

Before taking decisions about specific benefits, the design team must decide whether the firm is going to use a flexible benefit system, a fixed benefit system, or a semi-flexible system. Obviously, a firm with a flexible system can afford to make available a broader portfolio of benefits because employees will not be able to choose all of them.

Issue 4: Determine the Structure of Each Benefit

For each individual benefit, the organization must make decisions on four main structural issues: benefit coverage, funding of the benefit, eligibility for the benefit, and the flexibility of the benefit. In other words, what will the benefit provide? Who will pay for it? Who is eligible to receive it? And is it required or optional?

Coverage

A major decision for the design team is benefit coverage. How much coverage will be provided, how will it be based, and how far will it extend? Take dental insurance, for example. Should a particular dental insurance plan cover all dental expenses, only certain types of dental expenses, or all dental expenses up to a certain prescribed limit in a given period? Does it cover all the expenses of a given procedure, or does the employee need to pay a portion, say, 20 percent of each bill? Is there a deductible, in which an employee must pay the first 10 dollars of every claim? Do some employees receive a richer plan than others?

Moreover, is coverage restricted to the employee, or does it extend to family members? If it's a family plan, how will family members be defined? In an era of blended families and nontraditional relationships, defining such terms as "family member" or "spouse" may not be as straightforward as it first appears. At what point, for example, is a common-law partner accepted as a "spouse" for the purposes of benefit coverage? What status will children of that "spouse" (but not of the employee) receive? Will they be considered dependent children of the employee or not?

In addition, will coverage levels vary for different employees? For example, it is common for life insurance coverage to be provided as a multiple of salary. Pension contributions are also geared to salary. But other plans may be based on seniority, as in the case of Imperial Oil's savings plan, which matches 1 percent of salary the first year of employment and up to 5 percent of salary the fifth year. Will coverage continue after termination? Many firms do continue coverage of certain benefits for retirees and their immediate families.

A related issue is whether coverage will be geared to base pay only or to base pay plus performance pay. As Burns and Gherson note, many firms exclude performance pay as a basis for benefit calculations simply because they have never thought to include it.[57] Others exclude it because it raises benefit costs. But failure to include performance pay in benefit calculations actually serves to weaken performance pay and penalizes employees with a large component of performance pay. In contrast, including performance pay in calculations of benefit entitlements provides a way of linking indirect pay to performance, thereby reinforcing performance pay and making the indirect pay system more sensitive to performance.

Funding

The cost of the benefit (such as the premiums for health insurance) might be fully paid by the employer (i.e., it is non-contributory), by the employee (fully contributory), or it could be cost-shared (contributory). One option is for the basic level of the benefit to be employer-paid, and then higher levels of the benefit to be cost-shared or employee-paid. Of course, under a flexible benefit system, the employee could have the choice of whether the benefit would be employer- or employee-paid, as in the case of Mary Smith in Compensation Today 11.4.

Eligibility

A key issue for each benefit is to define which employee groups will be eligible to receive it. Although firms typically cover all full-time employees, there is often a waiting period before new employees become eligible for all benefits.

A more complex issue is the treatment of part-time, temporary, or contract employees. In many firms, part-time employees (defined by Statistics Canada as anyone working less than 35 hours a week) are offered few or no benefits, even if they have been employees of the firm for many years. Only one province has legislation regarding benefits for part-time employees. In 1996, Saskatchewan passed legislation that all employees who work an average of at least 15 hours a week must receive the same benefits as a comparable full-time employee, although these benefits can be prorated according to hours worked. Temporary full-time employees can be excluded if they do not meet the minimum employment period for inclusion in the benefit plan, and contract employees are typically excluded. In fact, some firms use part-time, temporary, and contract workers for the express purpose of avoiding having to pay benefits.

Some firms distinguish between two categories of part-time employees. Casual part-time employees work entirely at the will of the employer when their services are required. They receive no guarantee of weekly hours, and can be terminated at will. In contrast, permanent part-time employees are considered as permanent employees of the firm, and the firm has a commitment to provide these employees with a certain minimum number of hours on a weekly basis. These employees are often included in the benefits program, although on a prorated basis. Use of permanent part-time work has developed in organizations that want to enjoy the scheduling flexibility of part-time employees but also want to encourage a permanent relationship with these employees. Permanent part-time arrangements are particularly common in industries that depend on a large number of part-time employees on a continuing basis, such as banking (e.g., for tellers) or health care (e.g., for nurses).

Flexibility

The next issue is the degree of flexibility that is allowed for each benefit. Will the benefit be mandatory or optional? If it is mandatory, will there simply be a predetermined, fixed level or a minimum compulsory level, plus optional levels? If an organization has decided on a flexible plan, it will also need to decide if the benefit will be included in the core area of coverage or in the optional area. In addition, what value of flexible credits will be offered? Will employees be able to take unused credits as cash?

Issue 5: Develop Procedures for Administering, Communicating, and Evaluating the System

RPC 11.6

Once an organization has designed the benefit system, it must create a system for administering it and communicating it to employees. The complexity of these tasks depends on the complexity and flexibility of the system that has been designed.

Administration of Benefit System

Ongoing administration of the benefit system can be very complex. The key administrative tasks include enrolling employees in the benefit system; updating changes to employee records and benefit packages; dealing with employees when they terminate and after they terminate; handling the tax issues associated with benefits; dealing with the fiduciary responsibilities of funds held in trust; calculating employer and employee contributions; determining the validity of benefit claims and overseeing benefit payouts; advising employees on their benefit status and answering questions; and monitoring and evaluating the program and recommending changes. Another periodic administrative task is to select and replace sources for the various benefit products.

Virtually all organizations that offer benefits outsource some of this work. For some aspects, such as funds held in trust for pension plans, the law requires a separate trustee. Trust companies, banks, insurance companies, and investment firms are often used for this purpose. Most insurance firms handle the claims processing for insurance-based benefits. The degree to which the other aspects of the administrative process are outsourced varies dramatically, but as benefit systems have grown more complex, and as specialized providers of these services have emerged, use of outsourcing has been increasing.

An advantage of outsourcing routine benefits administration is that it frees the in-house HR staff to focus on the strategic issues of indirect pay and on the communications aspects. However, a disadvantage of outsourcing is that firms can lose touch with employees' needs and problems. That is why evaluation should be a key in-house function, as will be discussed shortly. Most firms believe that communication should also be an in-house function.

Communication of Benefit System

Ironically, although indirect pay may account for as much as one-quarter of an employee's total compensation, and the company pension plan may represent the largest financial asset an employee will ever own, employee understanding of this aspect of their compensation is generally limited.[58] In one striking example, a firm conducting focus groups to improve its benefit system discovered that employees in one location didn't even know they were covered by a pension plan.[59] It turned out that the firm had recently been acquired by another firm, and these employees mistakenly believed that their pension plan had been eliminated in the process.

If a benefit system is to shape behaviour and attitudes, then employees have to understand it. As discussed earlier, research shows that satisfaction with benefits increases directly in proportion with an understanding of the benefit system. There are two situations when communication and comprehension are especially important: when employees must make benefit selection decisions, and when they are in a situation where they may be eligible to receive their benefits.

Among the traditional methods used to communicate benefits are employee handbooks and periodic newsletters, along with an annual statement of pension coverage, which is required under law. But these approaches have generally enjoyed little success, due to the arcane and legalistic language that usually prevails in these documents, combined with a lack of motivation on the part of most employees to wade through the material. However, two events may help to improve employee comprehension of their benefits: the development of computer-based technology for communicating employee benefits, and the advent of benefit systems that require employees to make choices on their benefits, often on an annual basis.

Evaluating and Adapting the Benefit System

Once the system has been put into place, it needs to be evaluated on a regular basis to determine whether it is meeting objectives in the most cost-effective way. There are three main types of analysis. Cost analysis examines the cost of each individual benefit, and what is being received for that cost. Competitive analysis uses data from competitors to compare benefit plans. And benefits surveys examine employee satisfaction with each benefit and the value to them. The issue of evaluation is covered in more detail in Chapter 12.

Summary

This chapter has examined the third component of a compensation system: indirect pay. Although indirect pay is a very large and, until recently, growing component of many compensation systems, employers often have not carefully examined whether their mix between direct and indirect pay is optimal.

Employers vary dramatically in the extent to which they make use of indirect pay, and in the extent to which it is beneficial for them.

In this chapter, you have learned the advantages and disadvantages of indirect pay and the ways that a properly designed indirect pay component can play a role in meeting compensation objectives. You also learned that the most appropriate role for indirect pay to play depends on the characteristics of the firm, most notably managerial strategy.

You are now familiar with the six main categories of benefits: mandatory, retirement income, health benefits, pay for time not worked, employee services, and miscellaneous benefits; and the possible role of each type. You also understand the trend toward flexible benefit systems and the advantages and disadvantages of flexible systems. Finally, you learned about the five key issues in designing an effective indirect pay system: determining the role of indirect pay in the compensation strategy, choosing the process for plan design, identifying the benefit system and specific benefits to be included, determining the structure of each benefit, and developing procedures for administering, communicating, and evaluating the benefit system.

Key Terms

defined benefit plans, 426
defined contribution plans, 426
employee assistance programs (EAPs), 437
employee expense account, 441
fixed benefit system, 442
flexible benefit system, 442

health care expense account, 433
hybrid pension plans, 428
mandatory benefits, 425
pay for time not worked, 434
supplemental unemployment benefits
  (SUBs), 435

Web Links

To keep up to date on current issues in benefits management, check the websites of three publications: *Benefits Canada* (**http://www.benefitscanada. com/**), *Benefits and Pensions Monitor* (**http://www.bpmmagazine.com/**), and the *Canadian Human Resources Reporter* (**http://www.hrreporter.com/ home/**). (p. 424)

To find out the latest requirements for mandatory benefits, check the Human Resources Development Canada website at **http://www.hrsdc.gc.ca/en/ gateways/business/menu.shtml#labour**. (p. 425)

To see the impact of mental health problems from a business perspective, go to the website of the Global Business and Economic Roundtable on Addiction and Mental Health at **http://www.mentalhealthroundtable.ca/**. (p. 431)

To see what various firms are doing with their wellness programs, go to the Canadian Labour and Business Centre website at **http://www.clbc.ca/files/ Reports/summary_of_key_conclusions-final-e.pdf**. The Workplace Health

Strategies Bureau, a branch of Health Canada, offers various resources for workplace health promotion programs at **http://www.hc-sc.gc.ca/hecs-sesc/workplace/publications.htm**. Detailed case studies of wellness programs are also available from Health Canada at **http://www.hc-sc.gc.ca/hecs-sesc/workplace/pdf/healthysettings.pdf**. The following article, from the Canadian Association of Cardiac Rehabilitation, makes the business case for wellness programs: **http://www.cacr.ca/news/2004/Newsbeat12(1)0402Makrides.pdf**. (p. 438)

For information about the federal government's "work-life balance program," go to **http://www.hrsdc.gc.ca/asp/gateway.asp?hr=/en/lp/spila/wlb/06worklife_balance.shtml&hs=wnc**. (p. 439)

To find out more about benefits in Canada, check the website for the Canadian Pension and Benefits Institute (**http://www.cpbi-icra.ca/splash.ch2**) or the Canadian site of the International Foundation of Employee Benefit Plans (**http://www.ifebp.org/general/canadian.asp?canadian**). (p. 450)

RPC Icons

RPC 11.1 **Recommends benefits plan most suited to organizational objectives.**

RPC 11.2 **Ensures compliance with legally required programs.**

RPC 11.3 **Recommends pension plan most suited to organizational objectives.**

RPC 11.4 **Integrates the basic benefits program with disability management.**

RPC 11.5 **Performs a cost-benefit analysis of organizational and employee needs and preferences related to benefits plans, including taxation considerations and funding requirements.**

RPC 11.6 **Manages the transition to new plans, including communications, employee counselling, training, and discarding redundant practices.**

Discussion Questions

1. "Defined contribution pension plans are nothing more than an attempt by employers to shift risk from themselves to employees, who are much less able to bear this risk." Do you agree or disagree with this statement? Discuss why.
2. "Wellness and work-life balance programs are all very nice; but other than providing a safe working environment, why should it be up to the employer to look after an employee's health and wellness? Don't individuals have the responsibility to look after their own health and wellness?" Do you agree or disagree with this statement? Discuss why.
3. "Flexible benefits plans are beneficial to both employers and employees because they allow both groups to satisfy their needs." Do you think that the evidence supports this statement? Do you agree with this statement? Discuss why or why not.

Using the Internet

1. Go to the *Benefits Canada* and *Benefits and Pensions Monitor* websites (**http://www.benefitscanada.com/** and **http://www.bpmmagazine.com**), and make a list of the key issues that came up most frequently in the past two months. Which of these do you think is the most important?
2. The report on wellness programs produced by the Canadian Labour and Business Centre came to nine conclusions, listed on pages 31–32 of their report (**http://www.clbc.ca/files/Reports/summary_of_key_conclusions-final-e.pdf**). Which of these did you find the most interesting or surprising?

Exercises

1. In a small group, discuss how important benefits will be to you in choosing your next job. Then identify the three specific benefits listed in Compensation Notebook 11.1 that are most important to you. Do choices vary in your group? If so, discuss why.
2. Three firms are briefly described below. For each firm, identify the role (if any) that you believe indirect pay should play in the compensation system, and the specific benefits that it would make most sense to offer. Explain why.
   - A company offers lawn maintenance and yard clean-up services in the summer and snow removal services in the winter. It employs about 600 people at peak season (in the summer) and has branches in major cities across the prairies.
   - A retail clothing chain offers personalized service and caters to upscale customers. It is located in major cities across Canada and employs approximately 600 sales staff.
   - A computer software firm develops customized software for various specialized applications for individual clients. Located near Ottawa, it employs about 1000 people.

Case Questions

1. Analyze "The Fit Stop" in the Appendix, and identify the benefits system (including specific benefits) that would make the most sense for this firm.
2. Analyze "Plastco Packaging" in the Appendix, and identify the benefits system (including specific benefits) that would make the most sense for this firm.

Simulation Cross-Reference

If you are using *Strategic Compensation: A Simulation* in conjunction with this text, you will find that the concepts in Chapter 11 are helpful in preparing Section L of the simulation.

Endnotes

1. Chisholm, Patricia. 2001. "Redesigning Work." *Maclean's*, 114(10): 35.
2. Yerema, Richard W. 2005. *Canada's Top 100 Employers*. Toronto: Mediacorp, 352–355.
3. Babcock, Wafaa, and Clare Pitcher. 2000. "Building the Perfect Plan." *Benefits Canada*, May.
4. Conference Board of Canada. 2004. *Compensation Planning Outlook 2004*.
5. Statistics Canada. 2005: http://142.206.72.67/02/02b/02b_002_e.htm.
6. Statistics Canada. 2005. http://www.statcan.ca/english/freepub/82-401-XIE/2002000/tables/html/dt005_en.htm.
7. Scott, Sarah. 1997. "More Risk, Higher Rewards? The New Look of Company Pensions." *Maclean's*, 110(39): 46–48.
8. Brown, David. 2004. "Pension Crisis Has CFOs Reviewing Plan Design." *Canadian HR Reporter*, 17(10): 1–3.
9. Davies, Charles. 2004. "More DC Plans, More for Staff to Understand." *Canadian HR Reporter*, 17(11): G2–G8.
10. Coward, Laurence E. 1991. *Mercer Handbook of Canadian Pension and Benefit Plans*. Don Mills, ON: CCH Canadian Limited.
11. Coward, Laurence E. 1991. *Mercer Handbook of Canadian Pension and Benefit Plans*. Don Mills, ON: CCH Canadian Limited, 15.
12. Pitcher, H. Clare. 2004. "In Defence of the Much-Maligned DB Plan." *Canadian HR Reporter*, 17(4): G4.
13. Conference Board of Canada. 2004. *Compensation Planning Outlook 2004*.
14. Allen, Steven G., and Robert L. Clark, 1987. "Pensions and Firm Performance." In Morris M. Kleiner, Richard N. Block, Myron Roomkin, and Sidney W. Salsburg, eds. *Human Resources and Performance of the Firm*. Madison, WI: Industrial Relations Research Association, 195–242.
15. Allen, Steven G., and Robert L. Clark, 1987. "Pensions and Firm Performance." In Morris M. Kleiner, Richard N. Block, Myron Roomkin, and Sidney W. Salsburg, eds. *Human Resources and Performance of the Firm*. Madison, WI: Industrial Relations Research Association, 195–242.
16. Luchak, Andrew A., and Ian R. Gellatly. 2001. "What Kind of Commitment Does a Final Earnings Pension Plan Elicit?" *Relations industrielles/Industrial Relations*, 56(2): 387–418.
17. Mozill, Tracy U. 2001. "Benefits for Sale." *Benefits Canada*, 25(1).
18. Allen, Paula. 2004. "Mental Health Absenteeism Threatens to Break Disability Bank." *Canadian HR Reporter*, 17(6): 5–8.
19. Vu, Uyen. 2004. "Physical Disability Going Down, Mental Disability Going Up." *Canadian HR Reporter*, 17(6): 6.
20. See McKay, Robert J. 1996. *Canadian Handbook of Flexible Benefits*. New York: John Wiley and Sons.
21. Mozill, Tracy U. 2001. "Benefits for Sale." *Benefits Canada*, 25(1).
22. Rappit, Todd. 2004. "Need Help Being Creative with Perks?" *Canadian HR Reporter*, 17(21): 17.
23. England, Geoff, and Roderick Wood. 2001. *Employment Law in Canada*. Markham, ON: Butterworths.
24. For a full discussion of these issues and for recent awards by the courts, see Ball, Stacey R. 2004. *Canadian Employment Law*. Aurora, ON: Canada Law Book.
25. Litherland, Geoffrey J. 2000. *An Employer's Guide to Dismissal*. Aurora, ON: Aurora Professional Press.
26. Baarda, Carolyn. 2000. *Compensation Planning Outlook 2001*. Ottawa: Conference Board of Canada.
27. Rappit, Todd. 2004. "Need Help Being Creative with Perks?" *Canadian HR Reporter*, 17(21): 17.
28. Martin, Terry. 2005. "Building the Business Case for Wellness." *Canadian HR Reporter*, 18(6): 7.
29. Brown, David. 2005. "Benefits Providers Strive to Meet Clients Wellness Needs." *Canadian HR Reporter*, 18(6): 5–6.

30. Brown, David. 2004. "Finding Out Causes of Poor Health First Step to Cutting Benefits Costs." *Canadian HR Reporter*, 17(18): 5–7.

31. Baarda, Carolyn. 2000. *Compensation Planning Outlook 2001*. Ottawa: Conference Board of Canada.

32. Galt, Virginia. 2001. "Life and Profit on the Table in 'Family Friendly' Contracts." *The Globe and Mail*, July 16: A1.

33. Baarda, Carolyn. 2000. *Compensation Planning Outlook 2001*. Ottawa: Conference Board of Canada.

34. Vu, Uyen. 2004. "'Sandwich Generation' Challenges Big, and Getting Bigger." *Canadian HR Reporter*, 17(18): 1–8.

35. Extensive research on the nature of work-life conflict in Canada has been conducted by Professors Chris Higgins and Linda Duxbury, and the results of their work are available at the Public Health Agency of Canada website: http://www.phac-aspc.gc.ca/publicat/work-travail/index.html.

36. Rappit, Todd. 2004. "Need Help Being Creative with Perks?" *Canadian HR Reporter*, 17(21): 17.

37. McKay, Robert J. 1996. *Canadian Handbook of Flexible Benefits*. New York: John Wiley and Sons.

38. Carlyle, Nathalie B. 1996. *Compensation Planning Outlook 1997*. Ottawa: Conference Board of Canada.

39. Hackett, Brian. 1995. *Transforming the Benefit Function*. New York: The Conference Board.

40. McKay, Robert J. 1996. *Canadian Handbook of Flexible Benefits*. New York: John Wiley and Sons.

41. Brown, David. 2005. "Employers Approach Benefits Cost Containment with Caution." *Canadian HR Reporter*, 18(2): 2–4.

42. Conference Board of Canada. 2005. *Compensation Planning Outlook 2005*. Ottawa.

43. Dorrell, Kathryn. 2000. "Passing the Buck." *Benefits Canada*, 24(5): 19.

44. Brown, David. 2005. "Employers Approach Benefits Cost Containment with Caution." *Canadian HR Reporter*, 18(2): 2–4.

45. McKay, Robert J. 1996. *Canadian Handbook of Flexible Benefits*. New York: John Wiley and Sons.

46. Humber, Todd. 2004. "The Power to Change". *Canadian HR Reporter*, 17(11): G1–G10.

47. Charles, Julie. 1995. "Some Assembly Required." *Benefits Canada*, January: 25.

48. Sturman, Michael C., John M. Hannon, and George T. Milkovich. 1996. "Computerized Decision Aids for Flexible Benefits Decisions: The Effects of an Expert System and Decision Support System on Employee Intentions and Satisfaction with Benefits." *Personnel Psychology*, 49(4): 883–908.

49. Woolf, Daphne. 2005. "The Flux of Flex: How Flex Plans are Faring." *Canadian HR Reporter*, 18(2): 15.

50. Woolf, Daphne. 2005. "The Flux of Flex: How Flex Plans are Faring." *Canadian HR Reporter*, 18(2): 15.

51. Tremblay, Michel, Bruno Sire, and Annie Pelchat. 1998. "A Study of the Determinants and of the Impact of Flexibility on Employee Benefit Satisfaction." *Human Relations*, 51(5): 667–88.

52. Hewitt Associates. 1995. *Survey Findings: Canadian Flexible Benefit Programs and Practices*. Toronto: Hewitt Associates.

53. Sturman, Michael C., John M. Hannon, and George T. Milkovich. 1996. "Computerized Decision Aids for Flexible Benefits Decisions: The Effects of an Expert System and Decision Support System on Employee Intentions and Satisfaction with Benefits." *Personnel Psychology*, 49(4): 883–908.

54. For the most up-to-date and comprehensive source of benefits information, see McDonald, J. Bruce. 2005. *Carswell's Benefits Guide*. Toronto: Thomson Carswell. See also Koskie, Raymond, Mark Zigler, Murray Gold, and Roberto Tomassini. 2004. *Employee Benefits in Canada*. Brookfield, WI: International Foundation of Employee Benefit Plans.

55. Haslinger, John A., and Donna Sheerin. 1994. "Employee Input: The Key to Successful Benefits Programs." *Compensation & Benefits Review*, 26(3): 61–70.

56. Excellent guidance on the preparation of benefits surveys can be found in McDonald, J. Bruce. 2005. *Carswell's Benefits Guide*. Toronto: Thomson Carswell.

57. Burns, John M., and Diane Gherson. 1996. "Should Variable Pay Count Towards Benefits Calculations?" *Compensation & Benefits Review*, 28(5).

58. Luchak, Andrew, and Morley Gunderson. 2000. "What Do Employees Know about Their Pension Plan?" *Industrial Relations*, 39(4): 646–70.

59. Haslinger, John A., and Donna Sheerin. 1994. "Employee Input: The Key to Successful Benefits Programs." *Compensation & Benefits Review*, 26(3): 61–70.

PART FIVE

Implementing, Managing, Evaluating, and Adapting the Compensation System

Chapter

12

Managing the Compensation System

Chapter Learning Objectives

After reading this chapter, you should be able to:

- Describe the fundamentals of compensation administration.
- Identify the key issues in preparing to implement a compensation system.
- Describe the steps necessary for implementing the compensation system.
- Explain how to evaluate the effectiveness of the compensation system.
- Identify circumstances that may necessitate changes to the compensation system.
- Discuss the issues to be considered in adapting the compensation system.

In 1999, Canada Post had a big dilemma. It was trying to cope in the electronic age with HR systems that had originated decades earlier. It seemed that every HR process had its own system, none of which communicated well with the other systems or with users. Supervisors and employees had trouble getting basic information about pay and benefits, and making simple changes to employee hours or pay was an arduous process. Moreover, none of these systems connected well to the payroll function, which had been outsourced years before.

Like many firms, Canada Post decided to create a new HR system to integrate all their HR processes. But unlike many firms, they avoided what is known as the "customization trap," which is driven by the tendency of firms to want to customize off-the-shelf systems provided by HR systems venders to match their existing systems. Because these customized systems are very complex, customization takes far longer than implementing an off-the-shelf system. Moreover, unanticipated difficulties emerge, costs are much higher, program elements don't work well together, and upgrades are expensive because they too have to be customized. Instead, Canada Post went with an off-the-shelf integrated HR system from a major provider of HR software and customized only where they absolutely had to. This process was so successful that it even made economic sense to bring the payroll function back in-house, bucking a trend toward payroll outsourcing that has been evident for two decades or more.

Source: Humber, Todd. 2004. "Through Wind, and Sleet, and the Internet." *Canadian HR Reporter*, 17(19): G1–G8.

Introduction

At last! Your final destination on the road to effective compensation is in sight. You have formulated your compensation strategy. You have designed the technical processes for converting this strategy into a compensation system. What remains is to put this system in place, along with the infrastructure necessary to operate the system. Once in place, the system needs to be evaluated to ensure that it is achieving the goals set out for it and adapted to fit changing circumstances. The purpose of this final chapter is to deal with these issues.

The first section of this chapter outlines the fundamentals of compensation administration, including the key tasks that need to be carried out, and the ways they may be organized. Following that, you will learn about important issues in preparing to implement a new compensation system.

Without adequate preparation, the difficulties in effectively implementing a new compensation system are magnified dramatically.

Next, you will learn the main steps in the implementation process and ways to evaluate the compensation system. Then key circumstances that may create needs for change to the compensation system are briefly highlighted. The chapter concludes with a discussion of some of the key issues in effectively adapting the compensation system.

Compensation Administration

 12.1

For the compensation system to function, someone has to collect the necessary information, calculate gross earnings and deductions from earnings, prepare and distribute the paycheques or notices of direct deposit, and remit the proper amounts to various governmental agencies. In firms that offer employee benefits, someone must also keep track of who is entitled to what and ensure that proper payouts are made. In addition, employees need to be informed of any pay changes that affect them, and they need to have a reliable source of compensation information available to them, should they have questions or concerns. Taking care of these responsibilities is called **compensation administration**.

compensation administration

the process through which employee earnings are calculated and the appropriate remittances are forwarded to employees, governments, and other agencies

Mechanics of Compensation Administration

There are four basic steps in compensation administration: (1) collecting the necessary information, (2) performing the calculations, (3) preparing and distributing the remittances, and (4) detecting and correcting errors.

Collecting the Necessary Information

Compensation administration requires several types of information. The compensation unit must be informed of hirings, terminations, promotions, and transfers. If pay is based on an hourly or daily rate, number of hours or days worked must be collected for each pay period. If pay is based on output produced or units sold, this information must be provided for each pay period. If merit raises or bonuses have been granted, payroll must be informed. If new jobs have been created or jobs have been changed significantly, new pay rates must be established and applied. Where employees have options about their pay or benefits, their choices need to be ascertained.

Performing the Calculations

Once all the information has been collected, gross earnings for each employee can be calculated, followed by the relevant deductions for income taxes, the Canada or Quebec Pension Plan, Employment Insurance, and contributory benefits, resulting in the net pay for each employee for that pay period. Following that, the employer's contributions to EI, CPP/QPP, health taxes, and workers' compensation need to be calculated, as well as payments to private benefits providers, such as for life insurance.

Preparing and Distributing the Remittances

Once the calculations have been done, the remittances need to be prepared and distributed to employees, governments, and benefits providers. Increasingly, with electronic funds transfer, cheques are not physically prepared, but the amounts are simply deposited directly into the bank accounts of recipients.

Detecting and Correcting Errors

It is important for the compensation process to result in correct payments. A system for auditing the process and detecting errors needs to be built into the design of the overall compensation system.

ⓇⓅⒸ 12.2   Compensation Communication

Two types of ongoing communication are important. One type focuses on ensuring that all who have a role to play in operating the compensation system understand their roles. The other type focuses on ensuring that all who are subject to the compensation system understand it. Research has shown that employee satisfaction with their compensation is directly related to their understanding of the compensation system. For example, one study showed that 75 percent of employees with a "very good" understanding of their compensation system thought themselves fairly paid, compared with 33 percent of those with a "poor" understanding of the pay system.[1]

Keeping Managers Informed

An important aspect in compensation administration is to make sure that all those who play a role in operating the compensation system understand their role in the process. Some of the tasks may seem obvious, such as reporting hours worked or employee absences, but new supervisors may not be aware of these responsibilities. In addition, someone must keep track of overtime hours and report them, as well as changes in job status, including terminations and hirings. When merit pay or bonuses are used, supervisors must understand the criteria and procedures for awarding these. Of course, they must also understand the compensation system to be able to answer employee questions about pay accurately.

As well, managers and supervisors must be aware of less obvious pay issues. For example, they need to inform the compensation unit when job duties change significantly or the job needs to be reevaluated. They also need to be kept abreast of changes to the compensation system that affect them or their employees, and the reasons underlying these changes. And if the compensation system has been designed strategically, managers need to understand the intended links between compensation and organizational performance so that they can communicate this connection to their employees.

ⓇⓅⒸ 12.3   Keeping Employees Informed

If compensation is going to serve its intended role in shaping employee attitudes and behaviour, then employees have to understand the compensation that applies to them—the types of compensation provided, the amount, and the procedures for determining the amount. In addition, employees need to be informed of the compensation and benefits options available to them and may need guidance in selecting the options that are best for them. Employees may have questions about their pay and the way it was calculated and must have some avenues to discuss their concerns about pay. Of course, if pay is based on certain performance indicators, as in the case of profit sharing or gain sharing, employees should be kept up-to-date on this information.

Employee knowledge is particularly limited regarding pension plans, as Luchak and Gunderson found in a Canadian study.[2] This lack of awareness may cause employees to discount the value of this important component of the compensation system. Although certain types of information, such as an annual statement of pension contributions, are required by law, employers need to go beyond this minimal communication if they want employees to recognize the value of this reward.

As employee benefit choices become more complex, and as pensions move away from defined benefit plans toward defined contribution plans, the need for employee communication and education increases greatly. But most firms have been slow to respond to this need. For example, a recent study of firms using defined contribution pension plans found that most employees lacked the basic knowledge needed to make informed choices about the management of their pension funds.[3] For this reason, in 2004, pension regulators published new "Guidelines for Capital Accumulation Plans," which outlined employers' responsibilities for selecting and managing investments and for educating plan members.[4] While the extent to which employers can be held liable for poor pension choices by employees is unclear, making some effort to ensure that employees have the tools to make informed decisions in this very important matter is clearly in the employer's best interest.

Indeed, recent legal cases have found employers liable if they have failed to fully inform employees about benefits to which they may be entitled. In one case, an employee with behavioural problems quit his job after his employer threatened to fire him for unacceptable conduct.[5] Later, it was discovered that the employee's behaviour was due to mental illness. The court found that the employer was negligent in not informing the employee of his right to make a claim under the long-term disability policy that covered employees, and in failing to assist him in filing the claim.

This problem of keeping employees properly informed of their benefits rights can be particularly severe under flexible benefits plans, where there is much more potential for confusion than under fixed benefits plans. One legal expert suggests the following steps, as a minimum, to avoid legal liability in this area:

- Provide clear, concise information concerning each employee's entitlement to benefits;
- Review benefits with each employee to identify his or her obligations under each benefit;
- Ensure employees understand the timelines and processes for filing any claims.[6]

Use of Information Technology in Compensation Administration

Because of the large number of mechanical calculations needed, payroll was one of the first functions to be computerized in most organizations. Since then, many firms have also introduced integrated human resource information systems, in which compensation is just one part. Computers not only facilitate compensation administration but also transform complex compensation concepts—such as flexible benefit plans—into usable tools.

For most organizations, the question is not whether to use computers in compensation administration, but how far to extend their use. Possible uses include job documentation and evaluation, analysis of compensation survey data, communication, information collection, calculation of pay and remittances, record keeping, and compensation planning and research.

Job Documentation and Evaluation

Computers are very useful for data collection for job analysis purposes, particularly with a questionnaire approach (as discussed in Chapter 6). Computers can also play a role in developing factor weightings for job evaluation systems, as well as performing the routine calculations needed in the job evaluation process and computing market lines and pay policy lines.[7]

Labour Market Data Analysis

As discussed in Chapter 10, analysis of labour market and survey data is greatly facilitated by computers. A considerable amount of labour market data can be downloaded directly from a variety of governmental and other sources. As well, systems can be developed to store job matches from various surveys and then generate various "market rates" based on a number of different variables and assumptions.

Communication

Computers are being increasingly used to communicate compensation policies and information. For example, Telus claims to have cut human resources administrative overhead dramatically through use of an "intranet"—an internal communications network whereby employees can access compensation information via computer. Compensation Today 12.1 describes how Telus uses computers to provide the information base to facilitate compensation decision making. An effective intranet can also help firms deal with some of the communications responsibilities discussed earlier.[8]

Information Collection

Online computer systems can be used to capture a wide variety of compensation information. Departments can use direct entry for transactions such as new hires, terminations, and pay rate changes, as well as information such as hours worked and days absent. Appraisal and performance management

Compensation Today 12.1

Computers Ring Up Savings for the Phone Company

At Telus Corporation, computers are being used to decentralize compensation decision making to senior line management. Some 35 line managers now make decisions about the base pay of 2000 other management personnel. Telus has abandoned its job evaluation system for this group and now relies solely on market pricing. To make this work, all of the managers with compensation decision-making authority are provided access to an extensive computer database of benchmark jobs, using a commercially available software package known as "Comp Master." It is the job of the HR department to make sure this market database is kept up-to-date.

The corporation has a policy of matching the market on base pay. Within this policy, senior line managers have the latitude to set base pay for their subordinates as they wish, using the market database to guide them. The computer also allows managers to examine pay levels in other units of the corporation to determine whether their decisions are out of line with the decisions of other managers. To monitor this process, the computer allows the HR department to perform regression analysis on the pay structure for each business unit relative to the market and other business units.

Without computers, it would be virtually impossible to provide the information base managers need to make this system work. In the process, the corporation has greatly reduced the number of persons in the HR department handling compensation for the managerial group.

---

systems, such as 360-degree feedback, can be greatly facilitated with the use of an online system for data collection, compilation, and analysis.[9]

The computer can also be used to collect employee choices about aspects of pay, especially benefits choices. Not only can the computer guide employees through the process of benefits selection, but it can also serve as a tool to help them make choices most consistent with their own needs, as was noted in Chapter 11.

Pay and Remittance Calculation

Once properly programmed, computers excel at performing routine computations, such as calculating gross and net earnings, and calculating remittances to governmental agencies. Many "off-the-shelf" computer packages are available for such purposes.

Record Keeping

Accurate compensation records are essential for a wide variety of purposes. These include internal control, financial reporting, and external reporting, such as for income tax or pension purposes.

Compensation Planning and Research

Computers can be used to make projections of future compensation costs with a variety of assumptions and to prepare compensation budgets.[10] They can be used to analyze current pay structures or the distribution of merit money across departments. They can be also be used for analysis of labour productivity, absenteeism, or turnover rates. In addition, they are helpful for conducting online surveys of employee attitudes.

12.4

Privacy and Legal Issues

Online computer systems have the potential to dramatically reduce the amount of paperwork in compensation administration. However, in the past, "privacy concerns and legal restrictions on the use of electronic documents, including electronic signatures, have limited employers' ability to introduce electronic alternatives for payroll purposes."[11] To protect employee privacy in the face of electronic access to employee data, the federal government passed Bill C-6 in 2000, known as the Personal Information Protection and Electronic Documents Act (PIPEDA). As of January 1, 2004, this legislation required that no "personal health information" (such as employee medical or dental claims) can be released to anybody (including third-party benefits providers) without informed employee consent. This means that web-based benefits systems must be careful to limit access to employee records to only a few authorized persons. For example, an employee's supervisor cannot be allowed access to detailed information about the employee's health claims. This legislation applies in all jurisdictions that do not have equivalent provincial legislation, which includes all provinces except Quebec, Alberta, and British Columbia.

Another issue is the legality of electronic forms. For example, until 2000, Ontario employment standards legislation required that individualized employee pay statements be provided to each employee every pay period in paper format. However, with the passage of Bill 88 (the Electronic Commerce Act) by the Ontario legislature in 2000, employers are now allowed to provide electronic pay statements, as long as these comply with certain conditions. For example, simply making the statements available on a website does not comply with the law; the statements must be personally sent to each employee (i.e., through electronic mail), and the employee must be able to keep (i.e., print) a copy of the statement.

Organization of Compensation Administration

A major issue confronting employers is whether to perform all aspects of compensation administration in-house or to contract some or all of it to an outside agency, a practice which is becoming increasingly common.[12] In deciding whether to outsource compensation administration, organizations often distinguish between direct pay (payroll) and indirect pay (benefits). Depending on the nature and extent of employee benefits offered, benefits administration can be a very complex process; and most organizations outsource at least some aspects of their benefits administration, often to the product provider, such as an insurance company. Although processing of payroll is usually more straightforward than benefits administration, many companies also outsource this work; and there are several large companies—such as Ceridian or ADP—as well as numerous smaller companies that specialize in this type of service.

Until recently, there have been few, if any, providers able to supply the full range of compensation administration services. However, this changed in 2001, when the Canadian Imperial Bank of Commerce outsourced nearly half of its human resources department, including payroll and benefits administration, to EDS Corporation. In the process, some 200 of the bank's HR employees were moved to EDS. According to bank officials, the prime motive for the move was not to save money but to free the bank's HR department from the detailed administrative work that could be done better by a specialized service provider.[13]

However, although there have been some prominent examples of outsourcing, the outsourcing movement may be losing momentum. For example, a 2004 survey of the priorities of Canadian HR managers found that only 3 percent considered outsourcing of HR functions a priority—dead last on a list of 21 possibilities.[14] This may be at least partly due to the development and application of improved HRMS ("Human Resources Management Systems") software, as was demonstrated in the opening vignette. A survey of HR professionals conducted in 2005 suggested that about half of the respondents had an HRMS at their firm, and 79 percent reported that they were "somewhat" (54%) or "very" (25%) satisfied with it.[15] The predominant uses of HRM systems were for payroll (72 percent of respondents), benefits (67 percent), and time and attendance (57 percent).

Moreover, outsourcing is not necessarily an all-or-nothing proposition. For example, payroll can be done entirely in-house, it can be entirely outsourced, or it could be co-sourced, with the employer responsible for entering employee pay and attendance, and the outsourcer preparing the paycheques and other documentation. Trans Canada Credit, a Toronto-based consumer finance firm with 2200 employees, opted for a co-sourced model using an Application Source Provider (ASP) model.[16] Application service providers specialize in providing access to specialized business systems software over the Internet, eliminating the need for a firm to purchase and maintain its own applications software.[17] By paying a monthly fee, firms receive access to specialized payroll and benefits software, thus eliminating one reason to fully outsource compensation administration. At Trans Canada Credit, the ASP hosts and manages the payroll application off-site, while providing direct management access for purposes such as employee appraisals, and employee access to their own pay information.

Advantages of Outsourcing

Outsourcing payroll administration and benefits administration has several advantages. The first is cost. Outside providers generally have economies of scale that most employers cannot realize. For example, the costs of computerized benefits systems are very large for a single business, but an outside provider can spread these costs across numerous customers. Outside providers also achieve economies in terms of training, as their staff can specialize in compensation administration on a full-time basis, thus also reducing costs.

A second advantage is expertise. Outside providers may be in a position to employ specialized legal and professional experts that a single employer, especially a small or medium-sized one, simply could not afford. Third, when freed of the responsibility for day-to-day administration of the compensation system, in-house compensation managers may be able to spend more time on the strategic aspects of pay rather than on simply keeping the system running.[18] However, there is debate about whether that actually happens. For example, one U.S. researcher claims that "I have found no evidence that an

HR department becomes 'more strategic' after outsourcing major parts of the HR function. In fact, I found the exact opposite."[19]

Disadvantages of Outsourcing

One concern about the outsourcing of benefits administration is that the employer may lose touch with emerging problems and issues, or even lose the capacity to understand the benefit system. The firm may become overreliant on advice from the service provider, who may not understand the organizational context, especially if changes to managerial strategy are taking place. Moreover, service providers may not be concerned with looking for the mix of benefits that best serves the particular compensation objectives of a given employer.

Managing the relationship with the vendor can be a time-consuming and difficult process. If service contracts fail to specify all the details of who is responsible for what, within what time frame, and with what recourse if performance failures occur, then disagreements may materialize that take time and energy to resolve. For example, if paycheques are late, who covers the cost to employees of bounced cheques and late credit card payments?

One potential drawback to outsourcing is the impact on employee morale if it is necessary to lay off employees when their functions are contracted out. This is not much of an issue for classical firms; but for human relations and high-involvement firms, it is a serious consideration. Costs of severance and outplacement counselling also need to be considered. Although the Canadian Imperial Bank of Commerce avoided this problem by transferring its in-house employees to the service provider, this option is not available to all firms.

So when should outsourcing be considered? Four factors are key considerations: company size, internal capabilities, complexity and dynamism of the compensation system, and the strategic importance of compensation. Regarding company size, research has shown that many large firms believe that they can handle payroll and benefits more efficiently in-house because they can achieve economies of scale not available to smaller firms.[20] Internal capabilities can also influence outsourcing decisions: if the firm is already using a sophisticated human resources information system, and if computer systems and support are already in place, separating payroll and benefits from the system by outsourcing them may make little sense.

The more complex, unique, and dynamic the compensation system is, the more preferable it is to develop the expertise for running it in-house, since an outside provider may be reluctant to devote specialized resources to an individual customer, which reduces the provider's economies of scale and drives up costs. Dynamic systems also interfere with the provider's economies of scale if frequent changes are needed, which either drive up costs or cause provider resistance to system changes, thus increasing the rigidity of the compensation system.

A final consideration is the strategic importance of compensation. The more that compensation is regarded as a strategic variable, the more important it is to keep in-house control of the compensation system. However, as discussed earlier, some observers believe that the strategic focus of the compensation function is enhanced when routine administrative functions are outsourced. The proper balance between outsourcing and in-house provision of compensation services probably differs for each firm.

Preparing for Implementation

RPC 12.1

Even after the compensation strategy has been established and the technical processes determined, there is still much to be done before the new compensation system can be implemented. These tasks include identifying and dealing with remaining administrative details, assigning responsibilities and planning the infrastructure, documenting the system, developing a training and communications plan, developing the compensation budget, developing an evaluation plan, and developing the implementation plan itself.

Deciding the Administrative Details

After an organization has chosen its compensation strategy and main technical processes, it must deal with many other administrative details. Most of these are very mundane, sometimes so mundane that they are forgotten altogether, only to rear their heads during implementation.

For example, how often will employees be paid? Weekly, biweekly, monthly? Will cheques be distributed at work or mailed to employees' homes? Will direct deposit be available? If performance pay is used, how will the performance criteria be measured, how often, and by whom? When will performance appraisals take place, and when will pay raises take effect? If a profit-sharing committee is established, who will serve on it and how will they be selected?

If indirect pay is used, how and by whom will each of the employee benefits be provided? Will insurance claims be submitted through the employer or directly to the service provider? If an employee assistance program is available, which agencies are to be used? If company cars are to be provided, what will be the models and options, and will they be bought or leased? If a daycare facility is to be established at the workplace, where will it be located? Who will staff it?

Assigning Responsibilities and Planning the Infrastructure

Once all of the tasks and procedures for operating the compensation system have been identified, the organization needs to assign specific responsibilities for performing these tasks and plan the infrastructure to support the system. Who exactly will be responsible for inputting employee transactions? Who will develop the forms for recording these transactions and the computer systems for performing the pay calculations? Who will prepare the cheques: a payroll section in the human resources department, the accounting department, or an outside provider?

Documenting the Compensation System

If an organization is going to apply the compensation system uniformly, it must document the program. Two aspects of documentation are particularly

NEL

Chapter 12: Managing the Compensation System

473

important. First is the compensation system itself. If job evaluation is to be used, then manuals must be prepared describing the specific procedures to be used. If pay for knowledge is used, then procedures for assessing skill levels and competencies must be documented. Benefits must also be described, along with application procedures, limits, and the like.

Second, the organization must document assigned responsibilities for carrying out the various compensation processes, spelling out which departments are responsible for which tasks. It also needs to negotiate and draw up contracts with service providers. These contracts need to describe the services to be provided, including minimum performance standards and penalties for failure to meet them, as well as the employer responsibilities. Beyond addressing foreseeable tasks, contracts also need to be flexible enough to deal with unknown future events. Quite a challenge for any document!

ⓇⓅⒸ 12.2   Developing a Training and Communications Plan

Developing a training plan is also important for implementation of a new compensation system. First, key support people in the human resources department must fully understand the system and its components. They can then serve as trainers and advisers for the rest of the organization. Second, there must be sufficient training for supervisors, who will play a key role in many aspects of the system, from job description, to job evaluation, to performance appraisal, to approving salary increases. The third step is the training for all others who have a role in operating the systems, ranging from secretaries (who must submit departmental time cards) to recruiters (so that they will be able to explain the compensation system accurately to potential new employees).

Also, a plan to communicate the new system to all organizational members who are affected by it needs to be developed. As discussed earlier, a pay system has the desired impact on attitudes and behaviour only if it is understood (although it could have a negative impact on attitudes and behaviour if it is misunderstood). Not only should the new system be well communicated, but so should the underlying rationale and need for the new system. Employees are always sensitive about pay; so a misunderstanding of the motives underlying the new system may arouse suspicion, mistrust, and even resistance to the new system. Preventing this suspicion and mistrust is one reason why many experts recommend employee participation in compensation system development. Another advantage is that communicating the final system will be easier, since employees have been kept informed as it was being developed.

When developing the communications plan, organizations need to carefully plan the media and process for communications, along with the timing. In some cases, the communications process starts with a presentation by the CEO on the general features of the new system, the motives for introduction, and its objectives. This may be followed by small group meetings conducted by supervisors (once they have been trained in the new system) or by personnel from the human resources department. If the new system is complex, separate meetings may be planned for different aspects of the new system, with one meeting for direct pay and another for indirect pay, for example. Some firms also prepare videotapes for employees who could not attend these meetings and for new employees. Informational brochures typically need to be developed for each plan aspect. In addition, a telephone "hot line" for questions or a computer website may be set up.

If individual performance pay is part of the compensation package, then performance expectations also need to be communicated. If performance pay is going to be linked to departmental or organizational indicators, then management must not only communicate what these indicators are but also provide status reports on these indicators. Indeed, in some manufacturing plants, "electronic scoreboards" provide up-to-the-minute updates on achievement of organizational goals.[21] At Saskatoon-based Cameco Corporation, one of the world's largest producers of uranium, charts showing progress toward meeting divisional and corporate incentive goals are posted at every work unit and are updated throughout the year.

Finally, organizations need to consider how to communicate the reasons or the motives for changing the compensation system. Any change, no matter what it is, will be accepted more readily if people understand the need for the change. Not communicating the motives for the change is guaranteed to engender suspicion and mistrust of the changes, especially when the change concerns something that is so central for all employees—their compensation.

Budgeting for Compensation

A compensation budget for the coming year is usually an essential part of the planning process for most organizations. Such a budget can also serve as a way to control compensation costs (for example, by requiring departments to secure authorization to exceed their budgeted allocation) and as one benchmark against which to evaluate whether the compensation system is behaving as expected when it was formulated.

Traditionally, compensation budgeting has been done in one of two ways—either bottom-up or top-down. In the bottom-up approach, a budget is created by applying the compensation rates to employees, factoring in probable merit and seniority increases as well as expected turnover (turnover reduces compensation costs because new employees usually start at a lower rate than those who are retiring or quitting). In the top-down approach, management creates a budget by setting a limit on the total amount of compensation available for the coming year (usually based on some upward adjustment to the previous year's compensation bill) and then dividing the available funds among departments and units, who then divide it among their employees.

The approach advocated in this book is a top-down approach for the formulation of *compensation strategy*, to ensure that the compensation strategy dovetails with other key strategic aspects of the organization; but a bottom-up approach for *compensation budgeting*. A top-down approach to budgeting, where an arbitrary amount is allocated to compensation, undermines the whole notion of strategic pay. The main advantage of top-down budgeting is simplicity; but with new computer-based human resource management systems, this advantage disappears.[22]

Developing the Evaluation Plan

Prior to implementation, an organization needs a plan for evaluating the success of the compensation system, along with a system for monitoring conditions warranting changes to the compensation system. Evaluation criteria need to be set out, as well as procedures for collecting the evaluation information. Depending on the criteria, organizations may need to collect some evaluation information (such as employee attitudes) prior to implementation, to serve as a benchmark for evaluating consequences of the new system. Normally, these evaluation criteria are based on the strategic objectives for the compensation system. Each of these two crucial issues—developing evaluation criteria and monitoring organizational circumstances—are discussed in more depth later in the chapter.

Developing the Implementation Plan

Of course, someone or some group needs to be given responsibility for spearheading the implementation process. Depending on the magnitude and scope of the changes, several committees or task forces may be needed, each responsible for a particular aspect of the new compensation system, operating under the supervision of an umbrella group. For example, there may be one implementation task force for base pay, another for performance pay, and a third for indirect pay. There may even be separate task forces for specific programs, such as profit sharing. If the compensation plan is different for different employee groups, there may be a separate task force for each group.

The composition of these task forces is an important matter. Normally, the umbrella group is chaired by a senior executive, such as the head of human resources. It may even include the CEO if the changes are of sufficient magnitude. This body could conceivably be the same body that developed the new compensation system. Whether or not it includes employee representatives is a reflection of the managerial strategy pursued by the organization. But inclusion of a broad spectrum of employees would certainly be expected for high-involvement organizations, particularly on the subsidiary committees or task forces.

The schedule for implementation is a crucial matter. When will the system start? How long will it take to carry out the various steps in the implementation process? And are there other matters that need attention before implementation can begin?

For example, performance pay will be effective only if employees have control over performance. For employee control to occur, decentralization of decision making may be necessary. But decentralizing decision making will be irresponsible unless employees have the information to make effective decisions and the training to interpret and utilize that information. When will this training be done? When will the information systems be revamped? All of these considerations need to be taken into account when the implementation schedule is being developed. Of course, the greater the number of changes, the more complex this pre-implementation stage will be. But, the more that an organization gets the stage properly set, the larger the payoff will be later on.

Timing is another important implementation decision. If extensive changes are being made, should they be phased in? In theory, no. There is an old saying: "You can't leap a chasm in two jumps." To function effectively, all complementary parts of the organizational system need to be in place at the same time. But the reality is that a single implementation date simply may not be feasible for all the needed changes. Of course, this timing dilemma is one reason why many compensation changes fail to produce the intended results.

However, as long as everyone understands that all the pieces are coming, then phasing in these changes may not be a problem. For example, if jobs are changed to make them more challenging and interesting, the intrinsic motivation from this alone may be enough to keep employees motivated, at least for a while. But if employees do become more productive and contribute more to the organization, this enthusiasm will fade if the financial recognition fails to follow. Conversely, if performance pay is introduced, changes to the job structure to allow employees more control over their own performance cannot lag too far behind.

If the organization is very large and is divided into separate business units, it may be possible to implement the new system in one of these units first, in order to assess the consequences and to identify any adjustments that need to be made.

Implementing the Compensation System

R P C 12.1

Compared with the preparation, actual implementation of the new compensation system is relatively straightforward. The implementation task forces need to be staffed and the administrative infrastructure put in place and tested. Training of key actors in the system needs to be conducted, and the system must be communicated. Finally, the new system needs to be launched, and the wrinkles smoothed out.

Step 1: Establish the Implementation Task Forces

The first step in starting the implementation process is to appoint individuals to the implementation bodies and to provide the technical and administrative support for those bodies. Task force members need to fully understand the new compensation system as well as the key issues and steps in the implementation process.

Step 2: Put the Infrastructure in Place

Next, the compensation infrastructure must be put in place. Employees need to be hired or reassigned. Facilities need to be provided. The computer system has to be developed and tested. Additional hardware may need to be purchased. Human resources personnel must be trained in the system. The forms, brochures, and communications material should be developed. Trainers need to be selected and trained.

As well, necessary pre-implementation evaluation material needs to be collected. For example, it is often useful to conduct surveys of key employee attitudes before system implementation in order to have a baseline for future comparisons. Such a survey should ideally be done as early in the process as possible, since information about the new system may affect these preexisting attitudes.

Step 3: Test the System

It is crucial that the compensation system be tested before implementation. One approach is to run a computer simulation of how it would function. Employees would be put on the system, the data collected and input into the system, pay calculated, and so on—*before* the previous system is abandoned. This test allows time for identifying flaws and bugs in the system and double-checking the accuracy of the calculations.

Step 4: Conduct the Training

Once the infrastructure is in place and debugged, it is time to train all those outside the HR department who will play a role in the new system. This normally includes managers, supervisors, and other personnel who play an administrative role in the process. Training sessions have to be scheduled, trainees informed, and the training conducted.

Step 5: Communicate the System

The communications program should now be activated. But simply making sure that everyone has sat through the video from the company president and has received the plan brochures doesn't guarantee that communication has taken place. Communication does not actually occur until *understanding* passes from the sender to the receiver. Feedback is needed to check whether the key elements of the message were successfully communicated. Two-way communication greatly enhances the likelihood of effective communication.

Step 6: Launch and Adjust the System

After all this preparation, the actual launch of the system may seem anticlimactic. However, it is likely that the first "cycle" of the new compensation system will be extremely hectic, with many unanticipated problems and issues arising. No matter how careful the preparation, some elements of the plan will not work. Adjustments will need to be made just to keep the system running. Many of these changes will be short-term fixes, which will later be incorporated into the system. For example, the computer system may not correctly calculate the holiday pay of permanent part-time employees who are on medical leave. But this adjustment can be calculated by hand until the computer system is reprogrammed.

Ⓡ Ⓟ Ⓒ 12.5   Evaluating the Compensation System

Evaluating the effectiveness of the compensation system is no easy matter, and this aspect of compensation management is probably the most poorly done. There are two main reasons for this. The first is that separating out the precise impact of compensation on organizational performance with any degree of certainty is virtually impossible. There are just too many factors that affect overall organizational performance. The second reason is that most organizations don't even try to evaluate their compensation system, either because they don't know how, or because they consider it a futile effort.

But if the right information is collected, useful inferences about the effectiveness of the compensation system can be drawn, even if the exact role of compensation in organizational success is impossible to specify. However, a thorough evaluation takes a considerable effort, using multiple indicators; and a slipshod attempt at evaluation may do more harm than good. Only with a comprehensive set of relevant indicators can useful conclusions be drawn.

Evaluating the Impact of the Compensation System

⦗R⦘⦗P⦘⦗C⦘ 12.6

What is the best way to evaluate the compensation system? In general, the best design for assessing the impact of any organizational change is what is known as a "pre-test/post-test control group" design. What this means is that scores on important indicators are measured before and after implementation of the new system in a given organizational unit. These indicators are also measured at the same points in time in a comparable unit in which the new compensation system has not been applied. Use of this "control group" allows assessment of whether changes occurring in the "experimental group" were really due to the new compensation system, and not due to other changes.

Of course, using this design in real-life organizations is very difficult. Most organizations do not have units that are comparable to but independent of each other to use as control groups. And even if they did, they might not wish to exclude these groups from the new compensation system. (In fact, if the unit knows that it has been excluded from the new compensation system, this knowledge alone may actually change behaviour in the unit, diminishing its value as a control group.) Some organizations try to get around this problem by using other organizations as a type of control group, if the relevant data can be obtained from them.

Another problem with using this design is that for the results to be valid, only the compensation system—nothing else—should change during the evaluation period. Of course, for most organizations, the reality is that many things are changing all the time. The greater the extent of other changes, the less likely it is that any increases or decreases in performance can be attributed to the compensation system.

Timing of the evaluation is yet another critical element of an evaluation plan. Normally, the logical time for the first evaluation is one year after implementation, because one complete cycle will have been carried out. But is one year long enough to determine whether the desired consequences of the new compensation system are materializing? The answer depends on the magnitude of the changes being made and the types of consequences that are desired. Certain indicators, such as employee attitudes, change fairly quickly, while other indicators, such as organizational performance, change much more slowly. In fact, a phenomenon known as the **initial dip** often takes place; this is a tendency for performance to decline during the initial stages of any

initial dip

a tendency for performance to decline during the initial stages of any change

change, until people start to understand and become proficient in the new system. Moreover, costs of changes are usually immediate, while benefits are gradual. For example, a change in compensation strategy to lead the market increases costs immediately, but only increases productivity gradually, as the turnover rate declines, and as the firm is able to attract a higher calibre of employee.

On the other hand, some changes—such as slashing pay rates—may bring immediate gain but long-term pain, as the company's best performers gradually leave. But the key point is that it may take several years to really understand the impact of major changes to the compensation system, and thus evaluation should be carried out on a continuing basis.

The impact of the compensation system on organizational performance can be examined in three ways: through the impact on compensation costs, the impact on compensation objectives, and the impact on other organizational performance indicators.

Impact on Compensation Costs

One way of examining the impact of the new system on compensation costs is to compare actual compensation costs with budgeted costs. But what if you discover that actual compensation expenditures are much lower than budgeted? Great news, right? Not necessarily. Perhaps it means that senior employees hate the new system and are quitting in droves, only to be replaced by new employees who are much less qualified—and paid much less. This may make compensation costs look good but will probably have adverse consequences in terms of training costs and employee performance, which may well outweigh the compensation savings over the longer run.

Now, let's suppose the opposite has occurred, and total compensation expenditures are considerably *higher* than budgeted. This can only be bad news, right? Maybe not. Perhaps the system is doing even better than expected in retaining experienced employees, and the turnover rate is down, resulting in fewer savings from replacing senior employees with junior employees.

Another way of looking at compensation expenditures is average earnings per employee, which standardizes for any change in the number of employees. What if average earnings per employee are much higher than projected? In fact, this may be wonderful news, if these higher earnings are primarily a result of a gain-sharing plan. Since cost savings are split between the employer and employee in a gain-sharing plan, the more employees earn from it, the greater the savings to the company.

On the other hand, higher-than-budgeted compensation expenditures may not be wonderful news. Perhaps the job evaluation system has been overly generous in rating jobs, and too many jobs are in high pay grades. Perhaps supervisors are granting merit increases too readily. Perhaps the performance thresholds for individual bonus plans have been set too low. Perhaps one of the employee benefits is costing much more than expected.

Of course, still another possibility is that the budgeted compensation figures were not realistic in the first place, and comparisons to the budget would therefore be meaningless.

In medium to large organizations, examining compensation expenditures on a unit-by-unit basis makes a lot of sense. If one or two departments stand out from the others, this difference may warrant investigation. These differences may turn out to be justified, but they may also indicate inconsistency in the application of the new system. Other ways to assess compensation costs are to compare them with compensation expenditures in previous years, or with those of competitors.

But note that unless the goal of the new system was to reduce compensation costs, compensation costs alone do not give the whole picture. What is important is what the organization is receiving in return for its investment in compensation. So any evaluation that starts and ends with compensation costs may be worse than useless. Instead, the total impact of the system, including the impact on compensation objectives, must be assessed.

Impact on Compensation Objectives

While formulating the compensation strategy, the organization set out objectives for the compensation system. During the pre-implementation phase, it identified specific indicators and set up procedures to collect the necessary data. At this point, it can assess progress in meeting these objectives. If it has achieved them only partially, it needs to carefully examine the compensation system to determine whether modifications need to be made. Of course, the organization should also reexamine the objectives themselves to determine whether they are realistic.

Impact on Other Indicators

Let's suppose that our compensation objectives have been fully achieved. We should pat ourselves on the back, right? Not necessarily. We still need to examine whether there have been any unintended negative consequences. The following examples illustrate actual cases where compensation objectives were achieved, but the net impact of the new compensation system on company performance was actually negative.[23]

A retailer wanted store managers to improve their sales margins by introducing higher-value products, so the firm paid a bonus to managers based on the margin level obtained. Margins did increase to the desired levels. However, at the same time, overall sales volumes and market share dropped. Closer examination revealed that most store managers had raised their margins simply by increasing prices, rather than by introducing new products.

A consumer electronics firm wished to more rapidly reduce production costs of new products after their introduction. (Whenever a new product is introduced, production costs usually decrease over time.) So the firm instituted bonuses to managers based on how quickly after product launch these cost reductions were achieved. The objective was achieved: reduction in production costs occurred much more rapidly after the bonus system was put in place. However, the company eventually discovered that managers achieved this cost reduction by delaying product launch until they could work out ways of reducing production costs that could be quickly implemented after product launch. This process slowed the introduction of new products and translated into losses in sales and market share.

RPC 12.6

Organizational Performance Indicators

The following are some examples of the indicators that can be used in measuring the impact of the compensation system on the organization as a whole.

Compensation Cost Indicators

compensation cost ratio

the ratio of total compensation costs to total costs or to revenues

average employee earnings

total compensation divided by the number of full-time equivalent employees

There are two main indicators of compensation costs: compensation cost ratios and average earnings per employee. **Compensation cost ratios** are determined by taking total compensation costs as a percentage of total costs, or as a percentage of revenues. **Average employee earnings** takes total compensation and divides it by the number of full-time equivalent employees it covers. These two measures are not synonymous and tell us different things.

For example, it is possible for average employee earnings to go up but for the compensation cost ratio to go down. It is also possible for average employee earnings to go down but compensation cost ratio to go up. Finally, it is also possible for both average earnings and compensation cost ratio to go up and for profits to go up at the same time. How can this be?

Average employee earnings takes the perspective of the individual employee. If it goes up, then the typical employee is earning more money; if it goes down, the typical employee is earning less money. Compensation cost ratio takes the total of all compensation paid to all employees. It may increase for one of three reasons: if average employee earnings increase, if total number of employees increases, or if total costs or revenues decrease. Thus, it is possible for average earnings to increase but compensation cost ratio to decrease, if fewer employees are required to perform the work of the organization.

It is also possible for the compensation cost ratio to increase, even without any increase in total compensation or average earnings, if total costs or revenues go down. If the increase in compensation cost ratio is due to lower noncompensation costs, then the increase in compensation cost ratio is not necessarily bad news at all. However, if the increase in compensation cost ratio is due to declining revenues, then it *is* bad news. Conversely, a decrease in compensation cost ratio is not good news if it is due to increases in noncompensation costs, but it *is* good news if it is due to increases in revenues. In the latter case, the decreased compensation cost ratio is a sign of greater productivity.

Clearly, what happens to earnings and total compensation costs is just part of the picture. Also important is what happens to employee performance and productivity. Employee performance may be instrumental in reducing noncompensation costs or in increasing revenue. In addition, higher average earnings may increase the retention rate, thus reducing recruiting and training costs.

Financial Indicators

A variety of specific financial indicators can be used to assess overall organizational performance. These include profitability, return on equity, revenue growth, and total costs. Gross margins and sales margins can also be computed.

These can be analyzed by examining them for changes over time or by comparing them with industrial averages or those of competitors.

Other Indicators

The usefulness of other types of organizational performance indicators depends on the nature of the organization. In business organizations, market share is often considered a key indicator. Some firms may consider the number of new product introductions a key indicator; steel mills may use tonnes of product shipped; airlines may use average percentage of seats filled; hospitals may use average death rate in surgery; and universities may use number of awards won by faculty or number of research dollars generated.

Behavioural Indicators

RPC 12.6

A variety of indicators can be used to assess the extent to which the desired employee behaviour—whether membership, task, or citizenship behaviour— is taking place.

Membership Behaviour

Three key aspects of membership behaviour are attraction, retention, and attendance. Various indicators measure how effective the organization is at attracting new members. One indicator is simply the number of qualified applicants that job postings attract. Another is the percentage of offers made to potential new employees that are refused.

The main indicator of retention is employee turnover; however, some types of turnover are more serious than others. For example, is turnover spread across employees performing at different performance levels, or is it mainly high-performing employees who are quitting? Is turnover concentrated in certain departments or units? Reasons for turnover are also important. Some people quit because their spouse has been transferred to another province, and some people quit because they have received a better offer from another employer. It is important to know which of these is the reason for the turnover. Many organizations use exit interviews in an attempt to ascertain why employees are quitting the organization.

Another indicator of membership behaviour is absenteeism. Absenteeism can be measured in a variety of ways. One method is to simply tally up all the days missed by employees for any reason and divide by the number of employees. However, it should be noted that some absenteeism is unavoidable, due to reasons such as illness. Therefore, many experts argue that involuntary absenteeism should be excluded from the calculations. But while it might be theoretically correct to do this, actually doing so may be quite difficult. An alternative is to add up the number of occurrences and divide by the number of employees, thus yielding a statistic that is less likely to be skewed by long absences due to serious illnesses.

Task Behaviour

Employee performance has at least two dimensions: quantity and quality of work produced. Quantity of work can be measured in a variety of ways. For example, units produced or number of clients served can be divided by the number of employees, and compared over time or with competitors. Another measure is revenue divided by number of employees. Quality of performance can be measured by indicators such as customer feedback, number of errors made, or scrap losses.

Citizenship Behaviour

Citizenship behaviour is the most difficult of the three key behaviours to measure in a quantitative way. One indicator might be the number of useful employee suggestions that are submitted. In addition, indicators such as "shrinkage"—employee theft—would be expected to decline if citizenship increased. Other departments or customers can be surveyed to determine the degree of cooperativeness and citizenship practised by members of a given department. Feedback from customers about employees who go above and beyond the call of duty can be gathered.

⒭⒫Ⓒ 12.6 Attitudinal Indicators

Because attitudes condition behaviour, assessment of employee attitudes can play a major role in the evaluation process. For the purposes of compensation, there are two main sets of attitudes that are important: job attitudes and compensation attitudes.

Job Attitudes

Throughout the book, three key job attitudes have been discussed: employee job satisfaction, work motivation, and organizational identification. Over the years, numerous survey scales that measure these attitudes have been developed. Many firms conduct employee attitude surveys on an annual basis to assess the level of these attitudes. According to the Compensation Practices Survey, about half (48 percent) of Canadian firms conduct regular employee attitude surveys.

Compensation Attitudes

Employee attitudes toward the compensation system can also be surveyed. Several types of attitudes are important. One of these is satisfaction with the total amount of compensation being received (distributive justice). Another is satisfaction with the process by which compensation is determined (procedural justice). Both of these reflect the perceived fairness or equity of the system, as discussed in Chapter 3.

Attitudes for individual components of compensation can also be examined. For example, are employees satisfied with the amount and fairness of merit pay? What about the profit-sharing plan? Many organizations have a section on their internal compensation surveys dealing with employee benefits. Which benefits are employees most satisfied with? Least satisfied? Is the amount of the benefit satisfactory? Are benefits fairly allocated? Would employees prefer that certain benefits that are not being offered replace other benefits that are being offered?

Another important aspect to examine is employee understanding of the compensation system. Misunderstandings can cause dissatisfaction and complaints. Perhaps even more important, a system that is misunderstood will not have the desired effect on employee attitudes and behaviour, even if it is designed properly.

In addition, organizations can infer compensation attitudes from employee behaviours. For example, the number of employee calls to the compensation office may provide an index of understanding. The number of complaints and grievances that pertain to compensation can also be tallied and examined. Or if there is a formal appeals process for compensation, the number of appeals initiated and the number granted can also be examined.

Monitoring Changing Circumstances

Ⓡ Ⓟ Ⓒ 12.5

"Compensation systems don't suddenly break; instead they gradually become obsolete."[24] In some cases, this obsolescence is so gradual that nobody notices that the compensation system is no longer adding value to the organization. In order to prevent obsolescence and ensure maximum value, organizations need to watch for changing circumstances that signal a need for change to the system. These changing circumstances may be either external or internal to the organization.

Changes in External Circumstances

External circumstances that may trigger a need for changes in the compensation system include legislative and tax changes, labour market changes, changes in competitive conditions, and socioeconomic changes.

Legislative and Tax Changes

Provincial and federal legislation have a significant impact on compensation systems. Moreover, this legislation changes quite frequently, due to revisions made by legislators or court decisions. Examples include employment standards legislation, human rights legislation, and pay equity legislation. At the beginning of each year, organizations need to be aware of changes to RRSP limits, Canada/Quebec Pension Plan payments, Employment Insurance payments, and income tax and/or corporate tax provisions. Any of these changes may have implications for the compensation system.

Labour Market Changes

As the demand and supply of particular categories of workers change, attracting and retaining employees can become more—or less—difficult. The compensation system may need to change in response to this situation.

Competitive Environment Changes

Changes in the policies of competitors or the emergence of new competitors may have significant implications for compensation policies, either directly or indirectly. An example of a direct implication occurs when a competitor adds a very attractive new benefit to its compensation package, making it difficult for us to attract employees without offering a similar benefit. An example of an indirect implication occurs when new competitors force existing firms to adopt a new managerial strategy.

Socioeconomic Changes

Changes in either social attitudes or general economic conditions can also trigger a need for changes to the compensation system. For example, if economic conditions become more buoyant, an organization may decide to focus on non-economic types of rewards, such as advancement opportunities or intrinsic rewards. If social attitudes toward a particular industry become less favourable, the organization may need to boost pay levels.

Demographic changes may also be important. For example, an aging workforce will likely trigger a much greater focus on pension plans and health benefits than when the workforce was younger. Demographers point out that the baby boom generation (born from 1947 to 1966) has created a major blockage to career advancement in organizations, because the top end of hierarchies simply cannot accommodate so many people. This blockage will last until at least 2012, when the first of the boomers will finally start to reach retirement age.[25]

spiral career paths
career advancement marked by a combination of sideways and vertical progression

In the meantime, experts suggest that **spiral career paths** will become much more important, with most employees taking at least two sideways steps for each step up the hierarchy. This spiral pattern creates more pressure for firms to adopt pay-for-knowledge systems. However, whether or not a pay-for-knowledge system is implemented, employees will also value training and education opportunities highly as rewards (for both intrinsic reasons and because this makes employees more marketable), and organizations that offer these rewards will be much more attractive to employees than those that do not.

Changes in Internal Circumstances

Internal changes that can trigger a need to change the compensation system include changes in managerial strategy, in the workforce, in the organization's financial condition, and in the scope of the organization.

Changes in Managerial Strategy

Whenever the fundamental managerial strategy of the organization changes, the compensation strategy must also change. Factors that drive changes to managerial strategy have already been covered, including changes in the nature of the organization's environment, its technology, its competitive strategy, its size, and changes in its workforce. These changes themselves may also trigger a need for compensation changes.

Changes in the Workforce

Changes in the nature of an organization's workforce affect reward and compensation systems in a variety of ways. If the type of employee recruited by the firm changes over time, then the needs of these employees may be different from those of previous employees, and the compensation system may have to change to recognize that. For example, if the workforce ages, compensation will need more emphasis on pension plans and retirement income. Conversely, if the workforce becomes younger, more cash and more family benefits, such as dental plans, may be needed.

A trend in many organizations is toward a greater gender and ethnic diversity among employees. This makes it more difficult to define a single reward system that meets everyone's needs. Of course, some compensation elements, such as a flexible benefits plan, can accommodate changes in the workforce more easily than other systems.

Changes in Financial Circumstances

A decline in the organization's financial circumstances may trigger a need to cut costs, including compensation costs. The compensation strategy may be sound, but the organization may simply no longer have the funds to support it at its current level. In these circumstances, firms often ask for compensation concessions from their employees. As discussed later in the chapter, organizations have a variety of options for dealing with this problem. Of course, firms with a greater degree of variable pay are less vulnerable to these changes than firms with less variable pay.

Changes in Scope

One obvious circumstance requiring adaptation of the compensation system is a company merger or acquisition. The two organizations will almost certainly have different compensation systems. Merging these systems can be a very complex process, and there are no hard-and-fast rules for doing so. Of course, in some cases, integrating the compensation systems may not be necessary if the organizations are going to operate autonomously.

But when the units are to be integrated, a wide variety of compensation decisions will have to be made. The usual practice is to adopt the compensation system of the largest actor in the merger, but there are many constraints on this process, including legal obligations. However, not merging the compensation systems where employees will be working together doing similar work is a formula for inequity and dissatisfaction as well as an ongoing administrative nightmare.

Adapting the Compensation System

RPC 12.5

What do you do when your evaluation has indicated that your compensation system is not achieving the expected results, but you don't know what needs to be done? How do you identify the adaptations that will produce the desired results? Before you can answer this question, you need to know what exactly is going wrong with your current system. In fact, the problems might not have anything to do with your compensation system at all! This final section discusses some key considerations in making adaptations to the compensation system. It also considers three specific situations that may call for adaptations: adapting to financial crises, adapting to labour shortages, and accommodating individuals.

Identifying What to Adapt

Suppose that your compensation system does not seem to be producing the desired results. Your first reaction may be to ask yourself what changes to the compensation system should be made to correct this problem. But this should not be your first question.

Your first question should be: *Why* are the desired results not occurring? There are many possible answers. Perhaps the wrong compensation strategy was adopted. But maybe not. Perhaps the compensation strategy is correct, but the technical processes for transforming the strategy into a compensation system were poorly designed. Or maybe these two aspects are fine, but the system itself has been poorly implemented.

Maybe the necessary complementary policies have not been implemented. For example, a system for employee participation in decision making is necessary to realize the benefits of employee stock plans. Effective training programs are necessary for pay-for-knowledge systems to work. Or the lack of results could also simply be a problem of time. You are expecting too much too soon. Alternatively, maybe the problem is due to some cause completely unrelated to compensation, such as an aging plant or changes in quality of raw materials. Finally, perhaps your expectations for the compensation system were not realistic in the first place.

So how do you know which it is? All of this shows that compensation is less a science than an art, and that there is no substitute for understanding the organization and its people. This is why comprehensive evaluation data are so important. Evaluation data should allow you to rule out certain causes and perhaps pinpoint the problem. For example, if employees do not understand the compensation system, or they misperceive it, this should be corrected before making any changes to the compensation system itself.

The key point to remember here is that only when you have identified the cause of the perceived problem can you identify the proper adaptations. And when considering adaptations, they must be put in the context of the total system. Piecemeal changes to deal with specific problems may end up creating new problems, as will be seen shortly.

Adapting to Financial Crises

When a financial crisis hits an organization, compensation expenditures often look like a tempting target. The classical approach to cutting costs is either to lay off employees or to attempt to cut compensation. However, this approach may be shortsighted, depending on the cause of the crisis, its likely duration, and the nature of the organization. For example, if the crisis is not due to out-of-line compensation costs, or is likely to be short-term in duration, cutting compensation may not be a good solution.

In fact, if the organization practises either human relations or high-involvement management, then cutting compensation should be the solution of *last* resort. Cutting compensation will cause problems for most organizations, but these problems will be least severe for classical organizations, since they likely do not have positive job attitudes and citizenship behaviour to protect, and the organization is geared toward making employees replaceable. But cutting compensation will likely cause serious problems for human relations and high-involvement organizations, because this action may be seen as a violation of the psychological contract between employees and the firm.

If there seems to be no alternative to pay cuts, you can take five measures to minimize the damage. One is to provide full information on the crisis, showing that all other possible avenues for addressing the problem have been exhausted. Another is to seek employee input on ways to deal with the crisis. In some cases, this may produce a solution; but even if not, communication creates an organization-wide understanding of the crisis. The third measure is to ensure that compensation cuts are fairly shared throughout the organization. The fourth is to consult with employees on how best to achieve the necessary compensation reductions. For example, some employee groups may prefer reductions in certain benefits rather than decreases in base pay, while others may want to keep their benefits and reduce base pay. Some employee groups may prefer to go on a shortened workweek rather than accept layoffs. Early retirement programs may also be considered. The fifth measure is to try to boost nonfinancial rewards at the same time or make commitments to provide future rewards when circumstances permit. For example, some firms have implemented employee stock bonus plans when cutting other compensation as one way of guaranteeing that employees receive rewards from any upturn in the firm's fortunes.

Perhaps it is not necessary to actually cut compensation costs, but rather to contain them. Several possibilities are available:

- Extend the salary review period to a longer interval.
- Tighten controls to slow progress through the pay range.
- Tighten merit guidelines.
- Replace some raises with bonuses.
- Replace fixed pay with variable pay.
- Ensure that regional differences in wages are reflected in regional pay levels.
- Contain benefit costs.
- Create a two-tiered pay system for new employees coming in.[26]

Of course, the best approach to financial crises is to avoid them, or failing that, to have a system in place that will adjust to financial problems. Financial problems are less likely to arise if the compensation system adds maximum value to the organization. Variable pay systems may add not only value but also compensation flexibility. Some firms attempt to avoid having to cut compensation costs by maintaining production slightly below demand. Others keep a workforce of part-time employees or contingent employees to help protect core employees. Others have plans for sharing work. There are many possibilities.

 **12.6**

technical premiums

compensation measures that increase the compensation of technical employees

Adapting to Labour Shortages

One problem organizations frequently encounter is a shortage of particular types of labour. For example, several years ago, Canada experienced shortages of technical employees, particularly those skilled in computer applications and software development. One way of coping with this problem is the use of **technical premiums**, through which technical employees receive extra compensation.

According to a survey of Canadian firms, the most common approach to providing a technical premium is to place the needed employees higher in the pay range than would normally be justified. A third of the firms offering technical premiums offered one-time cash "signing bonuses." Some firms used the normal pay rates, but added a fixed percentage that would be carried along with these employees as they progressed through the pay range. A few firms offered special stock options to these employees.[27]

The danger of making many of these adjustments is that the overall integrity of the compensation system can be undermined. Equity concerns can arise if this group of employees is being treated significantly differently from other groups of employees. Moreover, because of compounding, compensation costs for these employees can easily spin out of control, especially if incentives and benefits are calculated as a percentage of base pay. There is also the issue of how to deal with these salaries when there is no longer a shortage of the particular skill in question.

Of course, rather than attempting to lure away each other's employees, organizations can deal with a skills shortage through internal training. Although training may not be feasible for all employers, especially if they need quick expansion, this approach has numerous benefits. It provides opportunities for training and development to current employees, shows commitment by the organization, is more likely to create employees with skills specific to employer needs, avoids skewing the compensation system, and helps to provide a solution to the labour shortage.

Accommodating Individual Employees

One dilemma every organization has to deal with occurs when an individual employee demands special treatment. For example, an employee may brandish a job offer from another organization, asking her or his current employer to "meet it or beat it." Of course, frequent occurrences of this sort suggests that your compensation system needs to be reassessed. But what do you do about the individual employee? The temptation is to match the competitor's offer, even if it puts the individual outside the pay range for that job.

However, the problem with this solution is that it undermines the integrity and equity of the total compensation system. To avoid doing so, it may well be preferable to let the employee go to the other job. This individual may be more valuable to the other employer, justifying the higher rate of pay the other employer is offering. Or the other job may not really be comparable—it includes different job duties not included in our job.

There may also be some other way of satisfying the employee, such as transferring him or her to more rewarding work or providing some promotion or training opportunities. In fact, sometimes presentation of a job offer may represent a cry for recognition, or some other problem, rather than a true desire to leave the firm.

A dilemma also occurs when recruiting new employees during brief, dramatic periods of shortage of certain kinds of expertise. If the firm responds by sweetening its offers to new employees, these employees may end up earning more than existing employees. Even if this inequity is subsequently corrected, this action may shake employees' confidence in the equity of the system. It is far better to address this issue before it becomes a problem, or to address it in a comprehensive way, rather than in a piecemeal fashion.

Summary

This chapter covered the final stretch of the road to effective compensation: the processes for implementing, managing, evaluating, and adapting the compensation system. You now understand the fundamentals of compensation administration, including the mechanics of payroll preparation and compensation communication. You also understand the key role information technology plays in this process, along with the issue of whether to perform all compensation administration in-house or to outsource some or all of it.

Next, you learned the process for implementing the compensation system. The key to successful implementation is proper preparation, including resolving administrative details, assigning specific roles and responsibilities, documenting the system, planning for training and communication, budgeting, developing evaluation procedures, and formulating the implementation plan. The implementation process itself consists of six steps: establishing the implementation bodies, putting the infrastructure in place, testing the system, conducting training, communicating the system, and launching and adjusting the system.

Following that, you learned the process for evaluating the compensation system. You also learned that evaluation of the compensation system is often done poorly or not at all. To truly understand the impact of the compensation system, you must use a variety of indicators, because simply reviewing the system against projected costs or goal attainment can give a misleading picture. Examples of possible organizational, behavioural, and attitudinal indicators were provided.

The chapter went on to note that compensation systems usually do not suddenly break, but gradually become ineffective. You always need to be vigilant about monitoring circumstances external and internal to the firm to prevent this occurrence. External circumstances include legislative, labour market, competitive, and socioeconomic changes. Internal circumstances include changes to managerial strategies, the workforce, financial conditions, and organization scope.

Even if the compensation system appears in need of change, the exact adaptations that need to be made are not always obvious. You first need to understand what is going wrong with the current system. It may turn out that what looked like a compensation problem is actually caused by something else.

A final issue is how to accommodate to financial problems, labour shortages, and individual employees who are threatening to quit. You learned that piecemeal adaptations made for the purposes of expediency can undermine the integrity of the entire compensation system, and so must be avoided.

With this chapter, you have now traversed the entire road map to compensation effectiveness. But that does not mean your learning is at an end. Unlike reading a book, the journey to effective compensation has no end, because compensation needs to evolve as the organization and circumstances change. In that respect, the road to effective compensation is more like an ever-changing maze than a speedy expressway. But that's what makes compensation so challenging and interesting!

Key Terms

average employee earnings, 482	initial dip, 479
compensation administration, 465	spiral career paths, 486
compensation cost ratio, 482	technical premiums, 490

Web Links

To learn more about the specialized field of compensation administration, check out the website of the Canadian Payroll Association at **http://www.payroll.ca/index.cfm**. (p. 465)

To learn the full requirements of the Personal Information Protection and Electronic Documents Act and how to comply, go to the Office of the Privacy Commissioner of Canada at **http://www.privcom.gc.ca/ekit/ekit_e.asp**. (p. 470)

The Canadian Privacy Institute provides a website that provides information on practical ways to comply with privacy legislation at **http://www.canadianprivacyinstitute.ca**. (p. 470)

Some websites that give useful advice on selecting an HRMS vendor are **http://www.ihrim.org/about/index.asp**, **http://www.pmihrm.com/realcosts.html** and **http://www.darwinmag.com/read/050103/hrsoft.html**. (p. 471)

RPC Icons

RPC 12.1 Ensures accurate and timely delivery of pay.

RPC 12.2 Manages the transitions to new benefits plans, including communications, employee counselling, training, and discarding redundant practices.

RPC 12.3 Manages the transition to a new or revised pension plan by providing information to plan participants, and providing appropriate training for administrative staff.

RPC 12.4 Ensures compliance with legally required benefits programs.

RPC 12.5 Monitors the competitiveness of the total compensation strategy on an ongoing basis.

RPC 12.6 Assesses the effectiveness of the compensation program in achieving the organization's goals, and its competitiveness in terms of attracting qualified candidates.

Discussion Questions

1. Why is compensation communication such an important aspect of an effective compensation system?
2. What issues should you consider when deciding whether to outsource compensation functions?
3. Why is it so important to have a process for evaluating the compensation system?
4. What are the key forces that could trigger a need to adapt or modify the compensation system? Which of these do you think are the most important?

Using the Internet

1. Go to the website of the Office of the Privacy Commissioner (**http://www. privcom.gc.ca/fs-fi/02_05_d_16_e.asp**) and review the 10 employer responsibilities under PIPEDA. What are the ways in which adhering to these responsibilities might affect the practice of compensation management?

Exercise

1. Form small groups. Each member of the group should check with a current or previous employer (or some other employer if this is not convenient) to determine whether the organization is outsourcing some or all of its compensation administration. Is the company happy with the current system? Why or why not?

Case Question

1. In previous chapters, you may have prepared compensation strategies for "The Fit Stop" or one of the other cases in the Appendix. If so, develop a detailed plan for implementing the new compensation strategy at one of these firms. If not, prepare a compensation strategy for one of these firms, design the technical processes, and develop the implementation plan.

Simulation Cross-Reference

If you are using *Strategic Compensation: A Simulation* in conjunction with this text, you will find that the concepts in Chapter 12 are helpful in preparing Sections N and O of the simulation.

Endnotes

1. Tyson, David E. 2001. *Carswell's Compensation Guide*. Toronto: Thomson Publishing.
2. Luchak, Andrew A., and Morley Gunderson. 2000. "What Do Employees Know About Their Pension Plan?" *Industrial Relations*, 39(4): 646–670.
3. Brown, David. 2001. "Employees Ill-Equipped to Make Pension Choices." *Canadian HR Reporter*, 14(10): 1, 12.
4. Nunes, Joe. 2005. How Pensions Got Tangled in Total Rewards." *Canadian HR Reporter*, 18(3): R10.
5. MacDonald, Natalie C. 2004. "Going Flex Comes with Obligations for Employers." *Canadian HR Reporter*,17(4): G5–G11.
6. MacDonald, Natalie C. 2004. "Going Flex Comes with Obligations for Employers." *Canadian HR Reporter*,17(4): G11.
7. Winter, Nadine. 2000. "Job Evaluation in a New Business Environment." *Canadian HR Reporter*, March 27: 17.
8. Ledden, Cathy, and Brenda McKinney. 2005. "Well-Made Intranet Offers Boundless Opportunity." *Canadian HR Reporter*, 18(2): 14.
9. Shetzer, Larry. 2000. "On-Line 360-Degree Feedback Encourages Bottom-Up Decision-Making." *Canadian HR Reporter*, November 6.
10. Ilsemann, Anne C., and Mark Simms. 2000. "Using Information Technology for Salary Budgeting and Planning." In Lance A. Berger and Dorothy R. Berger, eds. *The Compensation Handbook*. New York: McGraw-Hill, 189–96.
11. McEwen, Alan. 2001. "Privacy Concerns, Technology, Fuel the Debate over Electronic Forms." *Dialogue*, April/May: 16–19.
12. Murray, Vic. 1997. "Contracting Out HR Services: Passing Fad or Here to Stay?" *Human Resources Management in Canada*, July: 637–641.
13. Brown, David. 2001. "CIBC HR Department Halved as Non-Strategic Roles Outsourced." *Canadian HR Reporter*, 14(11): 1, 6.
14. Conference Board of Canada. 2005. *Compensation Outlook 2005*. Ottawa.
15. Humber, Todd. 2005. "The State of HR Technology." *Canadian HR Reporter*, 18(5): R2–R3.
16. Crowley, Lisa. 2004. "Outsourcing Payroll: How Much Do You Want to Give up?" *Canadian HR Reporter*, 17(15): G5.
17. Dobbs, Kevin. 2001. "Rightsourcing: Using a Mix of In-House and ASP Software." *Canadian HR Reporter*, 14(10): G5, G10.
18. Hackett, Brian, 1995. *Transforming the Benefit Function*. New York: The Conference Board.
19. Statement by John Sullivan, Professor of Management at San Francisco State University. Cited in Beamon, Karen, ed. 2004. *Out of Site: An Inside Look at HR Outsourcing*. Burlington, MA: IHRIM.
20. Harrison, Suzanne. 1996. *Outsourcing and the "New" Human Resource Management*. Kingston, ON: IRC Press.
21. Belli, Claudio. 1991. "Strategic Compensation Communication." In M.L. Rock and L.A. Berger, eds. *The Compensation Handbook*. New York: McGraw-Hill, 604–16.
22. Ilsemann, Anne C., and Mark Simms. 2000. "Using Information Technology for Salary Budgeting and Planning." In Lance A. Berger and Dorothy R. Berger, eds. *The Compensation Handbook*. New York: McGraw-Hill, 189–96.

23. Roberts, Alexander, 1994. "Integrating Strategy with Performance Measures." *Management Development Review*, 7(6): 13–15.
24. Britton, Paul B., and Christian M. Ellis. 1994. "Designing and Implementing Reward Systems: Finding a Better Way." *Compensation and Benefits Review*, 26(4): 44.
25. Foot, David K., and Rosemary A. Venne. 1990. "Population, Pyramids, and Promotional Prospects." *Canadian Public Policy*, 16(4): 387–98.
26. Sibson, Robert E. 1990. *Compensation*. New York: American Management Association: 356.
27. Allen, Ann. 1997. "Trolling for Technical Employees: Using Technical Premiums as Bait." *Human Resources in Canada*, June: 621–25.

Appendix

Cases for Analysis

The following cases, which reflect a range of compensation issues and organizational types, can be used in a variety of ways. They are presented here without any questions attached to them to allow instructors flexibility in their use. They can be used in conjunction with end-of-chapter case questions to illustrate compensation issues relevant to that chapter and to provide opportunities for applying compensation concepts. They can also be used as a basis for major term assignments or group projects. Some are short enough to be used as exam cases. And, of course, they can serve as a basis for lively class discussions of many important compensation issues.

Achtymichuk Machine Works

At the Achtymichuk Machine Works, each department has one or two clean-up employees who clean around the machines and also take care of the washrooms, hallways, and other areas. The cleaning job has the lowest status of any in the plant, although the pay is fairly good because the plant has had difficulty getting enough cleaners. The pay for cleaners is based on a flat hourly rate and provides only mandatory benefits.

There are 20 cleaners in all. They report to the supervisors of the departments in which they work, but the supervisors are very dissatisfied with them. A common complaint is that as soon as a cleaner knows what is expected of them and learns to do it right, they quit. Moreover, the cleaners are frequently absent and often come late.

Alliston Instruments

Alliston Instruments is a manufacturer of specialty medical instruments located in southern Ontario. Manufacturing involves two types of processes. First, individual workers produce the components for the medical instruments in batches of various sizes, using a variety of machine tools and equipment. Then other workers assemble the components into finished products. Assembly is done sequentially, with each product passing through four to six workstations before completion. The quality of the products, which is crucial, depends on both the quality of the component parts that are produced and the quality of the assembly process.

It is late January 2006, and the financial statements for 2005 have just been released. They are grim. For the first time in the company's 50-year history, the firm has shown a loss. The company's chief executive officer believes a lot of this has to do with production problems. The 2005 production reports indicate that although the number of units produced per employee showed a slight increase last year, the number of defective units reached an all-time high, along with a high rate of wastage in raw materials and other supplies. Although total sales (and therefore total production) are down from the previous year, total labour costs are up. As a result, costs per unit are at an all-time high.

Because you are an expert in management, the CEO has asked for your help. As background for your work, the CEO briefs you on industry conditions. Until two years ago, the firm had enjoyed increasing sales over many years. It had also had increasing profits, with a record profit of over $3 million in 2002. However, in the last two years, the medical instruments industry has suddenly become more competitive. High-quality medical instruments are now being produced by several Asian firms, two of which entered the Canadian market in 2003. (Previously, the main competitors in the Canadian market were U.S. and European firms; but they are not much of a problem because their products are very high-priced.)

Because of low labour costs, the Asian firms are able to price their products attractively; but buyers initially held back, concerned about potential quality problems. So for a while, it appeared as if Alliston's customers (mainly hospitals and health clinics) would remain loyal, even though they were themselves under pressure to cut costs, due to budget cuts. But in late 2003, an Asian competitor made a major sales push by slashing prices, and this cut dramatically into Alliston's 2004 sales. In mid-2004, Alliston laid off 50 employees. Although the firm had laid off employees from time to time in the past during production lulls, this was the largest layoff in company history.

In order to make up for the loss of sales, Alliston added a number of new products to its line. (Over the years, the company had tended to stick with the same set of products, although new products were being put into use in the hospitals.) While some of these new products sold well, they didn't really make money, because production costs were higher due to the need for new equipment and extensive employee training. Moreover, most employees preferred to work on the old products, so supervisors had to use a lot of pressure to get them to work on the new products.

Alliston's 250 production workers have been unionized since the 1960s. In 2002, they staged a short but bitter strike. Because product demand was so high, the company did not want a long work stoppage, and the union was able to win significant wage increases for 2003 and 2004 (a two-year contract was signed). Since then, union–management relations, never very good, have been quite strained. Relations between supervisors and workers are no better. Supervisors complain about lazy workers who don't care if they do a good job or not, and workers complain about overbearing supervisors who allocate work unfairly and spend all their time watching and harassing employees.

Interestingly, the employee turnover rate is low at Alliston. Pay at the firm is above average, and the benefits package, which increases with seniority, is very good, comprising about 25 percent of total compensation. Comparable alternative employment opportunities in the area are quite scarce.

In late 2004, in an effort to increase efficiency, the firm persuaded the union to accept an incentive system in which employees would receive, in addition to their hourly wages, a bonus based on individual output, rather than an increase in base pay for 2005. A standard per-hour production rate for each item or assembly operation was established,

based on estimated 2004 production levels. (However, because the firm had never kept detailed records, these standards were simply based on estimates of supervisors.)

Under the new system, if production per hour for a particular item exceeded 2004 levels, the employee would receive a fixed sum for each piece produced over that level, in addition to their normal hourly pay. Of course, employees would not receive a bonus for those items that were not of satisfactory quality, and supervisors were expected to deduct these from the employee totals. However, there were no set standards for quality, and each supervisor seemed to set different standards.

There seem to be many problems with this new pay system. For example, workers complain that the production standards for some tasks are set too high, and they have no chance of earning a bonus on these items. Everybody tries to avoid these jobs, and productivity on them is poor. On the other hand, there are some jobs that everybody wants to do, because substantial bonuses can be earned, and productivity is up dramatically on these jobs. But the net effect is that overall units produced per employee have not really changed at all, while substantial sums are being paid out in bonuses.

During the past year, 10 production workers retired or quit and were not replaced, but this workforce reduction was made possible by the drop in sales during the year, not by increased productivity. However, this reduction in the workforce was partially offset by the need to hire two additional supervisors to handle the increased needs for supervision, inspection, and administration for the bonus system, and one additional full-time clerical person in the payroll department just to handle the calculations for the new bonus system.

Supervisors have complained bitterly about the new system, saying it is creating additional pressure on them. They say it is causing increased conflict with employees because nobody wants the "bad" (poor-paying) jobs, and employees resent it when these "bad" jobs are assigned to them. They find that employees don't care about quality, as long as output meets minimum standards, nor about the high waste of raw materials. They have to supervise more closely to deal with these problems and try to keep quality and productivity up on the "bad" jobs.

And to top it off, supervisors are now making less money than some of the workers, since they are not eligible for the bonus system. The fact that none of the non-union employees received any pay increase last year does not help their mood either. During the year, three experienced supervisors quit. The firm had never had more than one or two supervisors quit in a single year before.

Although the union is generally opposed to individual performance pay plans, it had accepted this one in return for a clause in the collective agreement ensuring job security for the current unionized workforce. Any workforce reductions occurring from greater efficiency had to be achieved through attrition. Management agreed to this condition because they did not expect to have to lay employees off. They had expected the new bonus system to reduce unit costs of production so that Alliston could lower prices and win back the business that had been lost.

It hasn't worked out that way. Financial data for the last four years are shown below. As the table shows, sales peaked two years ago at $31 million but have since fallen to $24 million. Customers are complaining about both product price and quality. However, the company cannot afford to reduce prices, because unit costs are so high. It is clear to management that something needs to be done, and quickly, but exactly what it is that should be done is not so clear!

Eastern Provincial University

The following are the job descriptions that are used for compensation purposes at Eastern Provincial University, an institution that employs approximately 900 professors and 1500 non-academic staff and has about 20 000 undergraduate and graduate students. Descriptions are provided for the Clerk Stenographer, Draftsperson, Grounds Worker, and Medical Laboratory Technologist job classes.

Clerk Stenographer I

Kind and Level of Work

Employees of this class perform a variety of clerical tasks of limited complexity that may include the taking and transcribing of shorthand dictation. Vocabulary involved is usually free of technical terms and limited to the everyday language of business. Typing assignments, whether from copy, dictation, or machine transcription, require only normal speed and accuracy. Material copied may include scientific papers, theses, and special reports using technical language from any one of the University subjects; the employee is only responsible for the accurate transcription of material already written or typed. These employees maintain courteous and cooperative working relations with students and with faculty and other University staff for whom they provide typing, simple duplicating, telephone reception, and other services. While some positions are located away from the supervisors, preliminary detailed instructions and established procedures leave little responsibility for the exercise of initiative or the formation of independent judgments.

Year	Revenues	Total Employees	Labour Costs	Other Production Costs	Other Costs	Net Income (Loss)
2002	$27,000,000	320	$9,000,000	$13,500,000	$1,350,000	$3,150,000
2003	$31,000,000	350	$12,000,000	$15,500,000	$1,550,000	$1,950,000
2004	$25,000,000	300	$11,000,000	$12,500,000	$1,500,000	—
2005	$24,000,000	293	$12,000,000	$13,000,000	$1,444,000	($2,444,000)

Typical Duties and Responsibilities

1. Type correspondence, class assignments, and technical papers using special vocabulary, from copy.
2. Act as receptionist at the counter and on the telephone, relaying calls, recording messages, and answering simple questions.
3. File and retrieve materials arranged in simple alphabetical, numerical, chronological, or geographical order.
4. Reproduce copies of materials by photocopy or other simple duplicating methods.
5. Transcribe correspondence and other materials containing everyday language, from dictating machines.
6. Prepare form letters by inserting appropriate material from files or other sources.
7. Check forms for completeness.
8. Post figures to budget accounts or other simple statistical and accounting records.
9. Open, sort, route, and deliver mail according to predetermined patterns.
10. In some positions, take and transcribe correspondence and other materials requiring only a good vocabulary or ordinary language.

Desirable Qualifications

Previous office experience desirable but not required. Grade 12 and completion of a standard course in word processing, spreadsheets, and shorthand. Ability to meet test standards in typing and shorthand (for those positions requiring the use of shorthand).

Clerk Stenographer II

Kind and Level of Work

Employees of this class perform a variety of moderately complex clerical tasks, which may include taking and transcribing shorthand dictation and that requires knowledge of a technical vocabulary. Their work is supervised by academic, administrative, or senior clerical employees. This position is distinguished from Clerk Stenographer I in that it requires more knowledge of the organization, programs, and policies of the work unit; requires a higher degree of specialized clerical skills or knowledge of a technical vocabulary; or carries independent responsibility for the maintenance of significant records; or some combination of these attributes. These workers maintain helpful and courteous relations with students and staff, for whom they provide information and services.

Typical Duties and Responsibilities

1. From general instructions, compose and type routine correspondence, bulletins, and other materials requiring knowledge of the departments they serve.
2. Type from copy or dictating machine, class assignments, tests, research papers, and other materials requiring understanding of technical vocabulary, the use of special symbol keyboards, or judgment in the selection of format.
3. Answer students' inquiries concerning class schedules, timetables, general course content, class prerequisites, and similar matters requiring basic knowledge of calendars and departmental programs.
4. Train new employees by providing factual information on office routines, staff names and locations, work methods, and schedules.
5. Maintain records of budget expenditure, class attendance, class credits, grade distribution, and other data requiring accurate posting and simple calculations of totals, percentages, and balances, all subject to periodic review.
6. Compile simple statistical tables and graphs according to prescribed patterns, incorporating data flowing into or retained in their departments.
7. Organize, reorganize, and maintain filing systems based on alphabetic, numeric, or simple subject matter arrangement.
8. Act as receptionist for officials, screening telephone calls and visitors, providing answers to inquiries, making appointments, and referring callers to other officials.
9. Assist in the maintenance of counselling schedules at the time of student registration.

10. In some positions, take and transcribe short-hand dictation of correspondence, reports, research papers, and other materials containing technical language and concepts.

Desirable Qualifications

Several years of office experience, preferably in a university setting. Grade 12 and completion of a standard course in word processing, spreadsheets, and shorthand. Ability to meet test standards in typing and shorthand (for those positions requiring the use of shorthand).

Clerk Stenographer III

Kind and Level of Work

Employees of this class perform responsible, varied, and complex clerical tasks, which may include taking and transcribing shorthand dictation. Typically, their assignments require a broad understanding of the structure and division of responsibility, functions, and programs of the organizations they service. In most of these positions, they are secretaries to heads of larger departments and take initiative in relieving them of administrative details that do not require professional judgment. Their work is subject to supervision by academic or administrative supervisors, but they carry out a series of clerical operations calling for decisions without detailed instruction or review. The work of this class is distinguished from that of Clerk Stenographers I and II by broader knowledge requirements, greater latitude, and supervision of other clerk stenographers. In contacts with students, faculty and other staff, and the public at large, these employees attempt to promote public attitudes that support the work of the units.

Typical Duties and Responsibilities

1. For their superiors, compose and type correspondence that requires good knowledge of departmental organization, functions, and policies.
2. Maintain records pertaining to students' marks, credits, and degree requirements, or supervise the maintenance of such records.
3. Maintain records on budget allotments, expenditures, commitments, and residual balances, and notify department office of over-expenditures and balances, thus providing a measure of budget control.
4. Give elementary counselling services to students by advising them of degree requirements, class schedules, class prerequisites, and (in general terms) course content, using information from the calendars or from the faculty.
5. At the time of registration, schedule counselling interviews between students and professors and maintain records so that students are referred to the same counsellor each time.
6. Attend and record proceedings of faculty meetings or meetings between faculty and non-University groups, making shorthand notes summarizing discussions and transcribing the reports for the review of superiors.
7. Supervise assistants and participate in their selection, assign their duties, train them, reallocate work to meet deadlines, and exercise disciplinary control in minor matters.
8. Screen phone and office calls of visitors, setting up interviews with superiors as necessary, answering questions where possible, and referring visitors to other sources where appropriate.
9. Type tests and examinations for members of the faculty, assuring that contents are kept confidential and that papers are properly secured.

Desirable Qualifications

Approximately five years of office experience, including several years in a university setting and preferably including experience in a supervisory capacity. Grade 12 and completion of a standard course in word processing, spreadsheets, and shorthand. Ability to meet test standards in typing and shorthand (for those positions requiring the use of shorthand).

Draftsperson I

Kind and Level of Work

Employees of this classification use computer-aided design drafting (CADD) techniques to carry out assignments delegated by their supervisor, with direction from the project originator, where appropriate. They work from rough sketches and notes, verbal instructions, and other sources of information. While their day-to-day work is subject only to general supervision, completed assignments are reviewed. Although the projects on which they work may range across a variety of engineering and architectural fields, the more complex work is allocated to more senior positions. They may communicate with professional engineers and others who initiate the work they do in order to clarify certain requirements and detail.

Typical Duties and Responsibilities

1. Interpret existing records and information for the purpose of producing required CADD information.
2. Prepare finished CADD drawings from rough sketches, notes, and instructions.
3. Share in filing and managing inventory of records information.
4. Assist Physical Plant staff, professional engineers, and consultants in locating physical records information.
5. Use and be familiar with operating various equipment, including computer input/output devices, keyboards, digitizing equipment, and blueprint machine.
6. Assist in site verification of existing campus buildings and facilities.
7. Periodically assist in making site surveys with senior or surveying staff.
8. Participate in training programs relative to the CADD system.
9. Interact and communicate in a professional manner with Physical Plant staff, the University community, consultants, contractors, etc.

Desirable Qualifications

Previous related experience preferred. Grade 12 plus a two-year diploma in a related architectural/ engineering-associated technical program. Completion of computer-assisted design and drafting course work or equivalent experience required. Eligibility for membership as an Applied Science Technologist preferred.

Draftsperson II

Kind and Level of Work

Employees in this classification use more complex computer-aided design drafting techniques to carry out assignments delegated by their supervisor with direction from the project originator where appropriate. Their work is differentiated from that of junior positions by the complexity of their assignments, the judgment they use in completing their work, and their degree of independence. Delegated projects may range across a variety of engineering and architectural fields. They develop and maintain cooperative working relations with professionals and tradespersons in fulfilling their tasks.

Typical Duties and Responsibilities

1. Participate in production and design work of various projects as required.
2. Assist in the development, evaluation, implementation, and documentation of ongoing computer system procedures.
3. Assist in coordinating and supervising work of junior staff.
4. Complete site verification of existing campus buildings and facilities.
5. Participate in training in CADD system applications and in new and more complex portions of the system and support other staff as required.
6. Interact and communicate in a professional manner with Physical Plant staff, the University community, consultants, contractors, etc.

Desirable Qualifications

Minimum of two years' related experience in architectural and other engineering fields. An "operator" level of CADD and related computer operations is required. Grade 12 plus a two-year diploma in a related architectural/engineering associated technical program. CADD course work or equivalent experience required. Eligibility for membership as an Applied Science Technologist is also required.

Draftsperson III

Kind and Level of Work

Employees in this classification are responsible for directing the operation of a unit producing computer-aided design drafting information and drawings, under the general supervision of the Facilities Management Design and Information Systems Manager. Their work is differentiated from that of other operational staff in the unit on the basis of the skill level involved and the responsibility to supervise others. They develop and maintain cooperative working relations with professionals and tradespersons to facilitate project completion.

Typical Duties and Responsibilities

1. Supervise, allocate, assist, and participate in the work of subordinate staff.
2. Review work and ensure standards are maintained.
3. Assess incoming work, organize project priorities and flow, and plan and schedule workloads as appropriate.
4. Train and support Physical Plant staff in the use of system applications for records information access.
5. Assist in the design of computer system enhancements and general strategies.
6. Participate in the more complex design work of projects as required.
7. Interact and communicate in a professional manner with Physical Plant staff, the University community, consultants, contractors, etc.

Desirable Qualifications

A minimum of five years' experience in architectural and a variety of engineering fields, including some experience in a supervisory capacity. Must have experience in CADD and related computer operations at an "operator" and "systems" level. Grade 12 plus a two-year diploma in a related

architectural/engineering associated technical program. CADD course work or equivalent experience required. Eligibility for membership as an Applied Science Technologist is also required.

Grounds Worker I

Kind and Level of Work

The employees in this classification carry out routine gardening by maintaining the grass, flowers, and trees on the campus grounds. They either may be assigned an area on campus to look after or may work on a crew assigned to a task such as planting or pruning. These employees are responsible to a Grounds Worker II, who acts as a lead hand, assistant supervisor, or a supervisor.

Typical Duties and Responsibilities

1. Water lawns and flowerbeds in a particular area.
2. Trim lawns in areas where larger mowers cannot cut.
3. Hoe weeds in flowerbeds, shrubbery beds, and gravel parking lots.
4. Perform general clean-up work in an area.
5. Prune broken branches on shrubs and trees.
6. Use hand clippers to trim areas of lawn not accessible to machines, such as along buildings and ponds.
7. Assist in the planting of flowers, shrubs, trees, and grass.
8. Assist in sodding operation, which would involve removing old grass, preparing soil, laying new sod, spreading peat moss, and watering.
9. Do minor maintenance of small machinery.

Desirable Qualifications

Gardening experience preferred but not required. Grade 8 education.

Grounds Worker II

Kind and Level of Work

Employees in this class are responsible for a wide variety of gardening jobs involving many of those done by a Grounds Worker I. Generally, they are distinguished from the Grounds Worker I class in that they may be the lead person in a small group or may be a machine operator. These employees may be in charge of a specific operation, such as the greenhouse, a maintenance department, or the nursery. They are usually supervised by an assistant supervisor and supervisor.

Typical Duties and Responsibilities

1. Supervise the grounds maintenance in a particular area.
2. Supervise a special work crew engaged in an activity, such as sodding, planting, or pruning.
3. Supervise the work done in the greenhouse and the stocking of indoor planters.
4. Operate a mower for cutting playing fields and large areas of grass.
5. Operate a rototiller around trees and shrubs to kill weeds.
6. Operate a tractor or other large machine and all attachments such as front-end loader, grader blade, and backhoe.
7. Carry out maintenance on all equipment used in the department.
8. Train subordinates in all gardening operations.
9. Communicate instructions from the supervisor.

Desirable Qualifications
Several years' experience as a grounds worker. Grade 8 education.

Grounds Worker III
Kind and Level of Work
Employees in this classification collectively perform a wide variety of tasks related to the positions of ice making, machine operation, nursery management, irrigation, landscape maintenance, and tree and shrub pruning. Their work is distinguished from that of subordinate personnel by the degree of knowledge, skill, and understanding required to perform the duties, the extent of their supervisory and administrative responsibilities, or some combination of these factors. Their work is given general supervision and direction, usually by a supervisor or assistant supervisor; but these employees independently organize and supervise the work of the subordinates assigned to them.

Typical Duties and Responsibilities
The incumbent is expected to be able to perform all of the duties shown under the general listing below, and *one* of the specialties listed below that.

General

1. Supervise subordinate employees in their unit by training, allocating their work, assessing their performance, and ensuring acceptable standards.
2. Perform administrative work related to their units, such as recording time, maintaining stocks of supplies, setting up work schedules, and arranging for replacements when necessary.
3. Be familiar with the operation and general maintenance of all machines and tools in their area of responsibility.
4. Act as a lead hand and be familiar with all duties of subordinates and be prepared to carry them out, including shift work, when appropriate.
5. Liaise with supervisors and subordinates on a regular basis to ensure effective communication and coordinated operation.

Nursery/Landscaping/Pruning

1. Read and interpret blueprint information.
2. Supervise the application of herbicides or fungicides, or the landscaping of a specific area.
3. Perform a full range of skilled horticulture duties in areas such as pruning, tree surgery, landscaping, greenhouse, and nursery. Incumbents are expected to direct the work of and train subordinate staff in the operation of tree-pruning equipment, such as extension ladders, cranes, and pruners, and chemical applicators, such as hand-held sprayers, boom sprayers, and fertilizer spreaders.

4. Diagnose and treat various types of lawn and tree diseases in conjunction with the Horticulture Supervisor and Assistant Supervisor, using the proper application of appropriate chemicals.
5. Be familiar with all the duties required of a nursery person including all propagation practices, such as grafting, budding, seeding, transplanting, hardening, stratifying, etc.

Facilities

1. Oversee the operation of the skating and curling facilities in a cooperative spirit with the college of Physical Education to promote optimum facility usage and goodwill with patrons and staff.
2. Make ice in curling and skating rinks and paint markings on ice according to specifications.
3. Maintain ice surfaces with the use of appropriate equipment and tools.
4. Inspect mechanical rooms to ensure ice-making equipment is functioning correctly, and call service people as required.
5. Ensure that patrons conform to regulations governing behaviour in the rinks, and call for assistance from security personnel in case of serious problems.
6. Supervise personnel in ice maintenance and janitorial work.
7. Supervise gardening crews in the maintenance of playing fields, track and field facilities, and landscaped areas, parking lots, etc.
8. Be familiar with and supervise the operation of all gardening equipment used in the assigned area.
9. Inspect grounds and work areas regularly and take corrective action when required.

Machine Operator

1. Operate all the mowers for cutting playing fields and open areas.
2. Operate tree spade for tree transplanting.
3. Operate such equipment as large dump truck, front-end loader, bobcat, and snowplow.

4. Operate sanding truck in winter, including mixing sand and loading.
5. Do maintenance work on all equipment, but with primary emphasis on the maintenance of power machines (which this person normally operates).

Irrigation

1. Read and interpret blueprint information.
2. Troubleshoot and repair electric and electronic components, and hydraulic controls of automated irrigation system as well as mechanical components.
3. Be responsible for opening and shutting down the irrigation system in spring and fall, including the blowing out of all lines.
4. Liaise with the supervisor and assistant supervisor for the scheduling of irrigation throughout the campus.
5. Through liaison with the foreman and supervisor, ensure optimum water use efficiency when setting irrigation run times and repeat cycles, considering factors such as soil capacities, turf usage, and sprinkler and line capacities and pressure, etc.
6. Repair and/or install lawn water service including cutting and fitting pipe (PVC and poly) and placing or replacing all types of fittings including galvanized, brass, PVC, and plastic.

Desirable Qualifications
(A) Several years of work experience, including experience in supervision, and in the specialty skill area that is pertinent. This must include considerable knowledge of horticultural identification of plant materials for the nursery position, and several years' experience with the installation and maintenance of manual and automatic irrigation systems for the irrigation position. Additionally, an aptitude in electrical and electronic applications would be of value in the irrigation position. (B) The ability to do rigorous manual labour. (C) Possession of a diploma in horticulture or a related field for the nursery and irrigation positions. (D) Completion of Grade 12. (E) Driver's licence. (F) Pesticide Applicator's

Appendix: Cases for Analysis

Licence for those positions involved in the application of herbicides, insecticides, or fungicides.

Medical Laboratory Technologist I

Kind and Level of Work

This class comprises positions that require Medical Laboratory Technologist certification and involves positions that are generally located in the Medical, Dental, and Veterinary Medical colleges of the university. These are full working-level Technologists who are expected to conduct a variety of routine and semi-specialized tests and analysis in their areas of specialization, such as bacteriology, immunology, parasitology, virology, histology, etc. They are engaged in the examination of predominantly biological materials, such as blood, sera, tissue, urine, feces, etc., by chemical, bacteriological, or related techniques. After an initial orientation period, these employees work independently and are responsible for the accuracy of techniques and the reliability of results. Their work is subject to the general supervision of academic, technical, or administrative superiors.

Typical Duties and Responsibilities

1. Perform routine and semi-specialized diagnostic analysis using manual and automated techniques.
2. Prepare and standardize reagents, solutions, media, and cultures for study requiring special techniques.
3. Operate basic scientific or technical equipment, maintain as necessary, and monitor quality-control procedures to ensure reliability of results.
4. Perform sample entry, recording, reporting, and filing of results.
5. Assist with the teaching program by preparing materials and providing demonstration or explanation of equipment and/or diagnostic techniques and procedures to students.
6. Assist students with material identification and with projects as required.
7. Assist in the orientation and instruction of new staff; may also supervise student assistants, technical assistants, or first-level technicians.

8. Assist with research experiments by carrying out a variety of standardized quantitative and qualitative analyses by performing assays, routine spectroscopy and chromatography, and microbiological and other standard test procedures.
9. Prepare purchase requisitions, ordering, receiving, and storing supplies, tools, and equipment; care for materials and maintain required inventory and other records.

Desirable Qualifications

A minimum of one year of experience related to the position assignment. Completion of Grade 12 plus a related technical school diploma from a recognized technical institute. Current certification as a Registered Technologist with C.S.L.T.

Medical Laboratory Technologist II

Kind and Level of Work

This class comprises positions that require Medical Laboratory Technologist certification and involves positions that are generally located in the Medical, Dental, and Veterinary Medical colleges of the university. Employees in positions allocated to this class are experienced Technologists who conduct complex tests and/or provide supervision and training to Technologists assisting with complex tests or performing common tests. Their work involves the analysis of predominantly biological materials and processes in support of a variety of specialized areas, such as bacteriology, immunology, parasitology, virology, etc. This class is distinguished from the Medical Laboratory Technologist I by the complexity of tasks performed, judgment factors involved, responsibility for work output, and the involvement in training and supervision of junior staff. Their work is subject to general supervision and direction, usually by a member of faculty, but these employees independently organize and supervise the work of their assistants and laboratories.

Typical Duties and Responsibilities

1. Perform complex and specialized diagnostic analysis using manual and automated techniques.

2. Operate and maintain a variety of complex scientific equipment ensuring accurate calibration and reliability of results.
3. Verify procedures, evaluate effectiveness of experiments, and modify or develop techniques and/or procedures as required.
4. Provide demonstration and problem-solving consultation involving complex equipment and/or diagnostic techniques and procedures to students in an undergraduate or graduate teaching environment, or on a one-to-one basis with students as required.
5. Participate in the selection and assume responsibility for the training, assigning, and reviewing of the work of subordinate staff or less experienced staff engaged in semi-skilled or skilled work; supervise students in the use of equipment and facilities.
6. Assist individual faculty members with research projects by carrying out experiments, usually involving relatively advanced techniques and procedures, and analyze and report on results.
7. Search published scientific papers for information relating to specific projects.
8. Perform administrative work related to the units such as budgeting, advising on the purchase of material and capital equipment, maintaining appropriate inventory and records, etc.

Desirable Qualifications

Several years of work experience related to the position assignment including demonstrated supervisory experience. Grade 12 and either a technical school diploma in laboratory technology with A.R.T. standing, or a university degree relating to the position assignment. Current certification as a Registered Technologist with the C.S.L.T.

The Fit Stop

The Fit Stop Ltd. is a brand-new firm that will open its doors exactly four months from today. Their business objective is to sell all types of training, fitness, conditioning, and exercise equipment to the general public. They plan to become specialists in this equipment and to provide customers with personalized advice geared to a customer's specific training or conditioning needs (e.g., training for a particular sport, rehabilitation from injuries, strengthening of back muscles to deal with back pain, general conditioning and fitness), whether the customer is 8 or 80 years of age.

In order to provide high-quality advice, each store will employ a physiotherapist (to provide advice on problems such as injuries or chronic back pain) and a person with a bachelor's degree in kinesiology (to provide advice on training for various sports or other physical activities). In fact, a staff member will even sit down with customers and develop a personalized training or conditioning program that meets their own specific objectives and needs, at no cost to the customer.

The remainder of the staff in the store will consist of a manager, with a Bachelor of Commerce degree, and sales staff, who will have at least high school diplomas. Due to the long opening hours, it is expected that between 8 and 12 salespeople will be needed for each store. Because the stores are located in shopping malls, they will operate on a seven-day-a-week basis, open 9:00 to 9:00 weekdays, 9:00 to 6:00 Saturdays, and noon to 6:00 on Sundays.

Aside from personally helping customers, the roles of the physiotherapist and kinesiologist will be to train other employees in how each type of equipment can be used for various conditioning and rehabilitation purposes. Initially, sales staff will be given general training, but as time goes by, each salesperson will be expected to learn in depth about all the different pieces of equipment, to help customers diagnose their needs accurately, and to be able to explain proper usage of the equipment. Because of the high level of training required, all employees will be full-time.

The founder of the business is Susan Superfit, who has undergraduate degrees in kinesiology and commerce from the University of Saskatchewan. While at university she participated in numerous sports (and suffered numerous injuries due to her all-out style of play). She came up with the idea for this business while laid up with one of her injuries. While there were businesses that sold fitness and conditioning equipment, she often found that the people selling them had very limited knowledge about the equipment and often gave poor advice on what to buy and how to use it.

She has secured funding from private investors and from Working Ventures, a large, Canadian labour-sponsored investment fund. In order to get volume discounts on the equipment she will be purchasing and to beat competitors into the market, she wants to start off quite large, with stores in major cities in Ontario and the four western provinces, before expanding to Quebec and the Atlantic provinces. She knows that this is a risky strategy, and that cost control will be essential to keep the business going long enough to become well known and develop a stable clientele. She does not expect the business to make a profit for at least one year, or maybe even two.

Her main competitors will be sporting goods mega-stores, and department and discount stores, each of which sells some of the same equipment. Some of these outlets will be able to price their equipment lower than The Fit Stop will be able to, but none have the range of equipment that The Fit Stop will have, and none provide the personalized service that The Fit Stop will.

Susan believes that the key to her business success will be highly motivated and knowledgeable employees who have a strong concern for their customers and are able to work as a team with the other employees to provide the best possible customer service. Since no two customers are exactly alike, employees will have to be innovative in developing solutions that fit their needs. It will also be crucial to keep up with the latest fitness and training trends, as knowledge about fitness is continually increasing, along with different types of specialized equipment. A key aspect of company strategy is to be the most up-to-date and advanced supplier of new products and techniques.

Although Susan has given a lot of thought to her business, one thing she hasn't really given much thought to is how to compensate her employees. Since she doesn't really know much about compensation, she tends to feel that the safest thing would be to just do what her competitors are doing.

Henderson Printing

Henderson Printing is a small- to medium-sized manufacturer of account books, ledgers, and various types of record books used in business. Located in Halifax, the company has annual sales of about $10 million, mostly in the Atlantic Provinces.

The owner, George Henderson, is a firm believer in making a high-quality product that will stand up to many years of use. He uses only high-grade paper, cover stock, and binding materials. Of course, this has led to high production costs and high prices. He also believes in a high level of customer service and is willing to make the products to customers' specifications whenever they so request. However, resetting the equipment for relatively short production runs of customized products takes considerable extra time and, of course, also drives up costs.

The firm employs about 80 people, most of whom work in production. The firm has a few supervisors to oversee production, but their responsibilities are not clearly spelled out, so the supervisors often contradict each other. There is no system for scheduling production; in fact, there are few systems of any kind. Whenever there is a problem, everyone knows that you have to go to George if you expect a definite answer.

The company also has several salespeople who travel throughout the Atlantic region, mostly relatives of George or his wife. The company has one bookkeeper to keep records and issue the paycheques, and several office employees to handle routine administrative chores. The firm has no specialists in accounting, marketing, human resources, or production; George handles these areas himself, although he has no real training and little interest in any of them except production. He focuses most of his attention on ensuring product quality and on dealing with the countless problems that everyone brings to him every day. He has often been heard to exclaim, in his usual good-natured way, "Why am I the only one who can make decisions around this place?" as he deals with each of these problems.

When George was growing up, both his parents (his father was a printer and his mother was a seamstress in a garment factory) had to work hard in order to scratch out a living for their family. In those days, employers who showed little consideration for their employees were the norm, and George resolved that things would be different if he ever became an employer. Today, George tries hard to be a benevolent employer. Although he feels the organization cannot afford any formal employee benefits, he often keeps sick workers on payroll for a considerable time, especially if he knows the worker has a family to support. George is well liked by most employees, who have shown little interest in unionization during the few approaches made by union organizers.

George has no formal system for pay and tends to make all pay decisions on the spur of the moment, so almost everybody has a different pay rate. He has never gotten around to giving annual raises, so any employee who wants a raise has to approach him. He gives raises to most people who approach him, but the amount depends on his mood at the time and how well he knows the employee. For example, if the firm has just lost a major customer, raises are lower; and if the firm has just booked a large order, they are higher. They are also higher if he knows the employee has a family to support, or if the employee's spouse has been laid off, or if the employee has added a new member to the family.

George believes that a good employer should recognize the contributions made by employees during the year. So every Christmas, if profits allow, he gives a "merit bonus" to employees, which he says are based on their contribution to the firm. One day in early December, he sits down with his employee list, in alphabetical order, and pencils in an amount next to each name.

Everybody gets something, but the amounts vary greatly. If he can associate a face with the name (which is difficult sometimes, because new employees seem to turn over a lot), he tends to give larger bonuses; and if he can remember something such as a cheerful attitude, the bonuses are higher still. But if he remembers anyone complaining about that employee for some reason or another (he usually can't recall the exact reasons), the employee gets a smaller bonus. Not surprisingly, longer-term employees tend to receive much higher bonuses than new employees. He has noticed this tendency, but assumes that if an employee has been with the firm longer, that person must be more productive, so this is fair. He personally distributes the bonus cheques on the last working day before Christmas.

Since he has just turned 60, George is planning to retire in the next year or two, and turn the business over to his daughter, Georgette Henderson, who is just finishing her commerce degree at Dalhousie University. Ironically, it was on the day of his 60th birthday that his bookkeeper approached to inform him that there wasn't enough money in the bank account to meet payroll.

Multi-Products Corporation

It is early February. Late last year, the firm you work for, Multi-Products Corporation, acquired the rights to a new type of golf club, invented by a retired machinist who had been a lifelong golfer until his untimely demise (it turns out that golfing during a lightning storm is not such a great idea). The machinist had only produced a few sets of the clubs, but their superiority over existing clubs was so pronounced that word of his invention had spread far and wide. Fortunately for him (for his estate actually), he had patented the design of these clubs, so nobody could copy them.

Multi-Products Corporation has numerous divisions, each producing different products in the sporting goods field. They have never produced golf equipment of any kind, and plan to set up a separate division to produce and distribute the new clubs. You found out yesterday that you have been selected to head the new division. Corporate management will provide you with all the financial resources you need to get the division going and will also help you staff the division with experienced managers from the parent corporation. Because of their confidence in you, they have given you complete freedom to organize and operate the division as you see fit, as long as you attain the financial goals that have been set for the division.

Your first task is to design the organization structure. But before doing so, you recognize that you need to understand some key aspects about the organization and its context. Market research suggests that the demand for your product will be strong and stable. This demand will not be very price-sensitive, since golfers who want your

Appendix: Cases for Analysis

product will generally be willing to pay what it takes to get it. Therefore, it will be relatively easy for you to secure distributors. In fact, one distributor is willing to agree to a four-year sales contract for your equipment, with a fixed volume and a fixed price. This distributor is confident enough to make this offer because they believe that nobody else will be able to manufacture a similar club, due to the patent protection.

The production side also looks straightforward. Your production process includes readily available materials and there are many possible suppliers. You expect to be able to negotiate long-term contracts with suppliers at a fixed price. Acquiring the production equipment will also be straightforward, since the equipment is readily available in the marketplace.

The basic production technology, which will involve a sequential, step-by-step manufacturing process, has been in use for many years and has been refined to a high degree of efficiency. Since you know the likely volume of demand for your product, it is easy to decide on the optimum plant size, which will involve about 600 workers. The type of semi-skilled worker that you need is readily available; and since unemployment is quite high in your region, acquiring employees does not look to be very difficult. Employees in this industry are usually unionized; but the main union in the industry has not been highly militant in recent years, so labour disruptions don't seem likely.

Another possible factor that might affect your operations is government regulations. However, as long as your clubs meet CSA (Canadian Standards Association) standards, the government is unlikely to get involved with your product. Similarly, except for some groups opposed to the expansion of golf courses in ecologically sensitive areas (such as national parks), consumer and environmental groups are not likely to pose any concern.

Future technological change is another possible issue, but it does not appear to be of great concern. You will start out with the most up-to-date production equipment, which has not changed much in recent years. The product itself (golf clubs) is not likely to be replaced by anything radically different. The pace of technological change for golf clubs is quite slow, and some of the most popular clubs have been virtually unchanged in 30 years.

Plastco Packaging

Plastco Packaging Ltd. is a medium-sized manufacturer of plastic bags located on the west coast. These bags are used in the retail sector for purposes ranging from groceries to clothing and other goods. These bags are made from a variety of types of plastic and in a variety of sizes, depending on the intended purpose. Usually the retailer's name is printed on them.

There are three main phases in the bag manufacturing process: (1) producing the plastic sheeting (produced as rolls of tubing); (2) printing the retailer's name on the tubing; and (3) passing the rolls of tubing through bag-making machines that cut and seal the tubing into bag lengths.

This case focuses on the third step of the production process, the bag-making department. The department has 12 bag-making machines. Each machine operates semi-automatically but has to be manually loaded, set for the type of bag to be produced, started, monitored, and adjusted. The machines need frequent servicing to replace the cutting knives, adjust slipping belts, and lubricate the many moving parts. These functions and major repairs, when necessary, are carried out by mechanics from the maintenance department, a separate department reporting to the plant manager. The mechanics report machinery problems and future replacement and servicing needs to the maintenance supervisor, who reports significant problems to the plant manager. The plant manager then conveys any implications for production of bags to the bag-making supervisor.

There are six bag-making machine operators, with each operator tending two machines. There are also six inspectors/packers, who inspect bags for quality and pack them into boxes. Defective bags are thrown into waste bins based on the type of plastic. They are then melted down and remanufactured. Whenever an inspector/packer discovers poor-quality output, she must notify the operator to correct the problem. If the inspector/packer deems waste to be excessive, she is expected to report the operator to the bag-making supervisor.

In addition, four utility workers handle miscellaneous tasks, such as delivering rolls of plastic tubing and hauling boxes of finished bags to the shipping department. Traditionally, operators and utility workers have always been male, while inspectors/packers have always been female.

When a new operator is needed, the bag-making supervisor selects one of the utility workers and assigns him to an experienced operator for on-the-job training. It takes up to six months before a new operator is able to consistently produce an acceptable-quality product without supervision, since the machines are "finicky" to operate. The length of time needed to do bag changeovers also declines as the new operator gains experience.

The plant is unionized, and pay is based on an hourly wage. Operators receive approximately $22 per hour, utility workers $16 per hour, and inspectors/packers $11 per hour. Overall, benefits constitute about 20 percent of total compensation and increase with seniority.

The bag-making supervisor sees a number of problems at present. First is the high turnover among the inspectors/packers, as high as 100 percent a year. Turnover among the utility workers is about a third of that, and lower than that among operators, who quit or retire at the rate of about one a year. Second, while the department usually meets the minimum production levels, the bag-making supervisor believes that productivity could be much higher.

He also believes there's a high level of waste. However, whenever he questions an operator about this, the operator either blames maintenance for doing a poor job servicing the machines or the inspectors/packers for being unnecessarily fussy. It is also difficult to pinpoint specific operators for performing poor-quality work, since inspectors/packers seldom report an operator to the bag-making supervisor. When one does so, the operators usually accuse the woman of incompetence. All in all, there are very poor interpersonal relationships among the operators, mechanics, and inspectors/packers. Few members of the department appear to enjoy being at work.

Another problem is that customers are complaining about inconsistent quality in the products they receive. Sometimes the bags are of very high quality and sometimes many bags are defective. These complaints are a concern to the plant manager since a new competitor has recently opened up nearby and is aggressively competing for business. This competitor seems to be producing a product with fewer defects for a lower price.

Index

nonmonetary reward plans (*continued*)
    travel awards, 415
    types of, 415
nonroutine technology, 41
Nortel Networks, 371–372, 374, 375
not-for-profit organizations, goals of, 26
notice periods, 436–437
Nova Scotia Pay Equity Commission, 182
nurses, 274

O-Net, 250
objectives/results-based systems, 351
observation, 248
Old Age Security, 426
Oldham, Greg, 85
Ontario Pay Equity Act, 260
Ontario Pay Equity Commission, 260, 264
Ontario Securities Commission, 220
Ontario Teachers' Pension Fund, 224, 225
open book management. *See* high-involvement managerial strategy
operant conditioning, 89–90
opportunity costs, 100
optimal reward strategy, 8, 9
organization design, 24
organization of compensation administration, 470–473
organization size, 42
organization structure
    communication and information structure, 26
    control structure, 26
    coordination, 26
    decision-making and leadership structure, 26
    defined, 24
    departmentation, 26
    differentiation, 25
    integration, 25
    job design, 26
    managerial strategy, implications of, 29f
    organizational culture and, 37
    and size, 42
    structural variables, 25–26, 34–37
    substitute elements, 34
organizational citizenship behaviour
    altruism, 95
    cause of, 95–96
    civic virtue, 95
    courtesy, 95
    creating, 96–97
    defined, 66
    five dimensions, 95
    general compliance, 95
    measurement of, 484
    sportsmanship, 95
    understanding, 94–97
organizational commitment
    affective commitment, 80, 81
    continuance commitment, 80, 81

defined, 80
    reward system, role of, 81–82
organizational context, 101, 177
organizational culture, 37, 448
organizational identification
    consequences of, 67–68
    decision making, participation in, 96
    defined, 66
    as key attitude, 66–70
    membership feelings (belonging), 95–96
    shared organizational goals, 95
    as source of citizenship behaviour, 95–96
organizational justice, 74–76
organizational pay plans, 412
organizational performance indicators
    compensation cost indicators, 482
    financial indicators, 482–483
    other indicators, 483
organizational performance pay plans
    advantages and disadvantages, 165
    described, 117
    employee stock plans, 160–164
    long-term incentives (LTIs), 164–166
    performance share plan, 165
    performance unit plan, 164
    profit sharing, 156–160
organizational support, 101
organizational system, 23f
organizations
    defined, 23
    as systems, 23–24
outlier jobs, 287, 288
outplacement services, 439–440
output-related pay, 115, 134–135
    see also performance pay
outsourcing, 470–473
overtime pay rates, 180–181
owner-controlled firms, 223

painters, 274
paired comparison method
    of job evaluation, 253–254
    performance appraisals, 343
parental leaves, 435
part-time workers. *See* contingent workers
participation. *See* employee involvement
participatory mechanisms, 401–402
pay calculations, 469
pay cuts, 305–306
pay equity legislation, 126, 129, 133, 181–182, 256, 260
    see also pay equity requirements
pay equity maintenance
    changes, 266
    communication about changes, 267
    compensation changes, 267
    gender changes in workforce, 266
    job value changes, 267
    new job classes, 266–267

structural or bargaining agent change, 266
    vanishing job classes, 267
pay equity requirements
    adjustment of compensation, 265
    casual jobs, 264
    collection of job information, 262
    communication of results, 265–266
    determine what rules apply, 260–261
    establishment of body for conducting pay equity, 261–262
    female and male job classes, identification of, 261
    gender-neutral job comparison system, selection of, 262
    independent contractors, 265
    job comparisons, 262–263
    job evaluations and, 259–267
    job-to-job method, 262
    permissible differences, 263–265
    proportional value method, 263
    proxy comparison method, 263
    steps in Ontario process, 260
pay-for-knowledge system (PKS)
    advancing pay levels without promotion to management, 395
    advantages of, 130–131
    competency-based pay, 130, 376–377
    defined, 124
    described, 130–134
    disadvantages, 131–134
    high-involvement managerial strategy, 131, 134
    increase in adoption of, 54
    and pay equity legislation, 133
    skill-based pay, 130, 369–376
    and spiral career paths, 486
pay for time not worked
    bereavement leaves, 435
    compassionate leave, 434–435
    defined, 434
    educational leaves, 435–436
    holidays, 434
    parental leaves, 435
    personal absences, 434–435
    rest breaks, 434
    sabbatical leaves, 435–436
    severance pay, 436–437
    sickness, absences for, 434–435
    supplemental unemployment benefits (SUBs), 435
    vacations, 434
pay gap, 126
pay grade
    broadbanding, 298
    defined, 296
    equal increase approach, 298
    equal interval approach, 297
    equal percentage approach, 298
    establishing, 296–298
    number of, 297
    pay policy line, 299

Sterling Drug, 46
stock analysts, 159
stock options, 161, 225–226, 410–411
    see also employee stock option plan
stock ownership plans. *See* employee stock plans
stock plans. *See* employee stock plans
straight piece rate, 137
strategic framework for compensation
    contextual variables, 26–27
    contingency approach to organization design, 24
    described, 24–27, 25*f*
    fit, concept of, 23
    managerial strategy. *See* managerial strategy
    organizations as systems, 23–24
    structural variables, 25–26
Stronach, Frank, 222
structural changes, 266
structural variables, 25–26, 34–37
subordinate appraisals, 354–355
substance abuse, 437
substitute elements, 34
suggestion systems, 149, 392–393
supervisory appraisals, 353–354
supervisory reasons for performance appraisals, 338
supplemental health insurance, 430
supplemental unemployment benefits (SUBs), 435
survival needs, 83
Suzuki, 73
symbolic awards, 415
symbolic reasons for performance appraisals, 338

Taco Bell, 356
tangible costs, 100
targeted incentives, 148–149
task behaviour
    content theories of motivation, 82–88
    defined, 66
    dimensions of, 185–186
    measurement of, 483–484
    motivation, 188
    process theories of motivation, 83, 88–94
    quality of work, 484
    quantity of work, 483–484
    understanding, 82–94
task environment
    complexity of, 39
    defined, 27
    dynamic, 39
    and managerial strategy, 39
task forces, 476, 477
task identity, 85
task significance, 85
tax legislation, 183

taxes
    changes in, 485
    defined benefit plans, 428
    employee benefits, 442
    and employee stock plans, 407–408
    flexible benefit system, 445, 446
    health benefits, 431–433, 432*t*
    long-term disability insurance, 433
    pension plans, 431–433, 432*t*
    and profit-sharing plans, 404–405
    sabbatical leaves, 436
    stock options, 410–411
Taylor, Frederick Winslow, 136
team appraisals, 366–369
team-based merit pay, 155
technical ladders, 187, 395
technical premiums, 490
technology
    craft technology, 41
    defined, 24
    engineering technology, 41
    intensive technology, 40–41
    long-linked technology, 40
    and managerial strategy, 40–42
    mass/large batch technology, 42
    mediating technology, 40
    nonroutine technology, 41
    process technology, 42
    routine technology, 41
    unit/small batch technology, 42
telephone interviews, 322
telescopic approach, 298
Telus Corporation, 411, 443, 469
temporary workers. *See* contingent workers
termination of employment, 436–437
testing the system, 478
third-country nationals, 230–231
third-party surveys, 316–318
360-degree feedback, 356–358
time-based pay. *See* base pay
time not worked. *See* pay for time not worked
timing
    of evaluation of compensation system, 479–480
    of implementation, 477
tobacco products industry, 315
top-down approach, 359, 475
top hat plans, 404
topping out, 132–133
Toronto Maple Leafs, 313
total compensation costs, 288–289
total rewards, 6
Towers Perrin, 317
Toyota Motors, 69–70, 367, 415
tradeoffs, 188
training, 478
training opportunities, 373–374
training plan, 474–475
Trans Canada Credit, 471

travel awards, 415
trends
    in compensation system, 54–55
    in managerial strategy, 47–54
trust, 53, 140
tuition reimbursements, 441
turnover, 67, 82
two-factor theory of motivation, 85
two-tier wage system, 54, 218
Tylenol, 130
types of, 424–434

undesirable consequences, 64–65
UNICEF, 188, 189*f*
unilateral reduction of pay, 305
unionization
    and classical management firms, 52–53
    classical managers' opposition, 48
    indirect pay, 119–120
    job evaluation committee, 257
    pension plans and, 429–430
    and profit sharing plans, 157–158
    reduction of employee pay, 305
    severance pay, 436
    trade union legislation, 182
    unionized classical firms, 30
unit/small batch technology, 42
United Steelworkers, 395
United Technologies, 221, 228
University of Saskatchewan, 366
unjust dismissal, 391
utility analysis, 195–197

vacation buying or selling, 434
vacations, 434
valence, evaluation of, 99–100
validity, 282–283
Valley City Manufacturing, 406
values, 98, 100
Vancouver City Credit Union, 424
Vanderpol's Eggs, 4, 161
vice-president of human resources, 15
volatility, 184
volunteer workers, 180

wage
    defined, 115
    market wage, 126
wage freezes, 54
Watson Wyatt Worldwide, 317
websites, 317
weighted average, 323
weighted mean, 323
Welbourne, Theresa, 159
wellness programs, 438
whole job methods, 253
Wilkinson, Ian, 424
William M. Mercer, 317
Windsor Factory Supply, 176

women
  see also gender bias
  crossing guards, 182
  and pay equity legislation. *See* pay
    equity legislation
  pay gap, 126
work clothing or equipment,
    provision of, 441
work-life balance programs, 439
work motivation
  see also motivation
  consequences of, 67
  defined, 66
  and job satisfaction, 80
  as key attitude, 66–70
  two-factor theory of
    motivation, 85
work output, 249
work-related courses, 441
work-related disabilities, 430
workers' compensation
    benefits, 425
workforce
  changes in, 486–487
  diversity, and flexible benefit
    system, 445
  gender changes, 266
  nature of, 42–43
Workplace and Employee Survey
    (WES), 152
wrongful dismissal, 436

Zenon Environmental, 4
zero cost collars, 225